THE TUDOR CONSTITUTION

SECOND EDITION

THE
TUDOR CONSTITUTION

DOCUMENTS AND COMMENTARY

SECOND EDITION

EDITED AND INTRODUCED BY

G. R. ELTON

CAMBRIDGE UNIVERSITY PRESS

CAMBRIDGE

LONDON   NEW YORK   NEW ROCHELLE

SYDNEY   MELBOURNE

Published by the Press Syndicate of the University of Cambridge
The Pitt Building, Trumpington Street, Cambridge CB2 1RP
32 East 57th Street, New York, NY 10022, USA
296 Beaconsfield Parade, Middle Park, Melbourne 3206, Australia

First published 1960
Reprinted 1962, 1965, 1968, 1972, 1975, 1978
Second edition 1982

Printed in Great Britain at the University Press, Cambridge

Library of Congress catalogue card number: 81–15216

British Library Cataloguing in Publication Data

The Tudor constitution.—2nd ed.
1. Great Britain—History—Tudors, 1485–1603
I. Elton, G. R.
942.05 DA315

ISBN 0 521 24506 0 hard covers (1st edn 0 521 04891 5 hard covers)
ISBN 0 521 28757 X paperback (1st edn 0 521 09120 9 paperback)

CONTENTS

CONTENTS

TABLE OF DOCUMENTS

(References are to the numbers of the documents)

I. STATUTES

II. CASES

III. PRIVY COUNCIL PROCEEDINGS

IV. PROCEEDINGS IN PARLIAMENT

V. PUBLIC RECORDS

VI. LETTERS

VII. EXTRACTS

VIII. MISCELLANEOUS

Throughout the book figures in **bold** *type refer to documents*

PREFACE TO THE SECOND EDITION

When this book first appeared the spectacular expansion of Tudor studies had barely began. The work of the last twenty years therefore makes a new edition urgently necessary; on far too many points advancing knowledge has rendered what was said here badly out of date, though it is gratifying to find how much of it has survived the labours of innovation and revision. At the same time, the book could not, in the circumstances of the day, be much enlarged, and I have therefore restrained myself in altering the collection of documents. One has been replaced and five have been added, the original numbering being preserved: a modest exercise which leaves me still regretful about what has had to be left out, more especially the contemporary comments which, to some reviewers' annoyance, considerations of length forced me to remove from Tanner's book. The introductory passages, on the other hand, have been very much affected by revision, growing rather longer in the process; not one section has remained untouched, and some (especially those on the common law, on Parliament and on Puritanism) have changed out of recognition. The biggest alteration occurred in the footnotes and book-list, reflecting the formidable production of many scholars to whom I extend my respectful gratitude. By now it has become quite impossible to provide a complete bibliography in a book of this kind, but every effort has still been made to take the reader to the right sources and studies. I have pruned the original list with some ruthlessness, so that quite a few familiar friends have had to go; even so the list, which includes 178 new items, has grown by over 100.

Even more than in 1959, I am conscious how inadequate any treatment must be which confines itself to the analysis of institutions. I am very well aware that an understanding of the structure and working of Tudor government calls for an investigation of many problems that in this format cannot put in an appearance. I know how important patronage, faction, ideology and regional diversity are to such an understanding, but beyond drawing attention to these matters here and there I could see no way to do justice to them. At the same time, I remain equally convinced of the primary need to understand these

xiii

institutions correctly, for without that knowledge all answers derived from the evidence produced by the agencies of government are at best uncertain, more probably corrupt.

CAMBRIDGE   G.R.E.
January 1981

PREFACE TO THE FIRST EDITION

This book was originally intended as a revision of J. R. Tanner's *Tudor Constitutional Documents*, a work whose continued importance in the universities proved the necessity for keeping it in print. However, it soon became apparent that something more than a revised edition would be required: a book thirty-five years old and in a sense representative of a state of learning now over fifty years old could not just be overhauled but had to be replaced; and I therefore agreed, after consulting various people whose advice I valued (especially the Secretary of the Cambridge University Press), that it would be both simpler and more accurate to let this book appear over my name only. Thus it must be my first duty to discharge my debt to the scholar upon whose work I have rested my own. Dr Tanner was for many years one of the mainstays of historical teaching in Cambridge, a major figure in the University and in St John's College. Though he died in 1931, affectionate memories of him are still very much alive. He started lecturing as long ago as 1883; as late as 1926–7 he deputised from his retirement for the then Regius Professor (J. B. Bury). Though he devoted much of his energy to tutorial work in his College, he spared time for a great deal of productive research; in this his main interests were with Pepys and the seventeenth-century navy, but his long years of lecturing on Tudor and Stuart constitutional history resulted in three well-known books.[1]

Because it was my original commission to 'bring him up to date', I took from Tanner a number of things: the arrangement by topics (though I have changed these), a general guidance in the choice of documents (of the 216 documents here printed 127 appeared in Tanner, though not always in the same form), and above all the principle of introducing the documents with lengthy commentaries. Since there exists no comprehensive account of Tudor government I felt myself bound to provide as systematic and detailed a description as I could within the space at my disposal. The commentary is therefore in part designed as a guide to the bibliography of the topics discussed. This has

---

[1] *Tudor Constitutional Documents* (1922); *English Constitutional Conflicts of the Seventeenth Century* 1928); *Constitutional Documents of the Reign of James I* (1930).

made it unnecessary to append a classified book-list, while considerations of space and convenience have persuaded me to keep references in the body of the book as brief as is consistent with their easy identification in a general alphabetical list at the end. All documents—new and old—have been checked, a labour which discovered quite a few errors in Tanner's transcripts, one of them at least productive of a version which I am sorry to lose.[2] Such errors in a book of such length are inevitable; I do not doubt that some may have crept into this edition, too. I have also followed Tanner's example in modernising the spelling and punctuation of the documents. Though I am myself dubious about this, I have to admit that experience has proved the advantages of the practice to the student, and it is for undergraduate purposes that this book must in the first place be designed. All extracts, whether taken from print or manuscript, are therefore given in a standardised form. Unless it is stated otherwise, those taken from manuscript are from the Public Record Office.

I am aware of two weaknesses in the book which I saw no way of avoiding. Any selection of documents suffers from insufficiencies. Since it was the intention of the University Press that this book should take the place of Tanner's, I had to start with Tanner's collection; since I wished to include new topics and a more varied choice, while at the same time under instruction to produce a markedly shorter book than Tanner's, I had to leave out many pieces which I should have liked to put in. This does not matter so much if it is understood that no collection of sixteenth-century constitutional documents can be more than a bucket from the well. Because selection had to be so severe I have often given references to documents easily accessible in print elsewhere. This includes Tanner's book, which means that it retains independent value as a collection and helps to justify the omission of his name from the present title-page. More serious are the shortcomings of any method which deals exclusively in topics. For an understanding of institutions it is necessary that they should be discussed by themselves, but this unquestionably hides some of the realities of government which involve interacting institutions used differently from time to time. Unfortunately I could see no way of presenting the general con-

---

[1] The Treasons Act of 1534 fulminated (according to Tanner, 388) against those who ' . . . by crafty images invent, practice or attempt any bodily harm, etc.'. Alas for visions of premature Gillrays or wax-dolls with pins in them ! The passage really refers to those who 'by craft imagine, invent, etc.'.

stitutional developments in the compass of this book. I had to confine myself to an analysis of the parts. I believe that the topics into which Tudor government is here cut up are the ones that matter, though I could have wished for space to add something on the Royal Household and on war. But both these topics are a trifle marginal in a consideration of the Tudor constitution; in so far as the Household took part in running the ordinary government of the realm it is here included, and the study of military administration has not yet reached a state in which a summary can usefully be given in a book of this sort.

Thanks are due to the following for permission to print material not used by Tanner: to the Clarendon Press for extracts from R. B. Merriman's *Life and Letters of Thomas Cromwell*, from Conyers Read's *Mr Secretary Walsingham*, and from Stowe's *Survey of London*, ed. by C. L. Kingsford; to Messrs Longmans, Green & Co. Ltd., for two documents published in the *English Historical Review* (C. Hughes' 'Discourse of Nicholas Faunt', vol. xx, 1905, and J. E. Neale's 'Peter Wentworth', vol. xxxix, 1924), and for a document first published in R. R. Reid's *Council of the North*; to the Society for Promoting Christian Knowledge for parts of the 'First Admonition' from *Puritan Manifestoes*, by W. Frere and C. Douglas; to the Council of the Selden Society for documents from I. S. Leadam's *Court of Requests*; to the Early English Text Society for extracts from their Original Series, no. 186 (Harpsfield's *Life of More*), and no. 197 (Roper's *Life of More*).

I am most grateful to Lady Neale (Miss Elfreda Skelton) for permission to use and cite from her unpublished London M.A. thesis on the Star Chamber, and to Mr Christopher Morris for his help and advice, both in general and in particular. Many others have, without knowing it, contributed to the shaping of this book: I mean those who for ten years have suffered my teaching in lectures and supervisions. *Docendo didici.*

G.R.E.

CAMBRIDGE
March 1959

CHAPTER I

THE CROWN

I. THE TUDOR DYNASTY

The Tudors came to the throne as victors in a civil war; they held it because they fulfilled the first duty of kingship in governing effectively and to the satisfaction of the greater part of the realm. No Tudor, however, was ever altogether free from dynastic worries. They were an unhealthy and far from prolific stock; their rivals—especially the house of York—bred fast and lived long. The normal hazards of life in the sixteenth century would have caused anxiety enough; small families, matrimonial problems, and at last stubborn celibacy turned the anxiety into a standing political issue. Memories of disturbed successions, kept fresh by personal witness of such things in England and elsewhere, sufficed to make the misfortunes of the royal family a point of first importance to all who looked to it for a quiet and prosperous life.

Henry VII first had to assert a claim to the crown which was far from obvious. In the nebulous theory of the succession, hereditary right played the largest part, but in practice other factors were allowed to cut across it, provided some link in blood and descent existed. Exploiting this uncertainty, Henry VII took the simple line of describing himself as king once he had overthrown Richard III.[1] Victory in battle (as God's verdict) and the acclamation of his host at Bosworth were points to be used to underline the fact; they were not by any means the legal bases of his claim. Descent from Edward III (though afflicted by the specific exclusion of his line pronounced by Richard II and confirmed by the pope) and the later marriage to Elizabeth of York were ways of harnessing the dynastic principle. Yet none of these details should be called the foundation of the Tudor title. Nor was this parliamentary. The first Parliament of Henry VII—itself proof of his recognised kingship from the day of victory, since only a true king can summon a true Parliament—formally acknowledged Henry and his heirs as kings of England in a document which presents peculiar features (1). It is not strictly an act of Parliament, but rather a special petition of the Commons to which the king and Lords assented in an unusual formula; it has not even a chapter number and was not part of the statute. In fact, it simply followed the parliamentary proceedings by which Henry IV had had his claim confirmed in 1406.[2] Essentially, all Tudors rested their title on accomplished fact, which, they argued, announced God's choice. And when God had bestowed

[1] Or possibly even earlier: Pickthorn, 1, 10. (See 'List of Books' starting on p. 483)
[2] Chrimes, *Const. Ideas*, 25.

I

the crown on them, who was to deny their right to it? In this very real sense, Tudor monarchy was monarchy by divine right.

By 1495 Henry VII was safe on the throne; with pretenders overcome and European recognition obtained, he saw that the time had come to close the chapter of the civil wars. The long series of attainders came to an end,[3] while the so-called *de facto* act tried to reassure the king's late enemies (2). This act has been over-ingeniously explained.[4] It does not make a distinction between a king who was so by right and one who held the position in fact only, as has commonly been alleged; it speaks only of one kind of king who is so 'for the time being', a common Tudor phrase which means no more than 'at the time in question'.[5] Allegiance to any such king is protected from later charges of treason. In conjunction with section ii, the general clauses protected adherence to Henry VII even if he should be opposed by a pretender claiming to be king by right, and thus encouraged people to follow him without thought of the consequences. Secondly the act announced an end to vengeance by retrospectively justifying allegiance to Richard III while he was the king 'for the time being', even though such allegiance had been treated as treason between 1485 and 1495. But thanks to section ii, the act did not help a man who deserted Henry VII in any future renewal of the civil wars. The attempt to bind later Parliaments is discussed below.[6]

Even though Henry VII had done much to establish his dynasty, doubts about the future could not be avoided. After eighteen years of Tudor rule, trusted Crown servants could still seriously debate whether in the event of the king's death they should follow his young heir or prefer an older man (3). The death, in 1504, of Prince Arthur jeopardised the dynasty. However, Henry VIII came to the throne as an adult and to the music of general acclamation. He himself never had the faintest doubt about his right, by God's grace, to wear the crown. But his failure to provide heirs, and the matrimonial adventures which in part grew from that failure, introduced serious complications into the succession. The divorce from Catherine of Aragon and marriage to Anne Boleyn necessitated the first Act of Succession (4) which declared the Princess Mary illegitimate. (The measure was completed a year later by a statute which prescribed the oath mentioned in section ix.[7]) The act differed from earlier parliamentary dealings with the throne in that it enacted a precise devolution of the crown instead of simply accepting the present king and his heirs in general. This feature was even

---

[3] Below, p. 82 and Doc. 12.

[4] Bacon started it (*Henry VII*, 133). Holdsworth still thought that the act distinguished between *de facto* and *de jure* kings (IV, 500); and even Pickthorn (I, 151 ff.) goes astray on this point and others. For the best analysis of the act cf. Pollard in *Bull. Inst. Hist. Research*, VII, 1 ff.

[5] The temporary quality so often read into these words does not exist.

[6] P. 236.

[7] 26 Henry VIII, c. 2 (Gee and Hardy, 244 ff.).

more marked in the second Succession Act of 1536,[8] called forth by the failure of the second marriage: it secured the crown to the issue of Jane Seymour and declared all previous issue illegitimate. Section ix of this act seemed to go very far in increasing the power of the Crown when it authorised the king to bequeath the throne by will, but not too much should be read into this. The power was created to meet the possibility that there might be no heir from the third marriage, and therefore no legitimate heir at all when Henry died. His will was to be effective only in such circumstances. The clause really looks back to an older attitude which regarded the crown as a piece of private property subject to the laws applying to that;[9] it marks no absolutist increase of royal power. It acquires significance when seen against the contemporary legislation respecting wills: even as the law for the first time admitted a man's right to bequeath his lands, so (in a way) it recognised the king's right to dispose of his hitherto equally unwillable crown.[10] In any case, though the principle may seem extraordinary to an age which has depersonalised the Crown, this was a political and not a legal freak; the power ultimately depended on the Parliament which had granted it; and the king had no authority to leave his crown away from the heirs defined in the statute.

By 1544 the absence of a sufficiently large body of legitimate heirs demanded a third Succession Act.[11] This confirmed the king's right to bestow the crown by will but expressed a desire for more public definition. In fact it directed the crown to Mary and Elizabeth in that order (previous bastardisations being now ignored), if both Henry and Edward should die without further heirs. In December 1546 Henry drew up his will which—to simplify its complications—left the crown to his three children and their heirs in the manner established in the last act; if their lines all failed it was to go to the heirs of his younger sister Mary (the Suffolk line).[12] The only comment required is that the will did not come into operation until the death of Elizabeth in 1603 when the heirs of Henry's elder sister Margaret (the Stuart line, who had been ignored in 1546) succeeded without trouble or question. An earlier attempt to set both will and statute aside failed in 1553 when the duke of Northumberland tried to substitute the Suffolk line for Mary; thereafter Elizabeth's long life postponed the crisis until it had ceased to be one. Of course, the succession remained a vital issue through much of her reign,[13] and many both then and earlier had cause to regret blood links with the Tudors, but no further attempts were made to define the dynasty or its

[8] 28 Henry VIII, c. 7 (Tanner, 389 ff.).
[9] Cf. Plucknett, *Tudor Studies*, 161 ff.
[10] For the comparison see Pollock and Maitland, I, 505; for the Henrician legislation, Holdsworth IV, 465 f.
[11] 35 Henry VIII, c. I (Tanner, 397).
[12] *L.P.*, XXI, II, 634.
[13] Cf. below, pp. 316 ff., 321 f.

right publicly. Henry VIII's legislation drew attention to a basic problem which time rather than the law would solve. It also exemplified a new power in Parliament whose role in 1485 had been without significance to the nature of the Crown and of only marginal significance to its possessor; in 1534–44 it played a central and authoritative part. But it should be noted that the first two Succession Acts simply drew the necessary consequences from matrimonial vicissitudes outside the competence of Parliament, while the third in effect embodied the king's private intentions as later expressed in his will.

1. Act for the Confirmation of Henry VII (1485).

Item quedam Billa exhibita fuit prefato Domino Regi in presenti Parliamento per Communitates Regni Anglie in eodem Parliamento existentes, hanc seriem verborum continens.

To the pleasure of Almighty God, the wealth, prosperity and surety of this realm of England, to the singular comfort of all the king's subjects of the same, and in avoiding of all ambiguities and questions, be it ordained, established and enacted, by authority of this present Parliament, that the inheritance of the crowns of the realms of England and of France, with all the preeminence and dignity royal to the same pertaining, and all other seignories to the king belonging beyond the sea, with the appurtenances thereto in any wise due or pertaining, be, rest, remain and abide in the most royal person of our now sovereign lord king Harry the VIIth and in the heirs of his body lawfully come, perpetually with the grace of God so to endure, and in none other. Qua quidem billa in Parliamento predicto lecta, audita et matura deliberatione intellecta, eidem bille, de assensu dominorum spiritualium et temporalium in dicto Parliamento existentium ad requisitionem Communitatis predicte necnon auctoritate ejusdem Parliamenti respondebatur eidem in forma sequenti: Nostre Seigneur le Roy, de l'assent des Seigneurs Espirituelx et Temporelx esteauntz en cest Parliament et a la request des Comens avanditz, le voet en toutz pointz.   Rot. Parl., VI, 270

2. An Act that no person going with the King to the wars shall be attaint of treason (1495: 11 Henry VII, c. 1).

The King our sovereign lord, calling to his remembrance the duty of allegiance of his subjects of this his realm, and that they by reason of the same are bounden to serve their prince and sovereign lord for the time being in his wars for the defence of him and the land against every rebellion, power and might reared against him, and with him to enter and abide in service in battle if the case so require; And that for the same service what fortune ever fall by chance in the same battle against the mind and weal of the prince, as in this land some time past hath been seen; That it is not reasonable but against all laws, reason and good conscience that the said subjects going with their sovereign lord in wars, attending upon him in his person, or being in other places by his commandment within this land or without, any thing should lose or forfeit for doing their true duty and service of allegiance: It be therefore ordained, enacted, and established by the King our sovereign lord, by advice and assent of the Lords spiritual and temporal and Commons in this present Parliament assembled, and by authority of the same that henceforth no manner of person ne persons, whatsoever he or they be, that attend upon the King and sovereign lord of this land for the time being in his person and do him true and faithful service of allegiance in the same, or be in other places by his commandment, in his wars, within this land or without, that for the same deed and true service of allegiance he or they be in no wise convict or attaint of high treason ne of other offences for that cause by act of Parliament or otherwise by any process of law, whereby he or any of them shall or may forfeit life, lands, tenements, rents, possessions, hereditaments, goods, chattels or any other things, but to be for that deed and service utterly discharged of any vexation, trouble or loss; And if any act or acts or other process of the law hereafter thereupon for the same happen to be made contrary to this ordinance, that then that act or acts or other processes of the law, whatsoever they shall be, stand and be utterly void.

II. Provided alway that no person ne persons shall take any benefit or advantage by this act which shall hereafter decline from his or their said allegiance. *Stat. Realm*, II, 568

3. A Deposition: Conversations held at Calais (c. 1503).

'It is not long since his highness was sick and lay then in his manor of Wanstead. It happened the same time me to be amongst many great personages, the which fell into communication of the King's grace and of the world that should be after him if his grace happened to depart.' Then he[14] said that some of them spake of my lord of Buckingham, saying that he was a noble man and would be a royal ruler. Other there

[14] Sir Hugh Conway, treasurer of Calais.

were that spake, he said, in like wise of your traitor, Edmund de la Pole,[15] but none of them, he said, spake of my lord prince.[16] Then said Master Porter[17] to him, 'have ye never broken to the King's grace of this matter?' Then said Sir Hugh Conway to him again, 'I pray you, suffer me to tell forth my tale, for I am not yet at the end. . . . In like wise since my coming I have shewed the same to Sir Nicholas Vaux, lieutenent of Guisnes, and to Sir Anthony Browne, lieutenent of the castle here, and they answered me both this, that they had two good holds to resort unto, the which they said should be sure to make their peace, howsoever the world turn.' Then my master, your deputy,[18] and Master Porter both said to him that he could no less do but show these matters unto your highness. He said that 'it were good that the King's grace knew these sayings, but as yet I have not shewed him no part thereof, neither never I will do. . . . If ye knew King Harry our master as I do, ye would beware how that ye brake to him in any such matters, for he would take it to be said but of envy, ill-will and malice. Then should anyone have blame and no thanks for his truth and good mind; and that have I well proved heretofore in like causes . . .'.

Letters and Papers of Richard III and Henry VII, I, 233-4

4. An Act for the establishment of the King's succession, 1534 (25 Henry VIII, c. 22).

In their most humble wise show unto your Majesty your most humble and obedient subjects, the Lords spiritual and temporal and the Commons in this present Parliament assembled, that since it is the natural inclination of every man gladly and willingly to provide for the surety of both his title and succession, although it touch his only private cause; we therefore, most rightful and dreadful sovereign lord, reckon ourselves much more bounden to beseech and instant your Highness, although we doubt not of your princely heart and wisdom, mixed with a natural affection to the same, to foresee and provide for the perfect surety of both you and your most lawful succession and heirs, upon which dependeth all our joy and wealth, in whom also is united and knit the only mere true inheritance and title of this realm without any contradiction: Wherefore we your said most humble and obedient subjects

---

[15] Earl of Suffolk and Yorkist claimant.
[16] Arthur, prince of Wales.
[17] Sir Sampson Norton.
[18] Sir Richard Nanfan.

in this present Parliament assembled, calling to our remembrance the great divisions which in times past hath been in this realm by reason of several titles pretended to the imperial crown of the same, which sometimes and for the most part ensued by occasion of ambiguity and doubts then not so perfectly declared but that men might upon froward intents expound them to every man's sinister appetite and affection after their sense, contrary to the right legality of the succession and posterity of the lawful kings and emperors[19] of this realm, whereof hath ensued great effusion and destruction of man's blood, as well of a great number of the nobles as of other the subjects and specially inheritors in the same; And the greatest occasion thereof hath been because no perfect and substantial provision by law hath been made within this realm of itself when doubts and questions have been moved and proponed of the certainty and legality of the succession and posterity of the crown; By reason whereof the bishop of Rome and See Apostolic, contrary to the great and inviolable grants of jurisdictions given by God immediately to emperors, kings and princes in succession to their heirs, hath presumed in times past to invest who should please them to inherit in other men's kingdoms and dominions, which thing we your most humble subjects both spiritual and temporal do most abhor and detest; And sometimes other foreign princes and potentates of sundry degrees, minding rather dissension and discord to continue in the realm to the utter desolation thereof than charity, equity or unity, have many times supported wrong titles, whereby they might the more easily and facilely aspire to the superiority of the same; the continuance and sufferance whereof, deeply considered and pondered, were too dangerous and perilous to be suffered any longer within this realm and too much contrary to the unity, peace and tranquillity of the same, being greatly reproachable and dishonourable to the whole realm.

In consideration whereof your said most humble and obedient subjects the nobles and commons of this realm, calling further to their remembrance that the good unity, peace and wealth of this realm and the succession of the subjects of the same most specially and principally above all worldly things consisteth and resteth in the certainty and surety of the procreation and posterity of your Highness, in whose most royal person at this present time is no manner of doubt nor question, do therefore most humbly beseech your Highness, that it may please your Majesty that it may be enacted by your Highness with the assent of the

[19] See preamble of the Act of Appeals, 177 below.

Lords spiritual and temporal and the Commons in this present Parliament assembled that the marriage heretofore solemnised between your Highness and the Lady Catherine, being before lawful wife to Prince Arthur your elder brother, which by him was carnally known, as doth duly appear by sufficient proof in a lawful process had and made before Thomas, by the sufferance of God now archbishop of Canterbury and metropolitan primate of all this realm,[20] shall be by authority of this present Parliament definitely, clearly and absolutely declared, deemed and adjudged to be against the laws of Almighty God, and also accepted, reputed and taken of no value nor effect but utterly void and annulled, and the separation thereof made by the said archbishop shall be good and effectual to all intents and purposes, . . . and that the said Lady Catherine shall be from henceforth called and reputed only dowager to Prince Arthur and not queen of this realm. And that the lawful matrimony had and solemnised between your Highness and your most dear and entirely beloved wife Queen Anne[21] shall be established and taken for undoubtful, true, sincere and perfect ever hereafter, according to the just judgment of the said Thomas, archbishop of Canterbury, metropolitan and primate of all this realm[22], whose grounds of judgemnt have been confirmed as well by the whole clergy of this realm in both the Convocations, and by both the Universities thereof, as by the Universities of Bologna, Padua, Paris, Orleans, Toulouse, Angers and divers others, and also by the private writings of many right excellent well-learned men; which grounds so confirmed and judgment of the said archbishop ensuing the same, together with your marriage solemnised between your Highness and your said lawful wife Queen Anne, we your said subjects, both spiritual and temporal, do purely, plainly, constantly and firmly accept, approve and ratify for good and consonant to the laws of Almighty God, without error or default, most humbly beseeching your Majesty that it may be so established for ever by your most gracious and royal assent.

* * * * * *

IV. And also be it enacted by authority aforesaid that all the issue had and procreate, or after to be had and procreate, between your Highness

---

[20] Cranmer pronounced the marriage with Catharine of Aragon invalid in his archiepiscopal court at Dunstable, 23 May 1533.

[21] Anne Boleyn.

[22] Cranmer pronounced the marriage with Anne Boleyn to be valid, after a secret inquiry held at Lambeth, 28 May 1533.

and your said most dearly and entirely beloved wife Queen Anne, shall be your lawful children and be inheritable and inherit, according to the course of inheritance and laws of this realm, the imperial crown of the same, with all dignities, honours, preeminences, prerogatives, authorities and jurisdictions to the same annexed or belonging, in as large and ample manner as your Highness to this present time hath the same as king of this realm, the inheritance thereof to be and remain to your said children and right heirs in manner and form as hereafter shall be declared: That is to say, first the said imperial crown and other the premises shall be to your Majesty and to your heirs of your body lawfully begotten, that is to say to the first son of your body between your Highness and your said lawful wife Queen Anne begotten, and to the heirs of the body of the same first son lawfully begotten; And for default of such heirs, then to the second son of your body and of the body of the said Queen Anne begotten, and to the heirs of the body of the said second son lawfully begotten; and so to every son of your body and of the body of the said Queen Anne begotten, and to the heirs of the body of every such son begotten, according to the course of inheritance in that behalf. And if it shall happen your said dear and entirely beloved wife Queen Anne to decease without issue male of the body of your Highness to be gotten (which God defend) then the same imperial crown and all other the premises to be to your Majesty as is aforesaid, and to the son and heir male of your body lawfully begotten and to the heirs of the body of the same son and heir male lawfully begotten; And for default of such issue then to your second son of your body lawfully begotten and to the heirs of the body of the same second son lawfully begotten; And so from son and heir male to son and heir male, and to the heirs of the several bodies of every such son and heir male to be gotten, according to the course of inheritance in like manner and form as is above said; And for default of such sons of your body begotten, and the heirs of the several bodies of every such sons lawfully begotten, that then the said imperial crown and other the premises shall be to the issue female between your Majesty and your said most dear and entirely beloved wife Queen Anne begotten, that is to say: first to the eldest issue female, which is the Lady Elizabeth, now princess, and to the heirs of her body lawfully begotten, and for default of such issue then to the second issue female and to the heirs of her body lawfully begotten; And so from issue female to issue female and to their heirs of their bodies one after another by course of inheritance according

9

to their ages, as the crown of England hath been accustomed and ought to go in cases when there be heirs females to the same: And for default of such issue then the said imperial crown and all other premises shall be in the right heirs of your Highness for ever.

v. And be it further enacted by authority aforesaid that, on this side the first day of May next coming, proclamations shall be made in all shires within this realm of the tenor and contents of this act; And if any person or persons, of what estate, dignity or condition soever they be, subject or resiant within this realm or elsewhere within any the King's dominions, after the said first day of May by writing or imprinting or by any exterior act or deed maliciously procure or do, or cause to be procured or done, any thing or things to the peril of your most royal person, or maliciously give occasion by writing, print, deed or act whereby your Highness might be disturbed or interrupted of the crown of this realm, or by writing, print, deed or act procure or do, or cause to be procured or done, any thing or things to the prejudice, slander, disturbance or derogation of the said lawful matrimony solemnised between your Majesty and the said Queen Anne, or to the peril, slander or disherison of any the issues and heirs of your Highness being limited by this act to inherit and to be inheritable to the crown of this realm in such form as is aforesaid, whereby any such issues or heirs of your Highness might be destroyed, disturbed or interrupted in body or title of inheritance to the crown of this realm as to them is limited in this act in form above rehearsed, that then every such person and persons, of what estate, degree or condition they be of, subject or resiant within this realm, and their aiders, counsellors, maintainers and abettors and every of them, for every such offence shall be adjudged high traitors, and every such offence shall be adjudged high treason, and the offender and their aiders, counsellors, maintainers and abettors, and every of them, being lawfully convict of such offence by presentment, verdict, confession or process according to the customs and laws of this realm, shall suffer pains of death as in cases of high treason. And that also every such offender, being convict as is aforesaid, shall lose and forfeit to your Highness and to your heirs, kings of this realm, all such manors, lands, tenements, rents, annuities and hereditaments which they had in possession as owners or were sole seised of by or in any right, title or means, or any other person or persons had to their use, of any estate of inheritance at the day of such treasons and offences by them committed and done; And shall also lose and forfeit to your Highness and to your said heirs as well all manner such estates of freehold and interests for years of lands and rents as all their goods, chattels and debts which they had at the time of conviction or attainder of any such offence: Saving always to every person and persons and bodies politic, to their heirs, assigns and successors, and every of them, other than such persons as shall be so convict and their heirs and successors and all other claiming to their uses, all such right, title, use, interest, possession, condition, rents, fees, offices, annuities and commons which they or any of them shall happen to have in, to, or upon any such manors, lands, tenements, rents, annuities or hereditaments that shall so happen to be lost and forfeit by reason of attainder for any the treasons and offences above rehearsed at any time before the said treasons and offences committed.

VI. And be it further enacted by authority aforesaid, that if any person or persons, after the said first day of May, by any words without writing or any exterior deed or act, maliciously and obstinately publish, divulge or utter any thing or things to the peril of your Highness, or to the slander or prejudice of the said matrimony solemnised between your Highness and the said Queen Anne, or to the slander or disherison of the issue and heirs of your body begotten and to be gotten of the said Queen Anne or any other your lawful heirs which shall be inheritable to the crown of this realm as is afore limited by this act, that then every such offence shall be taken and adjudged for misprision of treason;[23] And that every person and persons, of what estate, degree or condition soever they be, subject or resiant within this realm or in any the King's dominions, so doing and offending and being thereof lawfully convict by presentment, verdict, process or confession, shall suffer imprisonment of their bodies at the King's will, and shall lose as well all their goods, chattels and debts as all such interests and estates of freehold or for years which any such offenders shall have of or in any lands, rents or hereditaments whatsoever at the time of conviction and attainder of such offence.

* * * * * *

IX. And for the more sure establishment of the succession of your most royal Majesty according to the tenor and form of this act, be it further enacted by authority aforesaid that as well all the nobles of your realm spiritual and temporal as all other your subjects . . . shall make a corporal oath in the presence of your Highness or your heirs, or

[23] See Glossary.

before such other as your Majesty or your heirs will depute for the same, that they shall truly, firmly and constantly without fraud or guile observe, fulfil, maintain, defend and keep to their cunning, wit and uttermost of their powers the whole effects and contents of this present act . . . ; And if any person or persons . . . obstinately refuse that to do in contempt of this act, that then every person so doing to be taken and accepted for offender in misprision of high treason . . .

Stat. Realm, III, 471–4

II. THE NATURE OF KINGSHIP

The Tudors inherited a kingship which in its own right enjoyed very considerable powers both defined and undefined.[24] England's medieval monarchy was by and large stronger in practice than any of its rivals in Western Europe, even if it made more moderate theoretical claims than that of France. Since the dynastic troubles of the fifteenth century never altered the potential power of the Crown, Henry VII found it necessary only to use afresh, not to recreate. The age was essentially monarchical: that is to say, the king was held to be the source and the centre of all political and social life (6). In their behaviour all the Tudor sovereigns stressed the semi-divine as well as the representative character of kingship: their courts and persons shone forth with a splendour which should be regarded as political propaganda rather than personal extravagance, and they insisted on ever greater deference. Even Henry VII employed new styles and placed a greater distance between himself and his subjects; his formidable son and remarkable granddaughter proved to have both the physical appearance and the mental make-up to justify the lavish and often slavish adulation which they received from the mass of their subjects.[25] From Henry VII onwards English kings gradually ceased to be 'their graces', and even 'their highnesses' came to enjoy more commonly the imported title of majesty. The Tudors added practical gains to kingship—especially the headship over the Church discussed below[26]—but their first striking achievement was to make the Crown appear glorious, untouchable, and yet accessible. With all their pomp and ceremonial, Henry VIII and Elizabeth never cut themselves off from their people; they could afford to condescend because they were so sure of their kingship.

The circumstances of the time—a disputed or uncertain succession, the weaknesses of a rudimentary police system, the problem of the Church,

[24] For fifteenth-century kingship see Chrimes, *Const. Ideas*, ch. 1.

[25] E.g. 5; and cf. for the significance of this display of emotion Morris, *The Tudors*, 34 f., 75 ff., 152 f., 165 ff.

[26] Pp. 338 ff.

foreign threats—combined to direct thinking about kingship into the channel of absolute obedience, a doctrine entirely summed up in the 1547 Homily on the subject (7). The burden of much teaching and preaching was that the prince, God's gift to the nation, must never be resisted.[27] In itself the doctrine formed part of the greater doctrine of order—of that divine order of the universe which men disturb at their peril;[28] but its specific application usually stressed the absolute need to obey the prince's command which even for conscience sake must not be resisted. In practice sixteenth-century Englishmen transgressed often enough against their duty of absolute obedience, and outside the pulpit and the pamphlet Tudor rulers were less concerned with the doctrine of obedience than the enforcement of order; but the principles of the Homily were at any rate representative of much conventional thought.[29] In the reign of Mary, John Ponet doubted whether these principles justified acquiescence in a popish triumph, and under Elizabeth men like Nicholas Sander or Robert Persons regarded their obedience as due first of all to Rome;[30] but, such interested exceptions apart, patriotism and king-worship combined to produce a general notion of unquestioning obedience to the divinely appointed king. The age held the notion the more fervently because in fact it was so full of lawless acts and ready disobedience.

However, the worst effects of byzantinism and adulation were subject to traditional modifications. Tudor kingship inherited not only potential absolutism (always implicit in medieval kingship) but also certain limitations. To be obeyed—in theory—a king needed only to be king; in practice it was tacitly assumed that he should be a just king. The tradition which looked back to Bracton's *debet rex esse sub lege* had recently received new formulation in the work of Chief Justice Fortescue which described the English Crown as *dominium politicum et regale*, constitutional monarchy, and not *dominium regale* or absolute monarchy.[31] Fortescue of course admitted the 'regal' elements in English kingship—discretionary powers outside the definition of the law— but while in this necessary practical reservation there lay the germs of Stuart absolutism, under the Tudors it remained simply an admitted exception which was not abused. Not only lawyers stressed the position of the Crown under the law; even in Hooker's hands (9) the point refers to the positive law of the realm rather than some nebulous law of nature to which all man-made law must conform. The law of nature was a sixteenth-century commonplace and to no one more important than to Hooker;[32] in this context it was more

---

[27] Baumer, *Theory of Kingship*, 85 ff.   [28] Morris, *Political Thought*, 68 ff.
[29] Cf. *The Mirror for Magistrates*, 65: all those who minister justice are called 'gods', and abuse of powers will be punished by God alone.
[30] Morris, *Political Thought*, 135 ff.; Baumer, *Theory of Kingship*, 112; Clancy, *Papist Pamphleteers*, chs. 2 & 3; Holmes, *Resistance and Compromise*.
[31] Fortescue, *Governance of England*, 109 ff.
[32] Baumer, *Theory of Kingship*, 128 ff.; Allen, *Political Thought*, 184 ff.

important that the king was thought of as subject to the common law of England and unable to tamper with it (9a).[33]

Even more significant was the growing conviction that though the king in person (rex solus) might be equipped with power he was yet subject to himself in Parliament. As is shown below,[34] a doctrine of parliamentary sovereignty—of an ultimate legislative supremacy vested in King-in-Parliament—was half-grasped and wholly practised after the constitutional revolution of the 1530's. Not everyone would have put the point with the frankness which the special circumstances of 1559 induced in John Aylmer (8),[35] but that the king assisted by Parliament was superior to the king in person was accepted by the Tudors themselves (129). Content with the reality of great political power, they never bothered to clothe it in a formal doctrine of absolutism. And capable though they were of arbitrary action, their deeds bore out the general tenet that monarchy exists under the law and is fully active only in co-operation with Parliament.

5. The Speaker's Oration, 1536 (Sir Richard Rich).

. . . Deinde Regie Maiestatis laudem enarrare exorsus est, eandem summis et meritis quidem laudibus extollens, dotesque Gratie et Nature prefati Domini Regis commemorans; quem ob Prudentiam et Iustitiam, *Salamoni*; ob Corporis Robur et Fortitudinem, *Sampsoni*; et ob Formam et Pulchritudinem, *Absaloni* digne et merito comparuit. . . .

Lords' Journals, I, 86

6. Sir Thomas Smith on the King (1565).

To be short, the prince is the life, the head and the authority of all things that be done in the realm of England. And to no prince is done more honour and reverence than to the king and queen of England; no man speaketh to the prince nor serveth at the table but in adoration and kneeling, all persons of the realm be bareheaded before him; insomuch that in the chamber of presence, where the cloth of estate is set, no man dare walk, yea though the prince be not there, no man dare tarry there but bareheaded. This is understood of the subjects of the realm: for all strangers be suffered there and in all places to use the manner of their country, such is the civility of our nation.

De Republica Anglorum, 62–3

[33] Cf. the debate between Hurstfield, *Trans. R. Hist. Soc.* 1967, 83 ff., and Elton, *Studies* I, 260 ff.   [34] Pp. 237 ff.
[35] Aylmer was concerned to play down the danger of a woman ruler in answer to John Knox and in support of the untried Elizabeth.

7. A Homily on Obedience (1547).

Almighty God hath created and appointed all things in heaven, earth and waters in a most excellent and perfect order. In heaven he hath appointed distinct orders and states of archangels and angels. In the earth he has assigned kings, princes, with other governors under them, all in good and necessary order. . . . Every degree of people, in their vocation, calling and office, has appointed to them their duty and order. Some are in high degree, some in low; some kings and princes, some inferiors and subjects, priests and laymen, masters and servants, fathers and children, husbands and wives, rich and poor. . . . Where there is no right order there reigneth all abuse, carnal liberty, enormity, sin, and babylonical confusion. Take aways kings, princes, rulers, magistrates, judges, and such states of God's order, no man shall ride or go by the highway unrobbed, no man shall sleep in his own house or bed unkilled, no man shall keep his wife, children and possessions in quietness; all things shall be common and there must needs follow all mischief and utter destruction. . . . God has sent us his high gift, our most dear sovereign lord, King Edward VI, with godly, wise and honourable council, with other superiors and inferiors, in a beautiful order. Wherefore let us subjects do our bounden duty . . . : let us all obey, even from the bottom of our hearts, all their godly proceedings, laws, statutes, proclamations and injunctions. . . . Let us mark well and remember that the high power and authority of kings, with their making of laws, judgments and officers, are the ordinances not of man but of God. . . . We may not resist, nor in any wise hurt, an anointed king which is God's lieutenant, vicegerent and highest minister in that country where he is king. . . . Yet let us believe undoubtedly, good Christian people, that we may not obey kings, magistrates or any other (though they be our own fathers) if they would command us to do anything contrary to God's commandments. In such a case we ought to say with the Apostles: we must rather obey God than man. But nevertheless in that case we may not in any wise resist violently or rebel against rulers or make any insurrection, sedition or tumults, either by force of arms or otherwise, against the anointed of the Lord or any of his appointed officers. But we must in such cases patiently suffer all wrongs or injuries, referring the judgment of our cause only to God. . . . Let us all therefore fear the most detestable vice of rebellion, ever knowing and remembering that he that resisteth common authority resisteth God and His ordinance, as it may be proved by many other more places of Holy Scripture. And here let us take heed that we understand not these . . . to be meant in any condition of the pretensed power of the bishop of Rome. For truly the scripture of God alloweth no such usurped power full of enormities, abuses and blasphemies. But the true meaning of these and such places be to extol and set forth God's true ordinance and the authority of God's anointed kings and of their officers appointed under them. . . .

Certain Sermons . . .

8. John Aylmer on Kingship (1559).

The regiment of England is not a mere monarchy, as some for lack of consideration think, nor a mere oligarchy, nor democracy, but a rule mixed of all these . . . the image whereof, and not the image but the thing indeed, is to be seen in the Parliament House, wherein you shall find these three estates: the king or queen, which representeth the monarch; the noblemen which be the aristocracy; and the burgesses and knights the democracy. . . . If the Parliament use their privileges, the King can ordain nothing without them. If he do, it is his fault in usurping it and their folly in permitting it; wherefore in my judgment those that in King Henry VIII's days would not grant him that his proclamations should have the force of a statute were good fathers of the country and worthy commendation in defending their liberty[36]. . . . To declare that it is not in England so dangerous a matter to have a woman ruler as men take it to be. For first it is not she that ruleth but the laws, the executors whereof be her judges, appointed by her, her justices of the peace and such other officers. . . . She maketh no statutes or laws but the honourable court of Parliament. . . . What may she do alone wherein is peril? She may grant pardon to an offender, that is her prerogative wherein if she err it is a tolerable and pitiful error to save life. She may misspend the revenues of the crown wantonly; so can kings do too, and commonly do, and yet they be kings. If on the other part the regiment were such as all hanged upon the king's or queen's will and not upon the laws written; if she might decree and make laws alone, without her senate; if she judged offences according to her wisdom and not by limitation of statutes and laws; if she might dispose alone of war and peace; if, to be short, she were a mere monarch and not a mixed ruler, you might peradventure make me to fear the matter the more. . .

An Harborowe . . .

[36] A reference to the debates which, it is reasonably supposed, reduced the Act of Proclamations (16) in scope and weight (cf. below p. 23).

9. Richard Hooker on Kingship (c. 1590).

In which respect I cannot choose but commend highly their wisdom by whom the foundations of this commonwealth have been laid; wherein, though no manner person or cause be unsubject to the king's power, yet so is the power of the king over all and in all limited that unto all his proceedings the law itself is a rule. The axioms of our regal government are these: 'Lex facit regem': the king's grant of any favour made contrary to the law is void: 'Rex nihil potest nisi quod iure potest'. . . .

Ecclesiastical Polity, VIII, c. 2 (13) (*Works*, III, 353)

9a. Anthony Brown J. in Willion v. Berkeley (1563).

If the land had been given to the king and to the heirs of his body, before the statute he could not have aliened in fee before issue had, for such alienation would have been a wrong in another person, and so should it have been in the king, if it were adjudged an alienation in fee, and therefore he could not do it: for the king cannot do any wrong, nor will his prerogative be any warrant to him to do an injury to another . . . It is a difficult argument to prove that a statute, which restrains men generally from doing wrong, leaves the king at liberty to do wrong.

Plowden, *Commentaries*, 247-8

III. THE POWERS OF THE CROWN

(i) THE ROYAL PREROGATIVE. It is commonly asserted that one of the major differences between the Tudors and Stuarts lay in their treatment of the royal prerogative: where the Stuarts spoilt acceptance by defining, the Tudors by not analysing reserved to themselves a large undefined power. But in truth the difference lay more profoundly in the content given to the term, not in any mere attitudinising over it. 'Prerogative' was the great Tudor word, stressed in particular by Henry VII and Elizabeth. The former needed it to restore the ascendancy and the finances of the Crown[37]; the latter opposed it to the interference of her subjects in delicate matters of policy.[38] Henry VIII, less in need of self-defence, also used the term more rarely: he was more likely to talk of the dignity and honour of his crown. But throughout the period prerogative did not lack precision or definition. As William Stanford explained (10), the Crown's prerogative comprised those rights enjoyed by the king which acknowledged his superior position and enabled him to discharge the task of governing. But—and this significant point would have been generally accepted in the century—this prerogative was granted by the

[37] Cf. Elton, *Studies*, 45 ff., 66 ff.   [38] Cf. below, pp. 312 ff.

laws of the realm. Addressing himself to law students, Stanford cited mainly legal examples; Thomas Smith (11) added rights of a political nature. Both, however, agreed that these privileges could be defined—were, in fact, defined by the common law of England. The lawyers (and Henry VII, too) regarded the rights arising out of the king's feudal overlordship as the most important, and these naturally had a peculiarly legal flavour.[39] But even Elizabeth, claiming that her marriage or the government of the Church were matters for her prerogative, was not extending the normal meaning of a term which accorded privilege to the personal concerns and possessions of the sovereign. Admittedly she refused to discuss how these matters came to fall within the prerogative, but that sensible policy—a refusal to bandy words—must not be regarded as an attempt to enlarge the field of privilege. In short, Tudor royal prerogative was a department of the law which conferred upon the ruler certain necessary rights not available to the subject. The Stuarts saw their prerogative very differently: to them it comprised those rights bestowed by God for which they were answerable to God only. Their prerogative was not part of the law: it was over and above it, or even over and against it. As Smith explained, *legibus solutus* meant to the Tudors a right to dispense with the law if equity required it, a necessary power of flexibility; to the Stuarts it meant true absolutism—freedom to disregard the law because that was under the king.

10. William Stanford on the King's Prerogative (1548).

Prerogativa is as much to say as a privilege or preeminence that any person hath before another, which, as it is tolerable in some, so it is most to be permitted and allowed in a prince or sovereign governor of a realm. For besides that that he is the most excellentest and worthiest part or member of the common body of the wealth, so is he also (through his good governance) the preserver, nourisher and defender of all the people, being the rest of the same body. . . . For which cause the laws do attribute unto him all honour, dignity, prerogative and preeminence, which prerogative doth not only extend to his own person but also to all other his possessions, goods and chattels. As that his person shall be subject to no man's suit, his possessions cannot be taken from him by any violence or wrongful disseisin, his goods and chattels are under no tribute, toll nor custom, nor otherwise distrainable: with an infinite number of prerogatives more, which were tedious here to recite. Howbeit, forasmuch as in every realm the king's prerogatives are no small part of the profits and commodities of the Crown of the same, and

[39] Cf. e.g. Constable, *Reading on Prerogativa Regis*.

namely within this realm of England it hath been thought good heretofore to declare and set forth in writing certain of the most highest and weightiest matters and articles touching the said prerogatives. And hereupon was there as declaration made in writing by the authority of Parliament holden in the 17th year of the reign of King Edward the 2nd[40]. . . . Howbeit, this Parliament maketh no part of the king's prerogative, but long time before it had his being by the order of the common law, as plainly may appear by them that have written before the making of the said statute of prerogative. [Citations from Glanvill, Bracton, Britton, and 21 Henry III, i.e. 1237.]   *An Exposition . . . fo. 5*

11. Sir Thomas Smith on the King's Prerogatives (1565).

The monarch of England, king or queen, hath absolutely in his power the authority of war and peace, to defy what prince it shall please him and to bid him war, and again to reconcile himself and enter into league or truce with him, at his pleasure or the advice only of his Privy Council. His Privy Council be chosen also at the prince's pleasure. . . . The prince doth participate to them all, or so many of them as he shall think good, such legations and messages as come from foreign princes, such letters or occurents as be sent to himself or his secretaries, and keepeth so many embassies and letters sent unto him secret as he will. . . . In war time and in the field the prince hath also absolute power, so that his word is law; he may put to death or to other bodily punishment whom he shall think so to deserve, without process of law or form of judgment. . . . The prince useth also absolute power in crying and decreeing the money of the realm by his proclamation only. The money is always stamped with the prince's image and title. The form, fashion, manner, weight, fineness and baseness thereof is at the discretion of the prince. . . . For all other measures and weights, as well of dry things as of wet, they have accustomed to be established and altered by the Parliament and not by the prince's proclamation only. The prince useth also to dispense with laws made, whereas equity requireth a moderation to be had, and with pains for transgression of laws where the pain of the law is applied only to the prince. But where the forfeit (as in popular actions chanceth

[40] I.e. 1324. The reference is to the so-called statute *Prerogativa Regis*, inserted by the old textbooks at the end of Edward II's reign, but now supposed to have been written in the second half of the fourteenth century. It is not a statute—i.e. not an act passed by Parliament—but probably an administrative summary of the king's common law prerogatives (cf. Holdsworth, 1, 473).

many times)[41] is part to the prince, the other part to the declarator, detector or informer, there the prince doth dispense for his own part only. Where the criminal action is intended by inquisition (that manner is called with us at the prince's suit)[42] the prince giveth absolution or pardon. . . . The prince giveth all the chief and highest offices or magistracies of the realm, be it of judgment or dignity, temporal or spiritual, and hath the tenths and first fruits of all ecclesiastical promotions, except in the Universities and certain colleges which be exempt.[43] All writs, executions and commandments be done in the prince's name. . . . The supreme justice is done in the king's name and by his authority only. The prince hath the wardship and first marriage of all those that hold lands of him in chief. And also the government of all fools natural, or such as be made by adventure of sickness and so continue, if they be landed. . . . Diverse other rights and preeminences the prince hath which be called prerogatives royal . . . which be declared particularly in the books of the common laws of England.   *De Republica Anglorum, 58–62*

(ii) THE CROWN AND LEGISLATION. In the sixteenth century, questions of the king's power tended to resolve themselves into the question of his relation to the law. What matters here is not so much his attitude to the existing law—an ancient issue really settled by the coronation oath crises of the middle ages[44]—as his behaviour towards new law. What powers had he over legislation enacted in Parliament, and what rights of independent legislation?

In the first place, the Crown could not, by prerogative action, abrogate, repeal or suspend any act of Parliament. When, for reasons of convenience or policy, the repeal of acts of attainder was released to Henry VII (**12**) or the enforcement of the first Act of Annates left to Henry VIII's letters patent (**176**), the significant point was that the authority to deal with statute—to annul it or make it effective—itself rested upon statute and could not rest elsewhere. Not even the king's tacit or express approval of an action could save the doer thereof from the operation of a statute which his deed might be

---

[41] Actions popular were actions started by private persons informing against those who offended against penal statutes, i.e. statutes which prohibited a stated offence on pain of a forfeiture or fine of which half went to the Crown and half to the informer (cf. Guth, 'Exchequer Penal Law Enforcement'; Beresford, *Econ. Hist. Rev.* 1957, pp. 221 ff.; Elton, *Star Chamber Stories*, ch. IV; Davies, *The Enforcement of English Apprenticeship*, 20 ff.; Holdsworth, IV, 355 ff.).

[42] The usual method for starting a criminal prosecution, by the inquest of a grand jury finding a 'true bill' against a named person.

[43] By statute 27 Henry VIII, c. 42.

[44] Cf. Schramm, *Hist. of the English Coronation*, ch. 7 (though he reads too much into Henry VIII's academic amendments and ignores the growth in this period of ideas of King-in-Parliament).

interpreted as offending. Gardiner's very interesting comment on this (13)—though inaccurate on the Act of Proclamations—demonstrates the acknowledged supremacy of statute over the king's will as well as the self-conscious attitude of the common lawyers in the matter. The Crown was therefore reduced to preventing the enactment of legislation displeasing to itself. Henry VII did this largely by a stringent control over parliamentary business,[45] though he sometimes went so far as to alter the finished product by adding provisos which had legal force despite their failure to receive the assent of Lords and Commons.[46] This method—more serious in its possibilities than in a substance which was always insignificant—might have been developed into a weapon of absolutism if anyone had wished to build one; instead it was abandoned. Henry VIII found influence and management sufficient to serve his purpose;[47] but Elizabeth needed the veto which she employed freely throughout her reign. Even after legislation got on the statute book, the Crown held one means of outflanking it. This was that power to dispense an individual from the effect of a law (whether common or statute) which Smith recognised as one of the royal prerogatives (11), and of which the pardoning of offenders, its sole survivor, was even then far the most common exercise. The clearest exposition of this prerogative and its effects is found in Francis Bacon's contribution to the 1601 monopolies debate (14). In practice, once again, a potentially sinister power was not abused by the Tudors to the derogation of statutory authority, though Elizabeth's employment of grants *non obstante* went well beyond her predecessors' practice. They had used it to ease the burden of the law on the subject; she seemed to come near to disposing of the law in the interests of the Crown. Still, only the Stuarts came to overwork a necessary prerogative and attempt its exploitation against the law rather than in aid of it.

Therefore, when parliamentary legislation had taken place, the Crown had only very limited means of evasion or amendment. Could it legislate on its own without seeking consent? This brings up the question of proclamations, legislative orders issued by the king, with or without the advice of his Council. Some such method was certainly necessary if the country was to be run efficiently: Parliament, after all, met only at considerable intervals, and even when it did meet many of its statutes assumed (and some specifically laid down) that the details and flexibility of the legislative programme should be left to royal proclamations. Three points remained somewhat uncertain about proclamations: the authority upon which they rested, the scope they covered, and their enforcement. All three received attention in the Act of

---

[45] Pickthorn, I, 129 f.

[46] Pollard, *Henry VII*, II, 16 f. Cf. Elton, *Hist. Journal*, XXII, 19 ff.: the practice lapsed after 1510, which indicates a new recognition of the supremacy of statute.

[47] Cf. below, pp. 292 ff.

Proclamations of 1539 (**16**). It used once to be held that this act marked the high-water mark of Tudor despotism,[48] but today few historians would regard it in that light.[49]

Proclamations were authorised by the act inasmuch as it specifically empowered the king (limited by the required consent of his Council, but this meant nothing in 1539) to 'set forth . . . his proclamations'. However, the legal validity of proclamations did not therefore begin with this act: not only had no one ever questioned the king's right to issue them, but eight years earlier Thomas Cromwell had been explicitly told by the lord chief justice what the king could do in the matter (**15**). Proclamations were one of the common law prerogatives of the Crown. The judge even used the phrase whose appearance in the act has caused so much annoyance: they were 'of as good effect as any law made by Parliament'. At most the act put aside such doubts as Cromwell himself had expressed; at the very least it deliberately grounded an existing royal prerogative in parliamentary authority.[50]

The scope and purpose of proclamations were given by practice, tradition and common law. Since they emanated from king and Council they were regarded as inferior to statute and common law. They could not (and did not) touch life or member; though they might create offences with penalties, they could not create felonies or treasons. Nor could they touch common law rights of property. All this was observed in Tudor practice. Their proclamations covered administrative, social, and economic matters—though they included religion, as the sphere of the supreme head's personal action—but never matters which both the judges and Parliament would regard as belonging to law and stature.[51] Here again the act, in section ii, only confirmed practice when it protected property and life against the attention of proclamations.

There remains the problem of enforcement. Issuing as they did from king and Council, proclamations had no force in the courts of common law. It was supposedly left to the Council, sitting as a court in Star Chamber, to do what it could to make a reality of the policy enunciated in them, but that this proved insufficient appears from the 1539 statute. Its ostensible and ultimate purpose was to secure obedience to proclamations. That purpose was proclaimed in its title and avowed in the famous and much-attacked phrase: the act did not say that proclamations could take the place of statute, but that they should be obeyed as though Parliament had made them. It has therefore been conjectured that the original bill introduced by the government in the

[48] E.g. Maitland, *English Law and the Renaissance*, 19.

[49] The best discussion of proclamations is found in Heinze and Youngs; the former (ch. 6) reviews the controversy over the 1539 act.

[50] Similar doubts may have been behind the specific authorisation of certain proclamations in the act of 1534 for customs on wine (**25**).

[51] For the texts of the documents cf. *Tudor Royal Proclamations*.

Lords wished to make proclamations enforceable in the ordinary courts and that the known opposition in Parliament was possibly directed against a reform which would free the Council of much judicial work but would also involve offenders in protracted and annoying litigation.[52] The Council set up by section iv was cumbersome and proved useless; in 1543 this part of the act had to be amended;[53] and the difficulties of the arrangement led to the repeal of both acts in 1547, leaving enforcement once again haphazard and ineffective.[54]

The act of 1539 was not, therefore, of very great significance; in large part it simply followed the common practice of Cromwell's administration by embodying in the surety of statute what had hitherto been only the uncertainty of judicial opinion, and where it was original (in its enforcement clauses) it proved unworkable. One need not be surprised that its repeal in 1547 made no difference to proclamations. Elizabeth, without the act, used them more freely than had Henry VIII with it. A treatise of the 1560's—which began by stating that 'all law which is positive consisteth either in proclamations or in acts of Parliament'—remarked that although the act of 1539 was 'now repealed' proclamations were good by the common law if they 'had been in supplement or declaration of a law that had been good'.[55] However, one can go too far in minimising the act: it did originally cause opposition in Parliament, and the version which now stands on the book was a revision produced in the Commons. The evidence is very slender and one must be careful of pressing it too far. However, the most reasonable interpretation of it would seem to be that the Lords displayed fears of arbitrary tendencies in the original act and modified it so as to stress the primary authority of statute, while the Commons concentrated on the dangers to common-law rights of life and property and may well have been responsible for the inclusion of section ii.[56] It is possible that the original draft, intent in the main on the question of enforcement, had been insufficiently nice on the problem of powers, though since the revised act readily received the royal assent one can hardly suppose really fundamental differences between the various parties. At any rate, the act as it stood—apart from its enforcement clauses—not only contented itself with giving statutory authority to an existing prerogative but went out of its way to stress the fact.

12. An Act authorising the King to repeal attainders by letters patent (1504: 19 Henry VII, c. 28).

The King our sovereign lord, considering that divers and many persons,

[52] Adair, op. cit., 42; Elton, Tudor Revolution, 344. But cf. Elton, Studies, I, 343 n. 3.

[53] 34 & 35 Henry VIII, c. 23. Some bills addressed to the statutory committee have, however, survived (Elton, Star Chamber Stories, 94).   [54] Heinze, ch. 9; Youngs, passim.

[55] Discourse upon the . . . Statutes, 103 ff.   [56] Elton, Studies, I, 345 ff.

whereof some of them . . . were and be attainted of high treason . . ., have made instant and diligent pursuit in their most humble wise to his Highness . . . to have the said attainders reversed . . ., the King's Highness of his especial grace, mercy and pity . . . is therefore inclined to hear and speed reasonably the said petitioners; So, if there were convenient time and space in the present Parliament (as it is not, for the great and weighty matters concerning the common weal of this land treated in the same and that the said Parliament draweth so near to the end, and that after the same his Highness is not minded, for the ease of his subjects, without great, necessary and urgent causes, of long time to call and summon a new Parliament), by which long tract of time the said suitors and petitioners were and should be discomforted and in despair of expedition of their suits, petitions and causes, unless convenient remedy for them were purveyed in this behalf. Wherefore, and in consideration of the premises, the King's Highness is agreed and contented that it be enacted by the Lords spiritual and temporal and the Commons in this present Parliament assembled, and by authority of the same, that the King's Highness from henceforth, during his life, shall have plain and full authority and power by his letters patent under his great seal to reverse, annull, repeal and avoid [all attainders made in the present reign or that of Richard III, down to and including the present Parliament]. And that the said letters patent . . . be as good, effectual and available in the law[57] . . . as if the same matters . . . were fully enacted, established and authorised by authority of Parliament.

Stat. Realm, II, 669

13. Stephen Gardiner to the Protector Somerset, 14 October [1547].

. . . Now whether the king may command against an act of Parliament, and what danger they may fall in that break a law with the king's consent, I daresay no man alive at this day hath had more experience what the judges and lawyers have said than I. First I had experience in my old master the Lord Cardinal,[58] who obtained his legacy by our late sovereign lord's request at Rome. . . . Yet because it was against the laws of the realm, the judges concluded the offence of the praemunire; which conclusion I bore away and take it for a law of the realm because the lawyers so said, but my reason digested it not. . . . Since that time, being of the Council, when many proclamations were devised

---

[57] I.e. pleadable in court and there to be accepted as valid evidence. [58] Wolsey.

against the carriers out of corn,[59] at such time as the transgressors should be punished the judges would answer—it might not be by the laws. Whereupon ensued the Act of Proclamations[60] at the passing of which many liberal words were spoken and a plain promise that, by authority of the Act of Proclamations, nothing should be made contrary to an act of Parliament or common law. When the bishop of Exeter and his chancellor were by one Body brought in a praemunire. . . . I reasoned with the Lord Audley, then chancellor, so far as he bade me hold my peace for fear of entering into a praemunire myself. Whereupon I stayed but concluded it seemed to me strange that a man authorised by the king (as since the King's Majesty hath taken upon him the supremacy every bishop is such one) could fall in a praemunire. After . . . the Lord Audley, then chancellor, to satisfy me familiarly. . . 'Thou art a good fellow, Bishop,' quoth he (which was the manner of his familiar speech), 'look upon the Act of Supremacy, and there the king's doings be restrained to spiritual jurisdiction; and in another act it is provided that no spiritual law shall have place contrary to a common law or act of Parliament. An this were not,' quoth he, 'you bishops would enter in with the king and by means of his supremacy order the laity as ye listed. But we will provide,' quoth he, 'that the praemunire shall ever hang over your heads, and so we laymen shall be sure to enjoy our inheritance by the common laws and acts of Parliament.'[61]

Letters of Gardiner, 390–2

14. Francis Bacon on the Prerogative and Statute.

[20 November, 1601] . . . Mr Francis Bacon said . . . I confess the bill as it is is in few words, but yet ponderous and weighty. For the prerogative royal of the prince, for my own part I ever allowed of it, and it is such as I hope shall never be discussed. The Queen, as she is our sovereign, hath both an enlarging and restraining power. For by her prerogative she may first set at liberty things restrained by statute law or otherwise; and secondly by her prerogative she may restrain things

---

[59] I.e. traders illegally exporting grain from the realm.

[60] Cf. below, Doc. 16.

[61] The complex of laws known as 'the praemunire' were passed between 1352 and 1393. They were intended to protect the king's rights against interference by foreign courts, i.e. in particular and solely against the papal court's interference with rights of ecclesiastical property in despite of action by the king's courts. Audley's argument demonstrates the expansion the laws had undergone: they were now to protect the secular courts of the realm against the action of the spiritual courts, even though the latter were also, since 1534, courts under the Crown. For praemunire, see also below, p. 339.

which be at liberty. For the first, she may grant *non obstante* contrary to the penal laws,[62] which truly according to my own conscience (and so struck himself on the breast) are as hateful to the subject as monopolies. For the second, if any man out of his own wit, industry or endeavour finds out anything beneficial for the commonwealth, or bring in any new invention which every subject of this kingdom may use; yet in regard of his pains and travail therein her Majesty perhaps is pleased to grant him a privilege to use the same only by himself or his deputies for a certain time. This is one kind of monopoly. Sometimes there is a glut of things when they be in excessive quantity, as perhaps of corn, and her Majesty gives licence of transportation to one man; this is another kind of monopoly. Sometimes there is a scarcity or a small quantity, and the like is granted also. These and divers of this nature have been in trial both at the Common Pleas upon actions of trespass, where if the judges do find the privilege good and beneficial to the commonwealth they then will allow it, otherwise disallow it. And also I know that her Majesty herself hath given commandment to her attorney-general to bring divers of them since the last Parliament to trial in the Exchequer, since which time at least fifteen or sixteen to my knowledge have been repealed, some by her Majesty's own express commandment upon complaint made unto her by petition and some by *quo warranto* in the Exchequer. But, Mr Speaker, said he (pointing to the bill) this is no stranger in this place but a stranger in this vestment; the use hath been ever to humble ourselves unto her Majesty and by petition desire to have our grievances remedied, especially when the remedy toucheth her so nigh in point of prerogative. . . . I say and say again that we ought not to deal, to judge or meddle, with her Majesty's prerogative. . .

D'Ewes, *Journals*, 644–5

15. Thomas Cromwell to the Duke of Norfolk, 15 July [1531].

. . . Mr Attorney and I both did intimate and declare the King's pleasure unto my lord chancellor who immediately sent for my lord chief justice of the King's Bench, the chief justice of the Common Pleas, the chief baron, and Mr Fitzherbert—Mr Attorney, Mr Solicitor, and I being present; and the case by my said lord chancellor opened, divers opinions there were, but finally it was concluded that all the statutes should be insearched to see whether there were any statute or

---

[62] Cf. above, p. 20. n. 41.

law able to serve for the purpose. And if there were, it was thought good that, if it should happen any accident to be whereby there might be any occasion that the money should be conveyed out of the realm, that then proclamation should be made grounded upon the said statute. . . . Upon which device search was made and a good statute found which was made in the fifth year of King Richard II[63]. . . But amongst all other things I moved unto my said lord chancellor, my lord chief justice and other that, if in case there were no law nor statute made already for any such purpose, what might the King's Highness by the advice of his Council do to withstand so great a danger. . . . To the which it was answered by my lord chief justice that the King's Highness by the advice of his Council might make proclamations and use all other policies at his pleasure as well in this case as in any other like for the avoiding of any such dangers, and that the said proclamations and policies so devised by the King and his Council for any such purpose should be of as good effect as any law made by Parliament or otherwise; which opinion, I assure your grace, I was very glad to have. . . .   Merriman, *Cromwell's Letters*, I, 409–10

16. An Act that proclamations made by the King shall be obeyed (1539: 31 Henry VIII, c. 8).

Forasmuch as the King's most royal Majesty for divers considerations by the advice of his Council hath heretofore set forth divers and sundry his Grace's proclamations, as well for and concerning divers and sundry articles of Christ's religion, as for an unity and concord to be had amongst the loving and obedient subjects of this his realm and other his dominions, and also concerning the advancement of his commonwealth and good quiet of his people, which nevertheless divers and many froward, wilful and obstinate persons have wilfully contemned and broken, not considering what a King by his regal power may do, and for lack of a direct statute and law to coarct offenders to obey the said proclamations, which being still suffered should not only encourage offenders to the disobedience of the precepts and laws of Almighty God, but also sin too much to the great dishonour of the King's most royal Majesty, who may full ill bear it, and also give too great heart and boldness to all malefactors and offenders; considering also that sudden causes and occasions fortune many times which do

[63] 5 Ric. II, c. 2.

require speedy remedies, and that by abiding for a Parliament in the meantime might happen great prejudice to ensue to the realm; and weighing also that his Majesty (which by the kingly and regal power given him by God may do many things in such cases) should not be driven to extend the liberty and supremacy of his regal power and dignity by wilfulness of froward subjects; It is therefore thought in manner more than necessary that the King's Highness of this realm for the time being, with the advice of his honourable Council, should make and set forth proclamations for the good and politic order and governance of this his realm of England, Wales and other his dominions from time to time for the defence of his regal dignity and the advancement of his commonwealth and good quiet of his people, as the cases of necessity shall require, and that an ordinary law should be provided, by the assent of his Majesty and Parliament, for the due punishment, correction and reformation of such offences and disobediences; Be it therefore enacted by the authority of this present Parliament, with the King's Majesty's, his Lords' spiritual and temporal and the Commons' assent . . . that always the King for the time being, with the advice of his honourable Council, whose names hereafter followeth, or with the advice of the more part of them, may set forth at all times by authority of this act his proclamations, under such penalties and pains and of such sort as to his Highness and his said honourable Council or the more part of them shall see[m] necessary and requisite; And that those same shall be obeyed, observed and kept as though they were made by act of Parliament for the time in them limited, unless the King's Highness dispense with them or any of them under his great seal.

II. Provided always that the words, meaning and intent of this act be not understood, interpretate, construed or extended, that by virtue of it any of the King's liege people . . . should have any of his or their inheritances, lawful possessions, offices, liberties, privileges, franchises, goods or chattels taken from them . . . nor by virtue of the said act suffer any pains of death, other than shall be hereafter in this act declared, nor that by any proclamation to be made by virtue of this act, any acts, common laws (standing at this present time in strength and force) nor yet any lawful or laudable customs of this realm . . . shall be infringed, broken or subverted; and specially all those acts standing this hour in force which have been made in the King's Highness' time; but that every such person . . . shall stand and be in the same state and condition, to every respect and purpose, as if this act or proviso had never been had or made. . . . Except such persons which shall offend any proclamation to be made by the King's Highness, his heirs or successors, for and concerning any kind of heresies against Christian religion.

* * * * * *

iv. And be it further enacted . . . that if any person or persons . . . which at any time hereafter do wilfully offend and break or obstinately not observe and keep any such proclamation . . . that then all and every such offender or offenders, being thereof within one half year next after their or his offence committed accused, and thereof within 18 months next after the same offence convicted by confession or lawful witness and proofs before the archbishop of Canterbury metropolitan, the chancellor of England, the lord treasurer of England, the president of the King's most honourable Council, the lord privy seal, the great chamberlain of England, lord admiral, lord steward (or grand master), lord chamberlain of the King's most honourable Household, two other bishops being of the King's Council such as his Grace shall appoint for the same, the secretary, the treasurer and controller of the King's most honourable Household, the master of the Horse, the two chief judges and the master of the Rolls for the time being, the chancellor of the Augmentations, the chancellor of the Duchy, the chief baron of the Exchequer, the two general surveyors, the chancellor of the Exchequer, the undertreasurer of the same, the treasurer of the King's Chamber for the time being, in the Star Chamber at Westminster or elsewhere, or at the least before the half of the number afore rehearsed, of which number the lord chancellor, the lord treasurer, the lord president of the King's most honourable Council, the lord privy seal, the chamberlain of England, the lord admiral, the two chief judges for the time being, or two of them, shall be two, shall lose and pay such penalties, forfeitures of sums of money . . . and also suffer such imprisonments of his body as shall be expressed, mentioned and declared in any such proclamation. . . .

v. And be it further enacted . . . that the lord chancellor, the lord privy seal, and either of them, with the assent of six of the forenamed, shall have power and authority by their discretions, upon every information to be given to them or to either of them touching the premises, to cause process to be made against all and singular such offenders by writs under the King's great seal or under his Grace's privy seal in form following, that is to say: first by proclamation under a pain or a penalty

29

by the discretion of the aforesaid councillors appointed for the awarding of process, and if he appear not to the same without a lawful excuse, then the said councillors to award out another proclamation upon allegiance of the same offender, for the due examination, trial and conviction of every such person and persons as shall offend contrary to this act, for the due execution to be had of and for the same in manner and form as is above remembered; Except it be within the liberty of the County Palatine of the Duchy of Lancaster, and in case it so be, then to pass by the chancellor of the King's Duchy of Lancaster under the seal of the said Duchy, with the assent of six at the least of the aforenamed councillors.

[VI. Offenders who 'obstinately, willingly or contemptuously avoid and depart out of' the realm, in order to escape the necessity of answering for offences against the act, are to suffer death as traitors and to forfeit their lands and goods.]

* * * * * *

VIII. And be it further enacted, that if it happen our said sovereign lord the King to decease (whose life God long preserve) before such time as that person which shall be his next heir or successor to the imperial crown of this realm shall accomplish and come to the age of eighteen years, that then all and singular proclamations which shall be in any wise made and set forth into any part of this realm or other the King's dominions by virtue of this act, within the foresaid years of the said next heir or successor, shall be set forth in the successor's name then being King, and shall import or bear underwritten the full names of such of the King's honourable Council then being as shall be the devisers or setters-forth of the same, which shall be in this case the whole number afore rehearsed, or at the least the more part of them, or else the proclamations to be void and of none effect.

* * * * * *

Stat. Realm, III, 726-8

(iii) SUPPRESSION OF RIVALS. Though the Tudors inherited a strong kingship, they could not simply be satisfied with reviving its powers and extending its impalpable aspects. To begin with especially, the Crown was not in sole control of the country. Recent events—the lack of governance for which the fifteenth century is so notorious—had greatly accentuated the problem of the 'overmighty subject', the individual with territorial and military power sufficient to rival the king's at least in his locality; while more troublesome in the long run were the ancient rights (liberties and franchises) enjoyed by many—individuals, corporations, even large tracts of land. In this double task of reducing all subjects, however great, to obedience to the Crown and of consolidating the realm into one unit under the king's sole jurisdiction, much progress was made in the century.

The elimination of the overmighty subject is the more familiar story.[64] The development of so-called 'bastard feudalism' had produced the great lord with his bands of retainers—followers (often armed) sworn to do his service and willing, despite ostensible reservations, to do it even to the detriment of the king's allegedly superior claim to their allegiance. To those he retained the lord would give his badge or livery as the visible sign of their interested obedience; he rewarded them with gifts of office, land or money; and he usually agreed to maintain their cause in any law-suit by his influence and power. This last evil, maintenance, led to the widespread decay of justice and the corruption of its machinery, both judges and juries being quite often in the pay (or at the mercy) of the maintainer. That is the traditional picture, and in large measure it is no doubt correct. But it must be remembered that the retaining of 'servants'—men lower in the social scale but often themselves lords to lesser men—merely represented the social structure of a hierarchical age which did not alter with the accession of the Tudors. The Crown did not attempt to interfere with this; it rightly contented itself with increasing the number of men sworn servants of the king and with eradicating the evils involved in retaining. What, therefore, was really at issue was not the existence of masters and men through the social scale but the abuse of the power bestowed by these relationships, as well as illicit retaining by indentures which failed to reserve the first allegiance to the king or (later) by failure to obtain a licence.[65] The problem could not be tackled with weapons which made the delicate distinctions implicit in social usage, and Henry VII's legislation spoke as though all retaining other than that of domestic servants was to be abolished.[66] In particular is this true of the act of 1504 (**18**). This, the last and most comprehensive Statute of Liveries, summed up a large body of law; its independent significance lies in the penalties imposed and the regularisation of enforcement. Sections vi and vii, which enabled prosecutions to be brought without the common law procedure of indictment and even empowered the officers of the Crown to act without information being laid before them, tackled the real problem, the problem of bringing notorious offenders to judgment. In actual fact, these clauses gave parliamentary authority to the habitual procedure of the Council which had certainly not been

[64] E.g. Tanner, 4, 7 ff., though his views must be modified by what follows here.

[65] For a discussion of lawful and unlawful retaining, cf. Dunham, *Lord Hastings' Indentured Retainers.*

[66] Holdsworth, IV, 520.

hampered in its work by the absence of such authority. The act lapsed in 1509. Decades of vigilance were needed to make the law fully effective; revivals of these quasi-feudal troubles came at intervals; but it was one problem which did prove amenable to the resources of the Crown.

The problem of consolidating the realm required more drastic, but in many ways also easier, action. Here established legal rights had to be withdrawn. By ancient prescription, or more commonly by explicit royal grant, many 'liberties' had grown up, from individual manors to such palatinates as Lancaster and Durham, whose characteristic it was that the king's writs did not carry exclusive—or sometimes any—authority there. The Tudors found the problem approaching solution, inasmuch as the great lay liberties had mostly fallen back to the Crown[67]; only Durham, as an ecclesiastical liberty, retained a palatine organisation over which the Crown had little control.[68] Several liberties, like Tynedale or Ripon, were notorious refuges for evildoers because they could keep out the king's sheriff. The lesser liberties had been reduced to order by a process of invasion carried on by the common law throughout the middle ages.[69] Rights of manorial jurisdiction mattered little now that all freemen could and did use the king's courts if they wished, while villeinage was nearly gone; and as a rule the liberty-holder could not stop the king's writ but only insist on his right to execute it.[70]

Nevertheless, there remained areas of jurisdiction—and therefore of power— where the king was rivalled or even replaced by a subject. Since these privileges rested on good title it was hard to see how they could be destroyed, until the weapon was found in the act of Parliament. Minor invasions of such rights were sanctioned by statute under Henry VII, as when the liberty of Tynedale was incorporated in the shire of Northumberland[71] or the law-making powers of borough-corporations subjected to the king's control (17).[72] Piecemeal tinkering was abandoned for sweeping measures in the act of 1536 (19) which in effect destroyed the difference between liberties and ordinary shire ground. Even though Lancashire and Durham continued to stand out in certain formal ways, all England was now one unit

[67] In the County Palatine of Lancaster all process was indeed in the name of the duke, but since after 1399 the ducal privileges were annexed to the Crown the distinction was one in name only (Somerville, *Duchy of Lancaster*, I, 142 ff.). Its sole remaining significance was that tenants of the duchy were regarded as mesne tenants of the Crown, with fiscal advantages to themselves (Elton, *Tudor Revolution*, 243).

[68] Cf. Tanner, 350 f.

[69] Holdsworth, I, 132 ff.

[70] If he failed, the king had further weapons. For an example cf. the Canterbury liberty of Hayes (Middx.) in 1530, obliged to admit royal writs which were, however, executed by the archbishop's bailiffs (Elton, *Star Chamber Stories*, 198).

[71] 11 Henry VII, c. 9.

[72] This was not the first act to concern itself with the rights of guilds and so forth: again, Henry VII was hardly engaged in a 'new' policy (Pickthorn, I, 137 f.).

subject in all matters of jurisdiction and administration to the power of the Crown.[73]

It remained to bring the non-English parts of the realm into the unitary state. The attempt was successful in Wales and failed in Ireland. By the mid-1530's the Welsh marches had been reduced to some order and more drastic steps had a hope of success. Thus two great statutes of 1536 and 1543 incorporated the old principality in England, reorganised the marcher lordships as shire ground, and extended the ordinary local administration of the English county to those regions.[74] Though they remained subject to special courts (the Court of Great Sessions in civil matters and the Council in the Marches of Wales in criminal) they had in effect lost their separate and extraordinary character and become part of the 'imperial' Crown of England.[75] Ireland, on the other hand, posed little except recurring problems, and it remains unclear whether the history of its government really belongs in a treatise on the Tudor constitution. It had its own important history of government, comprised of English attempts to exercise rule and Irish switches from compliance to resistance and back again, and it deserves a volume of its own. Earlier views, which spoke of a form of anarchy outside the Dublin Pale and a few towns, have been successfully controverted,[76] but for the rest the whole theme is at present beset by unresolved (though courteous) controversies. Was pre-1534 Ireland a successful example of delegated government or a denial of all English overlordship? Was a new start made in 1534 or 1541 or 1570? What was involved in the introduction of the Reformation into Ireland?[77] It can, however, be agreed that Henry VII made an unsustained attempt to govern through English officials, that Cromwell meant to bring Ireland within the unitary realm he was creating, that under Mary earlier efforts at peaceful assimilation gave way before the aggressive ambitions of new English settlers, and that Elizabeth in consequence faced disaffection and rebellion which made the problem a mainly colonial and military one, to be solved only by a comprehensive reconquest. Two points of constitutional importance may be noted. In 1494, Henry VII's deputy Edward Poynings secured the subjection of the Irish Parliament to the English Council (though the Council commonly responded to initiatives from Ireland), and in 1541 Henry VIII turned his lordship of Ireland into a kingship (through this was forced upon him by Irish politicians and long resisted by him).

[73] For the whole problem of franchises under the early Tudors see Thornley, *Tudor Studies*, 182 ff.

[74] 27 Henry VIII, c. 26, and 34 & 35 Henry VIII, c. 26.

[75] For Wales under the Tudors cf. the writings of P. R. Roberts (in List of Books) and Williams, *Welsh Reformation Essays*.

[76] Quinn, *Irish Hist. Studies*, I, 354 ff.; Ellis, 'Administration', and *Irish Hist. Studies*, xx, 235 ff.

[77] Bradshaw, *Irish Const. Revolution*; Ellis, *Hist. Journal*, xix, 807 ff. and xxiii, 497 ff.; Canny, *Elizabethan Conquest*; Bradshaw, *Hist. Journal*, xxi, 475 ff.

17. An Act that private and unlawful statutes shall not be made (1504: 19 Henry VII, c. 7).

[Recites 15 Henry VI, c. 6, compelling ordinances made by guilds and other corporations to be approved by the justices of the peace or mayors of towns and be entered before them as of record. This act having now expired]

... Be it therefore ordained, established and enacted ... that no masters, wardens, and fellowships of crafts or mysteries, nor any of them, nor any rulers of guilds or fraternities, take upon them to make any acts or ordinances, ne to execute any acts or ordinances by them here afore made, in disheritance or diminution of the prerogative of the King, nor of other, nor against the common profit of the people, but if the same acts or ordinances be examined and approved by the chancellor, treasurer of England, and chief justices of either Bench, or three of them, or before both the justices of Assizes in their circuit or progress in that shire where such acts or ordinances be made, upon the pain of forfeiture of £40 for every time that they do the contrary ...

[II. Corporations shall not make orders to restrain anyone from suing in the King's courts.] *Stat. Realm*, II, 652-3

18. *De Retentionibus Illicitis* (Statute of Liveries, 1504: 19 Henry VII, c. 14).

The King our sovereign lord calleth to his remembrance that where before this time divers statutes[78] for punishment of such persons that give or receive liveries, or that retain any person or persons or be retained with any person or persons ... have been made and established, and that notwithstanding divers persons have taken upon them some to give and some to receive liveries and to retain and be retained ... and little or nothing is or hath been done for the punishment of the offenders in that behalf, Wherefore our sovereign lord the King, by the advice [etc.] ... hath ordained, established and enacted that all his statutes and ordinances afore this time made against such as make unlawful retainers and such as so be retained, or that give or receive livery, be plainly observed and kept and put in due execution.

II. And over that, our said sovereign lord the King ordaineth, establisheth, and enacteth by the said authority, that no person, of what

---

[78] Statutes against retaining had been framed in 1399, 1401, 1406, 1411, 1429 and 1468.

estate or degree or condition he be . . . privily or openly give any livery or sign or retain any person, other than such as he giveth household wages unto without fraud or colour, or that he be his manual servant or his officer or man learned in the one law or in the other,[79] by any writing, oath, promise, livery, sign, badge, token, or in any other manner wise unlawfully retain; and if any do the contrary, that then he run and fall in the pain and forfeiture for every such livery and sign, badge or token, so accepted, 100s., and the taker and acceptor of every such livery, badge, token or sign, to forfeit and pay for every such livery and sign, badge or token, so accepted, 100s., and for every month that he useth or keepeth such livery or sign, badge or token, after that he hath taken or accepted the same, to forfeit and pay 100s., and every person that by oath, writing or promise, or in any other wise, unlawfully retain, privily or openly, and also every such person that is so retained, to forfeit and pay for every such time 100s., and as well every person that so retaineth as every person that is so retained to forfeit and pay for every month that such retainer is continued, 100s. . . .

III. And also it is ordained and enacted that no person of what estate [or] condition he be . . . name or cause himself to be named servant or retained to or with any person, or buy or cause to be bought or wear any gown as a livery gown, sign or token of the suit or livery of any person, or any badge, token or sign of any person, upon pain of forfeiture for every day or time that he doth, 40s., and also to have imprisonment by the discretion of the judges or persons afore whom he shall be thereof convicted, and that without bail or mainprize.

[IV–V. Justices of the peace shall make enquiry at their sessions of all persons suspected of unlawful retaining.]

VI. Moreover the King our sovereign lord, by the advice, assent and authority aforesaid, hath ordained, established and enacted, that every person that will sue or complain before the chancellor of England or the keeper of the King's great seal in the Star Chamber or before the King in his Bench, or before the King and his Council attending upon his most royal person wheresoever he be, so that there be 3 of the same Council at the least of the which two shall be lords spiritual or temporal, against any person or persons offending or doing against the form of this ordinance or any other of the premises, be admitted by their discretion to give information. . . . And that upon the same

---

[79] I.e., common or civil law.

all such persons be called by writ, subpoena, privy seal, or otherwise, And the said chancellor or keeper of the seal, the King in his Bench, or the said Council to have power to examine all persons defendants and every of them, as well by oath as otherwise, and to adjudge him or them convict or attaint, as well by such examination as otherwise, in such penalties as is aforesaid as the case shall require; . . . And also the same party plaintiff or informer shall have such reasonable reward of that that by his complaint shall grow to the King as shall be thought reasonable by the discretion of the said chancellor or keeper of the great seal, justices, or Council.

vii. And also it is enacted by the said authority that the said chancellor or keeper of the great seal, justices, or Council have full authority and power by this statute to do send by writ, subpoena, privy seal, warrant or otherwise by their discretion, for any person or persons offending or doing contrary to the premises without any suit or information made or put before them or any of them, and the same person or persons to examine by oath or otherwise by their discretions, and to adjudge all such persons as shall be found guilty in the premises by verdict, confession, examination, proofs or otherwise, in the said forfeitures and pains as the case shall require, as though they were condemned therein after the course of the common law, and to commit such offenders to ward and to award execution according.

viii. . . . And that all manner of writings or indentures between any person herebefore made, whereby any person is retained contrary to this act, that indenture or writing, as touching any such retainer only and no further, be void and of none effect: This act to take his effect and beginning for such retainers and offences and other misdemeanours as shall be done, had or made contrary to the form of this act after the Feast of Pentecost next coming only, and the same act to continue and endure during the life of our said sovereign lord the King that now is and no longer.

*   *   *   *   *   *

x. Provided also that this act extend not to the punishment of any person or persons the which by the virtue of the King's placard or writing signed with his hand and sealed with his privy seal or signet, shall take, appoint or indent with any persons to do and to be in a readiness to do the King service in war, or otherwise at his commandment, so that they that shall have such placard or writing for their part use not by that retainer, service, attendance, or any other wise the person or persons that they shall take, appoint or indent with, nor the persons that so do indent to do the King service use not themselves for their part in doing service or giving attendance to them that shall have authority by reason of the King's writing to take, appoint or indent with them, in any thing concerning the said act otherwise than shall be comprised in the same the King's placard or writing, and that placard or writing to endure during the King's pleasure and no longer.

XI. Provided also that this act extend not to any livery to be given by any serjeants at the law at their making or creation, or to be given by any executors at the interment of any person for any mourning array, or to be given by any guild, fraternity, or craft corporate, or by the mayors and sheriffs of the city of London, or by any other mayor or sheriff or chief officers of any city, borough, town or port of this realm of England, during their time of his office and by reason of the same, or to be given by any abbot or prior or other chief head or governor or officer of any monastery, abbey, or priory, or other places corporate, given to their farmers or tenants or otherwise, according as it hath been used and accustomed in the same monastery, abbey or priory.   *Stat. Realm*, II, 658–60

19. An Act for recontinuing of certain Liberties and Franchises heretofore taken from the Crown (1536: 27 Henry VIII, c. 24).

Where divers of the most ancient prerogatives and authorities of justice appertaining to the imperial crown of this realm have been severed and taken from the same by sundry gifts of the King's most noble progenitors, kings of this realm, to the great diminution and detriment of the royal estate of the same and to the hindrance and great delay of justice; For reformation whereof be it enacted by the authority of this present Parliament that no person or persons, of what estate or degree soever they be of, from the first day of July which shall be in the year of our Lord God 1536, shall have any power or authority to pardon or remit any treasons, murders, manslaughters or any kinds of felonies . . . or any outlawries for any such offences afore rehearsed, committed, perpetrated, done or divulged, or hereafter to be committed, done or divulged, by or against any person or persons in any parts of this realm, Wales, or the marches of the same; but that the

King's Highness, his heirs and successors kings of this realm, shall have the whole and sole power and authority thereof united and knit to the imperial crown of this realm, as of good right and equity it appertaineth, any grants, usages, prescription, act or acts of Parliament, or any other thing to the contrary thereof notwithstanding.

II. And be it also enacted . . . that no person or persons, of what estate, degree or condition soever they be, from the said first day of July shall have any power or authority to make any justices of eyre, justices of assize, justices of peace, or justices of gaol delivery, but that all such officers and ministers shall be made by letters patents under the King's great seal in the name and by authority of the King's Highness, his heirs kings of this realm, in all shires, counties, counties palatine and other places of this realm, Wales and marches of the same or in any other his dominions, at their pleasure and wills, in such manner and form as justices of eyre, justices of assize, justices of peace, and justices of gaol delivery be commonly made in every shire of this realm; any grants, usages, prescriptions, allowances, act or acts of Parliament, or any other thing or things to the contrary thereof notwithstanding.

III. And be it further enacted . . . that all original writs and judicial writs,[80] and all manner of indictments of treason, felony or trespass, and all manner of process to be made upon the same in every county palatine and other liberty within this realm of England, Wales and marches of the same, shall from the said first day of July be made only in the name of our sovereign lord the King, and his heirs kings of England, and that every person or persons having such county palatine or any other such liberty to make such originals, judicials, or other process of justice, shall make the teste[81] in the said original writs and judicial in the name of the same person or persons that have such county palatine or liberty. And that in every writ and indictment that shall be made within any such county palatine or liberty, after the said first day of July next coming, whereby it shall be supposed anything to be done against the King's peace, shall be made and supposed to be done only against the King's peace, his heirs and successors, and not against the peace of any other person or persons, whatsoever they be; any act of

---

[80] Writs in civil actions are either 'original' or 'judicial'. An original writ issues out of Chancery before the suit is begun and is the foundation of it. A judicial writ issues out of the court where the original is returned, after the suit is begun by original writ.

[81] The 'teste' was the final clause in a royal writ.

Parliament, grant, custom, usage or allowance in eyre before this time had, granted or used to the contrary notwithstanding.

IV. Provided alway that justices of assize, justices of gaol delivery, and justices of peace to be made and assigned by the King's Highness within the county palatine of Lancaster shall be made and ordained by commission under the King's usual seal of Lancaster, in manner and form as hath been accustomed; anything in this act to the contrary thereof notwithstanding.

[v–xviii elaborate the King's rights within liberties, reducing these last in effect to the same condition as parts not enjoying liberty.]

XIX. Provided alway and be it enacted, that Cuthbert now bishop of Durham,[82] and his successors bishops of Durham, and their temporal chancellor of the county palatine of Durham for the time being, and every of them, shall from henceforth be justices of peace within the said county palatine of Durham, and shall exercise and use all manner things within the same county palatine that appertaineth or belongeth to any justice of peace within any county of this realm of England to do, exercise and use, by virtue and authority that they be justice of peace, in as ample and large manner as any other justices of peace in any county within this realm have or might do, exercise or use; any thing or things in this act contained to the contrary notwithstanding.

[xx. The same proviso for the archbishop of York within the liberty of Hexham.]   *Stat. Realm*, III, 555–8

IV. THE REVENUES OF THE CROWN

The royal revenue was divided into ordinary and extraordinary, the former 'the king's own' either by prerogative right or permanent grant, the latter obtained when need arose. In theory the Crown was supposed to govern with the assistance of the ordinary revenue only; royal desire to remain independent of outside authority and national reluctance to pay taxes perpetuated a concept which rising prices and increasing government commitments had rendered invalid long before the century was out. Extraordinary revenue, supposedly collected only on special and by definition rare occasions, came in the 1590's to be common enough to make taxation a reasonably regular part of the royal income. But no one as yet admitted this. Thus the 1551 financial statement (**20**) took account only of the ordinary revenue, and even when more was sought Elizabethan administrators thought first of

[82] Tunstall.

increasing the yield of the ordinary sources and not of regularising parliamentary revenue.[83]

The ordinary revenue consisted of the Crown lands, the customs, the feudal revenue, the profits of justice, and after 1534 of income derived from the Church.[84]

The Crown lands formed the basis of Henry VII's restoration of the royal finances. Although some old-established land revenue came in from ancient demesne and the various farms (compositions) of shires and boroughs, this amounted to very little. The real Crown lands were those belonging to the Tudors by inheritance, confiscation and forfeiture. Thus Henry VII started with his own Richmond lands, with the duchy of Lancaster (the biggest single accumulation of land in the kingdom and annexed to the Crown since 1399), with the Yorkist lands (duchy of York, earldom of March), with the Warwick and Beauchamp lands acquired by Edward IV, and so forth. Fresh additions arose from resumptions, or as older grants fell in and traitors forfeited their property.[85] The biggest accession came from the Church, with the vesting of all monastic property in the Crown (1536–40).[86] Land revenue consisted overwhelmingly of the rents paid by tenants and leaseholders which the Crown found it difficult to expand to keep pace with rising prices, so that in the total picture of the royal finances the relative value of Crown lands declined steadily. In addition it proved fatally easy to realise capital by the sales which every emergency provoked. Much of the monastic gains was sold off in the crises of the 1540's and 1550's, while Elizabeth sold to establish her solvency in the 1560's and again in the 1590's to finance war. Even so, the lands remained a vital part of the Crown's finances. Henry VII increased their yield from about £3,700 in 1491 to about £40,000 at the end of the reign; Cromwell added something like £100,000 p.a.; and even after all the losses incurred in the next sixty years, Elizabeth's receiver-general of Crown lands still accounted for an average of over £60,000 p.a. at the end of the century.[87]

The customs revenue, on the other hand, should have more readily kept pace with inflation, and although Tudor governments never extracted all possible yield from this source they improved it steadily.[88] Down to the reign

[83] Docs. 70 and 72 throw some light on the classification of the finances. Administration is discussed below, pp. 129 ff.

[84] This leaves out some lesser and occasional sources, such as vacancies of episcopal sees or sales of woods, but it accounts for the regular bulk of the revenue.

[85] Wolffe, *Crown Lands*.

[86] Below, pp. 378 ff.

[87] All figures are approximate. Such tables as exist are neither fully reliable nor properly analysed. For land revenue, cf. Wolffe, *Crown Lands* and *Eng. Hist. Rev.*, LXXXIX, 225 ff.; Richardson, *Augmentations*; Dietz, *Exchequer in Elizabeth's Reign*, 86 ff.

[88] From £27,000 in 1505, to £40,000 round about 1540, £83,000 in 1559, and about £100,000 in the 1590's (Dietz, *Eng. Gov. Finance*, 80, 206, 208; *Exchequer in Elizabeth's Reign*, 86 ff.).

of Mary they enjoyed the established customs and subsidies[89] **(22)** which had developed in the later middle ages and were consolidated in the reign of Edward III.[90] The customs were in origin prerogative, while subsidies (tunnage and poundage) rested on a parliamentary grant, made under the Tudors for life in the first Parliament of each reign **(23)**. Despite a restatement in 1507, the rates at which they were levied remained pretty well unaltered until the books of rates of 1558, 1583 and 1590 raised the valuation on the average by 75 per cent.[91] However, new commerce as well as new needs called for additional levies, the so-called impositions. Such new duties were rarely resorted to before the reign of Mary, but thereafter the declining value of the Crown lands forced the government to extract more from trade. The favourite target was wine imports, but new duties were also levied on cloth and other goods exported.[92] Impositions were linked with a complicated system of customs farming,[93] but the more important issue here is their legality. Though there was no serious challenge until the reign of James I, it always remained uncertain by what right the Crown imposed such unparliamentary duties. The act of 1534 which empowered the Crown by proclamation to suspend or impose certain customs **(25)** justified these powers by citing the king's control over commercial treaties and therefore over the regulation of trade, and this became the classic Stuart argument for the prerogative of creating impositions. However, the act was limited to the life of Henry VIII and never revived for any of his successors. Moreover, the Crown's special powers were here confined to customs established by statute, while impositions proper must be defined as new customs created by the Crown. It therefore appears that Elizabethan activities in this matter rested simply upon the prerogative, and the precedents then established without challenge gave a strong case to James I.

The feudal revenues were those to which the king was entitled as feudal overlord. They included the two lawful aids of Magna Carta, on the knighting of his eldest son and the marriage of his eldest daughter; Henry VII was the last king to collect these, and he allowed Parliament to compound for them.[94] Rights which acquired much importance in the reign of Elizabeth, as inflation did its work, were purveyance and pre-emption—the privilege of obtaining supplies and transport for the royal Household at prices fixed arbitrarily below market rates.[95] More important were the dues owed by

[89] 'Subsidy' in this sense was a technical term for part of the customs.
[90] Cf. the chart in Gras, *Early English Customs*, 86.
[91] Gras, *op. cit.* 125, 694 ff.; Dietz, *Exchequer . . .* , 68.
[92] Cf. Gras, *op. cit.* 89 ff.; Dietz, *Eng. Public Finance*, 314 ff., 362 ff.
[93] Dietz, *Eng. Public Finance*, ch. XIV; Newton, 'The Great Farm of the Customs', *Trans. R. Hist. Soc.*, 1918, 129 ff.
[94] Tanner, 600 f.
[95] Woodworth, *Trans. Amer. Philos. Soc.*, 1945, 1 ff.

tenants-in-chief for their lands: relief (payable on the accession of an heir), escheats (return of lands if there was no heir), wardship of a minor heir, the marriage of a minor heiress, custody of the lands of widows and idiots. These latter—especially wardship—were profitable sources of revenue, whether administered directly or (as was more common) sold to interested parties.[96] They were thoroughly exploited by Henry VII and remained a vital part of the revenue, though Burghley as master of Wards was careful not to rouse anger by too energetic a use of the prerogative powers involved. In the last years of Elizabeth, Robert Cecil, succeeding his father, sharpened the policy and increased the yield. The total varied widely, around an average of £20,000 p.a. which rose towards the end of the century to £30,000 and over.[97]

Profits of justice, too, naturally varied a good deal from year to year. Among them must be included the fees taken for the issue of writs and letters under the great seal (collected by the Hanaper of Chancery), the fines and amercements levied in the common law and prerogative courts, and the profits obtained from enforcing penal legislation. Penal statutes—which imposed a specific fine or forfeiture for a given offence—increased greatly in number from Henry VII's reign onwards; their enforcement produced both cash and the bonds (obligations and recognisances) which played a great part under Henry VII, received attention under Cromwell, and intermittently brought gains even to the government of Elizabeth which could not afford to cause too much annoyance to the principal victims, enclosing gentry and smuggling merchants.[98]

The financial benefits of the supreme headship were embodied in 1534 in the grant to the Crown of the clerical first fruits and tenths (26). Every new incumbent of every benefice in England, from the highest to the lowest, was thereby compelled to pay one year's income to the Crown; at the same time he had to find an annual payment of one-tenth the clear value of his preferment (an income tax of 2s. in the £). This revenue, again, varied in the nature of things. It averaged approximately £40,000 p.a. under Henry VIII.[99] Mary gave it up, but Elizabeth resumed it, receiving between £15,000 and £25,000 a year from it.[100]

These, then, were the ordinary or regular revenues of the Crown. Totals cannot at present be given, but a rough estimate yields £100,000 p.a. down to 1530, £220,000 after Cromwell's additions, and between £200,000 and

[96] On wardship cf. Bell, *Court of Wards*; Hurstfield, *History*, 1952, 131 ff., and *Queen's Wards*; Constable, *Prerogativa Regis*, pp. XI ff. See also below, p. 133, on the Court of Wards.
[97] Bell, *Court of Wards*, table opposite p. 192.
[98] For penal statutes see the references cited above, p. 20 n. 41 and Dietz, *Eng. Gov. Finance*, 33 ff.; Richardson, *Tudor Chamber Admin.*, 141 ff.; Elton, *Studies*, I, 49 ff.
[99] Dietz, *Eng. Gov. Finance*, 221.
[100] Dietz, *Exchequer . . .* , 80 ff.

£300,000 throughout the reign of Elizabeth, the total increasing fairly steadily as prices rose but never remotely in step with them. In any case, what matters is whether income sufficed for expenditure, a happiness granted only to Henry VII after about 1494 and to Henry VIII for a short time after the Dissolution. War,[101] inflation, the cost of government, and at times extravagance saw to it that the Crown could never live of its own (e.g. **21**). The gap was filled by the extraordinary revenue: taxation, national loans in lieu of taxation, and genuine loans at interest.

Direct taxation could only be levied if assented to by Parliament: that principle was established by the middle of the fourteenth century. The traditional parliamentary tax was the Fifteenth and Tenth, a levy on movable property respectively rural and urban. Fixed in 1334 by composition with the localities, it yielded about £30,000 in the sixteenth century.[102] It was possible partly to overcome its insufficiency and rigidity by granting several Fifteenths and Tenths at one time; by Elizabeth's reign the grants nearly always consisted of two or three. However, there were also attempts to devise new taxes to trap the nation's wealth more accurately, such as the graduated poll tax of 1512 (**27**) and the various subsidies (proportionate levies on income, at a rate of between 1 and 4 shillings in the £) with which Wolsey experimented between 1514 and 1523.[103] Down to 1547, the subsidy, carefully assessed and collected, yielded up to £120,000 at a time, but tax evasion severely reduced yields thereafter. In Elizabeth's reign Parliament began granting several subsidies at once rather than contemplate an overhaul of the antiquated system. The clergy, too, paid subsidies by consent (which they granted in their Convocations), in the shape of 'dismes' (or tenths of income) and later at a rate of shillings in the £.[104] The total effect of direct taxation fell well short of the resources of the country; at the same time, all those ossified compositions led to an unequal distribution of the burden. Down to 1534, taxation was always justified on the traditional grounds (war or the threat of war); thereafter peacetime demands became commonplace.[105] Though the Commons could never be trusted not to get stubborn over their grants, it is notable that the two periods of most intensive taxation (the 1540's and 1590's) passed off with relatively little trouble on that score; the worst difficulty occurred in 1523.

---

[101] The far from serious operations of 1558–63 cost about £750,000 (Dietz, *Eng. Public Finance*, 16); four years of war with Spain after 1588 cost well over a million (Cheyney, *History*, II, 226); and the intensive last stage of the Irish conquest (1595–1603) was reckoned to have run to nearly two millions (Dietz, *Eng. Public Finance*, 433 n. 15).

[102] Dietz, *Eng. Gov. Finance*, 13 f.

[103] The only satisfactory study so far covers only the first half of the period: Schofield, 'Lay Taxation'.

[104] Scarisbrick, *J. Eccl. Hist.*, XI, 41 ff.; Heal, *Continuity and Change*, 92 ff.

[105] Elton, *War and Econ. Development*, 33 ff.

Not only were the taxes levied insufficient for the government's needs; worse, even when granted they usually took years to collect. Wolsey, in 1523, therefore experimented with an 'anticipation', offering easier terms to those who would pay their taxes earlier than Parliament had stipulated.[106] More commonly, the Crown used the security of subsidies to borrow either abroad or at home. All Tudor governments relied on interest-bearing loans from individuals, houses or companies, but beyond the fact that Henry VII and Elizabeth scrupulously maintained their credit by repayment while Henry VIII had his debts cancelled by Parliament in 1529, virtually nothing is yet known of this important aspect of government finance. The Crown would naturally have preferred to do without such borrowing and to circumvent Parliament's control over taxation. The Yorkist expedient of a benevolence—ostensibly a free gift, in fact a forced and unauthorised tax— was declared illegal by a statute of 1484; however, Henry VII, successfully pleading military needs, levied one in 1491, and Henry VIII (using a sporadic threat of force) got another in 1545.[107] More common were the so-called forced loans, or loans on privy seal.[108] These in effect were tax assessments not authorised by Parliament and justified by giving security for repayment in promissory notes under the privy seal. Wolsey's 'Amicable Grant' of 1525, abandoned in the face of violent opposition, was based on this notion;[109] several more were successfully collected by Henry VIII and Mary, whose last 'loan' in 1557 did not even pretend that the money would be repaid and was therefore a thinly disguised benevolence.[110] Elizabeth, too, employed privy seal loans several times, but though she did her best to repay as promised (28a) she met much individual opposition.[111] It was becoming ever more impossible to finance government without resort to Parliamentary taxation.

A word should be said about the use of casual income and windfalls. To a degree which was really disgraceful and illustrates the shaky financial position of Tudor governments, reliance was placed on such unrepeatable revenue as the pensions paid by France under treaty after 1492 and 1518, or on the praemunire fine of £118,000 imposed on the clergy in 1531. There was also the disguised revenue represented by Elizabeth's practice of conducting her policy abroad through joint-stock companies of which she was but one shareholder. Of all the aspects of Tudor government, finance was the most antiquated and most beset by problems, a situation for which governments and taxpayers were jointly responsible. Nevertheless, in spite of all these

---

[106] Pollard, *Wolsey*, 133 f.
[107] Dietz, *Eng. Gov. Finance*, 56, 165–6.
[108] *Ibid.*, 163.
[109] Pollard, *Wolsey*, 141 ff.
[110] Dietz, *Eng. Gov. Finance*, 211, and Doc. 28 which shows the method of collection.
[111] Dietz, *English Public Finance*, 17, 25–6, 62–3, 81.

problems the Tudors did not in fact go bankrupt and somehow managed; but this was achieved only by a mixture of rigid economy (especially under Elizabeth), some fiscal chicanery, and the abandonment of expensive though desirable policies.

20. Revenue and Expenditure in 1551.

The charge in:

Certainties in the courts of—

The Exchequer	£ 7557
Augmentations (in possession, £132080; in reversion, £12744)	£144825
Duchy of Lancaster (in possession, £16498; in reversion, £70)	£ 16568
First Fruits and Tenths	£ 15042
Wards and Liveries	nothing of certainty

Total: £183998

Casualties in the courts of—

The Exchequer	£ 31786[112]
Augmentations	£ 14370
Duchy of Lancaster	£ 1486
First Fruits and Tenths	£ 8521
Wards and Liveries	£ 31749

Total: £ 87914

Grand Total: £271912

Expenditure:

Fees, diets and allowances to officers[113]	£ 55815
The King's Great Wardrobe	£ 1163
Diets of ambassadors	£ 4927
Perpetual charges on revenue[114]	£ 10281
Expenses of audit	£ 3021

[112] Includes the customs. [113] I.e. the cost of the civil service.
[114] Payments made by collectors of revenue before delivery into the appropriate treasury (e.g. regular rents, alms, pensions etc.).

Decays and vacations of tenements etc.[115]	£ 6610
Repairs on royal lands	£ 7594
Payments to garrisons and fortresses	£ 9733
Assignments to the King's Household[116]	£ 41864
Jointures and dowers, etc. in the Court of Wards[117]	£ 15862
Pensions and annunities (monastic—£44861; ordinary—£14612; to officers pensioned in 1547—£3811)	£ 63285
Deductions in the Exchequer for years yet to come	£ 94
Pardon of amercements by Parliament	£ 881
Moiety forfeitures granted to King's servants[118]	£ 796
Diets and necessaries for the late duke of Norfolk in the Tower	£ 630
Lands granted for life	£ 12836
Total:	£235398

There remains (in possession—£36513; in reversion— £115037
£78523)

Against which are charged:[119]

The yearly charges of the Great Wardrobe above the revenue assigned thereunto

The yearly charges of the Admiralty

The yearly charges of the Ordnance

The yearly charges of the King's Purse

The yearly charges of the King's new year's gifts

The yearly charges of Calais above the revenue[120]

The yearly charges of Ireland above the revenue

---

[115] Items with which collectors are charged and which therefore appear as revenue, but which cannot be collected any longer because the rentable property they represent has ceased to exist.

[116] This figure differs slightly from that mentioned at the end of this summary for the same item. Such (and worse) discrepancies are common in sixteenth-century accounts.

[117] I.e. payments to widows, etc. charged upon lands that have come to the Crown by wardship.

[118] The half-value of forfeited property paid to customers and others bringing successful prosecutions against those breaking the penal statutes.

[119] These following items in practice represent the greater part of government expenditure on national matters but are irregular and cannot therefore be forecast.

[120] Calais (like Ireland) was supposed to pay for its administration out of local revenue, but neither dependency ever did. The gap between income and expenditure for Calais was reported here as £5286 in 1551, a sum which had to be made up from the central finances.

The yearly charges of the King's Household beside £41874 assigned to the same

Summarised from the Report of the Royal Commission of 1552 (B.M. Harl. MS 7383)[121]

21. The Budget of 1600.

Estimate of Her Majesty's domestical and foreign [expenditure].

The Privy Purse	£ 2000
Band of pensioners	£ 4000
Treasurer of the Chamber	£ 8000
Master of the Wardrobe	£ 4000
Cofferer of the Household	£ 4000
Master of the Jewelhouse	£ 2000
Master of the Posts	£ 2840
Ambassadors, etc.	£ 4000
Officers of the Works	£ 5000
Treasurer of the Navy (beside extraordinaries)	£ 2000
Victualling of the Navy	£ 15000
Lieutenant of the Ordnance, of ordinary	£ 6000
Master of the Armoury	£ 400
Lieutenant of the Tower and Keeper of the Gate-house	£ 2000
Castles, etc., forts	£ 4000
Justices' diets	£ 1600
Ireland	£320000
Low Countries	£ 25000
Fees and annuities	£ 26000

Total: £459840[122]

Besides sundry extraordinaries, as emptions and provisions for store in the offices of Admiralty, Ordnance and Armoury, and the charge of ships armed and set forth upon extraordinary occasions.

[121] For the best account of this much discussed Report cf. Alsop, *Hist. Journal*, xxii, 511 ff., which cites the earlier literature. The extract here printed is a summarised abstract of some eight pages which give a great deal more detail on individual items of expenditure. Sums are given in £s only, which accounts for apparent inaccuracies in addition. 'Certainties' are predictable sums, while 'casualties' are those that vary from year to year.
[122] Thus in the document; really £437840.

Estimate of Her Majesty's yearly revenues of the Exchequer.

Issues of sheriffs	£ 10000
Receivers of her Majesty's Possessions[123]	£ 60000
The Hanaper[124]	£ 4000
Alienations[125]	£ 4000
Customs and subsidies of ports	£ 80000
Imposts of wines, etc.	£ 24000
Licences, fines and casualties	£ 5000
Recusants	£ 7000
First Fruits and Tenths	£ 20000
Subsidy of the Clergy	£ 20000
Subsidy of the Laity	£ 80000
Fifteenths and tenths	£ 60000

Total: £374000

Which haply may in some of these natures and others, as of debts stalled[126] and arrearages of subsidies and fifteenths, and increase of revenue by recusants, may [sic] grow to the sum of £400000 yearly. State Papers Domestic, Elizabeth, vol. 276, fo. 99v

22. Details of the Customs, c. 1500.

The Rate of the King's Custom and Subsidy of Merchandises registered in the Exchequer.[127]

The custom of cloth without grain: the King's subjects pay for custom of a cloth 14d. The Spaniards pay for custom of a cloth 14d. The Hanse pays 12d. and aliens pay for a cloth 2s. 9d.

The custom of cloth in grain[128]: the King's subjects pays for every cloth 2s. 4d. The Spaniards pay 2s. 4d. The Hanse pays 2s. Other strangers pay 5s. 6d.

123 Crown lands.
124 Revenue of Chancery and payments for legal writs.
125 Sales of Crown lands.
126 Debts which had been converted into regular payments at stated intervals.
127 For the difference between customs and subsidies cf. Gras, *Early English Customs System*, ch. 11. In essence they had been charged in consolidated fashion from the later fourteenth century onwards, but certain differences continued to inhere in them. Historically, customs were generally imposed by the prerogative and subsidies granted by Parliament, though neither rule is without plenty of exception; technically, customs tended to be charged on a unit of merchandise and subsidies on poundage.
128 Cloth in grain—dyed scarlet.

The custom of cloth half-grained: the King's subjects pay for such cloth 21*d*. The Spaniards pay 21*d*. The merchants of the Hanse pay 18*d*. Other strangers pay 4*s*. 1*d*.

The subsidy of cloth as well in grain as ungrained, after the value of every £: the King's subjects for subsidy pay nothing. The Spaniards pay nothing. The Hanse pay nothing. Other strangers pay for subsidy of every £ 12*d*.

Custom of single worsted: the King's subjects, the Spaniards and the merchants of the Hanse pay for custom of every piece 1*d*. and all other strangers pay for custom 1½*d*.

The custom of the double worsted: the King's subjects, the Spaniards and merchants of the Hanse pay for every piece custom 2*d*. and all other strangers pay 3*d*.

The custom of every bed single worsted: the subjects of England, the Spaniards and the merchants of the Hanse pay for custom of every piece 5*d*. and all other strangers pay 7½*d*.

The custom of beds double worsted: the King's subjects, the merchants of the Hanse and the Spaniards pay for custom of every such piece 9*d*. and all other merchant strangers pay 13½*d*.

The subsidy of every £ value of worsted single and double, and of the worsted beds single and double: the King's subjects, the Spaniards and merchants of the Hanse pay for subsidy of the £ 1*d*. All other strangers pay 12*d*.

Custom of wax and subsidy: for every 100 wax all merchants pay for custom 12*d*. The King's subjects, the merchants of Spain and of the Hanse pay nothing for subsidy of no manner wax. All other merchants strangers pay for subsidy 12*d*.

Custom and subsidy of wines: the merchants of England and of Spain pay tunnage for every tun 3*s*. The merchants of the Hanse and other merchants strangers pay for custom of every tun 2*s*. And the other merchants strangers pay for subsidy 3*s*.

The custom and subsidy of every tun sweet wine: the merchants of England and of Spain pay tunnage 3*s*. The merchants of the Hanse and all merchant strangers pay for custom 2*s*. And the merchants strangers pay for subsidy 3*s*.

Custom and subsidy of tin by the £ value: the merchants of England and of Spain pay for subsidy 12*d*. The Hanse and merchants strangers pay custom 3*d*. And the merchants strangers for subsidy pay 3*d*.

Custom of pewter and subsidy by the £ value: the merchants of England and of Spain pay for subsidy 12*d*. And the merchants strangers pay for subsidy 2*s*. And the same merchant strangers pay for custom 3*d*.

The custom and subsidy of wool and fell[s] shipped to Calais: the merchant of the Staple pays for custom of a sack 6*s*. 8*d*. Item he paid for subsidy 33*s*. 4*d*. Item for every 240 woolfells for custom 6*s*. 8*d*. Item for subsidy of the same 33*s*. 4*d*.

Custom and subsidy shipped into other parts of wool and fell[s]: every merchant pays for custom of a sack 10*s*. Item for subsidy £3 6*s*. 8*d*. Item for the coming to Calais 8*d*. Item of every 240 skins of woolfell every merchant pays for custom 10*s*. and every merchant pays for subsidy £3 6*s*. 8*d*. Item for devoir[129] they pay 8*d*.

Custom and subsidy of leather: the merchant of England pays for every last leather tanned, for custom 13*s*. 4*d*. Item for the subsidy £3 6*s*. 8*d*. Item for devoir to Calais 16*d*. The merchant of Spain paid for custom 13*s*. 4*d*. Item for subsidy £3 6*s*. 8*d*. Item devoir, Calais, 8*d*. The merchant strangers pay for custom 20*s*. Item for subsidy £3 13*s*. 4*d*. Item for devoir, Calais, 16*d*.

The charges for the cockets[130] of merchandises: all manner of merchants shall pay for his cocket 2*d*.

The custom and subsidy of every £ value of all other merchandise: the English merchant paid for subsidy 12*d*. and the merchant of Spain 12*d*. The merchants of the Hanse pay for subsidy 2*d*. The same merchants pay for custom 3*d*. All other merchants pay for custom 3*d*. and for subsidy 12*d*.

Arnold, Customs of London, 193–6

23. An Act for a subsidy to be granted to the King—Tunnage and Poundage (1510: 1 Henry VIII, c. 20).

To the worship of God: We your poor Commons, by your high commandment come to this your present Parliament for the shires, cities and boroughs of this your noble realm, by the assent of all the Lords spiritual and temporal in this present Parliament assembled, grant by this present indenture to you our sovereign lord, for the defence of this your said realm and in especial for the safeguard and keeping of the sea, a subsidy called tunnage, to be taken in manner and form following,

[129] Duty.
[130] Seal of the customs house.

that is to say: 3s. of every tun of wine coming into this your said realm; and of every tun of sweet wine coming into the same your realm, by every merchant alien . . . 3s. over the said 3s. afore granted, to have and to perceive yearly the said subsidy from the first day of this present Parliament for time of your life natural. And over that, we your said Commons, by the assent afore, grant to you our said sovereign lord for the safeguard and keeping of the sea another subsidy called poundage, that is to say: of all manner merchandises of every merchant, denizen and alien . . . carried out of this your said realm or brought into the same by way of merchandise, of the value of every 20s., 12d., except tin, whereof the merchants strangers to pay for subsidy of the value of every 20s., 2s. and the merchants denizens 12d. And all such manner merchandises of every merchant denizen to be valued after that they cost at the first buying . . . by their oaths, or of their servants buyers of the said merchandise in their absence, or by their letters the which the same merchants have of such buying from their factors. All manner woollen cloth made and wrought within this your realm and by any merchant denizen not born alien to be carried out of the same realm within the time of this grant except; and all manner wool, wool fells and hides, and every manner of corn flour, every manner of fresh fish, bestial and wine into this realm coming also except; and beer, ale, and all manner victual going out of this your said realm for the victualling of your town of Calais and the marches there under your obeisance out of this grant alway except. To have and perceive yearly the said subsidy of poundage from the first day of your most noble reign during your life natural. . . .

*　　*　　*　　*　　*　　*

Stat. Realm, III, 21

24. Act against Smuggling 1559 (1 Eliz. I, c. 11).

Most humbly shewing, beseechen your Highness your Lords and Commons in this present Parliament assembled, that where the sums of money paid in the name of customs . . . is an ancient revenue annexed and united to your imperial crown and hath . . . amounted to great and notable sums of money, till of late years many greedy and covetous persons, respecting more their private gain and commodity than their duty and allegiance or the common profit of the realm, have and do daily, as well by conveying the same their wares and merchandises out of creeks and places where no customer is resident, as also by or through the negligence or corruption of the customer, searcher or other officer where they be resident, as by divers other fraudulent, undue and subtle practices and devices, convey their goods and merchandises, as well brought from the parts beyond the sea as transported out of this your realm of England, without payment . . . of the customs . . . therefor due; whereby the yearly revenue aforesaid is very much impaired and diminished. . . . That it may therefore be enacted by authority of this present Parliament that it shall not be lawful to or for any person or persons whatsoever . . . to lade or put, or cause to be laden or put, of or from any wharf, quay or other place on the land, into any ship . . . any goods, wares or merchandises whatsoever (fish taken by your Highness' subjects only excepted) to be transported into any place of the parts beyond the sea, or into the realm of Scotland, or to take up, discharge and lay on land . . . out of any ship . . . any goods, wares or merchandises whatsoever (fish taken by any your Highness' subjects and salt only excepted) to be brought from any parts beyond the sea or the realm of Scotland by way of merchandises, but only in the daylight . . . and in . . . some . . . open place, quay or wharf . . . where a customer, controller and searcher . . . or the servants of any of them have by the space of ten years last past been accustomably resident or hereafter shall be resident; upon pain of forfeiture of all such goods, wares or merchandises so laden or discharged contrary to the true meaning of this act, or the value thereof.

[II. Penalty on masters of vessels whose goods are unduly laden or discharged, £100.

III. Masters of ships exporting goods to give notice 'to the customer of the port where he ladeth and other officers there in the open Custom House' 'that he intendeth to lade, and to what place he intendeth to pass,' and to answer truly questions put to him by the customer concerning his cargo, under a penalty of £100.

IV. Similar clause with regard to unloading for masters of ships importing goods.

V. Goods imported or exported to be entered in the names of the true owners under penalty of forfeiture.

VI. Penalty on 'any wharfinger, crane-keeper, searcher, lighterman, weigher,' 'or other officer pertaining to the subsidy, custom or Custom House' concealing offences against the act, £100.

VII. Customers to appoint deputies in the several ports, and they and their deputies and servants to attend diligently under a penalty of £100 and loss of office.]

*   *   *   *   *   *

Stat. Realm, IV, 372-4

25. An Act whereby the King's Highness has authority to repeal the statute made for restraint of wines to come in afore Candlemas (1534: 26 Henry VIII, c. 10).

[Recites 23 Henry VIII, c. 7, sect. ii, concerning the importation of French wines at certain seasons, which act, like others, might conflict with commercial treaties made by the King.]

Be it therefore enacted by authority of this present Parliament that the King our sovereign lord shall during his life natural have full power and authority by his proclamations to be contained in letters patent under his great seal and enrolled in his court of Chancery, from time to time to repeal and make void as well the said article . . . as all other such acts and statutes in part or in the whole which hath been made since the beginning of this present Parliament for the restraint or let of any commodities of this realm or of other the King's dominions to be conveyed and uttered to and in any outward parts, realms or countries, or for restraint and let of any commodities or merchandise of outward parts, realms or countries to be conveyed, brought and uttered to or in this realm or elsewhere within the King's dominions; and by like proclamations from time to time shall have power and authority to revive and make effectual the said statutes and acts again. . . . And that every such repeal . . . and every such reviving . . . by proclamations under the great seal . . . shall be of the same quality, force, strength, condition and effect to all intents and purposes as if it had been done with all due circumstances by authority of Parliament; any thing or things contained in any such acts or any usage or custom of this realm to the contrary thereof notwithstanding.   *Stat. Realm*, III, 506

26. An Act concerning the payment of first fruits of all dignities, benefices and promotions spiritual; and also concerning one annual pension of the tenth part of all the possessions of the Church, spiritual and temporal, granted to the King's Highness and his heirs (1534: 26 Henry VIII, c. 3).

Forasmuch as it is and of very duty ought to be the natural inclination of all good people, like most faithful, loving and obedient subjects, sincerely and willingly to desire to provide not only for the public weal of their native country but also for the supportation, maintenance and defence of the royal estate of their most dread, benign and gracious sovereign lord, upon whom and in whom dependeth all their joy and wealth, in whom also is united and knit so princely a heart and courage, mixed with mercy, wisdom and justice, and also a natural affection joined to the same, as by the great, inestimable and benevolent arguments thereof being most bountifully, largely and many times shewed, ministered and approved towards his loving and obedient subjects hath well appeared, which requireth a like correspondence of gratitude to be considered according to their most bounden duties; Wherefore his said humble and obedient subjects, as well the Lords spiritual and temporal as the Commons in this present Parliament assembled, calling to their remembrance not only the manifold and innumerable benefits daily administered by his Highness to them all, and to the residue of all other his subjects of this realm, but also how long time his Majesty hath most victoriously by his high wisdom and policy protected, defended and governed this his realm and maintained his people and subjects of the same in tranquillity, peace, unity, quietness and wealth; And also considering what great, excessive and inestimable charges his Highness hath heretofore been at and sustained by the space of five and twenty whole years, and also daily sustaineth for the maintenance, tuition and defence of this his realm and his loving subjects of the same, which cannot be sustained and borne without some honourable provision and remedy may be found, provided and ordained for maintenance thereof, do therefore desire and most humbly pray that for the more surety of continuance and augmentation of his Highnesss' royal estate, being not only now recognised (as he always in deed heretofore hath been) the only supreme head in earth next and immediately under God of the Church of England, but also their most assured and undoubted natural sovereign liege lord and King, having the whole governance, tuition, defence and maintenance of this his realm and most loving, obedient subjects of the same: It may therefore be ordained and enacted by his Highness and the Lords spiritual and temporal and the Commons in this present Parliament assembled and by authority of the same in manner and form following. That is to say, that the King's Highness, his heirs and successors kings of this realm, shall have and enjoy from time to time, to endure for ever, of every such person and persons which at any time after the first day of January next coming shall be nominated, elected, prefected, presented, collated or by any other means appointed to have any archbishopric, bishopric, abbacy, monastery, priory, college, hospital, archdeaconry, deanery, provostship, prebend, parsonage, vicarage, chantry, free chapel, or other dignity, benefice, office or promotion spiritual within this realm or elsewhere within any of the King's dominions, of what name, nature or quality soever they be or to whose foundation, patronage or gift soever they belong, the first fruits, revenues and profits for one year of every such archbishopric, bishopric [etc.] . . . whereunto any such person or persons shall after the said first day of January be nominated, elected, prefected, presented, collated or by any other means appointed; and that every such person and persons, before any actual or real possession or meddling with the profits of any such archbishopric, bishopric, [etc.] . . . shall satisfy, content and pay, or compound or agree to pay, to the King's use at reasonable days upon good sureties the said first fruits and profits for one year.

*   *   *   *   *   *

VIII. And over this be it enacted by authority aforesaid that the King's Majesty, his heirs and successors kings of this realm, for more augmentation and maintenance of the royal estate of his imperial crown and dignity of supreme head of the Church of England, shall yearly have, take, enjoy and perceive, united and knit to his imperial crown for ever, one yearly rent or pension amounting to the value of the tenth part of all the revenues, rents, ferms[131], tithes, offerings, emoluments and of all other profits, as well called spiritual as temporal, now appertaining or belonging or that hereafter shall belong to any archbishopric, bishopric, abbacy, monastery, priory, archdeaconry, deanery, hospital, college, house collegiate, prebend, cathedral church, collegiate church, conventual church, parsonage, vicarage, chantry, free chapel, or other benefice or promotion spiritual, of what name, nature or quality soever they be, within any diocese of this realm or in Wales; the said pension or annual rent to be yearly paid for ever to our said Sovereign Lord. [Beginning at Christmas 1535.]

IX. And it is ordained and enacted by authority aforesaid that the said yearly rent and pension shall be taxed . . . in manner and form hereafter to be declared by this act, that is to say: that the chancellor of England . . . shall have power and authority to direct into every dio-

---

[131] Ferm or farm—a fixed yearly payment.

cese in this realm and in Wales several commissions in the King's name
under his great seal, as well to the archbishop or bishop of every such
diocese as to such other person or persons as the King's Highness shall
name and appoint, commanding and authorising the said commissioners . . . to examine, search and enquire . . . of and for the true and
just whole and entire yearly values of all the manors, lands [and other
property] . . . belonging to any archbishopric, bishopric [etc.] . . .

*　*　*　*　*　*

Stat. Realm, III, 493–9

27. An Act for the subsidy (1512: 4 Henry VIII, c. 19).

[The preamble recites the origins of the war with France which it
ascribes to Louis XII's defiance of the Pope and the latter's appeal for
assistance to the Christian princes. The King has therefore prepared his
armies, navies and defences 'which . . . cannot be supported, maintained and borne without right great costs and charges'.][132]

In consideration whereof, and also for that our said sovereign lord
many other divers and great charges for defence of this his realm in
divers sundry wise of late hath borne and sustained, and for the goodness, bounteousness, liberality, favour and tender zeal by his Highness
showed to his said Commons, as evidently is known, the same loving
Commons in this present Parliament assembled, with the assent of the
Lords spiritual and temporal in the same Parliament in like manner
assembled, have granted unto our said sovereign lord the King one
whole fifteenth and tenth to be had, taken, perceived and levied of
goods, moveables, chattels and other things to such fifteenth and tenth
usually contributory and chargeable within counties, cities, boroughs
and towns, and other places of this realm of England in manner and
form aforetime used. . . . The said fifteenth and tenth . . . to be paid
in the quindene of Easter which shall be in the year of our Lord God
1514.

*　*　*　*　*　*

IV. And for that the said one fifteenth and tenth . . . extendeth but
unto a small sum toward the said great charges, the said loving Commons after to their powers willing a greater sum toward the said
charges . . . as well in shorter time as in more easy, universal and in-

---

[132] The preamble in full in Tanner, 606–7.

different manner to be levied than such common tax of fifteenth and tenth hath or can be according to the ancient use thereof . . . have by the assent of the Lords . . . granted . . . one subsidy to be taken and paid of every person underwritten within this realm of England in manner and form as followeth, that is to say, of every duke, £6 13s. 4d.; of every marquis, earl, marchioness and countess, £4; of every baron, baronet[133] and baroness, 40s.; of every other knight not being lord of the Parliament, 30s.; of every person, man or woman, having lands, tenements or rents [etc.] . . . to the yearly value of £40 or above, 20s.; . . . of £20 or above, . . . 10s.; . . . of £10 or above, . . . 5s.; . . . of 40s. or above, . . . 2s.; . . . under 40s., 12d. Of every person, man or woman, . . . having goods or chattels moveable to the value £800 or above, 80s. 4d.; . . . £400 or above, . . . 40s.; . . . £200 or above, 26s. 8d., . . . £100 or above, . . . 13s. 4d.; . . . £40 or above, . . . 6s. 8d.; £20 or above, . . . 3s. 4d.; . . . £10 or above, . . . 20d.; . . . 40s. or above, . . . 12d. . . . Of every labourer, journeyman, artificer, handicraftman and servant, as well men and women, above the age of 15 years, taking wages or other profits for wages to the value of 40s. by the year or above . . . 12d.; . . . 20s. . . . . or above . . . 6d. Of every servant taking any wages or other profits under the value of 20s. . . . and also of every apprentice and of every other person . . . 4d.

[The remaining eleven sections deal with details of rating, collection and payment. The Commons shall appoint commissioners for every shire, city, town etc., none of whom shall be members of the present Parliament; a schedule of nominations is appended. The administration of the subsidy is to be in the charge of the Exchequer.]

Stat. Realm, III, 74–89

28. The Loan of 1556.

[At St James's, 5 October 1556] A letter to Thomas Mildmay, esquire, of thanks for his diligence and travail in the delivery of a privy seal sent unto him touching the Loan, and where he signifyeth that there be certain that have refused to pay and yet keep their privy seals with them, he is willed to deliver such letters as are addressed unto them and sent herewith and for the rest that have not paid and be not hitherto discharged he is also willed to keep a note in his book of their names, and

[133] Lesser baron.

to travail with them between this and his coming up for to make payments of the sums required of them.   *A.P.C.*, VI, 5

[At St James's, 19 November 1556] It was this day ordered that all such to whom privy seals have been addressed unto for the Loan and have detained the same in their hands and not paid the sums demanded of them, nor otherwise answered the same, notwithstanding divers of them have been eftsoons written unto herein, should be sent for to answer to their said doings.   *Ibid.*, VI, 19–20

[At Greenwich, 18 January 1557] These persons whose names do follow were ordered either to pay the money that they were heretofore appointed by privy seals to lend in such sort as was prescribed unto them, or else to give their continual attendance upon the Council till further order be taken with them by their Lordships. . . .   *Ibid.*, VI, 45

[At St James's, 21 October 1557] This day Alexander Wells, mayor of Rye, having heretofore been committed to the prison of the Fleet for his refusal to appear before the commissioners for the Loan in the county of Sussex when they sent for him, was this day discharged of the same imprisonment, having a good lesson given him to beware of the like disobedience hereafter.   *Ibid.*, VI, 188

[At St James's, 24 October 1557] Edmund Marshall, having been bound before the bishop of Lincoln and other commissioners for the Loan in the county of Lincoln to appear here, made this day his personal appearance.   *A.P.C.*, VI. 189

[At St James's, 25 October 1557] John Love of Winchelsea, merchant, having refused to receive the Queen's Majesty's privy seal for the Loan, was this day for his disobedience committed to the Fleet.   *Ibid.*, VI, 190

[At St James's, 2 November 1557] Henry Summers of Gloucestershire, being heretofore bound by the commissioners for the Loan in that shire to appear personally before the Lords of the Council, made this day his appearance accordingly and desired to have the same recorded, being contented to lend the sum required of him by the Queen's Highness' privy seal.   *Ibid.*, VI, 194

28a. A Privy Seal for a Loan, 1591.

By the Queen.

Trusty and well beloved, we greet you well. We doubt not but it is well known what great cause we have for the defence of our realm to be furnished with money. And therefore we require you, as other good subjects did this last year lend us sundry sums of money which have been duly repaid, so you will lend us in like manner the sum of £40, and the same to pay to such person as by order of our Privy Council shall be appointed our collector in that shire; which we promise to cause to be duly repaid to you or your assigns at the end of one year in our Receipt, upon the showing of this privy seal subscribed by the said collector. Given under our privy seal, at Basing the 13th day of September in the 33rd year of our reign.[134]

> Received of William Saxbie of Poynings, the 15th day of November 1591, the sum of £40 to the Queen's Majesty's use, according to this her Majesty's privy seal
>
> £40 *receptae per me* Henry Gorynge *Sexto die Novembris 1594:* repaid by Mr Killigrew[135] unto his assign subscribed
>
> William Peye
>
> Exchequer of Receipt, Miscellaneous Papers, 116

V. THE LAW OF TREASON

(i) EXTENSION OF TREASONS. The ultimate legal defence of Crown and realm depended on the treason law. High treason was regarded as the final denial of the divine order of things as established in the body politic and defined in the oath of allegiance. More soberly, it was the offence most dangerous to the person and powers of the monarch. At the accession of the Tudors the law stood approximately upon an act of 1352 which made it treason to compass the king's death, to levy war against him, or to adhere to his enemies. Even before the sixteenth century, this narrow definition had proved insufficient. The act required an overt deed, but in troubled times governments had found it easy to avoid this wise limitation. Thus the judges came to extend the operation of the law well beyond the terms of the 1352 statute. In particular the treason which (it is commonly alleged) was the most frightful of Henry VIII's additions to the law—treason by words—had a

[134] 1591.
[135] One of the tellers of the Receipt of the Exchequer.

much older history. Not only could even Henry VII's Council entertain a charge of alleged treasonable words,[136] but several times in the fifteenth century words were 'constructed' as treasonable by the courts.[137] Nor (despite some confident assertions) is it true that the Tudors fudged the whole meaning of treason by turning the supreme political offence into an emotional term for any heinous crime.[138] The act of 1531, which included murder by poisoning among treasons,[139] was in fact the dying echo of an older common law attitude which could at times be negligent of the real meaning of the word.[140] Typically, Tudor legislation extended treason to cover new aspects of the fundamental offence against king and realm. Sometimes it codified common law precedents, as in the case of treason by words; sometimes it acknowledged technological progress, as for instance treason rendered overt in print; but mostly it followed from the dynastic difficulties of the Tudors and the break with Rome. It is significant that statute was always used to expand or contract treason. The act of 1352 had not been regarded as exhaustive, leaving room for the doctrine and practice of constructive treasons. As in other fields so in this, Tudor reliance on statute restricted the operation of judicial interpretation. By the end of the century the best opinion allowed little scope for the construction of treasons additional to those specified in statute; in particular—because acts making words treason had all been repealed—it denied the existence of treason by words which had been a common law treason before Henry VIII's legislation.[141] Although the new precision might sometimes increase the force of an uncertain earlier construction, its chief effect was to draw limits where none had been before.

The ups and downs of the treason law have been well summarised elsewhere.[142] Under Henry VIII the various acts connected with his marriages protected each new wife and succession by treason clauses,[143] while the great act of 1534 (30) both brought the law up to date after the long interval since 1352 and provided the legal safeguards for the king's new position in the Church.[144] Another act (31) extended the principle that the Crown's executive powers must be protected by adding forgery of the privy seal, signet and

---

[136] Doc. 29. The terms of the accusation there strongly remind one of those later preferred against men who spoke for the pope and against the royal supremacy.

[137] Thornley, *Eng. Hist. Rev.*, XXXII, 556 ff.; Bellamy, *Later Middle Ages*, ch. 5.

[138] Tanner, 379; Pickthorn, II, 159 f.

[139] Tanner, 381 f.

[140] I am informed by Mr J. R. Lander that he has found a case in the reign of Edward IV in which a man was charged with treason *quod cognovit mulierem contra naturam*.

[141] Cf. Coke's opinion, cited in Tanner, 377 f.   [142] Bellamy, *Tudor Law*, chs. 1 & 2.

[143] 25 Henry VIII, c. 22 (4); 28 Henry VIII, c. 7 (Tanner, 389 ff.); 32 Henry VIII, c. 25 (*ibid.*, 395); 35 Henry VIII, c. 1 (*ibid.*, 397).

[144] For the history of this act cf. Elton, *Policy and Police*, ch. 4.

sign manual to the older treason of forging the great seal.[145] In 1547 Somerset repealed the Henrician treasons but at once re-enacted that denial of the supremacy in deed or writing should be treason at the first offence, in words at the third (32). Northumberland, who in 1552 added points concerning the royal succession and orthodoxy, returned very nearly to the straightforward position of the 1534 act (33). Mary began with a highminded return to 1352 (34), but soon found it necessary to guard against hostility to her Spanish marriage by penalties which in effect were those of praemunire and to protect Philip's person by the penalties of treason (35). Moreover, though mild enough in politics, she would suffer no disaffection in religion, and an act of 1555 made it treason to speak against the restored Roman connection.[146] Elizabeth at once enlarged her sister's acts to serve herself and her successors: words remained misprision of treason only.[147] Thereafter her treason legislation reflected nothing but her struggle with the Counter-Reformation. In 1571 one act (36) added further particulars to treasonable offences without changing the character of the crime, while another (13 Eliz. I, c. 2) made it treason to obtain a bull from Rome. Though other acts provided weapons in the fight at the level of felony, the Jesuit missions provoked a further treason act in 1585 (37). Other shortlived treasons appeared in the course of the century, like the violent reaction to the 1549 uprisings which in effect made every riotous assembly potentially treasonable.[148] But the main line of legislation was quite clear. It looked to give protection against the ultimate political crime to the Crown itself and to the Crown as the embodiment of the nation state.

29. Treasonable Words: an examination before the Council Learned, 25 April 1508.

Rowland Bowbank of Shouldham in the county of Norfolk, yeoman, of the age of 44 years or thereabouts, of his own voluntary will confesseth and saith that he was in service with Dan John Bray, then and yet prior of the house and canons of Shouldham in the said county; and that upon the Monday in the Rogation Week was three year,[149] as he remembereth, the said prior, being set down to his dinner at Shouldham aforesaid, and divers his brethren at [the] same board, whose names amongst other been called Dan Richard Stevenson, Dan Robert Wollislie, and Dan Robert Feeman, the said prior began to common what charge he had for payment of the dismes. And then uttered these words following:

---

[145] Despite Holdsworth (IV, 498) this act and others concerned with the coinage had a genuine political connotation.

[146] 1 & 2 Philip and Mary, c. 9 (Tanner, 407 f.).

[147] 1 Eliz. I, c. 5 (Tanner, 411).

[148] 3 & 4 Edward VI, c. 5.

[149] 28 April 1505.

'I marvel the King's Grace thus polleth us. I had liefer than we should be thus polled that yon gentleman beyond the sea, Edmund de la Pole, should come in, and I would spend with him my body and my goods.'

Memorandum, that the said prior hath confessed that he spoke these words: 'I marvel the King's Grace pillith us thus with these dismes.'

6 June 1508. Memorandum, that Robert Wollesley, Richard Stevenson and Robert Feeman abovewritten have been sent for by privy seal and sworn and examined to say the truth of this matter abovespecified. And by their oath they say and depose that they never heard the prior abovenamed utter any such words as in this bill is supposed, and so the said Robert Wollesley, Richard and Robert have licence to depart.

And after, the 9th day of August, the said prior was bound by obligation that under the convent seal of the priory of Shouldham he should bind himself and his successors in £100 to appear at Westminster in the Treseptimanam of St Michael the Archangel next etc.[150] and further, as in the said obligation appeareth more at large, etc.

Duchy of Lancaster Entry Books, 4, fo. 138v

30. An Act whereby divers offences be made high treason (1534: 26 Henry VIII, c. 13).

Forasmuch as it is most necessary, both for common policy and duty of subjects, above all things to prohibit, provide, restrain and extinct all manner of shameful slanders, perils or imminent danger or dangers which might grow, happen or arise to their sovereign lord the King, the Queen, or their heirs, which when they be heard, seen or understood cannot be but odible and also abhorred of all those sorts that be true and loving subjects, if in any point they may, do or shall touch the King, his Queen, their heirs or successors, upon which dependeth the whole unity and universal weal of this realm, without providing wherefor too great a scope of unreasonable liberty should be given to all cankered and traitorous hearts, willers and workers of the same; And also the King's loving subjects should not declare unto their sovereign lord now being, which unto them hath been and is most entirely both beloved and esteemed, their undoubted sincerity and truth; Be it there-

---

[150] Three weeks after Michaelmas (29 September) or a fortnight after the beginning of the Michaelmas Term, i.e. on 20 October.

fore enacted by the assent and consent of our sovereign lord the King
and the Lords spiritual and temporal and Commons in this present
Parliament assembled, and by authority of the same, that if any person
or persons, after the first day of February next coming, do maliciously
wish, will or desire by words or writing, or by craft imagine, invent,
practise or attempt any bodily harm to be done or committed to the
King's most royal person, the Queen's or their heir's apparent, or to
deprive them or any of them of the dignity, title or name of their royal
estates, or slanderously and maliciously publish and pronounce, by
express writing or words, that the King our sovereign lord should be
heretic, schismatic, tyrant, infidel or usurper of the crown, or rebelliously do detain, keep or withhold from our said sovereign lord, his
heirs or successors, any of his or their castles, fortresses, fortalices or
holds, within this realm or in any other the King's dominions or
marches, or rebelliously detain, keep or withhold from the King's said
Highness, his heirs or successors, any of his or their ships, ordnance,
artillery or other munitions or fortifications of war, and do not humbly
render and give up to our said sovereign lord, his heirs or successors, or
to such persons as shall be deputed by them, such castles, fortresses,
fortalices, holds, ships, ordnance, artillery and other munitions and
fortifications of war rebelliously kept or detained, within 6 days next
after they shall be commanded by our said sovereign lord, his heirs or
successors, by open proclamation under the great seal, that then every
such person and persons so offending in any the premises after the said
first day of February, their aiders, counsellors, consenters and abettors,
being thereof lawfully convict according to the laws and customs of
this realm, shall be adjudged traitors; and that every such offence in any
the premises that shall be committed or done after the said first day of
February, shall be reputed, accepted and adjudged high treason. And
the offenders therein, and their aiders, consenters, counsellors and abettors, being lawfully convict of any such offence as is aforesaid, shall
have and suffer such pains of death and other penalties as is limited and
accustomed in cases of high treason.

II. And to the intent that all treasons should be the more dread,
hated and detested to be done by any person or persons, and also because it is a great boldness and an occasion to ill-disposed persons to
adventure and embrace their malicious intents and enterprises, which
all true subjects ought to study to eschew; Be it therefore enacted by

the authority aforesaid that none offender in any kinds of high treasons, whatsoever they be, their aiders, consenters, counsellors nor abettors, shall be admitted to have the benefit or privilege of any manner of sanctuary; considering that matters of treasons toucheth so nigh both the surety of the King our sovereign lord's person and his heirs and successors.

* * * * * *

Stat. Realm, III, 508–9

31. An Act concerning the forging of the King's sign manual, signet and privy seal (1536: 27 Henry VIII, c. 2).

Forasmuch as by the laws of this realm small punishment has been hitherto provided for forging and counterfeiting of the King's sign manual or privy signet, by reason whereof divers light and evil-disposed persons now of late have taken the more boldness and courage to commit such offences. . . . For remedy whereof be it enacted by authority of this present Parliament that if any person or persons at any time hereafter falsely forge and counterfeit the King's sign manual, privy signet or privy seal, that then every such offence shall be deemed and adjudged high treason, and the offenders therein, their counsellors, procurors, aiders and abettors, being convict of any such offence according to the laws of this realm, shall be deemed and adjudged traitors against the King and the realm; and shall suffer and have such pains of death, forfeiture of lands, goods and chattels, and also lose the privilege of all sanctuaries, as in cases of high treason it is ordained.

Stat. Realm, III, 532

32. An Act for the repeal of certain statutes concerning treasons etc. (First Treasons Act of Edward VI, 1547: 1 Ed. VI, c. 12).

Nothing being more godly, more sure, more to be wished and desired, betwixt a prince the supreme head and ruler and the subjects whose governor and head he is, than on the prince's part great clemency and indulgency, and rather too much forgiveness and remission of his royal power and just punishment than exact severity and justice to be shewed, and on the subjects' behalf that they should obey rather for love, and for the necessity and love of a king and prince, than for fear of his strait and severe laws; yet such times at some time cometh in the commonwealth that it is necessary and expedient for the repressing of the insolency and unruliness of men and for the foreseeing and providing of remedies against rebellion, insurrection or such mischiefs as God, sometime with us displeased, for our punishment doth inflict and lay upon us, or the Devil at God's permission, to assay the good and God's elect, doth sow and set amongst us, the which Almighty God with his help and man's policy hath always been content and pleased to have stayed that sharper laws as a harder bridle should be made to stay those men and facts that might else be occasion, cause and authors of further inconvenience; the which thing caused the prince of most famous memory King Henry the Eighth . . . with the assent of the Nobles and Commons at divers Parliaments in their several times holden to make and enact certain laws and statutes which might seem and appear to men of exterior realms and many of the King's Majesty's subjects very strait, sore, extreme and terrible, although they were then when they were made not without great consideration and policy moved and established, and for the time to the avoidance of further inconvenience very expedient and necessary. But, as in tempest or winter one course and garment is convenient, in calm or warm weather a more liberal race or lighter garment both may and ought to be followed and used, so we have seen divers strait and sore laws made in one Parliament, the time so requiring, in a more calm and quiet reign of another prince by like authority and Parliament repealed and taken away; the which most high clemency and royal example of his Majesty's most noble progenitors, the King's Highness, of his tender and godly nature most given to mercy and love of his subjects, willing to follow, and perceiving the hearty and sincere love that his most loving subjects, both the Lords and Commons, doth bear unto his Highness now in this his Majesty's tender age, willing also to gratify the same therefore, and minding further to provoke his said subjects with great indulgency and clemency shewed on his Highness' behalf to more love and kindness towards his Majesty (if it may be) and upon trust that they will not abuse the same, but rather be encouraged thereby more faithfully and with more diligence (if it may be) and care for his Majesty to serve his Highness now in this his tender age, is contented and pleased that the severity of certain laws here following be mitigated and remitted. Be it therefore ordained and enacted by the King our sovereign lord with the assent of the Lords spiritual and temporal and the Commons in the present Parliament assembled, and by authority of the same, that from henceforth none act, deed or offence being by act of Parliament or statute made treason or petty treason[151] by words, writing, ciphering, deeds or otherwise whatsoever, shall be taken, had, deemed or adjudged to be high treason or petty treason but only such as be treason or petty treason in or by [25 Edw. III, st. 5, c. 2] and such offences as hereafter shall by this present act be expressed and declared to be treason or petty treason, and none other; nor that any pains of death, penalty or forfeiture in any wise ensue or be to any of the offenders for the doing or committing any treason or petty treason, other than such as be in the said statute made in the 25th year of the reign of the said King Edward III or by this present estatute ordained or provided; any act or acts of Parliament, statute or statutes, had or made at any time heretofore, or after the said 25th year of the reign of the said late King Edward III, or any other declaration or matter to the contrary in any wise notwithstanding.

[II repeals 'all acts of Parliament and estatutes touching, mentioning or in any wise concerning religion or opinions,' namely, 5 Rich. II, st. 2, c. 5; 2 Henry V, st. 1, c. 7; 25 Henry VIII, c. 14; 31 Henry VIII, c. 14, 34 & 35 Henry VIII, c. 1; and 35 Henry VIII, c. 5.]

[III repeals all new felonies created by statute since 23 April 1509.]

[IV repeals 31 Henry VIII, c. 8 and 34 & 35 Henry VIII, c. 23, giving statutory authority to royal proclamations.]

v. And be it enacted by the authority aforesaid, that if any person or persons at any time after the first day of March next coming, by open preaching, express words or sayings, do affirm or set forth that the King, his heirs or successors, kings of this realm for the time being, is not or ought not to be supreme head in earth of the Church of England and Ireland or of any of them immediately under God, or that the bishop of Rome or any other person or persons other than the King of England for the time being is or ought to be by the laws of God supreme head of the same Churches or of any of them, or that the King, his heirs or successors kings of this realm, is not or ought not to be king of England, France and Ireland, or any of them, or, after the said first day of March, do compass or imagine by open preaching, express words or sayings, to depose or deprive the King, his heirs or successors kings of this realm, from his or their royal estate or titles to or of the realms aforesaid, or do openly publish or say by express words or sayings that any other person or persons other than the King, his heirs or successors kings of this realm, of right ought to be kings of the realms aforesaid or of any of

---

[151] Petty treason is the killing of a natural superior other than the king—a master by his servant, a husband by his wife.

them, or to have and enjoy the same or any of them; That then every such offender, being thereof duly convicted or attainted by the laws of this realm, their aiders, comforters, abettors, procurers and counsellors, ... shall [suffer forfeiture of goods and imprisonment during the King's pleasure for the first offence: forfeiture of lands and imprisonment for life for the second: and the penalties of high treason for the third].

[VI. To affirm the same, in writing or printing or by overt act or deed, is to be high treason.]

* * * * * *

VIII. And be it further enacted by the authority aforesaid, that if any of the heirs of the King our said sovereign lord that now is, or any person or persons to whom the crown and dignity of this realm is limited and appointed by [35 Henry VIII, c. 1] or the heirs of any of them, do at any time hereafter usurp the one of them upon the other in the crown of this realm, or demand, challenge or claim the same otherwise or in any other form or degree of descent or succession, or in any other course, form, degree or condition but only in such manner and form as is declared by the said statute, or if any of the said heirs or persons aforesaid do interrupt or let the King's Highness that now is peaceably and quietly to keep, have and enjoy the said imperial crown, that then all and singular the offenders, their aiders, comforters, abettors, procurers and counsellors therein, shall be deemed and adjudged high traitors, and shall suffer and incur the pains of death, losses and forfeitures as is aforesaid in cases of high treason.

* * * * * *

XXII. Provided always and be it enacted by the authority aforesaid that no person or persons, after the first day of February next coming, shall be indicted, arraigned, condemned or convicted for any offence of treason, petty treason, misprision of treason, or for any words before specified to be spoken after the said first day of February, for which the same offender, speaker, offenders or speakers shall in any wise suffer any pains of death, imprisonment, loss or forfeiture of his goods, chattels, lands or tenements, unless the same offender, speaker, offenders or speakers be accused by two sufficient and lawful witnesses, or shall willingly without violence confess the same. _Stat. Realm_, IV, 18–22

33. An Act for the punishment of divers treasons (Second Treason Act of Edward VI, 1552: 5 & 6 Ed. VI, c. 11).

Forasmuch as it is most necessary for common policy and duty of subjects above all things to prohibit, restrain and extinct all manner of shameful slanders which might grow, happen or arise to their sovereign lord the King's Majesty, which when they be heard, seen or understood cannot be but odible and also abhorred of all those sorts that be true and loving subjects, if in any point they may, do or shall touch his Majesty, upon whom dependeth the whole unity and universal weal of this realm; without providing wherefor too great a scope of unreasonable liberty should be given to all cankered and traitorous hearts, and the King's loving subjects should not declare unto their sovereign lord now being, which unto them hath been and is most entirely both beloved and esteemed, their undoubted sincerity and truth: Be it therefore enacted by the assent and consent of our sovereign lord the King and the Lords spiritual and temporal and the Commons of this present Parliament assembled, and by authority of the same, that if any person or persons, after the first day of June next coming, by open preaching, express words or sayings do expressly, directly and advisedly set forth and affirm that the King that now is is an heretic, schismatic, tyrant, infidel or usurper of the crown, or that any his heirs or successors to whom the crown of this realm is limited [by 35 Henry VIII, c. 1] being in lawful possession of the crown, is an heretic [etc. . . .], that then every such offender, being thereof duly convicted or attainted by the laws of this realm, their abettors, procurers and counsellors, and all and every their aiders and comforters, knowing the said offences or any of them to be done [shall suffer forfeiture of goods and imprisonment during the King's pleasure for the first offence: forfeiture of profits of lands and spiritual promotions for life, and of all goods, and perpetual imprisonment for the second offence: and the penalties of high treason with forfeiture of lands and goods for the third offence].

II. And be it further enacted by the authority aforesaid, that if any person or persons, at any time after the said first day of June next coming, by writing, printing, painting, carving or graving, do directly, expressly and advisedly publish, set forth and affirm that the King that now is, or any his heirs or successors limited as is beforesaid, is an heretic [etc. . . .], that then every such offence and offences shall be deemed and adjudged high treason, and the offender and offenders, their abettors, procurers and counsellors, and all and every their aiders and comforters, knowing the said offences or any of them to be done, being thereof convicted or attainted according to the laws and statutes of this realm, shall be deemed and adjudged high traitors, and shall suffer pains of death, and lose and forfeit all their goods and chattels, lands and tenements, to the King as in cases of high treason.

[III. Detaining the King's ships and fortresses is declared high treason.

IV–VI. Treasons committed out of the realm may be tried by commission in any shire of the realm, with details as to process and punishment.]

* * * * * *

IX. Provided always and be it enacted by the authority aforesaid that no person or persons, after the first day of June next coming, shall be indicted, arraigned, condemned, convicted or attainted for any of the treasons or offences aforesaid, or for any other treasons that now be or hereafter shall be, which shall hereafter be perpetrated, committed or done, unless the same offender or offenders be thereof accused by two lawful accusers, which said accusers at the time of the arraignment of the party accused, if they be then living, shall be brought in person before the party so accused, and avow and maintain that that they have to say against the said party to prove him guilty of the treasons or offences contained in the bill of indictment laid against the party arraigned; unless the said party arraigned shall willingly without violence confess the same.

* * * * * *

Stat. Realm, IV, 144–6

34. An Act repealing certain treasons etc. (First Treason Act of Mary, 1553: 1 Mary, st. 1, c. 1).

Forasmuch as the state of every king, ruler and governor of any realm, dominion or commonalty standeth and consisteth more assured by the love and favour of the subject toward their sovereign ruler and governor than in the dread and fear of laws made with rigorous pains and extreme punishment for not obeying of their sovereign ruler and governor; and laws also justly made for the preservation of the common weal, without extreme punishment or great penalty, are more often for the most part obeyed and kept than laws and statutes made with great and extreme punishments, and in especial such laws and statutes so made whereby not only the ignorant and rude unlearned people, but also learned and expert people minding honesty, are often and many times trapped and snared, yea, many times for words only, without other fact or deed done or perpetrated: the Queen's most excellent Majesty, calling to remembrance that many, as well honourable and noble persons as other of good reputation within this her Grace's realm of England, have of late, for words only without other opinion, fact or deed, suffered shameful death not accustomed to nobles; her Highness therefore, of her accustomed clemency and mercy, minding to avoid and put away the occasion and cause of like chances hereafter to ensue, trusting her loving subjects will, for her clemency to them shewed, love, serve and obey her Grace the more heartily and faithfully than for dread or fear of pains of body, is contented and pleased that the severity of suchlike extreme dangerous and painful laws shall be abolished, annulled and made frustrate and void. Be it therefore ordained and enacted by the Queen our sovereign lady with the assent of the Lords spiritual and temporal and the Commons in this present Parliament assembled, and by authority of the same [that no act or offence shall be treason, petty treason, or misprision of treason but such as are so declared by 25 Edw. III, st. 5, c. 2].

* * * * * *

Stat. Realm, IV, 198

35. An Act whereby certain offences be made treasons (Second Treason Act of Mary, 1554: 1 & 2 Philip and Mary, c. 10).

Forasmuch as the great mercy and clemency heretofore declared by the Queen's Highness, in releasing the penal laws made by her progenitors, hath given occasion to many cankered and traitorous hearts to imagine, practise and attempt things stirring the people to disobedience and rebellion against her Highness, common policy and duty of subjects require that some law be eftsoons established to restrain the malice of such wicked and evil doers, whereby they may be prohibited to blow abroad such shameful slanders and lies as they daily invent and imagine of her Highness and of the King's Majesty her most lawful husband, which when they be heard cannot be but odible and detested of all good men, considering they touch their Majesties, upon whom dependeth the whole unity and universal wealth of this realm: In con-

sideration whereof be it ordained and enacted by the King's and the
Queen's Majesties, with the assent of the Lords spiritual and temporal
and of the Commons in the present Parliament assembled, and by
authority of the same, that if any person or persons, after the first day
of February next to come, during the marriage between the King's and
the Queen's Majesties, do compass or imagine to deprive the King's
Majesty that now is from the having and enjoying jointly together with
the Queen's Highness the style, honour and kingly name of the realms
and dominions unto our said sovereign lady the Queen's Highness
appertaining, or to destroy the King that now is during the said
matrimony, or to destroy the Queen's Majesty that now is, or the heirs
of her body begotten being kings or queens of this realm, or to levy
war [against the King or Queen or her heirs] or to depose [the Queen
or the heirs of her body] . . . and the same compasses or imaginations,
or any of them, maliciously, advisedly and directly shall or do utter by
open preaching, express words or sayings; or if any person or persons
after the said first day of February, by preaching, express words or
sayings, shall maliciously, advisedly and directly say, publish, declare,
maintain or hold opinion that the King's Majesty that now is, during
the said matrimony, ought not to have or enjoy jointly together with
the Queen's Majesty the style, honour and kingly name of this realm,
or that any person or persons, being neither the King or the Queen's
Majesty that now are, during the said matrimony between them, ought
to have or enjoy the style, honour and kingly name of this realm, or
that the Queen's Majesty that now is during her life is not or of right
ought not to be Queen of this realm, or after her death that the heirs of
her Highness' body being kings or queens of this realm of right ought
not to be kings or queens of this realm or to have and enjoy the same,
or that any person or persons other than the Queen's Majesty that now
is, during her life, ought to be queen of this realm, or after her death
other than the heirs of her body being kings or queens of this realm, as
long as any of her said heirs of her body begotten shall be in life, of right
ought to have and enjoy the imperial crown of this realm; That then
every such offender, being thereof duly convicted or attainted by the
laws of this realm, their abettors, procurers and counsellors, and all and
every their comforters, knowing the said offences or any of them be
done, and being thereof convicted or attainted as is abovesaid, for his or
their such offence shall forfeit and lose to the Queen's Highness, her heirs
and successors, all his and their goods and chattels and the whole issues

and profits of his and their lands, tenements, and other hereditaments for term of the life of every such offender or offenders, and also shall have and suffer during his or their lives perpetual imprisonment.

[II. Ecclesiastics offending shall be deprived of benefices and promotions; and all persons offending a second time shall be guilty of high treason.]

III. And be it further enacted by the said authority, that if any person or persons, at any time after the said first day of February next to come, during the said marriage, compass or imagine the death of the King's Majesty that now is and the same maliciously, advisedly and directly shall utter and attempt by any writing, printing, overt deed or act; or if any person or persons, at any time after the said first day of February next coming, shall maliciously, advisedly and directly, by writing, printing, overt deed or act [deny the title of the King or Queen or their issue, they shall be guilty of high treason].

[IV provides for the care of the realm and the King's and Queen's issue during minority under the guardianship of the King.]

V. And be it further enacted by the authority aforesaid, that if any person or persons, during the time that our said sovereign lord the King that now is shall and ought to have the order, rule, education and government of such issue or issues, being king or queen of this realm, according to the order and provision aforesaid, maliciously, advisedly and directly, by writing, printing, overt deed or act, do compass, attempt and go about to destroy the person of our said sovereign lord, or to deprive or remove his said Highness from the order, rule, education and government of the same issue or issues, being king or queen of this realm, contrary to the tenor, intent and true meaning of this present act, that then every such person or persons so offending, their procurers and abettors, being thereof lawfully convict or attainted by the laws of this realm, shall be deemed and adjudged high traitors, and that all and every such offence and offences shall be deemed and adjudged high treason. . . .

VI. And be it further enacted by the authority aforesaid, that all trials hereafter to be had, awarded or made for any treason shall be had and used only according to the due order and course of the common laws of this realm, and not otherwise.

*   *   *   *   *   *

XI. Provided always and be it enacted by the authority aforesaid, that upon the arraignment of any person which hereafter shall fortune to be arraigned for any treason mentioned in this act, all and every such person and persons, or two of them at the least, as shall hereafter write, declare, confess or depose any thing or things against the person to be arraigned, shall, if they be then living and within the realm, be brought forth in person before the party arraigned, if he require the same, and object and say openly in his hearing what they or any of them can against him for or concerning any the treasons contained in the indictment whereupon the party shall be so arraigned, unless the party arraigned for any such treason shall willingly confess the same at the time of his or their arraignment.

*　　*　　*　　*　　*　　*

Stat. Realm, IV, 255-7

36. An Act whereby certain offences be made treasons (Second Treasons Act of Elizabeth, 1571: 13 Eliz. I, c. 1).

Forasmuch as it is of some doubted whether the laws and statutes of this realm remaining at this present in force are vailable and sufficient enough for the surety and preservation of the Queen's most royal person, in whom consisteth all the happiness and comfort of the whole state and subjects of the realm, which thing all faithful, loving, and dutiful subjects ought and will with all careful study and zeal consider, foresee and provide for; by the neglecting and passing over whereof with winking eyes there might happen to grow the subversion and ruin of the quiet and most happy state and present government of this realm (which God defend): therefore at the humble suit and petition of the Lords and Commons in this present Parliament assembled, be it enacted, declared and established by authority of the same Parliament, that if any person or persons whatsoever, at any time after the last day of June next coming, during the natural life of our most gracious sovereign lady Queen Elizabeth (whom Almighty God preserve and bless with long and prosperous reign over this realm), shall, within the realm or without, compass, imagine, invent, devise or intend the death or destruction, or any bodily harm tending to death, destruction, maim or wounding of the royal person of the same our sovereign lady Queen Elizabeth; or to deprive or depose her of or from the style, honour or kingly name of the imperial crown of this realm or of any other realm or dominion to her Majesty belonging; or to levy war against her Majesty within this realm or without; or to move or to stir any foreigners or strangers with

73

force to invade this realm or the realm of Ireland or any other her
Majesty's dominions being under her Majesty's obeisance, and such
compasses, imaginations, inventions, devices or intentions or any of
them shall maliciously, advisedly and expressly utter or declare by any
printing, writing, ciphering, speech, words or sayings; or if any person
or persons whatsoever, after the said last day of June, shall maliciously,
advisedly and directly publish, declare, hold opinion, affirm or say by
any speech, express words or sayings, that our said sovereign lady Queen
Elizabeth during her life is not or ought not to be Queen of this realm
of England and also of the realms of France and Ireland; or that any
other person or persons ought of right to be King or Queen of the said
realms of England and Ireland or of any other her Majesty's dominions
being under her Majesty's obeisance, during her Majesty's life; or shall
by writing, printing, preaching, speech, express words or sayings,
maliciously, advisedly and directly publish, set forth, and affirm that the
Queen our said sovereign lady Queen Elizabeth is an heretic, schismatic,
tyrant, infidel or an usurper of the crown of the said realms or any of
them: That then all and every such said offence or offences shall be
taken, deemed and declared, by the authority of this act and Parliament,
to be high treason; and that as well the principal offender or offenders
therein as all and every the abettors, counsellors and procurers to the
same offence or offences, and all and every aiders and comforters of the
same offender or offenders, knowing the same offence or offences to be
done and committed in any place within this realm or without, being
thereof lawfully and duly indicted, convicted and attainted, according
to the usual order and course of the common laws of this realm, or
according to [35 Henry VIII, c. 2[152]] as the case shall require, shall be
deemed, declared and adjudged traitors to the Queen and the realm,
and shall suffer pains of death and also forfeit unto the Queen's Majesty,
her heirs and successors, all and singular lands, tenements and hereditaments, goods and chattels, as in cases of high treason by the laws and
statutes of this realm at this day of right ought to be forfeited and lost.

II. And be it also enacted by the authority aforesaid, that all and every
person and persons, of what degree, condition, place, nation or estate
soever they be, which shall, after the end of thirty days next after the
last day of this present session of this Parliament, at any time in the life
of our sovereign lady Queen Elizabeth in any wise claim, pretend, utter,

[152] This act provided that the trial of treasons committed outside the realm should be in King's
Bench or before a special commission.

declare, affirm or publish themselves or any of them, or any other than our said sovereign lady Elizabeth the Queen's Majesty that now is, to have right or title to have or enjoy the crown of England during or in the life of our said sovereign lady; or shall usurp the same crown or the royal style, title or dignity of the crown or realm of England during or in the life of our said sovereign lady, or shall hold and affirm that our said sovereign lady hath not right to hold and enjoy the said crown and realm, style, title or dignity, or shall not, after any demand on our said sovereign lady's part to be made, effectually acknowledge our said sovereign lady to be in right true and lawful Queen of this realm, they and every of them so offending shall be utterly disabled, during their natural lives only, to have or enjoy the crown or realm of England, or the style, title or dignity thereof, at any time in succession, inheritance or otherwise after the decease of our said sovereign lady as if such person were naturally dead; any law, custom, pretence or matter whatsoever to the contrary notwithstanding.

III. And be it further enacted, that if any person shall, during the Queen's Majesty's life, in any wise hold, affirm or maintain any right, title, interest or possibility in succession or inheritance in or to the crown of England, after our said sovereign lady the Queen, to be rightfully in or lawfully due or belonging unto any such claimer, pretender, usurper, utterer, declarer, affirmer, publisher or not-acknowledger, so that our said sovereign lady the Queen shall, by proclamation to be published through the realm, or else in the more part of those shires of this realm, as well on the south side as the north side of Trent, and also in the dominion of Wales, in which shires no war or rebellion then shall be, set forth, notify or declare such claiming, pretence, uttering, declaration, affirming, publishing, usurpation or not-acknowledging, then every person which after such proclamation shall during the Queen's Majesty's life maintain, hold or affirm any right in succession, inheritance or possibility in or to the crown or realm of England or the rights thereof to be in or to any such claimer, pretender, utterer, declarer, affirmer, usurper, publisher or not-acknowledger, shall be a high traitor and suffer and forfeit as in cases of high treason is accustomed.

IV. And be it further enacted, that if any person shall in any wise hold and affirm or maintain that the common laws of this realm not altered by Parliament ought not to direct the right of the crown of England, or that our said sovereign lady Elizabeth the Queen's Majesty that now is, with and by the authority of the Parliament of England, is not able to make laws and statutes of sufficient force and validity to limit and bind the crown of this realm and the descent, limitation, inheritance and government thereof, or that this present statute, or any part thereof, or any other statute to be made by the authority of the Parliament of England with the royal assent of our said sovereign lady the Queen for limiting of the crown, or any statute for recognising the right of the said crown and realm to be justly and lawfully in the most royal person of our said sovereign lady the Queen, is not, are not, or shall not, or ought not to be for ever of good and sufficient force and validity to bind, limit, restrain and govern all persons, their rights and titles, that in any wise may or might claim any interest or possibility in or to the crown of England in possession, remainder, inheritance, succession or otherwise howsoever, and all other persons whatsoever, every such person so holding, affirming or maintaining during the life of the Queen's Majesty shall be judged a high traitor and suffer and forfeit as in cases of high treason is accustomed; and every person so holding, affirming or maintaining after the decease of our said sovereign lady shall forfeit all his goods and chattels.

v. And for the avoiding of contentious and seditious spreading abroad of titles to the succession of the crown of this realm, to the disturbing of the common quiet of the realm, be it enacted by the authority aforesaid, that whosoever shall hereafter, during the life of our said sovereign lady, by any book or work, printed or written, directly and expressly declare and affirm, at any time before the same be by act of Parliament of this realm established and affirmed, that any one particular person, whosoever it be, is or ought to be the right heir and successor to the Queen's Majesty that now is (whom God long preserve) except the same be the natural issue of her Majesty's body, or shall wilfully set up in open place, publish, or spread any books or scrolls to that effect, or shall print, bind or put to sale, or utter, or cause to be printed, bound or put to sale or uttered, any such book or writing wittingly, that he or they, their abettors and counsellors and every of them, shall for the first offence suffer imprisonment of one whole year and forfeit half his goods, whereof the one moiety to the Queen's Majesty, the other moiety to him or them that will sue for the same by bill, action of debt, plaint, information or otherwise in any of the Queen's Majesty's courts, wherein no essoin or protection shall be allowed; and if any shall eftsoons offend therein, then they and every of them, their abettors and counsellors, shall incur the pains and forfeitures which in the statutes of provisions or praemunire are appointed and limited.

* * * * * *

[IX requires proof of the offences mentioned in the act by two witnesses in the presence of the party arraigned.]

[X. The aiders and comforters of offenders affirming that the Queen is 'an heretic, schismatic, tyrant, infidel or usurper of the crown' incur, for the first offence, the penalties of praemunire, and for the second offence the penalties of high treason.]

XI. Provided always and be it enacted by the authority aforesaid, that the giving of charitable alms, in money, meat, drink, apparel or bedding, for the sustentation of the body or health of any person or persons that shall commit any the offences made treason or praemunire by this act during the time that the same offender shall be in prison, shall not in any wise be deemed or taken to be any offence; anything in this act contained to the contrary thereof notwithstanding.

Stat. Realm, IV, 526–8

37. An Act for provision to be made for the surety of the Queen's most royal person (1585: 27 Eliz. I, c. 1).

Forasmuch as the good felicity and comfort of the whole estate of this realm consisteth (only next under God) in the surety and preservation of the Queen's most excellent Majesty; and for that it hath manifestly appeared that sundry wicked plots and means have of late been devised and laid, as well in foreign parts beyond the seas as also within this realm, to the great endangering of her Highness' most royal person and to the utter ruin of the whole common weal, if by God's merciful providence the same had not been revealed: therefore for preventing of such great perils as might hereafter otherwise grow by the like detestable and devilish practices, at the humble suit and earnest petition and desire of the Lords spiritual and temporal and the Commons in this present Parliament assembled, and by the authority of the same Parliament, be it enacted and ordained, if at any time after the end of this present session of Parliament any open invasion or rebellion shall be had or made into or within any of her Majesty's realms or dominions, or any act attempted tending to the hurt of her Majesty's most royal person, by or for any person that shall or may pretend any title to the crown of this realm after her Majesty's decease; or if anything shall be compassed or imagined tending to the hurt of her Majesty's royal person by any person or with the privity of any person that shall or may pretend title to the crown of this realm, that then by her Majesty's commission under her great seal the lords and others of her Highness' Privy Council and such other lords of Parliament to be named by her Majesty as with the said Privy Council shall make up the number of 24 at the least, having with them for their assistance in that behalf such of the judges of the courts of record at Westminster as her Highness shall for that purpose assign and appoint, or the more part of the same Council, lords and judges, shall by virtue of this act have authority to examine all and every the offences aforesaid and all circumstances thereof, and thereupon to give sentence or judgment as upon good proof the matter shall appear unto them. And that after such sentence or judgment given and declaration thereof made and published by her Majesty's proclamation under the great seal of England, all persons against whom such sentence or judgment shall be so given and published shall be excluded and disabled for ever to have or claim, or to pretend to have or claim, the crown of this realm or of any her Majesty's dominions; any former law or statute whatsoever to the contrary in any wise notwithstanding. And that thereupon all her Highness' subjects shall and may lawfully, by virtue of this act and her Majesty's direction in that behalf, by all forcible and possible means pursue to death every of such wicked person by whom or by whose means, assent or privity any such invasion or rebellion shall be in form aforesaid denounced to have been made, or such wicked act attempted, or other thing compassed or imagined against her Majesty's person, and all their aiders, comforters and abettors. And if any such detestable act shall be executed against her Highness' most royal person whereby her Majesty's life shall be taken away (which God of his great mercy forbid), that then every such person by or for whom any such act shall be executed, and their issues being any wise assenting or privy to the same, shall by virtue of this act be excluded and disabled for ever to have or claim, or to pretend to have or claim, the said crown of this realm or of any other her Highness' dominions; any former law or statute whatsoever to the contrary in any wise notwithstanding. And that all the subjects of this realm and all other her Majesty's dominions shall and may lawfully, by virtue of this act, by all forcible and possible means pursue to death every such wicked person by whom or by whose means any such detestable fact shall be, in form hereafter expressed, denounced to have been committed, and also their issues being any way assenting or privy to the same, and all their aiders, comforters and abettors in that behalf.

II. And to the end that the intention of this law may be effectually executed, if her Majesty's life shall be taken away by any violent or unnatural means (which God defend): be it further enacted by the authority aforesaid, that the lords and others which shall be of her Majesty's Privy Council at the time of such her decease, or the more part of the same Council, joining unto them for their better assistance five other earls and seven other lords of Parliament at the least (foreseeing that none of the said earls, lords or Council be known to be persons that may make any title to the crown), those persons which were chief justices of every Bench, master of the Rolls, and chief baron of the Exchequer at the time of her Majesty's death, or in default of the said justices, master of the Rolls and chief baron some other of those which were justices of some of the courts of record at Westminster at the time of her Highness' decease to supply their places, or any 24 or more of them, whereof eight to be lords of Parliament not being of the Privy Council, shall to the uttermost of their power and skill examine the cause and manner of such her Majesty's death, and what persons shall be any way guilty thereof, and all circumstances concerning the same, according to the true meaning of this act; and thereupon shall by open proclamation publish the same, and without any delay by all forcible and possible means prosecute to death all such as shall be found to be offenders therein and all their aiders and abettors. And for the doing thereof, and for the withstanding and suppressing of all such power and force as shall any way be levied or stirred in disturbance of the due execution of this law, shall by virtue of this act have power and authority not only to raise and use such forces as shall in that behalf be needful and convenient, but also to use all other means and things possible and necessary for the maintenance of the same forces and prosecution of the said offenders. And if any such power and force shall be levied or stirred in disturbance of the due execution of this law by any person that shall or may pretend any title to the crown of this realm, whereby this law in all things may not be fully executed according to the effect and true meaning of the same, that then every such person shall by virtue of this act be therefore excluded and disabled for ever to have or claim, or to pretend to have or claim, the crown of this realm or of any other her Highness' dominions; any former law or statute whatsoever to the contrary notwithstanding.

III. And be it further enacted by the authority aforesaid that all and every the subjects of all her Majesty's realms and dominions shall, to the uttermost of their power, aid and assist the said Council and all other the lords and other persons to be adjoined unto them for assistance as is aforesaid in all things to be done and executed according to the effect and intention of this law; and that no subject of this realm shall in any wise be impeached in body, lands or goods at any time hereafter for any thing to be done or executed according to the tenor of this law; any law or statute heretofore made to the contrary in any wise notwithstanding.

IV. And whereas of late many of her Majesty's good and faithful subjects have, in the name of God and with the testimony of good consciences, by one uniform manner of writing under their hands and seals and by their several oaths voluntarily taken, joined themselves together in one Bond and Association[153] to withstand and revenge to the uttermost all such malicious actions and attempts against her Majesty's most royal person: now for the full explaining of all such ambiguities and questions as otherwise might happen to grow by reason of any sinister or wrong construction or interpretation to be made or inferred of or upon the words or meaning thereof, be it declared and enacted by the authority of this present Parliament that the same Association and every article and sentence therein contained, as well concerning the disallowing, excluding or disabling of any person that may or shall pretend any title to come to the crown of this realm, and also for the pursuing and taking revenge of any person for any such wicked act or attempt as is mentioned in the same Association, shall and ought to be in all things expounded and adjudged according to the true intent and meaning of this act, and not otherwise nor against any other person or persons.

Stat. Realm, IV, 704–5

(ii) PROCEDURE IN TREASON TRIALS.[154] Even more helpful to the Crown than the extension of treason were the procedural advantages it enjoyed in the trials of people accused of the offence. The court could be rigged against them, and they were handicapped in the conduct of their defence. Treason was tried in King's Bench or at the Assizes, depending on the county in which it had allegedly been committed, though noblemen enjoyed the privilege of

153 A voluntary association of Englishmen sworn to protect the Queen and avenge her on the person of anyone who profited by her death (i.e. Mary Queen of Scots). It was formed after the assassination of William of Orange in July 1584.

154 Bellamy, *Tudor Law*, chs. 3 & 4; Elton, *Policy and Police*, chs. 7 & 8.

trial by their peers in the court of the lord steward.[155] The Assizes were empowered to try treasons and felonies by commissions of oyer and terminer, and since special commissions for particular cases could be issued the Crown could erect a court of handpicked nominees. Throughout the period most commoners, and indeed all important defendants, were arraigned before such special commissions, and though there was nothing novel or improper about the method it manifestly gave the prosecution a chance to select the judges. For state trials, the commission quite commonly consisted in effect of the Privy Council—the government against whose head the offence had allegedly been committed. The lord steward's court, though in theory composed of all the peers, could in practice be appointed by selective summons.[156] However, loyalty was so generally solid that in these matters very little artifice was required. At his trial, the accused had neither counsel nor a copy of the indictment; his witnesses (whose attendance he could not compel) were not allowed to depose on oath and thus tended to lose credit; and one sworn testimony against him was sufficient. All this was established in the law—pre-Tudor law—and it should be noted that strict legalism involved also some technicalities which on occasion benefited the accused: cases are known in which guilty men escaped the consequences of their treasons by such means.[157]

Developments during the century in the main continued the imbalance against the accused. Treason laws regularly deprived him of any benefit of clergy he might claim; but this was reasonable, since the privilege was so widely abused. The act which empowered the Crown to hold the trial before a special commission in any shire chosen (38) has been read as a move to avoid the common law under which all crimes had to be tried by a jury of the shire in which they were committed, but the act only confirmed lawful practice: even before its passage the trial of the northern rebels of 1537 was held before a commission 'for Yorkshire and Middlesex' (in fact, the Privy Council and judges) with a jury empannelled in Yorkshire and sent to Westminster.[158] The act's preamble has much reason on its side. Another Henrician statute (35 Henry VIII, c. 2), which provided for the trial of treasons committed outside the realm, was confirmed by Elizabeth (36): faced with Catholic subjects plotting abroad, she badly needed it. On the other hand, two Edwardian statutes (32 and 33) did something for the accused by demanding the testimony of two lawful witnesses; after Mary's repeal it remained a moot point whether this more equitable procedure stood or not, but opinion increasingly favoured what even in the 1530's had been a preference for more than one.[159]

[155] Harcourt, *His Grace the Steward*, ch. 12.
[156] Cf. Doc. 40 and Tanner, 448 ff.   [157] Elton, *Policy and Police*, 295 ff.
[158] *Deputy Keeper's Reports*, III, App. 2, 250 f. Mary, however, explicitly gave up the right to do this (35, sect. vi).
[159] Hill, *Amer. Journ. of Legal History*, XII, 95 ff.; Elton, *Policy and Police*, 308 f.

If all else failed, the Crown had one last weapon in the act of attainder, a parliamentary statute which could declare a man guilty of treason.[160] Originally, and most commonly, attainder was used to supplement a conviction in a court of law or guilt made manifest by death in battle against the king. It had been the means by which successive victors in the civil wars assured to themselves the property of the defeated: such acts 'attainted' a traitor's blood and thus deprived his now corrupted heirs of lands in tail which a conviction for treason did not touch.[161] However, after 1459 attainder was sometimes used without a conviction at law or manifest act of treason,[162] and this method of disposing of enemies whose offence fell short of treason, or who would have successfully defended themselves in a trial, recurred under Henry VIII. Among its victims were Elizabeth Barton and her accomplices (1534), the countess of Salisbury (1539), and Thomas Cromwell (1540), falsely accused of having invented it. This superiority of Parliament's legislative function to the forms of law was admitted, though with qualms of conscience,[163] and the precedents were not acted upon. Normally, the Crown could rely on the wide reach of the treason law and the bias of the trial; nor is it at all apparent that the vast majority of those executed as traitors were not in fact guilty in law. Charges of treason were usually investigated with great care, and escapes (by acquittal or otherwise) were not uncommon; the bad reputation of Tudor treason trials rests on the few in which high politics were involved, and in which indeed the fate of the accused was nearly always certain from the start.[164] It is a mistake to judge these matters solely by the famous cases—Sir Thomas More or Mary Queen of Scots.

38. An Act to proceed by Commission of Oyer and Terminer against such persons as shall confess treasons (1541: 33 Henry VIII, c. 23).

Forasmuch as divers and sundry persons upon great grounds of vehement suspicions as well of high treason, petty treasons, misprisions of treason, as of murders, be many times sent for from divers shires and places of this realm and other the King's dominions, to the King's Majesty's great charges and expenses, to be examined before the King's Highness' Council upon their offences, to the intent that convictions or declarations of such persons should speedily ensue, as the merits of

---

[160] That attainders had to be 'proper' statutes, assented to by all parts of the Parliament, was established in 1489 (Pollard, *Henry VII*, II, 19).

[161] E.g. **39**; and see **12** for Henry VII's endeavour to end the chain of attainders. In fact he was more inclined to intimidate potential trouble-makers by keeping such acts in being than the Yorkists had been (Lander, *Hist. Journal*, IV, 120 ff.). Lands in tail were held by a man and the heirs of his body, giving the existing tenant only a life interest; failure of heirs caused the lands to revert to the lord. The heirs' reversionary interest barred automatic forfeiture for treason.

[162] Bellamy, *Treason in the Middle Ages*, 197 ff.   [163] Holdsworth, IV, 185 and n. 4.

[164] Elton, *Policy and Police*, ch. 9, esp. the table on p. 387.

their cases should require; and albeit that after great travail taken in the examinations of such persons it appear to the said Council by confession, witness or vehement suspect that such persons be rather guilty of such offences whereof they be so examined than otherwise; yet nevertheless such offenders so examined by the course of the common law of this realm must be indicted within the shires and places where they committed their offences and also tried by the inhabitants or freeholders of such shires and places, although by their confessions or sufficient witness their offences be certainly known to the King's Council; [which results in trouble and expense and sometimes the escape of evildoers; be it therefore enacted] that if any person or persons, being examined before the King's Council or three of them upon any manner of treasons, misprisions of treasons or murders do confess any such offences, or that the said Council or three of them upon such examination shall think any person so examined to be vehemently suspected of any treason, misprisions of treasons or murder, that then in every such case, by the King's commandment, his Majesty's commission of oyer and terminer under his Highness' great seal shall be made by the chancellor of England to such persons and into such shires or places as shall be named and appointed by the King's Highness, for the speedy trial, conviction or deliverance of such offenders; which commissioners shall have power and authority to inquire, hear and determine all such treasons, misprisions of treasons and murders within the shires and places limited by their commission, by such good and lawful persons as shall be returned before them by the sheriff or his minister, or any other having power to return writs and process for that purpose, in whatsoever other shire or place, within the King's dominions or without, such offence of treasons, misprisions of treasons or murders so examined were done or committed. And that in such cases no challenge for the shire or hundred shall be allowed.

[II. Accused may challenge jurors for lack of freehold.

III. Peers to have trial by peers.]

* * * * * *

Stat. Realm, III, 863-4

39. The Act of Attainder of Edward, Duke of Buckingham (1523: 14 & 15 Henry VIII, c. 20).

Forasmuch as Edward, late duke of Buckingham, late of Thornbury in the county of Gloucester, the 24th day of April in the fourth year of the reign of our sovereign lord the King that now is and divers times after, imagined and compassed traitorously and unnaturally the destruction of the most royal person of our said sovereign lord and subversion of this his realm, and then traitorously committed and did divers and many treasons against our said sovereign lord the King, contrary to his allegiance, in the counties of Gloucester and Somerset, the city of London, the counties of Kent and Surrey, of the which treasons and offences the said late duke in the said counties was severally indicted. And afterward for and upon the same treasons the 13th day of May the 13th year of the reign of our said sovereign lord the King at Westminster in the county of Middlesex before Thomas, duke of Norfolk, for that time only being great steward of England by the King's letters patents, by verdict of his peers and by judgment of the said steward against the said late duke then and there given after the due order of the law and custom of England, was attainted of high treason, as by records thereof more plainly appeareth. Wherefore be it ordained, enacted and established by the King our sovereign lord, with the assent of the Lords spiritual and temporal and the Commons in this present Parliament assembled and by the authority of the same, that the said late duke for the offences above rehearsed stand and be convicted, adjudged and attainted of high treason, and forfeit to the King our sovereign lord and his heirs for ever all honours, castles, manors, lordships, hundreds, franchises, liberties, privileges, advowsons, nominations, knight's fees, lands, tenements, rents, services, reversions, remainders, portions, annuities, pensions, rights, possessions and other hereditaments whatsoever, in England, Ireland, Wales, Calais and marches of the same, or elsewhere, whereof the said late duke or any other person or persons to his use were seised or possessed in fee simple, fee tail, or for term of any other man's life or lives, or any estate of inheritance or otherwise the said 24th day of April or any time since, or in the which the said late duke or any other person or persons seised to his use had then or any time since lawful cause of entry within England, Ireland, Wales, Calais and marches of the same, or elsewhere. And over that, the said Edward to forfeit unto our said sovereign lord all goods and chattels, as well real as personal whatsoever, whereof the said Edward was possessed to his own use, or any other person or persons was possessed to the use of the same late duke, the said 13th day of May, or whereof the said late duke had lawful cause of seisure to his own proper use the said 13th day of May; and also to forfeit unto our said sovereign lord all debts which were owing by any person or persons unto the said late duke or unto any other person or persons to the use of the said late duke the said 13th day of May.

*   *   *   *   *   *

Stat. Realm, III, 246

40. The Trial for Treason of Thomas, fourth duke of Norfolk, 1572.[165]

... After the reading of the indictment, the clerk of the crown said to the duke: 'How sayest thou, Thomas duke of Norfolk, art thou guilty of these treasons whereof thou art indicted in manner and form as thou art thereof indicted, Yea or No?'

Thereupon the duke began, and said to this effect: May it please your grace, and you the rest of my lords here; the hearing of this indictment giveth me occasion to enter into the making of a suit which I meant not to have done before my coming hither. I beseech you, if the law will permit it, that I may have counsel allowed me for the answering of this indictment.

The lord chief justice answered that in case of high treason he cannot have counsel allowed; and that he was to answer to his own fact only, which himself best knew, and might without counsel sufficiently answer.

Duke. That you may understand I speak it not without some ground, these be the causes that move me to make this suit. I was told before I came here that I was indicted upon the statute of the 25th of Edw. III. I have had very short warning to provide to answer so great a matter; I have not had 14 hours in all, both day and night, and now I neither hear the same statute alleged, and yet I am put at once to the whole herd of laws, not knowing which particularly to answer unto. The indictment containeth sundry points and matters to touch me by circumstance, and so to draw me into matter of treason, which are not treasons themselves; therefore with reverence and humble submission I am led to think I may have counsel. And this I shew that you may think I move not this suit without any ground. I am hardly handled; I have had short warning and no books—neither books of statutes nor so much as the breviate of statutes. I am brought to fight without a weapon; yet I remember one

---

[165] Norfolk was tried before the earl of Shrewsbury as lord high steward and 26 lords triers, for treason committed under the statute of 1352, the overt act being his endeavour to marry Mary Queen of Scots and thus to encompass the Queen's death. The extracts are chosen to illustrate the difficulties experienced by accused in treason trials.

case in law—I think it is in the first year of King Henry VII. It is the case of one Humphrey Stafford, which was indicted of high treason and had counsel allowed him. If the precedent in his case be such as it may extend to me, I require it at your hands that I may have it allowed; I shew you my ground why I crave it; I refer me to your opinions therein.

Then Sir James Dyer, lord chief justice of the Common Pleas, said: My lord, that case of Humphrey Stafford *in primo* of Henry VII was about pleading of sanctuary, for that he was taken out of sanctuary at Culneham, which belonged to the abbot of Abingdon, so the question was whether he should be allowed sanctuary in that case, and with that form of pleading, which was matter of law; in which case he had counsel, and not upon the point or fact of high treason, but only for the allowance of sanctuary, and whether it might be allowed being claimed by prescription and without shewing any former allowances in eyre, and such like matters. But all our books do forbid allowing of counsel in the point of treason, but only it is to be answered guilty or not guilty.

Duke. Humphrey Stafford's case was high treason, and he had counsel. . . . If the law do not allow me counsel, I must submit me to your opinions. . . . I am now to make another suit to you, my lords the judges; I beseech you tell me if my indictment be perfect and sufficient in law, and whether in whole or in the parts, and in which parts, that I may know to what I should answer.

Lord Chief Justice Catlin. For the sufficiency of your indictment, it hath been well debated and considered by us all; and we have all with one assent resolved, and so do certify you, that if the causes in the indictment expressed be true in fact, the indictment is wholly and in every part sufficient.

Duke. Be all the points treasons?

L.C.J. Catlin. All be treasons, if the truth of the case be so in fact.

Duke. I will tell you what moveth me to ask you this. I have heard of the case of the Lord Scrope; it was in the time of Henry IV (the judges said Henry V), he confessed the indictment and yet traversed that the points thereof were no treasons.

L.C.J. Catlin. My lord, he had his judgment for treason upon that indictment, and was executed. . . . (pp. 965-7).

* * * * * *

Duke. I shall hardly come, after so smooth a tale as Mr Attorney of the Wards can tell; yet one good proof I have to my comfort, that they [*i.e.* the witnesses against him] be as please your Lordships to weigh them. If you would not have dealt thus untruly with me, I would not have taken exception against them, though I chiefly challenge none but Barker, in whom you may see what fear may do; besides that they have confessed themselves traitors, and so men of no conscience or credit. It is well known that Barker's stomach is nothing; he hath been known well enough. Fear hath done much in him. The bishop of Ross is also a fearful man. As touching Barker and the bishop of Ross, Bracton hath a saying that witnesses must be freemen and not traitors, neither outlawed nor attainted.

Catlin. None of them be outlawed, attainted, or indicted.

Duke. I mean not that they were indicted, but they be in as ill case, for they have confessed themselves traitors. . . (p. 1026.)

* * * * * *

Duke. You say my indictment is only upon the statute of 25 Edw. III. That statute standeth upon three points, compassing the death of the Prince's person, levying of war against the Prince, and aiding of the Prince's enemies; and all these must be proved overt-fact. If by any way, by any overt-fact, you can prove that I have directly touched the Prince's person, or done any of the said things that the statute extendeth to, I will yield myself guilty. If anything be doubtful, the statute referreth it to the judgment of the Parliament.[166]

Catlin. Usage is the best expounder of the law, that is, the common use how the statute hath been taken and expounded; and the same statute is but the declaration of the common law.

Duke. The preamble of the statute is to bring the laws of treason to a certainty, that men may certainly know what is treason.

Attorney-General. You complained of your close keeping, that you had no books to provide for your answer. It seemeth you have had books and counsel. You allege books, statutes, and Bracton. I am sure the study of such books is not your profession.

Duke. I have been in trouble these two years. Think you that in all this time I have not had cause to look for myself? . . . (p. 1027.)

* * * * * *

State Trials, 1, 957–1042

---

[166] The act of 1352, allowing for the possibility of treasons not specified in the statute, included a proviso reserving all such dubious cases to the determination of king and Parliament.

CHAPTER 2

THE COUNCIL

I. GROWTH AND COMPOSITION

The body which, under king or queen, governed the realm was the royal Council, chosen and appointed by the sovereign and responsible solely to him. However institutional and corporate it became, it never ceased in essence to be a collection of individuals; nor did it ever (except during the reign of Edward VI) escape the full control of the Crown. Together with the vagaries of the evidence, these facts make the Council a subject on which it is often difficult to be precise. The Council of Elizabeth was a small and select body properly called the Privy Council, while that of Henry VII comprised large numbers and displayed much less formality; but the exact nature of the latter and the way in which it grew into the former are still not absolutely clear. Although it has been suggested that the history of the early Tudor Council is obscured by the absence of evidence, it would be truer to say that the evidence is so bulky, so unsystematic, and so hard to interpret that it prevents clear-cut answers.[1] However, though a good deal remains to be done, enough work has by now been published on this important institution to make a reasonably confident account of its history possible.[2]

Henry VII inherited from his predecessors a well-defined institutional

---

[1] Elton, *Studies*, I, 308 ff.

[2] Older accounts should be forgotten, and little trust can be reposed in such summaries of inadequate analysis as Holdsworth, I, 495 ff.; IV, 56 ff.; or Pickthorn, I, 29 ff.; II, 13 ff. Pollard's articles in *Eng. Hist. Rev.*, XXXVII and XXXVIII cleared some errors out of the way but added new ones. A great advance was made possible by the discovery, at the Huntington Library in California, of Elizabethan transcripts from the lost early-Tudor registers, but Dunham (who found and first applied these documents) made less than totally convincing use of them (see List of Books). In particular, by misunderstanding some Tudor English, he invented a new institutional term—the 'Whole Council'—which still occasionally flickers through the literature. For the argument against these and other errors see the article cited in the previous note. The Ellesmere Extracts for Henry VII's reign are printed in Bayne, *Council of Henry VII*; the account there also fails to prove adequate (see Elton, *Studies*, I, 294 ff.). Guy has utilised these and further materials, discovered by himself, in his important *Cardinal's Court*. The history of the mid-Tudor Council has been thoroughly investigated by Hoak, Weikel and Lemasters. After 1558 the coverage remains patchy. MacCaffrey's work (*Shaping*, and *Government and Society*, 95 ff.) throws incidental but important light on the Council, and Pulman gives a plain account for the 1570's. The following description rests in the main on these recent contributions which I shall not cite at every point. For an attempt to place the Council in a general political and constitutional context cf. Elton, *Trans. R. Hist. Soc.*, 1975, 175 ff.

Council.[3] Chosen (when he could assert himself) at the king's discretion from nobility, clergy and gentry, it met regularly only during term-time, sat in one of the two rooms which made up the so-called Star Chamber in the palace of Westminster, dealt with any business of government put before it by the king but also with private suits for justice, and was attended by a clerk who kept a record of attendance and transactions. Though this body had fallen, during Henry VI's minority, into the hands of a small clique of nobles, the restoration of royal power by Edward IV, Richard III and Henry VII once again turned it into a Council of the king's trusted advisers. This fact was visibly expressed in its enlargement. Henry VII's councillors grew rapidly in number from an initial fifteen or sixteen to something like forty or fifty, and more, and many of the recorded meetings were attended by a great assembly of councillors.[4] Throughout the reign the Council consisted of some bishops (four to eight), a number of inferior clergy (dean of the Chapel Royal, the almoner, canon and civil lawyers, etc.), a fair representation of the English peerage,[5] some knights and esquires, and the law officers of the Crown (judges, attorney general, solicitor general, serjeants at law). Some held specific offices, but (except possibly for the non-noble laymen) this was no necessary condition. There can be absolutely no doubt that this body was an active Council—debating, advising, administering, judging—and that it is the only body at this time to be called the Council. The king employed several devices to increase the efficiency of what was essentially an overlarge committee. For one thing, he very frequently—perhaps usually—attended its meetings and clearly dominated its proceedings. There are signs that at times he did not expect the Council to do more than listen to him, though at other times he invited free discussion. For another, attempts were made to confine the hearing of suits, whether private or royal, to specified days and leave the Council free to govern at other times; but it does not appear that this sort of organisation worked well until much later.[6] Lastly the Council sometimes appointed committees, whether standing (like the committee of legal counsel, charged with enforcing the penal legislation, which sat from at least 1500 onwards)[7] or ad hoc (like the committee of lawyers, a bishop, and two lay councillors which in 1499 examined an alleged case of villeinage). The Council committees created by acts of Parliament—like the committee

---

[3] Mr Lander (Eng. Hist. Rev., LXXIII, 27 ff.) has shown that earlier views of the Council's 'disappearance' under the Yorkists are unsound.

[4] E.g. 39 on 15 June 1486, 33 on 30 January 1489, 49 on 6 November 1498, 40 on 26 November 1504 ('Ellesmere Transcripts'). At none of these meetings was the business in any way out of the ordinary.

[5] The first three years of the reign show the earl of Lincoln, later (1487) to be a rebel and defeated at Stoke, in regular attendance.

[6] This point is discussed more fully below, in the description of Star Chamber (pp. 163 ff.).

[7] Cf. Somerville, Eng. Hist. Rev., LIV, 427 ff.

of the so-called Star Chamber Act (78)—were also intended to assist the Council in managing its vast burden of work, though without much success. It remains true that there was in this period only one institution to be called the king's Council, whether it dealt with affairs or sat as a court to hear pleas, and that this Council had its active existence only during the sixteen weeks of the law terms.

However, this is not the whole story. Government had still to be carried on at other times, and well-attested tradition affirms that Henry chiefly relied on a few select councillors in his government—a variable part of the regular Westminster Council. When term ended the king usually went on his travels, while most of his councillors returned to their private avocations. Being on the king's Council was, in term time, no sinecure: great nobles like the duke of Buckingham or the marquess of Dorset, or the many bishops who attended so assiduously, had concerns of their own to look after which in term they were forced to neglect. The councillors who accompanied the king on his progresses and were intimately in his innermost counsels formed an 'inner ring' of office holders (especially holders of ostensibly Household offices), the really active and influential part of a government which was effectively in the king's own hands. This was the so-called 'council attendant', better described as 'the councillors attendant upon the king'. For these men did not compose an institutional Council either as against or as part of the Council proper; they were simply those special councillors whom the king wanted with him most of the time and who were sufficiently professional politicians and administrators to regard their work in government as an all-the-year-round affair. In term, when the king returned to the neighbourhood of Westminster, the Council assembled from all over the country, the attendant councillors naturally merging in the general body. When an act of 1504 (18) authorised prosecutions for illegal retaining either before the chancellor in the Star Chamber or 'the king and his Council attending upon his most royal person wheresoever he be', it was distinguishing not between two Councils but in effect between two different times of the year.

The accession of Henry VIII, by removing the active participation of the king, gave greater prominence to this 'inner ring'. Institutionally speaking his only Council, too, was that large body of councillors whose term-time meetings were recorded by the clerk of the Council, but there is some evidence that early in the reign the more active councillors began to meet with greater regularity and formality.[8] However, Wolsey's rise arrested any tendency that this group might show of developing into a genuine institution; until his fall, the only true Council remained that large, mixed and intermittent body which had been characteristic of the past. Wolsey in person usurped the functions of the inner ring (together with those of the king

[8] Elton, *Tudor Revolution*, 62 f.

himself); though the formal Council continued to meet nearly as often as in Henry VII's time, its work was much less political and more markedly judicial than before. Though it still quite regularly dealt with business that cannot be called Star Chamber matters, the bulk of the known transactions was either quite formal or curial.[9] At times Henry VIII grew restive at the absence of councillors from his court, and this together with the growing burden of business induced Wolsey to project reforms. More than once he tried to devolve some concerns on standing committees, some of which were to struggle through to a longer life after him.[10] In 1526 he went further when he proposed to reduce the Council to twenty members (all office holders but leaving out the law officers altogether) who were to be responsible both for the administrative work of a true Council and for the judicial work of what was already in effect the court of Star Chamber (41). The ostensible purpose of the reform—that the king might have sufficient councillors attendant upon him—was defeated by an arrangement which left Wolsey free still to make them attend upon himself at Westminster; but the significant part of the plan was the provision within the larger body of a smaller Council of twenty which was to do all the old Council's work. This would indeed have divided the Council into two, but the two parts were not respectively the ancestors of Privy Council and Star Chamber;[11] they were simply the leading councillors and the rest, a distinction which in practice had existed for a long time but had never had any meaning in institutional terms.

Though at the time nothing came of this reform, it formed the basis of Thomas Cromwell's reorganisation of the Council which at last produced the institutional Privy Council some time between 1534 and 1536[12]—most probably around the middle of 1536. By the latter date there existed a Council of nineteen, the sole body now and hereafter to be properly called the king's Council.[13] It simplifies things, though it cuts across the haphazardness of sixteenth-century terminology, to reserve the name 'Privy Council' for the product of Cromwell's reform. When this Privy Council met on 10 August 1540, to appoint a clerk and inaugurate a minute book (42), its institutional organisation was complete. Its clerk descended

---

9 'Ellesmere Transcripts'; and cf. Dunham, *Hunt. Lib. Quart.*, VII, 7 ff.

10 Cf. *ibid.*; also, for a more general account, Dunham in *Amer. Hist. Rev.*, vol. XLIX, 644 ff.

11 As Tanner thought (216 f.). The same idea is implicit in Holdsworth's erroneous statement (I, 495 ff.) that something called 'the Council at court' became the Privy Council, while the Council in Star Chamber developed into the court of that name.

12 Elton, *Tudor Revolution*, 317 ff.; *Trans. R. Hist. Soc.*, 1975, 200 ff.

13 Pollard (*Eng. Hist. Rev.*, XXXVIII, 49 ff.) has demolished the notion that even after 1540 there could exist two institutionally distinct Councils. However, it is true that Henry VIII's relative idleness and positive fear of plague induced him to keep part of the Council with him and away from Westminster even in term, with the result that for a few years the Privy Council tended to meet in two parts in different places. This had been foreshadowed towards the end of Cromwell's ministry (Elton, *Tudor Revolution*, 315).

from the junior, or assistant, clerk of the older Council whose senior clerk now continued as clerk of the Council sitting as a court in Star Chamber[14] The proceedings of the Privy Council (meeting all the year round and wherever was convenient) are recorded in its *Acts*; those of the court of Star Chamber in its lost *Books of Orders and Decrees*. But though the institutions were clearly distinct in every other way, they had very nearly the same membership.[15] The turning of the inner ring into the Privy Council had not left behind another part of the Council, now court of Star Chamber, as is sometimes suggested. The outer or 'ordinary' councillors not important or active enough to reach the eminence of the institutionalised ring were not replenished and disappeared in a short time; in Elizabeth's reign the only persons described as councillors and sworn of the Council were privy councillors.[16]

It was an essential part of Cromwell's reform that the Privy Council should be relatively small and in the main composed of office-holders (chancellor, treasurer, etc., secretary, and the so-called Household officers who were in fact ministers without portfolio). When royal control relaxed after Henry VIII's death problems arose, mainly because rival politicians wished to strengthen their factions in the Council. During the mid-Tudor period, while the Council was manifestly dominated by such leading personalities as the dukes of Somerset and Northumberland, or Bishop Gardiner and Cardinal Pole, it always contained enough powerful noblemen to ensure—in the absence of strong monarchs—plots and coups and battles for control. In administrative terms, however, its guiding spirit was its first clerk, William Paget (elevated to the peerage in 1549) who made it his concern to preserve the principles of the earlier reform through the upheavals of those years— upheavals in which he himself got caught up at regular intervals. His rules for the Council (43) represent a desired ideal rather than established practice, but they well illustrate the sort of organisation and routine that made the Tudor Privy Council such an effective instrument of government. Paget throughout aimed to prevent the Council from growing too large again, and in the reign of Edward VI he proved pretty successful—during Somerset's ascendancy because the Protector ignored the Council and ruled by himself, and during Northumberland's in despite of that duke's need for more

---

[14] The senior clerk had a salary of 40 marks a year (£26 13s. 4d.); the junior clerk got £20. By the reign of Elizabeth the Privy Council disposed of a staff of at least four clerks (Pollard, *Eng. Hist. Rev.*, XXXVIII, 56), but formally and in salary the clerk of the Star Chamber remained senior to them.

[15] Star Chamber continued to use the services of the chief justices and occasionally of others not privy councillors (below, pp. 162 f.).

[16] Pollard, *Eng. Hist. Rev.*, XXXVIII, 47 f. An exception should be made for the masters of requests (below, p. 189) who, because descended from lesser councillors, still took a kind of councillor's oath.

personal supporters on the Council.[17] In the next reign, the queen insisted on rewarding loyal friends with places on the Council while necessity required her to keep on the experienced men she inherited. This frustrated efforts to keep the body small. Paget tried to solve the resulting difficulties by confining policy-making to a small committee working in close contact with King Philip, but his own quarrel with Gardiner reduced his influence, and the Council declined in effectiveness. Its divisions and factiousness frustrated government (45), and attempts to cope with its unwieldiness resulted in the use of *ad hoc* committees (44), which gave but a spurious air of solidity to its work.[18] The true answer lay in reducing the size of the Council to below twenty, so that its membership and activities could be firmly under the control of the Crown and its work be once again efficient. On her accession, Elizabeth (no doubt on William Cecil's advice) immediately returned to Cromwell's principles, and her Privy Council fluctuated between eighteen and twelve. In the absence of standing committees the parties never grew into battling factions.[19] In general the Council grew smaller rather than bigger: the thirteen councillors of 1601 (46) represented a very select, and consequently very powerful, body. Most of the work was in fact done by a smaller group still: some four or five councillors, the lord treasurer and secretary prominent among them, attended with a regularity not observed by the rest. The queen was rarely present, as indeed had been practice since Henry VII's death. Characteristically the Privy Council excluded the judges and law officers[20]; its members held office under the Crown; and although Cromwell had retained the bishops, the remnant of Henry VII's dozen or more spiritual councillors, Elizabeth never appointed any ecclesiastic except Whitgift (1586) to her Council. Whether this was general or particular policy—whether she disliked bishops as councillors or did not take to the bishops available—is not clear. She was always able to assert the Crown's absolute freedom of choice in the appointment of her councillors; and so careful was she of this power that even acknowledged favourites like Essex waited years for

[17] For all this cf. Hoak who has, among other things, disposed of false views concerning the size of the Council and a supposed proliferation of committees which I expressed in the first edition of this book.

[18] The Council took one step under Mary towards better institutional organisation: in 1556 it acquired a seal of its own (Labaree and Moody, *Eng. Hist. Rev.*, XLIII, 190 ff.). Till then the Privy Council had either, like its medieval predecessor, employed the privy seal, or had relied on the signatures of members only. The last authentication continued to be the usual one, despite the new seal.

[19] The committees cited in Tanner, 224 f., were not, in fact, committees of the Council, but temporary commissions largely of non-councillors though appointed by the Council.

[20] Pollard suggested that chief justice Popham's elevation to the Council in 1601 was a presentiment of Stuart practice (*Eng. Hist. Rev.*, XXXVIII, 60), but it seems m ore likely that the shrinking of the Council compelled an addition and that Elizabeth, as usual, picked someone she had known for a long time.

membership of a body outside of which a man's influence on affairs barely existed.[22]

A word should be said about the office of president of the Council. As Pollard pointed out, in his definitive discussion of this side-issue,[22] the lord president had neither precise function nor place. When one can be sure that a man held the title (for some of the alleged presidents presided over such other bodies as the Court of Requests or the Council of the North) it is clear that he enjoyed a merely honorific distinction with no sort of duties. This was so with the duke of Suffolk, called president of the Council in an act of 1529,[23] though Northumberland used the title in 1552 to avoid the obnoxious protectorship held by his defeated rival Somerset. If the sovereign was present, he presided; if he was not, it would seem that the senior officer present (commonly the chancellor or treasurer) discharged this nominal function. From Cromwell onwards, the secretary was the least dispensable though not the most distinguished member of the Council.[24] In theory all councillors were equal.

41. The Eltham Ordinances, 1526.

Cap. 74. And to the intent that as well matters of justice and complaints touching the griefs of the King's subjects and disorder of his realm and otherwise which shall fortune to be made, brought and presented unto his Highness by his said subjects in his demur or passing from place to place within the same, as also other great occurrences concerning his own particular affairs, may be the better ordered and with his Grace more ripely debated, digested and resolved from time to time as the case shall require; it is ordered and appointed by his Highness that a good number of honourable, virtuous, sad, wise, expert and discreet persons of his Council shall give their attendance upon his most royal person, whose names hereafter follow, that is to say

> The lord cardinal, chancellor of England[25]
> The duke of Norfolk, treasurer of England
> The bishop of London, keeper of the King's privy seal[26]
> The duke of Suffolk, marshall of England
> The marquess Dorset
> The marquess Exeter

[21] For a general account of the Elizabethan Privy Council cf. also Cheyney, *History of England*, I, 65 ff.

[22] *Eng. Hist. Rev.*, XXXVII, 351 ff.

[23] 21 Henry VIII, c. 20.

[24] Cf. Elton, *Tudor Revolution*, 352 ff.

[25] Wolsey.

[26] Cuthbert Tunstall.

The earl of Shrewsbury, steward of the King's Household
The lord chamberlain[27]
The bishop of Bath[28]
The bishop of Lincoln[29]
The lord Sandys[30]
Sir William Fitzwilliam, treasurer of the King's Household
Sir Henry Guildford, controller
The secretary[31]
Sir Thomas More, chancellor of the Duchy
The dean of the King's Chapel[32]
Sir Henry Wyatt, treasurer of the King's Chamber
The vicechamberlain[33]
The captain of the Guard[34]
Doctor Wolman.[35]

Cap. 75. And forasmuch as the said lord cardinal, the lord treasurer of England, lord privy seal, lord steward, and divers other lords and personages before mentioned, by reason of their attendance at the terms for administration of justice, and exercising of their offices, and other reasonable impediments, shall many seasons fortune to be absent from the King's court, and specially in the term times; to the intent the King's Highness shall not be at any season unfurnished of an honourable presence of councillors about his grace, with whom his Highness may confer upon the premises at his pleasure, it is ordered that the persons hereafter mentioned shall give their continual attendance in the causes of his said Council unto what place soever his Highness shall resort; that is to say, the lord chamberlain, the bishop of Bath, the treasurer and controller of the King's Household, the secretary, the chancellor of the Duchy of Lancaster, the dean of the King's Chapel, the vice-chamberlain, the captain of the Guard, and for ordering of poor men's complaints and causes, Dr Wolman.

And because, per case, it may chance some of these aforenamed persons to be absent for some reasonable cause, be it always provided and foreseen that either the bishop of Bath, the secretary, Sir Thomas More and the dean of the Chapel, or two of them at the least, always be present, except the King's Grace give licence to any of them of the

[27] Earl of Oxford.
[29] John Longland.
[31] Richard Pace.
[33] Sir Richard Wingfield.

[28] John Clerk.
[30] Chamberlain of the Household.
[32] Richard Sampson.

[34] Sir William Kingston.

[35] Almoner.

contrary; which said councillors so appointed for continual attendance shall apply themselves effectually, diligently, uprightly and justly in the premises, being every day in the forenoon by ten of the clock at the furthest, and at afternoon by two of the clock, in the King's dining chamber, or in such other place as shall fortune to be appointed for the Council chamber, there to be in readiness, not only in case the King's pleasure shall be to commune or confer with them upon any cause or matter, but also for hearing and direction of poor men's complaints on matters of justice; which direction well observed, the King's Highness shall always be well furnished of an honourable presence of councillors about his grace, as to his high honour doth appertain.

Ordinances for the Royal Household, 159–60

42. Appointment of a Clerk to the Privy Council, 1540.

The 10th day of August in the 32nd year of the reign of our sovereign lord King Henry VIII [1540] . . . an order was taken and determined by his Majesty by the advice of his Highness' Privy Council, whose names hereafter ensue:

Thomas, archbishop of Canterbury[36]
Thomas Lord Audley of Walden, chancellor of England
Thomas duke of Norfolk, high treasurer of England
Charles duke of Suffolk, great master of the King's Household and president of the Council
William earl of Southampton, lord privy seal
Robert earl of Sussex, great chamberlain of England
Edward earl of Hertford[37]
John Lord Russell, great admiral of England
Cuthbert bishop of Durham[38]
Stephen bishop of Winchester[39]
William Lord Sandys, the King's chamberlain
Sir Thomas Cheyney, knight, lord warden of the Cinque Ports and treasurer of the King's Household
Sir William Kingston, knight, comptroller of the King's Household
Sir Anthony Browne, knight, master of the King's Horse
Sir Anthony Wingfield, knight, the King's vice-chamberlain
Sir Thomas Wriothesley, knight, the King's secretary

[36] Cranmer.
[38] Tunstall.
[37] Later the Protector Somerset.
[39] Gardiner.

Sir Ralph Sadler, knight, the King's secretary

Sir Richard Rich, knight, chancellor of the Augmentations of the
Revenues of the Crown

Sir John Baker, knight, chancellor of the Tenths and First Fruits

That there should be a clerk attendant upon the said Council to write,
enter and register all such decrees, determinations, letters and other such
things as he should be appointed to enter in a book, to remain always as
a ledger, as well for the discharge of the said councillors touching such
things as they should pass from time to time, as also for a memorial unto
them of their own proceedings; unto the which office William Paget,
late the Queen's secretary, was appointed by the King's Highness and
sworn in the presence of the said Council the day and year abovesaid.

Proceedings, VII, 3–4

43. Pagets' 'Advice to the King's Council', 1550.

In the name of God the Father, the Son, and the Holy Ghost.

First, the Council to love one another as brethren or dear friends, and
one to honour another in their degrees, whereby will come to pass that
others shall honour them and have them in great estimation.

Item, that none of them be contented to hear ill spoken of another,
and if he do hear any ill then to bring the matter and reporter to the
Council Board . . .

Item, that six at least of the Privy Council be continually attendant
in the court, whereof the lord chancellor or lord treasurer or lord great
master or lord privy seal or lord great chamberlain or lord chamberlain
to be two, and one of the secretaries to be a third, and that the six in the
absence of the rest may pass the affairs occurrent, and shall have their
proceedings ratified by the rest when they come.

Item, that the Council attendant in the court shall assemble themselves three days in the week at the least for the king's affairs, viz.
Tuesday, Thursday and Saturday, and shall meet in the Council
Chamber in the morning at 8 of the clock and sit till dinner, and after
noon at two of the clock and sit till four; and for private suits they shall
assemble upon the Sunday after dinner at two of the clock and sit till
four.

Item, that all letters shall be received by the secretary and brought to
the Council Board at the hours of meeting unless he shall see they
require a very hasty expedition, in which case he shall resort to the

highest of the Council then attendant, and he (the said highest), if he shall think so needful, to assemble the Council at what time soever it shall be.

Item, that every man do speak in convenable manner his opinion and conscience frankly in matters opened at the Council Board, without reproof, check or displeasure for the same of [by] any person.

Item, that all bills of supplication to the king's majesty or the Council shall be delivered to the master of the Requests, and he to deliver to the lord president all such that contain matter that cannot be determined but by the king or his Privy Council; and the lord president to exhibit them to the Council upon the Sunday, to be ordered as shall appertain; and the party to receive his answer at the lord president's hands . . .

Item, all offices and benefices of the king's gift to be preferred to the king to be disposed by the more voices of the Council present upon the Sunday at the Council Board, the more voices to be tried by two balls, a white and a black, to be put by every of the Council in two several pots . . . If they be found equal balls in either pot, then the lord president to prefer the suit, and so likewise if more than two do sue for one thing.

*   *   *   *   *   *

Item, that the clerk having charge of the Council Book shall daily enter all orders and determinations by the Council, all warrants for money, the substance of all letters requiring answer; and the next day following, at the first meeting, presenting the same by the secretary (who shall first consider whether the entry be made accordingly) to the Board, the Council shall the first thing they do sign the book of entries, leaving space for the councillors absent to sign their names when they come; and the clerk which keeps the book shall attend thereunto only and be burdened with no other charge.

Item, the secretary shall see to the keeping of all letters, minutes of letters to and from the king or the Council, instructions and such other writings as shall be treated upon by the Council.

Item, that none of the king's Privy Council shall in no wise speak or write for his friend in any matter of justice between party and party, nor in any other matter above one time: for that the request of a councillor is in a manner a commandment.

Hoak, *King's Council*, 273–5 (spelling modernised)

44. Council Committees under Mary, 1554.[40]

[At a Council meeting, held on 23 February 1554; present: the lords chancellor, admiral and chamberlain, the treasurer of the Household (Sir Thomas Cheyney), the comptroller (Sir Robert Rochester), Sir William Petre, Sir John Bourne, Sir Richard Southwell, Sir Thomas Wharton, Sir John Baker.]

The names of all such as be appointed for the purposes following:

To call in the debts and provide for money: my lord chancellor, my lord Paget, my lord chamberlain, Mr Comptroller.

To give order for supply of all wants at Calais, Guisnes and other pieces of those Marches; to give like order for Berwick and other places upon the borders of the north; to give the like order for Ireland, Portsmouth, the Isle of Wight and the islands: my lord treasurer, my lord steward, my lord privy seal, my lord of Sussex, my lord of Pembroke, Sir John Bourne, master of the Horse, Sir Richard Southwell, Sir Thomas Cornwallis.

To give order for the ships and to appoint captains and others to serve in them: my lord admiral.

To give order for victuals necessary to be sent to Calais, Berwick, etc.: Mr Comptroller, Sir Thomas Cornwallis, Sir William Drury.

To consider what laws shall be established in this Parliament and to name men that shall make the books thereof: my lord chancellor, my lord treasurer, my lord of Durham, my lord Paget, Mr Petre, Mr Baker, Mr Hare.

To appoint men to continue in the examination of the prisoners[41]:

To consider what lands shall be sold, and who shall be in commission for that purpose:

To moderate the excessive charges: my lord steward, etc., for the Household; my lord chamberlain, etc., for the Chamber.

To consider the patents and annuities payable in sundry places, so as the same may be paid all in one place: my lord chancellor, my lord treasurer, my lord steward, Mr Baker, my lord Paget, Mr Petre.

[40] For identifications see legend at the end.
[41] The prisoners taken in Wyatt's rebellion earlier that month.

To appoint a Council to attend and remain at London: my lord Rich, Mr Peckham, the master of the Rolls, Sir Thomas Pope, Sir John Mordaunt, the lieutenant of the Tower.

To give order for the furniture and victualling of the said Tower: the men aforesaid to give order.   *A.P.C.*, IV, 397–9

Explanatory legend of offices and names:

Lord chancellor	Stephen Gardiner
Lord treasurer	Marquess of Winchester
Lord steward	Earl of Arundel
Lord privy seal	Earl of Bedford
Lord admiral	Lord William Howard
Bishop of Durham	Cuthbert Tunstall
Lord chamberlain	Sir John Gage
Comptroller	Sir Robert Rochester
Principal secretaries	{ Sir William Petre { Sir John Bourne
Chancellor of First Fruits and Tenths	Sir John Baker
Master of the Horse	Sir Edward Hastings
Master of the Ordnance	Sir Richard Southwell
Master of the Rolls	Sir Nicholas Hare
Cofferer and treasurer of the Mint	Sir Edmund Peckham
Lieutenant of the Tower	Sir John Bridges
No identifiable office	{ Sir Thomas Pope { Sir William Drury { Sir John Mordaunt

45. The Privy Council under Mary: extracts from the letters of the imperial ambassador[42] to Charles V.

[14 November 1554] The limitation of the Council's membership is a somewhat invidious though necessary step, so the Queen herself had better decide to take it and let everyone realise that she has done so. . . . It certainly seems that the chancellor [Gardiner], Paget, the bishop of Norwich [Thirlby], and Secretary Petre are experienced statesmen whose services are indispensable. . . . As for the rest, they must be chosen in the light of knowledge of their characters. It would be a grave mistake to attempt to introduce any foreigners into the Council. . . .

[42] The first four extracts are from letters by Simon Renard, the last from one by Count Feria.

[23 November 1554] You may perhaps remember that I wrote some time ago with regard to . . . the reduction of the excessive number of councillors. It has proved impossible to achieve this measure, for it created too much bad feeling between the old and recent members of the Privy Council, especially as the new list did not include the high treasurer [Winchester], the controller [Sir Robert Rochester], Walgrave [Sir Edward Waldegrave], the lord warden [Sir Thomas Cheyney], [Sir Francis] Englefield, Southwell [master of the Ordnance], Baker [chancellor of the Exchequer], Peckham and Secretary Bourne who consider themselves to be as deserving as those who, as they say, rebelled against and resisted the Queen.

[10 February 1555] The split in the Council has increased rather than diminished; the two factions no longer consult together; some councillors transact no business; Paget, seeing that he is out of favour with the Queen and most of the Council, is often in the King's apartments.

[27 March 1555] The worst of it is that the Council is very much divided, and neither Arundel nor Paget attended because of their enmity for the chancellor and other councillors. When the chancellor reaches a decision, the others immediately endeavour to defeat it.

[10 March 1558] Pembroke, Arundel, Paget, Petre, the chancellor [Nicholas Heath], the bishop of Ely [Thirlby], and the controller are the leading members of the Council, and I am highly dissatisfied with all of them. . . . The Privy Council has so many members that it seems no one has been left out, except William Howard who was formerly admiral; and numbers cause great confusion.

Span. Cal., XIII, 91, 101, 139, 147, 367

46. The Privy Council, 21 December 1601.

The names of the Privy Councillors:

1. Doctor John Whitgift, Doctor of Divinity, lord archbishop of Canterbury.
2. Sir Thomas Egerton, knight, lord keeper of the great seal of England.
3. Sir Thomas Sackville, knight, Lord Buckhurst, lord high treasurer of England and knight of the honourable order of the Garter.
4. Charles earl of Nottingham, lord high admiral of England and knight of the Garter.
5. Gilbert earl of Shrewsbury, knight of the Garter.

6. Edward earl of Worcester, master of the Horse and knight of the Garter.
7. Sir George Carey, knight, Lord Hunsdon, lord chamberlain to her Majesty and knight of the Garter.
8. Sir William Knollys, knight, comptroller of her Majesty's Household.
9. Sir John Stanhope, vicechamberlain to her Majesty and treasurer of the Chamber.
10. Sir Robert Cecil, knight, principal secretary to her Majesty and master of the Wards and Liveries.
11. Sir John Fortescue, knight, chancellor and undertreasurer of the Exchequer.
12. Sir John Popham, knight, lord chief justice.
13. Mr John Herbert, Esq., one of her Majesty's secretaries.

A.P.C., xxxii, 485-6

II. BUSINESS

The outstanding characteristic of the Council, whether the pre-Cromwellian general king's Council or the Privy Council proper, was its all-pervasiveness: nothing that happened within the realm appeared to fall outside its competence. From this an impression has grown up that no reasonable classification can be made of its business. This is not so. The functions of the Council were, from time immemorial, to advise, administer and adjudicate. The king consulted it upon matters of policy, foreign and domestic; he employed it as a body or as individuals to see to the enforcement of that policy; and he used it to give reality to that residue of judicial power which remained in him even after the regular courts had been fully established. The subject who petitioned the Crown for redress expected to be heard by king and Council, which in practice meant by the Council presided over by the lord chancellor. It is at present difficult to see whether any marked differentiation took place in this threefold activity before the establishment of the Privy Council; the term time meetings of the older type of Council seem to have dealt indiscriminately with them all. This impression, however, may well spring only from an accident of record-keeping. Until Cromwell's reform, the Council at Westminster kept only one series of *Acta* in which both administrative and judicial decisions were entered,[43] a fact which has disguised the separate emergence of the conciliar court of Star Chamber during Wolsey's administration.[44] At any rate, the true Privy Council poses no such difficulties.

43 Elton, *Studies*, I, 330 ff.
44 Below, p. 164

Despite frequent statements to the contrary,[45] and even though the sixteenth century liked to call all government institutions courts, the Elizabethan Privy Council was not a court in any real sense and had no judicial functions. That is to say, unlike the court of Star Chamber it did not try cases. Admittedly it exercised what may be called quasi-judicial functions arising out of its political competence and illustrious standing; but in a matter which for too long has suffered from imprecision it is worth stressing that the difference between judicial and quasi-judicial is material to an understanding of the nature and doings of these institutions.

The best approach to the work of the Privy Council is provided by the analysis made in 1600 by one of its clerks (47). Though it, too, employs a tripartite division this is rather different from ours, and though (in accordance with custom) it smells strongly of curial predilections it does not describe a true court. In the first place there is business of state, which includes all deliberations and the administration of the realm, from such small matters as clothes for a prisoner in the Tower (48) to the embodiment of a considered policy of censorship in a Council order (49). Although Council warrants for payments are frequently entered, matters of financial policy (50) have left less trace in the record than one would suppose, but it must be remembered that of all kinds of business this first category would have the greatest difficulty in reaching the minutes. The clerk never recorded discussion but only decisions, and if really secret matters of state were toward he was often excluded from the meeting. It follows that the evidence for the Council's primary activities—policy and government—is far from exhaustive and comes as often from the letters of councillors and others as from the minute book. Herbert's second class of business concerned issues—lawsuits—between private persons, matters brought to the Council's attention by one of the parties. This, of course, was the sort of business that might make the Privy Council appear to act as a court in litigation, but—as Herbert indicates—it did nothing of the sort. A body composed of the kingdom's leading and most influential men, representing also the royal reservoir for the redressing of grievances, would naturally be bombarded with petitions by people seeking relief or hoping to exploit their contacts with great patrons. But though it received many petitions the Council, as Privy Council, did not deal with them in the manner of a court. In its early days it might settle a criminal issue by a species of administrative order, and later it might still interfere by bringing the parties to agreement (52), but in neither instance had it tried a case. Normally it reacted by referring the case to the proper court (53, 54), the

---

[45] E.g. Tanner, 226 ff.; Rowse, *England of Elizabeth*, 364, 367; Ogilvie, *King's Government*, 100 ff. Holdsworth (e.g., I, 478 f.; IV, 273 f.) is handicapped by his refusal to make a clear distinction between Council and Star Chamber: his examples of active jurisdiction by the Council turn out to be Star Chamber matters.

petitioners probably having hoped for this but seeing no prospect of speedy action without the Council's interposition. If a petitioner's patron did his work well, he might secure a formal arbitration by the Council, an action which did not represent a judicial trial but its evasion after consideration given to the points alleged.[46] All along the Privy Council found these private suits extremely irksome and repeatedly tried to unburden its agenda by ordering that petitions should be sorted and despatched to the appropriate court before reaching the Council table (51). The repetition of these orders testifies to their futility. Since the Council could influence the course of justice elsewhere, and since a patron would lose face unless he served his client, the stream of bills could at best be reduced, never dammed. But it is plain that the Council never acted as a true court and that it wished to be rid even of the quasi-judicial work which came to it in such quantity.

Lastly the Council concerned itself with matters 'betwixt some party . . . and the Queen's Majesty'. This would include really private disputes in which the Crown happened to be party (57), matters of internal security (58, 59), or matters of state, of which suspected treason was both the most important and the commonest.[47] In all these cases the Council acted rather in an administrative than a judicial way. It investigated, or ordered an investigation; it decided; it had powers to commit; but it did not adjudicate, render a verdict, or impose a sentence. If the Council's investigation of an alleged treason produced good grounds for suspicion, the resulting trial would have to be held in the proper court (60); if it did not, the Council would discharge the accused and could even order the accuser to make a public confession (61), but it had tried nothing and inflicted no legal punishment on anyone. It may well be held that these are distinctions with but little difference. The Council exercised a major and often extremely direct influence upon the whole machinery of justice, interfering in the conduct of cases and giving orders to the courts.[48] It summoned people, kept them in sometimes prolonged attendance while it investigated allegations against them, and either committed or discharged them in terms which would be appropriate for an established court.[49] In none of this, however, did this secret board with its haphazard procedure dictated by circumstances or convenience approach the publicity,

---

[46] Cf. 56, which illustrates the procedure in a really thorough arbitration. The Council would first commission legal experts to sift the evidence and might then have it argued before themselves, before giving its decision. Although this comes superficially near to a trial, it is entirely different from the typical procedure of a sixteenth-century court, lacking altogether in publicity, formality and enforceability.

[47] The nature of the complaint is not material. If the Council was not a court, the question of what kind of cases it could try does not arise. This makes Tanner's classification (229 ff.) irrelevant. But his examples may be read with profit from the point of view of Herbert's classification.

[48] Holdsworth, IV, 84 f.

[49] E.g. Cheyney, *History of England*, I, 75 f.

formality or powers of a true court, nor did anyone ever suppose that it did. The influence of a councillor, arbitration by the whole Council or someone deputed by it, the investigatory activities of a body charged with the security of the realm, might indeed involve the Council in matters which should have gone to a court, as did the desire of petitioners to go as high as possible; but it remains true that when Elizabethan councillors are seen acting as judges in a court they will be found to be, at that point, members of Star Chamber and not of the Privy Council.

The point has been argued at such length because the sixteenth-century habit of treating government as a matter of law-enforcement, and the reluctance of historians to be precise in these matters, have too often left it open whether the Privy Council had any true judicial functions or not, with consequent errors concerning its relation to the court of Star Chamber.[50] But it should not be forgotten that the political and administrative work of the Council was vastly more important both to the Crown and to the realm, and that it acted as the great centralising agent, with established lines of communication running from and towards it across the whole territory of the Crown.

47. John Herbert's Memorandum on Council business, 26 April 1600.

... Memorandum: That all causes to be treated on in Council and resolved are either only for her Majesty, or betwixt party and party, or betwixt some party (either subject or stranger) and the Queen's Majesty.

The first doth handle principally questions and consultations of state, growing from foreign advertisements or some extraordinary accidents within the realm.

The second (between party and party) are very seldom heard particularly, but rather ended by overruling an obstinate person who is made to acknowledge his fault, or else the parties are remitted to some court of justice or equity, or recommended by some letters to some justices in the country to compound the differences either by consent of the parties or by direction. Or, if the cause be great, the[n] to write letters to some principal persons to have some circumstances better understood and examined concerning matter of fact, whereof the Council cannot be so well informed when they have only the suggestions of one party against another; upon which report it often happeneth that quarrels

---

[50] That the distinctions which have been laboured are essential to an understanding of Star Chamber is a point taken up below, pp. 163 ff.

and differences are taken up by the Council when it appears clearly who is in default.

When there is anything in question wherein the Queen is a party, it is commonly either by the breach of peace or for some other title. If there be breach of peace the lords do either punish the offender by commitment, or do refer the matter to be further proceeded in in the Star Chamber, where great riots and contempts are punished. If it be matter of title, then the Lords refer it to the Queen's learned counsel, and recommend the same to the judges' care.

If there be some suits to the Queen of poor men, then do the lords endorse their petitions with their opinions, and recommend the dispatch to the secretary, or for the poorer sort to the master of the requests.

State Papers (Domestic), Eliz. CCLXXIV, No. 118. (fos. 259–60)

48. An example of minor administrative business.

[At Hampton Court, 1 March, 1541] . . . A letter was sent to — Malt, the King's tailor, to provide at convenient prices and make meet for the Lord Lisle, which remaineth at this time prisoner in the Tower, these parcels of apparel and other necessaries, and thereupon to bring unto the said Council a note of all particulars with the prices of the same, to the intent a warrant might be made for repayment unto him of the same.

In primis, a large gown of damask furred with black coney.

Item, a long nightgown of cloth at 10s. the yard furred with black lamb and faced with budge.[51]

Item, two jackets, one of damask, another of satin.

Item, two doublets of satin.

Item, four pair of hose.

Item, six pair of shoes and one pair of slippers.

Item, four shirts.

Item, two nightcaps of velvet and satin.

Item, two upper caps of cloth.

Item, two night-kerchiefs. . . .

Proceedings, VII, 146

49. Order against seditious books, 1566.[52]

1. That no person should print, or cause to be printed, or bring or

---

[51] Lamb-skin fur.

[52] This is not an original document, but Strype's summary of one that cannot now be found. The Privy Council register is missing for this period. It is given here because Doc. 89, a Star

procure to be brought into the realm printed, any book against the force and meaning of any ordinance, prohibition or commandment, contained or to be contained in any the statutes or laws of this realm, or in any injunctions, letters patents or ordinances passed or set forth, or to be passed or set forth, by the Queen's grant, commission or authority.

II. That whosoever should offend against the said ordinances should forfeit all such books and copies; and from thenceforth should never use or exercise, or take benefit by any using or exercising, the feat of printing, and to sustain three months imprisonment without bail or mainprize.

III. That no person should sell or put to sale, bind, stitch or sew any such books or copies, upon pain to forfeit all such books and copies, and for every book 20s.

IV. That all books so forfeited should be brought into Stationers' Hall. And there one moiety of the money forfeited to be reserved to the Queen's use, and the other moiety to be delivered to him or them that should first seize the books or make complaint thereof to the warden of the said Company. And all the books so to be forfeited to be destroyed or made waste paper.

V. That it should be lawful for the wardens of the Company for the time being or any two of the said Company thereto deputed by the said wardens, as well in any ports or other suspected places, to open and view all packs, dryfats,[53] maunds[54] and other things wherein books or paper shall be contained, brought into this realm, and make search in all workhouses, shops, warehouses, and other places of printers, booksellers and such as bring books into the realm to be sold, or where they have reasonable cause of suspicion; and all books to be found against the said ordinances to seize and carry to the Hall to the uses abovesaid, and to bring the persons offending before the Queen's commissioners in causes ecclesiastical.

VI. Every stationer, printer, bookseller, merchant, using any trade of book-printing, binding, selling or bringing into the realm, should before the commissioners or before any other persons thereto be assigned by the Queen's Privy Council enter into several recognisances of reasonable sums of money to her Majesty, with sureties or without, as to

Chamber decree, deals with the same subject as this, which is clearly a Privy Council ordinance: the differences are significant (cf. below, pp. 182 ff.).

[53] Cases or barrels for holding dry goods as opposed to liquids.
[54] Wicker baskets.

the commissioners should be thought expedient, that he should truly observe all the said ordinances, well and truly yield and pay all such forfeitures, and in no point be resisting but in all things aiding to the said wardens and their deputies for the true execution of the premises.

Upon the consideration before expressed and upon the motion of the commissioners, we of the Privy Council have agreed this to be observed and kept upon the pains therein contained. At the Star Chamber the 29th of June, anno 1566, and the eighth year of the Queen's Majesty's reign.

N. Bacon, C.S.,[55] Winchester, R. Leicester, E. Clinton, E. Rogers, F. Knollys, A. Cave, W. Cecil.

We underwrit think these Ordinances meet and necessary to be decreed and observed.

Matthew Cantuar., Ambrose Cave, Th. Yale, Edmund London, David Lewis, Rob. Weston, T. Huycke.[56]

Strype, *Life of Parker*, I, 442–3

50. Financial Administration.

[At St James', 8 September 1588] A letter to the lord treasurer[57] to signify that their lordships have appointed the merchants that lately set eight ships to the sea for the reinforcing of the strength of her Majesty's Navy under the charge of the lord admiral, to repair unto Mr Holstocke and Mr Borough[58] to cast up their accounts and reckonings, and therefore pray his lordship, by warrant of her Majesty's privy seal of the 13th of August last, to pay unto the said merchants such sums of money as shall be set down and brought unto his lordship under the hands of the said Holstocke and Borough to be due unto the merchants aforesaid.

A letter to the above mentioned Mr Holstocke and Borough to make a perfect book and account of the reckonings for the charge of the aforesaid eight ships set forth by the merchants and to send the same under their hands unto the lord treasurer who hath order tŏ see the same discharged accordingly . . .   *A.P.C.*, XVI, 271–2

---

[55] *Custos sigilli* = lord keeper of the great seal.
[56] These are the signatures of the members of the ecclesiastical commission who had asked the Privy Council to issue its order.
[57] Burghley, who was present at this meeting.
[58] Treasurers of the Navy.

51. Council Orders concerning private suits.

[15 April 1582] ... This day the lords and others of her Majesty's Privy Council considering what multitude of matters concerning private causes and actions between party and party were daily brought unto the Council Board, wherewith their lordships were greatly troubled and her Majesty's special services oftentimes interrupted, for remedy whereof it was agreed among them that from henceforth no private causes arising between parties for any action whatsoever which may receive order and redress in any of her Majesty's ordinary courts shall be received and preferred to the Board, unless they shall concern the preservation of her Majesty's peace or shall be of some public consequence to touch the government of this realm. . . .

A.P.C., XIII, 394-5

[8 October 1589] Whereas by reason of the multitude of private suitors resorting daily to her Majesty's Privy Council the lords and others of the same are continually so troubled and pestered with the said private suitors and their causes as at the times of their assembling for her Majesty's special services they can hardly be suffered (by the importunity of the said suitors) to attend and proceed in such causes as do concern her Majesty and the state of the realm, the said suits and causes being for the most part of such nature as either have been determined in other courts, or else such as ought to receive hearing and trial and order in the several courts of justice or of conscience within the realm ordained for those purposes. Their lordships therefore considering the inconvenience and hindrances growing to her Majesty's services commonly interrupted by giving audience to such private suitors, and that many times the judges and justices of sundry of the courts aforesaid, to whom the ordering and determining of many of the said suits do properly and naturally appertain, do thereby find cause of offence as derogating the lawful authority of the said courts and places of judgment. For these considerations their lordships this day, upon good deliberation, ordered and decreed that from henceforth no such private causes or suits which by due and ordinary course of law ought to receive their trial and determination in any of her Majesty's courts of justice or conscience, or in any court in corporate towns (where by charters such causes ought to be heard and determined) should be received and admitted to be heard and determined by the said Privy Council, and if any suitors shall at any time hereafter resort either to her Majesty's principal secretary, or to the clerk or clerks of the Council for the time attendant, or to the Council Board, as unacquainted with this order, whose causes shall manifestly appear to be of such kind as is aforesaid, that every such suitor and cause shall be addressed and directed either by her Majesty's principal secretary or in his absence from the court by any two of the Council, or when the Council shall not be assembled then by one of the clerks of the Council then attendant, either to the lord chancellor or masters of the Court of Requests (if the order thereof ought to be had in way of equity by course of those courts), or to such other courts of the common law or courts of equity or the courts for her Majesty's revenue, where the said causes are properly determinable; after which directions according to the nature of the suits, if the parties shall make complaint that notwithstanding such direction they cannot have their causes received to be heard and ordered according to the laudable usage of the courts whereunto they are addressed, then the parties complaining shall not be denied to be heard and their griefs remedied, as by proof it shall fall out that justice or usual help is denied unto them. And to the end that this order and decree may be duly and inviolably kept, observed and maintained, their lordships have promised and concluded among themselves that neither they in general nor any of them in particular will hereafter in regard of any private person or cause contrary to the form of this order move, require or do anything that shall impugn or violate the same, and for the better confirmation thereof they have severally subscribed the said order and decree and commanded the same to be entered into the Council Book, there to remain of record. Provided nevertheless that hereby is not meant to seclude any persons with their suits if they shall complain of any wrong, wilful delay, or denial of justice by any judge or judges in any court, or by any justice of peace in their jurisdictions, where they have made complaint in any ordinary sort, in which cases as their lordships will be willing to relieve them upon their complaints, so also if it shall be proved they have made their complaints without just cause it shall be reason to punish the said complainants. In like manner no man shall be barred by this order to give information against any persons for any fact tending to treason or conspiracy, or to any crime that may concern the safety or honour of her Majesty's royal person. *A.P.C.*, xviii, 181-3

[At Greenwich, 27 June 1591] An addition to the lords' order which was written and set down the 8th of October 1589. We seeing that notwithstanding this order the multitude of private suitors hath of late increased by reason of some intermission of the due execution of the same, whereby the public services of her Majesty are daily hindered and interrupted, do therefore will and require you, the masters of requests, that from henceforth when you shall have received the petitions exhibited at the Council Board you consider of several causes in them contained, and finding them such as by this order are not to be admitted, that you address the parties to the courts of justice and conscience where they are properly triable, and so provide that we be not troubled therewith, and for your better direction herein we have sent you a copy of our said order, whereby you may be directed for the nature and quality of the said causes. Hereof fail you not. *A.P.C.*, XXI, 240

52. Direct action in private suits.

[Grafton, 20 July 1541] . . . Nicholas Wentworth, of Livingstone in the county of Northampton, gentleman, exhibited a supplication as well against William Poyner of the said town, yeoman, accusing him to be a procurer of perjury, and a great embracer, and maintainer of brabbling matters and suits . . . whereupon the said Poyner, being convinced by the deposition of sundry witnesses to be guilty of the said crimes, was committed to the porter's ward, and for his further punishment adjudged to be set upon the pillory at Northampton, Stamford, Oxford and Aylesbury at four several market days, with a paper written in great letters declaring the cause of his punishment. . . .

Proceedings, VII, 217

[At Westminster, 30 April 1557] . . . Upon consideration of the matter in variance between Richard Michell, esquire, and William Penry, it was this day for a final end between them ordered, by the consent and agreement of the said Richard Michell, that the said Penry should at the next general sessions to be holden within the county of Carmathen, in open court before the justices there declare that he knoweth nothing touching the allegiance of the said Michell but honesty and truth, and that he, the same Penry, spake the words alleged against him in the action of the case brought by the said Michell rashly and unadvisedly, and that he cannot justify the same, for the which he is sorry and asketh him forgiveness; whereupon it is ordered that the said Michell, his attorneys and deputies, shall surcease from further proceedings against the said Penry in his action or in the execution of the same. . . . *A.P.C.*, VI, 82

53. Referring a case to the appropriate court.

[At Westminster, 31[59] June 1571] A letter to the vice-president and Council in the Marches of Wales, understanding lately of a great riot and assault made in the town of Bromyard upon the bishop of Hereford's officers and servants, and that the offenders therein be of such insolency as the bishop, being lord of the said town, cannot reform the same but is made afraid to see redress, and, as their lordships are informed, dare not well without a great guard travel from his dwelling-house; for the better meeting with the same they are required to give order that the principal offenders be apprehended and committed to prison, and thereupon appointing a private sessions, if the time of their general sessions be not near, to cause the riot to be enquired of, and to proceed with all due severity and by corporal punishment and fines, according to the quality of their offences. . . . *A.P.C.*, VIII, 33

54. Referring an appeal to its proper court.

[In the Star Chamber, 21 May 1588] Upon a petition exhibited to the lords of her Majesty's most honourable Privy Council by Nicholas Ridgley for the trial of an issue joined in an *ejectione firme*[60] now depending in her Majesty's court of Exchequer between John Mathew, the plaintiff, and the said Ridgley and one Strugnell, defendants, it is thought fit and ordered this present day by their lordships, for causes reasonable set forth in the said petition and in the presence of the parties to the said action, that the said cause shall be tried in the county of Wiltshire at the next assizes to be holden there, and that the barons of her Majesty's court of Exchequer shall take order for the said trial accordingly, and shall not suffer the same to be tried in the said court of Exchequer.[61] *A.P.C.*, XVI, 76

---

[59] *Sic*: probably 30.

[60] An action brought by a lessee for years against premature ejection by the lessor or a stranger.

[61] There is something highly suspicious about this: it need not be thought that the Council were necessarily assisting justice by their action. Commonly the reference of a case out of the Exchequer to the local assizes (by a writ of *nisi prius*: the trial at the assizes was therefore known as 'the nisi prius') brought local influences and chicaneries into play and was sought by the party which stood to lose by the impartial examination of a central court. On the other hand, the parties may just possibly have agreed here to such action because Exchequer trials were notoriously dilatory.

55. Transferring a prisoner.

[14 August 1579] A letter to Mr Justice Southcote that upon the humble suit of Mrs Trugeon, wife of Francis Trugeon lately condemned in the *praemunire* in the county of Cornwall, that he might from thence be removed, he should grant a writ of *habeas corpus* for the removing of him unto the prison of her Majesty's Bench,[62] there to remain under the marshal's custody until it should please Her Highness to dispose otherwise of him.   *A.P.C.*, XI, 237

56. Procedure by arbitration.

[Greenwich, 12 May 1575] This day their lordships having called before them Mr Doctor Humfrey, vicechancellor, and some other of the officers of the University of Oxford, Roger Taylor, mayor, and some other of the aldermen and burgesses of the said city, caused certain orders to be openly read before [them], the tenor whereof ensueth:

Whereas heretofore there hath been divers controversies, debates and strifes between the vicechancellor, masters and scholars of the University of Oxford on the one side, and the mayor, aldermen and commons of the said city on the other side, touching the use and exercise of sundry charters and privileges alleged by both parties for the maintenance of such liberties and other things as were claimed by them, whereby did and was daily more and more like to ensue great disquietness in the said University and town, not meet to be suffered; wherefore upon the repair hither of Mr Doctor Humfrey, vicechancellor, and certain other officers of the said University, and Roger Taylor, mayor, with some of the aldermen and the recorder, town clerk and other burgesses of the said city of Oxford, their lordships thought it convenient to move both parties to submit the hearing of the causes of their controversies in law to grave and indifferent men learned in the laws of the realm; whereupon both parties did assent that all and singular the said controversies and debates should be committed to the hearing, report and consideration of Roger Manwood and Roger Monson, two of the justices of the Common Pleas, Gilbert Gerrard and Thomas Bromley, her Majesty's attorney- and solicitor-general, who by order of their lordships sundry times called before them both parties, with their learned counsel, and fully heard and examined the charters

---

[62] The Marshalsea prison attached to King's Bench.

and privileges on each side, with all the allegations and answers of both parts, and thereupon the said four commissioners set down in writing their opinions concerning the said controversies as agreeable with law and justice, and afterwards their lordships having had at three several times the said vicechancellor and officers of the University with their learned counsel, the mayor, aldermen, recorder and town clerk of the said city before them with their learned counsel, whereof the one time was at the Star Chamber, where the lord keeper of the great seal of England and some others of the Privy Council, besides those above-named, were present, and with good deliberation considered not only the report of the said committees exhibited in writing, but also parti-cularly in presence of the said committees and all other parties heard the circumstance of the whole matter, the claims, answers and replies on both sides, what each party could allege, and so with great and advised deliberation their lordships have according to right and equity for the benefit and quiet of both of the said University and city, places neces-sary to be ordered always by the order and authority of the Privy Council, thought convenient and necessary to have these orders fol-lowing set down to be inviolably hereafter observed by both parties, and upon the return of the said vicechancellor and mayor within 14 days to be published and notified by them in the common places of the assemblies of the said University and city, to be by them appointed and called together for that purpose, so as in like solemn acts hath been here-tofore accustomed, as orders enjoined unto them from their lordships in the Queen's Majesty's name, and there to be registered in the com-mon book of the said University and city, to remain as a per-petual memory and record of such orders between them, as followeth:

[Here follows the Council order concerning the points in dispute.]

A.P.C., VII, 376–8

57. Crown *v.* Party: claims on the Crown.

[At Richmond, 13 October 1550] The chancellor of the Augmentations was spoken with for the suit of Thomas Knyvet to the intent the land might be surveyed, and the Council agreed to be suitors to the King's Majesty that the said Knyvet should have so much land as his father had paid for, and beside that £28 for the which the chancellor should either see ready payment or else good land delivered to the King's

Majesty; his suit was granted upon consideration that the bargain was made in the King's days that dead is [Henry VIII] and money paid.

A.P.C., III, 139

58. Crown v. Party: Scandalum Magnatum.

[15 December 1578] A letter to [three gentlemen of ? Lincolnshire] that where their lordships are given to understand that Robert Saville, esq., and his sons have not only misdemeaned themselves sundry ways heretofore towards the lord admiral and the Lord Clinton, his son, but also of late hath used slanderous speeches against his lordship, who bearing a great office of state in this realm and of her Highness' Privy Council, their lordships may [not] in justice and for example of so great a disorder neglect the redress thereof; and for the said lewd speeches [their lordships order the addressees to investigate the matter, calling the parties and witnesses before them] and accordingly to certify their examinations unto their lordships with as convenient diligence as they may.

A.P.C., X, 425–6

59. Crown v. Party: breach of the peace.

[13 April 1580] Robert Leveson and Laurence Dutton, servants unto the earl of Oxford, were committed to the Marshalsea for committing of disorders and frays upon the gentlemen of the Inns of Court.

A.P.C., XI, 445

60. Crown v. Party: Preliminary examination of alleged treason.

[At Greenwich, 13 April 1590] . . . A letter to the earl of Huntingdon,[63] that whereas certain articles had been exhibited unto the Queen's Majesty containing matter of treason and other heinous crimes wherewith Ralph Tankerd, of Arden in the county of York, his sons, servants and others of his confederacy stand charged, as might appear by the enclosed informations, his lordship is prayed and required to call before him the said malefactors and to examine the particular points of their accusation, and in case the allegations should appear to be true, and that the same were not prosecuted only of malice to defame the said persons, without any good pretence whereupon the informations were grounded, then to see the offenders to be forthcoming, and with convenient expedition to certify their lordships of his travail and the

[63] President of the Council of the North.

effects thereof, together with the names of the delinquents and the offences by them committed, to the intent they may be proceeded withal according to their deserts. . . .

A.P.C., XIX, 54

61. Crown *v.* Party: Dismissal of alleged treason.

[Westminster, 18 March 1541] . . . Whereas Thomas Dawes, of Ildersley in the county of Derby, labourer, had accused Sir Robert Moore, priest, parson of Bradley in the said county, and a certain woman being in house with the said priest, of sundry heinous and traitorous words supposed by the said Thomas to have been spoken by the said priest and woman, and thereupon certain letters were written from Hampton Court the 3rd of this present to the earl of Shrewsbury to apprehend the said parties and to examine the matter. Forasmuch it appeareth by the answer of the said earl and the examinations taken by him that the priest and woman were in no wise culpable of such things as were laid to their charge, the said earl was required by another letter not only to discharge the said priest and woman in case there could be no further evidence brought against them for the proofs of such matter as was objected unto them, but also to cause the said Thomas Dawes openly in the parish church of the said priest to ask him forgiveness upon his knees, acknowledging that he had falsely and maliciously slandered them; and if he refused so to do, then to cause him to be set upon the pillory the next market day, in example of such malicious false knaves as might hereafter attempt to do the semblable. . . .

Proceedings, VII, 158–9

CHAPTER 3

THE SEALS AND THE SECRETARY

For the conveying of the central government's orders to the scene of action the middle ages developed a series of royal seals, a new one being required for the king's immediate use as each older one came to be burdened with a large staff and a permanently settled office. By the end of the fifteenth century there existed three of them: the great seal of England in the charge of the lord chancellor, the privy seal in the nominal custody of its keeper (now called lord privy seal), and the signet held by the principal secretary.[1] These seals fulfilled a variety of functions which may, however, be briefly listed under two heads: they played a part in the disposal of the royal patronage (the making of grants), and they did direct and independent work of their own. By custom, and by a Council ordinance of 1444, all grants made by the Crown were supposed to follow a strict bureaucratic routine. The prospective grantee put in his petition which would receive the king's approval expressed by his signature; this signed bill was then a warrant to the signet office to make out a warrant to the privy seal office, which in turn authorised the Chancery to issue the actual grant under the great seal—for this alone carried legal force. In this laborious process only the original petition and the final letters patent were really necessary; the intervening stages simply copied twice over the terms of the proposed grant (already recited in the petition). In consequence petitioners usually tried for the favour of an 'immediate warrant' by which the signed bill became the chancellor's authority for the grant. This, however, meant a serious loss in fees to the clerks of the privy seal and signet, and in 1536 Thomas Cromwell promoted an act which (apart from placing the proper course of the seals on a statutory basis) secured them their payments even if they had done no work.[2] There are signs that after 1540 evasions by immediate warrant grew few;[3] with respect to this formal business of the seals—the bulk of their work—the sixteenth century simply confirmed and perpetuated a bureaucratic routine of little practical importance.

The independent work of the seals had had greater significance in the administration of the realm. The great seal, of course, was and remained essential to all royal grants, but in addition it was the seal used to authenticate

---

[1] This is to ignore, as in a discussion of the royal secretariats one must, the seals of the Exchequer and the common-law courts, which were smaller replicas of the great seal.

[2] 27 Henry VIII, c. 11. Cf. Elton, *Tudor Revolution*, 270 ff.

[3] Except that grants of monastic lands were usually made on the authority of petitions countersigned by the commissioners for sales. This explains the discrepancy between *ibid.*, 289 and Youings, *Devon Monastic Lands*, p. xiv, n. 1.

all original writs (writs originating actions at law) and several others, such as the writ of summons called a subpoena. From the 1530's onwards, at least, the Court of Star Chamber employed the great seal in all its work. The organisation which served this seal—the Chancery—was the oldest and most highly developed of the royal secretariats; this period made little difference in its organisation or activity.[4] Chancery had long lost the primacy in ordinary administration which it had once enjoyed, and apart from issuing the patents which disposed of the royal bounty in lands, favours and offices it now served entirely the needs of judicial administration, more especially in the lord chancellor's own two courts of Chancery and Star Chamber. It may be noted that in the reign of Henry VIII the stream of royal administrative orders enrolled on the Chancery series of Close Rolls at last dried up altogether; henceforward those rolls recorded the legal business of the subject.[5]

The place of Chancery as the centre of government had by the fifteenth century passed to the office of the privy seal which collected administrative orders from all the king's officers and redistributed them again to subordinate executive officers.[6] Now, as individual officers like the master of Wards or the general surveyors were equipped with courts and seals of their own, it lost this role.[7] Cromwell seems at one time to have contemplated its supersession by the signet, whose office routine he carefully reorganised: the act of 1536 required all administrative orders to follow the same chain of seals as did warrants for grants.[8] In practice no seal succeeded to the earlier position of the privy seal which continued to be employed for its own sake almost only in judicial matters: the Court of Star Chamber at first, and that of Requests throughout its life, relied on it in their work, and until 1556 the Privy Council, too, called upon it, especially for writs of summons. In addition it was the instrument used to seal promises to repay forced loans, a specialised and relatively short-lived career.[9] The decline of the privy seal did not make the fortunes of the signet. That seal enjoyed some authority in the authorisation of payments from the Household treasuries, and signet letters could at times be used for direct administrative orders.[10] But in the main the day of seals was past: they retained their place in the bureaucratic organisation, but they and their offices no longer played a major or originating part in the government of England.

[4] Cf. Maxwell-Lyte, The Great Seal, passim; Elton, Tudor Revolution, 129–33, 260–1.
[5] Giuseppi, Guide to the Public Records, I, 20.
[6] Tout, Chapters, v, 54 ff.; Elton, Tudor Revolution, 14 f.
[7] This was part of the administrative revolution of the 1530's: ibid., 286 ff.
[8] Ibid., 262 ff., 273 f.
[9] Cf. above, p. 44.
[10] It has been suggested (Hinton, Camb. Hist. J., XIII, 116 ff.) that an increased use of the signet under Elizabeth and especially the early Stuarts reflects attempts at a more autocratic exercise of the royal authority, but this article overlooked the fact that the survival of signet docket books from only 1580 biases the evidence.

That role now fell to what was virtually a new officer of the Crown, the principal secretary,[11] sometimes by the end of the century already described as secretary of estate (or state). Down to the reign of Henry VIII the secretary was what his name implies: a confidential servant employed about the king's correspondence, in charge of the seal which authenticated this (that is, the signet), always near the king and therefore likely to have a good deal of personal influence, commonly a specialist in diplomatic negotiations, but definitely not a man in the first rank of officers.[12] Henry VII's secretaries were sometimes on his Council, and so was at least one of Henry VIII's earlier secretaries, Richard Pace. The degree of influence possible, but also the effectively subordinate position occupied at this time, are displayed in a letter in which Pace defended himself against Wolsey's suspicions of one who had the king's ear (62).[13] The real career of the secretary as a foremost minister of the Crown began with the first layman to hold the office, Thomas Cromwell (1534–40). He not only exploited the potential of an office unburdened by traditional routine duties but more particularly developed the secretary's universal hold on the affairs of the realm.[14] By 1539 the office had reached such heights that in precedence it ranked below only the high dignitaries of state and Household, above unofficed bishops and barons (63). Its rise is well illustrated in the allowance of food and lodging at court made for the secretary in 1526 and 1544 respectively.[15] However, in 1540, when Cromwell gave up the office, it dropped in standing below the second rank of Household officers and below all peers. This was laid down in the famous warrant (64) which divided the secretaryship between two holders, partly because the work had grown too much but more particularly because Henry's continued absence from London even in term time made the presence of one secretary at court and one with the Council at Westminster desirable.[16] The division may originally have resulted from immediate needs, but it proved so useful that it came to be permanent. Although there were some times in the sixteenth century when only one secretary held office, it was now much more common for two to act together.[17] Technically they were equal, with equal

[11] Principal, because there existed also secretaries of the French and Latin tongues, employed to write diplomatic correspondence in those languages.

[12] For the secretary before 1530 cf. Otway-Ruthven, *King's Secretary . . . in the XV Century*; Elton, *Tudor Revolution*, 31 f., 56 ff.

[13] On the other hand, it is not true that really secret matters of state were kept from the secretary, as seems suggested by a letter of Henry VIII to Wolsey (*State Papers*, I, I) when only the first half is printed (as by Tanner, 211). The secret matters in question were personal: the queen's pregnancy and the king's fear of the plague.

[14] This is worked out at length in Elton, *Tudor Revolution*, 124 ff., 299 ff.

[15] Tanner, 207 f.

[16] For a discussion of this document and especially of the first two joint secretaries (Wriothesley and Sadler), cf. Elton, *Tudor Revolution*, 312 ff. For Sadler cf. Slavin, *Politics and Profit*, chs. 3 & 4.

[17] Cf. the list in Evans, *Principal Secretary*, 349 f. William Cecil exercised full power as sole secretary from 1558 to 1572, and Robert Cecil from 1596 to 1600. Walsingham's lonely tenure

duties and equal control of the signet. Both received the same fee of £100 and shared the profits of the signet, which augmented their meagre pay, in equal parts.[18] Though in fact one of them was quite often markedly senior to the other, the fiction of equality was maintained until the appointment as 'second secretary' of John Herbert (1600),[19] after which date a recognised difference in status came to be the rule under the Stuarts.

In the reign of Elizabeth the principal secretaries, building upon the foundations laid by Cromwell's use of the office, made themselves in practice the chief executive ministers of the Crown in domestic and foreign affairs, with particular responsibility for the security of the realm and the conduct of diplomatic negotiations. Both at home and abroad their activities reflect the newly grown needs of sixteenth-century government. The secretary was the usual channel between the queen and her subjects, and often between her and her Council, too. These arduous and multiplying duties could only be discharged because the secretaries were in fact creating a permanent office organisation out of their private staffs of clerks—the future departments of the secretaries of state. By the 1590's this organisation, first visible in Cromwell's private office,[20] had achieved a high degree of precision, bureaucracy and influence (66). The secretary remained, nevertheless, in a somewhat betwixt and between condition: definitely a leading officer of state, yet also a personal servant of the Crown, in close and constant contact with the sovereign, more frequently resident at court than other officials—a cross between a minister, a high civil servant, and a courtier. It is the less necessary to detail his many duties, unrestricted as they were by traditional definition, because we possess an excellent contemporary account of them from the hand of Robert Beale, for many years Walsingham's confidential clerk and chief assistant (67).[21] The principal secretary's role in the management of patronage is well illustrated by the work of Michael Hickes, confidential secretary to both William and Robert Cecil.[22]

62. Richard Pace[23] to Cardinal Wolsey, 29 October 1521.

. . . I never rehearsed your Grace's letters, diminutely or fully, but by the King's express commandment, who readeth all your letters with great diligence, and mine answers made to the same not by my device

from 1587 to 1590 resulted from the fact that the second secretary, Davison, though disgraced, still received the emoluments of the office (Wernham, *Eng. Hist. Rev.*, XLVI, 632 ff.).

[18] For the secretary's income cf. Tanner, 210; Elton, *Tudor Revolution*, 125 f.

[19] Evans, *op. cit.* 57.

[20] Elton, *Tudor Revolution*, 304 ff.; Smith, *Eng. Hist. Rev.*, LXXXIII, 481 ff.

[21] For the secretary under Elizabeth cf. also Evans, *op. cit.* 43 ff.; Rowse, *England of Elizabeth*, 287 f. Much detail is to be found in Conyers Read's studies of *Walsingham* and *Cecil*, though neither book discusses the institutional problems of the office or the administrative activities of these two outstanding Elizabethan secretaries.

[22] Smith, *Servant of the Cecils*, esp. ch. 3.   [23] Principal secretary, 1516–26.

but by his instructions. And as for one of my letters . . . I had at that time devised a letter in the same matter far discrepant from that ye received; but the King would not approve the same and said that he would himself devise an answer to your grace's letters sent to him at that time; and commanded me to bring your said letters into his privy chamber, with pen and ink, and there he would declare unto me what I should write. And when his grace had your said letters, he read the same three times, and marked such places as it pleased him to make answer unto, and commanded me to write and rehearse as liked him, and not further to meddle with that answer. So that I herein nothing did but obeyed the King's commandment as to my duty appertaineth, and especially at such time as he would upon good grounds be obeyed, whosoever spake to the contrary. As touching untrue information to be made by me to the King of your grace's letters, I am sorry ye do lay that to my charge; for if I did untruly inform his Highness of any part of the same letters which be of so great weight and importance, I should not only deal unkindly and falsely with your grace but also be a manifest traitor to the King. . . . Furthermore, if I would inform the King otherwise of your grace's letters than the truth is, I cannot so do without great shame and to mine own evident ruin, for his grace doth read them all himself, and examine the same at leisure with great deliberation, and hath better wit to understand them than I to inform him. . . .   *State Papers*, I, 79–80

63. An Act for the placing of the Lords in the Parliament (1539: 31 Henry VIII, c. 10).

Forasmuch as in all great councils and congregations of men having sundry degrees and offices in the commonwealth it is very requisite and convenient that an order should be had and taken for the placing and sitting of such persons as be bound to resort to the same, to the intent that they knowing their places may use the same without displeasure or let of the council; therefore the King's most royal Majesty, although it appertaineth unto his prerogative royal to give such honour, reputation and placing to his counsellors and other his subjects as shall be seeming to his most excellent wisdom, is nevertheless pleased and contented for an order to be had and taken in this his most High Court of Parliament. . . .

*   *   *   *   *   *

vi. And it is also enacted by authority aforesaid that the King's chief secretary being of the degree of a baron of the Parliament shall sit and be placed afore and above all barons not having any of the offices aforementioned; and if he be a bishop, that then he shall sit and be placed above all other bishops not having any of the offices above remembered.

* * * * * *

viii. And it is further enacted that if any person or persons which at any time hereafter shall happen to have any of the said offices of lord chancellor, lord treasurer, lord president of the King's council, lord privy seal, or chief secretary, shall be under the degree of a baron of the Parliament, by reason whereof they can have no interest to give any assent or dissent in the said House, that then in every such case such of them as shall happen to be under the said degree of a baron shall sit and be placed at the uppermost part of the sacks in the midst of the said Parliament Chamber, either there to sit upon one form or upon the uppermost sack, the one of them above the other in order as is above rehearsed.

* * * * * *

x. And it is enacted by authority aforesaid that as well in all Parliaments as in the Star Chamber, and in all other assemblies and conferences of Council, the lord chancellor, the lord treasurer, the lord president, the lord privy seal, the great chamberlain, the constable, the marshal, the lord admiral, the grand master or lord steward, the King's chamberlain, and the King's chief secretary, shall sit and be placed in such order and fashion as is above rehearsed and not in any other place, by authority of this present act.   *Stat. Realm*, iii, 729–30

64. Warrant for the appointment of two secretaries, 1540.

First, that Thomas Wriothesley and Ralph Sadler, and every of them, shall have the name and office of the King's Majesty's principal secretaries during his Highness' pleasure; and shall receive, to be equally divided between them, all such fees, droits, duties and commodities, not hereafter specially limited, as have, do or ought to belong to the office of his Majesty's principal secretary.

Item, his Highness hath resolved that every of the said Thomas Wriothesley and Ralph Sadler shall, for the time of their being in the said office, have and keep two his Grace's seals called his signets, and with the same seal all such things, warrants and writings, both for inward and outward parties, as have been accustomed to be passed heretofore by the same; every of the said Thomas Wriothesley and Ralph Sadler nevertheless to keep a book containing all such things as shall pass by either of their hands, and the one to be made ever privy to the other's register.

Item, his Majesty is contented that every of the said Thomas Wriothesley and Ralph Sadler shall have an ordinary chamber or lodging within the gates of his Grace's house, in all places where the same may be, conveniently furnished; and every of them to have like bouche of court[24] in all things as is appointed to the secretary.

Item, his Majesty is pleased and ordaineth that all such times as the lord privy seal[25] shall be present in the court, the said Thomas Wriothesley and Ralph Sadler shall accompany him at his table; and when he shall be absent out of court, then they to have his diet for themselves and such other as be appointed to that table.

Item, his Majesty ordaineth that in all Councils, as well in his Majesty's Household as in the Star Chamber and elsewhere, all lords, both of the temporalty and clergy, shall sit above them; and likewise the treasurer, comptroller, master of the Horse, and vice-chamberlain of his Highness' Household; then next after to be placed the said principal secretaries, and so after them all such other councillors as shall resort and have place in any of the said Councils. And albeit that by a statute lately made,[26] the office of the principal secretary should be and sit continually in the Upper House of the Parliament upon one of the woolsacks, yet his Highness, considering the good service that the said Thomas Wriothesley and Ralph Sadler may do him in the Nether House, where they have now places, doth ordain that during his pleasure they shall use themselves as hereafter ensueth; that is to say, on all such days as the Speaker shall be present, or that the King's Majesty shall be present in person, they shall attend on his Highness, and shall both have their places upon the said woolsack according to the said statute; and at all other times the one of them to be one week in the High House and the other in the Low House, and so he that was in the Lower House to be the next week in the Higher House, changing their

---

[24] Free allowance of some food, fuel and light while resident at court.
[25] Thomas Cromwell.
[26] See Doc. 63.

places by course, unless it be upon some special day for matters to be treated in the Nether House, at which time they shall may[27] both be present there accordingly; and in all other places within his Grace's Household and elsewhere his pleasure is that they and every of them shall have, enjoy and use the place of principal secretary as heretofore hath been accustomed. *State Papers*, II, 623-4

65. The secretary's control of the Privy Council, 1554.

[Paget said] that if [Sir William] Petre wished to retire he ought not to be allowed to do so but kept in office, for he had been there so long that he was as good as a Council register and reminded the members of everything that had occurred in the past. . . . *Span. Cal.*, XIII, 89

66. Nicholas Faunt's 'Discourse touching the office of principal secretary of estate', April 1592.

* * * * * *

Now amongst all particular offices and places of charge in this state, there is none of more necessary use, nor subject to more cumber and variableness, than is the office of principal secretary, by reason of the variety and uncertainty of his employment. . . .

* * * * * *

[The secretary should avoid recourse to other officers, higher or lower, so as to guard the secrecy of his office; instead he should employ a principal servant or chief clerk whom he can trust] . . . It shall be also convenient to be provided of another for the dispatch of ordinary matters and chiefly for continual attendant [*sic*] in the chamber where the papers are whose particular charge may be to endorse them or give them their due titles as they daily come in of all sorts, which (to reduce them into a few heads) are noted to be of three kinds, namely *home letters* which are the greatest multitude, *Council matters* concerning any private or public cause, and *divers matters* which contain petitions to the secretary, discourses, projects, relations, declarations, or informations of private and public causes etc.; and every morning to set them in several bundles for the present use of them and when they grow to be many, those that have been most dealt in and dispatched to be removed

[27] *Sic.*

into some chest or place, lest confusion or loss of some of them grow through an exceeding and unnecessary multitude of papers, as hath been seen in that place. . . . The other servant, whom I first described, will be chiefly charged with foreign matters and others that more nearly [touch] his Majesty and the state. . . .

*   *   *   *   *   *

[The books to be kept should include a daily diary of things to be done and an entry book for registering the dates of receiving and sending all despatches; also registers and letter books divided into foreign and home affairs, the former including 'a book of treaties' and a 'book (or books) of present negotiations'. Among the latter there should be: a survey of the lands with the commodities thereof (i.e. a description of England), the sea causes (navy, munitions, guns), the defence of the realm within the land (musters, training, equipment, ordnance), the revenues of the land, the charges of the Crown, the courts of justice.] Many other books might be hereunto annexed . . . as books of coinage and mint causes, of rates for victualling, of weights and measures, of orders touching her Majesty's Household, of precedents of all matters that concern the service, of discoveries and new inventions, of descriptions most exactly taken of other countries as well by maps and cards as by discovering the present state of their government, their alliances, dependents etc. . . . Thus I have in some sort discovered my poor conceit touching the necessary servants and books that the secretary is to provide as instrumental means for the better discharge of his weighty office. . . .   Printed by Hughes, *Eng. Hist. Rev.*, xx, 499–508

67. Robert Beale's 'Treatise of the office of a councillor and secretary to Her Majesty', 1592.

Of such things as the secretary is to proffer to the Council, let him first have in a several paper a memorial or docket of those which he mindeth to propound and have dispatched at every sitting. . . . When the Council meeteth, have a care that the time be not spent in matters of small moment, but to dispatch such things as shall be propounded unto them, for you shall find that they will not meet so often as you would desire, sometimes for sickness and sometimes for other employment. . . . Favour not secret or Cabinet Councils which do but cause jealousy and envy. . . . When there shall be any unpleasant matter to be imparted to her Majesty from the Council, or other matters to be done of great importance, let not the burden be laid on you alone but let the rest join with you . . . for if anything be misliked it will be said that it was the secretary's doing, that they signed for company, that the letter was brought to them, etc.

*　*　*　*　*　*

Take heed to whom you give any warrant for the apprehension of any man or searching of houses; they may abuse you and use it for other purposes . . . and unless there be great cause or you be so specially commanded by her Majesty, take heed of any letters that may stay or hinder the ordinary course of justice between party and party or be against the law and liberty of the land whereto the prince is sworn . . .

When any business cometh into the secretary's hands, he shall do well for the ease of himself to distribute the same and to use the help of such her Majesty's servants as serve underneath him, as the clerks of the Council, the clerks of the signet, the secretary of the Latin and French tongues, and of his own servants.

*　*　*　*　*　*

Burden not yourself with too many clerks or servants, as Sir Francis Walsingham did. Let your secret services be known to a few; the lord treasurer Burghley, being secretary, had not above two or three. . . .

*　*　*　*　*　*

A secretary must have a special cabinet whereof he is himself to keep the key, for his signets, ciphers and secret intelligences, distinguishing the boxes or tills rather by letters than by the name of the countries or places, keeping that only unto himself, for the names may inflame a desire to come by such things. . . . I could wish that the secretary should make himself acquainted with some honest gentlemen in all the shires, cities and principal towns and the affection of the gentry. . . . It is convenient for a secretary to understand the state of the whole realm; to have Sir Thomas Smith's book,[28] though there be many defects which by progress of time and experience he shall be able to spy and amend. Then to have a book or notice of all the noblemen, their pedigrees and alliances among themselves and with other gentlemen. . . .

[28] *De Republica Anglorum.*

[Pp. 429–31 give a detailed list of subjects with which the secretary should be familiar.]

*   *   *   *   *   *

Things to be done with her Majesty:

Have in a little paper note of such things as you are to propound to her Majesty and divide it into the titles of public and private suits, as the lord treasurer and Mr Secretary [Walsingham] were wont to do. . . .

Learn before your access her Majesty's disposition by some of the privy chamber, with whom you must keep credit, for that will stand you in much stead. . . .

When her Highness is angry or not well disposed, trouble her not with any matter which you desire to have done, unless extreme necessity urge it.

When her Highness signeth it shall be good to entertain her with some relation or speech whereat she may take some pleasure.

*   *   *   *   *   *

If it shall be needful to publish any proclamations, consider well of the matter and look unto former precedents, and therefore it shall be needful for you to have the book of proclamations printed in the time of King Edward 6 and all the rest as many as you can get. . . . If the matter be according to law, then urge it. . . . As new evils require new remedies, so if no provision hath been heretofore made that may be enforced by law, then her Majesty by her prerogative may take order in many things by proclamation.[29] And herein it is good to see what hath been done in like cases in other countries; and to this purpose the books of the edicts and ordinances of France and the pragmatics of Spain may stand you in some stead. But be circumspect in applying of those precedents to this state, to avoid opinion of being newfangled and a bringer-in of new customs. . . .

Be not dismayed with the controlments and amendments of such things which you shall have done, for you shall have to do with a princess of great wisdom, learning and experience. It is reported of King Henry 8 that when Sir William Petre, at the first time that he was secretary, seemed to be dismayed for that the King crossed and blotted out many things in a writing which he had made, the King willed him not to take it in evil part, 'for it is I,' said he, 'that made both Cromwell,

[29] Cf. above, p. 22.

Wriothesley and Paget good secretaries, and so must I do to thee'.[30] The princes themselves know best their own meaning and there must be time and experience to acquaint them with their humours before any man can do any acceptable service.

* * * * * *

Yelverton MS 162, printed in Read, *Walsingham*, I, 423–43

[30] A pretty tale, but (if not apocryphal) proof only of Henry VIII's inflated opinion of himself. The surviving draft letters of Cromwell's and Wriothesley's secretarial periods show no sign of the King teaching them their business. In any case, all these three statesmen had served long periods of apprenticeship before they came into direct contact with the King.

CHAPTER 4

FINANCIAL ADMINISTRATION

Ordinarily, the royal finances were in the hands of the Exchequer. Established by the end of the twelfth century as an independent department of state, it had age, experience and reputation on its side. Above all, it could claim to be immune to peculation. It contained within itself the two departments which any financial organisation needs: a treasury for the receipt and disbursement of revenue (the Lower Exchequer or Exchequer of Receipt) and an office for the scrutiny and audit of accounts (the Upper Exchequer or Exchequer of Account); its officers and records often acted as a check upon each other, and safety was the watchword of its famous 'course', as the rules governing the passing of accounts were called. On the other hand, it suffered from serious drawbacks. For one thing, by the later fifteenth century it had almost ceased to handle cash and dealt practically only in the peculiar credit instruments known as tallies: its records had become rather a register of tallies than a statement of money transactions.[1] Receivers of revenue found that just about all the incoming money had been anticipated for payment, and the Crown rarely received any actual coin. Administratively, too, the slow processes of the Exchequer were very unsatisfactory. Audits took a very long time, two years being the average rather than the exception; the account rolls were not designed to give a clear picture of income and expenditure; it was very difficult to discover the state of the finances at a given moment, the more so because much of the royal revenue appeared as technical 'debts' or outstanding items whose collection might take years. The Exchequer had never really been the royal treasury in the simplest sense; at all times the Crown had disposed of cash in coffers kept somewhere in the royal Household, though the sophisticated department of state normally retained responsibility over all accounts. For reasons of administrative convenience, or sometimes because a baronial opposition kept its hand on the Exchequer, medieval monarchs had at intervals developed Household departments into secondary financial offices. Henry III and Edward I relied on the Wardrobe; Edward II and Edward III exploited the potentialities of the Chamber.[2] It is

---

[1] For the fifteenth-century Exchequer cf. Steel, *Receipt of the Exchequer*, esp. ch. 1. Tallies were wooden sticks, notched to represent a given sum and split, the Exchequer retaining one half by way of record. The other half could either be used in the process of accounting, as a receipt for money paid in, or as a 'tally of assignment' authorising payment of royal money by a specified collector of revenue who would later produce the tally to prove his payment.

[2] The story of medieval Exchequer and Household finance is the main subject of Tout's *Chapters*. Cf. also Chrimes, *Administrative History*, esp. 96 ff., 179 ff., 189 ff.

important to think of these offices as organised treasuries, staffed by clerks who kept accounts, receiving and paying money which might either be assigned to them by the Exchequer or (especially in the case of the Chamber) come from sources which they controlled without rivalry.

The revival of monarchy by the Yorkists and Henry VII relied in great part on the renewed exploitation of the Household as a means of administration. In particular this meant the development of the Chamber as a financial department.[3] Though Henry VII carried through a few minor reforms in the Exchequer, his chief concern was to make his Chamber the centre of all revenue administration. To this end he ordered that the bulk of the ordinary revenue—with the exception of the customs, retained by the Exchequer—should be paid directly to the treasurer of the Chamber. This officer's revenues consisted essentially of two kinds: the Crown lands whose yield went straight to him, and such other sources (the seals, justice, wardship) as yielded a surplus paid to him by the primary agency of control. Expenditure from the Chamber remained under the king's hand, being authorised either by word of mouth or at best a signet warrant.[4] The treasurer's accounts were checked by the king in person, as his frequent initialling of pages proves, and he appointed leading members of the Household for a more formal audit at the end of the year.[5] This administration without rules worked so well only because the king gave it his constant attention, and because his authority prevented complaints from the Exchequer. In one respect, however, a little more organisation was required. Henry VII needed in the first place to discover what in fact was available by way of revenue; his problem lay less in the collection of a known and regular supply than in the reassertion and expansion of rights neglected during the period of monarchic decline. Originally he followed Yorkist practice (though he improved on it) by appointing temporary commissions of enquiry, charged with the discovery of prerogative rights, rights in lands, and fine-bearing offences. There are signs that later on he began to prefer less temporary arrangements, though he could still issue such commissions in 1504 and 1508. But from 1500, anyway, a regular committee looked after the collection of fines on penal statutes.[6] In 1503 there appeared a regular master of wards, with an organisation designed to make sure of the consistent and complete administration of this

[3] Wolffe, *Eng. Hist. Rev.*, LXXI, 1 ff. and LXXXIX, 225 ff.; Richardson, *Tudor Chamber Administration*, 79 ff.; Elton, *Tudor Revolution*, 20 ff.

[4] The Exchequer required writs under the great or privy seal.

[5] Mr Richardson has argued that something to be called an 'office of audit' was created by Henry VII (*Tudor Chamber Administration*, 176 ff.). But his own account shows that he has overstated the degree of formal elaboration achieved: e.g. as late as 1508 accounts were audited by councillors assigned to the duty as occasion arose (*ibid.*, 178). For his general tendency to see more precision than existed cf. also Hooker, *Speculum*, XXXIII, 69 ff.

[6] Somerville, *Eng. Hist. Rev.*, LIV, 427 ff.

valuable source of profit (**68**). Finally, in 1508, all the policies designed to make the most of the king's prerogative rights culminated in the short-lived office of surveyor of the king's prerogative.[7] The whole system, inescapably 'Household' in its details, centred upon the treasurer of the Chamber as the officer responsible for collecting and administering the money obtained. Its modernity consisted in the new accounting methods—straightforward books of receipts and payments—and the rapid auditing which the absence of the Exchequer's rolls, bills and tallies made possible. The Duchy of Lancaster provided the model, but this itself was only the outstanding example of private administrative methods which could be found on other estates and also in the offices of merchants. In one respect, the central government remained very oldfashioned: it retained Roman numerals until late in the seventeenth century.

Henry VII's death jeopardised his system, partly because he had maintained it in so personal and unorganised a way, and partly because it had roused opposition in the Exchequer and elsewhere. It was argued, not without justice, that without the 'course of the Exchequer' the king could not be sure that he was not defrauded by his receivers and that a satisfactory record of outstanding items was kept. Outposts of the 'Chamber system' came under attack—Belknap avoided Empson's fate by allowing his activities as surveyor of the prerogative to lapse—but the core of it, the use of the Chamber as the leading revenue department, was too convenient to be abandoned. Between 1512 and 1515, accompanying the rise of Wolsey and illustrating his reliance on Henry VII's Household methods, a series of commissions and acts gave the system a little more permanence and organisation by the creation of two general surveyors of Crown lands, responsible for the Chamber revenue administered by its treasurer but also appointed to take the accounts of other revenue officers.[8] The reform, which replaced the total informality of specially appointed councillors by the relative certainty of statutory officers, culminated in an act (**69**) defending and authorising their activities. In essence, no doubt, Henry VIII's general surveyors did no more and had no less power than his father's councillors in charge of Chamber finance, but greater definition, more bureaucratic detail, and a growing organisation reduced the need for the king's personal participation as well as the chance that the system might lapse. However, the possibility still existed: until 1535, when it was made permanent, the Act for the General Surveyors only operated from one Parliament to the next. At the same time, the internal office organisation of the treasurer of the Chamber grew more complex, especially in the hands of Sir Brian Tuke who succeeded Sir Henry Wyat in 1528.[9] As the Chamber system lost many

---

[7] Richardson, *Eng. Hist. Rev.*, LVI, 52 ff.

[8] Elton, *Tudor Revolution*, 45 f.; Richardson, *Tudor Chamber Administration*, 248 ff.

[9] Cf. Elton, *Tudor Revolution*, 177 ff.; *Star Chamber Stories*, 114 ff.

of the advantages of flexibility and informality, it approximated more closely to a proper department. Yet the general surveyors continued to rely on the Exchequer and privy seal for much of their work; the treasurer of the Chamber remained unmistakably a personal servant; the whole structure was still characteristically the royal Household active in national affairs.

A document of 1531 (70) describes the organisation of the finances on the eve of Thomas Cromwell's accession to power. Listing the various sources of revenue, it allots their receivers to one of the three auditing departments. The Exchequer controlled the 'old' revenues—the customs and sheriffs' farms—with a supervisory and collecting function in profits of justice. The Duchy of Lancaster, run by its own Council, administered the lands belonging to it. All the rest—Crown lands, feudal profits, butlerage, vacant sees, Calais, the Hanaper of Chancery—fell within the general surveyor's province.[10] Though there was system and order in this situation, nothing could alter the fact that the bulk of the royal revenue remained in a but partially organised Household office: what was growingly a centralised national state depended for its financial structure on the uncertainties of the royal will and entourage. Cromwell's reforms, which put an end to this, sprang from two motives: new revenue coming to the Crown had to be administered, and he had a preference for bureaucratic and statutory departments of state. Whether he deliberately set himself against Household methods will perhaps remain a subject for debate, but his activities in the administration seem certainly to add up to a definite policy.[11] It is true that at first he was content to operate a kind of private Household system, supplanting the treasurer of the Chamber at the centre of affairs either by his own activities as a treasurer for the king's

[10] The document added the self-administering mint (for which see now Challis, *Tudor Coinage*) and the Council Learned who had not quite ceased to function. However, if their activities resulted in profit, the general surveyors and Chamber took charge of it.

[11] My analysis of these changes has several times been questioned, especially in the general debate initiated by Harriss and Williams in *Past and Present*, xxv (see my answer, *ibid.*, xxix). While I have somewhat broadened my views (cf. *Reform and Reformation*, 215 ff.) I remain persuaded that I was right in *Tudor Revolution* about Cromwell's intentions and the ultimate effects of his intervention. My distinction between Household administration and departments of state (which I was not the first to make: cf. Newton, *Tudor Studies*, 232) may have been misunderstood: of course, both were equally the king's government and equally capable of efficiency (or inefficiency). However: in the 14th–15th centuries both styles of administration are found coexisting; by the 17th only the second survived, covering now all the ground; the change began in the 1530's. It is true that the discovery in the reigns of the two Henries of a new Household department with sometimes national tasks (Starkey, 'Privy Chamber') shows that I overestimated Cromwell's immediate success in eliminating the 'medieval' element, but I would stand by two central points: (a) There is a fundamental difference between administration moved from within the royal Household, subject to the personal vagaries of the monarch and capable of producing from the Household by prerogative action further administrative organs to rival the national machinery, and one in which the role of the Household has atrophied to the occasional participation of individuals, while government is really and truly in the hands of established departments often resting on statute. (b) Cromwell's administration witnessed a self-conscious attempt to reorganise the government on the principle of public as against royal administration.

money or through the use of the treasurer of first fruits as, so to speak, his personal treasurer of the Chamber.[12] However, the addition of the monastic land revenue drew his attention to the need for more fundamental reform, and he proceeded thereafter along the lines of a new policy which reduced the scope of the Chamber system, broke the link between it and the Household, and created organised departments (courts) modelled on the Duchy of Lancaster, for specified sections of the revenue.[13] The first of these courts was that of Augmentations (71),[14] and by 1542 reforms sponsored by Cromwell and those he had trained resulted in a financial administration reorganised in six great departments of state. The Exchequer continued untouched in charge of the revenue it had controlled in 1531, as did the Duchy of Lancaster. The general surveyors, reduced to the fixity of a court,[15] administered the Crown lands collected by Henry VII and Wolsey. Augmentations dealt with all new Crown lands, while First Fruits and Tenths (also now a proper court)[16] handled the ecclesiastical revenue. Lastly, the Court of Wards and Liveries was responsible for the feudal revenue—the revenue of the fiscal prerogative.[17] Each court was independent in itself, capable of enforcing its will, summoning defaulters, and adjudicating upon disputes arising out of the revenue under its charge; each had its own local organisation of receivers and central organisation of head officers and auditors. None of them depended on the action of the king or was capable of the indeterminate extension and contraction characteristic of Household government. Unity was provided by the ultimate control of the Privy Council, which was also responsible for financial policy.

The obvious weakness of Cromwell's system lay in its diversity, a consequence of its gradual creation, and in the multiplying of officials which it produced. The fiscal crisis of the 1540's—itself caused by war, inflation and the disastrous debasement of the coinage—compelled further reforms which always aimed primarily at reducing the cost of the administration but usually attempted also to apply considered administrative principles. Largely the work of Sir William Paulet, marquess of Winchester, assisted by other experts trained in the Cromwell era, they resulted in the final elimination of the Household and the restoration of Exchequer supremacy.[18] But it was a

[12] Elton, *Tudor Revolution*, 139 ff., 190 ff.

[13] *Ibid.*, 203 ff. The degree of bureaucratic organisation is apparent from Doc. **72**.

[14] For Augmentations cf. *ibid.*, 204 ff.; Richardson, *Augmentations*; Youings, *Devon Lands*, pp. viii, seqq.

[15] 33 Henry VIII, c. 39 (1542).

[16] 32 Henry VIII, c. 45 (1540).

[17] 32 Henry VIII, c. 46 (1540) and 33 Henry VIII, c. 22 (1542). Cf. Bell, *Court of Wards*, 14 f.

[18] Elton, *Tudor Revolution*, 223 ff. From the administrative point of view much of the interest of these reforms lies in their procedure: enquiry by a royal commission which took evidence and rendered a report, sometimes followed by action which, since statutory courts were involved, had to be based on statute but relied on letters patent (prerogative action) for the detail. For one such commission cf. Doc. **20**.

different Exchequer. The reformers proceeded by amalgamating courts. In 1547 General Surveyors and Augmentations were combined into one office for the Crown lands (second Court of Augmentations). In 1554, after prolonged discussion, all the new courts disappeared by absorption into the Exchequer (73). The original intention had been to reduce the revenues of Augmentations and First Fruits to the normal process of the Exchequer, but in practice there were created within the Exchequer specialised subdepartments which administered these matters according to the modern accounting methods introduced by Henry VII and embodied in Cromwell's bureaucratic organisation. The essential additions to the Exchequer machinery were the seven auditors of the land revenue (usually the same men as acted as auditors for the old revenue, accounted for according to the 'course' of the Exchequer) who in a sense continued the work of Augmentations, and the two auditors of the prests (revived in 1560)[19] who controlled the 'declared accounts', that is those of all revenue neither ancient nor Crown lands. These last inherited the general auditing capacity of Wolsey's general surveyors which in turn had passed to officials of the same name in the second Augmentations Court.

Outside the Exchequer there remained, for reasons partly political and partly administrative, the Court of Wards and the Duchy of Lancaster; but by the side of the Exchequer's turnover their part was small. From 1554 onwards the bulk of the Crown's resources was once more administered in the Exchequer. The Lower Exchequer now dealt again largely in cash which reforms in its organisation and records enabled it to handle with greater efficiency; and the Upper Exchequer contained both modern and old-fashioned auditing machinery. The solution represented a compromise which often enough hampered efficiency; since in part at least it marked a surrender to the jealousies of the Exchequer hierarchy, this is not to be wondered at. From the Crown's point of view, the reformed Exchequer was never so satisfactory as Henry VII's Chamber system or Cromwell's revenue courts had been; but, provided the three key officers were men of ability it could do its work well enough. These three were the lord treasurer, now once more minister of finance; the chancellor of the Exchequer, an officer who only at this time acquired real importance;[20] and the auditor of the Receipt who rapidly established a powerful position of control over receipts and issues.[21] Winchester and Burghley, treasurers from 1550 to 1598, ensured that the Crown's finances should be handled as soundly as their general insufficiency and the selfishness of the closed Exchequer shop would permit.[22]

[19] George, Eng. Hist. Rev., XXXI, 41 ff., and cf. Elton, Tudor Revolution, 255.
[20] Cf. Elton, Tudor Revolution, 117 ff., 256 f.
[21] Ibid., 252 ff.; Studies, I, 355 ff.
[22] The history of Elizabethan financial administration remains to be unravelled; Mr C. H. D. Coleman is at present engaged upon that very complicated task.

68. Henry VII's machinery for administering wardships.

. . . Wherefore it is to be remembered that in the time of our late sovereign lord King Henry VII (whose soul God pardon) divers officers were appointed for the due ordering of the said wards, that is to say a master, a general receiver, an auditor, and particular receivers in every shire. And the said master for the time being did deliver every term to the said auditor a bill of such names as were the king's wards and a titling of every office,[23] by reason whereof the particular receivers had knowledge of the same, which answered the issues and profits of their lands every year by way of account. . . . And since that time hitherto[24] there hath no like order been taken. . . .

State Papers Henry VIII, vol. 159, fo. 47 (printed in Bell, Court of Wards, 187)

69. The Act concerning the King's General Surveyors (1515: 6 Henry VIII, c. 24).

Forasmuch as in the time of the late right noble and famous prince, King Henry VII, father unto the right noble King that now is, by his high wisdom, providence and circumspection divers and many his chamberlains of his principalities of Wales and other receivers . . . of divers his honours, castles, lordships, manors, lands, tenements and other hereditaments as well in England and Wales as in Calais and the marches of the same, which then were in his hands and possession as well by the ancient inheritance of his crown as by rebellion or forfeiture of divers and sundry persons, as by reason of the nonage of all and singular his wards, or by purchase of himself, or by any other mean of occasion of his prerogative royal, accounted by his commandment by mouth before then his trusty servants and councillors Sir Reginald Bray, Sir Robert Southwell, knights, and other whom the said late King in that behalf at several and divers times appointed as well for the more speedy payment of his revenues to be had and for the accounts of the same more speedily to be taken than his Grace could or might have been answered of after the course of his Exchequer, as for the greater ease and less charge of all and singular the foresaid accountants, farmers, fee farmers and other officers. . . . And that divers and many sums of

---

[23] Inquisition *post mortem*.
[24] This undated document was probably written *c.* 1520 (cf. Elton, *Tudor Revolution*, 220).

money which were due by divers and sundry the foresaid accountants ... were paid unto the said late King and his Chamber either to his
own hands or to some other person or persons to his use, as it may appear
by bills or books signed with his sign manual, or to the hands of then
his trusty servant John Heron, as also it may appear by bills signed with
the hand of the same John Heron;[25] [which processes and accounts,
being of no effect in the Exchequer, will cause trouble to the
said accountants and their heirs whom the Exchequer is suing for
these sums]—

The right high and mighty prince, our sovereign lord the King that
now is ... by the assent of the Lords spiritual and temporal and the
Commons in this present Parliament assembled, and by authority of
the same, hath ordained, established and enacted that the said persons
that hereafter shall be executors of this act shall have full power and
authority to call before them all and singular officers accountable [listed
in the attached schedule]; and that the said executors of this act shall
take the accounts of all things contained in the said schedule or sche-
dules ... and that the said officers nor none of them shall never be
chargeable to account before the barons of the said Exchequer nor in
none other court or place nor before other persons but only before the
said persons, executors of this act. ...

[II. The executors of the act may order process under privy seal for
appearance in the Prince's Council Chamber at Westminster, the keeper
of the privy seal to act upon their fiat.

III. No other process is to lie against any accountants out of the
Exchequer].[26]

IV. And where it is considered that neither by course of the King's
Exchequer nor by this present act or acts any officer or officers accountable ... be discharged of their accounts or payments in the said
Exchequer but only by or upon several accounts either to be made and
engrossed in the said Exchequer or by the said executors of this act ...
which now by experience is not possible to be accomplished forasmuch
as many and most part of the said accounts, which were of long time
past by the commandment of our late sovereign lord King Henry VII
taken by divers several auditors thereunto appointed, which auditors

---

[25] For Bray, Southwell and Heron cf. Richardson, *Tudor Chamber Administration*, 160 ff.,
451 ff.

[26] 'Process' is the issue of summons and orders, and the right here conferred equipped the general
surveyors with executive power to enforce their decisions.

be deceased and not only the said accounts allowed be broken, lost and otherwise embezzled, so that no sufficient matter may be had to make new the said accounts according to the continue and purport of the said act; and so the said officers accountable be without remedy to their extreme loss, danger and utter undoing [it is enacted that all accounts shall be quit by certificate of the general surveyors for all sums, arrears, etc. down to Michaelmas 1508].

[v–xviii. Detailed elaboration of the duties and scope of the general surveyors of Crown lands.]

xix. Also be it ordained, established and enacted by the authority of this present Parliament that the King's forenamed trusty servant John Heron be from henceforth treasurer of the King's Chamber . . . and that he and every other person whom the King hereafter shall name and appoint to the said room and office of the treasurer of his Chamber be not accountable in Exchequer for any such his or their receipt, or any part or parcel of the premises as before is expressed, but to the King's Highness or his heirs, or before such as his Grace shall thereunto limit and appoint.

[xx. Acquittance from treasurer of the Chamber to be valid in the Exchequer.

xxi. The executors of this act to be called general surveyors of Crown lands.

xxii. Appointment of clerk, messenger and usher.

xxiii–xxvi. Further details of the working of the office.]

xxvii. Provided always that if any time hereafter the King's Highness . . . shall think it more expedient and profitable for his Grace that the account of any officer . . . may be more surely taken before any other person . . . that then the King . . . by his . . . letters of privy seal shall have authority to ordain and depute the said other person or persons, or the barons of the Exchequer for the time being, to hear and determine the accounts of all such officers. . . . This act to endure unto the Feast of the Annunciation of Our Lady[27] which shall be in the year of our Lord God 1516.

$$* \quad * \quad * \quad * \quad * \quad *$$

Stat. Realm, III, 145–52

---

[27] 25 March.

70. **A Memorial for the King's Highness, declaring the kind of things wherein riseth yearly as well his certain revenues as his casual revenues, and who be officers to his Highness in that behalf (c. 1531).**

The treasurer of England	First, the yearly revenues and profits growing of the King's customs and subsidies, accounted for in his Exchequer by the customers of his ports.
The master of the wards	Item, the profits and yearly revenues growing of his wards and of their lands and tenements, accounted before the general surveyors by the master of the wards.
The surveyors of the liveries	The issues, profits and sums of money yearly growing to the King by the surveyors of the King's liveries,[28] accounted before his general surveyors.
The butler of England	The yearly profits growing to the King of his butlerage, received and taken by the butler of England and accounted before the general surveyors.
The surveyors of vacations of bishoprics and abbacies	The yearly profits and revenues growing to the King by the surveyors of the vacations of bishoprics, abbacies and priories, accounted before the general surveyors.
The surveyors of the restitution of the temporalties of bishops, abbots and priors	The yearly profits and revenues growing yearly to the King's Highness for the restitution of the temporalties of bishops, abbots and priors, accounted before the general surveyors.
The surveyors of the King's woods	The surveyors of the King's woods for wood sales made yearly on this side and beyond Trent, accounted before the general surveyors.
The clerk of the Hanaper	The issues, profits and yearly revenues growing to the King in the office of the clerk of the Hana-

[28] Livery—here the sum paid by an heir on attaining his majority to redeem his lands from wardship.

per[29] for his great seal, for writs of entries, fines and other writs and patents, accounted for before the general surveyors.

The chancellor of the Duchy of Lancaster	The yearly issues, revenues and profits growing to the King by the receivers general and particular of the Duchy of Lancaster, accounted before the auditors of his said Duchy.
The general surveyors	The yearly issues, profits and revenues growing to the King by the hands of his receivers general, particular and all other his officers being charged with his lands, being accounted before the King's general surveyors; that is to say, Warwick lands, Spencer lands, Buckingham lands, the Duchy of Cornwall, the chamberlain of Chester, the chamberlain of North and South Wales, and the whole Principality of the same.
The Exchequer	The fines, amercements and recognisances taken, forfeited and assessed yearly, growing in the King's courts of his Chancery, the Star Chamber, the King's Bench and his Common Pleas. should be estreated and accounted for in the Exchequer.[30]
The Exchequer	The yearly profits which should grow to the King by his escheators for the profits coming of outlawries, instructions and other escheats of lands, tenements and movable goods and chattels should be accounted for in the Exchequer.
The Exchequer	The profits and revenues with the proffers of his sheriffs which grow unto his Grace of his counties and fee farms of his cities and towns, yearly accounted for by his said sheriffs in the Exchequer.
The Exchequer	Recognisances, fines and amercements forfeited and assessed before his justices of assize, justices

[29] The financial department of Chancery responsible for collecting the fees paid 'for the seal', i.e. due to the Crown upon the issue of any writ or letters patent.

[30] I.e. the court which imposes the fine, etc. must make a return to the Exchequer which is responsible for the collection of the money (estreat—extract from the records of one department for communication to another).

sewers,[31] justices of the peace, justices of
quorum,[32] and justices of oyer and terminer[33]
should be estreated into the Exchequer and
there accounted for.

[Profits from recognisances and bonds taken and forfeited before the
officers already listed, and from debts yet owing in these various departments; also the profits of Calais and its environs, accounted before
the general surveyors.]

The warden and masters of the King's Mint	The yearly profits growing to the King's High-ness of his Mint within the Tower of London and other places within this realm would be enquired for; and to know what profits hath grown to his Highness this six years past, which I[34] think do amount to a great sum of money.
The King's Learned Council[35]	The revenues and yearly profits growing to the King's Highness of statutes penal,[36] and also of ends taken with his Highness or Council by obligation, indenture, payment or otherwise, for any manner offence or forfeiture, would be declared by a book, so that his Highness might be ascertained thereof yearly.

State Papers Henry VIII, vol. 67, fos. 32–37 (printed Elton, *Tudor Revolution*, 433–8)

71. An Act establishing the Court of Augmentations (1536: 27 Henry VIII, c. 27).

[The preamble recites the act for the annexation of the lesser monasteries, 27 Henry VIII, c. 28.]

For the more surety and establishment whereof, and to the intent
that the King's Majesty, his heirs and successors shall be yearly as well
truly and justly answered, contented and paid of the rents, farms, issues,
revenues and profits rising, coming and growing of the said manors,
lands, tenements and other hereditaments before specified, as of the
goods, chattels, plate, stuff of household, debts, money, stock, store and
other whatsoever profit and commodity given, granted or appointed

---

[31] Commissioners of sewers were appointed at intervals, with powers to survey and repair
waterways or drain marshes.

[32] For the quorum cf. below, p. 465.

[33] Cf. Glossary.

[34] Thomas Cromwell.   [35] Cf. above, p. 81.   [36] Cf. pp. 20 nn. 41, 42.

to the King's Majesty by the same . . . be it enacted, ordained and established by the assent of the King's Majesty, his Lords spiritual and temporal, and the Commons in this present Parliament assembled, and by authority of the same, in manner and form as hereafter followeth in articles, that is to say:

I. First, the King our sovereign lord, by authority aforesaid, ordaineth, maketh, establish and erecteth a certain court commonly to be called the Court of the Augmentations of the Revenues of the King's Crown; which court by authority aforesaid continually shall be a court of record[37] and shall have one great seal and one privy seal . . .

II. Also it is enacted by authority aforesaid that there shall be one certain person to be named and assigned by the King's Highness which shall be chancellor of the said court and shall be the chief and principal officer of the same court . . . and shall have the keeping of the said great seal and privy seal. . . . Also that there shall be one person to be named by the King's Highness which shall be called the King's treasurer of the Court of the Augmentations of the Revenues of the King's Crown and shall be the second officer of the same court.

III. Also it is ordained by authority aforesaid that there shall be one person learned in the laws of the land to be named by the King's Highness which shall be called the King's attorney of the said court and shall be the third officer of the same court. Also that there shall be one person to be named by the King's Highness which shall be called the King's solicitor of the said court and shall be the fourth officer of the court. Also that there shall be ten particular auditors to be named by the King's Highness which shall be called auditors of the revenues of the said Augmentations. Also there shall be sixteen particular receivers to be named by the King's Highness which shall be called receivers of the said revenues. Also that there shall be one person to be named by the King's Highness which shall be called clerk of the said court; and one other person which shall be usher of the same court; and one other person which shall be called messenger of the same court; which usher and messenger shall be named by the King's Highness; and every of them shall have such yearly fees, rewards and profits as the usher and messenger of the Duchy Chamber of Westminster have and perceive.

* * * * * *

[37] Strictly a court which keeps a plea roll—i.e. a court of common law—but used more generally for any court which kept a record of proceedings that would be recognised as valid evidence in another court.

v. Also . . . that all the said monasteries, priories and other religious houses which be dissolved and come or shall come to the King's Highness by the act aforesaid . . . shall be in the order, survey and governance of the said court and of the officers and ministers thereof . . . except always and reserved such and as many of the same monasteries, priories and houses . . . which the King's Majesty by his letters patent under his great seal shall declare and limit to continue and be in their essential state and to persevere in the body and corporation as they were before the making of the said act.

vi. Also . . . that all those manors, lands, tenements and hereditaments which the King's Highness hath purchased . . . and which hereafter his Highness shall purchase, shall be and remain in the order, survey and governance of the said court. . . .

[vii–viii. The court to have power to make grants, leases etc., reserving tenure of knight's service in chief and a yearly rent of one tenth of the annual value.[38]]

*　*　*　*　*　*

xi. Also that the said chancellor for the time being shall have full power and authority to award, under the privy seal appointed to the said court, in the King's name such process and precepts with reasonable pains to be therein limited as be now commonly used in the court of the King's Duchy Chamber of Lancaster being at Westminster.[39] . . .

*　*　*　*　*　*

[xv. The receivers to pay all receipts to the treasurer whose signed acquittance shall be an effective discharge.

xvi. The treasurer to account yearly before the chancellor and two or more of the auditors; each receiver to account before one of the ten auditors assigned to him by the chancellor; receivers to complete their accounts for the year ending each Michaelmas by 20 March next following; the treasurer to complete his account by 1 April.]

*　*　*　*　*　*

[38] Tenure-in-chief was at first imposed as a condition of sale, in order to preserve for the Crown the profits of wardship, etc.; because of the burden of prerogative rights, it ultimately proved impossible to sell land on such terms and socage was progressively substituted for larger and larger amounts (cf. Hurstfield, *Law Quart. Rev.*, 1949, 72 ff.). The reserved rent was intended to compensate the Crown for the loss of the clerical tenth derived from the now secularised lands.

[39] The Duchy Chamber was the Council of the Duchy in its judicial capacity.

XXII. Also . . . that all manner of process that shall be made out of the King's Exchequer to or against any person or persons for any farms, rents, issues or profits concerning the premises or any part thereof limited by this act to be in the survey, order and governance of the said court and the ministers thereof shall be clearly void and of no effect.

XXIII. Also . . . that the said chancellor and treasurer shall yearly declare to the King's Highness the state of the clear yearly value of the said houses [etc.], and how, where and to whom they be employed, and what remaineth thereof in the hands of the said treasurer.[40]

[XIV. Provided that all royal lands in the county of Lancaster, and all the lands of monasteries of which the King is founder as duke of Lancaster, shall come under the administration of the Duchy of Lancaster and not of this court.] *Stat. Realm*, III, 569–74

72. Memoranda concerning the financial administration, 1537.

* * * * * *

Item, a commandment to be given to the chancellor of the Augmentations, and to the attorney, treasurer, solicitor, auditors and receivers of the said office, to make full declaration of the whole yearly value of all monasteries suppressed. And also of all other the honours, castles, lands and tenements being within the charge of their offices. And of all the profits and sums of money growing and coming to the King's Highness . . . accountable within the said office. And of all such sums of money as have been received to the King's use since the first establishment of the said office. What profit hath grown to the King of the lead, bells, plate, jewels, implements of household, ornaments of the church, corn, cattle, iron, glass, timber, stone. . . . What ready money hath been received, how the same hath been employed; what debts be stalled and owing by whom, and what it amounteth to. What lordships, lands and tenements the King's Highness hath given to any person or persons, and what the yearly value thereof doth amount unto. What offices, fees or annuities ordinary goeth out yearly of the said office; what extraordinary charges doth also go out of the same office. And what the whole yearly charges of the whole doth amount, and what the whole remainer to the King's use will yearly amount unto.

[40] There is no evidence that this instruction was ever observed.

Item, a like commandment to be given to the treasurer of the First Fruits and Tenths and to all others officers and ministers of the same office, to make a full declaration of the whole yearly value of all the tenths and first fruits and of all other things being within the charge of their offices. [Further to the same effect as in the previous paragraph.]

Item, a semblable commandment to be given to the treasurer of the Chamber and all other the King's officers of the King's surveyors and to all auditors and receivers of the same office, to make full declaration of the whole yearly value of all the honours, castles, manors, lands and tenements being within the charge of their offices. . . .

Item, a like commandment to be given to the barons, auditors, clerks and other officers and ministers of the King's Exchequer, to make a full declaration of the whole yearly value of all the honours, castles, manors, lands, tenements and hereditaments, being within the charge of their offices . . . and of all other things accountable within the said office whereof any profit hath or might be made to the King's use. . . .

Item, a like commandment to be given to the chancellor of the Duchy, auditors and receivers of the same office, to make full declaration of the whole yearly value of all the honours, castles, lands, tenements and hereditaments being within the charge of their offices. . . .

By means whereof the King's Highness may know his estate, and by means thereof may establish all his affairs; and thereby to put an order how a certain treasure yearly may be laid up for all necessities.

State Papers Henry VIII, vol. 119, fos. 106–7

73. Letters Patent dissolving the second Court of Augmentations, January 1554.

(i) Mary, by the grace of God Queen [etc.] to all and singular our loving subjects of what estate, degree or condition so ever they be, greeting. [Recites the erection of the courts of Augmentations and General Surveyors, and their amalgamation in 1546.] And where also in the Parliament begun and holden at Westminster the 1st day of October in the 1st year of our reign amongst many other things in the second session of the same Parliament it was enacted, ordained and established by the authority of the same Parliament that we should or might at any time hereafter during our natural life by our letters patents under our great seal of England at our will and pleasure alter, change, unite, transpose, dissolve or determine all or any of the courts commonly called the Court of the Augmentations and Revenues of the King's Crown, the Court of the First Fruits and Tenths, the court commonly called the Court of the King's Wards and Liveries, the Court of General Surveyors of the King's Lands, and the Court of the Duchy of Lancaster, and to reduce the same courts or any of them into one, two or more court or courts . . . as to us from time to time shall be thought most convenient and best for the better, surer and more speedy answering of our yearly revenues. . . . And forasmuch as we are informed and do directly understand that a great part of the possessions and hereditaments which were limited and appointed to be under the order and survey of the said Court of the Augmentations and Revenues of our Crown are since the making of the said statute for the erection of the said court, and since the erection thereof, as well by gifts and grants of our said late father as our said dear brother dispersed, cut away and greatly dismembered . . . and yet neverthele ssthe yearly allowances, fees, diets, rewards and other superfluous charges of our said court appear unto us to remain and rather to be augmented than diminished, to our great and excessive charges. For the which causes and for divers other great and weighty considerations us specially moving, we have presently resolved and determined by our royal power, and by force and authority of the said statute, wholly, absolutely and fully to dissolve, determine and extinguish the same court commonly called the Court of the Augmentations and Revenues of the King's Crown, and the jurisdiction and authority of the same . . . In witness whereof we have caused these our letters to be made patents. Witness ourself at Westminster, the 23rd day of January the first year of our reign.

(ii) [Recites the above letters patent.] We by these our letters patents do for us, our heirs and successors, unite, transpose and annex the same court so dissolved to our Court of the Exchequer, there to be and continue as a member and parcel of the same Court of the Exchequer. And further by the authority of these presents we do also limit and appoint all our honours, manors, lands, tenements, farms, issues, revenues, profits and all other our hereditaments, of what nature, kind or quality so ever they be, which at the time of the dissolution of the said court so by us dissolved was or ought to be in the order, survey, rule and governance of the same court shall remain and continue from the time of the said dis-

solution in the order, survey, rule and governance of our said Court of
the Exchequer, in such manner, order and form as is used and had of
other our manors, lands, tenements and hereditaments now in the order
and governance of our said Court of the Exchequer, and according to
such articles, ordinances and devices as in a schedule unto these our
letters patents annexed and signed with our hand is further limited,
appointed, mentioned and devised. . . . Witness ourself at Westminster,
the 24th day of January the first year of our reign.

(iii. The Schedule).[41]

1. First, all honours, manors [etc.] which is within the survey, rule
and order of the Augmentations . . . shall be perceived, levied and
gathered from henceforth by the sheriff of any shire . . . where the said
honours, manors [etc.] doth lie, or by any other person or persons that
shall be appointed by the lord treasurer and the Court there. After
which receipt the said sheriff . . . or other accountant so appointed
shall content and pay the revenue thereof at the Receipt of the Exchequer in manner and form as hereafter shall be declared.

* * * * * *

4. Item, that every sheriff . . . or other accountant aforesaid shall be
charged with the revenues aforesaid in his account from Michaelmas to
Michaelmas, according to the ancient laws and custom of the said
Exchequer.

* * * * * *

8. Item, that every sheriff or other accountant shall appear to his
account in his own proper person or by his sufficient deputy authorised
in writing . . . in Hilary Term, and there to take an oath according to
the ancient usage of the said Exchequer. . . .

* * * * * *

21. Item, that all records of the said Court of the Augmentations
that doth concern execution of any process . . . and all records of
books of orders and decrees . . . shall remain in the charge of the
queen's remembrancer of the said Exchequer.

* * * * * *

[41] The passages extracted from this very long Schedule are chosen to illustrate the desire to
allow Augmentations to be fully absorbed by the Exchequer and its old way. In addition these
extracts show (as the full schedule would demonstrate more clearly still) the power that accrued
to the lord treasurer as a consequence of the reforms.

24. Item, that all sealed indentures, rentals, court rolls and other writings and muniments whatsoever, touching the same revenues, to be placed in the treasury house that shall be appointed for that purpose by the lord treasurer and other the head officers of the Court.

25. Item, the account of the revenues taken every year and the engrossing in form aforesaid to remain in the charge of the clerk of the Pipe. . . .

* * * * * *

29. Item, that the accounts of the Hanaper, the Butlerage, the Staple of Calais and the revenues of the counties there, the Prests, the Mint, the Great Wardrobe, the customers of the ports of Chester, Berwick and Calais, be yearly taken and engrossed by the auditors of the Exchequer according to the ancient laws of the same Court and as heretofore they have been accustomed before the erection of the Courts of Survey and Augmentations of the Revenue.

* * * * * *

Close Roll, 1 Mary, part 7, mm. 3–4

CHAPTER 5

THE ANCIENT COURTS[1]

The law of England was the common law, common because it applied to all parts of the king's dominions.[2] Grown from ancient (Germanic) custom upon which the scientific principles of the Roman law had played in the twelfth and thirteenth centuries, developed by legislation both royal and parliamentary and by the decisions of judges (case-law), it had long before the sixteenth century acquired great antiquity and profound respect. In its history the sixteenth century represented an era of major transformation. The scholar who once called it 'the dark age of English legal history'[3] has since explained the revolution which the law underwent during the half-century before Henry VIII's death, a revolution produced largely from within itself through the actions of counsel and judges anxious to accommodate outdated concepts to a changing society.[4] Much legislation from the 1530's onwards was engaged in affirming and codifying the new principles and practices thus devised. The revolution especially transformed the law of landed property, the ancient core of the system.[5] The common law commanded the services of a professional class, the only professional class of laymen known to the medieval West; its practitioners were trained at the Inns of Court in London by experienced lawyers from among whom the king picked his judges. This professional class grew markedly in size, probably out of proportion to the general increase in population; its reputation varied from high respect to conventional dislike, but it provided not only practitioners of the law but also a managerial group of stewards and surveyors of lands, and of advisers to landowners, town corporations and merchant companies.[6] Members of the gentry increasingly acquired at least a superficial acquaintance with the law (useful to them in their duties as justices of the peace and on other royal commissions), and the language of the law

---

[1] A full exposition of all courts in the realm will be found in Holdsworth, vol. 1; here it is only possible to list and discuss the most important central courts. The reader should, however, be aware of the existence of others (such as the Court of the Constable and Marshal—cf. Squibb) and of the manner in which the central courts transferred their authority to the localities by delegation. In particular, the criminal jurisdiction of King's Bench was commonly exercised by commissioners of oyer and terminer, authorised to hear cases locally.

[2] For a good guide to the history of the law, cf. Baker, *Introduction*.

[3] Baker, *Legal History Studies 1972*, 1 ff.

[4] Baker (ed.), *Spelman's Reports*, Introduction.

[5] Simpson, *Land Law*, chs. 7 & 8.

[6] Ives, *Law Quart. Rev.*, LXXV, 348 ff., *Univ. of Birmingham Jour. of History*, VII, 130 ff., *Trans. R. Hist. Soc.*, 1968, 145 ff.; Prest, *Inns of Court*; Brooks, *Legal Records*, 41 ff. The essays collected in Prest (ed.), *Lawyers*, provide a good summary introduction.

penetrated into many forms of literature. Law and lawyers stand among the most pervasive features of the sixteenth-century social scene. All this gave the law great corporate strength and powers of resistance to attack.

By the end of the fifteenth century, three central courts had come into being, all originally grown from the king's entourage—for all jurisdiction stemmed from him—but now established as independent and separate institutions in Westminster Hall.[7] Of these the Court of King's Bench was the most distinguished and superior; though as late as the fourteenth century it had been virtually a court 'coram rege' and hard to distinguish from the Council, it was now no more than one of the ordinary courts.[8] Its jurisdiction covered pleas of the Crown—matters in which the king was concerned and especially criminal cases of all kinds—and it also exercised a jurisdiction in error. This was the nearest that the medieval common law came to the practice of appeals. Since it was a principle that a case once decided stood unalterable, it was possible to remedy manifest injustice only by a tacit review which could only be made on proof of a technical error (verbal or procedural) in the previous trial. Even ingenuity could not make this a satisfactory substitute for real appeal jurisdiction, but it helped a little. As the century opened, the King's Bench was in decline, its business (and income) dwindling and its future darkening.[9] Thereafter it dealt with this problem by developing a practice in civil matters between private parties by offering better remedies than were available in the court which should really have dealt with these, the Court of Common Pleas.[10] This, the oldest of the common law courts, covered all suits between party and party; it was far and away the busiest fifteenth-century court, but also in consequence the most dilatory and expensive. From the reign of Elizabeth onwards its monopoly in actions over property was threatened by the various fictitious devices used by King's Bench to extend the quasi-criminal action of trespass into a general civil jurisdiction.[11] Common Pleas thereafter lost ground steadily, which in turn drove it to recover its share of litigation (and fees) at the expense of the new conciliar courts. The third common-law court was the Exchequer of Pleas, a court presided over by the treasurer and barons of the Exchequer and originally concerned only with revenue cases.[12] This court achieved its full

---

[7] The way in which, in the reign of Elizabeth, the various courts shared out amongst themselves the space offered by Westminster Hall and the adjoining chambers is described in Doc. 74.

[8] Holdsworth, I, 35* ff., 204 ff.

[9] Blatcher, King's Bench, chs. 1 & 2.

[10] Holdsworth, I, 195 ff.

[11] Especially the action by bill of Middlesex (Blatcher, Elizabethan Gov., 188 ff.) which established the court's rights over any action concerning a particular defendant by pretending a fictitious custody of his person in the Marshalsea, the prison of the court. Although used as early as the fifteenth century (Hastings, Court of Common Pleas, 25 f.), the fiction came to full growth in the seventeenth.

[12] Holdsworth, I, 231 ff.

development in this century when, by offering speedier justice in private suits than was available in Common Pleas, it extended its competence to a sphere wider than the Crown's claims for money. In 1579 it was finally altogether acclimatised to the common-law courts: from thenceforth all the barons, some of whom had hitherto been financial experts, were to be lawyers chosen (like the judges in King's Bench and Common Pleas) from the ranks of the serjeants-at-law, and out of term sent on circuit like the rest.[13]

Although these three courts existed side by side in jealous isolation, their judges were men of the same stamp, and movement from one court to another was possible. Moreover, the whole body of judges and barons composed the king's legal advisers whose counsel was frequently sought by the Tudors; whenever any business came up that might involve legal or legislative action, the first instinctive step was to seek the advice of these experts.[14] The judges were therefore used to working together, and from this habit there developed the use of the Exchequer Chamber as a meeting place for formal consultation and the discussion of problems arising in the regular courts. In fact, it is possible to distinguish three bodies to which the name Exchequer Chamber has been applied.[15] The medieval court of that name consisted simply of all the judges withdrawn in private to consider a difficulty arising in any one court; the decision arrived at by this assembly was then promulgated in the court in which the problem had occurred. Strictly, this gathering was not really a court at all. The Exchequer Chamber seems to have served this purpose rarely as the Tudors developed the Council's jurisdiction which could sort out the problems of the common law by the application of common sense. However, two statutes of Elizabeth's reign set up Courts of Exchequer Chamber for the correction of errors. In 1585 the Court of King's Bench, whose errors had hitherto been amenable only in the intermittent High Court of Parliament, was subjected to a procedure of error in Exchequer Chamber before the judges of the other two courts[16]; and in 1589 the Exchequer's refusal to submit to King's Bench, and the inadequacy of earlier procedure, led to the erection of another court of this name for the correction of Exchequer errors, which consisted essentially of the two chief justices.[17]

This system of courts covered the ground pretty well, and the common law administered in them was a highly developed, well established body of law. But the system had major drawbacks. For one thing, the law had ossified, in the sense that by the late fifteenth century it was difficult to provide new

[13] For circuit jurisdiction cf. Cockburn, *Assizes*.

[14] King's Bench and Common Pleas had a chief justice and five puisne judges each; there were one chief baron and four lesser barons in the Exchequer. The chief justice of King's Bench was lord chief justice of England and the effective head of the judiciary.

[15] Holdsworth, I, 41* f., 242 ff.

[16] 27 Eliz. I, c. 8 (Tanner, 343 f.).

[17] 31 Eliz. I, c. 1 (Tanner, 345 f.).

remedies for new ills, except by the relatively rare and far from flexible intervention of parliamentary statute. Here the revolution described by Dr Baker
marked a breakthrough: by the seventeenth century the new actions for
settling disputes had altogether superseded those employed in the middle
ages, even though they still remained available. For another, the procedure of
the common law often worked against the true interests of justice; and it was
this second deficiency which particularly called for reform. Procedure at law
consists essentially of four stages: the methods used to bring the case to the
court's notice and call the parties before it, the investigation of the case, the
proof (or trial, as it was known at common law), and the decision with enforcement. In civil cases, a common-law action began with plaintiff suing out
a writ from Chancery (the 'original' writ) which enabled the court to take
cognisance of his case; but these 'forms of action', being very specific, might
not serve the needs of a particular case, and errors in their technicalities could
defeat a good cause.[18] The machinery evolved for bringing defendant
into court—the 'mesne process'—was exceedingly cumbersome and afforded
vast opportunities for dilatory tactics.[19] Next, when the case came to be
tried, it was originally opened (in a form of French) before the judges;
though these pleadings were being replaced by documents, the earlier oral
discourses had compelled the adoption of the principle that the whole case
be reduced to one specific point in dispute (the issue), so that the full complex
of troubles was never considered or settled. If plaintiff's counsel chose the
wrong issue, he could do his client much harm. The common law employed
several methods of proof, but of all these only trial by jury now survived.[20] In
civil cases the jury composed supposedly a body of expert witnesses—the men
of the locality who knew the truth about the matter in dispute, though in fact
sixteenth-century juries were in principle no different from modern ones.
Since it was pretty well impossible to bring the jury to the central court it had
become almost invariable practice to dismiss the case to the locality by the
procedure of *nisi prius* which called the jury to Westminster unless the matter
had previously been settled at the assizes (which it always was).[21] This brought
local politics and powers into play; and during the troubles of the fifteenth
century the jury, easily bribed, packed or intimidated, became suspect as a
means of proof. In addition the whole procedure was spiky with technicalities of the most recondite and absurd kind, offence against which, however

[18] The common law held, as Maitland put it, that 'where there is no remedy there is no wrong'
(*Equity*, 299). This precisely inverts the principle of natural justice that no wrong should be without its remedy.
[19] Cf., e.g., Hastings, *Court of Common Pleas*, 169 ff.
[20] 'Wager of law'—i.e. compurgation or the use of oath-helpers—was still available in some
actions, but it played little part in litigation.
[21] For the civil jury, cf. Holdsworth, I, 327 ff., and for examples of *nisi prius* actions and local
influences, cf. Elton, *Star Chamber Stories*, 78 ff.

immaterial, could lose a good case. In criminal matters procedure was less open to complaint, but also liable to perversions. It consisted essentially of an indictment presented at the king's suit to the grand jury of the shire which would then 'find a true bill', that is, declare the person indicted to be suspected of the crime; the Crown would then have to prove the case before a petty or trial jury[22]. One grave weakness of criminal procedure lay in the fact that at common law offences had to be tried in the shire in which they had been committed; this led to virtual extradition problems between counties, while the disruptive tendencies of the fifteenth century turned the whole business into an obstacle to law-enforcement. It is also true that the common law in effect (though probably not originally by intent) protected the interests of the accused, which in times of central weakness meant that the guilty got off. In short, common-law procedure in civil cases tended to deprive plaintiff of a remedy; in criminal cases it handicapped the Crown.

The latter problem was to be solved in part by a more energetic control over criminal actions and the use of the Council;[23] the former resulted in the growth of new courts to help the deficiencies of the common law. Of these the earliest, the most enduring, and the most important was the Court of Chancery.[24] Its jurisdiction had grown out of the demands made by the king's subjects on the king's justice; in the course of the fourteenth century, the chancellor, usually an ecclesiastic and the head of the writ-issuing department, came to be thought of as the specialist in people's petitions, and by the fifteenth he headed a formal enough court of law, sitting at Westminster and charged with remedying lack of justice in civil matters. His scope was mainly threefold: he could deal with matters outside the common law (such as maritime or ecclesiastical problems), could assist the common law if ordinary process was unable to overcome the power of the defendant, and could supplement it where it had failed to adapt itself to changing circumstances. In the sixteenth century the first two sorts of activity were drawn into other courts, leaving the Chancery with the last which had, in any case, always been its most important. It was here—in the needs of men which the law, unchanging and rigid, refused to satisfy—that the Chancery's peculiar jurisdiction best developed, and it is for this reason that its law was given the name of equity (74a).[25] The chancellor applied principles of natural justice, common sense and common fairness, and originally equity meant no more than that. Cases coming before him required that the hardships of the law or its deficiencies be overcome, and he treated them on their merits.[26] Chancery took

---

[22] Baker, *Crime in England*, 15 ff.   [23] Below, pp. 173 f.

[24] Jones, *Chancery*; Dawson, *Lay Judges*, esp. III/5.

[25] The Introduction to *St German's Doctor and Student* provides a valuable analysis of the whole concept.

[26] By the side of its equity jurisdiction Chancery also had a common law, or 'Latin', jurisdiction

great strides forward when, in the fifteenth century, it enlarged its business enormously by offering to protect copyhold (outside the sphere of Common Pleas because technically an unfree tenure) and enfeoffment to uses (called 'the use'). This latter was an attempt to evade the common law's ban on the devising of lands by will and to escape the feudal incidents which occurred on the death of a tenant-in-chief. At its simplest it consisted of the creation of a trust (which need never die) to whom the legal seisin (possession) was conveyed on condition that the use and profits of the lands should lie with a third party known as the *cestui qui use* (e.g. the testator's heir). Breach of obligation by the trustees (feoffees to uses) could find no remedy at common law which refused to recognise the whole transaction. Enfeoffment to uses became the commonest mode for holding land because it defeated all the limitations which the common law placed on landownership, but by avoiding death duties it also, of course, gravely affected the fiscal prerogative of the Crown. In consequence, attempts were made to legislate against it, but its advantages protected it and left the Chancery as its sole controller until Henry VIII in 1536 secured the Statute of Uses (**76a**) which incorporated the system into the common law and destroyed its attractions by turning the *cestui* into the legal owner of the estate, liable to everything that the use had guarded him against. The harshness of this law had before long to be modified by the Statute of Wills of 1540 (**76b**) which permitted the bequeathing of two thirds of a man's lands.[27] In the course of the century, the common law also extended its sway over copyhold, so that Chancery came to lose its grip on actions over land and turned more to work on the law of fraud, contract and charities, but even in disputes over land equitable remedies continued to be used.

The medieval concept of equity—natural justice applied to individual problems—reached its apogee under Wolsey who employed himself eagerly as chancellor in helping all who sought assistance that the law could not give —quite a few of them apparently without good cause.[28] After his day, and starting with Sir Thomas More, chancellors were nearly always common lawyers, a fact which eased the coexistence of law and equity. Though More's use of equity did not differ from Wolsey's, the Elizabethan chancellors began the process by which equity, too, became a developed system of rules, principles and precedents supplementary to the law, and soon as rigid as

in cases in which the subject sought a remedy against the Crown. Since the king could not be sued at law (the meaning of the phrase that 'he can do no wrong'), it was possible for him to do an injury to a party—e.g. by wrongfully seizing property for a non-existing debt or lands for a non-existing escheat—which required amendment. Here Chancery provided a remedy by accepting petitions of right asking the king, as a matter of voluntary restitution, to investigate the complaint (cf. Maitland, *Equity*, 4; Giuseppi, *Guide to the Public Records*, I, 46).

[27] Ives, *Eng. Hist. Rev.*, LXXXII, 673 ff.
[28] Metzger, *Law-Making and Law-Makers*, 79 ff.

its elder brother.[29] Symbiosis assisted the survival of Chancery when, in the reign of James I, the Court of Common Pleas (led by Sir Edward Coke) tried to destroy this rival jurisdiction. On the other hand, in its procedure, as Sir Thomas Smith points out (75), the Chancery leant heavily on the civil law, and it was here that, from the plaintiff's point of view, it most remedied the defects of the common law. Procedure was not by writ but by English bill. That is to say, plaintiff put in a petition called his bill in which he could elaborate any set of circumstances and rehearse all the details at issue between him and defendant. To this defendant entered his written answer, and the parties exchanged further documents called replication and rejoinder in which they usually did no more than repeat their earlier assertions. If it was desired, the process could be repeated in the rebuttal and surrebuttal. These written proceedings, unlike the single issue of the common law, made possible a full investigation of the case.[30] The method of proof relied on the examination of witnesses named by the parties; these made written depositions in response to written interrogatories, and on oath. In this way, trustworthy evidence could be collected in a manner unknown to the common law. Chancery disposed of two vital weapons to prevent evasions and delays: by the writ of subpoena, which ordered an appearance in answer to 'whatsoever may be objected', no details being necessary at this stage, it could readily secure the attendance of parties to a dispute, and by injunction it could prevent people nullifying the effects of a decree of judgment by premature action. Altogether, the procedure of Chancery resulted in a speedier and more exhaustive investigation, in a more certain establishment of the truth, and in a more flexible jurisdiction. But the law administered in the court was that of England, not that of Rome.[31]

Civil law,[32] in fact, served only two purposes in England: after 1535, when the study of canon law was forbidden at the universities, it was (more or less) the law practised in the declining courts of the Church, and it was necessarily the law of the one court which dealt with matters involving foreigners and foreign goods, the Court of Admiralty.[33] What had been an intermittent

[29] Guy, *Public Career*, pt II; Jones, *Chancery*, pt II. One effect was that other courts could adopt equity, as did the Exchequer which during Elizabeth's reign added an equity side to its normal common-law proceedings (Bryson, ch. 2).

[30] Though in due course common-law influences added verbal arguments on top of the written procedure and compelled counsel in this court, too, to 'arrive at the issue', the advantages of the bill and answer procedure were never totally lost.

[31] For the details of equity in the sixteenth century, cf. Holdsworth, v, 278 ff.

[32] *Ibid.*, IV, 228 ff. This is the place to draw attention to the fact that Maitland's thesis of a near victory for the civil over the common law in the early sixteenth century (*English Law and the Renaissance*) will not stand up to investigation. To Holdsworth's careful analysis (IV, 253 ff.) there could be added other facts showing the vitality of the common law at this time. Cf. also Elton, *Studies*, II, 223 f.

[33] Holdsworth, I, 544 ff.

and uncertain jurisdiction over maritime and commercial affairs exercised by occasional admirals, became in the reign of Henry VIII the settled operation of a permanent court. Under the Tudors it covered a wide variety of mercantile causes and had much business and power; practice in it, and especially judicial appointment to it, were the chief ambitions of men trained in the civil law who in 1511 formed themselves into a society (Association of Doctors of Law) modelled on the Inns of Court and formally incorporated in Doctors' Common in 1565.[34] The old admirals' jurisdiction had, however, been chiefly criminal, concerned with the suppression of piracy, and here the sixteenth century altered the position completely. On the interesting grounds that the civil law procedure of Admiralty, with its demand for witnesses' evidence, allowed piracy to be committed with impunity if only it was sanguinary enough, an act of 1536 (**76**) transferred the criminal jurisdiction of the court to special commissions which were to try cases by the common law and as though the alleged crimes had been committed not on the high seas but in the coastal shire adjoining. The commissioners were usually common-law judges,[35] so that criminal cases were in effect transferred from Admiralty to something like special commissions of oyer and terminer. The assertion that the civil law was too careful of accused's interests should be taken into account when considering the usual encomia on the common law's protection of the innocent.

A brief word should be said about the franchisal jurisdictions. As has already been pointed out,[36] in the sixteenth century the great franchises were subordinated to the authority of the Crown. But this did not abolish the courts which had once exercised the independent jurisdiction; it only made them agents of the king's justice instead of the franchise-holder's. The great counties palatine of Lancaster and Durham harboured a whole system of courts duplicating the royal courts at Westminster; and though this had no political significance in the one after 1399 and in the other after 1536, it made a considerable difference to the way in which people pursued their litigious interests.[37] The only one of the institutions set up by palatine lords which had wider implications and interests—so that it was almost a national court—was the Court of Duchy Chamber. The palatine jurisdiction of Lancaster covered only the county palatine; the Duchy of Lancaster, on the other hand, included lands in every part of England, and the duke's administrative Council, responsible for running this very large complex of estates, developed easily, by the familiar method of response to petitions, into an equitable court for all his lands (**77**).[38] After the duchy fell to the Crown in 1399, this court remained

---

[34] *Ibid.*, IV, 235 ff.   [35] *Ibid.*, 551.   [36] Above, pp. 32 f.

[37] For the franchises, cf. Holdsworth, I, 21* f., 109 ff. Cf. also Tanner, 350 ff., especially for the Stannary Courts of Cornwall, a minor peculiarity in the English system; and Jones, *Tudor Men*, 123 ff., for Chester.   [38] Cf. Somerville, *Trans. R. Hist. Soc.*, 1941, 159 ff.

as a special jurisdiction for duchy tenants, doing for them the work of the king's Chancery and draining off some of the vast bulk of litigation which the sixteenth century produced.

74. The Courts at Westminster.

In [Westminster] Hall [Henry III] ordained three judgment seats, to wit, at the entry on the right hand, the Common Pleas where civil matters are to be pleaded, specially such as touch lands or contracts; at the upper end of the Hall, on the right hand or south-east corner, the King's Bench where pleas of the Crown have their hearing; and on the left hand or south-west corner sitteth the lord chancellor, accompanied by the master of the rolls and other men learned for the most part in the civil law and called masters of the Chancery, which have the King's fee. The times of pleading in these courts are four in the year which are called terms. The first is Hilary Term, which beginneth the 23rd of January (if it be not a Sunday) and endeth the 12th of February. The second is Easter Term and beginneth seventeen days after Easter Day and endeth four days after Ascension Day. The third term beginneth six or seven days after Trinity Sunday and endeth the Wednesday fortnight after. The fourth is Michaelmas Term which beginneth the 9th of October (if it be not Sunday) and endeth the 28th of November. . . .

Within the port or entry into the Hall on either side are ascendings up into large chambers without the Hall adjoining thereunto where certain courts be kept: namely, on the right hand is the Court of the Exchequer, a place of account for the revenues of the Crown. . . . In this court be heard those that are delators or informers in popular and penal actions.[39] . . . On the left hand above the stair is the Duchy Chamber wherein is kept the court for the Duchy of Lancaster by a chancellor of that Duchy and other officers under him. Then is there in another chamber, the office of the receipts of the Queen's revenues for the Crown; then is there also the Star Chamber where in the term time every week once at the least (which is commonly on Fridays and Wednesdays) and on the next day after the term endeth the lord chancellor and the lords and other of the Privy Council and the chief justices of England, from 9 of the clock till it be 11 do sit. . . . There be plaints heard of riots, routs and other misdemeanours which, if they be found by the King's Council, the party offender shall be censured by

39 Cf. above, p. 20, n. 41.

these persons (which speak one after another) and he shall be both fined and commanded to prison. Then at the upper end of the great hall by the King's Bench is a going up to a great chamber called the White Hall wherein is now kept the Court of Wards and Liveries, and adjoining thereunto is the Court of Requests.   Stow, *Survey of London*, II, 118-20

74a. Christopher St German on Equity

Equity is righteousness that considers all the particular circumstances of the deed, the which also is tempered with the sweetness of mercy. And such an equity must always be observed in every law of man and in every general rule thereof, and that knew he well that said thus—'laws covet to be ruled by equity'. And the wise man says: be not overmuch righteous, for the extreme righteousness is extreme wrong—as who says, if thou take all that the word of the law gives then shalt thou sometime do against the law. And for the plainer declaration what equity is, thou shalt understand that since the deeds and acts of men for which laws be ordained happen in divers manners infinitely, it is not possible to make any general rule of the law but that it shall fail in some case. And therefore makers of laws take heed to such things as may often come and not to every particular case, for they could not though they would. And therefore to follow the words of the law were in some case both against justice and the commonwealth: wherefore in some cases it is good and even necessary to leave the words of the law and to follow that reason and justice require. And to that intent equity is ordained.   *St German's Doctor and Student*, 97

75. The purpose of the Court of Chancery.

. . . Our law, which is called of us the common law . . . is and standeth upon . . . *ius summum*; and their maxims be taken so straitly that they may not depart from the tenor of the words, even as the old civil law was. And therefore as that lacked the help of a *praetor* (which might *moderari illud ius summum*, give actions where none was, mitigate the exactness and rigour of the law written, give exceptions . . . and maintain always *aequum & bonum*)—the same order and rank holdeth our Chancery. . . . So he that putteth up his bill in the Chancery, after that he hath declared the mischief wherein he is, has relief as in the solemn *forum*. And for so much as in this case he is without remedy in the common law, therefore he requireth the chancellor according to equity and reason to provide for him and to take such order as to good conscience shall appertain. And the Court of the Chancery is called of the common people the court of conscience, because that the chancellor is not strained by rigour or form of words of law to judge but *ex aequo* and *bono* and according to conscience, as I have said. And in this court the usual and proper form of pleading of England is not used, but the form of pleading by writing which is used in other countries according to the civil law; and the trial is not by twelve men, but by the examination of witnesses as in other courts of the civil law.

Smith, De Republica Anglorum, 70–1

76. An Act for punishment of pirates and robbers of the sea (1536: 28 Henry VIII, c. 15).

Where traitors, pirates, thieves, robbers, murderers and confederators upon the sea many times escape unpunished because the trial of their offences hath heretofore been ordered, judged and determined before the admiral or his lieutenant or commissary, after the course of the civil laws, the nature whereof is that before any judgment of death can be given against the offenders, either they must plainly confess their offences (which they will never do without torture or pains), or else their offences be so plainly and directly proved by witness indifferent, such as saw their offences committed, which cannot be gotten but by chance at few times because such offenders commit their offences upon the sea, and at many times murder and kill such persons being in the ship or boat where they commit their offences which should witness against them in that behalf, and also such as should bear witness be commonly mariners and shipmen, which because of their often voyages and passages in the seas depart without long tarrying and protraction of time, to the great costs and charges as well of the King's Highness as such as would pursue such offenders; For reformation whereof be it enacted by the authority of this present Parliament that all treasons, felonies, robberies, murders and confederacies, hereafter to be committed in or upon the sea, or in any other haven, river, creek or place where the admiral or admirals have or pretend to have power, authority or jurisdiction, shall be enquired, tried, heard, determined and judged in such shires and places in the realm as shall be limited by the King's commission or commissions to be directed for the same, in like form and condition as if any such offence or offences had been committed or done in or upon the land; And such commissions shall be had under the King's great seal directed to the admiral or admirals or to his or their lieutenant, deputy or deputies, and to 3 or 4 such other substantial persons as shall be named or appointed by the lord chancellor of England for the time being from time to time and as often as need shall require, to hear and determine such offences after the common course of the laws of this land, used for treasons, felonies, robberies, murders and confederacies of the same done and committed upon this land within this realm.

II. And be it enacted . . . that such persons to whom such commission or commissions shall be directed, or 4 of them at the least, shall have full power and authority to enquire of such offences and every of them by the oaths of twelve good and lawful inhabitants in the shire limited in their commission, in such like manner and form as if such offences had been committed upon the land, within the same shire. . . . And that the trial of such offence or offences, if it be denied by the offender or offenders, shall be had by 12 lawful men inhabited in the shire limited within such commission. . . .

[III. Offenders shall not have benefit of clergy or sanctuary.]

* * * * * *

Stat. Realm, III, 671

76a. Statute of Uses (1536: 27 Henry VIII, c. 10)

Where by the common laws of this realm lands, tenements and hereditaments be not devisable by testament, nor ought to be transferred from one to another but by solemn livery and seisin . . . yet nevertheless divers and sundry imaginations, subtle inventions and practices have been used whereby the hereditaments of this realm have been conveyed from one to another by fraudulent feoffments, fines, recoveries and other assurances craftily made,[40] to secret uses intents and trusts, and also by wills and testaments sometimes made by nude parols[41] and words, sometimes by signs and tokens and sometimes by writing, and for the most part made by such persons as be visited by sickness, in their extreme agonies and pains or at such time as they have had scantly any good memory or remembrance; at which time they, being provoked by greedy covetous persons lying in wait about them,

[40] Various devices for creating uses.
[41] Bare words.

do many times dispose indiscreetly and unadvisedly their lands and inheritances: By reason whereof, and by occasion of which fraudulent feoffments . . . divers and many heirs have been unjustly at sundry times disinherited, the lords have lost their wards [etc.], and scantly any person can be certainly assured of any lands by them purchased nor known surely against whom they shall use their actions or executions for their rights, titles and duties . . . For the extirping and extinguishment of all such subtle practised feoffments . . . it may please the king's most royal majesty that it may be enacted by his highness, by the assent of the Lords spiritual and temporal and the Commons in this present Parliament assembled, and by authority of the same, in manner and form following, that is to say:

1. That where any person or persons stand or be seised, or at any time hereafter shall happen to be seised, of and in any honours, castles, manors, lands, tenements, rents, services, reversions, remainders or other hereditaments, to the use confidence or trust of any other person or persons or any body politic . . . that in every such case all and every such person and persons and bodies politic . . . shall from henceforth stand and be seised, deemed and adjudged in lawful seisin, estate and possession of and in the same honours [etc.] to all intents, constructions and purposes in the law . . . . *Stat. Realm*, III, 539-40

76b. Statute of Wills (1540: 32 Henry VIII, c. 1)

Where the king's most royal majesty in all the time of his most gracious and noble reign has ever been merciful, loving and benevolent . . . in such wise as all his said subjects be most bounden to the uttermost of all their powers and graces by them received of God to render and give unto his majesty their most humble reverence and obedient thanks and services, with their daily and continual prayers to Almighty God for continual preservation of his most royal estate in most kingly honour and prosperity; yet always his majesty, being replete and endowed by God with grace goodness and liberality, most tenderly considering that his said obedient and loving subjects cannot use or exercise themselves according to their estates, degrees, faculties and qualities, or to bear themselves in such wise as that they may conveniently keep and maintain their hospitalities and families nor the good educations and bringing up of their lawful generations (which in this realm, laud be to God, is in all parts very great and abundant), but that in manner of necessity . . . they shall not be able of their proper goods, chattels and, other movable substance to discharge their debts and after their degrees set forth and advance their children and posterities: Wherefore our said sovereign lord, most virtuously considering the mortality that is to every person at God's will and pleasure most common and uncertain, of his most blessed disposition and liberality, being willing to relieve and help his said subjects in their said necessities and disabilities, is contented and pleased that it may be ordained and enacted by authority of this present Parliament in manner and form as hereafter follows; that is to say:

[1. Lands held in socage may be devised by will without restriction.]

II. And it is further enacted by the authority aforesaid that all and singular person and persons having any manors, lands, tenements or hereditaments of estate of inheritance held of the king's highness in chief by knight's service . . . shall have full power and authority by his last will, by writing or otherwise by any act or acts lawfully executed in his life, to give dispose will or assign two parts of the said manors, lands, tenements or hereditaments in three parts to be divided, or else as much of the said manors, lands, tenements or hereditaments as shall extend or amount to the yearly value of two parts of the same three parts . . . to and for the advancement of his wife, preferment of his children, and payment of his debts, or otherwise at his will and pleasure; any law, statute, custom or other thing to the contrary notwithstanding . . . .

Stat. Realm, III, 744-5

77. The Court of the Duchy Chamber of Lancaster.

. . . It is called *Comitatus Palatinus*, a County Palatine, not *a Comite*, in respect of the dignity of an earl, but a *Comitatu* and *a Palatio Regis*, because the owner thereof, be he duke or earl, etc., hath in that county *jura regalia* as fully as the King had in his palace, from whence all justice, honours, dignities, franchises and privileges, as from the fountain, at the first flowed. . . . The power and authority of those that had county palatines was king-like, for they might pardon treasons, murders, felonies and outlawries thereupon. They might also make justices of eyre, justices of assize, of gaol delivery and of the peace. And all original and judicial writs, and all manner of indictment of treasons and felony, and the process thereupon, were made in the name of the persons having such county palatine. And in every writ and indictment within any county palatine, it was supposed to be *contra pacem* of him that had the county palatine. . . .

. . . The proceeding in this Court of the Duchy Chamber at Westminster is as in a Court of Chancery for lands, etc., within the survey of that Court, by English bill, etc., and decree; but this Chancery Court is not a mixed court as the Chancery of England is, partly of the common law and partly of equity. . . . The process is by privy seal, attachment, etc., as in the Chancery. The officers of this Court be the chancellor, the attorney, the receiver-general, clerk of the Court, the auditors, surveyors, the messenger. There is an attorney of the Duchy in Chancery and another in the Exchequer. There be four learned in the law assistants, and of counsel with the Court. . . .

. . . The seal of the Duchy of Lancaster remains with the chancellor at Westminster. And the seal of the County Palatine remains always in a chest in the County Palatine under the safe custody of the keeper thereof. All grants and leases of lands, tenements, offices, etc., in the County Palatine of Lancaster shall pass under that seal and no other; and all grants and leases of lands, tenements, offices, etc., out of the County Palatine and within the survey of the Duchy, shall pass under the seal of the Duchy and no other; otherwise such grants and leases shall be void. . . .   Coke, *Fourth Institute*, 204–5, 206, 210

CHAPTER 6

CONCILIAR COURTS

I. STAR CHAMBER

(i) HISTORY.[1] The early history of the Court of Star Chamber used to be enveloped in a variety of myths, the first and most persistent of which ascribed its beginning to an act of 1487 (**78**). That legend, current by 1563 at the latest,[2] proved useful when the Long Parliament, anxious to abolish the Court, used its supposedly statutory foundation to justify a repealing act. In truth, the Court differed in every particular from the body set up in 1487 which was no more than a belated example of Lancastrian methods of government, attempting to provide for the enforcement of public order by means of a high-powered ministerial tribunal. It is known to have acted occasionally, was still potentially in existence in 1529,[3] but never achieved either prominence or permanence.[4] The Court itself, however, mainly engaged in civil pleas, was simply the whole of the king's Council sitting to hear litigation brought before it either by private parties or occasionally by the Crown through the attorney-general. It represented a further stage in the process which had already created the Court of Chancery, and indeed the High Court of Parliament. The king's powers to remedy grievances being unexhausted by the setting up of regular courts, the subject was free to petition him and his advisers for relief. Throughout its history the Council was therefore inundated with such petitions and looked for machinery to deal with them. By the reign of Henry VII, the Parliament (which had handled a mass of them under Edward I) had long since ceased to be useful for the purpose, while the chancellor had quite recently so far specialised in his work as to leave much material to which he could not attend. Thus once again the Council found itself saddled with the hearing of complaints in ever increasing numbers and once more driven to find a way out: this time, it looked to machinery developed from within its own structure of meetings. There thus resulted a specialisation of the functions engaged in by

[1] The first edition of this book included a long discussion of various errors concerning the origin and early history of Star Chamber, as well as some suggestions of my own based on then unfinished researches. The former has been rendered superfluous by the thorough investigations of Guy's *Cardinal's Court* which has settled just about all the questions. As for the latter, that book confirms some and demolishes others. There is therefore no need to preserve an outdated argument and analysis. The present discussion in the main summarises Dr Guy's conclusions.

[2] Bayne, *Council of Henry VII*, p. xxviii.

[3] 21 Henry VIII, c. 20, which adds the president of the Council to the three members of the 1487 tribunal; no practical consequences resulted (Guy, *Cardinal's Court*, 133).

[4] *Ibid.*, esp. 20.

this one body, a specialisation which in due course gave to one of the Council's activities the characteristics of a true court (regularity, known procedure, public proceedings). Under Henry VII this activity took place, but neither the amount of work done nor the degree of specialisation achieved entitles us to speak of the Court of Star Chamber at this time. Instead we find the king's councillors, meeting in the Star Chamber at Westminster when occasion offered, to take care of petitions presented. Their role resembled more that of arbitrators than that of a court. In the technical language of the documents, this is what they remained throughout, but that language hides the thorough institutionalisation which was to come.

In fact, the Court proper, as Sir Thomas Smith knew (79), was the creation of Cardinal Wolsey whose eagerness to serve the common weal made him expand the Council's activities by inviting private persons to seek there the settlement of their disputes. Wolsey provided regularity of proceedings, a growth in clerical organisation, and a degree of consistency in handling matters, so that by the time of his fall a genuine court had come into existence. By this time, therefore, the Council sitting as a court adjudicating upon matters brought before it by litigants can be clearly distinguished from the same body of men sitting as a council of state to administer the realm and advise the Crown. (The distinction, of course, is one of activities, not of people.) Three facts have combined to disguise the extent of the development achieved. Coincidence of membership between the Court and the Council was to trouble historians, though no one at the time. The use of one single register for both kinds of business must have been confusing for everybody: it awaited remedy by the institution of a separate register for Privy Council business in the time of Thomas Cromwell, which left the old book of entries to survive as the (now lost) books of Star Chamber Decrees and Orders. Lastly, Wolsey's penchant for setting up temporary committees to handle the abundance of work could look like the creation of courts separate from the Council proper and confuse the issue by suggesting that what happened involved a distinction of personnel, not of areas of activity: and yet no such distinction existed when the Star Chamber was manifestly in existence. While these problems indicate the weakness of Wolsey's methods—an insouciant lack of system—they can no longer hide his real achievement, which was to turn the judicial functions of the Council into the work of a court.

The institutional history of the Court after the departure of the cardinal, who had both given it existence and by his personal management prevented its clear emergence as an institution, amounted to a definition of that emergence. This, which involved a firmer distinction between the various activities of the Council, a settling of the regularity of curial meetings, and an increase in professionalism in the clerical staff, was the work of Cromwell.

His creation of the restricted Privy Council enabled Star Chamber to become a visibly separate court: he provided 'the professionalism and continuity that could only stem from a settled constitution'.[5] The reform also altered the composition of the Court, though not its nature. Older views, holding that the two institutions (Star Chamber and Privy Council) represented institutionalised branches of the earlier Council, have caused endless confusion.[6] The Court of Star Chamber was always the whole of the Council sitting as a court, which meant that after 1536 fewer people were available to staff it. Too few, in fact: since the Privy Council excluded the judges, whose expert skill was essential to a court of law like Star Chamber, the two chief justices, though not privy councillors, always sat in Star Chamber as full and ordinary members (80). There has, however, been much doubt whether the Star Chamber was confined to the Privy Council and the two judges; it has commonly been held that others could sit in it, although councillors 'by birth' (nati) only inasmuch as they were peers of the realm. This was asserted by Sir Thomas Smith early in Elizabeth's reign (79), and Pollard thought that the Crown could afforce the court at will.[7] James I seems to have thought so, too,[8] but his opinions on the English constitution are notoriously unreliable. As Coke's writings show (81), some idea survived in his day that non-councillors could sit in the court, but they were not treated as on a par with councillors and did not in fact appear. A study of the court under Elizabeth has demonstrated that, though early in the reign others may have attended the court, it progressively and rapidly shed all these supernumeraries.[9] In 1563, in a case concerning the earl of Hertford, non-conciliar barons who tried to assert a right to sit were refused admission by the lord keeper. Long before the accession of the Stuarts (whom Pollard made responsible for identifying the two institutions),[10] the Court of Star Chamber consisted simply of the Privy Council and the two chief justices. It is more than probable that the attendance, earlier on, of men who were not privy councillors had nothing to do with politics or pressure,[11] but resulted from the difficulty of finding a sufficiently impressive 'presence' without resorting to such outsiders. According to Coke (81), eight constituted a quorum; yet many meetings of the Privy Council were attended by three or four.

[5] Ibid., 136.
[6] Cf. Holdsworth, I, 496: 'It is this branch of the Council which sat at Westminster which developed into the court of Star Chamber'. Here the word 'branch' is fatal to a correct understanding. False expectations have led to devastatingly false conclusions: cf. ibid., 495 f., where it is argued, on no evidence at all, that lesser councillors did Star Chamber work and composed a branch of the Council.
[7] Eng. Hist. Rev., xxxvii, 536 ff. Much of his evidence there does not bear out his statement; the best (Hudson's) proves that the Crown could prevent a regular member from attending, not that it could add to the membership.
[8] Cf. Holdsworth, I, 500.   [9] Skelton, 'Star Chamber', 21 ff.   [10] Eng. Hist. Rev., xxxvii, 338.
[11] Miss Skelton shows that there was no deliberate packing (op. cit., 28).

This Star Chamber—the Council, old or new, sitting as a court—therefore composed a perfectly defined and precise institution from the 1530's onwards. It was simply one of the courts of the realm, dealing largely with cases between parties, though sometimes engaged upon matters put before it by the Crown. It was highly regarded and very popular with litigants because it was relatively speedy, flexible and complete in its work. It met in term time only, except that sometimes a meeting was held on the day after term ended, at which the lord chancellor delivered an address on the state of the realm and the policy of the queen to the Council, the judges and such justices of the peace as could be collected.[12] Under Elizabeth, times of meeting were on Wednesdays and Fridays at 9 o'clock; it is reasonably clear that earlier in the century the court had sat more often. By the last quarter of the century it was sufficiently one of the ordinary courts to have become affected by dilatoriness and inefficiency.[13] Henry VII was often present himself at the Council sessions which dealt with cases[14]; but as the court developed into a separate institution the monarch came very rarely, leaving the court in the hands of the lord chancellor. All present, whether councillors or chief justices, were judges in the court and delivered judgment, but the chancellor and justices usually made the decisive pronouncements, the rest following their lead. Since these operative experts were common lawyers, the court (like Chancery) did not develop into the sort of rival to common law jurisdiction which it might so easily have been.

78. An Act giving the Court of Star Chamber authority to punish divers misdemeanours (1487: 3 Henry VII, c. 1).

The King our sovereign lord remembereth how by unlawful maintenances, giving of liveries signs and tokens, and retainders by indenture promises oaths writing or otherwise, embraceries of his subjects, untrue demeanings of sheriffs in making of panels and other untrue returns, by taking of money by juries, by great riots and unlawful assemblies, the policy and good rule of this realm is almost subdued, and for the non-punishment of this inconvenience and by occasion of the premises nothing or little may be found by inquiry, whereby the laws of the land in execution may take little effect, to the increase of murders, robberies, perjuries, and unsureties of all men living and losses of their lands and goods, to the great displeasure of Almighty God; Be

---

[12] Skelton, 20. The custom, observed during the unsettled early years of Elizabeth's reign, then lapsed until the equally unsettled last years (Hawarde, *Reportes*, 19, 56 ff., 101 f., 159 f.).

[13] Barnes, *Amer. Jour. of Legal History*, VI, 221 ff., 315 ff.

[14] Cf. Bayne, *Council of Henry VII*, 1 ff.

it therefore ordained for reformation of the premises by the authority of this Parliament, That the chancellor and treasurer of England for the time being and keeper of the King's privy seal, or two of them, calling to him a bishop and a temporal lord of the King's most honourable Council and the two chief justices of the King's Bench and Common Pleas for the time being, or other two justices in their absence, upon bill or information put to the said chancellor for the King or any other against any person for any misbehaving afore rehearsed, have authority to call before them by writ or privy seal the said misdoers, and them and other by their discretions to whom the truth may be known to examine, and such as they find therein defective to punish them after their demerits, after the form and effect of statutes thereof made, in like manner and form as they should and ought to be punished if they were thereof convict after the due order of the law.

[II. Justices of the peace to enquire into any who hold lands to the value of 40s. a year and have concealed earlier inquests; and to punish such concealments.]

Stat. Realm, II, 509–10

79. Sir Thomas Smith on Star Chamber.

There is yet in England another court, of the which that I can understand there is not the like in any other country. In the term time . . . every week once at the least (which is commonly on Fridays and Wednesdays, and the next day after that the term doth end), the lord chancellor and the lords and other of the Privy Council, so many as will, and other lords and barons which be not of the Privy Council and be in the town, and the judges of England, specially the two chief judges, from nine of the clock till it be eleven do sit in a place which is called the Star Chamber, either because it is full of windows or because at the first all the roof thereof was decked with images of stars gilded. There is plaints heard of riots. Riot is called in our English term or speech, where any number is assembled with force to do anything. . . . If the riot be found and certified to the King's Council, or if otherwise it be complained of, the party is sent for, and he must appear in this Star Chamber, where seeing (except the presence of the prince only) as it were the majesty of the whole realm before him, being never so stout he will be abashed; and being called to answer (as he must come, of what degree soever he be) he shall be so charged with such gravity, with such reason and remonstrance, and of those chief personages of

England, one after another handling him on that sort, that, what courage soever he hath, his heart will fall to the ground, and so much the more when if he make not his answer the better, as seldom he can so in open violence, he shall be commanded to the Fleet, where he shall be kept in prison in such sort as these judges shall appoint him, lie there till he be weary as well of the restraint of his liberty as of the great expenses which he must there sustain, and for a time be forgotten, whilst after long suit of his friends he will be glad to be ordered by reason. Sometime, as his deserts be, he payeth a great fine to the prince, besides great costs and damages to the party, and yet the matter wherefor he attempteth this riot and violence is remitted to the common law. For that is the effect of this court, to bridle such stout noblemen or gentlemen which would offer wrong by force to any manner men and cannot be content to demand or defend the right by order of law. This court began long before, but took great augmentation and authority at that time that Cardinal Wolsey, archbishop of York, was chancellor of England, who of some was thought to have first devised the court because that he, after some intermission by negligence of time, augmented the authority of it, which was at that time marvellous necessary to do, to repress the insolency of the noblemen and gentlemen of the north parts of England, who being far from the King and the seat of justice made almost as it were an ordinary war among themselves and made their force their law. . . . *De Republica Anglorum, 115–8*

80. Sir Edward Coke on the origin of Star Chamber.

That which now is next to be considered *in serie temporis* is the statute of 3 H. 7. . . . Upon this statute and that which formerly hath been said, these six conclusions do follow. The first conclusion is that this act of 3 H. 7 did not raise a new court, for there was a Court of Star Chamber, and all the King's Privy Council judges of the same. For if the said act did establish a new court, then should those four[15] or any two of them be only judges, and the rest that they should call to them should be but assistants and aidants and no judges: for the Statute of 31 E. 3, cap. 12, which raiseth a new court and before new judges, is introductory of a new law, by having conusance[16] of error in the

[15] The lords chancellor, treasurer and privy seal of 3 Henry VII, c. 1, with the president of the Council added by 21 Henry VIII, c. 20.
[16] Cognisance.

Exchequer which shall be reversed in the Exchequer Chamber[17] before the chancellor and treasurer, or calling to them two judges, there the chancellor and treasurer are only judges in the writ of error, and so in the like. But it is clear that the two justices in the Star Chamber are judges and have voices, as it hath been often resolved and daily experience teacheth. And further, to clear this point, if the justices should be but assistants and no judges in the Star Chamber, for that they are to be called, etc., then and for the same reason should neither lord spiritual nor temporal nor other of the Privy Council be judges nor have voices in the Court of Star Chamber. And therefore the sudden opinion in 8 H. 7 and of others not observing the said distinction between acts declaratory of proceedings in an ancient court and acts introductory of a new law in raising of a new court, is both contrary to law and continual experience.

The second conclusion is, that the act of 3 H. 7, being in the affirmative, is not in some things pursued. For where that act directeth that the bill or information should be put to the lord chancellor, etc., all bills and informations in that court are constantly and continually directed to the King's Majesty, as they were before the said act; and it is a good rule that where the act of 3 H. 7 is not pursued, there (if there be many judicial precedents in another sort) they must have warrant from the ancient court, and yet it is good (as much as may be) to pursue this act, there being no greater assurance of jurisdiction than an act of Parliament. And where there be no such precedents, then the statute as to the judges must be pursued; and that was the reason that in default of others, Sir Christopher Wray, chief justice of England, for a time was made lord privy seal to sit in the Star Chamber, *ne curia deficeret in justitia exhibenda.*

Thirdly, that this act being (as hath been said) in the affirmative, and enumerating divers particular offences, albeit 'injuries' is a large word, yet that court hath jurisdiction of many other, as is manifest by authority and daily experience, and this must of necessity be in respect of the former jurisdiction.

Fourthly, this act in one point is introductory of a new law which the former court had not, *viz.* to examine the defendant, which being understood after his answer made, to be upon oath upon interrogatories, which this ancient court proceeding in criminal causes had not nor

---

[17] Cf. above, p. 150.

could have but by act of Parliament or prescription, the want whereof, especially in matters of frauds and deceits (being like birds closely hatched in hollow trees) was a mean that truth could not be found out, but before the statute the answer was upon oath.

Fifthly, where it is said in this act, *And to punish them after their demerits after the form and effect of statutes made, etc.*, the plaintiff may choose whether he will inform upon such statutes as this act directeth or for the offence at the common law, as he might have done before this act; which proveth that this act taketh not away the former jurisdiction.

Lastly, that the jurisdiction of this court dealeth not with any offence that is not *malum in se*, against the common law, or *malum prohibitum*, against some statute.   *Fourth Institute, 62–3*

(ii) PROCEDURE AND BUSINESS. Procedure in the Court of Star Chamber underwent a good deal of development, growing more rigid and formal throughout the century. Basically, however, it remained much the same, being typical of that practised in the old Council and therefore closely resembling the procedure of Chancery.[18] Suits were started either by plaintiff's bill (addressed to the king instead of the chancellor, and requesting a remedy by the lords of the Council),[19] with all the exchange of documents thereafter which was also used in Chancery; or by information laid by the attorney-general. The ensuing process might be short-circuited by the *ore tenus* procedure—by proceeding upon the offender's sworn confession, a method which could be helpful in notorious cases but was subject to abuses and disliked by many.[20] Normally the action started either with a bill or an information. Next the court would either non-suit the plaintiff, or more probably take note of the complaint and issue process (that is, summon the defendant). This was done by writ of subpoena. In its early days the court used a writ of privy seal to the same effect, but later it employed the Latin writ under the great seal, as did Chancery.[21] If defendant failed to obey, a writ of attachment followed by a commission of rebellion (raising the hue and cry) could be used to compel attendance.[22] Once summoned, the defendant would either acknowledge the authority of the court and make his answer (which nearly always safeguarded him by formally claiming that the case was determinable at common law), or he could enter a demurrer, which meant that he denied the court's right to cognisance of a case which should have gone to common

[18] Above, p. 154. Cf. Guy, *Cardinal's Court, passim.*
[19] For examples of bills cf. **87, 88.**
[20] Holdsworth, v, 165 ff., and cf. Coke's opinion in **81.**
[21] Cf. **82** and note.
[22] Skelton, 90.

law. However, the Star Chamber usually overrode these evasions, compelled an answer (which, unlike the bill, was made on oath), and the business continued through written pleadings, the examination of witnesses named by the parties, and the public hearing of a case already investigated to the judgment and decree. All written pleadings had to be signed by one of the attorneys authorised to practise in the court. Judgment was given by the individual members in turn, the judges as inferiors speaking first and thereafter the councillors in ascending order of seniority (84). The earlier stages of taking answers and depositions were handled by the clerks and examiners of the court, often out of term. The decision was embodied in a formal decree, a document given to the victorious party and entered (though in the absence of registers we do not know whether fully transcribed) in the order books of the court. The decree briefly recited the case and recorded the judgment, but for the rest it seems to have changed a little in course of time. The normal form would appear to have begun with the words 'In the matter of variance between etc.' and to have announced the decision with some such phrase 'it is ordained and decreed by the same Council' or 'the said Council have awarded, ordered and decreed'.[23] At the beginning of the period the judges seem to have acted only as assessors: the decree, just cited, of 1508 speaks of the Council's award 'by the advice and consent of all the king's judges', and a decree of 1524 (85) is similarly phrased. This is not the case in the fully developed procedure (e.g. 89). Wolsey's decree of 1524 incidentally illustrates most graphically the cardinal's personal ascendancy in an institution which he treated as an emanation of his greatness; but the form of the document is certainly not typical.

In theory every case went through these various stages in court, but in practice the Star Chamber found it impossible to cope with the flood of work without delegating some of it. Occasionally it resorted to drastic steps, as when Wolsey in 1516 and 1525 attempted to decentralise business by establishing a series of tribunals at the centre and in the localities.[24] These experiments produced little result, though the existence of provincial Councils in the North and the Welsh marches certainly helped the Star Chamber.[25] More common and more useful was the practice of delegating part or even all of a case to special commissioners. It was obviously easier for local magistrates to administer interrogatories to witnesses, but at least in the reign of Henry VIII the Council often went further and committed even decisions in a case

[23] E.g. Leadam, *Star Chamber*, I, 188, n. 2 (1508); Star Chamber Proc., 2/28/135 (1532). This last could conceivably be a decree of the Court of Requests.

[24] Guy, *Cardinal's Court*, 40 ff.

[25] Cf. below, section III. It did not always help. Thus some time in the 1530's the Star Chamber had to consider a case previously heard by the Council in the Marches because (allegedly) new evidence had come to light. They referred it back to the lesser Council (Star Chamber Proc., 2/19/178).

to gentlemen of the shire (83). In practice, a good deal of the preparatory work was commonly done locally under such commissions of *dedimus potestatem*, but it appears that commissioners often took advantage of the escape clause which permitted them to avoid making up their own minds and returned the case they had investigated for decision to the court.

Star Chamber usually punished with imprisonment and fines.[26] From first to last these latter tended to be very great but were almost always reduced before payment. The great fines both expressed the indignation of the amateur judges who sat in the court and a warning to offenders; the later 'taxing', which towards the end of the century might cut the nominal penalty by as much as nine-tenths,[27] took account of the realities of the situation. The court could not inflict loss of life or property; these most sacred rights of the individual were subject only to the common law. However, Star Chamber—especially if defendants were too poor to be worth fining—frequently resorted to unusual punishments. Juries convicted of rendering false verdicts were commonly imprisoned for a spell; at other times whipping, the pillory (with perhaps such mutilations as loss of ears), public confessions (sometimes accompanied by the wearing of a paper specifying the offence), and such like painful and humiliating punishments were inflicted (86). It looks on the whole as though the court acquired a growing taste for exotic penalties as time went on. But in the vast majority of cases it either fined or contented itself with an order to the loser to obey an earlier decision, often an earlier decree made in Star Chamber. The court was probably the most effective of Tudor courts, but that did not stop it from failing to make its will felt in a good many instances. One thing must be stressed: the court did not use torture in the course of the trial, though some of the corporal punishments inflicted might be regarded as coming within the category. Not a single example is known in which Star Chamber employed the rack to extract confessions or obtain information about accomplices, and statements to the contrary arise from a total confusion between Star Chamber and Privy Council, between this court of law and the security services of the state.[28]

[26] For Star Chamber punishments cf. Bayne, *op. cit.* pp. clxx seqq.; Guy, *Cardinal's Court*, 63 ff., 115 ff.; Cheyney, *History of England*, I, 101 ff.

[27] Hawarde, *Reportes*, pp. lxii, 411 ff.

[28] Holdsworth, v, 185, says (revealingly): 'that torture was used all through this period [i.e. in the Star Chamber] is conclusively proved by the Acts of the Privy Council'. His examples (one seems to be an error, as the page quoted does not deal with torture at all) accordingly turn out what one might expect: orders of the Privy Council investigating either serious crimes or treasons and using torture (as all governments of the day did) to obtain the details. Not only does the Court of Star Chamber never enter into any of this, but the instances concern offences which it was not competent to try. Thus, to say that 'torture was freely used' in this court (*ibid.*, 184) is a very bad error.

The scope of the court was defined negatively and approximately defined positively. Unable to touch life or property, it could not deal with felonies or treasons which involved loss of both.[29] Moreover, the court never dealt with any business other than judicial. Assertions that its business remained 'miscellaneous' rest upon a misunderstanding, on the confusion—once again—between court and Council.[30] An apparent exception to this rule was the occasional issue of formal orders which look like Orders in Council or proclamations. In truth, however, these (if issued by Star Chamber) were always the outcome of a law-suit involving larger principles and worth embodiment in a formal and public pronouncement because they might affect both policy and other suits. Commonly they arose from the trial of a breach of earlier proclamations.[31] The only non-curial survival in the doings of Star Chamber were those occasional meetings on the day after the end of term, with the address delivered by the lord chancellor or keeper, which have already been mentioned—'official pronouncements of royal policy and political discourses upon contemporary circumstances, combined with wholesome advice'.[32]

Apart from this insignificant point, the court was simply a court, dealing with matters of law and justice. These fell into three major categories. In the first place the Star Chamber heard pleas of riot and cognate offences (87, 88). This was its original and remained its chief purpose: it enforced the king's peace. However, it proved easy enough to include a charge of riot or assault in the bill and thereby bring the matter within the purview of the court, and some phrase alleging riotous proceedings 'with force and arms, that is to say with staves and bills, and other weapons invasive and defensive' is usually to be found in a Star Chamber complaint. It should be treated as a formality, though no doubt on occasion rioting had taken place.[33] By dint of this trick every sort of issue could be brought before the court, though it is true that in its maturity its business was largely concerned with disturbances of peaceful possession, attacks on the person, and the like. During its earlier days, the bulk of its work dealt with property (title to land), a province which by 1558 it had returned to the common law.[34] Libel and slander came into its competence, as likely to lead to a breach of the peace (and also ill provided for at common law). Even if the violence alleged was often imaginary, it does

[29] According to Miss Skelton (*op. cit.*, 93), felony was no bar since the court was limited only in punishments and not in the matter tried. Though this may be true, it is a fact that its inability to inflict the penalties appropriate to felonies left these cases in practice to the common law.
[30] Holdsworth, I, 502; Tanner, 257 f. The point is well made by Cheyney, *History of England*, I, 106 f.
[31] Skelton, *op. cit.*, 198: these orders represented 'another attempt at widespread remedy'.
[32] *Ibid.*, 199.
[33] The phrase was borrowed from indictments at common law where it had also become so purely formal that an act of 1545 (37 Henry VIII, c. 8) made it unnecessary to include it.
[34] Guy, *Cardinal's Court*, ch. 4.

not alter the fact that the court was essentially occupied with crimes: it came to be effectively the chancellor's court of criminal jurisdiction. Secondly, Star Chamber protected law enforcement in all the courts of the realm. It punished contempt of court, wherever committed, and offences which led to an absence or denial of justice, as perjury, false jury verdicts, conspiracy, subornation and maintenance. Some of its most important work was connected with this jurisdiction which it enjoyed as the heir to the old Council and the executant of the king's vigilance over justice. Lastly, it occasionally enforced royal proclamations and adjudicated upon their breach. After the failure of the 1539 Act of Proclamations to provide machinery for their application,[35] the Council in Star Chamber willy-nilly retained this branch of law-enforcement, though in practice it did far less of this kind of work than one might have supposed. Proclamations remained unenforced in the main. Its so-called order concerning printers (**89**) arose out of a judgment in a case based on a breach of the proclamation of 1566 (**49**) and developed into a general statement of rules governing censorship.

The law which the court administered in all these cases was the law of England—common and statute law, with the addition of proclamations which had no force in the ordinary courts.[36] Its procedure—swift, simple and equitable—offered advantages over the common law courts upon which litigants were not slow to seize. If Wolsey meant anything by his famous statement that he would teach some offenders 'the new law' of the Star Chamber,[37] he can only have been thinking of the effectiveness in enforcing the existing law which conciliar jurisdiction represented. Star Chamber 'law' was new inasmuch as the court swept aside the delays of the common law and made itself felt, but in substance it was not new. Unlike Chancery, the Council in Star Chamber did not develop a new body of rules to cope with deficiencies in the criminal law. At the same time, its willingness to adjudicate impartially upon violence or acts likely to lead to violence was, in that violent age, of the greatest advantage to the subject and left its mark upon the common law itself which, taught by Star Chamber, grew more developed on its hitherto very primitive criminal side, and more rational and efficient in its procedure.[38]

81. Sir Edward Coke on the procedure of Star Chamber.

The proceeding in this Court is by bill or information, by examination of the defendant upon interrogatories, and by examination of witnesses,

---

[35] Above, p. 23.
[36] Holdsworth, v, 163.
[37] Guy, *Cardinal's Court*, 34.
[38] This is discussed at length by Holdsworth, v, 188 ff., 197 ff.

and rarely *ore tenus*, upon the confession of the party in writing under his hand, which he again must freely confess in open court, upon which confession in open court the Court doth proceed. But if his confession be set down too short, or otherwise than he meant, he may deny it, and then they cannot proceed against him but by bill or information, which is the fairest way.

The informations, bills, answers, replications, etc., and interrogatories are in English, and engrossed in parchment and filed up. All the writs and process of the Court are under the great seal: the sentences, decrees, and acts of this Court are engrossed in a fair book with the names of the lords and others of the King's Council and justices that were present and gave their voices.

* * * * * *

This Court sitteth twice in the week in the term time, *viz.* on Wednesdays and Fridays, except either of those days fall out to be the first or last day of the term, and then the court sitteth not, but it constantly holdeth the next day after the term ended; but if any cause be begun to be heard in the term time and for length or difficulty cannot be sentenced within the term, it may be continued and sentenced after the term.

It is the most honourable court (our Parliament excepted) that is in the Christian world, both in respect of the judges of the Court and of their honourable proceeding according to their just jurisdiction and the ancient and just orders of the court. For the judges of the same are (as you have heard) the grandees of the realm, the lord chancellor, the lord treasurer, the lord president of the King's Council, the lord privy seal, all the lords spiritual, temporal and others of the King's most honourable Privy Council and the principal judges of the realm, and such other lords of Parliament as the King shall name. And they judge upon confession, or deposition of witnesses; and the Court cannot sit for hearing of causes under the number of eight at the least. And it is truly said, *Curia Camerae Stellatae, si vetustatem spectemus, est antiquissima, si dignitatem, honoratissima.* This Court, the right institution and ancient orders thereof being observed, doth keep all England in quiet.

Albeit the style of the court be *coram Rege et Concilio*, yet the King's Council of that Court hear and determine causes there, and the King in judgment of law is always in court; as in the King's Bench the style of the court is *coram Rege* and yet his justices, who are his council of that court, do hear and determine, and so *coram Rege in Cancellaria*, and the like.

So this Court, being holden *coram Rege et Concilio*, it is or may be compounded of three several councils. That is to say, of the lords and other of his Majesty's Privy Council, always judges without appointment. . . . 2. The judges of either Bench and barons of the Exchequer are of the King's Council for matter of law, etc., and the two chief justices, or in their absence other two justices, are standing judges of this Court. 3. The lords of Parliament are properly *de magno concilio regis*, but neither these, being not of the King's Privy Council, nor any of the rest of the judges or barons of the Exchequer are standing judges of the Court.   *Fourth Institute*, 63-4, 65

82. Writ of summons (temp. Henry VIII).[39]

By the King.

For certain causes and considerations us and our Council moving, we will and charge you that, all manner excuses and delays utterly set apart, ye be and personally appear afore us and our said Council wheresoever we shall be within this our royaulme in the quindene of Easter next coming, to answer to such things as then shall be laid and objected against you on the behalf of Thomas Bedford of Newbury, clothier. Not failing hereof upon pain of £100 and as ye will answer unto us at your further peril. Given under our privy seal at our manor of Greenwich the last day of March.

Star Chamber Proceedings Henry VIII, bundle 20, no. 37

83. Commission out of Star Chamber.[40]

By the King.

Trusty and wellbeloved, we greet you well. And whereas matter of controversy is depending before us and our Council between John Hare and Joan his wife, party plaintiffs on the one part, and John

---

[39] Writs of privy seal usually omitted the year; hence this writ cannot be dated. It is, however, peculiar in some respects and almost certainly belongs early in the reign. It would appear that after Wolsey's administration the Court invariably used the great and not the privy seal (with the result that its summons or subpoenas were in Latin), and summoned offenders to Westminster, the regular seat of the Court, instead of to the peripatetic Council 'wheresoever we shall be'.

[40] Like 82, this, being a privy seal, is in English; the common practice later in the century was to issue commissions under the great seal and in Latin.

Tanner, party defendant on the other part; like as by bill of complaint, answer, replication and rejoinder (which we send unto you here enclosed) ye may perceive more at large; whereupon we, trusting in your wisdoms and indifferences for the due administration of justice, will and desire you and by these presents authorise you that, calling the said parties and such witnesses as they shall name and bring afore you in our name, ye will groundly[41] examine the said witnesses upon their oaths and depositions in form of law sworn upon the contents of the said bill, answer, replication and rejoinder with interrogatories and circumstances of the same. And thereupon to order and determine the same according to justice if ye can; or else to certify unto us and our said Council the truth and plainness of the said matter and depositions in writing under your seals by the quindene of the Holy Trinity next coming; to the intent that we, by the advice of our said Council, may further do therein as the case shall rightfully require. And that ye conform you thus to do, as ye tender our pleasure and the good advancement of justice. Given under our privy seal at our manor of Greenwich, the 11th day of March.

Star Chamber Proceedings, Henry VIII, bundle 20, no. 121

84. Judgment in Star Chamber, 8 February 1594.

[In the case of Parsons *v.* Herne, concerning perjury and other misdemeanours,] the Court went to sentence as follows.

John Fortescue, knight[42]: checked Herne for his rash deposing and speaking regarding his oath, but this notwithstanding acquitted him as to the perjury and every part of it; and also as to the misdemeanour. And so did John Woolly, knight,[43] but he blamed Herne for giving counsel to a usurer. These two did not give any charges.

Lord Anderson, chief justice of the Common Bench,[44] acquitted Herne of everything and would restore his good fame in the best sort that could be, and delivered some words in dislike of what John Woolly had uttered regarding usury.

The chief justice of the Bench[45] also acquitted Herne of everything, and he to have restoration of his good name. He would have this done

---

41 Thoroughly.
42 Chancellor of the Exchequer and privy councillor.
43 Latin secretary and privy councillor.
44 Sir John Anderson, chief justice of Common Pleas.
45 Sir John Popham.

by the plaintiff's confession in Lincoln's Inn or in this Court; and the said Parsons to be examined who were the maintainers of this suit and if they be of ability to pay costs to Herne.

Lord Buckhurst[46] said that, perjury being the greatest offence, and that as the simplest man living ought to esteem [his good name] rather than his goods or his life, we ought not to proceed to sentence this without proofs *luce clariores* and witnesses *omni exceptione maiores*. And thus he agreed in all points with the chief justice of the Bench.

The bishop of Worcester[47] agreed with them and argued some *divinitas*, but the whole cause was opened by the chief justice of the Queen's Bench.

The archbishop[48] agreed with them, and so did the lord keeper.[49] And he ordered that according to the precedents . . . the plaintiff, if his ability be such, shall pay costs to the defendant and shall make confession in this court of his slanderous complaint against Herne, and he shall be specially examined who were his procurers, aiders or assisters in this suit.   Hawarde, 8–9

85. A Star Chamber decree of Wolsey's, 1524.

Thomas, by the sufferance of God of the title of St Cecily beyond Tiber of the Holy Church of Rome priest cardinal, legate of *latere*, archbishop of York, primate of England and chancellor of the same; to all people to whose sight, reading, hearing or knowledge this present writing shall come, sendeth greeting in our Lord God Everlasting. It is ordained, deemed, awarded and decreed by the said most reverend father in God and the King's most honourable Council, and by the advice of the King's judges and justices, the 29th day of November the 16th year of the reign of our sovereign lord King Henry VIIIth, between George Blundell, gentleman, plaintiff, on the one part, and Edward Molyneux, clerk, parson of Seston, and Brian Morecroft, clerk, with other defendants, on the other part, in manner and form hereafter following; that is to wit . . . [the decree orders the defendants to observe an earlier Star Chamber decree made against them and binds them in sureties of £1000].   Star Chamber Proceedings, Henry VIII, vol. 5, fo. 51

[46] Thomas Sackville, Lord Buckhurst, privy councillor and Burghley's successor as lord treasurer (1599).

[47] Richard Fletcher.

[48] John Whitgift.

[49] Sir John Puckering, lord keeper of the great seal (an office of less dignity than the chancellorship and correspondingly cheaper to the Crown, but equipped with equivalent powers).

86. Star Chamber decree, 22 April 1597.

The Queen's attorney[50] informed against Johnes and Thomas, gold-smiths of London, for that it was ordained in the time of Edward III that all plate should be thus alloyed sterling of the standard, the wardens of the company should view weekly what plate is made, and there is an assayer sworn to take assay and set on the company's mark; which is the alphabetical letter, the leopard's head appointed by Edward III, the lion appointed by Henry VIII, and every goldsmith's mark which remaineth in their Hall, and all these are commanded to be upon all plate which is sold. But Johnes and Thomas had made divers pieces of plate and alloyed them with copper alloy, twelve pennyweight in every ounce, and had counterfeited the alphabetical letter, the leopard's head, the lion, the mark of the company, and set them all to and sold them without assay; and every freeman is sworn to the contrary, so [that] they might be proceeded withal for perjury. But for these deceits and falsehoods they were sentenced by the whole Court to wear papers here upon the pillory,[51] and to lose either of them an ear on the pillory at Cheapside, and to go with papers where they dwell, and to pay either £100, and imprisonment; for this was condemned for a greater fault than robbery, for by this we know not how many nor who was robbed; and to coin money is treason, *ideo* this is a great offence.

Hawarde, 73

87. A bill in Star Chamber (riot, 1500): Joyfull *v.* Warcoppe.

To the King our Sovereign Lord

In humble wise complain to your most noble grace your faithful subjects and true liegemen Richard Joyfull, John Mercer of Warcop in your county of Westmorland, yeomen, Gabriel Warcoppe, Thomas Mosse the elder, Robert Gibson and Robert Mosse, of the same, yeomen. That where your said beseechers were in God's peace and yours, one Robert Warcoppe the elder, of Warcop, Robert Warcoppe the younger, and other riotous and misruled people, to the number of 53 persons and more, the 14th day of the month of October last past, with force and arms, that is to say with bows, arrows, bills, swords and buck-lers, at Warcop forsaid in the county of Westmorland riotously assembled, made assault upon your said beseechers and there beat, wounded

---

50 Sir Edward Coke, attorney-general,

51 I.e. to stand in the pillory with a paper around their necks specifying their offence.

and put in jeopardy of their lives without occasion on their part giving, to the great peril of your said beseechers and to the worst example of other like offending unless due punishment be had for reformation of the premises. In consideration whereof, and that your said poor subjects might there live in God's peace and yours, sovereign lord, that it might please your most noble grace to grant to your said beseechers your gracious letters of privy seal to be directed to the said misdoers, commanding them by the same to appear before your highness and your honourable Council at a day by your grace to be limited, and to bring with them such other of the said offenders as shall like your grace; to answer to the premises and therein further to do and receive after their demerits, as shall accord with right and good conscience. And your said beseechers shall pray to God for the preservation of your most noble estate in joy long to endure. Leadam, *Star Chamber*, I, 106

88. A bill in Star Chamber (case of assault and riot, temp. Henry VIII): Cappis *v*. Cappis.

To the King our Sovereign Lord

In most humble wise complaineth to your Highness your daily oratrix and poor bedewoman, Philippa Cappis, widow, late wife of James Cappis, esquire, deceased, That where John Rowe, serjeant-at-the-law, and other were and yet be seized of and in six messuages and 500 acres of land lying in East Whitfield and West Whitfield in your county of Somerset in their demesne as of fee to the use of your said oratrix for term of her life as for her jointure to her by her said late husband willed and put in surety, which lands and tenements since the decease of her said husband your said oratrix hath peaceably had, used and occupied by the sufferance of the said John Rowe and other. . . . So it is, most dread sovereign lord, that one Robert Cappis, one of the sons of the said James, being a person of most ragious and wilful condition, nothing dreading the punishment of your laws as concerning his wilful and ragious acts, wrongfully, forcibly and in riotous manner, accompanied with three like ragious and riotous persons apparelled with weapons of warfare defensible . . . upon the feast of St Luke last past came into the town of Wivelscombe in your said county, and perceiving that your oratrix was at dinner within an honest man his house within the said town, came into the said house where your said oratrix was at dinner and seeing her there suddenly plucked out his sword, having these words to her as hereafter followeth, that is to wit: 'Ah, thou stepdame, by God's Blood I care not though I thrust my sword through thee,' and he intending so to have done in most eager manner, one of his said riotous company, being somewhat better advised, plucked him aback, saying to him these words: 'Master Cappis, beware what ye do; kill her not.' And furthermore, before the said riotous persons coming into the said house, the said oratrix had with her in the said house one of her sons called Sir Roger Cappis, being a priest, brother to the said Robert Cappis, which Roger shortly perceiving the sudden coming of the said riotous persons, unto whom the said Robert had a long time borne his deadly malice for no other quarrel but for assistance and defence of his said mother's lawful quarrel and title in the premises, and dreading the danger of his life or bodily hurt suddenly to be to him done by the said riotous persons, conveyed himself and avoided from their presence, before their said coming in, at a backside of the said house, and so departed out of their danger; after whose departing and after the said ragious demeanour of the said Robert to your oratrix as is aforesaid, the said Robert demanded by these words following: 'Where is that whoreson the priest? If I had him I would hew him in small gobbets to sell him at the market ere I went.' And this done, the said riotous persons departed, leaving your said oratrix in such dread and agony that she was and hath been since in peril of her body and life, and ever shall be the worse while she liveth. Yet the said malefactors, not contented with their said ragious demeanour, perceiving your oratrix to be from home, in like ragious and riotous demeanour incontinent entered into the said lands and there took and drove away a cow in the name of an heriot, saying there and publishing himself to be very lord and heir of the same lands, and in like manner he hath used himself upon the premises divers times before this, and hath received with menacing and threatening of your oratrix's poor tenants of the said premises divers sums of money of the rents of right belonging to your oratrix, the said Robert Cappis having no manner of colour of title to the premises, neither as heir to the same nor otherwise; which is not only great dread as well to her person but also of the vexation for her said poor tenants and danger of their lives, and by occasion whereof she is in such confusion, what for lack of receipts of the profits of the said lands which is her whole living, and what for the wild and furious rage of the said Robert and his adherents, that she being a woman in extreme age and impotent, and cannot without extreme charges defend herself, knoweth not what to do without the merciful succour of your most gracious Highness in such case requisite to be administered to poor, impotent and succourless widows; wherefore may it please your Highness of your most abundant grace to grant to your said suppliant your gracious writs of subpoena to be directed to the said Robert and other the said riotous persons with him before named, commanding them by virtue of the same to appear before your Highness and your most honourable Council in your High Court of Star Chamber, there to answer to the premises, and further commanding the said Robert by any of the said writs to him to be delivered by way of injunction, to avoid his possession of the premises and to suffer your said oratrix in the mean time peaceably to occupy the same till such time as the title in the premises be tried before your said honourable Council.

Bradford, *Proceedings in Star Chamber*, 264–6

89. Star Chamber decree concerning printers, 1586.

Whereas sundry decrees and ordinances have upon grave advice and deliberation been heretofore made and practised for the repressing of such great enormities and abuses as of late (more than in times past) have been commonly used and practised by divers contemptuous and disorderly persons professing the art or mystery of printing and selling of books; and yet, notwithstanding, the said abuses and enormities are nothing abated, but (as it is found by experience) do rather more and more increase, by the wilful and manifest breach and contempt of the said ordinances, to the great displeasure and offence of the Queen's most excellent Majesty; by reason whereof sundry intolerable offences, troubles and disturbances have happened, as well in the Church as in the civil government of the state and commonweal of this realm, which seem to have grown because the pains and penalties contained and set down in the same ordinances and decrees have been too light and small for the correction and punishment of so grievous and heinous offences, and so the offenders and malefactors in that behalf have not been so severely punished as the quality of their offences have deserved:

Her Majesty therefore of her most godly and gracious disposition, being careful that speedy and due reformation be had of the abuses and disorders aforesaid, and that all persons using and professing the art, trade or mystery of printing or selling of books should from henceforth be ruled and directed therein by some certain or known rules or ordinances which should be inviolably kept and observed and the breakers and offenders of the same to be severely and sharply punished and corrected, hath straitly charged and required the most reverend father in God the archbishop of Canterbury, and the right honourable the lords and others of her Highness' Privy Council, to see her Majesty's said gracious and godly intention and purpose to be duly and effectually executed and accomplished.

Whereupon the said reverend father and the whole presence sitting in this honourable Court this 23rd day of June in the 28th year of her Majesty's reign, upon grave and mature deliberation, hath ordained and declared that the ordinances and constitution, rules and articles, hereafter following, shall from henceforth by all persons be duly and inviolably kept and observed, according to the tenor, purpose and true intent and meaning of the same, as they tender her Majesty's high displeasure and as they will answer to the contrary at their utmost peril.

I. *Imprimis*, That every printer and other person ... which at this time present hath erected ... any printing press, roll or other instrument for imprinting of books, charts, ballads, portraitures, paper called damask paper, or any such matters or things whatsoever, shall bring a true note or certificate of the said presses ... already erected, within ten days next coming after the publication hereof, and of the said presses ... hereafter to be erected or set up from time to time, within ten days next after the erecting or setting up thereof, unto the master and wardens of the Company of Stationers of the City of London for the time being; upon pain that every person failing or offending herein shall have all and every the said presses and other instruments utterly defaced and made unserviceable for imprinting for ever, and shall also suffer twelve months' imprisonment without bail or mainprize.

II. *Item*, That no printer of books nor any other person or persons whatsoever shall set up, keep or maintain any press or presses ... for imprinting of books [etc.] ... but only in the City of London or in the suburbs thereof (except one press in the University of Cambridge and one other press in the University of Oxford, and no more); and that no person shall hereafter erect, set up or maintain in any secret or obscure corner or place any such press ... but that the same shall be in such open place or places in his or their house or houses as the wardens of the said Company of Stationers for the time being, or such other person or persons as by the said wardens shall be thereunto appointed, may from time to time have ready access unto to search for and view the same. And that no printer . . . shall at any time hereafter withstand or make resistance to or in any such view or search, nor deny to keep secret any such press . . . upon pain that every person offending in anything contrary to this article shall have all the said presses . . . defaced and made unserviceable for imprinting for ever, and shall also suffer imprisonment for one whole year without bail or mainprize, and to be disabled for ever to keep any printing press . . . or to be master of any printing-house, or to have any benefit thereby other than only to work as a journeyman for wages.

III. *Item*, That no printer or other person whatsoever that hath set up any press . . . within six months last past shall hereafter use or occupy the same, nor any person or persons shall hereafter erect or set up any press . . . till the excessive multitude of printers having presses already set up be abated, diminished and by death given over, or otherwise brought to so small a number of masters or owners of printing-houses being of ability and good behaviour as the archbishop of Canterbury and bishop of London for the time being shall thereupon think it requisite and convenient, for the good service of the realm, to have some more presses . . . erected and set up. And that when and as often as the said archbishop and bishop . . . shall so think it requisite and convenient, and shall signify the same to the said master and wardens of the said Company of Stationers . . . , that then and so often as the said master and wardens shall (within convenient time after) call the assistants of the said Company before them, and shall make choice of one or more (as by the opinion of the said archbishop and bishop . . . need shall require) of such persons, being free stationers, as for their skill, ability and good behaviour shall be thought by the master, wardens and assistants, or the more part of them, meet to have the charge and government of a press or printing-house; and that within fourteen days next after such election and choice, the said master, wardens, and four other at the least of the assistants of the said Company shall present before the high commissioners in causes ecclesiastical, or six or more of them whereof the said archbishop and bishop to be one, to allow and admit every such person so chosen and presented, to be master and governor of a press and printing-house according to the same election and presentment; upon pain that every person offending contrary to the intent of this article shall have his press . . . defaced and made unserviceable and also suffer imprisonment by the space of one whole year without bail or mainprize.

IV. *Item*, That no person or persons shall imprint or cause to be imprinted or suffer by any means to his knowledge his press, letters or other instruments to be occupied in printing of any book, work, copy, matter or thing whatsoever except the same book . . . hath been heretofore allowed, or hereafter shall be allowed, before the imprinting thereof according to the order appointed by the Queen's Majesty's Injunctions[52] and be first seen and perused by the archbishop of Canterbury and bishop of London for the time being, or one of them, (the Queen's Majesty's printer for some special service by her Majesty or by some of her Highness' Privy Council thereunto appointed, and such as are or shall be privileged to print the books of the common law of this realm for such of the same books as shall be allowed of by the two chief justices and chief baron for the time being, or any two of them, only excepted); nor shall imprint or cause to be imprinted any book, work or copy against the form or meaning of any restraint or ordinance contained in any statute or laws of this realm, or in any injunction made or set forth by her Majesty or her Highness' Privy Council, or against the true intent and meaning of any letters patents, commissions or prohibitions under the great seal of England, or contrary to any allowed ordinance set down for the good governance of the Company of Stationers within the City of London; upon pain to have all such presses, letters and instruments as in or about the imprinting of any such books or copies shall be employed or used to be defaced and made unserviceable for imprinting for ever, and upon pain also that every offender and offenders contrary to this present article or ordinance shall be disabled (after any such offence) to use or exercise or take benefit by using or exercising of the art or feat of imprinting, and shall moreover sustain six months' imprisonment without bail or mainprize.

V. *Item*, That every such person as shall sell utter or put to sale wittingly, bind stitch or sew, or wittingly cause to be sold uttered put to sale bound stitched or sewed, any books or copies whatsoever printed contrary to the intent and true meaning of any ordinance or article aforesaid, shall suffer three months' imprisonment for his or their offence.

VI. *Item*, That it shall be lawful for the wardens of the said Company

---

[52] The Injunctions of 1559: Prothero, 188.

for the time being or any two of the said Company thereto deputed by the said wardens, to make search in all workhouses, shops, warehouses of printers, booksellers, bookbinders, or where they shall have reasonable cause of suspicion, and all books . . . contrary to . . . these present ordinances to stay and take to her Majesty's use, and the same to carry into Stationers' Hall in London; and the party or parties offending . . . to arrest, bring and present before the said high commissioners in causes ecclesiastical, or some three or more of them, whereof the said archbishop of Canterbury or bishop of London for the time being to be one.

VII. *Item*, That it shall be lawful to or for the said wardens for the time being, or any two of them appointed, . . . to enter into any house, workhouse, warehouse, shop, or other place or places, and to seize, take and carry away all presses, letters and all other printing instruments set up, used or employed contrary to the true meaning hereof, to be defaced and made unserviceable as aforesaid. And that the said wardens shall, so often as need shall require, call the assistants of their said Company, or the more part of them, into their said Hall and there take order for the defacing, burning, breaking and destroying of all the said presses, letters and other printing instruments aforesaid; and thereupon shall cause all such printing-presses or other printing instruments to be defaced, melted, sawed in pieces, broken or battered at the smith's forge, or otherwise to be made unserviceable. And the stuff of the same, so defaced, shall re-deliver to the owners thereof again within three months next after the taking or seizing thereof, as aforesaid.

VIII. *Item*, That for the avoiding of the excessive number of printers within this realm it shall not be lawful for any person or persons being free of the Company of Stationers or using the trade or mystery of printing, bookselling or bookbinding, to have, take and keep hereafter at one time any greater number of apprentices than shall be hereafter expressed. That is to say, every person that hath been or shall be master or upper warden of the Company whereof he is free, to keep three apprentices at one time, and not above. And every person that is or shall be under warden or of the livery of the Company whereof he is free, to keep two apprentices, and not above. And every person that is or shall be of the yeomanry of the Company whereof he is or shall be free, to keep one apprentice (if he himself be not a journeyman) and not above. Provided always, that this ordinance shall not extend to the Queen's Majesty's printer for the time being for the service of her

Majesty and the realm, but that he be at liberty to keep and have apprentices to the number of six at any one time.

IX. *Item*, That none of the printers in Cambridge or Oxford for the time being shall be suffered to have any more apprentices than one at one time at the most. But it is and shall be lawful to and for the said printers and either of them, and their successors, to have and use the help of any journeymen, being freemen of the City of London, without contradiction; any law, statute or commandment contrary to the meaning and due execution of these ordinances or any of them in any wise notwithstanding.

Strype, *Whitgift*, I, 423–4; III, 160–5

II. THE COURT OF REQUESTS

The Court of Requests, which by the later 1530's existed as a court of equity in civil matters rivalling Chancery's work in that field, was a true offspring of the king's Council. For once it is not difficult to establish the distinction: though its judges continued to take a Council oath, though process in it was of the king's Council, and though all bills were addressed to the king, the institution and its staff were entirely separate from the parent stem. The history of the court, on the other hand, is less clear-cut. Its origins are now reasonably clear. Though the appointment of individual councillors to attend to the complaints of poor petitioners, seeking relief in small matters and for minor legal problems, had a long history,[53] the turning of that practice into the provision of a regular court began in Henry VII's reign, received encouragement under Wolsey, and was settled by Cromwell. Thus the junior Council court developed very much alongside its elder brother in Star Chamber. The Court of Requests sprang from two roots. Its records (books of orders and decrees) went back to the register kept on progress by the councillors attendant upon Henry VII away from Westminster: for this reason the established Court was commonly described as 'the Council Attendant', even though by then it had its permanent venue at Westminster and never attended the king.[54] The other official name for the Court, 'the Council in the White Hall at Westminster', spoke more truly; for the Court did indeed use the room of that name as its regular meeting place. This association derived from its second root—the assignment of the room to one of the Council committees (undercourts) which Wolsey set up in 1517–20 (**92**), with frequent and bewildering rearrangements thereafter,

[53] Leadam, *Requests*, pp. ix seqq.

[54] Elton, *Studies*, I, 331. As early as 1523 the customary summons to 'wherever the king might be' could cause a man to turn up at the king's migratory court while the body that had summoned him was sitting at Westminster (Guy, *Cardinal's Court*, 43).

to relieve the burden on the Council in Star Chamber.[55] By 1529, only the White Hall committee still existed; it formed the parent body of the Court of Requests proper which took over the attendant Council's register.[56] When Cromwell reduced the size of the Council he caused a minor crisis because the White Hall committee included only councillors left out of the reformed Council; this raised the question of the authority by which they might continue to offer their judicial services. In 1538–9 Cromwell solved this problem by firmly establishing the Court under two judges called masters of requests (replacing the eight to ten members of the earlier committee) and allowing them various trappings to signify descent from Council membership even though they themselves were never again members of the Privy Council.[57] The orders issued in 1543 (93), which sum up these reforms, show the Court in full flower; by this time it even had to guard against litigants who resorted to it after losing their case in another court. Requests sat formally in term time only but its origins in the Council Attendant survived in its willingness to accept complaints throughout the year and wherever the sovereign might be. This rapidly increased its workload, and in about 1562 Elizabeth found it advisable to add two masters of requests extraordinary to the two ordinary masters appointed under Cromwell's reform. This made it possible to continue the work of the court at Westminster while people were able to hand their bills also to officers of the court accompanying the queen on progress. The ordinary masters received £100 each and the extraordinary ones nothing;[58] however, one need not echo the sarcasms wasted by historians on Elizabeth's parsimony because all these officers did very well out of fees and perquisites.[59]

From the first the councillors in Requests included men trained in the civil law; bishops, doctors of law and almoners were its leading judges. A court which always remained one of equity and conscience in the broadest sense could not do without them, but it was significant that from at least the 1530's one expert in the common law was always a member of the court, and one of the most assiduous at that.[60] This remained true even when the number of

[55] *Ibid.*, 41–5.

[56] Elton, *Tudor Revolution*, 135; Guy, *Cardinal's Court*, 49. 'Requests' was never really a technical term; rather, it signified any tribunal concerned to help the poor and plug holes in the administration of justice. Bodies going by the name are found, e.g., in various towns.

[57] Cf. for all this Knox, 'Requests', which has settled many questions touching the early days and established practice of the Court.   [58] Leadam, *Requests*, p. xx.

[59] Masterships of Requests were among the more avidly sought appointments in the reigns of Elizabeth and James I. For the general scheme of things which relied for the payment of Crown servants by official fees and unofficial gratuities rather than by salaries cf. Neale, 'The Elizabethan Political Scene', *Essays in Elizabethan History*, 59 ff.

[60] Elton, *Tudor Revolution*, 136, n. 11; Holdsworth, IV, 277. Thomas More, active on Wolsey's undercourts from 1519, probably represented an early example of that practice: in 1520 he was the only common lawyer on quite a powerful committee otherwise composed of civilians (Guy, *Cardinal's Court*, 42 f.).

masters had been fixed; there were then usually three civilians and one common lawyer whose presence assured that the court should be able to deal with matters of property along common law lines.[61] In theory the lord privy seal was alleged to be president of Requests (91), but little enough evidence exists to support this notion. Though Pollard thought that Bishop Foxe, during his long tenure of the privy seal (1487–1516) 'established a seemingly permanent association' of that office with Requests,[62] there is no real sign that he ever had anything to do with a court which even under Henry VII was often managed by the lord president.[63] Certainly after Foxe's day and until the coming of the Stuarts no lord privy seal treated Requests as his proper court, in the way in which the lord chancellor regarded Chancery.[64] In all probability the idea was a piece of bad history on Coke's part. It was the more plausible because the court had close links with the office of the privy seal. The senior clerk of that department was always *ex officio* clerk of Requests, and after Star Chamber took to using the great seal for its process the privy seal became something like the special seal of Requests.[65]

Procedure in Requests was very like that of Chancery and Star Chamber, except that it was swifter and cheaper. These last qualities naturally attracted litigants, so that the original purpose of the court tended to be lost to sight. It had grown out of the king's duty and willingness to give justice to men too poor and uninfluential to secure their ends in the ordinary courts, and in name it always remained a special court 'for poor men's causes'. Since it was also a Council court active at first in the king's Household, Crown servants enjoyed the privilege of having their suits tried there. However, its attractions proved too strong to make this restriction to king's servants and the poor practicable. In 1543 the court tried to confine the privilege to Household servants proper (93), many others who could claim to be in the position of Crown servants having taken up too much of its time. Lambarde recalled that at one time bills in Requests always stated that the plaintiff fell into one of the recognised categories, but he also knew that from the first others had managed to get their troubles heard by this branch of the Council (90). Its business was nearly exclusively civil, concerned with disputes over rights; sometimes, it seems, mercantile cases were also referred to it for lack of some other competent tribunal.[66] Though it used to be thought of as particularly active in protecting tenants' rights (copyhold tenures) in a time of agrarian upheaval,[67] this was almost certainly an impression created out of the socio-political prejudices of

---

[61] Cheyney (*History of England*, I, 110) maintained that all the masters were civilians, but the two whom he did not identify as such (Rokeby and Wilbraham) were common lawyers (cf. Leadam, *Requests*, p. cxx, n. 140 and p. cxxi, n. 144).

[62] Pollard, *Wolsey*, 83.

[63] Cf. Bayne, *op. cit.*, p. xxxviii.

[64] Elton, *Tudor Revolution*, 136 ff.

[65] *Ibid.*, 297 f.; and cf. 90.

[66] Holdsworth, I, 413; V, 139.

[67] Leadam, *Requests*, pp. xvi seqq.

certain historians and their selection of evidence: cases involving tenants' rights got printed out of a mass that had nothing to do with such matters. Requests did no more for copyholders than did Chancery,[68] and both did no more than apply the law, arbitrating between claims that were often morally suspect on both sides. As Common Pleas extended its hand over coyphold, Requests began to lose a justification for its existence though not, for a long time, its business. It is, however, worth emphasising that in all questions touching title to land the conciliar courts, and Chancery too, could never achieve a final end because security of title was obtainable only at law. Everything depended on whether a party defeated at equity would decide to call it a day or insist on going further in a common-law court. No wonder, therefore, that by the early seventeenth century the common-law courts had recovered their monopoly over the trial of title.

In this reversal of fortunes, Requests, the weakest of the new courts, became the obvious victim. It had always been more vulnerable than Star Chamber because its judges were less exalted and its services in civil matters less indispensable than Star Chamber's in criminal. Moreover, the court upon whose province it was encroaching—Common Pleas— already suffered the depredations of Chancery and even King's Bench.[69] It is therefore small wonder that during the common law's counter-attack late in Elizabeth's reign the Court of Requests came under heavy attack.[70] The argument against it concentrated on proving that as a tribunal it did not possess the powers of a court and rested upon no known basis (91); its enemies produced a wealth of historically invalid points. In the case of Stepney v. Flood (1599), Common Pleas expressly declared that Requests 'had no power of judicature'. This did not abolish the court which continued to serve the needs of large numbers of litigants, but it threw all its decisions in doubt and enabled a stubborn loser to evade his responsibilities by denying that the case had been tried in a proper court.[71] The quarrel got more violent in the next century, but the court struggled on under constant fire from the common-law judges until it simply ceased to be in 1643.

90. William Lambarde on the Court of Requests (c. 1580).

In that the Court of Requests handleth causes that desireth moderation of the rigour which the common law denounceth, it doth plainly participate with the nature of the Chancery; but in that the bills here

---

[68] Gray, Copyhold, 51–2.

[69] Above, p. 149.

[70] The story is told at length in Leadam, Requests, pp. xxiii seqq.; and cf. Ogilvie, King's Government, 124 ff.

[71] Leadam, Requests, pp. xliii seqq.; as he shows, in 1607 even perjury in Requests was declared by all the judges to be not punishable.

be exhibited to the Majesty of the King only and to none other, and in that it hath continually been served with a clerk that was ever therewithal one of the clerks of the King's privy seal, it seemeth to communicate with the Star Chamber itself, and to derive the authority immediately from the royal person as that doth. . . .

. . . It is out of all doubt therefore that as our kings have used personally to receive complaints of criminal condition, and have adjudged thereof of themselves or by their Council of Estate, so have they also from time to time taken knowledge of civil suits especially offered by the poorer sort of subjects or by their own Household men, and have for the most part recommended the same to the care of some of their said Council assisted with the advice of men learned both in the civil and common laws, so as some one temporal lord or bishop, two doctors, and two common lawyers have been many times known to have sitten here together. . . .

Now albeit there can no other beginning therefore be conceived than together with the very regality and kingdom itself, yet forasmuch as they of this court have not always had their standing place of resort, but have, until the age next before this, remained and removed with the King wheresoever he went, travelling between the prince and petitioners by direction from the mouth of the King, I have in this, as in the Star Chamber, also taken the first apparent settling and manifest continuance thereof for the very spring and original itself.

And I have lately seen that from the eighth year of King H. 7, ever since which time this Court hath rested in the place called the White Hall, the books of the acts of entries there have been orderly digested and kept, in which you may read the handling of the causes, not only of poor men and King's servants, but also of sundry abbots, knights, esquires and other rich and wealthy complainants. Howbeit I do well remember that within these 40 years the bills of complaints presented there did ordinarily carry one or the other of these two suggestions, namely, that the plaintiff was a very poor man, not able to sue at the common law, or the King's servants ordinarily attendant upon his person or in his Household. But because enlargement of jurisdiction is not proper to [this] court alone but common to it with all the rest, I will not now stand to object it, but hasten to an end.

The masters of the requests are neither called by writ nor appointed by commission nor created by patent, but only have letters patent for their fees and salary; and do take the same oath which the councillors do conceive.

The clerkship of this court hath, as I said, beyond all memory been committed to a clerk of the privy seal. . . .

The attorneys were in my first knowledge of them but two only, and now are three, whose places are at the disposition of the clerk.

The usual process is by privy seal . . . attachment and writ of rebellion if the contumacy of the defendant do so deserve; in the rest of the proceedings the course is not much different from the order of the Chancery. *Archeion, 224–31*

91. Sir Edward Coke against the Court of Requests.

. . . It shall be fit in this place to treat of the jurisdiction of the Court of Requests, wherein the lord privy seal at his pleasure and the masters of requests do assemble and sit. And the original institution hereof was, that such petitions as were exhibited to the King and delivered to the masters of the requests should be perused by them, and the party directed by them to take his remedy, according to their case, either at the common law or in the Court of Chancery. And thereupon they were called *Magistri a libellis supplicum*; and in this respect this meeting and consultation was called the Court of Requests, as the Court of Audience and Faculties are called Courts albeit they hold no plea of controversy.

Those which in former times would have this Court to be a court of judicature took their aim from a court in France. . . . But others, taking this jurisdiction to be too narrow, contend to have it extended to all cases in equity equal with the Chancery and their decrees to be absolute and uncontrollable. But neither of these are warranted by law, as shall evidently appear.

In the reign of H. 8 the masters of requests thought (as they intended) to strengthen their jurisdiction by commission to hear and determine causes in equity. But those commissions being not warranted by law (for no court of equity can be raised by commission) soon vanished, for that it had neither Act of Parliament nor prescription time out of mind to establish it.

Mich. 40 & 41 Eliz. In the Courts of Common Pleas, upon a bill exhibited in the Court of Requests against Flood, for default of answer an attachment was awarded against Flood under the privy seal to Stepney, then sheriff of Carnarvon, who by force of the said writ attached Flood and would not let him go until he had entered into an obligation to the sheriff to appear before his[72] Majesty's Council in the Court of Requests; upon which obligation the sheriff brought an action of debt for default of appearance, and all this matter appeared in pleading. And it was adjudged upon solemn argument that this which was called a Court of Requests or the White Hall was no court that had power of judicature, but all the proceedings thereupon were *coram non judice*, and the arrest of Flood was false imprisonment. . . .

The punishment of perjury in the Court of White Hall by the Statutes of [32] H. 8, cap. 9[73] and 5 Eliz., cap. 9[74] doth not give it any jurisdiction of judicature, no more than the statutes that give against a gaoler an action for an escape, or punisheth a gaoler of his own wrong for extortion, an officer of his own wrong shall be punished by the statutes in that case provided, and yet the statutes thereby make them no lawful officers, for it is one thing to punish and another to give authority. So it was justice in the Parliaments to punish perjury in the White Hall although the court were holden by usurpation, and so before it appeareth to be by the judgment in Stepney's case. . . . And as gold or silver may as current money pass, even with the proper artificer, though it hath too much allay, until he hath tried it with the touchstone, even so this nominative court may pass with the learned as justifiable in respect of the outside by vulgar allowance, until he advisedly looketh into the roots of it and try it by the rule of law; as (to say the truth) I myself did. . . .

. . . And although the law be such as we have set down, yet in respect of the continuance that it hath had by permission, and of the number of decrees therein had, it were worthy of the wisdom of a Parliament, both for the establishment of things for the time past and for some certain provision with reasonable limitations (if so it shall be thought convenient to that High Court) for the time to come; *et sic liberavi animam meam.*

Coke, *Fourth Institute*, 97–8

92. Orders for the Council, c. 1516.

For the expedition of poor men's causes depending in the Star Chamber, It is ordered by the most reverend father, etc., Thomas, lord cardinal,

---

[72] *Sic.*

[73] 32 H. 8, c. 9, prohibits unlawful maintenance 'in any action . . . in any of the King's Courts of Chancery, the Star Chamber, the White Hall, or elsewhere.'

[74] 5 Eliz. I, c. 9, recites 32 H. 8, c. 9, § 3, and imposes a penalty for suborning witnesses to commit perjury in any of the courts mentioned in that act or in other courts now enumerated.

chancellor of England, and the other lords of the King's most honour-able [Council] that these causes here mentioned shall be heard and determined by the King's councillors hereunder named. The which councillors have appointed to sit for the same in the White Hall here at Westminster, unto the which place the pleasure of the said most reverend father, etc., and the other etc., is that the said poor suitors shall resort before the said commissioners for the decision and deter-mination of their said causes as appertaineth, where they shall have hearing with expedition.

That is to say

My lord of Westminster[75]
Mr Dean of Paul's
My lord of St John's[76]
Sir Thomas Neville[77]
Sir Andrew Windsor[78]
Sir Richard Weston[79]
Mr Doctor Clerk[80]
Mr Roper[81]

Leadam, *Requests*, p. lxxxi

93. Orders appointed for the Court of Requests, 1543.

1. First that all makers of bills brought into the court subscribe their names, both to answers, replications and rejoinders, and every person omitting the same to repay the fee by him received to the parties there-by hurt and damnified. And in case the same maker for lack of learning or knowledge shall otherwise pen or set forth any poor men's causes contrary to the truth or matter afore him showed in writing, or other good and sufficient information to him evidently given, whereby the parties so grieved shall be compelled of reason to reform and make new matter by that occasion only; then the maker to repay his fee received, with such other charges as shall be thought requisite for his negligence or remiss doing in that behalf.

2. Item, that every person upon his appearance by the King's privy seal or otherwise bring their answer at the day to them assigned by the

[75] The abbot of Westminster.
[76] Thomas Docwra, the prior of the Order of St John of Jerusalem.
[77] A common lawyer and councillor; Speaker of the Commons in 1515.
[78] Keeper of the Great Wardrobe; (probably) a common lawyer.
[79] Courtier and revenue official.
[80] LL.D. of Bologna; later master of the Rolls and bishop of Bath and Wells.
[81] William Roper (Thomas More's son-in-law and biographer), a common lawyer, afterwards clerk of the pleas in the King's Bench.

court; and in like case the replication and rejoinder. . . . The court days therefore appointed of common course to be Monday and Wednesday and Friday. . . .

3. That all gentlemen which bring complaints to the King's Grace or his Council, not being his Grace's Household servants attendant upon his person . . . be remitted to the common law, and in default of remedy there to the King's High Court of Chancery, considering their suits to be greatly to the hindrance of poor men's causes admitted to sue to the King's grace. . . .

4. Item that all persons contemning the King's privy seal to them delivered be from henceforth charged and chargeable with the payment of the second process against them sued out. . . .

* * * * * *

6. Item, that all persons presenting complaints to the King's Grace or his Council which prosecute not the same during the space of one whole term neither by himself neither his counsel learned, nor showing cause sufficient to the contrary, be compelled to pay the defendant's costs and the matter remitted to the common law.

7. Item, it is ordered that no person after his appearance made before the King's Council depart before his answer made and to them presented, and licence to them given in the court, where they shall in like case enter the name of his attorney and counsel learned to speak in his absence, so thereby no delay from henceforth be made and used to the hurt and prejudice of any party. . . .

8. Item, that all persons which refuse or wilfully disobey any decrees made by the King's Council, supposing them to have matter or title sufficient to disprove the same, be upon the said surmise so alleged charged to pay all such costs as in the decree were awarded. . . . And over this that the same party so disobeying as aforesaid be examined who was his counsellor or provoker to do the same. And that proved and found, his counsellor to be compelled to pay all such costs as shall be awarded and further to be punished as by the Council shall be devised.

* * * * * *

10. Item, that all persons . . . which do of their wilful minds provoke and bring afore the King's Council such causes as against them have been determined, either by the courts of the King's common laws,

the Courts of Chancery, Star Chamber, or otherwise . . . as now is daily practised by wilful persons, be discharged of their suits and commanded to pay the party's costs being so grieved and wilfully vexed without just cause. . . .

11. Item, that all bills concerning copyhold lands (no default alleged against the lord or his steward) be always remitted to the lord's officers of the manor whereof the lands are holden, there to be tried according to the custom of the same. And if default be supposed against the lord or his steward, then a commission to be awarded to some indifferent gentlemen by the Council nominated, to sit with the steward for knowledge of the truth in that behalf.

* * * * * *

13. It is finally ordered by the King's Council, to the intent that all manner of causes afore them depending may be well and indifferently heard without any exclamation or interruptions of any persons standing or being present at the hearing of the same, that they and every of them, not being counsellors in the same case, do keep silence without interrupting thereof. . . . Leadam, *Requests*, pp. lxxxv–lxxxvii

94. A case in Requests: Burges *v.* Lacy (temp. Henry VIII).

To the King our Sovereign Lord

In most humble wise sheweth and complaineth unto your Grace your daily orator Sir William Burges, priest. That where he hath continued in service with one Mistress Luce Lacy of the said city[82] by the space of one whole year, according to his promise and covenant, and now at his year's end would lawfully depart for his most profit, so it is, most gracious lord, that the said Mistress Luce wrongfully and untruly surmiseth that your said orator should grant to serve her another year, which is untrue and but matter feigned of malice, as your said orator can and will evidently prove and justify by sufficient records and proofs; and over this, gracious lord, the same Mistress Luce, of her royal power without cause or matter of right, wrongfully withholdeth and keepeth from your said orator all his quarter's wages, 13*s.* 4*d.*, and his gown, the price thereof is 23*s.* 4*d.*, and his letters of his orders, contrary to right and good conscience. Please it therefore your noble Grace the premises tenderly to consider, and that your said orator is but lately come to the

---

[82] Of London.

city and have small acquaintance and very few friends, and also is of none power to sue for his right and remedy by the course of the law, of your most godly and blessed disposition and at the reverence of God and in the way of charity to command the said Mistress Luce personally to appear before your Grace there to answer to the premises, and further to be ordered in the same as by your Grace shall be thought most according with right, law, equity, justice and good conscience; and your said orator shall daily pray to God for your prosperity and state long to endure. . . .

The answer of Luce Lacy to the bill of complaint of Sir William Burges, priest.

The said Luce saith that the said bill of complaint is untrue, uncertain and unsufficient to be answered unto, and the matter therein contained determinable by course of the common law, whereof she prayeth allowance. Notwithstanding, for the further declaration of the truth, the said Luce saith that for a truth the said Sir William was in service and retained with the said Luce for 2 years, and the said Sir William promised, covenanted and granted to serve the said Luce by the space of 2 years, and not for one year in manner and form as is in the said bill specified. And as touching the said wages and gown, the said Luce saith that she is and at all time hath been ready to deliver it to the said Sir William so that the said Sir William will do his service according to the covenant made with the said Luce. Without that that anything effectual in the said bill contained is true otherwise than is specified in this present answer. All which matters the said Luce is ready to prove as this court will award, and prayeth to be dismissed out of the same with her reasonable costs for her wrongful [vexation] and trouble in that behalf.

Leadam, *Requests*, 59–60

95. Decree of the Court of Requests, 17 November 1539.

Be it remembered that the cause in controversy depending at the common law between the brewers and other inhabitants of Holborn against one William Bobye, for the withdrawing and keeping from them the water being in the well or dike at Holborn near Gray's Inn . . . is now by the King's Council, considering the withdrawing the same to be much hurtful and prejudicial to the foresaid brewers and inhabitants . . . ordered: that two labourers by the said Council appointed shall immediately make upon the head of the said dike or well after such rate and manner that it may hold and keep water as afore the breaking up of the same it did; and so the said Bobye it to suffer to continue and remain without breaking or any other hurt doing to the said head, either by himself or by any other by his procuring to the contrary; to whom it is commanded by way of injunction upon pain of £100 that he not only observe the same but peacably and quietly permit and suffer the said brewers to pass and repass to the same well. . . .

Leadam, *Requests*, 48

96. Order of the Court of Requests, 5 Edward VI (1552).

Well-beloved, we greet you well. Letting you wit that John Perkins, *alias* Wolman, late of Farnborough in our county of Kent, which not only for his great and urgent contempts by him committed and done, as well in disobeying our letters under our privy seal, upon penalties of great sums of money, faith and allegiance, attachments, proclamations, with writs of rebellion;[83] but also a decree and all our orders by our Council made and determined for the quieting and pacifying of the cause in traverse between him and Robert a Rice; was committed to the prison of the Fleet where he yet remaineth and of long time hath done according to his deserts. Yet nevertheless, he being called afore our said Council and being by them advertised for his conformity to be had in that behalf, in no wise would be persuaded thereunto. Wherefore we, considering his obstinacy and disobedience, and fully perceiving his perverse mind to continue in prison rather than to perform the decrees and orders of our said Council, being thereunto gently persuaded, will that ye by authority of this our express commandment, for that ye be steward and bailiff in the hundreds and liberties called Rokesby hundred, that immediately with convenient celerity ye resort and go to the tenement called the sign of the George in Farnborough, and all other lands belonging to the said Perkins *alias* Wolman, and of the same to put the plaintiff in full and quiet possession, so that they may therein peacably continue and have the same, until the whole rents thereof shall amount and extend to the sum of £15 specified and recited in the decree thereof made, and the arrearages that is and shall be due by force of the said annuity, and unto such time they shall have received, collected

---

[83] This is the full gamut of legal process to secure the attendance of a party defendant: summons (here by privy seal specifying penalties for disobedience), a writ of attachment to the sheriff, proclamation of outlawry by the sheriff (writs of rebellion being an extreme element in the last stage).

and taken £15 with the sum of 20s. awarded for the process and writs sued by the said Robert with other great charges for execution of the same . . . without failing the due execution hereof, upon pain of £100 and as ye will further answer at your utmost peril.[84] Given under our privy seal. . . .

[Caesar], *Court of Requests*, 150–1

III. LOCAL COUNCILS

The special needs of certain regions provoked special remedies. Both in the north, on the border against Scotland, and in the west, in the marches of Wales,[85] the power of the Crown was always weaker than elsewhere. Both areas had had to be developed as centres of defence against permanent foes. In the north, Scottish hostility and frequent inroads (repaid in kind on many occasions) compelled the construction of a military system based on the wardens of the East, Middle and West marches and covering the three shires of Northumberland, Cumberland and Westmorland. Although these wardens were royal officers it proved in practice impossible to appoint anyone to the office except powerful local feudatories; throughout the fourteenth and fifteenth centuries the border was in the hands of the three great and semi-independent families of Percy, Neville, and Dacre. The frontier against Wales had, before Edward I's conquest, produced its familiar consequence: the growth of a number of border barons (the lords marcher) equipped with special franchises and unusual military and jurisdictional powers.[86] Turbulence in these regions demanded specially privileged authorities; they in their turn became dangerous in their independence; and in the fifteenth century the powers and rivalries of northern and western barons involved the whole country in prolonged civil war. Even after this was ended by Henry VII's triumph, the frontier regions remained unsettled. Henry's Welsh descent and hold over Welsh feelings gave him a chance of establishing the royal authority there, but in the north the word of a Percy or Neville remained more influential than the king's, down to the defeat of the 1569 rebellion anyway. Furthermore, both these areas exercised a disturbing influence on their hinterlands. The lawlessness of the Welsh marches—the lords' franchises acting as refuges for criminals—affected the adjoining shires, and

[84] This whole phrase, enjoining obedience to the writ, is common form, though it is somewhat surprising to find a money penalty and 'utmost peril' (in place of 'upon your allegiance') used in a writ ordering the execution of a court order; such stringent phrases are more usual in writs of summons or orders to a party in the case. It almost looks as though the addressee had before this failed the court, being perhaps in collusion with the contumacious defendant.

[85] I.e. the area between the English border shires and the principality of Wales (cf. the map in Elton, *England under the Tudors*, 177). For its social scene cf. Pugh, *Marcher Lordships*, and Lloyd. *Gentry*.

[86] Cf. Otway-Ruthven, *Trans. R. Hist. Soc.*, 1958, 1 ff.

even Cheshire and Lancashire had always been difficult to control. North of the Trent, remoteness from London left to a powerful collection of noble and gentle families too many chances to go their own way. The solution inherited and developed by the Tudors lay in the creation of special councils with wide powers of jurisdiction and extensive territorial reach. It must be stated at once that these councils were in no sense 'offshoots' of the central king's Council, and their origin, development and competence differed in many respects from this latter.

The Council of the North had a history going back to Yorkist days.[87] It appears to have originated in the private council of Richard, duke of Gloucester, who administered the north for his brother, Edward IV. On succeeding to the throne, Richard III remembered the value of such a council and equipped his nephew Lincoln, whom he appointed his lieutenant, with an efficient body to govern the north parts.[88] The degree to which this was to be a settled court of law is shown in the instructions drawn up for it (97). Henry VII's accession interrupted the council's history; unlike Richard III he had no natural links with the north and was at first forced to rely on the Percies. The murder of Northumberland in 1487 gave him a freer hand, but it is far from clear that he exploited his freedom properly. Possibly an intermittent council, ostensibly attached to his mother's territorial possessions in the north, may have existed. Whatever there was had lapsed by 1509, and until 1522 nothing much was thereafter done to bring the north into order and obedience. In that year needs of defence against the Scots called Wolsey's attention to the problem, and by 1525 a council staffed largely by lawyers and administrators was established for the new lieutenant, Henry VIII's illegitimate and infant son, the duke of Richmond.[89] This council administered the Tudor lands in the north, but was also to exercise wide civil and criminal jurisdiction, on the model of Lincoln's council. It went beyond this precedent when its powers were extended outside Yorkshire into the marches, Durham being excepted. However, it failed in the face of the northern magnates' hostility; the wardenships, originally concentrated in Richmond, were allowed to go back to the local bosses, and the council did little. Wolsey's fall led to reforms. Richmond and his lands were removed from the council in 1530; Tunstall, bishop of Durham, took charge as president; and the council was once again restricted to Yorkshire only.[90] Tunstall proved incompetent and far too weak, and in 1533 the lamentable sixth earl of Northumberland was appointed lieutenant. At the same time, the Crown took steps to subdue

---

[87] Cf. Reid, *Council of the North*, and a valuable short account in Brooks, *Council of the North*.
[88] Reid, *op. cit.*, 61 ff.
[89] Reid, 102 ff.
[90] It is difficult to agree with Miss Reid (*op. cit.*, 113 f.) that this emasculated and ineffective council marked a vital step in institutional development.

the magnates of the north by extending its own territorial possessions at their expense, and by 1535 the great Percy interest was broken.

This did not solve the administrative problem, and the outbreak of the northern rebellion, the pilgrimage of grace, in the autumn of 1536 compelled drastic action. As soon as the risings were suppressed and the duke of Norfolk, lieutenant of the north during the troubles, could be recalled, Cromwell set about reorganising the Council of the North on a permanent and institutional basis.[91] The council thus established was a body of administrators and judges under a lord president, responsible for the whole of the north and freed from any responsibility for any royal lands. It was simply an instrument of government, controlled from the centre, a bureaucratic machine designed for a specific purpose; and the proper history of the institution began with this reform. Its structure and powers are well described in the detailed instructions of 1543 (98). It rested upon royal commission and was in no sense a delegation from the central Council. Its jurisdiction covered matters civil (between party and party) and criminal and derived not from the Privy Council but from commissions of the peace and of oyer and terminer. Unlike the central Council, therefore, it had a common-law jurisdiction and could deal with felonies and treasons. The growing habit of Chancery later in the century of dismissing northern cases to York developed also a jurisdiction in equity. At the same time, and in a way more fundamentally, the council had a Star Chamber competence in riots and the supervision of administration.[92] These wide powers were qualified by two things. The Council of the North was generally subordinated to the Privy Council which kept a watchful eye on its doings,[93] and it was no more thoroughly successful in establishing the royal authority in the face of local resistance than was Star Chamber itself. All these Tudor bodies achieved much but, especially in the conservative decline of Elizabethan administration, much less than had been hoped. Though properly organised in 1537, the Council of the North remained somewhat at the mercy of politics, and the outbreak of the rebellion of the earls in 1569 did not show it at its best.[94] However, the defeat of that rising gave Elizabeth and Cecil a chance of completing the work of Henry VIII and Cromwell. In 1572 the earl of Huntingdon became president of the northern council, and his twenty-three years of rule established both the council and its work as ordinary parts of the administration of the realm.[95] Holding its sessions, from 1582, invariably at York, the council proved generally effective enough in enforcing the Crown's policy upon the northern

[91] Brooks, *op. cit.*, 16 f.; Reid, *op. cit.*, 147 ff.
[92] Cf. for all this Reid, *op. cit.*, 280 ff.; Brooks, *op. cit.*, 21 ff.
[93] Holdsworth, IV, 74.
[94] Reid, *Trans. R. Hist. Soc.*, 1906, 174 ff.
[95] Cross, *The Puritan Earl*, ch. 5.

gentry and in providing justice for private parties. Its importance declined as its work took hold, though Thomas Wentworth, when he became president in 1628, was to find the north still worthy of attention and the council still a flexible instrument of policy. His work should warn one not to over-estimate the success of the Tudor presidents. Naturally, as the council's immediate importance lessened and its occupation of ground taken from the common law came to be resented by the lawyers, it fell under the sort of attacks which had been launched against other conciliar jurisdiction. The outbreak of the civil war simply brought it to an end, without formal dis-solution.[96]

The history of the Council in the Marches of Wales was more straight-forward.[97] It grew out of the council which administered Edward IV's marcher lands for him and was revived under Henry VII as a council for his son Arthur, prince of Wales, with competence over Wales and the Tudor lands in the marches. Wolsey found it moribund and in 1525 reconstituted it as the Princess Mary's council under Bishop Veysey of Exeter. Veysey proved weak in the face of the Welsh gentry's lawlessness, and it was not until the 1530's that a more formal council court, similar to that developed in the north, was created by Cromwell for the establishment and confirmation of order in Wales and the marches.[98] The appointment in 1534 of an effective president in Rowland Lee, bishop of Coventry, coincided with an act (101) which, among other things, gave the council power to supervise the execution of justice in the franchises of the marcher lords. Lee busied himself with the suppression of theft and murder throughout the principality even before the union of 1536[99] facilitated the council's activity by granting it competence in the whole of Wales and the border shires. The act of 1543 which summarised and consolidated all Henry VIII's legislation for Wales specifically mentioned a president and council in Wales and its marches 'as hath heretofore been used and accustomed' (102); thus, though this council, like that of the north, originally rested simply on the king's commission, it could from that time onward claim statutory authority. Once again, it was not an offshoot of the centre, though it came under the Privy Council's general surveillance. From its seat at Ludlow it controlled the seventeen shires of Wales, Monmouth, Hereford, Worcester, Shropshire, and Gloucester; until 1569 Cheshire, too, was subject to it.[100]

The Council in the Marches exercised in the first place conciliar jurisdiction; it was, even more than its northern brother, a local Star Chamber and

[96] Brooks, *op. cit.*, 28 ff.; Reid, *op. cit.*, 360 ff., 436 ff. The blackmail act of 1601 (100) not only alleged continued lawlessness in the north but also failed to mention the council as such among the authorities empowered to act under it.

[97] P. Williams, *Council in the Marches of Wales under Elizabeth*, pretty well supersedes Skeel, *Council in the Marches*, even for the earlier history of the institution.

[98] Williams, *Council* 28 f.   [99] Above, p. 33.   [100] Williams, *Council*, 47.

Chancery, though the Star Chamber proper both withdrew cases from it and remitted cases to it at the instance of parties. In addition it had competence in common law matters since it, too, was equipped with commissions of the peace and of oyer and terminer. Its instructions empowered it to hear cases not only of felony but even of treason; and unlike every other court of the realm it was specifically authorised to use torture.[101] However, an act of 1543 (34 & 35 Henry VIII, c. 26) set up four courts of Great Sessions under permanent judges which in practice exercised all common-law jurisdiction in the twelve shires of Wales.[102] The council's civil and criminal—though not its Star Chamber—powers thus conflicted in Wales with the Great Sessions and in the border shires with the Westminster courts. It therefore suffered the fate of all these conciliar courts and got involved in quarrels with the common law which from about the turn of the century onwards rendered its work more and more difficult.[103] However, as the Council in the Marches had been the oldest of these royal experiments, so it lived the longest. In abeyance during the civil war and Interregnum, it performed the astonishing feat of returning at the Restoration and was not abolished until 1689. From the reign of Henry VIII onwards it had in effect been simply a law-court of wide competence and considerable and effective usefulness to Crown and subject alike. In that reign the independence of the marcher lords was destroyed, and the council never afterwards played the political role which the continued restiveness of the north forced upon its brother at York. Like that other council, however, it had many administrative tasks to carry out, of which the organisation of the armed forces and a variety of preventive police duties were the most important.[104]

A third such council, the Council of the West, was set up in 1539 when Henry VIII's suppression of the Devon magnate interest of the Courtenays, marquesses of Exeter, suggested the desirability of taking a firmer hold upon the south-west.[105] Covering the four shires of Cornwall, Devon, Somerset, and Dorset, it was clearly modelled on the reformed Council of the North. This new council did not last long: abolished in 1540, about the time of Cromwell's fall, it demonstrated that his predilection for such regional boards was not shared by the king. The Council had proved expensive, ineffective and unnecessary.

97. Regulations for the Council of the North, 1484.

These articles following be ordained and established by the King's Grace,[106] to be used and executed by my lord of Lincoln and the lords

---

[101] Ibid., 49, 55. [102] Holdsworth, I, 123 ff.
[103] Ogilvie, King's Government, 126 ff.; Williams, Council, 225.
[104] Williams, Council, 106 ff. [105] Youings, Trans. R. Hist. Soc., 1960, 41 ff.
[106] Richard III.

and other of his Council in the north parts, for his surety and wealth[107] of the inhabitants of the same.

1. First, the King will that none lord ne other person appointed to be of his Council, for favour, affection, hate, malice or meed, do not speak in the Council otherwise than the King's laws and good conscience shall require, but be indifferent and in no wise partial, as far as his wit and reason will give him, in all manner matters that shall be ministered afore them.

2. Item, that if there be any matter in the said Council moved which toucheth any lord or other person of the said Council, then the same lord or person in no wise to sit or remain in the said Council during the time of the examination and ordering of the said matter, unless he be called; and that he obey and be ordered therein by the remnant of the said Council.

*　*　*　*　*　*

4. Item, that the same Council be, wholly if it may be, once in the quarter of the year at the least at York, to hear, examine and order all bills of complaint and other there before them to be shown, and oftener if the case require.

5. Item, that the said Council have authority and power to order and direct all riots, forcible entries, distress takings, variances, debates and other misbehaviours against our laws and peace committed and done in the said parts; and if such be that they in no wise can thoroughly order, then to refer it unto us and thereof certify us in all goodly haste thereafter.

*　*　*　*　*　*

9. Item that all letters and writings by our said Council to be made for the due executing of the premises be made in our name, and the same to be endorsed with the hand of our nephew of Lincoln underneath by these words, *Per Consilium Regis.*

10. Item, that one sufficient person be appointed to make out the said letters and writings and the same put in register from time to time; and in the same our said nephew and such with him of our said Council then being present set their hands; and a seal to be provided free for the sealing of their said letters and writings.

*　*　*　*　*　*

Brit. Mus., Harl. MS. 433, fo. 264v, (printed Reid, Council of the North, 504–5)
107 Welfare.

98. Instructions given by the King's Highness to . . . the archbishop of York[108] and such other as shall be named hereafter, whom his Majesty has appointed to be of his Council resident in the North parts . . . (c. 1544).

His Majesty, much desiring the quietness and good governance of the people there, and for speedy and indifferent administration of justice to be had between party and party, intendeth to continue his right honourable Council called the King's Council in the North Parts. And his Highness, knowing the approved truth, wisdom and experience of the said archbishop of York, with his assured discretion and dexterity in executing of justice, hath first appointed him to be president of the said Council so established, and by these presents do give unto him the name and title of lord president of the said Council; and with the said name, power and authority to call all such others as shall be named of the said Council, at this time or hereafter, together, at all such seasons as he shall think the same expedient, and otherwise by his letters, when they shall be absent, to appoint them and every of them to do such things for the advancement of justice and for the repression and punishment of malefactors as, by the advice of such part of the said Council as then shall be present with him, he shall think meet for the furtherance of his Grace's affairs and the due administration of justice between his Highness' subjects. And further, his Majesty by these presents giveth unto the said lord president, in all council where things shall be debated at length for the bringing out of the most perfect sentence—which his Majesty's pleasure is shall be observed in all cases where the same shall be such as may abide advisement and consultation—a voice negative, to the intent nothing shall pass but his express commandment, consent and order. And his Highness also willeth and commandeth that all and every of the said councillors to be hereafter named shall exhibit to the said lord president as much honour, obedience and reverent behaviour in all things (kneeling only excepted) as they would exhibit unto his own person if he were there present amongst them; and in like sort receive and execute all his precepts and commandments to be addressed unto them or any of them, for any matter touching his Majesty or any process or thing to be done or served in his Grace's name.

And to the intent the said president, being thus established as head and director of such Council as his Highness hath erected and established

---

[108] Robert Holgate.

there for the purposes abovesaid, may be furnished with such assistants and members as be of wisdom, experience, gravity and truth, meet to have the name of his Grace's councillors, his Majesty upon good advisement and deliberation hath elected and chosen these persons whose names ensue hereafter to be his councillors joined in the said Council in the North Parts with the said president, that is to say . . . the earls of Westmorland and Shrewsbury;[109] . . . William, Lord Dacre of the North; William, Lord Eure; Thomas, Lord Wharton; John Hynde,[110] serjeant-at-law; Edmund Molyneux,[111] serjeant-at-law; . . . Sir Marmaduke Constable the elder, Sir Henry Savile, knights; Sir Robert Bowes,[112] knight; William Babthorpe, knight; Mr Thomas Magnus, clerk,[113] Robert Challoner, Thomas Gargrave,[114] Richard Norton, and John Uvedale, esquires; the which John Uvedale his Highness doth also appoint to be both secretary to the said Council and to keep his Grace's signet where he is with the said president and Council and not in his absence—wherewith nevertheless he shall seal nothing but by express warrant of the said lord president, or of two other of the Council by the consent of the said president—and also to be sworn a master of the Chancery for taking of recognisance in such cases as by the said president and such of the said Council as shall be from time to time present with him shall be thought convenient, the case so requiring. . . .

His Majesty ordaineth that . . . the earl of Westmorland, the Lord Dacre, the Lord Eure, the Lord Wharton, John Hynde, Edmund Molyneux, Sir Marmaduke Constable, Sir Henry Savile, Mr Thomas Magnus and Richard Norton shall give their attendance at their own pleasure, that is to say, go and come when their will is, unless they shall be otherwise by the said president appointed, saving only at four general sittings where every of the said Council shall be present unless they have some just necessary impediment to the contrary. And because it shall be convenient that a number shall be continually abiding with the said president, to whom he may commit the charge and hearing of such matters as shall be exhibited unto him for the more expedition of the same, by these presents his Highness doth also ordain that William Babthorpe, Robert Challoner, Thomas Gargrave and John

109 The earl of Cumberland was added 11 December, 1546.
110 Judge of the Common Pleas, 1545–50; knighted, 1545.
111 Knighted, 1547; judge of the Common Pleas, 1550.
112 Warden of the East and Middle Marches, 1550; master of the Rolls, 1552.
113 Archdeacon of the East Riding, 1504.
114 Knighted, 1549; Speaker of the House of Commons, 1559.

Uvedale shall give their continual attendance upon the said president, or at the least two of them, so as none of this number appointed to give his continual attendance shall in any wise depart at any time from the said president without his special licence, and the same not to extend above six weeks at one season. And for the better intreatment of the said president and all the said Council of both sorts when they or any of them should be present in the said Council, his Highness doth give a yearly stipend or salary of £300 . . . to the said president towards the furniture of the diets of himself and the rest of the said councillors, with such number of servants as shall be hereafter allowed to every of them, that is to say, every of the said Council himself to sit with the president at his table, or at a place in his house to be by him prepared conveniently for him after his degree and haviour. . . .

And to furnish the said president and Council in all things with authority sufficient and ready to execute justice as well in causes criminal as in matters of controversy between party and party, his Majesty hath commanded two commissions to be made out under his great seal of England by virtue whereof they shall have full power and authority in either case to proceed as the matter occurrent shall require. And for the more speedy expedition to be used in all cases of justice, his Majesty's pleasure is that the said president and Council shall cause every complainant and defendant that shall have to do before them to put their whole matter in their bill of complaint and answer, without replication, rejoinder or other delay to be had or used therein, which order the said president and Council shall manifest to all such as shall be counsellors in any matter to be intreated and defined before them, charging all and every the said counsellors, upon such penalty as their wisdoms shall think convenient, to observe duly this order as they will eschew the danger of the same: no attorney to take for his fee at one sitting above 12*d.* nor any counsellor above 20*d.* To the which president and Council the King's Majesty by these presents doth give full power and authority, as well to punish such persons as in anything shall neglect or contemn their commandments as all other that shall speak any seditious words, invent rumours, or commit any such offences, not being treason, whereof any inconvenience might grow, by pillory, cutting their ears, wearing of papers, or otherwise at their discretions; and to poor suitors having no money, at their discretions to appoint counsel and other requisites without paying of any money for the same. And likewise his Highness giveth full power and authority to the said president and

Council, being with him, to cess fines of all persons that shall be convict of any riots, how many soever they be in number, unless the matter of such riot shall be thought unto them of such importance as the same shall be meet to be signified unto his Majesty, and punished in such sort, by the order of his Council attendant upon his person, as the same may be noted for an example to others. And semblably, his Grace giveth full power and authority unto them by their discretions to award costs and damages, as well to the plaintiff as to the defendants, and execution of their decrees, all which decrees the said secretary shall be bounden, incontinently upon the promulgation of every of the same, to write or cause to be written fair in a book, which book shall remain in the hands and custody of the said president.

And to the intent it may appear to all people there what fees shall be taken of them for all manner of process and writings that shall be used by this Council, like as his Majesty straitly chargeth the said president and Council upon their allegiance to suffer no more to be taken for anything the nature whereof shall be expressed hereafter than shall be taxed upon the same, so his Highness will, and by these presents appointeth, that there shall be a table affixed in every place where the said president and Council shall sit at any sessions, and a like table to hang openly, that all men may see it, in the office where the said secretary shall commonly expedite the said writings, what shall be paid for every of the same: that is to say, for every recognisance wherein one person and sureties are bound for him, 12*d.*; for cancelling of one like recognisance, 12*d.*; for entering of one decree, 6*d.*; for the copy of the same decree, if it be asked, 6*d.*; for every letter, commission, attachment or other precepts sent to any person, 4*d.*; for every dismission before the said commissioners, if it be asked, 4*d.*; for the copies of bills and answers, to have for every 10 lines reasonably written, 1*d.*; for every subpoena, 4*d.*; for letters of appearance under the signet, 4*d.*; for every leaf of paper written in copy, so that the same contain 20 lines, 2*d.*; for examination of every witness, 4*d.* And his Grace's pleasure is that there shall be no examiner of witness nor writer of either bills, answers, copies or other process in the said court but by the special licence of the said president and some of the Council, so that the said president may ever have a voice negative in the same.

And for the more certain and brief determination of all matters that shall chance in those parts, his Majesty by these presents ordaineth that his said Council shall by the space of one whole month in the year at least remain at York, by the space [of] one other month at Newcastle, by the space of one other month at Kingston-upon-Hull, and by the space of one other month at Durham, within the limits whereof the inhabitants there shall be called and to none other place. And they shall in every of the said places keep one gaol delivery before their departure from thence. His Grace nevertheless referreth it to their discretion to take such other place or places for the said four months or four general sittings as they shall think most convenient for the time, if by death or any other occasion they shall think the towns appointed or any of them not meet for them; so that they keep the full term of one month in every place where they shall sit, if they can in any wise conveniently so do.

And forasmuch as the King's Majesty, calling to his remembrance how that the great number of his tenants in this realm have been heretofore retained, either by wages, livery, badge or cognisance, with divers persons of the countries where the same do inhabit, by reason whereof when his Majesty should have had service of them they were rather at commandment of other men than, according to their duties of allegiance, of his Highness of whom they had their livings; his Majesty's express pleasure and high commandment first is, that none of his said Council shall by any livery, wages, badge, token or cognisance, retain or entertain any of his Grace's tenants in such sort as whereby he should account himself bounden to do unto him or under him any other than as his Highness' officers, if he be so in any manner of service.

And further, his Majesty's like pleasure and commandment is, that the said president and Council shall in any of their principal sittings give special notice and charge that none other nobleman, gentleman or other person presume to retain any of his Grace's said tenants in such wise as is aforesaid and as hath been accustomed; charging all the said tenants, upon pain of forfeiture of their holdings and incurring of his Majesty's further displeasure and indignation, in no wise to agree to any such retainder with any other man, but wholly to depend upon his Highness and upon such as his Majesty shall appoint to be his officers, rulers and directors over them.

And semblably, his Grace's express pleasure and commandment is, that in every such sitting, and in all other places where the said president and Council shall have any notable assembly before them, they shall give strait charge and commandment to the people to confirm themselves in all things to the observation of such laws, ordinances and determinations as be made, passed and agreed upon by his Grace's

Parliament and clergy, and specially the laws touching the abolishing of usurped and pretended power of the bishop of Rome, whose abuses they shall so beat into their heads by continual inculcation as they may smell the same, and perceive that they declare it with their hearts and not with their tongues only for a form. And likewise they shall declare the order and determination taken and agreed upon for the abrogation of such vain holy days as be appointed only by the bishop of Rome to make the world blind, and to persuade the same that they might also make saints at their pleasure, do give occasion by idleness of the increase of many vices and inconveniences. Which two points his Majesty doth most heartily require and straitly command the said president and Council to set forth with dexterity; and to punish extremely, for example, all contemptuous offenders in the same. . . .

Furthermore, the said president and Council shall from time to time make diligent inquisition who hath taken and enclosed commons, called intakes; who be extreme in taking of gressoms[115] and onering of rents;[116] and so call the parties that have so used themselves evil herein before them; and . . . they shall take such order for the redress of the enormities used in the same as the poor people be not oppressed, but that they may live after their sorts and qualities.

And if it shall chance that the said president and Council shall be variant in opinion, either in law or for any order to be taken upon any fact, that like as if the case be not of very great importance, that part wherein shall be the greater number of the councillors appointed to give continual attendance shall determine, or else, if they be of like number, that part whereunto the president shall consent and lean who in all causes as is aforesaid shall ever have a voice negative; so, being the case of great importance, if the question be of the law, the said president and Council shall signify the case to the judges at Westminster who shall with diligence advertise them again of their opinions in it. And if it be an order to be taken upon the fact, the said president and Council shall in that case advertise the King's Majesty, or his Council attendant upon his person, upon the same; whereupon they shall have knowledge how to use themselves in that behalf. And the said president and Council shall specially take regard that in cases between party and party, where the question and complaint shall be of any spoil, extortion or oppression, that the part grieved may have due and undelayed

---

115 A premium or fine paid to a feudal superior on entering upon a holding.
116 I.e. raising of rents so as to be onerous or burdensome.

restitution, or for want of ability thereunto the offenders to be punished to the example of others, as well in things that may hereafter be complained of as of such as be passed heretofore at any time for the which agreement is not already made. And if it happen that any man, of what degree soever he be, shall, upon such a ground and cause as the law will allow for good and reasonable, and shall so appear unto the said president and Council, demand surety of peace or justice against any great lord of the country, the said president shall in that case grant the petition of the poorest man against the richest and greatest lord, whether he be of his Council or no, as he would grant the same, being lawfully asked, of men of the meanest sort, degree and haviour.

And forasmuch as it may chance the said lord president to be sometime diseased, that he shall not be able to travail for the direction of such matters as shall then occur, or to be called to the Parliament, or otherwise to be employed in the King's Grace's affairs or about necessary business for good reformation within his rule; to the intent the said Council may be ever full, and that there may be at all times in the same a personage to direct all things in such sort, order and form as the said president shall do by virtue of these instructions, his Majesty's pleasure is, that when the said lord president shall be in any wise so diseased or absent as is aforesaid that he cannot supply his room, he shall name one of the number of such councillors as be appointed to give continual attendance to supply his room for that season, to whom, for so long time as the said lord president shall be diseased that he cannot execute his office or otherwise to be absent as is aforesaid, his Highness giveth the name of vice-president, which name nevertheless he shall no longer have than the said president shall be recovered, there present, or returned home again. So his Majesty's pleasure is that for the time only that any of the said Council shall occupy the room and place of a vice-president by assignment of the said lord president as is aforesaid, all the rest of the Council shall in all things use him in like sort and with like reverence as they be bounden by these instructions to use the lord president himself; whereunto his Grace doubteth not every of them will conform themselves accordingly.

Furthermore, his Majesty by these presents giveth full power and authority to the said president and Council that when the condition of any recognisance taken before them shall be fulfilled they shall at their discretions in open court cause the same to be cancelled for the discharge of the parties; provided ever that no recognisance be in any wise cancelled but before the president, or a vice-president in time of his disease and sickness or absence, and three others of the Council at least sitting in court with him.

And whereas in an article before written it is contained that every of the said Council shall be present at every of the said four general sittings; forasmuch as the King's Majesty doth consider that it should be much tedious and chargeable to divers of the lords and some others of the said Council to come to every of the said sittings, their habitations being far off, his Highness is contented that those councillors which be not bounded to continual attendance shall be only present at the sitting or sittings that shall be near unto their dwelling-places, unless they shall be commanded by the president to attend upon him at the other sittings that be further off from them, in which case they shall obey his commandment therein, all excuses set apart, as appertaineth. And where in another article it is also provided that no person shall retain any of the King's tenants by any livery, wages, badge or cognisance, his Grace doth intimate to the said president and Council that the meaning of his Grace is that no man shall retain any such his Grace's tenants as is aforesaid, unless he shall keep the same continually in household with him and give unto them meat, drink, wages and lodging; in which case his Majesty is contented that his tenants may be retained, so as the same be not such persons as have any office or certain authority amongst their neighbours. *State Papers*, v, 402–11

99. An Act for the increase of tillage, etc. (1571: 13 Eliz. I, c. 13).

For the better increase of tillage and for maintenance and increase of the navy and mariners of this realm, be it enacted that . . . it shall be lawful to all and every person and persons being subjects of the Queen's Majesty, her heirs and successors, and inhabiting within her Highness' realms and dominions [to export corn and other foodstuffs to friendly countries from certain ports] at all such times as the several prices thereof shall be so reasonable and moderate in the several counties where any such transportation shall be intended as that no prohibition shall be made . . . by the Queen's Majesty . . . by proclamation to be made in the shire town or in any port towns of the county, or else by some order of the lord president and Council in the North, or the lord president and Council in Wales, within their several jurisdictions, or of the justices of Assizes at their sessions in other shires out of the jurisdiction of the said two presidents and Councils, or by the more part of the justices of the peace of the county at their Quarter Sessions. . . .

Stat. Realm, IV, 547

100. An Act for the more peacable government of the parts of Cumberland, Northumberland, Westmorland and the bishopric of Durham (1601: 43 Eliz. I, c. 13).

Forasmuch as now of late years very many of her Majesty's subjects dwelling and inhabiting within the counties of Cumberland, Northumberland, Westmorland and the bishopric of Durham have been taken, some forth of their own houses and some in travelling by the highway or otherwise, and carried out of the same counties or to some other places within some of the said several counties as prisoners, and kept barbarously and cruelly until they have been redeemed by great ransoms; and where now of late time there have been many incursions, rodes, robberies, and burning and spoiling of towns, villages and houses within the said counties, that divers and sundry of her Majesty's loving subjects within the said counties, and the inhabitants of divers towns there, have been enforced to pay a certain rate of money, corn, cattle or other consideration, commonly there called by the name of black mail,[117] unto divers and sundry inhabiting upon or near the Borders, being men of name and friended and allied with divers in those parts who are commonly known to be great robbers and spoil-takers within the said counties, to the end thereby to be by them freed, protected and kept in safety from the danger of such as do usually rob and steal in those parts. By reason whereof many of the inhabitants thereabouts, being her Majesty's tenants or other good subjects, are much impoverished, and theft and robbery much increased, and the maintainers thereof greatly encouraged, and the service of those borders and frontiers much weakened and decayed, and divers towns thereabouts much dispeopled and laid waste, and her Majesty's own revenue greatly diminished; which heinous and outrageous misdemeanors there cannot so well by the ordinary officers of her Majesty in those parts be speedily prevented or suppressed without further provision of law. For remedy whereof be it enacted by the authority of this present Parliament that whosoever shall at any time hereafter, without good and lawful warrant or authority, take any of her Majesty's subjects against his or their wills

---

[117] Mail here means a rent; black mail is therefore illegal rent obtained by oppression.

and carry them out of the same counties, or to any other place within any of the said counties, or detain, force, or imprison him or them as prisoners, or against his or their wills to ransom them or to make a prey or spoil of his or their person or goods upon deadly feud or otherwise, or whosoever shall be privy, consenting, aiding or assisting unto any such taking, detaining, carrying away, or procure the taking, detaining or carrying away of any such person or persons prisoners as aforesaid, or whosoever shall take, receive or carry, to the use of himself or wittingly to the use of any other, any money, corn, cattle or other consideration, commonly called black mail, for the protecting or defending of him or them or his or their lands, tenements, goods or chattels from such thefts, spoils and robberies as is aforesaid, or whosoever shall give any such money, corn, cattle or other consideration called black mail for such protection as is aforesaid, or shall wilfully and of malice burn or cause to be burned, or aid, procure or consent to the burning of, any barn or stack of corn or grain within any the said counties or places aforesaid, and shall be of the said several offences or of any of them indicted and lawfully convicted, or shall stand mute,[118] or shall challenge peremptorily above the number of twenty,[119] before the justices of assizes, justices of gaol delivery, justices of oyer and terminer, or justices of peace within any of the said counties at some of their general sessions within some of the said counties to be holden, shall be reputed, adjudged and taken to be as felons, and shall suffer pains of death without any benefit of clergy, sanctuary or abjuration, and shall forfeit as in case of felony.

*   *   *   *   *   *

v. Provided always that this act nor anything therein contained shall not extend to abridge or impeach the jurisdiction or authority of any the lords wardens of any the Marches of England for and anenst Scotland; anything in this present act to the contrary notwithstanding.

Stat. Realm, IV, 979

101. An Act that murders and felonies done or committed within any lordship marcher in Wales shall be enquired of at the sessions holden within the shire grounds next adjoining, etc. (1534: 26 Henry VIII, c. 6).

Forasmuch as the people of Wales and marches of the same, not dread-

---

[118] Refuse to plead.

[119] A prisoner had the right to challenge a given number of jurors without stating a reason.

ing the good and wholesome laws and statutes of this realm, have of long time continued and persevered in perpetration and commission of divers and manifold thefts, murders, rebellions, wilful burning of houses and other scelerous deeds and abominable malefacts, to the high displeasure of God, inquietation of the King's well-disposed subjects and disturbance of the public weal; which malefacts and scelerous deeds be so rooted and fixed in the same people that they be not like to cease unless some sharp correction and punishment for redress and amputation of the premises be provided according to the demerits of the offenders; Be it therefore enacted by the King our sovereign lord, and the lords spiritual and temporal and the Commons in this present Parliament assembled, and by authority of the same that all and singular person and persons dwelling or resiant within Wales or in the lordships marches of the same, from time to time and at all times hereafter, upon such monition or warning given for the court to be kept in Wales or in any of the lordships marches aforesaid, as before this time hath been used, shall personally repair, resort and appear before the justice, steward, lieutenant or other officer, at all and every sessions, court and courts, . . . And then and there shall give his and their personal attendance to do, execute and accomplish all and every thing and things which to him or them shall affeir and appertain, upon pain of such fines, forfeitures and amerciaments as shall be affeired, assessed and taxed by the justice, steward, or other officer, to the King's use if it be within any of the King's lordships marchers, and if it be within any other lordships marches then to the use of the lord of the said lordship marcher for the time being. . . .

II. And forasmuch as the officers in the lordships marchers in Wales have oft and sundry times heretofore unlawfully exacted the King's subjects within such lordships where they have had rule or authority by many and sundry ways and means, and also committed them to strait duress and imprisonment for small and light feigned causes, and extortiously compelled them thereby to pay unto them fines for their redemptions, contrary to the law, Therefore be it further enacted that if any steward, lieutenant or any other officer of any lordship marcher do feign, procure or imagine any untrue surmise against any person or persons that shall so give their personal attendance before them at such court or courts, and upon the same untrue surmise commit them to any duress or imprisonment contrary to the law, or contrary to the true and laudable custom of that lordship, that then upon suit made unto the King's commissioners or Council of Marches . . . the same commissioners or Council shall have full power and authority to send for such steward, lieutenant or officer, and also for the person or persons so imprisoned; and if the same person or persons so imprisoned can evidently prove before the said Council . . . that his imprisonment was upon any feigned surmise, without cause reasonable or lawful, that then the same commissioners shall have full power and authority to assess the said officer to pay to the said person or persons wrongfully imprisoned 6s. 8d. for every day of their imprisonment, or more by the discretions of the said commissioners according to the hurts and behaviour of the person or persons imprisoned; and that the same commissioners shall set further fine upon the said officer to be paid to the King's use as by their discretions shall be thought convenient. And in case the same officer do refuse to appear before the same commissioners incontinent after any commandment to them directed and delivered after any such complaint made to the same commissioners, that then the same commissioners shall have full power and authority [to fine the officer and to imprison him if he refuse to pay]. . . .

* * * * * *

VI. And for the punishment and speedy trials . . . of all and singular felonies [etc.] . . . committed within any lordship marches of Wales, Be it enacted by authority aforesaid that the justices of gaol delivery and of the peace and every of them for the time being, in the shire or shires . . . next adjoining to the same lordship marcher or other place in Wales . . . shall from henceforth have full power and authority . . . to enquire by verdict of twelve men of the same shire . . . to cause all such counterfeiters, washers, clippers of money, felons, murderers and accessories to the same to be indicted according to the laws of the land. . . .

[VII. Justices may award process into the marches, and officers there shall arrest offenders and convey them into England.]

* * * * * *

Stat. Realm, III, 500–3

102. An act for certain ordinances in the King's Majesty's dominion and principality of Wales (1543: 34 & 35 Henry VIII, c. 26).

* * * * * *

III. Item, that there shall be and remain a president and Council in the said dominion and principality of Wales and the marches of the same, with all officers, clerks and incidents to the same, in manner and form as hath heretofore been used and accustomed; which president and Council shall have power and authority to hear and determine by their wisdoms and discretions such causes and matters as be or hereafter shall be assigned to them by the King's Majesty, as heretofore hath been accustomed and used.

*   *   *   *   *   *

Stat. Realm III, 926

CHAPTER 7

ECCLESIASTICAL COURTS

I. THE ORDINARY COURTS

Apart from the various secular courts there existed also a comprehensive system of Church courts, or courts Christian. Their functions were essentially threefold. They supervised the affairs of the clergy, punished their misdemeanours, and adjudicated in disputes among them; they protected the clergy in their relations with the laity; and they exercised jurisdiction over the laity in matters of religion, morals and certain causes which were reserved from the secular courts.[1] Among the first kind of matters we may mention neglect of duties, worldly behaviour, crimes, heresy or lesser offences against conformity in doctrine and ritual. The second covered the enforcement of lay payments to the Church, especially tithe but also oblations, mortuaries and other fees, as well as the punishment of riotous behaviour in church, contempt of the clergy, and attacks on ecclesiastics. The last involved the detection and punishment of heresy and the like among the laity; of adultery, incontinence and other sexual offences; a vast jurisdiction over matrimonial and testamentary affairs; and jurisdiction over such matters as perjury and defamation which in the sixteenth century came to be handled by the Star Chamber. The law administered was the canon law of Rome, until the Reformation ended its study in England. Thereafter (from about 1540) the English Church courts did not quite seem to know what their law was, though after the repeated failure to promulgate canons for the Church of England a body of law based partly on the old canons and partly on statute was used.[2] Practitioners in the courts came to be civilians instead of canonists.[3] Procedurally the cases before the courts were of three kinds: instance cases between party and party; *ex officio* cases which represented the corrective action of the judge, acting on information obtained either in periodic visitations or in the constant contact between clergy and their flocks; and probate. Instance jurisdiction, at its height in the late fifteenth century, declined in the sixteenth, probably because parties found better remedies in Chancery and the conciliar courts; but *ex officio* jurisdiction received a stimulus from the Reformation's demand for a better clergy and a more moral laity. Probate remained a vital ecclesiastical preserve until it was removed into a new secular

---

[1] There is now a sizable body of work on this subject. Cf. esp. Woodcock, *Medieval Eccl. Courts*; Houlbrooke, *Church Courts* (with an exhaustive bibliography); Lander, *Continuity and Change*, 215 ff.

[2] Holdsworth, IV, 488 ff.

[3] *Ibid.*, IV, 232, 238.

court in 1857.[4] The courts could inflict only three punishments—forbidding attendance at church, and lesser and greater excommunication—but since all these were redeemable by penance the infliction of various forms of penance (quite often commuted for money payments) is a frequent entry in the records.

In theory the activity and effectiveness of this jurisdiction, vigorous in the later middle ages, continued unabated throughout the sixteenth century. With the Reformation, of course, the courts lost their independence, becoming subject to the authority of the king as supreme head and, more significantly, to that of statutes made by the king-in-Parliament.[5] Increasingly the secular courts interfered by means of prohibitions which arrested actions in the Courts Christian, especially in tithe cases. The courts' jurisdiction over heresy was taken over by the special commissions set up by the supreme head.[6] On the other hand, they appear to have increased their activity in the sphere of the laity's moral delinquencies, in matrimonial causes, and in the probate of testaments. In early-Tudor England, fear and dislike of the courts played its part in the age's notorious anticlericalism, with heresy and tithe the issues that caused most trouble.[7] Their jurisdiction interfered in the private lives of the laity; their procedure differed from that of the common law, and though it was not so different from that of the conciliar courts it was conducted in incomprehensible Latin; they were held to be particularly oppressive and expensive; and it was freely alleged that vexatious suits promoted by clerics or even by counsel eager for business were common. The archdeacons' courts, ever the authority which impinged most directly on people at large, employed themselves in enforcing the standards which we call puritan and thus maintained their unpopularity.[8] How far the whole system deserved the evil reputation enshrined in the pamphlet literature remains uncertain, but that the laity did not love it need not be doubted.[9] Despite the courts' continued and ever increasing activity, it looks very much as though they came to be less regarded as time went on, especially by the laity. Not all of them were so sunk in corruption as those of Gloucester in the reign of Elizabeth,[10] but as the secular courts ceased to assist them in their decisions they seem generally to have passed into a state of abstraction—active in a vacuum, vexatious but no longer dangerous or

[4] Holdsworth, I, 73*, 629; and especially Woodcock, *Medieval Ecclesiastical Courts*, 79 ff.
[5] Cf. Houlbrooke's summaries: pp. 83 ff., 114 ff., 148 ff., 266 ff.
[6] Below, sect. II.
[7] For heresy cf. the Commons' Supplication of 1532 (**170**) and Cooper, *Eng. Hist. Rev.*, LXXII, 636 ff. For tithe cf. Elton, *Star Chamber Stories*, 174 ff.; Hill, *Economic Problems*, 77 ff.; Purvis, *Select Tithe Causes*.
[8] Anglin, *Tudor Men and Institutions*, 171 ff.
[9] Bowker, *Trans. R. Hist. Soc.*, 1971, 61 ff., argues that the courts owed their unpopularity to their effectiveness, not their corruption: but that still leaves them unpopular.
[10] Cf. Price, *Eng. Hist. Rev.*, LVII, 106 ff.; *Church Quarterly Review*, CXXVIII, 94 ff.

powerful. Probate jurisdiction must be excepted from this; that remained real and important enough.

The courts composed a reasonably ordered hierarchy.[11] At the bottom was the archdeacon's court, kept by him for his archdeaconry. From there lay an appeal to the bishop's or consistory court, which, however, also had a jurisdiction in first instance. The consistory court met under the bishop's deputy or 'official', usually his chancellor; the bishop retained a power to withdraw cases from the court and hear them in person. Certain parishes in a diocese enjoyed exemption from episcopal jurisdiction; these were known as peculiars and came under specially constituted courts of their own.[12] Above this diocesan organisation there stood the provincial organisation of the archbishop. Each province contained three metropolitan courts. The archbishop of Canterbury heard appeals from the diocesan courts (including the consistory court of the diocese of Canterbury presided over by his commissary-general) and entertained pleas of first instance in a court, originally called the Court of Canterbury, which came to be known as the Court of the Arches because it met in the London church of St Mary-le-Bow over a row of arches. Its president was the archbishop's official principal, also named dean of the Arches.[13] The York equivalent was known as the archbishop's Court of Chancery. Both archbishops also had Courts of Audience, originally an expression of their residual judicial authority and essentially courts of appeal; by the later middle ages what had been an informal supervisory and personal activity had become formalised in a true court under a professional judge. Lastly, each archbishop claimed a special (prerogative) jurisdiction in probate where the property bequeathed belonged into more than one diocese; for this business there existed the Prerogative Courts of Canterbury and York.[14]

The Church courts were thus sufficiently organised—even over-organised —up to provincial level, but no English authority completed the pyramid by hearing appeals from both provinces. Canterbury's ancient claim to primacy over York had never been admitted in matters of jurisdiction, though when a will came up for probate covering both provinces (a longstanding bone of contention) Canterbury usually won. Down to the Reformation the lack was remedied by the universal authority of the court of Rome which heard English cases both by appeal from one of the parties and by provocation or the calling up to Rome of a case depending in a lower court, a privilege obtained by a litigant for heavy payments. The Act of Appeals of 1533 (**177**) cut off this

[11] Holdsworth, I, 68* ff., 599 ff.

[12] Cf. Holdsworth, I, 600.

[13] Originally the dean of the Arches was the official in charge of the archbishop's court for his thirteen London peculiars; but the two courts, sitting in the same place, coalesced and in the fifteenth century the two judgeships came to be merged.

[14] Kitching, *Continuity and Change*, 191 ff.

further appeal from the archbishop's court whose decision was to be final in private suits; in cases involving the Crown an appeal to the upper house of Convocation was permitted. This proved unsatisfactory, and next year the Act for the Submission of the Clergy (**175**) provided for appeals in private cases to a commission out of Chancery, that is to the Crown.[15] Such a commission, specially appointed and therefore different for each appeal, was known as the High Court of Delegates; it tended to consist of ecclesiastical lawyers only, though at first bishops and judges were sometimes added.[16] In 1833 this cumbrous machinery was replaced by the Judicial Committee of the Privy Council.

II. THE HIGH COMMISSION

By the side of the ordinary Church courts there existed throughout special courts created by commissions under royal letters patent.[17] In the reign of Elizabeth such commissions issued irregularly for particular dioceses, while permanent courts were set up from 1559 for the two provinces of Canterbury (sitting at London) and York.[18] Both diocesan and provincial commissions acted independently for their territories; even the Canterbury High Commission in practice interfered rarely outside the province or with diocesan matters within it. These bodies were meant to strengthen the disciplinary machinery of the bishops and archbishops, so that unlike the ordinary ecclesiastical courts they usually acted upon their own initiatives, especially in major cases of disobedience. They have been described as the Church's criminal courts, civil matters—cases between party and party—being left to the normal machinery.[19] In the usual Tudor manner, private parties soon attempted to use the commissioners for their own purposes, but the consequent loss of business by the other courts led to steps being taken against the accepting of private suits, steps which, though never totally successful,

---

[15] It had at first been intended to include this provision in the act of appeals, but opposition from the Church forced the government to wait a year (Elton, *Studies*, II, 96 ff.).

[16] Duncan, *Delegates*.

[17] Usher's *High Commission*, a pioneer work when first published in 1913, is now known to be frequently wrong on the origins, history and functions of the institution. Nevertheless, it remains important but must be used in the 1968 reprint which contains an important corrective introduction by Philip Tyler. This exploits material not known to Usher, especially the act books of the Northern High Commission which survive nearly complete for the period 1561–1641: the importance of that discovery is obvious. In my view Tyler overstates the continuity between pre- and post-Reformation arrangements; that there was some is, however, true and important.

[18] The supposition that the Northern High Commission was identical with the Council of the North (Reid, *Council of the North*, 188, 194) has been disproved (Tyler's Introduction to Usher, p. ii). The Council in the Marches of Wales at times held commissions for ecclesiastical causes (Williams, *Council*, 88 ff.). For an example of a diocesan commission cf. Price, *Bristol & Glos. Transactions*, LIX, 61 ff.

[19] Tyler's Introduction to Usher, p. xxx.

nevertheless achieved something like a set of demarcation lines. The Commission courts, diocesan or provincial, in the main attended to enforcing the spiritual law upon transgressors, especially in heresy cases and notorious misbehaviour. They were thus much better suited than the bishops' consistory courts for the maintenance of uniformity in the Church, and for our understanding of that much debated subject it is very unfortunate that, except for those of the Northern High Commission, their records have nearly all vanished.

The Commissions were from the first proper courts, composed of both clergy and laity; they used the normal procedures of the Church courts but were more ruthless in the employment of oaths and cautionary imprisonment.[20] They were not linked one with another: no chain of appeals existed between them, or between them and the ordinary courts.[21] Their powers, which were very wide, they derived solely from the letters patent setting them up. That is to say, they emanated from the Crown, but the question is whether the Crown possessed such powers only as a consequence of the creation of the royal supremacy. The king's duty to assist in the enforcement of the spiritual law went back into pre-Reformation times, and examples of royal commissioning for such purposes can be found in the fourteenth and fifteenth centuries.[22] The very fact that Mary, in 1557, sought to assist the restoration of the papal obedience and Catholic orthodoxy by setting up such commissions sufficiently disposes of Usher's notion that the power to commission in matters ecclesiastical sprang solely from the Reformation.[23] However, as in most things to do with the royal supremacy, the case is by no means clear-cut. Though Elizabeth's first commission of 1559 (**103**)[24] copied an established form also used by her sister, it embodied a determination to provide for the royal rule over the Church where Mary had been merely concerned to extirpate heresy. Furthermore, the 1559 Act of Supremacy (**184**) complicated things when it expressly authorised the queen, 'by virtue of this act', to appoint commissions for the exercise of the spiritual jurisdiction.[25] It was later held that this only confirmed powers inherent in the Crown and did not constitute a parliamentary grant,[26] and at first sight this might equate Elizabeth's commissioning activity with what her pre-Reformation ancestors had occasionally practised. However, the view expressed in that decision arose from the assumption that the royal supremacy was immemorially inherent: the powers spoken of belonged to those which the Crown had

---

[20] Usher, *High Commission*, 56 ff., was wrong in supposing that regular courts grew by stages out of commissions acting as visitors rather than judges.

[21] *Ibid.*, 96 ff.   [22] Tyler's Introduction to Usher, pp. xiii seqq.

[23] Usher, *High Commission*, 23.

[24] Changes of personnel and policy compelled periodic reissues (cf. the list, *ibid.*, 361 ff., and extracts in Prothero, 232 ff.) but until 1611 none in the terms of the commission.

[25] Below, p. 374.   [26] Below, p. 231.

'restored' to itself under Henry VIII. In other words, Elizabethan opinion viewed the royal control over the spiritual jurisdiction as something recovered from the papacy and thus as essentially different from the support given to papally derived powers before 1534. To this extent—which in practice is both fundamental and total—the commissions issued by Elizabeth originated in the royal supremacy and differed entirely from any commissions issued by monarchs not claiming the supreme headship. In addition, the mention of this power in a statute did introduce parliamentary authority into the Crown's powers (however determinedly Elizabeth endeavoured to avoid that conclusion), opened the way to the testing of their exercise in the courts, and ultimately facilitated their destruction in 1641.[27]

The problem is further complicated by the confusion between judicial and visitatorial functions, a confusion found in Usher's book where it is more venial than Tyler, for instance, seems to think.[28] The two cannot really be kept separate, as the position taken by Thomas Cromwell indicates. From first obtaining the supremacy in the Church, Henry VIII had found it convenient to devolve its functions upon others by delegation, but when he made Cromwell his deputy he bestowed upon him two separate offices whose conjunction shows that they were necessarily associated, but whose separation indicates that clearer distinctions should be made than usually are. As the king's vicar-general, Cromwell possessed general powers of visitation which he used to investigate the monasteries in preparation for their destruction; as the king's vicegerent in spirituals he held the powers of a supreme judge in causes ecclesiastical which he embodied in a regular court. That the vicegerent's court existed and acted in cases both promoted by itself and brought by parties is sufficiently proved even by the pitiful evidence which has managed to survive.[29] It was modelled on the court which Wolsey set up as legate for all England (and especially copied its model by its interference with the probate jurisdiction of the episcopal courts), because like Wolsey's legateship the vicegerency was designed to provide a single unifying authority over the two provinces of the English Church. No one after Cromwell ever again occupied that position, but that did not dispose of the need to give effect to the Crown's supremacy throughout the realm. This need was not well served either by the ordinary ecclesiastical organisation or by the system of particular commissions. Out of this deficiency grew the claims of the Canterbury Commission, always equipped with powers that extended

[27] In 1580, the Privy Council, writing to Grindal, spoke of the queen's 'Commission Ecclesiastical warranted by the laws of this realm' (Usher, *High Commission*, 49), a phrasing which shows that the powers were thought to rest on both prerogative and statute. No such phrasing could have been employed before 1559.

[28] Tyler's Introduction to Usher, p. xxi.

[29] Elton, *Reform and Renewal*, 134 f.; *Policy and Police*, 247 f. Cf. also Lehmberg, *Eng. Hist. Rev.*, LXXXI, 225 ff.

beyond its provincial boundaries, to act as *the* High Commission.[30] Though this territorial reach may not often have been brought into action, it always existed as an available potential. And part of the High Commission's claim to authority consisted in its link with royal visitations. While indeed it took separate commissions to carry these out,[31] it was the Court of High Commission that used the material discovered in its initiatives against suspects and evildoers. If the Cromwellian example had ever been followed, the manner in which the two functions inescapably linked together would have remained plainer.

There is thus much justice in the traditional view which treated the High Commission of the Province of Canterbury as the supreme high court of the English Church. The court was certainly useful. It was ready to entertain pleas which were either pending or had been decided elsewhere as though they had never been heard, and grieved or impatient parties freely took advantage of this. Its wide competence included all matters affecting the Church as well as the traditional moral jurisdiction of the spiritual courts, except that it applied to persons only; the court could not deal with matters touching property, even such ecclesiastical property as tithe or Church lands.[32] It offered remedies *in forma pauperis* and it offered speed, qualities which were particularly welcome because litigation in the Church courts tended to be even more expensive and dilatory than in the lay courts. Moreover, it could inflict punishments not available to the ordinary courts Christian; it could fine and imprison. In an age increasingly contemptuous of spiritual sanctions such powers were useful and made the court attractive to the winning side. It carried the authority of the Crown and could depend upon the support of Star Chamber and Privy Council at a time when the ordinary courts were losing whatever hold they had once had over the lay power. In fact, it did for the Crown's ecclesiastical jurisdiction very much what Star Chamber did on the secular side; and like Star Chamber it was barred from the ultimate issues and punishments. In theory, at least, excommunication (the death of the soul) was worse than any fine or imprisonment; and in good solid fact the High Commission's inability to touch property deprived it of a vital field of action.

Popular with many, it was however hated by some, especially after Whitgift turned it into the chief instrument for his war on nonconformity (1583). Its political activity against Puritanism naturally provoked counterattacks, and the alliance between Puritanism and the common law was in part assisted by

[30] All the commissions for Canterbury spoke of all England, and some mentioned Ireland as well. Usher was right in treating the Southern Commission as one for the province of Canterbury, but wrong to ignore the fact that its powers enabled it to cover the other province too.
[31] Tyler's Introduction to Usher, pp. xxiii seqq.
[32] For the details of High Commission's jurisdiction cf. Usher, *High Commission*, 102 ff.

their joint dislike of an institution which harried the one and encroached upon the other.[33] The attacks tended to concentrate not upon the court itself—this would have meant questioning the authority of both queen and statute—but upon aspects of its procedure, and especially upon its use of oaths and its power to imprison. Procedure[34] in the court began with articles put in either by a plaintiff (in private suits—*ex officio promoto*) or on behalf of the Commission (in a case started by the court—*ex officio mero*). The accused was then summoned by letters missive and, before knowing the charges, compelled to take an oath (the *ex officio* oath) that he would truthfully answer everything that was to be preferred against him. Although Star Chamber, for instance, demanded answers and depositions on oaths taken beforehand,[35] selfincrimination in matters of heresy or ecclesiastical dissent had so much more devastating consequences that the *ex officio* oath became the chief stumbling block to enemies of the High Commission. It worked both ways, as was discovered in Cartwright's case in 1591–2: if the accused refused to take the oath the whole procedure of the court, which depended upon it, came to a standstill. The court possessed only one means of compelling a man to plead: it could imprison him for contempt until he should surrender and swear. But this did not always work; Puritans were notoriously obstinate in such matters, and in any case such action only produced a further attack which questioned the court's power to commit on the grounds that it had no authority to do so.

Ultimately, therefore, the hostility of Puritans and common lawyers was bound to result in a general assault on the court's activity, and in 1591 the whole problem was brought into the open in Cawdrey's Case.[36] Cawdrey was a Puritan clergyman who had been deprived for nonconformity by the High Commission and later brought a Queen's Bench action for trespass against his successor in the benefice. The details of his plea may be read elsewhere; its essence was that the High Commission had exceeded the powers it possessed under the Act of Supremacy. By taking his case to common law he was also inviting the judges to claim a supervisory function over High Commission in a matter which beyond question was purely spiritual. He lost his case, and the judges in their decision went a long way to approve and define

---

[33] For the opposition under Elizabeth cf. *ibid.*, 121 ff. Burghley's famous charge that the High Commission behaved too much like 'the Romish Inquisition' (Tanner, 373 f.) shows how widespread dislike of its proceedings could be. But he exaggerated.

[34] Cf. Usher, 106 ff., for the full details. Essentially procedure in spiritual courts was not dissimilar to that of the conciliar courts (though the technical terms differed), which is small wonder since both rested on that of the Roman law. It was, however, exclusively in writing, secret, and dependent upon oaths to an extent which Star Chamber, influenced by the common law, did not copy.

[35] Bayne, *Council of Henry VII*, pp. xciv seqq., shows that the Star Chamber employed something like an *ex officio* oath, but that (since the court did not touch life or property) a defendant was 'not bound to answer questions which . . . touched him in life or limb'.

[36] 104; discussed at length by Usher, *High Commission*, 79 ff. and 136 ff.

the authority of the Court of High Commission. They maintained that the 1559 act, being declaratory, only affirmed the powers of the Crown without in any way circumscribing them. Virtually quoting the Act of Appeals (177) they spoke of the two jurisdictions of Church and state vested in the Crown and conceded that the queen could create ecclesiastical commissions by the prerogative. Consequently the powers of the commission would depend upon the terms of the letters patent, and these, as has been said, were about as wide as could be wished. Cawdrey's Case in effect established the Court of High Commission as a proper and lawful court, and it endured through further attacks until abolished in 1641. In the abolition, at least, the grant of authority included in the act of 1559 could be used to full effect.[37]

103. The ecclesiastical commission of 1559.

I. Elizabeth by the grace of God, etc., to the reverend father in God Matthew Parker, nominated bishop of Canterbury, and Edmund Grindal, nominated bishop of London, and to our right trusted and right well-beloved councillors, Francis Knowles our vice-chamberlain and Ambrose Cave, knights, and to our trusty and well-beloved Anthony Cooke and Thomas Smith, knights, William Bill our almoner, Walter Haddon and Thomas Sackford, masters of our requests, Rowland Hill and William Chester, knights, Randall Cholmely and John Southcote, serjeants-at-the-law, William May, doctor of law, Francis Cave, Richard Goodrich and Gilbert Gerard, esquires, Robert Weston and Thomas Huick, doctors of law, greeting.

II. Where at our Parliament holden at Westminster the 25th day of January . . . there was two acts and statutes made and established[38] . . . and where divers seditious and slanderous persons do not cease daily to invent and set forth false rumours, tales and seditious slanders, not only against us and the said good laws and statutes, but also have set forth divers seditious books within this our realm of England, meaning thereby to move and procure strife, division and dissension amongst

---

[37] The judgment in Cawdrey's Case seems to me to have evaded the question whether the granting of authority by the Act of Supremacy affected the liberty of the prerogative in this matter (cf. below, p. 231). But since the judges were really asked to decide the powers rather than the basis of ecclesiastical commissions, their caution on the point was natural. What is less acceptable is the interpretation of Tudor *dicta* as confirming that the commissions emanated from 'the traditional duty of the Crown to safeguard the Church and the Christian community' (Tyler's Introduction to Usher, esp. p. xxiv). In its endeavour to downgrade the Reformation, this interpretation simply swallows Tudor propaganda. The powers which the judges held to be 'declared' in 1559 were those of the royal supremacy (as the act itself makes plain), treated in doctrine as always inherent in the Crown but, in historical truth, acquired by it only in 1534. The judges spoke of powers that before the Reformation had not existed.

[38] I.e. the Act of Supremacy and Uniformity.

our loving and obedient subjects, much to the disquieting of us and our people.

III. Wherefore we, earnestly minding to have the same acts before mentioned to be duly put in execution, and such persons as shall hereafter offend in anything contrary to the tenor and effect of the said several statutes to be condignly punished; and having especial trust and confidence in your wisdoms and discretions, have authorised, assigned and appointed you to be our commissioners, and by these presents do give our full power and authority to you, or six of you, whereof you the said Matthew Parker, Edmund Grindal, Thomas Smith, Walter Haddon, Thomas Sackford, Richard Goodrich, and Gilbert Gerard to be one, from time to time hereafter during our pleasure to enquire, as well by the oaths of twelve good and lawful men as also by witnesses and other ways and means ye can devise, for all offences, misdoers and misdemeanours done and committed, and hereafter to be committed or done, contrary to the tenor and effect of the said several acts and statutes and either of them; and also of all and singular heretical opinions, seditious books, contempts, conspiracies, false rumours, tales, seditions, misbehaviours, slanderous words or showings, published, invented or set forth . . . by any person or persons against us, or contrary or against . . . the quiet government and rule of our people and subjects, in any county, city, borough or other place or places within this our realm of England, and of all and every the coadjutors, counsellors, comforters, procurers and abettors of every such offender.

IV. And further, we do give power and authority to you or six of you . . . from time to time hereafter during our pleasure, as well to hear and determine all the premises as also to enquire, hear and determine all and singular enormities, disturbances and misbehaviours done and committed, or hereafter to be done and committed, in any church or chapel, or against any divine service or the minister or ministers of the same, contrary to the laws and statutes of this realm; and also to enquire of, search out, and to order, correct and reform all such persons as hereafter shall or will obstinately absent themselves from church and such divine service as by the laws and statutes of this realm is appointed to be had and used.

V. And also we do give and grant full power and authority unto you and six of you . . . from time to time and at all times during our pleasure to visit, reform, redress, order, correct and amend, in all places within this our realm of England, all such errors, heresies, crimes, abuses, offences, contempts and enormities, spiritual and ecclesiastical, where-soever [*sic*], which by any spiritual or ecclesiastical power, authority or jurisdiction can or may lawfully be reformed, ordered, redressed, corrected, restrained or amended, to the pleasure of Almighty God, the increase of virtue, and the conservation of the peace and unity of this our realm, and according to the authority and power limited, given and appointed by any laws or statutes of this realm.

vi. And also that you and six of you . . . shall likewise have full power and authority from time to time to enquire and search out [all masterless] men, quarrellers, vagrant and suspect persons within our city of London and ten miles compass about the same city, and of all assaults and affrays done and committed within the same city and compass aforesaid.

vii. And also we give full power and authority unto you and six of you, as before, summarily to hear and finally to determine, according to your discretions and by the laws of this realm, all causes and complaints of all them which in respect of religion, or for lawful matrimony contracted and allowed by the same, were injuriously deprived, defrauded or spoiled of their lands, goods, possessions, rights, dignities, livings, offices, spiritual or temporal; and them so deprived, as before, to restore into their said livings and to put them in possession, amoving the usurpers in convenient speed, as it shall seem to your discretions good, by your letters missive or otherwise; all frustatory appellations clearly rejected.

viii. And further, we do give power and authority unto you and six of you . . . by virtue hereof not only to hear and determine the same and all other offences and matters before mentioned and rehearsed, but also all other notorious and manifest advoutries, fornications, and ecclesiastical crimes and offences within this our realm, according to your wisdoms, consciences and discretions.

ix. Willing and commanding you or six of you . . . from time to time hereafter to use and devise all such politic ways and means for the trial and searching out of all the premises as by you or six of you, as aforesaid, shall be thought most expedient and necessary; and upon due proof had, and the offence or offences before specified, or any of them, sufficiently proved against any person or persons by confession of the party or by lawful witnesses or by any due mean, before you or six of you . . . that then you or six of you, as aforesaid, shall have full power and authority to award such punishment to every offender by fine, imprisonment or otherwise, by all or any of the ways aforesaid, and to take such order for the redress of the same as to your wisdoms and discretions [shall be thought meet and convenient].[39]

x. [And further we do give full power and authority unto you] or six of you . . . to call before you or six of you, as aforesaid, from time to time all and every offender or offenders, and such as by you or six of you, as aforesaid, shall seem to be suspect persons in any of the premises; and also all such witnesses as you or six of you, as aforesaid, shall think [meet] to be called before you or six of you, as aforesaid; and them and every of them to examine upon their corporal oath, for the better trial and opening of the premises or any part thereof.

xi. And if you or six of you, as aforesaid, shall find any person or persons obstinate or disobedient, either in their appearance before you or six of you, as aforesaid, at your calling and commandment, or else not accomplishing or not obeying your order, decrees and commandments in anything touching the premises or any part thereof; that then you or six of you, as aforesaid, shall have full power and authority to commit the same person or persons so offending to ward, there to remain until he or they shall be by you or six of you, as aforesaid, enlarged and delivered.

xii. And further we do give unto you and six of you . . . full power and authority by these presents to take and receive by your discretions of every offender or suspect person to be convented or brought before you a recognisance or recognisances, obligation or obligations, to our use, in such sum or sums of money as to you or six of you, as aforesaid, shall seem convenient, as well for their personal appearance before you or six of you, as aforesaid, as also for the performance and accomplishment of your orders and decrees, in case you or six of you, as aforesaid, shall see it so convenient.

xiii. And further, our will and pleasure is that you shall appoint our trusty and well-beloved John Skinner to be your register of all your acts, decrees and proceedings by virtue of this commission, and in his default one other sufficient person, and that you or six of you, as aforesaid, shall give such allowance to the same register for his pains and his clerks, to be levied of the fines and other profits that shall rise by force of this commission and your doings in the premises, as to your discretions shall be thought meet.

[39] In order to make sense of this and the next clause it is necessary to adopt the emendations suggested in Prothero, 230.

xiv. And further, our will and pleasure is that you or six of you, as aforesaid, shall name and appoint one other sufficient person to gather up and receive all such sums of money as shall be assessed and taxed by you or six of you, as aforesaid, for any fine or fines upon any person or persons for their offences; and that you or six of you, as aforesaid, by bill or bills signed with your hands, shall and may assign and appoint, as well to the said person for his pains in recovering the said sums as also to your messengers and attendants upon you for their travail, pains and charges to be sustained for or about the premises or any part thereof, such sums of money for their rewards as by you or six of you, as aforesaid, shall be thought expedient: willing and commanding you or six of you, as aforesaid, after the time of this our commission expired, to certify into our Court of Exchequer as well the name of the said receiver as also a note of such fines as shall be set or taxed before you; to the intent that upon the determination of the account of the said receiver we be assured of that that to us shall justly appertain: willing and commanding also our auditors and other officers, upon the sight of the said bills signed with the hand of you or six of you, as aforesaid, to make unto the said receiver due allowances according to the said bills upon his accounts.

xv. Wherefore we will and command you our commissioners with diligence to execute the premises with effect; any of our laws, statutes, proclamations, or other grants, privileges or ordinances which be or may seem to be contrary to the premises notwithstanding.

xvi. And more, we will and command all and singular justices of the peace, mayors, sheriffs, bailiffs, constables and other our officers, ministers and faithful subjects to be aiding, helping and assisting, and at your commandment in the due execution hereof, as they tender our pleasure and will answer to the contrary at their utmost perils.

xvii. And we will and grant that these our letters patents shall be a sufficient warrant and discharge for you and every of you against us, our heirs and successors, and all and every other person or persons, whatsoever they be, of and for or concerning the premises or any parcel hereof, of or for the execution of this our commission or any part thereof. Witness the Queen at Westminster, the 19th day of July.

PER IPSAM REGINAM.

Prothero, *Select Statutes*, 227-32

104. Cawdrey's Case, 1591.

. . . It was resolved, That the said act of the first year of the said late Queen concerning ecclesiastical jurisdiction was not a statute introductory of a new law, but declaratory of the old; which appeareth as well by the title of the said act, viz., 'An act restoring to the Crown the ancient jurisdiction over the state ecclesiastical and spiritual, etc.,' as also by the body of the act in divers parts thereof.[40] For that act doth not annex any jurisdiction to the Crown but that which in truth was, or of right ought to be, by the ancient laws of the realm parcel of the King's jurisdiction and united to his imperial crown, and which lawfully had been or might be exercised within the realm; the end of which jurisdiction and of all the proceeding thereupon was, that all things might be done in causes ecclesiastical to the pleasure of Almighty God, the increase of virtue, and the conservation of the peace and unity of this realm, as by divers parts of the said act appeareth. And therefore as by that act no pretended jurisdiction exercised within this realm, being either ungodly or repugnant to the prerogative or the ancient law of the Crown of this realm, was or could be restored to the same Crown, according to the ancient right and law of the same, so that if that act of the first year of the late Queen had never been made, it was resolved by all the judges that the King or Queen of England for the time being may make such an ecclesiastical commission as is before mentioned, by the ancient prerogative and law of England. And therefore by the ancient laws of this realm this kingdom of England is an absolute empire and monarchy consisting of one head, which is the King, and of a body politic compact and compounded of many and almost infinite several and yet well agreeing members; all which the law divideth into two general parts, that is to say, the clergy and the laity, both of them, next and immediately under God, subject and obedient unto the head. Also the kingly head of this politic body is instituted and furnished with plenary and entire power, prerogative and jurisdiction to render justice and right to every part and member of this body, of what estate, degree or calling soever, in all causes ecclesiastical or temporal, otherwise he should not be a head of the whole body. And as in temporal causes the King by the mouth of the judges in his courts of justice doth judge and determine the same by the temporal laws of England, so in causes ecclesiastical and spiritual, as namely blasphemy, apostasy

[40] Doc. 184.

from Christianity, heresies, schisms, ordering admissions, institutions of clerks, celebration of divine service, rights of matrimony, divorces, general bastardy, subtraction and right of tithes, oblations, obventions, dilapidations, reparation of churches, probate of testaments, administrations and accounts upon the same, simony, incests, fornications, adulteries, solicitation of chastity, pensions, procurations, appeals in ecclesiastical causes, commutation of penance, and others (the conusance whereof belong not to the common laws of England) the same are to be determined and decided by ecclesiastical judges, according to the King's ecclesiastical laws of this realm. . . .   Coke, *Fifth Report*, 344-5

CHAPTER 8

PARLIAMENT[1]

I. THE NATURE OF PARLIAMENT AND STATUTE

By the early sixteenth century Parliament was an accepted part of the constitution, a known and established element in the king's government, though not as yet a regular or necessary part.[2] Strictly it is wrong to speak of Parliament; there were only Parliaments, each meeting, called and ended by the Crown, having its own identity. No one then supposed that Parliaments should meet as regularly as, for instance, the law courts, though that sort of notion had prevailed in the early days when Parliament was little more than the king's most eminent court. By 1485 it was taken for granted that Parliament met occasionally and only if it was needed for a special purpose, usually the granting of money; both Henry VII and Elizabeth took credit to themselves for not overburdening their subjects with frequent meetings.[3] It must not be thought that longish intermissions between Parliaments implied a deliberate attempt to suppress the institution. It is possible that Wolsey, who could not manage Parliament, would have welcomed its lapse; and Elizabeth, who had to deal with Parliaments very different from her grandfather's, looks at times to have so conducted her affairs that she could keep sessions to a minimum. Only Henry VIII, after 1529, displayed absolutely no reluctance to meet his subjects in Parliament, and he had special advantages in complete self-assurance and considerable unity of purpose. But no Tudor ever supposed that he would call no more Parliaments. In the twenty-four years of Henry VII there met seven Parliaments sitting for a total of about sixty weeks; in Henry VIII's thirty-seven years, nine Parliaments, one of which had seven sessions, assembled for 183 weeks (five of them comprising 136 weeks, met in the last eighteen years of the reign); Edward VI in six years summoned two Parliaments which sat for five sessions and forty-six weeks; Mary in her four years faced five Parliaments, totalling twenty-eight weeks; and in her forty-five years Elizabeth called ten Parliaments which met for rather less than 140 weeks altogether in their thirteen sessions.

This intermittent institution was generally described as a court—the king's High Court of Parliament. The medieval Parliament had certainly been very frequently a true court; in its beginning it had often been the occasion for

---

[1] The history of the Tudor Parliament is at present in flux. The interpretation associated with Sir John Neale has collapsed, and the revised views are still emerging. My account here therefore relies in part on my own unfinished researches.

[2] Cf. Elton, *Studies*, II, 19 ff., for a general survey; and *Hist. Journal*, XXII, 255 ff., for a new look at the role of Parliament. [3] Pickthorn, I, 97; Neale, *House of Commons*, 381.

dispensing the king's justice in doubtful, novel or urgent cases, and in the fifteenth century a theoretical definition of the assembly as a court grew universal.[4] However, the purely curial character of the earlier Parliament has been exaggerated; its form and nomenclature might be those of a court, but it also—and perhaps primarily—discharged political functions.[5] More particularly, far too much has been made of the idea that medieval Parliaments could not make law but merely declare it. It is more significant, as we shall see, that until the Tudor period Parliament's 'judgments'—which like all judgments could make as well as declare law—were not thought of as essentially different from those of other courts. If medieval Parliaments did not legislate, much in the *Rolls of Parliament* becomes incomprehensible; and so does the further development of legislative functions in the sixteenth century. Of course, in that age, too, oldfashioned talk of Parliament as a court was common. As late as 1550 a chief justice of Common Pleas could call it 'nothing but a court',[6] though the stress he placed on his aside makes one wonder if he was perhaps contradicting a novel view that it was a great deal more. Concentration on name-calling obscures the issues.[7] The sixteenth-century Parliament was much less of a court than its predecessors, in part because it was never used as one: its functions in the settlement of legal difficulties (if they did not require legislation) were discharged by the new conciliar courts, and no occasion arose for the trial of great offenders by impeachment.

In fact, after much revision and new research, it remains evident that a marked change came over the nature of Parliament as a consequence of the long and vital sessions of the Reformation Parliament (1529–36), and that this change remains hard to describe except by resorting to the traditional phrases about the emergence of a true legislative assembly.[8] Even before 1529 Parliament had often discussed matters of moment (**107**), though never anything quite so overwhelming as the Reformation; this was an ancient thing, for from Edward I's reign onwards kings of England, like other kings, had often called their Parliaments because they wanted advice on 'great matters'. Parliamentary statute had long been regarded as the highest expression of law in the realm. Nevertheless, the changes produced by the 1530's gave to Parliament a permanent place of political importance and, so to speak, finally incorporated it in the English system of government; they recognised the

[4] The classic argument for Parliament as a court is found in McIlwain, *High Court*; for the fifteenth century cf. Chrimes, *Constitutional Ideas*, 70 ff.

[5] Edwards, *Bull. Inst. Hist. Research*, XXVII, 35 ff.

[6] Quoted by McIlwain, *Constitutionalism Ancient and Modern*, 116.

[7] Cf. Tanner, 511: some of his examples, moreover, show the House of Commons claiming to be a court in itself, a very different matter from the traditional notion of the whole Parliament as the king's court.

[8] Cf., *inter alia*, Pollard, *History*, 1936–7, 219 ff.

principle of legislation and extended the operation of statute virtually to omnicompetence; and they resulted in the emergence of the modern Parliament, its three parts all equally necessary to its authority. Smith's description of the powers of Parliament (105), though it includes both legislative and ostensibly curial functions, in practice recognises it as a body which makes laws overriding all other laws.

This opinion, dear to Tudor historians, has not pleased medievalists who rightly regard the pre-Tudor Parliaments as both institutionally well developed and politically effective enough.[9] The disagreement has in the main arisen because traditional discussions of Parliament have seized on the wrong point: they have concentrated on the Commons and their supposed role in limiting the power of the Crown, instead of looking at the whole body (king, Lords and Commons) and its proper function in giving effect to the common will in legislation.[10] As maintainers of conflict with the monarch, Tudor Parliaments probably did less well than many a medieval assembly, but that means only that political life was a little more settled and political strife took place elsewhere. As bearers of legislative sovereignty they acquired a 'modern' competence for which pre-Tudor events had been a preparation, no more. The history of the institution's records offers a guide to better understanding. Between the accession of Henry VII and the end of Wolsey's rule, the Roll of Parliament (the old master-record) lost all significance; the Lords acquired a Journal and the Commons a clerk's book, and the printed sessional statute came to define the legislation passed.[11] During these same years the old imbalance between the two Houses was redressed as the Lords came to treat the Commons with the same courtesy that they had hitherto expected from the Lower House;[12] a High Court of Parliament, in which the Commons brought the grievances of the realm before the Lords sitting as a Council, was replaced by a legislative body containing two equipollent chambers. This was therefore a formative period, and the long endurance of the Reformation Parliament (1529–36) brought these incipient transformations to a conclusion, especially by so noticeably enlarging the omnicompetence of parliamentary statute.[13]

In the first place, Parliament acquired an entirely new reputation. By the beginning of Elizabeth's reign, Smith (105) ascribed to it 'the most high and absolute power in the realm', and even before this Aylmer saw in it the 'image' of England's government (8). A legal writer, though he calls it 'the

---

[9] Cf. esp. Roskell, *Bull. John Rylands Library*, XLVI, 448 ff.

[10] For the argument against the concentration on political conflict cf. Elton, *Studies*, II, 7 ff.; *Trans. R. Hist. Soc.*, 1974, 183 ff.; *Hist. Journal*, XXII, 257 ff. Cf. also Russell, *History*, LXI, 1 ff.

[11] Elton, *Eng. Hist. Rev.*, LXXXIX, 481 ff.; *Hist. Journal*, XXII, 1 ff; *Wealth and Power*, 68 ff. For the Commons' book, which does not survive before 1547, cf. 140.

[12] Elton, *Studies*, 53 ff.

[13] For the Henrician Parliaments cf. Lehmberg, *Reformation Parliament* and *Later Parliaments*.

most ancient court', asserts that its authority 'is absolute' (that is, subject to no one's control) 'and bindeth all manner of persons'.[44] The overriding authority of Parliament was a commonplace by the second half of the century. So also was the reason advanced for it: Parliament was supreme and bound all men because in it all members of the realm, from the king downwards, were regarded as being present—they are 'privy and parties' to all its doings.[15] It is interesting and possibly significant that there is no trace of such a view in Edmund Dudley's *Tree of Commonwealth* (1509), though the writer's intention was to stress the organic unity of king and realm. But in 1525 a common councillor of London told Wolsey that Richard III's acts were good despite that king's delinquency because they were made 'by the consent of the body of the whole realm, which is the Parliament'.[16] In 1542 Henry VIII hinted at the notion when he spoke of all members of the Parliament, himself included, being 'knit together in one body politic' (129). One of the significant steps taken in incorporating parts of his dominions in the unitary kingdom being built in his reign consisted in asking these hitherto separate territories (Wales, Chester, Calais) to send elected members to Parliament.

Thus the notion of the king's high court whose decisions overrode everything else precisely because it was the king's ultimate seat of judgment, gave way before the developed idea of a representative institution—king-in-Parliament (three partners in one body)—whose decisions bound everyone because everyone was present in it either in person or by proxy. At the same time statute came to be seen as an expression of free legislative authority, and the limitations surrounding it came to be removed. As late as 1495, the *de facto* Act (2) had implicitly denied the free authority of Parliament by prohibiting its own repeal in any later assembly. Politically speaking, the prohibition was of course meaningless, though it was probably provoked by political considerations: the reassurances embodied in the act would look better still if doubts about the future could be thus ruled out. But that such a statement—so pointless by the standards even of the later sixteenth century[17]—could be included strongly suggests that at this time it was still possible to treat a judgment in Parliament as final because it made immutable law. Whether the century ever arrived at a full doctrine of legislative sovereignty vested in the king-in-Parliament remains disputed because it depends whether one looks at the theorists or at the practitioners.[18] It is also noticeable

---

[14] *Discourse upon the Statutes*, 108.

[15] *Ibid*. So also Smith (105), Aylmer (8), Hooker (106), etc. The *Discourse* (p. 110) makes the old exception of tenants in ancient demesne (who did not take part in elections), but this was virtually a piece of antiquarianism (cf. *ibid.*, 13 ff.).

[16] Hall, *Chronicle*, 698.   [17] Cf. 112.

[18] Thus McIlwain (e.g. *Constitutionalism and the Changing World*, 26 ff.) denied any true theory of sovereignty before the seventeenth century because doctrines of fundamental law and the like tended to persist. But cf. for a different interpretation of the writers, Mosse, *Struggle for Sovereignty*, ch. 1.

that a rapid advance in that direction was arrested by the end of the century. But that an expansion of Parliamentary competence—an enlargement of the field touched by statute—occurred is beyond doubt. The best definition of the scope of statute (the positive law of the realm of England) as it stood on the eve of the Reformation is to be found in St German's *Doctor and Student* (**109**). High and even exalted as its place there is, it is subjected to a vital condition: it must be consonant with the law of nature (or reason) and the law of God. If one thing was quite certain before the Reformation it was that statute could not touch matters spiritual because by the law of God these were reserved to the Church. A notorious case of 1506 led to the dictum that Parliament cannot make the king a parson because 'no temporal act can . . . make a temporal man have spiritual jurisdiction'.[19] Yet after 1529 acts of Parliament habitually dealt with the spiritual jurisdiction exercised by the king (a layman) as supreme head, and though Parliament did not create this position it certainly altogether ignored the limitations which before 1529 no one had questioned. On a lesser plane it also liberated itself from bonds of rights properly established in law, for it constantly overrode title; though this had occasionally happened before, the exercise of such powers to sweep away all franchises came as near as no matter to asserting omnicompetence, a universal claim to obedience, and therefore full legislative sovereignty.[20]

People naturally recognised the problems raised by this sudden extension of Parliament's sphere and the power of statute. It was possible to take up one of three positions to it. A true conservative like Sir Thomas More (**110**) denied the validity of an act which went counter to the established law of Christendom; he held that there existed criteria for judging acts good (and therefore valid) or bad (and therefore void). The rather embarrassed ruling produced in reply by the lord chief justice suggests that he saw the point. Secondly, it was possible to agree with the general tenor of the Reformation statutes, to accept their claim that they were in accord with truth and God's law, and thus preserve the old sanctions in a changed world. That was the reaction of St German, overtaken by the Reformation in his eighties, who in 1535 could still assert that certain things, if done by Parliament, were void because they offended the law of God: 'for if the Parliament erred therein there were no man bounden to obey the Parliament in that behalf'.[21] Lastly, some men, as logical as More but as convinced as St German of the justness of the Reformation, could go very near to admitting full sovereignty and un-

[19] Quoted McIlwain, *High Court*, 277 f. The issue (property) was minor; the argument provoked by it led much further.

[20] Cf. above, p. 32, and docs. **17, 19**.

[21] St German, *Answer*, sig. B. VI. The argument maintains itself by making an ingenious but unconvincing distinction between things called spiritual which really are and others which are not, though so called. It causes no surprise to find that the second group includes all the points touched on in the Reformation statutes.

limited competence in statute. Cromwell not only based his practice on this conviction but hinted at a theoretical opinion in accord with it (**111**).[22] An act of 1534 explicitly denied that canon law (in which More saw the law of Christendom) had any validity in England unless accepted by the positive law;[23] statute stood above everything else. This last view, therefore, held that the sanction of a statute rested not in its being consonant with some other superior law but in the authority behind it, in the sovereign will of the legislative body. Statute was good, and therefore to be obeyed, if properly made, not if it fitted a moral scheme.

This view prevailed in practice, and statesmen so recognised it. Gardiner was no whit behind his enemy Cromwell in this, though it is true that he tried to use the overriding authority of an act of Parliament as a shelter for his resistance to Somerset's policy in 1547.[24] Mary was constrained to imply acknowledgment of the sovereignty of statute when she had to resort to Parliament for the abrogation of the royal supremacy, even though she regarded the title as inimical to the law divine and the statute affirming it as for that reason void.[25] According to James I, Burghley often remarked that he did not know what an act of Parliament could not do in England;[26] and when Bacon came to consider the quality of statute he called Parliament 'supreme and absolute' and recognised that a statute overrode everything until in its turn it might be overridden—but only by another statute (**112**). This was precisely the point made long before by lord chancellor Audley, in conversation with Gardiner, who 'never knew or read of any act of Parliament in this realm broken till the same had been by like authority of Parliament repealed'.[27] To all these men, and in practice to all Englishmen, any argument about limitation by abstract laws meant nothing once Parliament had been called upon to legislate widely in the spiritual sphere. That they did not speak of sovereignty and even continued to use the old formulae does not affect the practical sphere of statute,[28] the new authority and competence of Parliament, or the remarkable addiction to legislation which this release from old shackles called forth.[29]

There remained, however, one possible obstacle to Parliamentary sovereignty. Abstract laws might mean nothing, but the positive law of the realm was another matter. Statutes had to be applied, and in applying them the

---

[22] Cf. Elton, *Trans. R. Hist. Soc.*, 1956, 69 ff.

[23] 25 Henry VIII, c. 14. Canonical sanctions are here declared 'but human', i.e. they do not represent a superior law by which statute must be judged.

[24] *Letters*, 370, 377.

[25] Pollard, *Pol. Hist.*, 102; Muller, *Stephen Gardiner*, 226, 234.

[26] James I, *Political Works*, 329.

[27] *Gardiner's Letters*, 319 f.

[28] Cf. Hooker in **106**.

[29] Cf. Elton, *Reform and Renewal*, ch. 4.

judges might either refuse to admit a statute which, in their view, contradicted the existing law or contravened natural justice; or if they did not go so far, they might by 'interpretation' twist the statute out of all recognition.[30] Here, too, the constitutional changes of the 1530's made a profound difference. Down to that time the judges appear to have treated statute with respect but not as differing in essence from other judicial pronouncements.[31] In consequence they handled acts of Parliament with ease, needing no justification or argument in their modification and selective application. But after the Reformation the position changed. Now statute clearly bore a new force, and the judges were faced, for the first time, with the problem of authority involved in their practice of 'interpreting'. In consequence they began to make distinctions between affirmative statutes (which, not being destructive of existing rights, could be interpreted generously) and negative (which, being mandatory, required strict interpretation); or between 'penal', which punished and must be treated strictly, and 'beneficial' which assisted and merited expansion or contraction so as to procure their benefit for as many people as possible. Paradoxically enough, the new position of statute was itself responsible for equipping the judiciary with equitable powers of interpretation; they never thought it necessary to develop or define such powers as long as statute was no less subject to their freedom of decision than any other form of law. Medieval judges ignored or illtreated statutes which they thought might lead to injustice; Tudor and later judges, no longer able to act so cavalierly yet still constrained in the interests of justice to avoid rigid construction, resorted to a variety of definitions and rules to assist themselves out of the dilemma created by their novel respect for Parliament.

The most extreme control which the common law could exercise over the sovereignty of Parliament was to disallow an act altogether on grounds of natural reason or justice. This would have restored the principle that sanctions exist superior to the law of Parliament, and Coke is often regarded as having held this. However, it does not seem to be the case that such powers were claimed in the fifteenth century;[32] and, as we have seen, Audley, in the 1530's, regarded any statute as good until repealed by another. The view that in the sixteenth and seventeenth centuries statute was 'often' declared null

---

[30] All earlier discussions of the 'judicial interpretation' of statutes down to c. 1600 are superseded by S. E. Thorne's introduction to his edition of the *Discourse upon the Statutes*. This paragraph is based on it.

[31] *Ibid.* 9: 'Statutes were regarded in the courts as essentially isolated rulings, supplementing or modifying common law, enacted to aid the judiciary in deciding the questions of *meum et tuum* . . . as subsisting, like the rules of the common law itself, wholly within a private-law scheme.'

[32] McIlwain, *High Court*, 270 ff., thought they were; but he is effectively answered by Chrimes, *Constitutional Ideas*, 289 ff. On the other hand, Chrimes is probably mistaken in ascribing to the judges any view that they were bound by statute because of any 'principle of reference to the intentions of the legislature' (*ibid.*, 298 f.); the real reason seems to have lain in the difficulty of operating the particular statute in question (cf. Thorne in *Discourse upon the Statutes*, 74 f.).

'if against reason or fundamental law' will not stand up.[33] The only valid example of any such action is Bonham's Case of 1609 in which Coke seemed to say that acts of Parliament could be void if they conflicted with law and reason. He also remarked that 'in many cases the common law will control acts of Parliament'. It has, however, been shown that his meaning was not to judge statute by some abstract standard represented by the common law, but rather (in the manner of his fifteenth-century predecessors) that if a statute, strictly applied, led to injustice or manifest impossibility it was the judges' duty to remedy the deficiencies of the legislature.[34] Though this asserts a greater power of interpretation than modern judges would claim, it is in strict accord with that claimed from the sixteenth to the nineteenth centuries and recognises the supremacy of statute to the full.

Thus the political events and constitutional expansion of the 1530's produced major changes in the position of Parliament. Long and frequent sessions, fundamental and far-reaching measures, revolutionary consequences, governmental leadership—all these combined with the Crown's devotion to statute and use of Parliament to give that institution a new air, even to change it essentially into its modern form as the supreme and sovereign legislator. That aspects of its history qualified it for the part, and that the revolutionary change was not immediately recognised everywhere, not only goes without saying but does nothing to derogate from the fundamental facts.

105. Sir Thomas Smith on Parliament (1565).

The most high and absolute power of the realm of England consisteth in the Parliament. For as in war, where the King himself in person, the nobility, the rest of the gentility and the yeomanry are, is the force and power of England: so in peace and consultation where the prince is to give life and the last and highest commandment, the barony for the nobility and higher, the knights, esquires, gentlemen and commons for the lower part of the commonwealth, consult and show what is good and necessary for the commonwealth, and to consult together and upon mature deliberation (every bill or law being thrice read and disputed upon in either House) the other two parts first each part and after the prince himself in presence of both the parts doth consent unto and alloweth. That is the prince's and whole realm's deed; whereupon justly no man can complain but must accommodate himself to find it good and obey it. That which is done by this consent is called firm,

---

[33] Pollard, *Evolution*, 232 f. He does not, in fact, cite a single case, and his references only demonstrate certain dicta, not actual decisions.

[34] Cf. *Discourse upon the Statutes*, 85 ff. Also Thorne, *Law Quart. Rev.*, LIV, 542 ff.

stable and *sanctum*, and is taken for law. The Parliament abrogateth old laws, maketh new, giveth orders for things past and for things hereafter to be followed, changeth rights and possessions of private men, legitimateth bastards, establisheth forms of religion, altereth weights and measures, giveth forms of succession to the Crown, defineth of doubtful rights whereof is no law already made, appointeth subsidies, tallies, taxes and impositions, giveth most free pardons and absolutions, restoreth in blood and name as the highest court, condemneth or absolveth them whom the prince will put to that trial. And, to be short, all that ever the people of Rome might do either in *Centuriatis comitiis* or *tributis*, the same may be done by the Parliament of England which representeth and hath the power of the whole realm, both the head and the body. For every Englishman is intended to be there present, either in person or by procuration and attorneys, of what preeminence, state, dignity or quality soever he be, from the prince (be he king or queen) to the lowest person in England. And the consent of the Parliament is taken to be every man's consent. *De Republica Anglorum,* 48–9

106. Richard Hooker on Parliament (c. 1595).

... The Parliament of England, together with the Convocation annexed thereunto,[35] is that whereupon the very essence of all government within this kingdom doth depend; it is even the body of the whole realm; it consisteth of the king and of all that within the land are subject unto him; for they all are there present, either in person or by such as they voluntarily have derived their very personal right unto. The Parliament is a court not so merely temporal as if it might meddle with nothing but only leather and wool. Those days of Queen Mary are not yet forgotten, wherein the realm did submit itself unto the legate of Pope Julius: at which time had they been persuaded as this man seemeth now to be, had they thought that there is no more force in laws made by Parliament concerning the Church affairs than if men should take upon them to make orders for the hierarchies of angels in heaven, they might have taken all former statutes in that kind as cancelled, and by reason of nullity abrogated in themselves. ... Had they power to repeal laws made and none to make laws concerning the regiment of the Church? *Eccles. Polity,* VIII, c. 6 (11) (*Works,* III, 408–9)

[35] The mention of Convocation may be thought reasonable in a treatise concerned with the government of the realm as a Church, but the fact is that the 'essence of government' in Tudor England was quite independent of the Convocations of the archiepiscopal provinces; for, in addition, there was and is no such thing as *the* Convocation of England.

107. Thomas Cromwell to John Creke, 17 August [1523].

. . . Supposing ye desire to know the news current in these parts, for it is said that news refresheth the spirit of life, wherefore ye shall understand that by long time I amongst other have endured a Parliament which continued by the space of seventeen whole weeks; where we communed of war, peace, strife, contention, debate, murmur, grudge, riches, poverty, penury, truth, falsehood, justice, equity, deceit, oppression, magnanimity, activity, force, attemprance, treason, murder, felony, conciliation, and also how a commonwealth might be edified and also continued within our realm. Howbeit, in conclusion we have done as our predecessors have been wont to do; that is to say, as well as we might and left where we began. . . . Merriman, *Cromwell's Letters*, I, 313

108. Stephen Gardiner on Parliament.

[21 May 1547] I beseech your grace[36] to pardon me, for I am like one of the Commons' House that, when I am in my tale, think I should have liberty to make an end. . . .

[Sept. 1547] I reasoned once in the Parliament House, where was free speech without danger. . . .

[Nov. 1547] I cannot discuss by conjecture why evidence is thus put off in my case that hath been wont commonly to be granted to all men. If it should be of any man through policy to keep me from the Parliament, it were good to be remembered whether mine absence from the Upper House, with the absence of those I have used to name in the Nether House, will not engender more cause of objection, if opportunity serve hereafter, than my presence with such as I should appoint were there. . . . *Letters*, 282, 392, 424

109. Christopher St German on the positive law (*c.* 1528).

[Cap. 4, the doctor:] The law of man, the which sometimes is called the law positive, is derived by reason as a thing which is necessarily and probably following of the law of reason and of the law of God. . . . In every law positive well made is somewhat of the law of reason and of the law of God; and to discern the law of God and the law of reason from the law positive is very hard. And though it be hard yet

---

[36] The protector Somerset.

it is much necessary in every moral doctrine and in all laws made for the commonwealth . . . . And that the law of man be just and righteous two things be necessary: that is to say, wisdom and authority . . . . But the sentence of a wise man doth not bind the community if he have no rule over them. Also to every good law . . . be required these properties, that is to say that it be honest, righteous, possible in itself, and after the custom of the country, convenient for the place and time, necessary, profitable, and also manifest that it be not captious by any dark sentence ne mixed with any private wealth but all made for the common wealth. . . . As the cardinal of Camer' writeth[37] . . . every man's law must be consonant to the law of God. And therefore the laws of princes, nor the commandments of prelates, the statutes of communities, ne yet the ordinance of the Church is not righteous nor obligatory but it be consonant to the law of God. . . .

[The student states that the law of England is grounded upon the law of reason, the law of God, divers general customs of the realm, certain principles called maxims, divers particular customs, and statutes made in Parliament.]

[Cap. 5, the student:] It is not used among them that be learned in the laws of England to reason what thing is commanded or prohibit by the law of nature and what not; but all the reasoning in that behalf is under this manner: as when anything is grounded upon the law of nature they say that reason will that such a thing be done, and if it be prohibit by the law of nature they say it is against reason or that reason will not suffer that it be done.

[Cap. 6, the student:] It is enquired in many courts in this realm if any hold any opinions secretly or in any other manner against the true Catholical faith. And also if any general custom were directly against the law of God, or if any statute were made directly against it; as if it were ordained that no alms should be given for no necessity, that custom and statute were void. . . . And by the authority also of this ground the law of England amitteth the spiritual jurisdiction of dismes, oblations and offerings and of all other things that of right belong unto it. And receiveth also all laws of the Church duly made and that exceed not the power of them that made them. Insomuch that in many cases it behoveth the King's justices to judge after the law of the Church.

[Cap. 7, the student:] . . . And so all the ground and beginning of the

[37] Pierre d'Ailly, cardinal of Cambrai (1350–1420). I owe this identification to Prof. T. F. T. Plucknett.

said courts depend upon the custom of the realm, the which custom is of so high authority that the said courts ne their authorities may not be altered ne their names changed without Parliament. . . .

[Cap. 11, the student:] The sixth ground of the law of England standeth in divers statutes made by our sovereign lord the King and his progenitors, and by the Lords spiritual and temporal and the Commons of the whole realm in divers Parliaments, in such cases where the law of reason, the law of God, customs, maxims ne other grounds of the law of England seemed not to be sufficient to punish evil men and to reward good men. *Doctor and Student*, 27–9, 31–3, 39–41, 47, 73

110. Thomas More on Statute (1534).

. . . And forasmuch as this indictment is grounded upon an act of Parliament directly repugnant to the laws of God and His Holy Church, the supreme government of which or of any part whereof may no temporal prince presume by any law to take upon him, as rightfully belonging to the see of Rome, a spiritual preeminence by the mouth of our Saviour himself personally put upon earth, only to St Peter and his successors, bishops of the same See, by special prerogative granted; it is therefore in law amongst Christian men insufficient to charge any Christian man. . . . [Worried by this argument, lord chancellor Audley, presiding at the trial, asked the lord chief justice's opinion; who replied:] My lords all, by St Julian (that was ever his oath) I must needs confess that, if the act of Parliament be lawful, then the indictment is good enough. Harpsfield, *Life of More*, 193, 196–7

111. Thomas Cromwell to Bishop Fisher [February 1534].

[Concerning the Nun of Kent] . . . And here I appeal your conscience and instantly desire you to answer. Whether, if she had showed you as many revelations for the confirmation of the King's Grace's marriage which he now enjoyeth as she did to the contrary, ye would have given as much credence to her as ye have done and would have let the trial of her and of her revelations to overpass these many years where ye dwelt not from her but twenty miles, in the same shire where her trances and disfigurings and prophecies in her trances were surmised and counterfeit. And if percase ye will say (as it is not unlike but ye will say, minded as ye were wont to be) that the matters be not like, for the law of God in your opinion standeth with the one and not with the other:

surely, my lord, I suppose this had been no great cause more to reject the one than the other. For ye know by histories of the Bible that God may by his revelation dispense with his own law, as with the Israelites spoiling the Egyptians and with Jacob to have four wives, and such other. . . . Your thinking shall not be your trial, but the law must define whether you oughted to utter it or not. . . .

Merriman, Cromwell's Letters, I, 376

112. Francis Bacon on Statute.

[Commenting on the Treasons Act, 1495 (Doc. 2)]. But the force and obligation of this law was in itself illusory as to the latter part of it; (by a precedent act of Parliament to bind or frustrate a future). For a supreme and absolute power cannot conclude itself, neither can that which is in nature revocable be made fixed; no more than if a man should appoint and declare by his will that if he made any later will it should be void. And for the case of the act of Parliament, there is a notable precedent of it in King Henry the Eighth's time; who, doubting he might die in the minority of his son, procured an act to pass that no statute made during the minority of a king should bind him or his successors, except it were confirmed by the king under his great seal at his full age.[38] But the first act that passed in King Edward the Sixth's time was an act of repeal of that former act; at which time nevertheless the king was a minor.

Works, VI, 160

II. COMPOSITION

Parliament consisted of three parts, Crown, Lords and Commons. The consent of all three was necessary for the validity of an act: in 1489 the judges unanimously agreed that a certain act of attainder was no act because, though it rested on the king's will and the assent of the Lords, 'nothing was said of the Commons'.[39] This superseded the doctrine, occasionally found in the fifteenth century, that the Lords by themselves could make a statute.[40] A more extraordinary view, propounded early in the reign of Elizabeth, maintained that the Lords were superfluous: 'The king with his commonalty may keep the Parliament alone, for the Commons have everyone of them a greater voice in Parliament than hath a lord or bishop.'[41] However, this view

[38] 28 Henry VIII, c. 17.
[39] Pollard, *Henry VII*, 19.
[40] Chrimes, *Constitutional Ideas*, 156.
[41] *Discourse upon the Statutes*, 113.

seems to rest on the unsatisfactory authority of that fourteenth-century will-o'-the-wisp, the *Modus tenendi Parliamentum*,[42] and it certainly went counter both to sound contemporary opinion and invariable contemporary practice. Parliament was a gathering of three partners, and in matters of lawmaking all three were equal to the extent of having to give their assent. As has been said, this equal partnership was a new development of the sixteenth century. Parliament originated in an enlarged meeting of the king's Council to which representatives of the communities might also be summoned, and a full meeting of Parliament (at the opening and close of the session) consisted of the monarch on the throne, surrounded by both the peers and the professional Council in their appointed places, with the Commons at the bar—that is, outside the Parliament Chamber proper. These arrangements are significant: they tell us something about the history of the institution. But they are also misleading because in this century they ceased to reflect the true composition of the sovereign body.

By about 1530 the king's Great Council in Parliament had grown into the House of Lords; the Lords, once the Parliament proper, became simply one 'House', one part of the composite institution.[43] This was particularly noticeable in their membership. The king's permanent Council, originally the core of Parliament, continued to be represented in the Tudor Lords by the judges, serjeants-at-law, and masters in chancery who took their places upon three of the four woolsacks which formed a square in the centre of the chamber;[44] though these councillors had no voice they played an important role in the House as advisers and assistants; they often drafted bills.[45] On the other hand, an attempt was made to retain the presence of the king's leading privy councillors. An act of 1539, which arranged the 'precedence' or order of sitting in the House,[46] provided for the presence of leading officers (lord chancellor, lord treasurer, lord privy seal, lord president, and principal secretary) as well as of certain great household officials, whether they were noblemen or not;[47] but except for the lord chancellor, who throughout the century presided over the House, none of these attended unless they were peers. Indeed, many of them came to seek election to the House of Commons, a fact which amply illustrates the new position of that body where the presence of leading ministers came to be common practice and (from the Crown's point of view) essential. With the disappearance of non-noble members went a growth in the concept of peerage in Parliament.

[42] On the *Modus*, cf. Pronay and Taylor, chs. 1 & 2.

[43] The term House of Lords has not been found before 1544 (Pollard, *Henry VII*, I, p. xxxiii). It should be noted that the institutional equality between the Houses did not deprive the Lords of a social and political superiority.

[44] Elsynge, *Manner*, 111.

[45] For the Upper House cf. in general, Graves, *House of Lords*.

[46] 31 Henry VIII, c. 10 (63).   [47] Cf. Pike, *House of Lords*, 351 f.

Although individual summons, which distinguished members of the Upper House, had not yet become a matter of right, in practice no one after Henry VII refused summons to all the nobility; they contented themselves with private instructions to stay away to those whose presence was not desired.[48] In the critical years of Henry VIII's reign, the growing self-consciousness of the peerage—a new thing, for as late as the reign of Henry VII the line between a baron and a knight banneret had been hard to discern[49]—was reflected in attempts to define the class and turn it into a caste; but nothing came of this.[50] However, in the course of the century it became possible to identify nobility with peerage of Parliament.

Though the Lords in Parliament were both temporal and spiritual they composed but the one House and formed between them one of the assenting partners in the making of statute. This is the modern doctrine which was fully established by the reign of Henry VIII.[51] As early as 1516 the judges laid it down that the presence or assent of the spiritual lords was not required to make an act valid;[52] since lords temporal and spiritual were all members of one House, the voice of the House rested with the majority of those present, of whatever kind. This point has been of some importance in assessing the legality of the Elizabethan Church Settlement, but it mattered more before the Reformation when the spiritual peers outnumbered the lords temporal. Bishops and abbots in Parliament numbered forty-nine under Henry VII and fifty-two under Henry VIII; the removal of thirty-one abbots by the dissolution of the monasteries was ill-balanced by the addition of five bishops, and the twenty-six spiritual lords of Elizabeth's reign had definitely fallen into a minority. At Henry VII's accession, the effects of attainder, absenteeism, and suspension had reduced the lay lords to twenty-nine, but after the restoration of peace and by judiciously infrequent creations their numbers rose to between fifty and sixty from about 1530 onwards.[53] The House of Lords was thus effectively secularised. Both lay and spiritual peers tended to be amenable to the influence of the Crown. They were not an absolutely 'safe' House, as opposition in 1529 to attacks on ecclesiastical liberties, in 1539 to the Act of Proclamations, and in 1559 to the Elizabethan settlement showed well enough; but for the most part the government could rely on the cooperation of bishops appointed by the Crown and lords either subdued or created by the Tudors.[54]

[48] Pickthorn, I, 95; Pollard, *Evolution*, 302; and cf. for the established practice under the Stuarts, Elsynge, *Manner*, 59. It was alleged in 1531 that peers who opposed the king found it easy to get licence for absence (*L.P.* v, 120).

[49] Chrimes, *Constitutional Ideas*, 146. On the whole problem of the growth of an hereditary peerage, cf. Pike, *House of Lords*, ch. VI.

[50] Plucknett, *Trans. R. Hist. Soc.*, 1936, 121 ff.

[51] For some remarks on this cf. Maitland, *Historical Essays*, 251 f.

[52] Pike, *House of Lords*, 326 f.   [53] For all these figures cf. Tanner, 513 f.

[54] Cf. in general Miller, *Bull. Inst. Hist. Research*, XXIV, 88 ff., and *Hist. Journal*, X, 325 ff.

If the Lords in Parliament became a House, it is not too much to say that the established House of Commons in this period became a House of Parliament. They had been a 'House'—an organised institution—from the later fourteenth century, and by the fifteenth had certainly been an accepted part of Parliament. Yet they had remained outside the Parliament proper and occupied no position equal to king and Lords.[55] Under the Tudors they achieved precisely this standing in the constitution. The majority of bills started in the Commons; money grants had to originate there; and on occasion they replaced the Lords as the arena for the debating of matters of state. The Reformation Parliament, during which most of the great matters were first debated in the Commons, marked the beginning of this development; the presence there of the king's leading ministers signified what had happened; and when in 1549 they acquired a meeting place (St Stephen's Chapel) within the palace of Westminster[56] they announced their arrival as equals on the parliamentary scene.[57] A most striking development took place in their numbers. The Commons had always been more numerous than similar institutions in more populous countries of the continent, but in the sixteenth century they grew vastly—from 296 to 462, or by some fifty-six per cent. Some of these additions occurred when Henry VIII called members from the hitherto unrepresented boroughs and shires of Wales and Cheshire (thirty-one seats); the two burgesses for Calais called after 1536 disappeared in 1558. But most additions were due to the enfranchisement (new or restored) of English boroughs. Thirty-four new members under Edward VI, twenty-five under Mary, and sixty-two under Elizabeth (who made no new boroughs after 1586)—such figures represent what looks like a remarkable activity on the part of the Crown to enlarge representation.[58] Especially since the increase took place in borough seats—more amenable to electoral influence and often already quite like rotten boroughs—it used to be supposed that the Crown wished to pack Parliament; but it is now established beyond doubt that this expansion arose from entirely different causes.[59] The creation of new seats came in response to pressure from boroughs themselves, and especially from landed gentlemen interested in the enfranchisement of places in which they had influence. Great patrons at the centre—men like Leicester or Burghley—would be pressed by towns with which they were connected to assist in these moves; there is no evidence that they, any more than the Crown, were concerned to create a Parliamentary interest by such means.

[55] This is not to deny their practical influence and standing but merely to define their constitutional position. Cf. Chrimes, *Constitutional Ideas*, 157 ff.

[56] Neale, *House of Commons*, 364.

[57] When as late as 1546 the Commons were described as 'inferior members' of Parliament (Pike, *House of Lords*, 327), this meant little more than our use of 'lower house'.

[58] Neale, *House of Commons*, 140 f., 146.

[59] For this point and what follows cf. *ibid.*, 141 ff.

The real reason for all these new seats is to be found in a novel desire to enter Parliament and a consequent competition for seats. The century witnessed what has been called 'the invasion' of Parliament by the country gentry. In strict law no one was to represent a borough unless he resided in it; this ought to have resulted in a House one-fifth gentry (sitting for the shires) and four-fifths burgesses. In reality, the proportions were just about reversed by the last quarter of the century.[60] Country gentlemen had long taken over some borough seats. As early as 1422 about a quarter of these had been occupied by non-residents and half the burgesses were only technically so, being socially connected with the gentry;[61] and in the reign of Edward IV there had been a notable influx of gentlemen and Crown officials into seats which should have been occupied by true burgesses.[62] But from the latter part of Henry VIII's reign, the trickle became a flood, as the creation of new boroughs testifies; and by the reign of Elizabeth the House of Commons, largely composed of men belonging to the landed gentry, at long last truly represented the dominant section of the community. Local ties snapped as more and more men sat for boroughs with which they had no personal links; borough seats became little more than means of entering Parliament and politics, and ceased to be the means of bringing the localities into contact with the centre.[63] Thus the House not only acquired men of social standing, independence, political training and experience, but could also fairly claim to speak for the political nation, a role which down to the Wars of the Roses had been more properly filled by the Lords. In that transformation of the House of Commons from a body of local representatives, charged with communicating the locality's grievances to the king's government, into an aspiring partner in the political government of the nation, which is its history in the sixteenth century, the 'invasion of the gentry' played a most vital part.

III. PROCEDURE

Parliament was above all a working institution, producing acts out of bills, and the efficient conduct of business depended on the observation of a reasonably regular procedure. Some rules for it evidently, and necessarily, existed before the sixteenth century,[64] and though developments unquestionably occurred thereafter their meaning has been traditionally misjudged. Procedural change aimed to improve the discharge of business, not perhaps to advance the purposes of an opposition: 'as a temperature chart for

[60] *Ibid.*, 146 ff.

[61] Roskell, *Bull. Inst. Hist. Research*, XXIV, 152 ff., and *Commons of 1422*, 49, 130.

[62] McKisack, *Representation of English Boroughs*, 113.

[63] By c. 1600 two boroughs out of three were represented by two non-residents (Neale, *House of Commons*, 162 f.).

[64] Elton, *Studies*, II, 49 f.

political or constitutional developments the history of procedure is suspect.'[65] We need to understand procedure in order to understand what went on, not in order to track 'the rise of the House of Commons'; the entrenched conviction that the history of procedure reflects some sort of 'maturing' (growth to political dominance) on the part of the Commons is not supported by what happened,[66] for changes manifestly resulted from the initiatives of Crown managers. The available evidence, which becomes reasonably full only in Elizabeth's reign, can also mislead and suggest 'growth'. In fact, both Houses had evidently been able long before this to conduct their affairs according to sensible rules—rules which they treated with great flexibility and in the Commons at least never reduced to order. The Lords, always more 'mature' and more businesslike, led the way.[67] Conferences between committees of both Houses (118), which offered an opportunity to prevent misunderstandings and disagreements, also assisted the influence of the Upper House upon the Lower. We hear of such meetings ('intercommunings') in the middle ages and of a conference proper in 1515;[68] once the Journals assist us, we find them in frequent use, at least down to 1581.[69] At this point there is some evidence that members of the Lower House grew apprehensive of the Lords' ability to overawe their representatives: it was resolved that the Commons' committee could not agree to anything in a conference that had not previously been in their instructions from the House.[70] In the second half of the reign conferencing grew rare, though it is not advisable to seek the reason in any supposed growth of power in the Commons. In sessions already very short of time, conferences took up too much of it,[71] and though the Commons on occasions before and after 1581 displayed a mild corporate resentment against the peers they mostly continued to take their cue from the Upper House.

In the reign of Henry VIII bills were still quite frequently introduced on parchment, a practice which made amendment difficult;[72] thereafter it became the rule that they should be on paper.[73] Their promoters presented

---

[65] Elton, *Hist. Journal*, XXII, 268. The outstanding treatment of procedure is Lambert, *Eng. Hist. Rev.*, XCV, 753 ff., which demonstrates what really happened.

[66] This conviction mars Neale's account (*House of Commons*, chs. 18–22) which is otherwise still useful.

[67] Graves, *House of Lords*, ch. 7.

[68] Edwards, *Commons*; Pollard, *Wolsey*, 49. Pollard's mention of a conference in 1529 (*ibid.*, 354) is baffling: I cannot trace his evidence.

[69] Neale, *Elizabeth and her Parliaments*, I, 235 f., 287, 386 f., 412 f. [70] *C. J.*, I, 123.

[71] Cf. an expert opinion expressed in 1572: 'conference may do and does good, but much of it sometimes does more hurt . . . Over-many conferences work many courses to prolong the session' (British Library, Harleian MS 253, fo. 35v).

[72] Lehmberg, *Eng. Hist. Rev.*, LXXXV, 2 f.

[73] Except for bills signed by the queen to signify her recommendation and approval. The problem of 'sign manual' bills is much too complex to be discussed here, but cf. Miklovich, *Bull. Inst. Hist. Res.*, LII, 23 ff.

them at the beginning of the session to the Speakers or clerks of either House who became responsible for seeing them opened in the House. They were supposed to be taken in the order received (**113**), but that proved impossible in practice. The fortunes of a bill depended on its promoter, especially in the case of private bills which inevitably got stuck unless 'followed' in the House (with the obligatory payments made to the clerks). Private bills, which for those who introduced them represented the major interest of the session, included strictly private concerns (repeals of attainders, settlements of estates, denizations and naturalisations) and the affairs of particular groups (bills for tanners or vintners); they always occupied more time than suited the managers of business, so that efforts (always unavailing) were made to confine dealing with them to particular hours. Much skill was displayed in forwarding them: members of either House were retained of service or at least lobbied, and pressure was applied outside Parliament especially to councillors.[74] However, after 1529 the growing amount of public business cut down the time spent on private matters, and important government bills tended to be taken first.

Bills were normally read three times in each House (**114, 119**); though very contentious or very difficult bills could receive more readings as contents were hammered out, this must not be interpreted as indicating a 'primitive' state of development but as a sign of the Commons' usual flexibility in accommodating rules of procedure to the needs of the moment.[75] After the second reading, the bill would either be engrossed on parchment or sent to a committee for revision in detail. Bill committees, described in 1536 as being 'as the manner is',[76] certainly grew more customary but never became universal for all bills. Bills could be rejected at any reading or upon the report of a committee. Those received from the other House passed through the same stages except that they were, of course, already on parchment; amendments had to be made either by the addition of a proviso or by means of a list of points to be entered on the bill by the first House if it was willing to agree. Both Houses commonly produced revised bills (*nove bille*) if they did not like what had been sent, or even simply if they wanted changes which could not be conveniently squeezed onto the parchment bill.[77] Within the rules, flexibility always dominated; precedents at best guided and never governed; and comment, even by contemporaries, about

---

[74] Lobbying of the Commons by peers promoting private bills occurred in 1485 (Pronay and Taylor, 186); this would not have been acceptable even by 1523 when Wolsey was told that it was against the liberty of the House to debate in his presence (Roper, *More*, 17 ff.).

[75] Elton, *Hist. Journal*, XXII, 268. Fewer than three readings also occurred: acts for general pardons were always read once only, and in 1485 the bill for tunnage and poundage passed the Commons after two readings (Pronay and Taylor, 186).

[76] *L.P.*, X, 336.

[77] Elton, *Studies*, 272.

the rules should be treated with the caution reserved for statements meant to serve a secret purpose.[78]

Bill committees should be distinguished from committees appointed in either House for other purposes. The first certain mention of committees in the Commons occurs in 1529 when the machinery was used for the drafting of bills to remedy grievances raised in the House (115). This device remained available (e.g. 116) even after Thomas Cromwell initiated the practice of preparing a programme of bills before the session. In 1571, a number of issues raised in debate were referred to a committee which produced a few bills.[79] Bills on cognate topics could be referred to one committee which thus became a standing committee for the session; so-called 'grand' committees to receive proposals touching specified topics came to be appointed session after session, though they did little or no work.[80] In the Commons, committees grew larger, mainly because members could not be trusted to turn up, and during sessions afternoons came increasingly to be occupied with committee meetings.[81] All this resulted demonstrably from managerial initiatives. It certainly looks as though members, especially of the Commons, grew busier during Elizabeth's reign, a fact easily accounted for by the very large number of bills handled of which no more than about a third could ever be brought to a conclusion in the short sessions preferred by the queen.[82] Bill committees added to the burden on members and the pressure on time; special and standing committees were devices to improve the handling of business. The former proved useful in improving bills, while the latter never really did much good. Neither in any way represented efforts by an opposition or even independently minded men to take the running of the House out of the Council's hands.[83]

In the Lords, members voted in person and had their vote recorded. In the Commons, too large an assembly for this practice, voting was by majority, and originally by acclamation.[84] The growing lack of satisfaction with this simple method, which enabled the louder-voiced to carry the day, illustrates growth in competence and procedure. Before 1558 divisions seem to have been rare. The earliest known example occurred in 1532 when the king was allegedly present in both Houses to see his supporters win.[85] Under Elizabeth it became ever more common to divide the House,

---

[78] Lambert, *Eng. Hist. Rev.*, xcv, 755 f.

[79] *C.J.*, i, 83.

[80] Lambert, *Eng. Hist. Rev.*, xcv, 759 f.

[81] The Houses sat normally from 8 to 11 in the morning, though they could meet earlier and sometimes rose at a later hour (Neale, *House of Commons*, 367 f.).

[82] Elton, *Hist. Journal*, xxii, 260.

[83] The Elizabethan Commons, like the House of Commons throughout its long history, never really acquired the right to control its own affairs. The House's reputation for power and ascendancy is one of the major legends of English history.

[84] Neale, *House of Commons*, 397 ff.   [85] *L.P.*, v, 898.

the Ayes (as the innovators) leaving the chamber while the Noes (who wished to maintain the *status quo*) sat tight. This in a House too small to accommodate more than a minority of members with comfort favoured the Noes; not only did it take some courage to signify one's views by rising, but members were also reluctant to lose their seats.[86]

One essential point of parliamentary procedure received early attention. The House of Commons could hardly have done its business efficiently unless it restricted freedom of debate by some rules of order. It was established by the middle of the century that language must be decorous, that members must give way to one another, that they must address the Speaker, and that in full session (though not in committee) no man could speak more than once a day to any given bill (**119**).[87] In theory the Commons presented the picture of an orderly and courteous assembly which, under the Speaker's vigilant eye, discharged its business with speed and decorum. In truth this was not necessarily so; the Elizabethan House of Commons was only too adept at expressing its disapproval of some members' speeches (**120**), and the Speaker often had difficulty in controlling debates (**121**).

Two aspects of parliamentary affairs deserve inclusion in an account of procedure. At all times, members' absenteeism has presented a problem both to ardent parliamentarians and to the government.[88] In 1515 an act of Parliament transferred the control over members to the Speaker: licences for absence, hitherto obtained from the Crown, were now to be issued by him (**140**). During the Reformation Parliament protests were sometimes heard about the length of sittings, and in 1532 a deputation headed by the Speaker asked that the Parliament might be sent home.[89] Usually, however, protests were individual and took the form of unlicensed departure home on private business, or unexplained absence from the House. Lawyers were notorious for the readiness with which, to follow their profession, they slipped off into Westminster Hall next door. In extreme cases, the House could be 'called': that is, the roll was read by the clerk, and every member present answered his name by going into the lobby (**122**). This slow and cumbersome method was rarely used, and as a rule the Crown had to accept a thin attendance even on days of important business, though Elizabeth used some strong language on the subject. The problem was one with which managers of government parties remained only too familiar. Lastly we may note that proceedings in Parliament were secret, and that anyone proved to have discussed them outside the House could get into serious trouble. In 1555 Sir William Cecil escaped imprisonment by Mary's Council only because he had been careful to avoid involvement in other men's extra-parliamentary discussions (**123**), and in Elizabeth's day complaints that

[86] Cf. Neale, *House of Commons*, 398.
[87] On rules of debate cf. *ibid.*, 404 ff.
[88] *Ibid.*, 413 ff.
[89] Hall, *Chronicle*, 784.

matters of Parliament were the talk of every tavern grew frequent.[90] It no doubt signified much about the standing of the House that affairs there should excite so much interest, but it also led to centuries of wrangling over the need to protect secrecy.

113. Matters of the Parliament (1571).

The matters whereof the Parliament is holden or kept ought to be delivered into the Parliament and to be called upon in manner of a calendar according to every man's petition, and no respect to be had to any man's person, but that he who layeth first his bill in shall be first heard. In the calendar of the Parliament every matter ought to be had in memory under this manner and form: First, of wars if there be any, of matters concerning the king's and queen's person and of their children. Secondly of matters concerning the common weal and to ordain new laws, debarring the old laws made in times past whose execution have been prejudicial. Thirdly the matters concerning the private weal, and these to be examined according to the file or calendar, as is before written.
John Vowell (al. Hooker), in Somers Tracts, I, 179

114. William Lambarde on the passage of bills (temp. Elizabeth, though printed in 1641).

. . . Upon the first reading of a bill the Speaker, taking the bill in one hand, may say: 'You have heard the bill the contents whereof are these etc.' . . . without suffering any man . . . to speak unto it, but rather to advise thereof until the next reading; which is a means not only to hear effectual speech but also to save a great deal of time. A bill may not be committed upon the first reading. . . . At the second reading of a bill it ought to be either engrossed, committed or rejected; . . . and if the more voices will have it engrossed it must be done accordingly. And if the more voices will have it committed, then the Speaker entreats them to appoint the committees,[91] and, that done, their names and the time and place of meeting and the day of their report shall be endorsed upon it. . . . When a bill is engrossed and hath received the third reading, it must either pass or be rejected by the more voices; if it pass, then it must be endorsed *Soit baillé aux Seigneurs*; and if it be rejected, it must not come any more in the House.
Harleian Miscellany, V, 241–3

[90] Neale, *House of Commons*, 416 ff.
[91] In Elizabethan usage, one to whom a bill is committed is called a committee; i.e. an Elizabethan committee is a member of what we should call a committee.

115. Committees in 1529.

When the Commons were assembled in the Nether House, they began to common of their grieves wherewith the spiritualty had before time grievously oppressed them, both contrary to the law of the realm and contrary to all right. . . . Whereupon the burgesses of the Parliament appointed such as were learned in the law, being of the Common House, to draw one bill of the probates of testaments, another for mortuaries, and the third for non-residence, pluralities and taking of farms by spiritual men.   Hall, *Chronicle*, 765–6

116. Committees in 1555: (a) Imperial ambassador to Charles V, 12 January 1555.

. . . The bill on the security of the realm and its administration is still being discussed. . . . Yesterday, several member of the two Houses were chosen to draw up the act in suitable form and in terms appropriate to the authority and reputation of the King.   *Span. Cal.*, XIII, 133

(b) James Basset to the earl of Devonshire, 27 October 1555.

The Nether House of themselves devised that it should be committed to twenty of them to devise upon some subsidy for the Queen's relief, which they did and agreed that the self-same subsidy should be granted unto her which she had when she came to her estate, and two fifteenths when that is done; which yesterday, being declared by the committees to the House, was [liked or disliked?] of more. . . . This day it will be brought into the House, and I think we shall have a short Parliament.

Ven. Cal., VI, 233

117. Imperial ambassador to Charles V, 21 December 1554.

Yet another bill . . . had passed the Upper House, but intrigues in the Lower succeeded in throwing it out and having a different measure adopted in its stead, which is to be sent up once more to the House of Lords. It was suspected that the bill had been devised by wicked authors to an evil end . . . to the hurt of the King and the realm. A member called Pollard, who was Speaker of the last Parliament, protested vehemently that the realm had a debt of gratitude toward the King, to serve whom was his object, and that the bill contained some obscure matter. Then one Brown, a lawyer, spoke to the same purpose, and their opinion prevailed. Baker,[92] a treasury official, was of opinion that the Upper House ought to be consulted before a new bill was framed, but the majority went against him and the new measure ... was passed.

Span. Cal., XIII, 125

118. Committee procedure, 26 March 1589.

Mr Vicechamberlain and the residue of the committees returning from the Lords, he showed that according to the commission of this House they prayed conference with their lordships touching such parts in the bill concerning houses of husbandry and tillage as this House had thought meet to be considered of; and that thereupon their lordships asked them if they were ready for conference. Whereunto he and the residue answered they were. And thereupon (the committees of this House being sequestered) their lordships did send unto them a committee of themselves, unto whom he and the residue of the committees of this House did impart the opinion of this House touching the said bill, together with such amendments of the same as this House prayed their lordships' assent and good liking unto. And that thereupon the committees of the Lords, willing the committees of this House to stay awhile for answer, went in again to the Lords, and some of them shortly after returning brought from their lordships this answer: that we of this House were possessed of the said bill and might do therewith as should seem good unto us, and that when it should come back again to them their lordships would then likewise do therewith as they should think good.

D'Ewes, Journals, 453

119. Sir Thomas Smith on the rules of debate (1565).

All bills be thrice in three divers days read and disputed upon, before they come to the question. In the disputing is a marvellous good order used in the Lower House. He that standeth up bare-headed is understanded that he will speak to the bill. If more stand up, who that first is judged to arise is first heard; though the one do praise the law, the other dissuade it, yet there is no altercation. For every man speaketh as to the Speaker, not as one to another, for that is against the order of the House. It is also taken against the order to name him whom ye do confute but by circumlocution, as 'he that speaketh with the bill,' or 'he that spake against the bill and gave this and this reason.' And so with

[92] Sir John Baker, chancellor of the Exchequer and of First Fruits.

perpetual oration, not with altercation, he goeth through till he do make an end. He that once hath spoken in a bill, though he be confuted straight, that day may not reply; no, though he would change his opinion. So that to one bill in one day one may not in that House speak twice, for else one or two with altercation would spend all the time. The next day he may, but then also but once.

No reviling or nipping words must be used. For then all the House will cry, 'It is against the order': and if any speak unreverently or seditiously against the prince or the Privy Council, I have seen them not only interrupted but it hath been moved after to the House and they have sent them to the Tower. So that in such a multitude, and in such diversity of minds and opinions, there is the greatest modesty and temperance of speech that can be used. Nevertheless, with much doulce and gentle terms they make their reasons as violent and as vehement the one against the other as they may ordinarily, except it be for urgent causes and hasting of time. . . . The Speaker hath no voice in the House, nor they will not suffer him to speak in any bill to move or dissuade it. . . .   *De Republica Anglorum*, 54–5

120. Interrupting of speeches.

[2 December 1584] This bill had been much argued upon before it was committed; and it seems, some arguments not being liked, divers of the House had endeavoured by coughing and spitting to shorten them. Whereupon Sir Francis Hastings made a motion (that as upon like occasion offered others had moved that words of note, as townclerk and such like, should not offensively be applied to the persons of such as had formerly spoken) that in like manner it were now to be wished that in respect of the gravity and honour of this House, when any member thereof shall speak unto a bill, the residue would forbear to interrupt or trouble him by unnecessary coughing, spitting or the like.

[9 November 1601] . . . Then Serjeant Heyle stood up and made a motion saying: 'Mr. Speaker, I marvel much that the House will stand upon granting of a subsidy, or the time of payment, when all we have is her Majesty's, and she may lawfully at her pleasure take it from us. . . .' At which all the House hemmed and laughed and talked. 'Well,' quoth Serjeant Heyle, 'all your hemming shall not put me out of countenance.' So Mr Speaker stood up and said: 'It is a great disorder that this should be used, for it is the ancient use of every man to be silent when anyone speaketh, and he that is speaking should be suffered to deliver his mind without interruption.' So the said serjeant proceeded, and when he had spoken a little while the House hemmed again, and so he sat down. . . .

D'Ewes, Journals, 335, 633

121. Order of debate.

[18 February 1589] Mr Speaker, noting the great disorder in this House by some that standing up and offering to speak, sometimes three or four together, and persisting still without offering to give place one of them to another, knowing well nevertheless which of themselves did first stand up and so by the order of this House ought to be first heard, but yet expecting by acclamation of the residue of the House, growing for the most part to a great confused noise and sound of senseless words, do stand still continuing their offer to speak first, and do also many times in their motions and arguments utter very sharp and bitter speeches, sometimes rather particularly offensive than necessarily with such great vehemency delivered—putteth them in remembrance that every member of this House is a judge of this court, being the highest court of all other courts, and the Great Council also of this realm, and so moveth them in regard thereof that as in all other courts, being each of them inferior to this high court, such confused courses, either of contention, acclamations or reciprocal bitter and sharp speeches, terms or words are not any way either used or permitted amongst the judges of the said inferior courts or the counsellors admitted in the same courts, so they would hereafter forbear to attempt the like disorders, as the honour and gravity of this House justly requireth.

[7 March 1593] . . . Now stood up two or three to have spoken, striving who might speak first. Then the Speaker propounds it as an order in the House in such a case, for him to ask the parties that would speak on which side they would speak—whether with him that spake next before, or against him; and the party that speaketh against the last speaker is to be heard first. And so it was ruled. Where it may seem that the Speaker did give admonishment sitting in the House as a member thereof, and not sitting in his chair as Speaker, which he never doth at any committee, although it be of the whole House.

D'Ewes, Journals, 434, 493-4

122. Controlling attendance of members.

[30 May 1572] . . . Martin Cole, one of the burgesses for the borough of Sudbury in the county of Suffolk, was for his great business and affairs licensed to be absent for eight days.

[26 March 1589] The House was this day called and the defaults noted . . . by her Majesty's pleasure, upon some intelligence given to her Highness of the small number of the members of this House presently attending the service of the same, the one half at least supposed to be absent.

[1 December 1601] . . . Mr Wiseman moved the House to remember two things: one, that it had been an ancient custom in Parliament sometimes to call the House, which as yet was not done; the other, that whereas heretofore collection had been used for the poor, those which went out of town would ask leave of the Speaker and pay their money.

Sir Edward Hobby said . . . May it please you, it hath been a most laudable custom that some contribution or collection should be made amongst us *in pios usus*, and I do humbly pray we do not forget our Parliamental charity. Every knight paid 10s., every burgess 5s. . . .

Mr Fettiplace said, It is true, Mr Speaker, I was collector the last year. There was paid out of the money collected, to the minister, £10, to the serjeant, £30, to Sir John Leveson for the redemption of Mr Foxe his son that made the Book of Martyrs, £30; there was money given to prisons, that is the two Counters, Ludgate and Newgate in London, in Southwark two, and Westminster one. How old the custom is I know not; but how good it is I know. . . .   D'Ewes, *Journals*, 220, 453, 661

123. Discussing Parliament matters outside the House (1555).

After [Sir William Cecil's] return in the Parliament time, there was a matter in question for something the Queen would have to pass. Wherein Sir Anthony Kingston, Sir William Courtney, Sir John Pollard and many others of value, especially western men, were opposite. Sir William Cecil being their speaker and having that day told a good tale for them, when the House rose they came to him and said, 'they would dine with him that day'. He answered, 'they should be welcome, so they did not speak of any matters of Parliament': which they promised. Yet some began to break promise, for which he challenged them. This meeting and speech was known to the Council. And all the knights and gentlemen were sent for and committed. Sir William Cecil was also sent for to my Lord Paget and Sir William Petre. When he was brought before them he desired they would not do by him as by the rest, which he thought somewhat hard. That was, to commit them first and to hear them after. But prayed them first to hear him and then to commit him if he were guilty. 'You speak like a man of experience,' quoth my Lord Paget. And upon their hearing the circumstances, he cleared himself. And so at once escaped both imprisonment and disgrace.   'Life of Burghley' in Peck, *Desiderata Curiosa*, I, 9

IV. PRIVILEGES

The rights appertaining to members of both Houses, which we commonly collect under the heading of parliamentary privilege, were in the sixteenth century more precisely distinguished into privilege and liberties. Privilege, in the legal sense, meant a special protection granted to a person in a court of law, and parliamentary privilege meant more particularly the right of every peer, knight and burgess (and their servants) to avoid arrest by the order of any court inferior to the Parliament, during the time that Parliament was sitting. Liberties, on the other hand, a term in later years loaded with principled meaning, at this time signified protection of the practices which enabled both Houses to discharge the functions for which they had been summoned—counselling the Crown and conducting legislative business. These were the liberties of the Lords and Commons, not the liberties of the subject against whom they might well be asserted. Parliamentary privilege had a pre-Tudor history; parliamentary liberties would appear to have had virtually none. The issue was defined in the request which the Speaker addressed to the sovereign at the beginning of every Parliament. Medieval Speakers asked for special protections for themselves in communicating the voice of the House to the king, though they might add some general and unspecified phrase touching the Commons.[93] In the sixteenth century, this conventional address underwent a very significant change. In 1542 the Speaker still asked only for protection for himself, while in 1559 he concentrated on the liberties of the House (**124**). Sir Thomas Smith, writing in 1559, supposed that the whole speech attended solely to these latter, and according

[93] In 1401 the Speaker added a request that the Commons might have their liberties in Parliament, but there was no indication what these might be (Chrimes and Brown, 201). To judge from Young's Case of 1455 (*ibid.*, 309), they might comprise 'the freedom to speak and say in the House of their assembly as to them is thought convenient', but this isolated assertion proves very little. Neale (*Tudor Studies*, 265) was right to devalue the case.

to him they fell into two parts.[94] There were the old liberties and privileges on the one hand, sufficiently established not to need description, and on the other particular rights listed (free speech, the right of the House to punish offending members itself, the right to seek advice from queen and Lords). I know of no recorded Speaker's address which answers exactly to this description, but it helps to confirm that by the beginning of Elizabeth's reign the privileges and liberties asked for were those of the House, whereas traditionally they had been those of the Speaker. The address delivered by Thomas More in 1523 (**125**) had most fruitfully departed from convention, but if there was an effect it was much delayed; his immediate successors all followed the old pattern.[95]

Thus there is reason for thinking that the history of parliamentary privilege really began, and to some extent ended, in the sixteenth century. More especially, the formal appearance, which pretended a grant by royal grace, by the end of the century quite manifestly disguised a reality in which both Houses could consider their privileges and liberties to be theirs by right. Unlike James I, Elizabeth avoided the touchy question of grace and right. On the other hand, just what those privileges amounted to could still be disputed.

The privilege of freedom from arrest (privilege properly so called) posed the fewest problems: it had been long established. It rested on the principle that a man called by the king to his Parliament must be free to obey and must not be hindered by the actions of private persons. The privilege extended to his servants, on the grounds that without suitable attendance he would be equally incapable of doing his duty. In this century the history of the privilege turned largely upon the manner of its enforcement. Until the reign of Henry VIII it was recognised that a member improperly arrested could only be released upon the issue of a writ of privilege addressed to the jailer, which writ was granted by Chancery upon the Speaker's request. However, in Ferrers' Case of 1542 (**129**) the Commons released their member by sending their own serjeant-at-arms and claiming that his mace (the badge of his office) was sufficient authority. Such action was described as being 'by warrant of the mace'. The difficulty encountered over Ferrers suggests that the method **may** then have been new.[96] Ferrers' Case was significant in another respect:

---

[94] *De Republica*, 52.

[95] *L.J.*, I, pp. clii, 86.

[96] The full story of Ferrers' Case is found only in the extract from Holinshed's *Chronicle*, printed as Doc. **129**; this is not a source of first-rate reliability. The main facts are vouched for by a shorter entry in Hall's contemporary *Chronicle* (p. 843). However, what has always attracted special attention to the case was the king's personal intervention and his famous statement about the position of the king in Parliament (below, p. 277). His remarks were addressed to a deputation of the Lower House, but they do not seem to have been written down till perhaps thirty years after; they may well have got distorted in the transmission. I should be prepared to relegate the whole speech—no doubt only partially remembered—to a position of little moment; but

in it, as in nearly every case, the privilege was claimed by a member attached for debt at the suit of his creditors. A man so arrested and then set at large by privilege could not be re-arrested, so that he escaped the debt; this was in the lord keeper's mind in 1593 when he alluded to those who might try to use the liberties of the House to defraud others of their rights (128). He may in particular have remembered Smalley's Case of 1576 (131).[97] Edward Smalley, servant to Arthur Hall, the unpopular burgess for Grantham, procured his own arrest for a debt which was really Hall's. Hall then moved for privilege to free his servant. A Commons' committee, reluctant to assist in what they suspected was trickery, at first ignored the precedent of Ferrers' Case and maintained that Smalley could only be freed by writ out of Chancery; but Hall's obstinacy secured his release by warrant of the mace, thus confirming the Commons' right to enforce their privilege by their own powers. Though released from the Counter, Smalley was by the House committed to the Tower till the debt was paid, and both he and Hall were severely censured for their attempted fraud. In 1572 the Lords similarly protected their freedom from arrest in Lord Cromwell's Case (130); but when privilege was moved in 1584 for one alleged to be the servant of a peer (131) they denied it to him because he was no servant in the strict sense. The Commons, always more assertive in their claims, tended to be generous in their estimate of what constituted service, but it was as well that the Lords, whose nominal servants, thanks to the social system of clientage, were very many, should have been more precise.[98]

The reign produced also several attempts to extend freedom from arrest by claiming the protection of the House against judicial process which stopped short of arrest. Thus in 1585 a member served with a subpoena out of Chancery tried to evade it by maintaining that during the sitting of the House members could not be summoned into an inferior court; the Commons, standing on their 'ancient liberties', tried to support him, but were courteously rebuffed by the lord chancellor who asked them to produce their non-existent precedents (133). On the other hand, they provided that members involved in *nisi prius* actions at local assizes should be assisted with writs of supersedeas, by which action was stayed until further notice (134). This was reasonable: a sitting member would be prevented from doing his first duty if he had to attend an assize. A last case in the reign led to some limitation of freedom from arrest. In 1593 Thomas Fitzherbert, an elected

Holinshed does assert that he had taken great pains to discover the truth, and George Ferrers was still alive in 1577 when the *Chronicle* appeared.

[97] Fully discussed in Neale, *Elizabeth and her Parliaments*, I, 333 ff.

[98] Henry VIII's alleged remark in Ferrers' Case (below, p. 277) that privilege of Parliament covered both him and his servants may have been one of his little jokes; taken seriously, it would have spread the claim beyond all reason, for those entitled to call themselves the king's servants numbered many hundreds.

member, was arrested at the queen's suit (for a debt) before the sheriff had received the return; it was decided that privilege did not extend to him because he was technically not yet a member, but more particularly because the arrest had been procured by the Crown (**135**). In fact, the whole history of freedom from arrest under Elizabeth concerned cases of private action and did not settle what the Crown might do. After Strickland's Case of 1571 (**163**), Elizabeth was careful not even to give the impression that she was arresting a member for things done in the House; no one in her reign raised the cry of privilege on this issue. Wentworth, in 1576, was imprisoned on the Commons' own authority;[99] in 1587 he and other members were arrested during the session ostensibly for their strictly unconstitutional dealings before the opening of Parliament;[100] and the same excuse served for his final arrest in 1593.[101]

The so-called liberties of the House raise difficulties. In the Commons' minds they comprised certain powers which they thought necessary for the conduct of business. In 1581, Sir Walter Mildmay (chancellor of the Exchequer) told the Lords that the liberties of the Lower House included their right to call a conference when the bill in dispute was in their hands and their right to amend a bill signed by the queen—a warning not to overestimate the import of the term.[102] Taken seriously, however, these liberties could produce a claim that the Commons by themselves were a 'court' equipped with powers to summon and to try, but despite some loose references to the House as a court (e.g. **121**) it never came near to achieving that position. Its insistence, in 1549, to hear the evidence put before the Lords in Seymour's Case arose justifiably out of its legislative function: it ought to know what was alleged before it could agree to an act of attainder.[103] If this was a claim to curial status, which seems doubtful, it had no consequences. The Commons Journal never acquired the character of a 'record' in the legal sense; though it was recognised and ultimately supervised by the House, and though it recorded its orders which constituted precedents, it could not be alleged in another court.[104] When the Commons ordered the commitment to prison of any person, only the queen's writ could release him.[105] The House could not even compel the attendance of people before bill committees whom yet it called by Speaker's warrant: that warrant conveyed information, not a summons, and people came because it was in their interest to do

[99] Neale, *Elizabeth and her Parliaments*, I, 325 ff.
[100] Neale, *Elizabeth and her Parliaments*, II, 157.
[101] *Ibid.*, 260 ff.
[102] British Library, Cotton MSS, Titus F.i, fos. 216v–217r.
[103] Tanner, 513.
[104] For the Journal cf. Neale, *Trans. R. Hist. Soc.*, 1920, 136 ff., and the corrections offered in Elton, *Hist. Journal*, XXII, 262 ff.
[105] In Wentworth's Case (below, pp. 285 f.) the Commons could not get the prisoner out of the Tower until the queen offered them the chance to do so.

so. But though the House, unlike the Lords, was no court, it established some measure of control over its internal affairs which may be included among its 'liberties'. Involved in this general notion were several specific rights. Though as late as 1536, Thomas Cromwell, created a peer before the session of Parliament began, had been authorised by the king, without reference to the House and contrary to proper rules of qualification, to continue in the Commons for that session,[106] the power to decide whether a man was qualified for membership of the House was by mid-century vested in the Commons themselves (**136**). From this they soon progressed to a claim to decide disputed elections. Traditionally everything to do with elections was within the authority of Chancery which issued the writs, received the returns, and compiled the official (Crown Office) list of members; naturally any disputed or irregular election had always been referred to it as well. A case of 1581 (**137**) shows how the Commons crept into this business through their established claim to judge the qualifications of elected members. On that occasion the chancellor would not issue a writ for a new election until the Commons had decided to remove from his place a member who, though lawfully elected, had afterwards been convicted of felony. It was a short step from the chancellor's refusal to issue a writ until notified by the Commons of a vacancy, to the Commons' demand that they should authorise all writs arising out of uncertain elections. The point came up in the 1586 Parliament when a dispute arose in the election of knights for the shire of Norfolk.[107] After a possibly rigged election the Privy Council had ordered the issue of a new writ. The matter was raised at once when the Commons met, and although the queen told them not to interfere they appointed a committee and decided for the first election (**138**). Although the case was not clear enough for an unmistakable precedent—the chancellor and judges independently came to the same conclusion—the Commons had in effect asserted a right to decide disputed elections in spite of the queen's attempt to prevent this extension of privilege. Already in 1581 and 1584 committees had been set up to examine returns;[108] after the Norfolk election case, it became customary to appoint a standing committee of privileges at the beginning of a new Parliament and to commit all election disputes to it (**139**). In practice the Chancery had lost, though the House still had to assert their right against James I in Goodwin's Case in 1604.

The internal government of the House also became a private matter in this period. In 1515 an act empowered the Speaker, in place of the Crown, to license members to absent themselves (**140**). More significantly, in the reign of Elizabeth the Commons employed their 'curial' character to take punitive

106 Dugdale, *Summons*, 500.
107 Neale, *Elizabeth and her Parliaments*, II, 184 ff.
108 Tanner, 595.

action against a member. Peter Wentworth's speech on liberty led to his imprisonment and examination by order of the House; he had to make 'humble submission' before they would receive him back (**141**). But this case at least concerned proceedings in the House, as did that of Dr Parry who in 1584 was sequestered and forced to submit for speaking violently against the bill against Jesuits (**143**). That of Arthur Hall in 1581 went much further (**142**).[109] Hall, a cantankerous and excitable man, had not forgiven the Commons for his defeat in Smalley's Case; unfortunately for himself he unloaded his spleen in two pamphlets published in 1579–80. In these he not only revealed proceedings in Parliament, thus bringing himself within the clutches of privilege; he made sure that the Commons would act by attacking their excessive claims to privilege and disproving their happy notions of age-old precedent. Right as he was in telling the Commons that they were 'a new person in the Trinity', he did himself little good by the truth. In the 1581 Parliament, of which he was a member, he was fined, imprisoned and expelled the House. Though the queen quietly remitted the first two punishments as soon as the session ended, Hall, the champion of history against the innovatory notions of the Commons, had only succeeded in presenting them with a splendid precedent for their powers to fine and imprison and in general to sit in judgment on a member for things done outside Parliament.[110]

Lastly we may note that the Commons also secured recognition of a right to deal with non-members who had offended them (**145**). There were no major or outrageous cases in this period, such as occurred in later centuries. That the Commons should be able to admonish and briefly imprison outsiders who had somehow managed to sneak into the House and listen to debates, or to punish noisy and troublesome pages making a nuisance of themselves near the door of the House, was proper enough. Nor were these powers used at all frequently, and the precedents proved totally inadequate when in the next century the Commons wished to assert their independence against the Crown.

That leaves liberty of speech—that famous supposed right which entitled members to speak freely and without fear of the consequences in the Parliament.[111] It is this freedom which comes most readily to mind when parliamentary privilege is mentioned, but at the time it was not comprehended within that term, being assigned to the liberties (e.g. **127**). While, of course, it is true that without some such liberty Parliament could not have gained political influence or independence of mind, it is worth stressing that the Crown conceded it, and the occasional protesters claimed it, on

---

[109] Cf. Elton, *History and Imagination*, 88 ff.
[110] Hall had enough effrontery to get himself re-elected in 1584, but not enough to take his seat.
[111] The classic discussion is Neale, *Tudor Studies*, 257 ff., which, subject to some corrections and changes of perspective, remains acceptable.

the grounds that Parliament would not be useful to the monarch unless it freely gave its advice and opinion. Freedom of speech, like everything about Tudor Parliaments, arose from cooperation, not from conflict. Despite Young's Case of 1455, whose implications are doubtful, there is no good evidence that the issue was ever raised as a matter of liberty before the reign of Henry VIII. In that time, however, several decisive steps were taken. For one thing, in Strode's Case (1513) the Commons got formal recognition of the obvious point that, as part of the High Court of Parliament, they and their doings were privileged against inferior courts in the realm.[112] The real problem, of course, was the protection of speech against interference by the Crown. As far as is known, the first request by a Speaker for free speech in the proper sense—members' right to say what they liked, within the limits of decorum and respect, about any matter put before them—was made by Speaker More in 1523 (125),[113] and it is not without significance that the Parliament of 1523, notoriously a troublesome one, apparently discussed a wide variety of contentious matters (107). Certainly, Henry VIII respected the Commons' right to speak freely. He allowed attacks on his policy and even on his private concerns to pass without action more drastic than an explanatory address,[114] and we have Gardiner's word for it that by the 1540's parliamentary insistence on liberty of speech had become proverbial (108).[115] In fact, by 1558 the petition for freedom of speech had become regular, and the privilege was firmly established as one of right in practice, however much theory might insist on grace.

However, the extent and precise meaning of the privilege were quite another matter. No one doubted that the Commons enjoyed the right to say what they liked on matters before them, provided they avoided excess ('licence'); but neither More's petition nor Henry VIII's general practice supposed that they could demand to discuss anything they liked without leave from the Crown. The problem became acute in the reign of Elizabeth when every session produced a clash over issues which some members wished to discuss while the queen wanted them kept from Parliament.[116] What was new in the reign was not so much that some members had ideas on

[112] Cf. Tanner, 558 f. Richard Strode, a Devonshire burgess, had joined in promoting a bill hostile to the tin interests of the shire; for this he was fined and imprisoned by the Stannary Court until freed by writ of privilege out of the Exchequer. An act was passed (4 Henry VIII, c. 8) indemnifying him in particular but also enacting in general that utterances and doings in Parliament could not be made the basis of an action in other courts. The real importance of Strode's Case lies in the recognition of the Commons as a full partner in Parliament.

[113] Cf. above, p. 261 n. 95.

[114] Neale, *Tudor Studies*, 269 f. Cf. Hall, *Letter*, 78 f., who speaks of the 'contented minds lately shown by kings and queens' 'in matters of Parliament when things have not fallen out current to their expectations'.

[115] Gardiner had the Lords in mind.

[116] Cf. below, pp. 307 f.

policy, but that the Crown meant to stand still while other men wanted to move on. Since a few, at least, realised that the political and religious ambitions for which they stood could not be furthered unless they could raise them in the House, the constitutional question of freedom of speech became a battleground. The lead was taken by the brothers Wentworth, Paul and Peter, who attacked at two points. On the one hand, they resented the queen's attempts to inhibit free speech by what Peter Wentworth called 'rumours and messages'. It was put about that the queen liked this or misliked that, and that members would do well to heed her desires. Furthermore, Wentworth alleged that some in the House—he meant the privy councillors—revealed to the queen what had been said, so that freedom of speech was endangered by members' fears of the consequences. In these ways, even the old liberty of speech was limited beyond the point accepted by Henry VIII who had never used the weight of authority to inhibit discussion. It cannot be denied that in this matter Elizabeth was less generous than her father,[117] though it may be argued that she could not afford his willingness to let members have their say. The Wentworths were on less sure ground in their second and more fundamental attack. They maintained that free speech meant not liberty to discuss what was put before the House, but liberty to discuss anything which to the Commons seemed necessary for the good of the realm. In other words, they contended that freedom of speech also involved freedom to initiate debate on any issue. The argument was developed in three stages. In 1566 Paul Wentworth put three questions to the House in which he suggested that the queen's ban on a discussion of the succession problem was a breach of privilege.[118] In 1576 Peter Wentworth delivered his celebrated speech on liberty in which he rehearsed a general claim to the right to discuss all matters; here he took free speech to the limits of its possible definition (126).[119] And in 1587 Peter prepared a list of ten questions to be put to the House which elaborated his basic argument that the House of Commons, being a council of the realm, could not properly discharge its functions unless his interpretation of freedom of speech were accepted (127).[120]

That Wentworth had much logic on his side is as undeniable as that precedent was dead against him. In any case, he represented a minority view; in 1576 the House itself stopped him from continuing, and in 1587 the Speaker had no difficulty in preventing his questions from reaching the light of day. His extremism must not lead one to think that he was right. The queen had her own reasoned opinion of what constituted freedom of speech in Parliament, the best exposition of which is found in the lord keeper's reply to the

117 Cf. Neale, *Tudor Studies*, 284 f.
118 Neale, *Elizabeth and her Parliaments*, I, 152 ff.
119 *Ibid.*, I, 318 ff.
120 *Ibid.*, II, 154 ff.

Speaker's petition in 1593 (**128**). Members were free to speak without hindrance to any bill before them, but the initiative in introducing anything depended on the nature of the matter. 'Matters of state'—those touching the prerogative—could not be raised in the House unless the monarch had given express permission; and such matters of state included all those issues which concerned the queen in her person (her marriage, or the succession to the throne) and in her office as supreme governor in things spiritual and temporal (the settlement of religion, the conduct of foreign policy, the regulation of trade, the issue of letters patent such as those for monopolies). Needless to say, those were exactly the issues which ardent men of Wentworth's persuasion insisted on discussing. Elizabeth's distinction appears to have been her own invention: it did involve a principled restriction on freedom of speech. However, she could claim to be following the spirit of the precedents, and she managed to maintain her position. No monarch in the sixteenth century ever admitted anything so extreme as freedom of speech in the fullest sense, while none denied that such speech on proper topics as was used in Parliament should be entirely free and privileged. This particular privilege therefore reached the point where it was established but still involved in controversy over its precise meaning. Of all parliamentary liberties this alone arose from political rather than constitutional or procedural issues, and its further development therefore depended on changes in the political relationship between Crown and Commons.

No more, therefore, than the history of procedure does that of privilege offer proof that the House of Commons 'rose' in the sixteenth century. However, both procedure and privilege demonstrate a consolidation and elaboration of existing practices which testify to the institutional development of both Parliament as a whole and the Commons in particular. Though no one intended to set up a claim to ascendancy, or to dispute the essential unity of the tripartite sovereign body, precedents and practices were created which could be used in a more aggressive way, and the Lower House certainly acquired a very good opinion of itself.

124. The Speaker's petition for privilege.

[20 January 1542] . . . Hodie Communes presentabant Regie Majestati *Thomam Moyle*, singulorum suffragiis electum Prolocutorem suum. . . . Supplicavit Regie Majestati 'Ut in dicendis sententiis quivis libere et impune eloqui posset quid animi haberet et quid consilii.' Itaque, finiens orationem, nomine Communium petiit, 'Accedendi veniam ad Regiam Personam in causis magis perplexis et gravioribus quam ut ipsi inter se definire sufficerent.'

Cui quidem orationi Regia Majestas, maxima cum humanitate, sic respondit per Cancellarium. . . . 'Honestam dicendi libertatem non negare Regiam Majestatem, tum etiam accessum permittere ad suam personam, quoties usus postulaverit; ita tamen ut perplexas hujusmodi causas non per universam multitudinem sed per pauculos aliquot cordatiores viros, ejus Majestati significare satagerent. . . .' *Lords' Journals, I, 167*

[28 January 1559] . . . And lastly [Sir Thomas Gargrave] came, according to the usual form, first, to desire liberty of access for the House of Commons to the Queen's Majesty's presence upon all urgent and necessary occasions. Secondly, that if in anything himself should mistake or misreport or overslip that which should be committed unto him to declare, that it might without prejudice to the House be better declared, and that his unwilling miscarriage therein might be pardoned. Thirdly, that they might have liberty and freedom of speech in whatsoever they treated of or had occasion to propound and debate in the House. The fourth and last, that all the members of the House, with their servants and necessary attendants, might be exempted from all manner of arrests and suits during the continuance of the Parliament, and the usual space both before the beginning and after the ending thereof, as in former times hath always been accustomed.

To which speech of the said Speaker . . . the lord keeper . . . replied . . .

. . . To these petitions the Queen's Majesty hath commanded me to say unto you that her Highness is right well contented to grant them unto you as largely as amply and as liberally as ever they were granted by any her noble progenitors; and to confirm the same with as great an authority. Marry, with these conditions and cautions: first, that your access be void of impunity, and for matters needful, and in time convenient. For the second, that your diligence and carefulness be such, Mr Speaker, that the defaults in that part be as rare as may be; whereof her Majesty doubteth little. For the third, which is liberty of speech, therewith her Highness is right well contented, but so as they be neither unmindful or uncareful of their duties, reverence and obedience to their sovereign. For the last, great heed would be taken that no evil-disposed person seek of purpose that privilege for the only defrauding of his creditors and for the maintenance of injuries and wrongs. These admonitions being well remembered, her Majesty thinketh all the said liberties and privileges well granted. . . . *D'Ewes, Journals, 16–17*

125. Sir Thomas More's request, 1523.

. . . Forasmuch as there be of your Commons, here by your high commandment assembled for your Parliament, a great number which are . . . appointed in the Common House to treat and advise of the common affairs among themselves apart; and albeit . . . there hath been as due diligence used in sending up to your Highness' Court of Parliament the most discreet persons out of every quarter that men could esteem meet thereunto, . . . yet, most victorious prince, since among so many wise men neither is every man wise alike, nor among so many men like well witted, every man like well spoken. And it often happeneth that, likewise as much folly is uttered with painted polished speech, so many, boisterous and rude in language, see deep indeed and give right substantial counsel. And since also in matters of great importance the mind is often so occupied in the matter that a man rather studieth what to say than how, by reason whereof the wisest man and the best spoken in the whole country fortuneth among, while his mind is fervent in the matter, somewhat to speak in such wise as he would afterward wish to have been uttered otherwise, and yet no worse will had when he spake it than he hath when he would so gladly change it; therefore, most gracious sovereign, considering that in your High Court of Parliament is nothing entreated but matter of weight and importance concerning your realm and your own royal estate, it could not fail to let and put to silence from the giving of their advice and counsel many of your discreet Commons, to the great hindrance of the common affairs, except that every of your Commons were utterly discharged of all doubt and fear how anything that it should happen them to speak should happen of your Highness to be taken. . . . It may therefore like your most abundant Grace, our most benigne and godly King, to give to all your Commons here assembled your most gracious licence and pardon, freely, without doubt of your dreadful displeasure, every man to discharge his conscience and boldly in every thing incident among us to declare his advice; and whatsoever happen any man to say, that it may like your noble Majesty, of your inestimable goodness, to take all in good part, interpreting every man's words, how uncunningly so ever they be couched, to proceed yet of good zeal towards the profit of your realm and honour of your royal person, the prosperous estate and preservation whereof, most excellent sovereign, is the thing which we all, your must humble loving subjects, according to the most bounden duty of our natural allegiance, most highly desire and pray for. *Roper, Life of More, 14–16*

126. Peter Wentworth's speech, 1576.

Mr Speaker, I find written in a little volume these words in effect: Sweet is the name of liberty, but the thing itself a value beyond all inestimable treasure. So much the more it behoveth us to take care lest we, contenting ourselves with the sweetness of the name, lose and forego the thing, being of the greatest value that can come unto this noble realm. The inestimable treasure is the use of it in this House. . . .

. . . Sometime it happeneth that a good man will in this place (for argument sake) prefer an evil cause, both for that he would have a doubtful truth to be opened and manifested, and also the evil prevented; so that to this point I conclude that in this House, which is termed a place of free speech, there is nothing so necessary for the preservation of the prince and state as free speech, and without, it is a scorn and mockery to call it a Parliament House, for in truth it is none, but a very school of flattery and dissimulation, and so a fit place to serve the devil and his angels in, and not to glorify God and benefit the commonwealth. . . .

. . . Amongst other, Mr Speaker, two things do great hurt in this place, of the which I do mean to speak. The one is a rumour which runneth about the House, and this it is, 'Take heed what you do; the Queen's Majesty liketh not such a matter; whosoever preferreth it, she will be offended with him': or the contrary, 'Her Majesty liketh of such a matter; whosoever speaketh against it, she will be much offended with him.' The other: sometimes a message is brought into the House, either of commanding or inhibiting, very injurious to the freedom of speech and consultation. I would to God, Mr Speaker, that these two were buried in hell, I mean rumours and messages, for wicked undoubtedly they are; the reason is, the devil was the first author of them, from whom proceedeth nothing but wickedness. . . .

. . . Now the other was a message Mr Speaker brought the last sessions into the House, that we should not deal in any matters of religion but first to receive from the bishops. Surely this was a doleful message, for it was as much as to say, Sirs, ye shall not deal in God's causes, no, ye shall in no wise seek to advance his glory. . . . Truly I assure you, Mr Speaker, there were divers of this House that said with grievous hearts immediately upon the message, that God of his justice could not prosper the session; . . . God . . . was the last session shut out of doors. But what fell out of it, forsooth? His great indignation was therefore poured upon this House, for he did put into the Queen's Majesty's heart to refuse good and wholesome laws for her own preservation, the which caused many faithful hearts for grief to burst out with sorrowful tears, and moved all papists, traitors to God and her Majesty . . . in their sleeves to laugh all the whole Parliament House to scorn. . . . So certain it is, Mr Speaker, that none is without fault, no, not our noble Queen, since then her Majesty hath committed great fault, yea, dangerous faults to herself. . . .

. . . It is a dangerous thing in a prince unkindly to abuse his or her nobility and people, and it is a dangerous thing in a prince to oppose or bend herself against her nobility and people. . . . And how could any prince more unkindly intreat, abuse, oppose herself against her nobility and people than her Majesty did the last Parliament? . . . And will not this her Majesty's handling, think you, Mr Speaker, make cold dealing in any of her Majesty's subjects toward her again? I fear it will. . . . And I beseech . . . God to endue her Majesty with his wisdom, whereby she may discern faithful advice from traitorous, sugared speeches, and to send her Majesty a melting, yielding heart unto sound counsel, that will may not stand for a reason; and then her Majesty will stand when her enemies are fallen, for no estate can stand where the prince will not be governed by advice. And I doubt not but that some of her Majesty's Council have dealt plainly and faithfully with her Majesty herein; . . . I have heard from old Parliament-men that the banishment of the pope and popery and the restoring of true religion had their beginning from this House and not from the bishops. . . . And I do surely think, before God I speak it, that the bishops were the cause of that doleful message, and I will shew you what moveth me so to think: I was, amongst others, the last Parliament sent unto the bishop of Canterbury for the Articles of Religion that then passed this House. He asked us why we did put out of the book the articles for the homilies, consecrating of bishops, and such like? 'Surely, sir,' said I, 'because we were so occupied in other matters that we had no time to examine them how they agreed with the word of God.' 'What?' said he, 'surely you mistook the matter; you will refer yourselves wholly to us therein?' 'No, by the faith I bear to God,' said I, 'we will pass nothing before we understand what it is; for that were but to make you popes.'

'Make you popes who list,' said I, 'for we will make you none.' And sure, Mr Speaker, the speech seemed to me to be a pope-like speech, and I fear lest our bishops do attribute this of the pope's canons to themselves, *Papa non potest errare.* . . . D'Ewes, *Journals*, 236–40

127. Peter Wentworth's questions, 1587. [121]

1. First, whether the prince and state can be maintained without this Court of Parliament.

2. Item, whether there be any council that can make or abrogate laws, but only this Court of Parliament.

3. Item, whether free speech and free doings or dealings be not granted to every one of the Parliament House by law.

4. Item, whether that great honour to God and those great benefits may be done unto the prince and state without free speech and doings in this place that may be done with them.

5. Whether it be not an injury to the whole state and against the law that the prince or Privy Council should send for any member of this House in the Parliament time, or after the end of the Parliament, and to check, blame or punish them for any speech used in this place, except it be for traitorous words.

6. Item, whether this be a place to receive supplications of the griefs and sores of the commonwealth, and either that we should be humble suitors unto the Queen her Majesty for relief or else to relieve them here, as the case requires.

7. Item, whether it be not against the orders and liberties of this House to receive messages either of commanding or prohibiting, and whether the messenger be not to be reputed as an enemy to God, the prince and the state.

8. Item, whether it be not against the orders and liberties of this House to make anything known to the prince that is here in hand to the hurt of the House, and whether the tale-carrier be not to be punished by the House and reputed as an enemy unto God, the prince and the state.

9. Item, whether we do show ourselves faithful unto God, the prince and the state in receiving such messages and in taking such tales in good part without punishing of the messenger and tale-carrier by the order and discretion of this House.

[121] This is a better version of the paper than that given in D'Ewes, *Journals*, 410–11.

10. Item, whether he or they may be not to be esteemed, reputed and used as enemies unto God, the prince and state that should do anything to infringe the liberties of this honourable Council.

Printed by Neale, *Eng. Hist. Rev.*, XXXIX, 48

128. The lord keeper's statement, 1593.

... I ∴ . will therefore descend to your last part, wherein I noted three petitions for your company and a fourth for yourself. Her gracious Majesty is well pleased to grant them so far as they be grantable. She sayeth there be two things in a man most behoveful if they be well used, and most deadly if they be ill used: wit and tongue, they are those; they be most happy possessions and needful helps, and all as they be placed. Having therefore especial care that that may never hurt you which she by her grant doth yield you, she wills you take good heed in what sort she permits it. She would be sorry that folly past should by new redouble the faults, and chargeth you, Mr Speaker, if any shall deliver to you any bill that passeth the reach of a subject's brain to mention, that same you receive not but with purpose to shew it where it best becometh you. Next, if any speech undecent or matter unfit for that place be used, remember them of this lesson: Your petitions ... must be ruled, and that her Majesty granteth you liberal but not licentious speech, liberty therefore but with due limitation. For even as there can be no good consultation where all freedom of advice is barred, so will there be no good conclusion where every man may speak what he listeth, without fit observation of persons, matters, times, places and other needful circumstances. It shall be meet therefore that each man of you contain his speech within the bounds of loyalty and good discretion, being assured that as the contrary is punishable in all men, so most of all in them that take upon them to be counsellors and procurators of the commonwealth. For liberty of speech her Majesty commandeth me to tell you that to say yea or no to bills, God forbid that any man should be restrained or afraid to answer according to his best liking, with some short declaration of his reason therein, and therein to have a free voice, which is the very true liberty of the House; not, as some suppose, to speak there of all causes as him listeth, and to frame a form of religion or a state of government as to their idle brains shall seem meetest. She saith no king fit for his state will suffer such absurdities, and though she hopeth no man here longeth so much for his ruin as that he mindeth to make such a peril to his own safety, yet that you may better follow what she wisheth, she makes of her goodness you the partakers of her intent and meaning. Access to her Majesty's most sacred presence her Highness is likewise pleased to vouchsafe, so that the same be desired only in matters of the greatest exigency and weight, and with due respect of times, that her Majesty's more important cogitations be not interpelled thereby. Neither is the mind of her gracious Majesty to deny you those other good privileges of the Court of Parliament which the Commons of the realm heretofore have usually enjoyed, howbeit with this caution, that the protection of your House be not worn by any man for a cloak to defraud others of their debts and duties. . . . Printed by Neale, in *Eng. Hist. Rev.*, xxxi, 136–7

129. Ferrers' Case, 1542.

In the Lent season, whilst the Parliament yet continued, one George Ferrers, gentleman, servant to the King, being elected a burgess for the town of Plymouth in the county of Devonshire, in going to the Parliament House was arrested in London by a process out of the King's Bench at the suit of one White for the sum of 200 marks or thereabouts, wherein he was late afore condemned as a surety for the debt of one Weldon of Salisbury; which arrest being signified to Sir Thomas Moyle, knight, then Speaker of the Parliament, and to the knights and burgesses there, order was taken that the serjeant of the Parliament, called St John, should forthwith repair to the Counter in Bread Street (wither the said Ferrers was carried) and there demand delivery of the prisoner.

The serjeant (as he had in charge) went to the Counter and declared to the clerks there what he had in commandment. But they and other officers of the City were so far from obeying the said commandment as after many stout words they forcibly resisted the said serjeant, whereof ensued a fray within the Counter gates between the said Ferrers and the said officers, not without hurt of either part; so that the said serjeant was driven to defend himself with his mace of arms and had the crown thereof broken by bearing off a stroke, and his man stricken down. During this brawl the sheriffs of London . . . came thither, to whom the serjeant complained of this injury and required of them the delivery of the said burgess, as afore. But they, bearing with their officers, made little account either of his complaint or of his message, rejecting the same contemptuously with much proud language, so as the serjeant was forced to return without the prisoner. . . .

The serjeant, thus hardly intreated, made return to the Parliament House, and finding the Speaker and all the burguesses set in their places declared unto them the whole case as it fell, who took the same in so ill part that they all together (of whom there were not a few as well of the King's Privy Council as also of his Privy Chamber) would sit no longer without their burgess, but rose up wholly and repaired to the Upper House, where the whole case was declared by the mouth of the Speaker before Sir Thomas Audley, knight, then lord chancellor of England, and all the lords and judges there assembled, who, judging the contempt to be very great, referred the punishment thereof to the order of the Common House. They returning to their places again, upon new debate of the case, took order that their serjeant should eftsoons repair to the sheriff of London and require delivery of the said burgess without any writ or warrant had for the same, but only as afore.

And yet the lord chancellor offered there to grant a writ which they of the Common House refused, being in a clear opinion that all commandments and other acts of proceeding from the Nether House were to be done and executed by their serjeant without writ, only by show of his mace, which was his warrant. But before the serjeant's return into London, the sheriffs, having intelligence how heinously the matter was taken, became somewhat more mild, so as upon the said second demand they delivered the prisoner without any denial. But the serjeant, having then further in commandment from those of the Nether House, charged the said sheriffs to appear personally on the morrow by eight of the clock before the Speaker in the Nether House and to bring thither the clerks of the Counter and such officers as were parties to the said affray, and in like manner to take into his custody the said White which wittingly procured the said arrest in contempt of the privilege of the Parliament.

Which commandment being done by the said serjeant accordingly, on the morrow . . . the said sheriffs and the same White were committed to the Tower of London, and the said clerk (which was the occasion of the affray) to a place there called 'Little Ease', and the officer of London which did the arrest . . . with four other officers to Newgate, where they remained from the 28th until the 30th of March, and then they were delivered, not without humble suit made by the mayor of London and other their friends. And for so much as the said

Ferrers, being in execution upon a condemnation of debt and set at large by privilege of Parliament, was not by law to be brought again into execution, and so the party without remedy for his debt . . . after long debate of the same by the space of nine or ten days together, at last they resolved upon an act of Parliament to be made and to revive the execution of the said debt against the said Weldon . . . and to discharge the said Ferrers. But before this came to pass, the Common House was divided upon the question; howbeit, in conclusion, the act passed . . . by fourteen voices.

The King then being advertised of all this proceeding, called immediately before him the lord chancellor of England and his judges, with the Speaker of the Parliament and other of the gravest persons of the Nether House, to whom he declared his opinion to this effect. First commending their wisdoms in maintaining the privileges of their House (which he would not have to be infringed in any point) he alleged that he, being head of the Parliament and attending in his own person upon the business thereof, ought in reason to have privilege for him and all his servants attending there upon him. So that if the said Ferrers had been no burgess, but only his servant, yet in respect thereof he was to have the privilege as well as any other. 'For I understand,' quoth he, 'that you not only for your own persons but also for your necessary servants, even to your cooks and horsekeepers, enjoy the said privilege. . . . And further we be informed by our judges that we at no time stand so highly in our estate royal as in the time of Parliament, wherein we as head and you as members are conjoined and knit together into one body politic, so as whatsoever offence or injury (during that time) is offered to the meanest member of the House is to be judged as done against our person and the whole Court of Parliament. Which prerogative of the court is so great (as our learned counsel informeth us) as all acts and processes coming out of any other inferior courts must for the time cease and give place to the highest. . . .'

Holinshed, III, 824–6

130. Lord Cromwell's Case, 1572.

[30 June 1572] . . . Whereas upon complaint and declaration made to the said Lords spiritual and temporal by Henry, Lord Cromwell, a lord of the Parliament, that in a case between one James Tavernor against the said Lord Cromwell depending in the Court of Chancery, for not obeying to an injunction given in the said Court of Chancery, in the absence of the lord keeper of the great seal, at the suit of the said Tavernor the person of the said Lord Cromwell was by the sheriff of the county of Norfolk attached, by virtue of a writ of attachment proceeding out of the said Court of Chancery, contrary to the ancient privilege and immunity time out of memory unto the lords of Parliament and peers of this realm in such case used and allowed, as on behalf of the said Lord Cromwell was declared and affirmed, wherein the said Lord Cromwell as a lord of Parliament prayed remedy.

Forasmuch as, upon deliberate examination of this case in the said Parliament Chamber in the presence of the judges and other of the Queen's Majesty's learned counsel there attendant in Parliament, and upon declaration of the opinions of the said judges and learned counsel, there hath been no matter directly produced or declared whereby it did appear or seem to the said lords of Parliament there assembled that by the common law or custom of the realm, or by any statute law, or by any precedent of the said Court of Chancery, it is warranted that the person of any lord having place and voice in Parliament in the like case in the said Court of Chancery before this time hath been attached, so as the awarding of the said attachment at the suit of the said Tavernor against the said Lord Cromwell, for anything as yet declared to the said lords, appeareth to be derogatory and prejudicial to the ancient privilege claimed to belong to the lords of this realm.

Therefore it is . . . ordered by consent of all the said lords in Parliament there assembled, that the person of the said Lord Cromwell be from henceforth discharged of and from the said attachment. . . .

D'Ewes, Journals, 203

131. Smalley's Case, 1576.

[20 February 1576] . . . Upon the question, and also upon the division of the House, it was ordered that Edward Smalley, yeoman, servant unto Arthur Hall, esquire, one of the burgesses for Grantham, shall have privilege . . . (p. 249).

[22 February 1576] . . . Report was made by Mr Attorney of the Duchy . . . that the committees found no precedent for setting at large by the mace any person in arrest, but only by writ, and that by divers precedents of records perused by the said committees it appeareth that every knight, citizen and burgess of this House which doth require privilege, hath used in that case to take a corporal oath before the lord chancellor or lord keeper . . . that the party for whom such writ is prayed came up with him and was his servant at the time of the arrest made; and that Mr Hall was thereupon moved by this House that he should repair to the lord keeper and make oath in form aforesaid, and then to proceed to the taking of a warrant for a writ of privilege for his said servant according to the said report of the said former precedents . . . (p. 249).

[27 February 1576] . . . After sundry reasons and arguments, it was resolved that Edward Smalley, servant unto Arthur Hall, esquire, shall be brought hither to-morrow by the serjeant, and set at liberty by warrant of the mace and not by writ . . . (p. 250).

[28 February 1576] . . . Edward Smalley . . . being this day brought to the bar in the House by the serjeant of this House and accompanied with two serjeants of London, was presently delivered from his imprisonment and execution according to the former judgment of this House, and the said serjeants of London discharged of their said prisoner; and immediately after that, the said serjeants of London were sequestered out of this House, and the said Edward Smalley was committed to the charge of the serjeant of this House. And thereupon the said Edward Smalley was sequestered till this House should be resolved upon some former motions, whether the said Edward Smalley did procure himself to be arrested upon the said execution in the abusing and contempt of this House or not . . . (p. 251).

[7 March 1576] . . . Upon the question, it was ordered that Mr Hall be sequestered the House while the matter touching the supposed contempt done to this House be argued and debated. Edward Smalley, upon the question, was adjudged guilty of contempt and abusing of this House by fraudulent practice of procuring himself to be arrested upon the execution of his own assent, and intention to be discharged as well of his imprisonment as of the said execution. . . . Upon another question it was adjudged by the House that the said Smalley be for his misdemeanour and contempt committed to the prison of the Tower . . . (p. 254).

[10 March 1576] . . . Edward Smalley . . . appearing in this House this day at the bar, it was pronounced unto him by Mr Speaker, in the name and by the appointment and order of this House, for execution of the former judgment of this House awarded against him, that he the said Edward Smalley shall be forthwith committed prisoner from this House to the Tower of London, and there remain for one whole month next ensuing from this present day, and further after the same month expired, until such time as good and sufficient assurance shall be had and made for payment of £100 [to his creditor] . . . and also forty shillings for the serjeant's fees . . . (p. 258). D'Ewes, *Journals*, 249–58

132. Case of Robert Finnies, 1584.

[7 December 1584] . . . Whereas the Lord Viscount Bindon moved the Lords for the privilege of the House for Robert Finnies, alleging that he was his servant, the Lords gave commandment to the gentleman usher to go to the Counter in Wood Street, where the said Robert Finnies then lay upon an execution, and to bring him and the parties that arrested him before them. And this day the said Lords, after hearing of the cause, thought it not convenient that the said Robert Finnies should enjoy the privilege of this House, as well because he claimed not the privilege when he was first arrested nor in the Counter when he was charged with the execution, as also for that he was not a menial servant nor yet ordinary attendant upon the said viscount. . . .

D'Ewes, *Journals*, 315

133. Case of Richard Cook, 1585.

[10 February 1585] . . . Upon a motion this day made touching the opinion of this House for privilege in a case of subpoena out of the Chancery served upon Richard Cook, esquire, a member of this House. . . . It was ordered, That Mr Recorder of London, Mr Sandys and Mr Cromwell, attended on by the serjeant of this House, shall presently repair in the name of the whole House into the body of the Court of Chancery and there to signify unto the lord chancellor and the master of the Rolls that by the ancient liberties of this House the members of the same are privileged from being served with subpoenas. . . .

[11 February 1585] . . . Mr Recorder of London, Mr Cromwell and Mr Sandys, being returned from the Chancery, did declare unto the House that they have been in Chancery within the court and there were very gently and courteously heard in the delivery of the message and charge of this House committed unto them; and were answered by the lord chancellor that he thought this House had no such liberty of privilege for subpoenas as they pretended, neither would he allow of any precedents of this House committed unto them formerly used in that behalf, unless this House could also prove the same to have been likewise thereupon allowed and ratified also by the precedents in the said Court of Chancery. . . . D'Ewes, *Journals*, 347

134. Procedure by supersedeas, 1589.

[21 February 1589] . . . Upon a motion made by Mr Harris, that divers members of this House having writs of *nisi prius* brought against them to be tried at the assizes in sundry places of this realm to be holden and kept in the circuits of this present vacation, and that writs of supersedeas might be awarded in those cases in respect of the privilege of this House due and appertaining to the members of the same; It is agreed, that those of this House which shall have occasion to require such benefit of privilege in that behalf may repair unto Mr Speaker to declare unto him the state of their cases, and that he upon his discretion (if the cases shall so require) may direct the warrant of this House to the lord chancellor of England for the awarding of such writs of supersedeas accordingly.   D'Ewes, *Journals*, 436

135. Fitzherbert's Case, 1593.

[7 March 1593] . . . Sir Edward Hobby, moving the cause of Mr Fitzherbert his bringing up into this House by a writ of *habeas corpus cum causa* from the lord keeper, sheweth, That he hath moved the lord keeper touching the said writ, and that his lordship thinketh best, in regard of the ancient liberties and privileges of this House, that a serjeant-at-arms be sent by order of this House for the said Mr Fitzherbert at his own charge, by reason whereof he may be brought hither to this House without peril of further being arrested by the way, and the state of this cause to be considered of and examined when he shall be come hither: which was thereupon well liked and allowed by this House.

[5 April 1593] . . . The business so much before agitated touching Mr Fitzherbert received this day the final resolution of the House . . . which said case was singly this. Thomas Fitzherbert being elected a burgess of the Parliament, two hours after his election and before the return of the writ to the sheriff with the indenture of his election, the said sheriff arresteth him upon a *capias utlagatum* in an outlawry after judgment at the Queen's suit. . . . Upon all which matters there grew two questions: First, whether the said Mr Fitzherbert were a member of the House; and secondly, admitting he were, yet whether he ought to have privilege. . . . The judgment of the House was that Thomas Fitzherbert was by his election a member thereof, yet that he ought not to have privilege in three respects. First, because he was taken in execution before the return of the indenture of his election; Secondly, because he had been outlawed at the Queen's suit and was now taken in execution for her Majesty's debt; Thirdly and lastly, in regard that he was so taken by the sheriff neither *sedente Parliamento*, nor *eundo*, nor *redeundo*.

D'Ewes, Journals, 490, 518

136. Qualifications of members.

[21 January 1550] . . . It is ordered, That Sir Francis Russell, son and heir-apparent of the now earl of Bedford, shall abide in this House in the state he was before. . . .

[13 October 1553] . . . It is declared by the commissioners that Alex. Nowell, being prebendary in Westminster, and thereby having voice in the Convocation House, cannot be a member of this House; and so agreed by the House, and the Queen's writ to be directed for another burgess in that place.

Commons' Journal, I, 15, 27

137. Election writs, 1581.

[21 January 1581] Mr Broughton also this forenoon made a motion to know the mind of the House touching his companion or fellow-burgess, who now stood indicted of felony, whether he ought to remain of the House or forbear coming, or that a new one should be elected in his place. Whereupon after the matter had been a while agitated and disputed of in the House, it was adjudged that he ought to remain of the House till he were convicted: for it may be any man's case who is guiltless to be accused and thereupon indicted of felony or a like crime. After which judgment given by the House, Mr Norton did further inform them that the lord chancellor willed him to signify unto the House that this matter had been moved to him and that a new writ had been desired of him for the election of another in the place of the said burgess; but that his lordship had refused to yield thereunto and had further alleged that he ought first to be removed by the judgment of the House; and that thereupon, the House signifying so much to his lordship, he would thereupon grant a new writ for a second election to be made. The judgment of the lord chancellor, who was both learned in the laws and had been an ancient Parliament man,[122] was much commended by the House, and the rather because it so opportunely concurred at this time with the judgment of the House. Which

---

[122] Sir Thomas Bromley.

resolution seemeth cross to that former opinion before-given in the House on Thursday last the 19th day of this instant January, *viz*. that new burgesses being returned in the place of others living were to be allowed and received in the House.

D'Ewes, *Journals*, 283

138. The Norfolk Election, 1586.

[3 November 1586] ... Mr Speaker shewed unto the House that he received commandment from my lord chancellor from her Majesty to signify unto them, that her Highness was sorry this House was troubled the last sitting thereof with the matter touching the choosing and returning of the knights for the county of Norfolk: a thing in truth impertinent for this House to deal withal, and only belonging to the charge and office of the lord chancellor, from whence the writs for the same elections issued out and are thither returnable again. And also that her Majesty had appointed the said lord chancellor to confer therein with the judges; and so thereupon examining the said returns, and the sheriff touching the matter and circumstances of his proceedings in the said elections, to set down such course for making the true return as to justice and right shall therein appertain.

[11 November 1586] Mr Cromwell, one of the committees for the examination of writs and the returns for the knights of the county of Norfolk ... maketh report: ... They do find that the first writ and return, both in manner and form, was perfect and also duly executed, and the second writ not so; and that besides it might also be a perilous precedent ... to the liberty and privilege of this House to admit or pass over any such writ or return in such manner and course as the said second writ carrieth; ... the lord chancellor and the judges had resolved, that the said first writ should be returned as that which was in all parts duly and rightly executed, and not the second. ... One of the committees, assenting with the residue in opinion of [the] validity of the said first writ and return and of the invalidity of the second, and also in resolution that the explanation and ordering of the case as it standeth appertaineth only to the censure of this House, moved notwithstanding in the committee that two of the committees might be sent to the said lord chancellor to understand what his lordship had done in the matter; which the residue thought not convenient, first, for that they were sufficiently satisfied therein by divers of themselves, but principally in respect they thought it very prejudicial and injurious to the privilege and liberties of this House to have the said cause decided or dealt in in any sort by any others than only by such as are members of this House; and that albeit they thought very reverently (as becometh them) of the said lord chancellor and judges, and know them to be competent judges in their places, yet in this case they took them not for judges in Parliament in this House; and so further required that (if it were so thought good) Mr Farmer and Mr Gresham might take their oaths, and be allowed of and received into this House by force of the said first writ, as so allowed and admitted only by the censure of this House and not as allowed of by the said lord chancellor or judges. Which was agreed unto accordingly by the whole House, and so ordered also to be set down and entered by the clerk.   D'Ewes, *Journals*, 393, 398–9

139. Scrutiny of elections, 1593.

[26 February 1593] Ordered that all the members of this House being of her Majesty's Privy Council [with thirty others] shall, during all this present sessions of Parliament, examine and make report of all such cases touching the elections and returns of any of the knights, citizens, burgesses and barons[123] of this House, and also all such cases for privilege as in any wise may occur or fall out during all the same sessions of Parliament; to the end this House upon the reports of the same examinations may proceed to such further course in every the same cases as to this House shall be thought meet. And it is further ordered that the said committees do meet upon Wednesday next in the Exchequer Chamber at three of the clock in the afternoon to examine the manner of the said election of the said Richard Hutton, and also any other case of elections, returns or privileges whatsoever in question, which shall be moved unto them by any member of this House at their pleasure. And notice was then also given in the House to all the members of the same that in all these cases they might from time to time repair to the said committees as occasion shall serve accordingly.   D'Ewes, *Journals*, 471

140. An Act concerning burgesses of the Parliament (1515: 6 Henry VIII, c. 16).

For so much as commonly in the end of every Parliament divers and many great and weighty matters . . . are to be treated, commoned of

---

[123] The members for the Cinque Ports were styled barons.

and by authority of Parliament to be concluded, So it is that divers knights of shires, citizens for cities, burgesses for boroughs, and barons of the Cinque Ports long time before the end of the said Parliament of their own authorities depart and go home into their countries, whereby the said great and weighty matters are many times greatly delayed, In consideration whereof be it enacted by the King our sovereign lord, the Lords spiritual and temporal and the Commons in this present Parliament assembled, and by authority of the same, that from henceforth none of the said knights, citizens, burgesses and barons . . . do not depart from the same Parliament nor absent himself from the same till the same Parliament be fully finished, ended or prorogued; except he or they so departing have licence of the Speaker and Commons in the same Parliament assembled, and the same licence to be entered or record in the book of the clerk of the Parliament appointed . . . for the Commons' House. [Unauthorised departure is to be punished by loss of member's wages.]   *Stat. Realm*, III, 134

141. Punishment of a member (Peter Wentworth, 1576).

[9 February 1576] This day, Mr Treasurer,[124] in the name of all the committees yesterday appointed for the examination of Peter Wentworth, burgess for Tregoney, declared that all the said committees did meet yesterday in the afternoon in the Star Chamber . . . and there examining the said Peter Wentworth touching the violent and wicked words yesterday pronounced by him in this House touching the Queen's Majesty, made a collection of the same words; which words so collected the said Peter Wentworth did acknowledge and confess. And then did the said Mr Treasurer read unto the House the said note of collection, which being read, he declared further that the said Peter Wentworth, being examined what he could say for the extenuating of his said fault and offence, could neither say anything at all to that purpose, neither yet did charge any other person as author of his said speech, but did take all the burden thereof unto himself; and so the said Mr Treasurer thereupon moved for his punishment and imprisonment in the Tower as the House should think good and consider of; whereupon, after sundry disputations and speeches, it was ordered upon the question that the said Peter Wentworth should be committed close prisoner to the Tower for his said offence, there to remain until such

---

[124] Sir Francis Knollys, treasurer of the Household.

time as this House should have further consideration of him. And thereupon immediately the said Peter Wentworth, being brought to the bar by the serjeant, received his said judgment accordingly by the mouth of Mr Speaker in form above recited; and so Mr Lieutenant of the Tower was presently charged with the custody of the said Peter Wentworth. . . .

[12 March 1576] . . . Mr Captain of the Guard did first shortly declare and make report unto the House that whereas a member of the same had [on 8 February] uttered in a prepared speech divers offensive matters touching her Majesty, and had for the same been sent prisoner to the Tower by the House, yet that her Majesty was now graciously pleased to remit her just-occasioned displeasure for the said offence and to refer the enlargement of the party to the House, which was most thankfully accepted by the same upon the said report. . . .

Mr Peter Wentworth was brought by the serjeant-at-arms that attended the House to the bar within the same, and after some declaration made unto him by Mr Speaker in the name of the whole House both of his own great fault and offence and also of her Majesty's great and bountiful mercy shewed unto him, and after his humble submission upon his knees acknowledging his fault and craving her Majesty's pardon and favour, he was received again into the House and restored to his place, to the great contentment of all that were present.

D'Ewes, *Journals*, 244, 259–60

142. Case of Arthur Hall, 1581.

[14 February 1581] . . . Where it was informed unto this House . . . that Arthur Hall, of Grantham in the county of Lincoln, esquire, had, since the last session of this Parliament made, set forth in print and published a book, dedicated unto Sir Henry Knyvet, knight, a good member of this House, without his privity, liking or allowance, in part tending greatly to the slander and reproach not only of Sir Robert Bell, knight, deceased, late Speaker of this Parliament, and of sundry particular members of this House, but also of the proceedings of this House in the same last session of Parliament in a cause that concerned the said Arthur Hall and one Smalley, his man;[125] and that there was also contained a long discourse tending to the diminishment of the ancient authority of this House. And that thereupon by order of this

125 Cf. above, pp. 278 f.

House the said Arthur Hall was sent for by the serjeant of this House to appear . . . which he did accordingly. Whereupon being called to the bar and charged by the Speaker with the information given against him, he confessed the making and setting forth thereof. Whereupon the said Arthur Hall being sequestered, the House did presently appoint divers committees to take a more particular examination of the said cause, and of all such as had been doers therein. . . .

. . . It was . . . resolved and ordered that he should remain in the said prison of the Tower by the space of six months and so much longer as until himself should willingly make a particular revocation or retractation under his hand in writing of the said errors and slanders contained in the said book, to the satisfaction of this House, or of such order as this House shall take for the same, during the continuance of this present session of Parliament. And . . . it was also . . . resolved and ordered, that a fine should be assessed by this House to the Queen's Majesty's use upon the said Arthur Hall for his said offence . . . and . . . that the same fine should be 500 marks. . . . It was likewise resolved and ordered that the said Arthur Hall should presently be removed, severed and cut off from being any longer a member of this House during the continuance of this present Parliament, and that the Speaker by authority from this House should direct a warrant from this House to the clerk of the crown office in the Chancery for awarding of the Queen's Majesty's writ to the sheriff of the said county of Lincoln for a new burgess to be returned into this present Parliament for the said borough of Grantham, in the lieu and stead of the said Arthur Hall so as before disabled any longer to be a member of this House. . . .

D'Ewes, *Journals*, 296, 298

143. Case of Dr Parry, 1584.

[17 December 1584] . . . The bill against Jesuits, seminary priests, and such like disobedient subjects . . . passed the House with little or no argument, except it were from one Doctor Parry, who in very violent terms spake directly against the whole bill, affirming it to savour of treasons, to be full of blood, danger, despair and terror or dread to the English subjects of this realm, our brethren, uncles and kinsfolks, and also full of confiscations. . . . Whereupon Dr Parry, by order of this House, was appointed to be sequestered into the outer room of this House into the serjeant's custody. . . . And afterwards being brought to the bar and there kneeling upon his knee, he was told by Mr Speaker, in the name of the whole House, that if he thought good the House was contented to hear him what reasons he could yield for himself in maintenance of his said speeches against the aforesaid bill [and the contempt shown in attacking a bill on third reading without explaining his reasons]. Whereupon . . . he answered . . . that as before when he spake to the bill . . . he then concealed his said reasons from this House, so he would now conceal the same still. Whereupon being sequestered again, it was resolved, that for that he did speak to the bill and gave his negative voice so directly and undutifully, and in contempt of this House would not shew his reasons for the same, being merely against the ancient orders and usage of this high court . . . that he should be committed to the serjeant's ward till the matter shall be further considered of by this House, the day being then very far spent. . . .

[18 December 1584] . . . Mr Vice-Chamberlain also declared unto this House that her Majesty having been made privy unto the misbehaviour of Mr Doctor Parry yesterday shewed in this House, and of the order of this House taken therein with him for the same, her Highness doth not only deem him to have given just cause of offence unto this House in the same his misdemeanour, but also doth very well allow of the grave discretion of this House in forbearing for the time to use any sharp course of correction against him for his said offence, in respect that he had said he reserved his reasons to be imparted to her Majesty only; which as he had discovered unto some of the lords of the Council by her Highness' appointment, and that partly to the satisfaction of her Majesty, so her Highness did think that upon his humble submission unto this House, with a dutiful acknowledgment of his fault, this House would the rather dispense with him therein. Which done, Mr Doctor Parry was called to the bar. . . . And then kneeling upon his knee in very humble manner, affirmed directly that he had very undutifully misbehaved himself, and had rashly and unadvisedly uttered those speeches he used, and was with all his heart very sorry for it. . . . Whereupon, being sequestered again out of the House, it was, after some arguments and speeches had, resolved that upon his said acknowledgment of his fault and his humble submission he should be received into this House again as a member of the same and take his place as before, so that he would afterwards use himself in good sort as he ought to do. . . .   D'Ewes, *Journals*, 340–2

144. Preserving secrecy of proceedings, 1589.

[15 February 1589] . . . Sir Edward Hobby moved (he said) upon good cause, that Mr Speaker do give admonition unto this whole House that speeches used in this House by the members of the same be not any of them made or used as table-talk, or in any wise delivered in notes of writing to any person or persons whatsoever not being members of this House, as of late (is thought) hath been done in this present session. And thereupon, by consent of this House, admonition was given by Mr Speaker in that behalf accordingly, shewing unto them that they are the common council of the realm. . . .   D'Ewes, *Journals*, 432

145. Dealings with non-members.

On Thursday the 5th day of April [1571] Thomas Clark and Anthony Bull, of the Inner Temple, London, gentlemen, were by this House committed to the serjeant's ward . . . for that they presumed to enter into this House and were no members of the same, as themselves at the bar confessed.

[1 February 1581] It is ordered that Mr Speaker, in the name of this House, do require the warden of the Fleet, being a member of this House, that he do cause from henceforth two of his servants to attend at the stair-head near unto the outer door of this House, and to lay hands upon two or three of such disordered serving-men or pages as shall happen to use such lewd disorder and outrage as hath been accustomed to be exercised there this Parliament time, to the end they may thereupon be brought into this House and receive such punishment as to this House shall seem meet.

[27 March 1593] Matthew Jones, gentleman, being found sitting in this House and no member of the same, was brought to the bar, and there being charged by Mr Speaker for his said offence humbly excused himself by ignorance; and appearing unto the House to be a simple ignorant old man was upon his humble submission pardoned to be discharged tomorrow, paying his fees, and ordered in the meantime to remain in the serjeant's ward of the House. [28 March: after admonition by the Speaker—] this House doth discharge him paying his fees.

D'Ewes, *Journals*, 156, 290–1, 511–2

V. MANAGEMENT

The growth of Parliament in the sixteenth century, and especially its new importance in the conduct of the king's affairs, raised new problems in the relationship between it and the Crown. More particularly, if the ultimate activity of the polity consisted in a legislative act agreed to by three separate partners, it followed that nothing could get done unless harmony between them was somehow secured. At times, of course, the three partners co-operated because they were at one in interest and opinion; the general anti-papal policy of Henry VIII, for instance, met with approval from a majority of both Lords and Commons. But one cannot rely on fate or accident to produce such agreement as a regular feature of political life. The sixteenth century therefore witnessed at the least a vast intensification, and in many ways a novel exploration, of those arts of politics by which a government influences and manages a representative assembly. At no time did these arts amount to packing, dictation or coercion; nor were they ever so successful that opposition could always be discounted. There was absolutely nothing improper in the idea of management, any more than there is in any system which enables leadership to be exercised in any large body of men; nor did the practices of the sixteenth-century managers, on any reasonable inter-pretation, exceed the bounds of respectability. It would be truer to say that those (like the early Stuarts) who ignored the need for management were guilty of a major political error and even dereliction of duty. The task applied more particularly to the House of Commons, if only because the Lords could on the whole be expected to follow the government's lead with-out special management; but it is also true that the evidence is fuller for the Commons. It suggests very strongly something like a serious beginning in these matters in the Reformation Parliament; this, again, might in part be the consequence of selective survival, but since both the duration and the competence of that Parliament were something quite new it is probable that the impression left by the record is accurate.

Management works in two ways: influence over elections and influence over the House when elected. Elections were always held to be free, but what this meant is another question. In the shires, the electorate consisted of the freeholders with an annual income of 40s. from freehold property; but in the boroughs the franchise came more and more to be concentrated in a small group of town officials.[126] Shire elections were thus harder to influence from outside, though this did not always prove impossible;[127] on the other hand, matters were usually in the management of the leading shire families who exercised supreme control, or divided seats by agreement, or—if necessary—

[126] Pickthorn, I, 99. f.
[127] Cf. Doc. 148 (vi and vii).

entered into a contest.[128] The shire was the chief battleground of local politics whose sum amounted so often, in the three centuries dominated by the old House of Commons, to an apparently national conflict at Westminster. Government influence could be more active in the boroughs where, as has been seen, patronage played a great part in determining the choice of members.[129] Basically, the government's task was to secure the election of suitable members in the few constituencies in which Crown influence predominated, and so to organise matters that elsewhere the personal and local influences of prominent men associated with the Crown and Council were properly deployed. Boroughs which kept one or both their seats for the nominees of patrons were in effect pocket boroughs in which either the individual or his patron or the Crown could place suitable or ambitious men.[130] The operations of government managers, from Thomas Cromwell through Burghley, Danby, Walpole, and the rest, to the dying days of the 'unreformed' system in the nineteenth century, depended upon the social and electoral structure of the country, the existence of local (shire and borough) magnates, the influence of the centre over these, and on patronage spreading through office and reward bestowed by the Crown. Of this last there is little sign under the Tudors: the centre here weighed upon the localities through sheer force of authority and the pervasive feeling of loyalty among the gentry and the nobility. One undoubted consequence of the new interest in managing elections was the increase of king's servants—ministers and lesser men—in the House of Commons. It was remarked in 1529 as a disturbing fact that many members were the sworn servants of the king, which was reckoned to weaken their independence, and the northern rebels of 1536 mentioned this among their grievances.[131] In 1555 the Commons even discussed a bill prohibiting any paid servant or dependent of the Crown from sitting as a member, but nothing came of this.[132] Such fears exaggerated and distorted the truth, for the House had never been without those who owed their first allegiance to the king, nor was it as full of them now as disgruntled observers might think. Nevertheless, it is quite clear that something like the nucleus of a government party was created when councillors, civil servants and household officers began habitually to seek election and form themselves into an influential group, and there is little doubt that deliberate policy accentuated the tendency.[133]

[128] For a full discussion of the shire cf. Neale, *House of Commons*, chs. 1–6.

[129] Above, pp. 248 f., and cf. esp. Neale, *House of Commons*, chs. 9–13.

[130] The whole business if so fully analysed in *ibid.*, that no more than this brief summary is needed here.

[131] Hall, *Chronicle*, 767; *L.P.*, XI, 504.

[132] Or so we are always told on the strength of *Ven. Cal.*, VI, 252. No such bill can be identified in *C.J.* where the only one to concern members of the House apparently meant to improve attendance (pp. 42 f.). The Venetian ambassador may have been badly informed.

[133] Elsynge (*Manner*, 81 f.) commented upon the lapse of the ancient privilege of exemption

Systematic concern with elections began really in the 1530's; Thomas Cromwell was the first minister of the Crown deliberately to devote himself to this necessary task. His own election in 1529 (**146**) suggests how haphazard the business was at that point: although he specifically sought the king's approval for his entry into Parliament he relied for a seat entirely on private connections.[134] But the length and purpose of the Parliament produced novel problems, and in 1534 we find him busy revising the list of members and contemplating bye-elections.[135] The first election he managed in full occurred in 1536; it is unfortunate that we have only one clear piece of evidence for government influence in that year—the notorious Canterbury election when the city was compelled by orders from Cromwell on the king's behalf to rescind its election and choose instead two men named by the Crown (**147**). What little is known of the inwardness of this unique case of direct compulsion suggests that some interests in the city had broken a genuine engagement. At any rate, when Cromwell wrote to Canterbury in 1537 on the private behalf of one of the rejected members, he was told that the man had been dismissed from his office as town clerk because in 1536 he had 'presumed' to arrange for his own election.[136] In 1539 the fuller evidence displays Cromwell hard at work organising the influence which he and other councillors commanded in the localities to prepare what he called a 'tractable' Parliament (**148**).[137] Here we find nothing remotely improper, but only the full managerial skills of the old parliamentary system. As far as is known, no other statesmen of the century copied Cromwell's painstaking attention to this business. Instead it became customary for the Council to send a round-robin to sheriffs, mayors and influential men in the locality, asking them in general terms to see to the return of suitable men—men both substantial enough to avoid firebrands and reliable enough in the various changes of religious policy (**149–154**). Only Northumberland, desperate for his policies, tried to secure a general acceptance of government nominees (**150**). No doubt more informal influences were at work in individual constituencies

from parliamentary service enjoyed by the king's servants; he linked it with the early years of the sixteenth century. Not enough work has yet been done on the subject, but it looks as though from Edward IV onwards at least the Crown was concerned to build up a government interest in the House, similar (and possibly as a counterweight) to those private interest groups or 'affinities' which controlled the Lancastrian House of Commons (cf. Roskell, *Commons of 1422*, esp. 69 ff.). The Parliament of 1523 contained a sizeable body of 'king's servants' (**157**).

134 The point is discussed in Elton, *Tudor Revolution*, 77 ff. Cromwell's 'election' at Taunton at a very late date was possible because the borough had kept one seat vacant for the convenience of the patron.

135 Pollard, *Bull. Inst. Hist. Research*, IX, 31 ff.

136 *L.P.*, XII, II, 1324; this seems to dispose of a good many customary strictures on this famous case (even Neale, *House of Commons*, 284). The electoral history of Canterbury has its strange patches. Thus in 1429 an election was overridden by the sheriff who put in a nominee of the bishop of Rochester (Roskell, *Commons of 1422*, 30).

137 For a discussion of this election cf. Elton, *Studies*, I, 201 ff.

and at court among the borough patrons who in their turn depended upon the government, and late in Elizabeth's reign the personal struggle between Essex and Robert Cecil expressed itself also in the systematic construction of parliamentary interests.[138] But it does not appear that any later Tudor statesman set himself to manage elections as Cromwell did and as was again to be practice after the Restoration. It is not impossible that Elizabeth's parliamentary difficulties were connected with this absence of a strong Crown faction in the House.[139]

The effects of these manoeuvres are not easy to estimate. As we shall see, they did not prevent frequent clashes in Parliament and never, indeed, produced anything remotely resembling subservience in the House.[140] All that could be hoped for, and was, was the creation of a reliable supporting group. Especially when it took to writing general letters, the government had to be careful. These circulars—which were not, of course, used at every election—could be taken for dictation. At times an agent acted tactlessly and put the freeholders' backs up, as in the election for Kent in 1547 (**149**). For the rest it is difficult to know whether Council letters had much influence on elections at all. On the one occasion when a check is possible the result does not suggest that the missives did much good. In 1586 the queen, compelled to call Parliament before the date to which the existing assembly stood prorogued, had to order the election of a new one; hoping to get back much the same House, she tried for the re-election of sitting members (**153**). Yet few boroughs seem to have taken much notice.[141] All told, Tudor electoral management had severe limits. Cromwell may have succeeded in building up a court group, and the Parliaments of the 1540's look surprisingly amenable. Ordinarily, government could at best obtain the return of leading Crown servants, exercise scattered (no doubt often widespread) influence through its links with patrons, and make hopeful suggestions in general terms. But not even Cromwell's careful management came anywhere near to packing; throughout the century elections were essentially free—that is, influenced or even arranged by local powers.

In any case, Tudor governments relied more on managing the House once it was elected. Here again, no improper means were used; it was a question

---

[138] Neale, *House of Commons*, 233 ff.

[139] Professor Neale (*ibid.*, 282 ff.) describes Cromwell's organising and Northumberland's letters as 'blatant electoral devices'; he praises Elizabeth's government for restricting itself to general letters and occasional assistance to individual candidates. However, this seems to me part of the general Elizabethan reluctance to assert central authority against local interests—Burghley's famous 'caution'—which can be read at least two ways; it may also have been a result of Elizabeth's deliberate promotion of balancing faction in her Council which kept the government from being single-minded on these occasions. Nor can I agree that the Council letters of Elizabeth were less particular, and therefore less of an interference, than Mary's.

[140] Below, pp. 307 ff.

[141] Neale, *House of Commons*, 291 f.

of providing guidance, not domination. What the absence of such methods could produce was demonstrated by Wolsey's ham-handed treatment of the 1523 Parliament, and later again by the early Stuarts. The essential weapons in the task were three: the preparation of parliamentary business; the presence in the House of privy councillors who guided debate and conveyed to the Commons the desires of the monarch; and the use of the Speaker to control the House. The first two methods between them amounted simply to the maintenance of a government front bench charged with the carrying through of a specific legislative programme. Not surprisingly, we first find evidence for such necessary practices in the first Parliament called upon to put through a planned programme, in the Reformation Parliament. Cromwell was the prototype of all those English statesmen who have regarded membership of the Commons, management of business there, and leadership in its debates as an essential part of their equipment. We know, for instance, how he prepared bills for the House and manipulated things there so as to get his plans accepted.[142] His papers are full of entries concerning the affairs of Parliament, and many parliamentary drafts bear plentiful corrections in his hand. Nor was he alone in this; rather he presided over a team of draftsmen, among whom the king's legal counsel—judges, attorney-general, even the lord chancellor—were prominent. The guiding hand of the privy councillors is notably displayed in a dispute of 1548 when they were forced to make concessions and yet retained their ascendancy (155). The part played by the councillors of Mary and Elizabeth is a commonplace, though it is possible that they found the House less easy to manage than Cromwell had done. But they continued active about the preparation of business and the guiding of the House, effectively composing a government group in the Commons who commanded respect and sometimes obedience by their knowledge and skill.[143] As committees became common, councillors usually dominated them too. Nor were they alone. The Council relied heavily on non-councillors, 'men of business', for getting its business done in the House.[144]

In the sixteenth century the Speaker, though formally, of course, elected by the Commons who had no corporate existence until they had chosen him, was as a rule a Crown nominee. In the reign of Elizabeth, the queen and Council are known to have decided beforehand on the person of the Speaker, and privy councillors in the House saw to his election.[145] But though no explicit evidence survives for earlier reigns, it is plain both from the necessary

---

[142] Elton, *Studies* II, 82 ff., 107 ff. For my present views on the events of 1523, revised in response to various criticisms, cf. *Reform and Reformation*, 150, n. 27.

[143] Holdsworth, IV, 96 ff.; Neale, *House of Commons*, 364 f., 395 ff., etc.; for an example of legislation prepared by the Council cf. *A.P.C.*, VII, 28. Parliamentary matters occur often in the State Papers and the Council Registers.

[144] Graves, *Hist. Journal*, XXIII, 17 ff.

[145] Doc. 156; Neale, *House of Commons*, 354 ff.

circumstances and the men chosen that the later practice differed in no way from what was done earlier.[146] When the House first met to elect a Speaker, it would be nothing but a collection of individuals waiting for a lead; and naturally that lead would always come from one of the experienced men, the councillors in the House. As for the Speakers themselves, a few examples will demonstrate the true position. Sir Thomas Lovell (1485), Sir Reginald Bray (1496), Edmund Dudley (1504), Sir Thomas More (1523), Sir Thomas Audley (1529), Sir Richard Rich (1536), Sir John Baker (1545 and 1547), Sir John Popham (1581), Sir John Puckering (1584 and 1586), Sir Edward Coke (1593)—all these men were to have prominent careers in the government service, and the rest, though less well-known, were of the same stamp. Ostensibly the servant as well as the ruler of the House of Commons, the Tudor Speaker felt obliged to the Crown and assisted in the management of the House. Thus he acted as a useful ally to the privy councillors, especially because he could arrange the order of business and sometimes see to it that disagreeable matters were not raised, or were raised in such a way that they had no chance of being pushed too far.[147]

In the last resort, it was possible to bring the monarch into play. Henry VIII very occasionally attended both Houses in person, though he was more inclined to have deputations wait upon him through which he could directly influence members.[148] A report has it that in 1536 he went so far as to present a bill to them himself; this sounds very unlikely.[149] Elizabeth used those 'rumours and messages' which so annoyed Peter Wentworth.[150] As privy councillors had a duty in managing the House, so the sovereign, from a greater distance, had to employ himself in promoting the transaction of business. Those who wish to read improper threats, pressure and control into all this are mistaken. Of course there was pressure—there could even be the hint of threats. Elizabeth especially never hid her frequent anger or contempt for the Commons' 'idle brains' and for mischief-making members. But does anyone suppose that a body like the Commons ever existed free from every kind of pressure or influence? What would have been improper—as signifying a total misunderstanding of the political scene—was aloofness, reluctance to manage, failure to get results. Everybody worked hard during a session of Parliament, and if things did not go entirely as intended one took that in one's stride. In 1545 Sir William Petre was surprised to find that Henry VIII did not particularly mind when a bill in which he was interested failed in the Commons;[151]

---

[146] Pickthorn, I, 108.

[147] Neale, *House of Commons*, 395 ff. In 1587, e.g., the Speaker blocked Peter Wentworth's move by refusing to put his ten questions to the House; he showed them to the Council instead (Neale, *Elizabeth and her Parliaments*, II, 156).

[148] Above, p. 277.

[149] *L.P.*, x, 462.

[150] Above, p. 267.
[151] *L.P.*, xx, II, 1030.

he forgot that a man grown old in parliamentary management—and Henry excelled at it—would take the occasional reverse without turning a hair.

146. Ralph Sadler to Thomas Cromwell, 1 November 1529.

... A little before the receipt of your letter I came from the court where I spake with Mr Gage and according to your commandment moved him to speak unto my lord of Norfolk for the burgess's room of the Parliament on your behalf. And he accordingly so did without delay, like a faithful friend. Whereupon my said lord of Norfolk answered the said Mr Gage that he had spoken with the King his Highness and that his Highness was very well contented ye should be a burgess, so that ye would order yourself in the said room according to such instructions as the said duke of Norfolk shall give you from the King. .... As touching Mr Rush,[152] I spake with him also at the court; if I then had known your pleasure, I could now have sent you answer of the same. Howbeit, I will speak with him this night, God willing, and know whether ye shall be burgess of Orford[153] or not. And if ye be not elect there, I will then according to your further commandment repair unto Mr Paulet[154] and require him to name you to be one of the burgesses of one of my lord's[155] towns of his bishopric of Winchester accordingly. Sir, me thinketh it were good, so it may stand with your pleasure, that ye did repair hither tomorrow as soon as ye conveniently may, for to speak with the duke of Norfolk by whom ye shall know the King his pleasure how ye shall order yourself in the Parliament House. ....

Merriman, *Cromwell's Letters*, I, 67–8

147. The Canterbury Election, 1536.

(i) *John Hobbys, Sheriff of Canterbury, to Thomas Cromwell, 12 May* [1536].

Pleaseth it your mastership to understand that the 11th day of this present month of May, between the hours of 8 and 9 before noon of the same day, I held the county at Canterbury in the place thereunto accustomed where by virtue of the King's writ of summons to the Parliament in the full county there, according to the said writ and

[152] Thomas Rush, M.P. for Orford (Suff.) in 1529.
[153] For this correction from 'Oxford', cf. Elton, *Tudor Revolution*, 78.
[154] Sir William Paulet, master of the Wards, later marquess of Winchester.
[155] Wolsey.

statute, assembled the number of 80 persons and above, citizens of the said city. And there, so gathered for the election of new burgesses, I made open proclamation of the same, whereupon the said citizens freely and with one voice chose two burgesses. The one is chamberlain and alderman of the same city whose name is John Starky, and the other is a citizen and common clerk of the same city whose name is Christopher Levyns. Which two burgesses then newly chosen, the commons gave them their full power and authority to do and consent for themselves and the said city in every thing and matter that shall be treated of and ordained at the said Parliament, as by mine and their certificate indented and sealed plainly shall appear, and the which shall be certified according to the tenor of the King's writ of summons. After which election thus ended, about 12 of the clock the same day, Mr Mayor of the same city sent for me and showed me a letter sent unto him and me by my lord chancellor and your mastership, whereby it appeared then that the King's pleasure and yours was that John Bryges and Robert Darknall should fulfil the said rooms. And if your said letter had come to me before the said election passed, I would have done the best that had been in my power to accomplish our sovereign lord the King's pleasure and your request in the premisses. And forasmuch as the King's pleasure and yours at the time of the said election to me was unknown, I beseech you accept this my humble certificate which is true in all points, by the oath that I have made to our said sovereign lord the King, as Almighty God be my help who preserve you in honour. Written the 12th day of May.

State Papers, Henry VIII, vol. 103, fos. 276v–277

(ii) *Cromwell to the Mayor, Sheriff and Commonalty of Canterbury, 18 May* [1536].

(Endorsed: the copy of the King's letter.)

In my hearty wise I recommend me unto you. These shall be: forasmuch as the King's pleasure and commandment is that Robert Darknall and John Bryges should be elect and chosen citizen or burgesses for that city, by reason whereof my lord chancellor and I by our letters written unto you advertised you thereof, and ye, the same little or nothing regarding but rather contemning, have chosen other at your own wills and minds contrary to the King's pleasure and commandment in that behalf, whereat the King's Highness doth not a little marvel; wherefore, in avoiding further displeasure that might thereby ensue, I require you on the King's behalf that notwithstanding the said election ye proceed to a new and elect those other, according to the tenor of the former letters to you directed for that purpose, without failing so to do as the King's trust and expectation is in you and as ye intend to avoid his Highness' displeasure at your peril. And if any person will obstinately gainsay the same, I require you to advertise me thereof that I may order him as the King's pleasure shall be in that case to command. Thus fare ye well. At the Rolls, the 18th day of March.

Merriman, Cromwell's Letters, II, 13–14

(iii) *The Mayor, Sheriff and Commonalty of Canterbury to Cromwell, 20 May* [1536].

In humble wise certify you that the 20th day of this present month of May at 6 of the clock of the morning, I, John Alcock, mayor of Canterbury, received your letter directed to me, the said mayor, sheriff and commonalty of the said city, signifying to us thereby the King's pleasure and commandment is that Robert Darknall and John Bryges should be burgesses of the Parliament for the same city of Canterbury. By virtue whereof, according to our bound duty, immediately upon the sight of your said letters and contents thereof perceived, caused the commonalty of the said city to assemble in the County Hall there where appeared the number of four score and 17 persons, citizens and inhabitants of the said city, and according to the King's pleasure and commandment freely with one voice and without any contradiction have elected and chosen the foresaid Robert Darknall and John Bryges to be burgesses of the Parliament for the same city, which shall be duly certified by indenture under the seals of the said citizens and inhabitants, by the grace of the Blessed Trinity who preserve you. Written at Canterbury at 12 of the clock the foresaid 20th day of May.

State Papers, Henry VIII, vol. 104, fo. 39v

148. The election of 1539.

(i) *Christopher More to Thomas Cromwell, March* 1539.

. . . My lord admiral[156] has showed me that your pleasure is to have a friend of yours to be one of the burgesses of the Parliament for the borough of Gatton in the shire of Surrey, whereof Sir Roger Copley is owner; wherein your lordship shall have your pleasure. Albeit, upon

---

[156] Sir William Fitzwilliam, earl of Southampton.

the refusal thereof by my lord admiral, which instantly desired me to have the same, I had promised it unto a very friend of mine, which, since I know your lordship's pleasure, at my desire is contented to leave it. So that now, if I might know the name of your lordship's friend, I shall send it to Mr Copley to the intent he may cause the indentures to be made between the sheriff and him for the same. And I must beseech your lordship that whosoever have it that he may take no wages therefor; for so my promise is made to Mr Copley in that behalf, and the cause is there is but one house in the town to be any relief and help to the same. . . .   State Papers, Henry VIII, vol. 144, fos. 217-8

(ii) *The earl of Southampton to Cromwell, 10 March 1539.*
Sir, touching the burgess of Farnham, albeit I fear my lord of Winchester[157] at his being there hath already done something therein and moved men after his own desires, yet I shall adventure to do somewhat. So that, if I may do anything at all, I intend to advance one Mores of Farnham and some other honest man for that town who, I put no doubts, will serve the King's intent in all points. . . . We have picked out certain of the best of the country whose names be in the schedule herewith sent, to the intent ye shall prick his head whom you would have chosen, which my lord[158] and I will advance and prefer the best we can; and for that cause have thought meet to defer the election till the next county day. . . .   Brit. Mus., Otho E., ix, fo. 77v

(iii) *Cromwell to Henry VIII, 17 March 1539.*
. . . In the meantime I and other of your Grace's Council here do study and employ ourselves daily upon those affairs that concern your Grace's Parliament, and to prepense and prepare in the same and other all that we may think to your Highness' satisfaction . . . Amongst other, for your Grace's Parliament, I have appointed your Majesty's servant Mr Morison to be one of them; no doubt he shall be ready to answer and take up such as would crake or face with literature of learning or by indirect ways—if any such there shall be, as I think there shall be few or none. Forasmuch as I and other your dedicate councillors be about to bring all things so to pass that your Majesty had never more tractable Parliament. . . .   Brit. Mus., Tit. B., I, fos. 265-6

(iv) *Sir William Godolphin to Cromwell, 25 March 1539.*
. . . Pleaseth it you to be advertised that I have received your honour-

---

[157] Stephen Gardiner.   [158] Sir William Paulet, Lord St John.

able letter . . . wherein I do perceive your pleasure in the preferment
of your servant, my son, to be one of the knights of the shire of Cornwall for the King's most honourable Court of Parliament; whereof I
most humbly thank your good lordship. Notwithstanding, before the
receipt of your honourable letter there was great suit made by Sir
Piers Edgecomb, Sir John Chamond and John Arundel, son and heir
unto Sir John Arundel kt. As yet the writ came not to my hands; when
I do receive the same I shall do the uttermost of my power in fulfilling
of your pleasure in the advancement of my said son. . . .

State Papers, Henry VIII, vol. 144, fos. 169–70

(v) *John Kingsmill*[159] *to Thomas Wriothesley*, 1 *April* 1539.
. . . To certify you for the choice of the knights of the shire [for
Hampshire]: surely and truly the more part of the shire was very glad
to have you knight of the shire and so they have chosen you, and likewise I pray you inform my lord privy seal[160] they have chosen Mr
Worseley. . . . It pleased my lord privy seal at my now last being at
London with his lordship that I should be a burgess to have a place in
this Parliament House of some borough in some other shire where I am
not sheriff. I think his lordship may have a place at Lurgershall in Wiltshire the which is in rule of Mr Richard Bridges (I hear say, knight of
Berkshire for the Parliament), whose father in his life, and he, were ever
burgesses there; and this I would fain be working to good opinion if I
may have place. . . . If you think good also, you may have John
Dalle who is a goodwitted fellow and says he will follow your advice
if it please you to get him place. . . . *Ibid.*, vol. 146, fos. 237–8

(vi) *Sir Edmund Knyvet to Cromwell*, 2 *April* 1539.
. . . In the election of the knights within this shire of Norfolk, appointed
to be chosen at Norwich the fourteenth day of this month, at which
day and place I shall not fail to be in readiness with such my tenants
and friends as I can make there, to give my voice and consent with all
my company unto any such as by your lordship shall be ensigned me;
doubting no deal but that I . . . shall cry so loud on him that the voice
of the other shall ill be heard. Notwithstanding that the bruit yet only
doth run on Mr Southwell and Mr Wyndham, named (as Mr Southwell
told me) by the King's Highness . . . whereunto I have and do think

---

[159] Sheriff of Hampshire.   [160] Cromwell.

not best to give over-firm credence till your further pleasure known in this behalf. Whereunto, what so it be, I shall so earnestly and diligently confer me as I would do if that with your pleasure it stood thereto to name and appoint me. . . .

Ibid., fo. 242

(vii) *Cromwell to Knyvet, 6 April* 1539.

. . . Having received your letters of the second of this present, I perceive by the same your gentle affection towards me with your desire to know my advice touching the knights of the shire for Norfolk. . . . For answer whereunto . . . I have thought meet to signify unto you that of truth the King's Majesty is well inclined to have Mr Southwell and Mr Wyndham elected and chosen to supply those rooms at this Parliament; whereunto my advice shall be that you shall conform yourself, not for that I do think either of them more able for the office than yourself, but because (they being also convenient for the same and partly minded by his Highness) I would all my friends, in the number whereof I do accept you, should in all things apply themselves to satisfy his Grace as appertaineth. . . .

Ibid., fos. 274–5

149. The election of 1547.

[28 April 1547] To Sir Thomas Cheney, lord warden of the Cinque Ports, to recommend Sir John Baker so to those that have the naming of knights of the shire as at the next Parliament he may be made knight of the shire of Kent accordingly.

[28 September 1547] To the sheriff of Kent, that, where the lords wrote to him afore to the end to make his friends for the election of Sir John Baker to be knight of the shire, understanding that he did abuse towards those of the shire their request into a commandment, their lordships advertise him that as they meant not nor mean to deprive the shire by any their commandment of their liberty of election whom they would think meet, so nevertheless if they would in satisfaction of their lordships' request grant their voices to Mr Baker they would take it thankfully.

A like letter written to the lord warden of the Cinque Ports, with this addition that, being informed he should abuse their request to menace them of the shire of Kent, as they would not believe it, so they advised him to use things in such sort as the shire might have the free election.

A.P.C., II, 516, 518–19

150. The election of 1553: the King's letter to the sheriffs for Parliament men.

Trusty and well-beloved, we greet you well. Forasmuch as we have, for divers good considerations, caused a summonition for a Parliament to be made, as we doubt not but ye understand the same by our writs sent in that behalf unto you; we have thought it meet for the furtherance of such causes as are to be propounded in the said Parliament for the common weal of our realm, that in the election of such persons as shall be sent to the Parliament . . . there be good regard had that the choice be made of men of gravity and knowledge in their own countries and towns, fit, for their understanding and qualities, to be in such a great council. And therefore . . . we do . . . at this present will and command you that ye shall give notice as well to the freeholders of your county as to the citizens and burgesses of any city or borough which shall have any of our writs by your direction . . . that our pleasure and commandment is, that they shall choose and appoint (as nigh as they possibly may) men of knowledge and experience . . . so as by the assembly of such we may by God's goodness provide . . . for the redress of the lacks of our commonweal more effectually than heretofore hath been. And yet nevertheless our pleasure is, that where our Privy Council or any of them within their jurisdictions in our behalf shall recommend men of learning and wisdom, in such case their directions be regarded and followed, as tending to the same which we desire—that is, to have this assembly to be of the most chiefest men in our realm for advice and good counsel.

Strype, *Ecclesiastical Memorials*, II (2), 64–5

151. The election of 1555: the Queen to the sheriffs.

Trusty and well-beloved, we greet you well, and where among other matters . . . we intend principally the restitution of God's honour and glory whom we acknowledge our chief author and helper as well in bringing us to the right of our estate as also in this most noble marriage. . . . These shall be to will and command you that, for withstanding such malice as the devil worketh by his ministers for the maintenance of heresies and seditions, ye now on our behalf admonish such our good loving subjects as by order of our writs should within that county choose knights, citizens and burgesses to repair from thence to this our

Parliament, to be of their inhabitants, as the old laws require, and of the wise, grave and Catholic sort, such as indeed mean the true honour of God, with the prosperity of the commonwealth. The advancement whereof we and our dear husband the King do chiefly profess and intend, without alteration of any particular man's possessions, as, among other false rumours, is spread abroad to hinder our godly purpose. . . .

Strype, *Ecclesiastical Memorials*, III, 245

152. The election of 1571: the Privy Council to Archbishop Parker and Lord Cobham (warden of the Cinque Ports), 17 February 1571.

After our hearty commendations to your lordships. Where the Queen's Majesty hath determined for divers necessary great causes concerning the state of the realm to have a Parliament holden at Westminster this next April; . . . upon some deliberation had by her Majesty with us . . . her Majesty hath called to her remembrance (which also we think to be true) that though the greater number of knights, citizens and burgesses for the more part are duly and orderly chosen, yet in many places such consideration is not usually had herein as reason would, that is, to choose persons able to give good information and advice for the places for which they are nominated, and to treat and consult discreetly upon such matters as are to be propounded to them in their assemblies. But contrariwise that many in late Parliaments (as her Majesty thinketh) have been named, some for private respects and favour upon their own suits, some to enjoy some immunities from arrests upon actions during the time of the Parliaments, and some other to set forth private causes by sinister labour and frivolous talks and arguments, to the prolongation of time without just cause, and without regard to the public benefit and weal of the realm; and therefore her Majesty, being very desirous to have redress herein, hath charged us to devise some speedy good ways for reformation hereof at this time, so as all the persons to be assembled in this next Parliament for the cities, shires and boroughs may be found (as near as may be) discreet, wise and well-disposed, according as the intention of their choosing ought to be. And therefore, as we have thought meet to give knowledge hereof to such as we think both for their wisdoms, dispositions and authorities in sundry counties in the realm can and will take care hereof, so have we for this purpose made special choice of your lordships, requiring you in her Majesty's name to consider well of these premises, and to confer with the sheriff of that shire of Kent by all such good means as you shall think meet, and with such special men of livelihood and worship of the same county as have interest herein, and in like manner with the head officers of cities and boroughs, so as by your good advice and direction the persons to be chosen may be well qualified with knowledge, discretion and modesty, and meet for those places. . . .

Parker, *Correspondence*, 379–81

153. The election of 1586.

[At Windsor, 19 September 1586) Letters unto the several counties concerning the new summons of the Parliament: that whereas her Majesty had thought good for especial and urgent causes to hasten the High Court of Parliament with a new summons . . . forasmuch as in the last election as well for the knights of the shire as the citizens and burgesses of the cities and borough towns there was a very good and discreet choice made of sundry wise and well affected gentlemen and others, their lordships have thought good to require the sheriff of that county that, calling unto him three or four of the well affected gentlemen thereabouts in that county, he send to or for the principal of the cities and boroughs and let them understand that in their lordships' . . . opinion they shall do very well, considering the good choice made before, to nominate in their free elections for this present Parliament those citizens and burgesses they did then make election of; unless some of them may since be deceased . . . in which case their lordships doubt not but they will have especial care to supply their rooms with discreet persons and known to be well affected in religion and the present state. . . .

A.P.C., XIV, 227

154. The election of 1597.

[22 August 1597] Another minute of letters to the high sheriffs of all the several counties of the realm. Whereas the Queen's Majesty hath upon great considerations . . . determined to hold her Parliament at Westminster . . . her Majesty meaning to have this her intended Parliament to be served with men of understanding and knowledge for the particular estate of the places whereunto they ought to be chosen, and of discretion also requisite in consultation for causes concerning the public weal of the realm, hath commanded us of her Privy Council to admonish you to whom her Majesty's writs of summons are now directed to have good regard how this her Majesty's good meaning may be observed and fulfilled. And to that intent, though we doubt not much but the principal persons of that county will have good regard to make choice without partiality or affection, as sometimes hath been used, of men meet for all good respects to serve as knights for that shire, yet in the choice of burgesses for borough towns we doubt (except better regard be had herein than commonly hath been) there will be many unmeet men and unacquainted with the state of the boroughs named thereto, and therefore we require you that shall have the direction of the writs to any boroughs in that county to inform them by your letter (or otherwise) of the contents of this her Majesty's good meaning for the choice of persons meet for the service of the said boroughs in this intended Parliament, which if it shall otherwise appear to be evil supplied, we shall have occasion to enquire and find out by whose default the same hath happened. . . .   *A.P.C.*, xxvii, 361

155. The influence of councillors, 1548.

[At Westminster 6 May 1548] Whereas in the last Parliament . . . among other articles contained in the act for colleges and chantry lands etc., to be given unto his Highness, it was also inserted that the lands pertaining to all guilds and brotherhoods within this realm should pass unto his Majesty by way of like gift, at which time divers then being of the Lower House did not only reason and argue against that article for the guildable lands, but also incensed many others to hold with them, amongst the which none were stiffer nor more busily went about to impugn the said article than the burgesses for . . . Lynn . . . and . . . Coventry. . . . In respect of which their allegations and great labour made herein unto the House, such of his Highness's Council as were of the same House there present thought it very likely and apparent that not only that article for the guildable lands should be dashed, but also that the whole body of the act might either sustain peril or hindrance, being already ingrossed and the time of the Parliament prorogation hard at hand, unless by some good policy the principal speakers against the passing of that article might be stayed; whereupon they did participate this matter with the lord protector's grace and others of the lords of his Highness' Council, who, pondering on the one part how the guildable lands throughout this realm amounted to no small yearly value, which by the article aforesaid were to be accrued to his Majesty's possessions of the Crown, and on the other part, weighing in a multitude of free voices what moment the labour of a few setters-on had been of heretofore in like cases, thought it better to stay and content them of Lynn and Coventry by granting to them to have and enjoy their guild lands, etc., as they did before, than through their means, on whose importune labour and suggestion the great part of the Lower House rested, to have the article defaced, and so his Majesty to forgo the whole guild lands throughout the realm; and for these respects, and also for avoiding of the proviso which the said burgesses would have had added for the guilds to this article, which might have ministered occasion to others to have laboured for the like, they resolved that certain of his Highness' councillors being of the Lower House should persuade with the said burgesses of Lynn and Coventry to desist from further speaking or labouring against the said article, upon promise to them that if they meddled no further against it, his Majesty, once having the guildable lands granted unto him by the act as it was penned unto him, should make them over a new grant of the lands pertaining then unto their guilds, etc., to be had and used to them as afore. Which thing the said councillors did execute as was devised, and thereby stayed the speakers against it, so as the act passed with the clause for guildable lands accordingly. . . .

A.P.C., II, 193–5

156. Electing the Speaker.

[25 January 1559] Whereupon the knights, citizens and burgesses departing to their own House did there take their several places, and most remaining silent or speaking very submissively, Mr Treasurer of the Queen's House,[161] standing up uncovered, did first put the House in remembrance of the lord keeper's late speech, and of his declaration of her Majesty's pleasure that they should choose a Speaker, and therefore in humble obedience to her Majesty's said pleasure, seeing others remain silent, he thought it his duty to take that occasion to commend to their choice Sir Thomas Gargrave, knight, one of the honourable Council in the North Parts, a worthy member of the House and learned in the laws of this realm; by which commendations of his of the aforesaid worthy member of the House to their consideration he said he did

[161] Sir Francis Knollys.

not intend to debar any other there present from uttering their free opinions and nominating any other whom they thought to be more fitting, and therefore desired them to make known their opinions, who thereupon did with one consent and voice allow and approve of Mr Treasurer's nomination and elected the said Sir Thomas Gargrave to be the Prolocutor or Speaker of the said House. . . .

[24 October 1597] . . . The . . . lord keeper . . . delivered unto the said Commons the causes of her Majesty's calling of this Parliament; and so in the end willed them . . . to make choice of their Speaker . . . which done, the said Commons presently repaired unto their own House, and there being assembled and sitting some space of time very silent, at last . . . Sir William Knollys, one of her Highness' most honourable Privy Council and controller of her Majesty's Household, stood up and spake to the effect following: Necessity constraineth me to break off this silence and to give others cause for speech . . . I will . . . deliver my opinion unto you who is most fit for this place, being a member of this House, and those good abilities which I know to be in him (here he made a little pause and the House hawked and spat, and after silence made he proceeded) unto this place of dignity and calling in my opinion (here he stayed a little) Mr Serjeant Yelverton (looking upon him) is the fittest man to be preferred (after which words Mr Yelverton blushed and put off his hat, and after sat bare-headed), for I am assured that he is, yea, and I dare avow it, I know him to be a man wise and learned, secret and circumspect, religious and faithful, no way disable but every way able to supply this place. Wherefore in my judgment I deem him, though I will not say best worthy amongst us, yet sufficient enough to supply this place; and herein if any man think I err, I wish him to deliver his mind as freely as I have done; if not, that we all join together in giving general consent and approbation to this motion. So that the whole House cried, 'Aye, aye, aye, let him be.'. . .

D'Ewes, Journals, 40, 548–9

VI. CONFLICT

If, in the conditions produced by the constitutional revolution of the 1530's, management was necessary because the work of government now required co-operation between king, Lords and Commons, the difficulties encountered also showed up the limitations of management. Parliament was so little packed, subservient or submissive that it could never be relied upon with real certainty to support the policy of the Crown. Naturally enough, conflict was not the standing order of the day, and only a perverted reading of history would suppose that it should have been.[162] Since Parliament represented various interests in the nation, disagreement naturally showed up there; since the politics of Court and Council were dominated by faction, the politics of Lords and Commons naturally were faction-ridden too. Three fundamental errors have marked the received story.[163] In the first place it is supposed that the strains ran between the three parts of the Parliament, so that we hear of conflicts between government and Commons, or between Lords and Commons, hundreds of heads being treated as one; in fact, such lines of political conflict as existed ran vertically through Council, Lords and Commons. The most spectacular 'conflicts' occurred when the monarch's policy, or lack of it, united all the factions, as in 1566 when the queen stood alone on the succession question, in opposition to not only both Houses of Parliament but the Privy Council too. On such occasions the lead tended to be taken by the Council who then used parliamentary protest to put pressure on the queen. Secondly, it has been held that conflict was ideological—that in the reigns of both Mary and Elizabeth advanced Protestants in the Lower House used Parliament to promote their concepts of a true Church. Here a few genuine cases have been allowed to misrepresent the real minds and purposes of parliamentary debates, so that all moves (even by bishops) towards improvement, for instance, in the quality of the clergy have automatically been interpreted as stemming from a Puritan opposition.[164] And thirdly, all this distortion has arisen quite naturally because historians have picked out occasions of supposed conflict from the whole series of events—the passing of bills—which really occupied Parliament.

Nevertheless, these erroneous interpretations have had their uses: they have once and for all exploded still earlier notions which made Tudor Parliaments into nothing except obedient or coerced instruments of the royal will. A great deal of work is still needed to discover all that went on, but at least we now know that we cannot reduce policy-making to the actions of

[162] English constitutional history has been written so much from the point of view of the early Stuart period that every age has been judged by the extraordinary standard of that time; the Commons have received praise or blame inasmuch as they have opposed or supported the Crown, irrespective of circumstances. But the total failure of co-operation which became progressively apparent between 1603 and 1640 was uncharacteristic.

[163] The two volumes of Neale's *Elizabeth I and her Parliaments* tell little of harmony and concentrate on discord which they allege arose out of differences over policy. The interpretation misjudges the nature of such disputes as did occur, mainly because the author persuaded himself of the existence of a virtually continuous Puritan opposition party in the Commons, leaving the Lords out altogether. There was no such party, and the Lords matter.

[164] For Mary's reign cf. Loach, *Mid-Tudor Polity*, 9 ff., and Graves, *House of Lords*. For that of Elizabeth, first attempts to revise Neale's interpretation are found in Elton, *Hist. Journal*, XXII, 255 ff., and Graves, *ibid.*, XXIII, 17 ff.

kings and queens. Parliaments were real occasions when real interests were pursued and sometimes clashed. The relative peace in Parliament, so necessary to effective legislation and to government in general, was maintained only by conscientious attention to management—by argument, cajolery and influence, by carrying out the proper tasks of responsible government.

The one issue over which the Commons could be relied on to prove difficult was that of money. Even in the reign of Henry VII—if the story of Thomas More's successful resistance in 1504 is true—they seem to have been capable of thwarting the king's financial demands.[165] It was money that caused the vigorous and partially successful opposition to Wolsey in 1523.[166] The Reformation Parliament, ready enough to follow the royal lead against the Church and the pope, stuck for years over the government's plans to reinforce prerogative fiscal rights by legislation against the 'uses' which evaded them (**160**).[167] On the other hand, when the king, in 1529, asked for a statutory repudiation of his debts—a more drastic invasion of property rights, but then repayment looked very unlikely—opposition seems to have been confined to a few (**158**). Much of the vigorous resistance to Mary rested on fears for the newly acquired monastic lands (**161**), and the troubles encountered by Elizabeth in the 1590's were closely linked with the increasing demands of war finance and the oppressive burdens of monopolies (**167**).[168] Altogether, the Commons were never so united as on financial issues and the Crown never more careful than when asking for money. At the same time it should be remembered that after 1540 taxes were always granted with great readiness: supply was never an occasion of real trouble under Elizabeth.

It would not be right to suppose that Parliament proved difficult only on this one issue. The Parliament of 1515 quarrelled violently with the clergy and promoted petitions against them, despite Wolsey's hold over the government.[169] Even in 1523, when supply dominated the session, Cromwell at least (then a private member) either spoke or contemplated speaking at length against the whole foreign policy which necessitated the taxation demanded.[170] The Reformation Parliament did not pass without occasional words or murmurs against the king's religious policy and even his personal affairs, though the reports, usually from the hostile imperial ambassador, must be treated with some caution.[171] Both Lords and Commons resisted the

[165] Roper, *More*, 7. I have my doubts.

[166] **157**, and cf. Hall, *Chronicle*, 655 ff.

[167] Cf. above, p. 153.

[168] Neale, *Elizabeth and her Parliaments*, II, 198 ff., 352 ff., 376 ff., 411 ff.

[169] Cf. below, p. 329.

[170] Merriman, *Cromwell's Letters*, 30 ff. The speech there printed may be ascribed to Cromwell with every confidence, but whether it was ever delivered is another matter.

[171] E.g. **159**; and cf. *L.P.*, V, 171, 941, 1202. The bill of annates in 1532 caused difficulties (*ibid.* 898) and that against appeals in 1533 was held up by fears for the trade with the Netherlands (*ibid.*, VI, 296). Cf. Elton, *Studies*, I, 155 ff.

Act of Proclamations in 1539.[172] The reign of Edward VI, when the gentry, dominant in Parliament, also controlled the Council, not surprisingly offers few examples of energetic opposition,[173] but Mary encountered difficulties both over the return to Rome and her Spanish marriage.[174]

In the reign of Elizabeth—even though Neale's Puritan opposition did not exist—religion and the consequences of religious strife could divide queen from Commons, or more properly speaking from the few men there whom ardour, assurance and arrogance encouraged to stand out against their sovereign. Even so, they made a serious impact only when their extreme views looked useful to the real leaders of both Houses (the official element of councillors and men of business), and they often looked useful in the years before the Spanish war when the threat of Catholicism loomed large. Since only Elizabeth judged that threat as soberly as it deserved ardent Protestants—her most loyal subjects—could, in their passion for preventing the destruction of the true faith, sometimes look like an effective opposition. However, that was never the truth of the situation. The allegation that in 1559 a 'Puritan' opposition forced through a more Protestant religious settlement than Elizabeth wanted has been disproved,[175] while Strickland's attempts in 1571 to introduce a reformed Prayer Book (163) was read as a nearly successful move only because a concomitant campaign by Council and bishops for reforming statutes was interpreted as a Puritan move.[176] The presbyterian movement of the 1570's and 1580's did produce parliamentary manoeuvres of a genuine kind in the *Admonitions* campaign[177] and the unpromising attempt in 1587 to overthrow the Settlement at one fell blow (164). However, such extravagances never had any hopes of success, any more than had the introduction in 1593, when Puritanism had lost its revolutionary urges, of bills for religion contrary to the official policy by one who was himself a government official (166). None of this did any good to either religious reform or to its promoters, and concentration on it has distorted the history of Parliament under Elizabeth. It was not Puritanism but Protestantism that animated those who feared that the queen might misjudge the dangers of her own position. Such religion—the fear of a popish succession—underlay the issues over which the Commons really united to harass the queen. In 1572, 1584 and 1587 they tried hard to be rid of Mary Queen of Scots whom only Elizabeth, determined to protect a crowned head against

---

[172] Above, p. 23.

[173] But cf. 155 for a case in which the Council had to appease protests.

[174] Loach, *Mid-Tudor Polity*, 9 ff., shows how much the difficulties emanated from Council and Lords.

[175] Against Neale, *Elizabeth and her Parliaments*, I, 51 ff., cf. Jones, *Parliament*, and Hudson, chs. 6 & 7.

[176] Neale, *Elizabeth and her Parliaments*, I, 191 ff.

[177] Below, p. 445.

these plebeian attacks, saved for so long.[178] Apprehensions for the future of the Protestant Church played their part in the agitation of 1563 and 1566 when the Council encouraged both Houses to press the queen for a settlement of the succession which Elizabeth was resolved not to concede, both because she better realised the difficulties involved and because she could never bring herself to contemplate her own demise (**162**).[179] When Peter Wentworth revived the succession question in 1593 (**165**), he found that interest had died before the queen.[180]

As has already been shown, these issues of religion and policy, which the queen obstinately reserved for herself as 'prerogative matters', also produced in this reign a novel kind of opposition—opposition on points of constitutional principle. In particular, freedom of speech became a battleground.[181] But it did so because a few men recognised—Peter Wentworth in the van—that unless their unlimited definition of that privilege was accepted the Crown would always be able to arrest discussion and silence criticism on all really contentious matters. What they wanted was not so much freedom of speech itself as the promotion of Puritanism and the protection of Protestant England. On these issues the House was much less united than it was on money and monopolies, and the opposition under Elizabeth, down at least to 1593, should be seen as a variable group of determined men making a lot more noise than numbers or success justified, assisted by the political dangers of the years when the queen of Scots acted as a resident centre for all disaffection. Since, in any case, sittings were often thinly attended,[182] the influence of a group of men who knew what they wanted might have made itself more effectively felt than their numbers would have warranted. Throughout those sometimes troubled sessions, however, the truly regular attenders were the managers of business, not the so-called leaders of opposition. If the Commons had been as united over religion, the succession, or the queen of Scots as the rather one-sided evidence of diaries kept by Puritan members would suggest, Elizabeth would have had quite a different task in staving off their interference. What could be achieved when the House was at one, the monopoly debates of 1597 and 1601 demonstrated with some insistence. Although there was less of principle involved in them, and although the opposition lacked leaders comparable to those of the previous three decades, the queen had to give way entirely.

It thus appears that opposition in Parliament was possible throughout

---

[178] Neale, *Elizabeth and her Parliaments*, I, 247 ff.; II, 28 ff., 103 ff.

[179] The story as told *ibid.*, I, 101 ff., 129 ff., must be corrected by removing Neale's Puritan 'choir'. The evidence from which he constructed this chimaera proves only the existence of a very mixed, and highly temporary, group of noisy debaters (cf. Elton, *Hist. Journal*, XXII, 272).

[180] Neale, *Elizabeth and her Parliaments*, II, 251 ff.

[181] Above, pp. 266 ff.

[182] Neale, *House of Commons*, 413 f.

the century and encountered by all the Tudors, but that it grew more persistently troublesome in the reign of Elizabeth. The reasons may be found in part in the developing selfconsciousness of the Commons and the presence there of an eager Protestant group, in part in the fact that from 1558 the Crown ceased to lead the country into new ways but tried to prevent change, and in part perhaps in the nature of our evidence—scanty before Elizabeth, relatively full during her time. But this last point cannot be taken very seriously, except that one must not suppose opposition and conflict to have been new things after 1558. Their increase should not be in doubt. Elizabeth's difficulties in parliamentary management were unquestionably greater than her father's, but it may be suggested that she was also a little less skilful at handling her Commons. She was good enough, but Henry had, by all accounts, been superb. He had the advantage of being a man possessed of a kind of hearty (and often genuine) joviality, which Elizabeth, a woman and necessarily more on her dignity, could not copy. There were, however, also differences of temperament. Parliamentary opposition to Henry VIII, even when it touched his private concerns, met with no more than courteous argument or jocular respect (**158, 159**). Elizabeth, on the other hand, was always increasing her difficulties by some piece of sharp, sometimes waspish, comment. Her father would never have referred to idle brains among his Commons or thought it monstrous that the feet should presume to direct the head,[183] though it is, of course, arguable that he never had occasion to feel so provoked. In 1571, over Strickland's attempt to introduce a bill for religion, Elizabeth made a bad mistake when she sequestered him and then had to restore him to the House (**163**). In any case, she had to learn her job and clearly got better at it as the years passed. But both the vigour of opposition and her outspoken determination to keep her prerogative intact led to many a difficult moment, though in the end she always knew how to restore harmony. It remains true that her 'golden speech' of 1601 (**168**) symbolises the essential unity of Crown and Commons, of queen and people, upon which the Tudor constitution rested.

157. Opposition in 1523: a letter to the earl of Surrey.

. . . Since the beginning of the Parliament there hath been the greatest and sorest hold in the Lower House for payment of 2s. of the £ that ever was seen, I think, in any Parliament. The matter hath been debated and beaten fifteen or sixteen days together: the highest necessity alleged on the King's behalf to us that ever was heard of: and of the contrary

---

[183] Neale prints the queen's speeches to Parliament in full, at the end of each session. Skilful and affectionate as they often are, they also contain some needlessly sarcastic stuff. Her scolding, which some liken to that of a mother, seems to me to reek of the governess.

the highest poverty confessed, as well by knights, esquires and gentlemen of every quarter, as by the commoners, citizens and burgesses. There hath been such hold that the House was like to have been dissevered; that is to say, the knights being of the King's Council, the King's servants and gentlemen of the one party, which in so long time were spoken with and made to say yea, it may fortune contrary to their heart, will and conscience. Thus hanging the matter, yesterday the more part, being the King's servants, gentlemen, were there assembled; and so they, being the more part, willed and gave to the King 2s. of the £ [etc.]. . . . I have heard no man in my life that can remember that ever there was given to anyone of the King's ancestors half so much at one grant. . . . I think now that this matter is so far passed that the Parliament will soon be ended.

Ellis, I, I, 220–1

158. Opposition in 1529.

This John Petite . . . was twenty years burgess for the city of London and free of the grocers, eloquent and well spoken, exactly seen in histories, song and the Latin tongue. King Henry VIII would ask in the Parliament time, in his weighty affairs, if Petite were of his side. For once, when the King required to have all those sums of money to be given to him by act of Parliament which afore he had borrowed of certain persons, John Petite stood against the bill, saying, 'I cannot in my conscience agree and consent that this bill should pass, for I know not my neighbour's estate. They perhaps borrowed it to lend to the King. But I know mine own estate, and therefore I freely and frankly give the King that I lent him.' . . .

Narratives of the Reformation, 25

159. The imperial ambassador (Eustace Chapuys) to Charles V, 2 May 1532.

. . . The King has again applied to Parliament for a subsidy in money to fortify the frontiers of Scotland. During the debate two worthy members of that assembly were bold enough to declare openly and in plain terms that there was no need at all of such military preparations . . . for the Scotch would never declare war or invade England without having an ally on the continent, and that the best fortifications against the enemy consisted in maintaining justice in the kingdom and keeping on friendly terms with your Imperial Majesty. . . . Parliament ought at once to petition the King to take back his legitimate wife and treat

313

her kindly. . . . These sentiments of the two members meeting with the approbation of the whole Parliament with the single exception of two or three present, nothing was then resolved about the said subsidy; but the King, exceedingly displeased at the turn the affair was taking, sent for the majority of the members and made them a marvellously long speech in justification of his intended divorce, representing to them that this was not a matter for them to consider and discuss. . . . This the King said in the most gracious and amiable terms, promising the members that they should be thoroughly supported against the encroachments of ecclesiastical power. . . .   *Span. Cal.*, IV, 440–1[184]

160. Opposition to the Statute of Uses, 1532.

[A first draft of the bill, which freed half a man's land from prerogative demands provided the other half was not conveyed away, causing much opposition, Henry VIII addressed a delegation from the Commons:] 'I much commend you that you will not contend nor stand in strife with the spiritual men . . . but much more me thinketh that you should not contend with me that I am your sovereign lord and king, considering that I seek peace and quietness of you; for I have sent to you a bill concerning wards and primer seisin in the which things I am greatly wronged; wherefore I have offered you reason, as I think, yea, and so thinketh all the Lords, for they have set their hands to the book; therefore I assure you, if you will not take some reasonable end now when it is offered, I will search out the extremity of the law and then will I not offer you so much again.' With this answer the Speaker and his company departed. . . . When this bill came first among the Commons, Lord, how the ignorant persons were grieved and how shamefully they spake of the bill and of the King's learned counsel but the wise men which understood and saw the mischief to come would gladly have had the bill assented to, or at the least to have put the King in a surety of the third or fourth part; which offer I am credibly informed the King would have taken. But many forward and wilful persons, not regarding what might ensue (as it did indeed) would neither consent to the bill as the Lords had agreed and set to their hands, nor yet agree to no reasonable qualification of the same; which they sore repented. For after this the King called the judges and best learned

---

[184] The translations of *Span. Cal.* are at times a trifle wild, and I have therefore used the abstract in *L.P.*, v, 989 in constructing the rendering of this passage.

men of his realm, and they disputed the matter in the Chancery and agreed that land could not be willed by the order of the common law; whereupon an act was made that no man might declare his will of no part of his land.   Hall, *Chronicle*, 785

161. Opposition under Mary: the Venetian ambassador (Giovanni Michieli) to the Doge and Senate of Venice.

[18 November 1555] None of the proposals made in Parliament have as yet been decided, either with regard to compelling the absentees to return[185] or about confirming the cession made by the Queen of the Church property,[186] both matters (it is said) having been sharply debated, many members opposing the recall of the absentees, as no one ought to be deprived of his liberty to go and reside wherever he pleased ... with the Queen's permission ... ; if in future her Majesty chose not to concede it, in order to prevent anyone from living abroad, it was in her power to do so. Touching the second proposal, about the cession, by no means would they give their assent to the alienation of anything, however insignificant, which had been incorporated with and annexed to the Crown, to the prejudice of its heirs, for the advantage solely of an alien and foreigner (meaning the Pope), although the Queen, they say, during her lifetime, may do what she pleases with the revenues of the realm ... ; but as to alienating them with their consent, they would not open this door, lest in the event of the succession of a new king they incur disgrace and perhaps punishment. In this they still persist, these contradictions proceeding (as told me by a person well acquainted with the present tactics) from the fact that the present House of Commons, whether by accident or from design, a thing not seen for many years in any Parliament, is quite full of gentry and nobility (for the most part suspected in the matter of religion) and therefore more daring and licentious than former Houses which consisted of burgesses and plebeians, by nature timid and respectful. ...

[3 December 1555] Members of the committee for the revision of the articles stipulating the cession, having reported their opinion this morning in Parliament, after great disputes and contention in the Lower House, from daybreak, when they met, until 3 p.m., during which time the doors were closed, no one being allowed egress either

---

[185] I.e. those who had fled England for religion's sake.
[186] I.e. the Queen's proposal to return the first fruits and tenths to the Church.

to eat or for any other purpose; at length, this evening, the bill was carried by 183 ayes against 120 noes, the Lords being unanimously content. . . .

Ven. Cal., VI, 251, 270

162. Opposition in 1566.

On Friday the 18th day of October [1566] . . . a motion was made by Mr Molineux for the reviving of the suit touching the declaration of a successor, in case her Majesty should die without issue of her own body, which suit had been first moved by the House and their petition preferred therein in the first session of this Parliament . . . and that the said business touching the declaration of a successor and the Subsidy Bill might proceed together; which motion was very well approved by the greater part of the said House. And thereupon divers propositions and reasonings ensued, this great business being once moved, although it should seem in the conclusion thereof that the greater part of the House were resolved to recontinue the said suit and to know her Highness' answer; although Sir Ralph Sadler, knight banneret, one of her Privy Council, had declared and affirmed unto the House that he had heard the Queen say, in the presence of divers of the nobility, that for the wealth of the realm her Highness was minded to marry. . . . On Saturday, the 19th day of October, . . . Mr Secretary Cecil and Sir Francis Knollys, her Majesty's vice-chamberlain, declared unto the House that the Queen's Majesty was, by God's special providence, moved to marriage, and that she mindeth for the wealth of her commons to prosecute the same. Sir Ambrose Cave, chancellor of the Duchy, and Sir Edward Rogers, controller of her Majesty's Household, affirmed the same, and thereupon persuaded and advised the House to see the sequel of that before they made further suit touching the declaration of a successor. But against this opinion divers lawyers of the House . . . did argue very boldly and judiciously, and so prevailed with the greatest part of the House as that it was resolved, contrary to the foregoing motion of those of her Majesty's Privy Council, to recontinue their suit touching the declaration of a successor and to get the Queen's answer. And to that end it was ordered, that all the Privy Council being members of this House, with 44 others . . . should meet to-morrow to consult and advise in what manner they might move the lords of the Upper House to join with them in this matter. . . .

On Wednesday the 6th day of November . . . Sir Edward Rogers, knight, controller of her Highness' Household, and Sir William Cecil, knight, her Majesty's principal secretary, read in writing notes of the Queen's Majesty's saying before the Lords and committees of this House; tending that her Grace had signified to both Houses by words of a prince that she by God's grace would marry and would have it therefore believed; and touching limitation for succession, the perils be so great to her person, and whereof she hath felt part in her sister's time, that time will not yet suffer to treat of it. Whereupon all the House was silent. . . .

On Friday the 8th day of November . . . Mr Lambert began a learned oration for iteration of the suit to the Queen's Majesty for limitation of succession, and thereupon strongly reasoned for both parts: whence it appeareth plainly, that though her Majesty satisfied the Lords by her former answer on Tuesday the 5th of this instant November preceding (the effect of which was that she was desirous to incline her mind to marriage, but could not declare a successor in respect of the great danger thereof) yet those of the House of Commons rested not contented therewith, but only resting upon her Majesty's promise touching her marriage, they still discoursed of and resolved to press further that other part of their former suit touching the declaration of a successor. . . .

On Saturday the 9th day of November . . . Sir Francis Knollys, knight, her Majesty's vice-chamberlain, declared the Queen's Majesty's express commands to this House that they should no further proceed in their suit, but to satisfy themselves with her Highness' promise of marriage. After whom Mr Secretary Cecil and Mr Controller severally rehearsed the like matter. So that by this it may be gathered that her Majesty, understanding of Mr Lambert's motion made yesterday and fearing that the House should fall afresh upon the discussion of this business, did now send her express inhibition to prevent it by these forenamed honourable personages. . . .

On Monday the 11th day of November . . . Paul Wentworth, a burgess of the House, by way of motion, desired to know whether the Queen's command and inhibition that they should no longer dispute of the matter of succession (sent yesterday to the House) were not against the liberties and privileges of the said House. And thereupon arose divers arguments, which continued from nine of the clock in the morning till two of the clock in the afternoon. But then, because the time was far spent, all further debate and reasoning was deferred until the next morning. . . .

On Tuesday the 12th day of November, Mr Speaker being sent for to attend upon the Queen's Majesty at the court about nine of the clock, sent word to the House where he was, requiring the House to have patience; and at his coming after ten of the clock began to show that he had received a special command from her Highness to this House, notwithstanding her first commandment, that there should not be further talk of that matter in the House (touching the declaration of a successor in case that her Majesty should die without issue) and if any person thought himself not satisfied but had further reasons, let him come before the Privy Council and there shew them. . . .

On Monday the 25th day of November . . . Mr Speaker, coming from the Queen's Majesty, declared her Highness' pleasure to be that for her good will to the House she did revoke her two former commandments requiring the House no further to proceed at this time in the matter. Which revocation was taken of all the House most joyfully, with most hearty prayer and thanks for the same.

[Queen's Speech at the Dissolution of Parliament, 2 January 1567]

. . . I have in this assembly found so much dissimulation, where I always professed plainness, that I marvel thereat; yea, two faces under one hood, and the body rotten, being covered with two visors, succession and liberty, which they determined must be either presently granted, denied, or deferred. . . .

. . . But do you think that either I am unmindful of your surety by succession, wherein is all my care, considering I know myself to be mortal? No, I warrant you. Or that I went about to break your liberties? No, it was never in my meaning, but to stay you before you fell into the ditch. For all things have their time. And although perhaps you may have after me one better learned or wiser, yet I assure you none more careful over you; and therefore henceforth, whether I live to see the like assembly or no, or whoever it be, yet beware however you prove your prince's patience as you have now done mine. And now to conclude, all this notwithstanding (not meaning to make a Lent of Christmas) the most part of you may assure yourselves that you depart in your prince's grace.   D'Ewes, *Journals*, 124, 127-30, 116-7

163. Opposition in 1571: Strickland's Bill.

[14 April 1571] The bill for reformation of the Book of Common Prayer was read the first time, after which (the bill being preferred by Mr Strickland) ensued divers long arguments. . . . After which arguments, it was upon the question agreed that a petition should be made by this House unto the Queen's Majesty for her licence and privity to proceed in this bill before it be any further dealt in. . . . The Parliament was then by the consent of the House, for that it was Easter Eve, adjourned until Thursday next . . . during which said time of Easter Mr Strickland . . . was called before the lords of the Privy Council and required to attend upon them, and to make stay from coming to the House in the mean season.

[20 April 1571] Mr Carleton, with a very good zeal and orderly show of obedience, made signification how that a member of the House was detained from them (meaning Mr Strickland), by whose commandment or for what cause he knew not. But forasmuch as he was not now a private person, but to supply the room, person and place of a multitude, specially chosen and therefor sent, he thought that neither in regard of the country, which was not to be wronged, nor for the liberty of the House, which was not to be infringed, we should permit him to be detained from us. But whatsoever the intendment of this offence might be, that he should be sent for to the bar of that House, there to be heard and there to answer.

Mr Treasurer in some case gave advertisement to be wary in our proceedings, and neither to venture further than our assured warrant might stretch, nor to hazard our good opinion with her Majesty on any doubtful cause. Withal he wished us not to think worse than there was cause. For the man (quoth he) that is meant, is neither detained nor misused, but on considerations is required to expect the Queen's pleasure upon certain special points; wherein (he said) he durst to assure that the man should neither have cause to dislike or complain, since so much favour was meant unto him as he reasonably could wish. He further said that he was in no sort stayed for any word or speech by him in that place offered, but for the exhibiting of a bill into the House against the prerogative of the Queen, which was not to be tolerated. Nevertheless, the construction of him was rather to have erred in his zeal and bill offered, than maliciously to have meant anything contrary to the dignity royal. . . .

Mr Yelverton said he was to be sent for, arguing in this sort. First, he said, the precedent was perilous, and though in this happy time of lenity, among so good and honourable personages, under so gracious a prince, nothing of extremity or injury was to be feared, yet the times might be altered, and what now is permitted hereafter might be construed as of duty and enforced even on this ground of the present permission. He further said that all matters not treason, or too much to the derogation of the imperial crown, were tolerable there where all things came to be considered of, and where there was such fulness of power as even the right of the Crown was to be determined, and by warrant whereof we had so resolved. That to say the Parliament had no power to determine of the Crown was high treason. He remembered how that men are not there for themselves but for their countries. He shewed it was fit for princes to have their prerogatives; but yet the same to be straitened within reasonable limits. The prince, he showed, could not of herself make laws; neither might she by the same reason break laws. . . .

Mr Fleetwood [citing precedents] resolved that the only and whole help of the House for ease of their grief in this case was to be humble suitors to her Majesty, and neither send for him nor demand him of right. During which speech the council whispered together, and thereupon the Speaker moved that the House should make stay of any further consultation thereupon. . . .

. . . The above-mentioned Mr Strickland did this forenoon [21 April 1571], upon an advertisement (as it should seem) from her Majesty's Council, repair again to the said House soon after it was set. And coming just upon the time when the foregoing bill for coming to church and receiving the communion was in the referring to committees, the said House did, in witness of their joy for the restitution of one of their said members awhile from them restrained, presently nominate him one of the said committees. . . .   D'Ewes, *Journals*, 166-8, 175-6

164. Opposition in 1587: Cope's Bill and Book.

On Monday the 27th day of February [1587] . . . Mr Cope . . . offered to the House a bill and a book written; the bill containing a petition that it might be enacted that all laws now in force touching ecclesiastical government should be void, and that it might be enacted that the book of common prayer now offered, and none other, might be received into the Church to be used. The book contained the form of prayer and administration of sacraments, with divers rites and ceremonies to be used in the Church. And desired that the book might be read. Whereupon Mr Speaker in effect used this speech: For that her Majesty before this time had commanded the House not to meddle with this matter . . . he desired that it would please them to spare the reading of it. Notwithstanding, the House desired the reading of it. Whereupon Mr Speaker willed the clerk to read it. And the clerk[187] being ready to read it, Mr Dalton made a motion against the reading of it, saying that it was not meet to be read . . . and thought that this dealing would bring her Majesty's indignation against the House, thus to enterprise the dealing with those things which her Majesty especially had taken into her own charge and direction. . . . And so the time being passed the House brake up, and the petition nor book read.

This done, her Majesty sent to Mr Speaker as well for this petition and book as for that other petition and book for the like effect that was delivered the last session of Parliament; which Mr Speaker sent to her Majesty. . . .

D'Ewes, Journals, 410

165. Opposition in 1593: the succession.

[24 February 1593] This day Mr Peter Wentworth and Sir Henry Bromley delivered a petition unto the lord keeper, therein desiring the lords of the Upper House to be suppliants with them of the Lower House unto her Majesty for entailing the succession of the Crown, whereof a bill was readily drawn by them. Her Majesty was highly displeased therewith after she knew thereof, as a matter contrary to her former strait commandment, and charged the Council to call the parties before them. Sir Thomas Heneage presently sent for them, and after speeches had with them, commanded them to forbear the Parliament and not to go out from their several lodgings. The day after being Sunday, . . . though the House sat not, yet they were called before the lord treasurer, the Lord Buckhurst, and Sir Thomas Heneage. The lords intreated them favourably and with good speeches; but so highly was her Majesty offended that they must needs commit them, and so they told them. Whereupon Mr Peter Wentworth was sent prisoner unto the Tower; Sir Henry Bromley and one Mr Richard Stevens, to whom Sir Henry Bromley had imparted the matter, were sent to the Fleet, as also Mr Welch, the other knight for Worcestershire. . . .

[187] 'Court' in the text, which is probably a misprint.

[10 March 1593] Mr. Wroth . . . desired that we might be humble and earnest suitors to her Majesty that she would be pleased to set at liberty those members of the House that were restrained. To this was answered by all the privy councillors that her Majesty had committed them for causes best known to herself, and for us to press her Majesty with this suit, we should but hinder them whose good we seek. And it is not to be doubted but her Majesty of her gracious disposition will shortly of herself yield to them that which we would ask for them, and it will like her better to have it left unto herself than sought by us. . . . D'Ewes, *Journals*, 470, 497

166. Opposition in 1593: Morice's bills.

[27 February 1593] Mr Morice, attorney of the Court of Wards, moveth the House touching the hard courses of the bishops and ordinaries and other ecclesiastical judges in their courts, used towards sundry learned and godly ministers and preachers of this realm by way of inquisition . . . compelling them upon their own oaths to accuse themselves . . . and offereth unto Mr Speaker two bills, the one concerning the said inquisitions, subscriptions and offering of oaths, and the other concerning the imprisonments upon their refusal of the said oaths. . . .

[28 February 1593] . . . Mr Speaker stood up and said, That he had a message to deliver from her Majesty to the said House. . . . The message delivered me from her Majesty consisteth in three things: First, the end for which the Parliament was called; secondly, the speech which the lord keeper used from her Majesty; thirdly, what her pleasure and commandment now is. For the first, it is in me and my power (I speak now in her Majesty's person) to call Parliaments; it is in my power to end and determine the same; it is in my power to assent or dissent to anything done in Parliaments. . . . Her Majesty's pleasure being then delivered unto us by the lord keeper, it was not meant we should meddle with matters of state or causes ecclesiastical, for so her Majesty termed them. She wondered that any could be of so high commandment to attempt (I use her own words) a thing so expressly contrary to that which she had forbidden; wherefore with this she was highly offended. And because the words then spoken by my lord keeper are not now perhaps well remembered, or some be now here that were not then present, her Majesty's present charge and express commandment is that no bill touching the said matters of state or reformation in causes ecclesiastical be exhibited. And upon my allegiance I am commanded, if any such bill be exhibited, not to read it. . . .   D'Ewes, *Journals*, 474, 478

167. Opposition in 1601: Monopolies.

[20 November 1601] Dr Bennet said: He that will go about to debate her Majesty's prerogative royal had need walk warily. In respect of a grievance out of the city for which I come, I think myself bound to speak that now which I had not intended to speak before—I mean, a monopoly of salt. It is an old proverb, *Sal sapit omnia*; fire and water are not more necessary. But for other monopolies, of cards (at which word Sir Walter Raleigh blushed), dice, starch and the like, they are (because monopolies) I must confess very hurtful, though not all alike hurtful. I know there is a great difference in them, and I think if the abuses in this monopoly of salt were particularised this would walk in the fore rank. . . .

. . . Mr Francis Moore said . . . We have a law for the true and faithful currying of leather; there is a patent sets all at liberty, notwithstanding the statute. And to what purpose is it to do anything by act of Parliament when the Queen will undo the same by her prerogative ? . . . There is no act of hers that hath been or is more derogatory to her own Majesty and more odious to the subject, more dangerous to the commonwealth, than the granting of these monopolies.

Mr Martin said, I do speak for a town that grieves and pines, for a country that groaneth and languisheth under the burden of monstrous and unconscionable substitutes to the monopolitans of starch, tin, fish, cloth, oil, vinegar, salt, and I know not what, nay, what not? The principalest commodities both of my town and country are ingrossed into the hand of those bloodsuckers of the commonwealth. . . .

[21 November 1601] . . . Sir Robert Wroth said . . . There have been divers patents granted since the last Parliament; these are now in being, viz. the patents for currants, iron, powder, cards, ox shin-bones, train oil, transportation of leather, lists of cloth, ashes, aniseeds, vinegar, sea-coals, steel, *aqua vitae*, brushes, pots, saltpetre, lead, accidences, oil, calamine stone, oil of blubber, fumathoes or dried pilchards in the smoke, and divers others.

Upon the reading of the patents aforesaid, Mr Hakewill, of Lincoln's Inn, stood up and asked thus: Is not bread there ? Bread, quoth

one. Bread, quoth another. . . . This voice seems strange, quoth a
third. No, quoth Mr Hakewill, if order be not taken for these, bread
will be there before the next Parliament. . . .

[24 November 1601] . . . Upon some loud confusion in the House
touching some private murmur of monopolies, Mr Secretary Cecil
said . . . I have been (though unworthy) a member of this House in six
or seven Parliaments, yet never did I see the House in so great confusion.
I believe there never was in any Parliament a more tender point
handled than the liberty of the subject, that when any is discussing this
point he should be cried and coughed down. This is more fit for a
grammar-school than a Court of Parliament. I have been a councillor
of state this twelve years, yet did I never know it subject to construction
of levity and disorder. Much more ought we to be regardful in so great
and grave an assembly. Why, we have had speeches upon speeches,
without either order or discretion. One would have us proceed by bill
and see if the Queen would have denied it; another, that the patents
should be brought here before us and cancelled—and this were bravely
done. Others would have us to proceed by way of petition, which
course doubtless is best; but for the first, and especially for the second,
it is so ridiculous that I think we should have as bad success as the devil
himself would have wished in so good a cause. Why, if idle courses had
been followed, we should have gone forsooth to the Queen with a
petition to have repealed a patent of monopoly of tobacco pipes . . .
and I know not how many conceits; but I wish every man to rest
satisfied till the committees have brought in their resolutions.

[25 November 1601] . . . Mr Speaker (after a silence, and every man
marvelling why the Speaker stood up) spake to this effect: It pleased her
Majesty to command me to attend upon her yesterday in the afternoon, from whom I am to deliver unto you all her Majesty's most
gracious message. . . . She yields you all hearty thanks for your care
and special regard of those things that concern her state . . . , for
our . . . making of so hasty and free a subsidy . . . and for our loyalty. . . .
She said that partly by limitation of her Council, and partly by divers
petitions that have been delivered unto her both going to the chapel
and also to walk abroad, she understood that divers patents which she
had granted were grievous to her subjects, and that the substitutes of the
patentees had used great oppressions. But she said she never assented to
grant anything which was *malum in se*; and if in the abuse of her grant
there be anything evil . . . she herself would take present order of

reformation. . . . Further order should be taken presently and not *in futuro* . . . and that some should be presently repealed, some suspended, and none put in execution but such as should first have a trial according to the law for the good of the people. . . .

Mr Francis Moore said, I must confess, Mr Speaker, I moved the House both the last Parliament and this touching this point, but I never meant . . . to set limits and bounds to the prerogative royal. But now, seeing it hath pleased her Majesty of herself, out of the abundance of her princely goodness, to set at liberty her subjects from the thraldom of those monopolies from which there was no town, city or country free, I would be bold in one motion to offer two considerations to this House: The first, that Mr Speaker might go unto her Majesty to yield her most humble and hearty thanks and withal to show the joy of her subjects for their delivery and their thankfulness unto her for the same; The other, that where divers speeches have been made extravagantly in this House, which doubtless have been told her Majesty and perhaps all ill-conceived of by her, I would therefore that Mr Speaker not only should satisfy her Majesty by way of apology therein but also humbly crave pardon for the same.

. . . So it was put to the question and concluded, That thanks should be returned by the Speaker, and some twelve were named to go with him as a convenient number, and entreaty made to the Privy Council to obtain liberty to be admitted. . . .   D'Ewes, *Journals*, 645–54

168. The Queen's speech to a Commons' deputation, 30 November 1601.

. . . In the afternoon, about three of the clock, some seven score of the House met at the great chamber before the Council Chamber in White-hall. At length the Queen came into the Council Chamber, where, sitting under the cloth of state at the upper end, the Speaker with all the company came in, and after three low reverences made [he delivered his speech] . . . And after three low reverences made, he with the rest kneeled down, and her Majesty began thus to answer herself, *viz.* . . .

. . . Mr Speaker, you give me thanks, but I doubt me I have more cause to thank you all than you me; and I charge you to thank them of the House of Commons from me, for had I not received a knowledge from you, I might have fallen into the lap of an error only for lack of true information. Since I was Queen yet did I never put my pen to any grant but that upon pretext and semblance made unto me that it was both good and beneficial to the subjects in general, though a private profit to some of my ancient servants who had deserved well. But the contrary being found by experience, I am exceeding beholden to such subjects as would move the same at first. And I am not so simple to suppose but that there be some of the Lower House whom these grievances never touched; and for them I think they speak out of zeal to their countries, and not out of spleen or malevolent affection as being parties grieved; and I take it exceeding grateful from them, because it gives us to know that no respects or interests had moved them other than the minds they bear to suffer no diminution of our honour and our subjects' love unto us. The zeal of which affection tending to ease my people and knit their hearts unto me, I embrace with a princely care; for above all earthly treasure I esteem my people's love, more than which I desire not to merit. . . . I have ever used to set the last judgment day before mine eyes, and so to rule as I shall be judged to answer before a Higher Judge. To whose judgment seat I do appeal, that never thought was cherished in my heart that tended not to my people's good. . . . And though you have had and may have many princes more mighty and wise sitting in this seat, yet you never had or shall have any that will be more careful and loving. . . . And so I commit you all to your best fortunes and further counsels. And I pray you, Mr Controller, Mr Secretary, and you of my Council, that before these gentlemen depart into their countries you bring them all to kiss my hand.

D'Ewes, *Journals*, 658–60

CHAPTER 9

THE CHURCH

The sixteenth-century Church was an institution of government, a system of rule by itself and also a part of the national constitution. That it was also something else—a spiritual body, a ministry of religion—goes without saying but cannot here concern us. In constitutional matters the history of the Church under the Tudors is at heart straightforward: it was turned into an adjunct of the state, removed from the spiritual and jurisdictional supremacy of the pope, and subjected to a similar dominion exercised by the Crown. These were the constitutional aspects of the English Reformation. Some of its consequences—secularisation of lands, settlement of religion, the preservation of the Church so established against attacks—must also be considered because they display the reformed government of the Church in action. One must, perhaps, avoid overstating the extent of the revolution which took place. Unquestionably the Crown had large enough powers in and over the Church before the Reformation, and the relationship of Church and state in the fifteenth century was not that which had prevailed in the thirteenth. The importance of changes which in part amounted to a formal confirmation of past developments will always be variously assessed by different people and parties; but, as shall be shown, it is hard to avoid the conclusion that the English Reformation in its constitutional aspect—the creation of a national Church under the king's supremacy—was a genuine revolution.[1]

I. GRIEVANCES AGAINST THE CLERGY

The changes which came over the Church were in part the result of political accidents; Anne Boleyn should not be forgotten. Yet it is quite certain that they sprang from much deeper causes, from the condition of the Church and the anomaly of its privileged position within a growingly more centralised national state. The existing situation proved untenable because the laity feared, resented and despised much about the Church, its officers, its courts and its wealth, and because, in the last resort, its 'liberties' could not be permitted to survive to the detriment of the state's omnicompetent control. That the pre-Reformation Church was not in the best of health is well enough known.[2] The sort of grievances voiced against it were not always so extreme as Simon Fish's (169) whose foul mouth and nascent Protestantism

---

[1] For the outline, cf. Dickens, *English Reformation*; Elton, *Reform and Reformation*; Cross, *Royal Supremacy*. For an interesting critique cf. Haigh, *Stadtbürgertum*, 88 ff.

[2] For a judicious review, which hides an indictment, cf. Hughes, *Reformation*, I, 31 ff.

make him perhaps an unfair representative of the aggrieved people. Others expressed themselves more moderately, though they did not spare their criticisms.[3] A poverty-stricken and ignorant lower clergy, wealthy bishops and abbots, a wide ramification of jurisdiction,[4] a mixture of high claims and low deeds, did not make for respect or love among a laity which, though formally very devout, showed few signs of spiritual or evangelical leanings. The bishops were mostly trained administrators, ministers or ex-ministers of the Crown, and—while often respectable, able and upright—little qualified to shepherd their flocks.[5] The presence of notorious abuses (especially pluralism and the taking of excessive fees from the laity) caused constant irritation. The clergy seemed not only wealthy but greedy. In short, anticlericalism was the unmistakable order of the day, more particularly among the gentry but often also found lower down the social scale.[6] This remains true even though it has been shown that the pamphleteers wildly exaggerated and that in actual fact the condition of the Church was improving on the eve of the break with Rome.[7]

Wolsey not only typified and concentrated these problems in his person; by his avowed policy he brought home to England the dangers of an international papal power which exercised jurisdiction over matters English and extracted money from the English Church.[8] Hostility to clergy and papacy drew support from various intellectual and religious movements—remnants of Lollardy, noticeable among the lower orders,[9] humanist dissatisfaction with the existing condition of the Church,[10] the beginnings of Lutheranism in the English universities[11]—but it is more to the point that they came to involve the interests of the Crown. Enforcement of law and order came up against two notorious clerical privileges which in themselves only represented the general existence of a state within a state. Benefit of clergy was originally the right enjoyed by a man in holy orders to be tried for his crimes in a spiritual court which could inflict only spiritual penalties. In course of time it developed into a complicated set of rules which in effect protected a wide variety of people claiming at least minor orders against the consequences of their crimes. An act of 1489 limited 'clergy' by inflicting branding in the thumb on any criminals claiming it if they were not in major orders; this was intended to prevent the mass of clergiable persons from enjoying the privilege

---

[3] Cf. e.g. the extracts from More and Starkey printed by Tanner, 73 ff., 82 ff.
[4] Cf. above, p. 219.
[5] Hughes, *Reformation*, I, 74 ff.
[6] Cf. Elton, *Star Chamber Stories*, ch. VI.
[7] Heath, *Parish Clergy*; Bowker, *Secular Clergy*.
[8] Elton, *Reform and Reformation*, 92 ff.
[9] Thomson, *Later Lollards*; Aston, *History*, XLIX, 149 ff.
[10] Cf. McConica.
[11] Rupp, *Protestant Tradition*; Porter, ch. I.

more than once.[12] During the reigns of Henry VIII and Edward VI the privilege was further reduced to manageable proportions by removing some classes of people and more classes of offences from it;[13] though later legislation modified the energy of these laws and benefit of clergy was allowed to survive, it ceased to be a serious obstacle to effective law-enforcement and became rather a necessary mitigant of the vicious criminal code that ruled in the seventeenth and eighteenth centuries.[14] Sanctuary—the right of refuge in certain places enjoyed by escaping criminals—was altogether dealt with in the reign of Henry VIII when the greater sanctuaries (usually ecclesiastical liberties) were brought under the king's writ;[15] there only survived the forty days' protection offered by churches and churchyards to those who afterwards abjured the realm (or, later, agreed to stay in a recognised place), and this no longer served for greater crimes, especially treason.[16] Benefit of clergy and sanctuary provoked much legislation, but they cannot be regarded as more than minor manifestations of the greater problem—the liberties of the Church.

The first crisis under the Tudors in the relations between Church and state occurred in 1515 when two problems simultaneously disturbed the peace. One arose out of benefit of clergy. The act of 1513 (4 Henry VIII, c. 2) which had limited it came under attack, and in the subsequent struggle between clerical protagonists the king ominously acted as arbiter, taking occasion to remark that 'kings of England had never had superiors but God alone'. The other case, that of Richard Hunne, involved the laity, especially that of London, who expressed themselves violently in Parliament. Hunne's Case combined a wide variety of combustible material: grievances against clerical exactions (Hunne had refused to pay a mortuary fee), disputes over jurisdiction (he had sued a praemunire to stop the Church courts from exacting payment), matters of heresy (he was arrested for possessing a Lollard Bible), not to mention the basic issue whether Hunne, found hanged in the bishop of London's prison, had died of murder or suicide.[17] Wolsey procured peace by a general submission to the royal will and the rapid dissolution of Parliament, but he could only postpone the reckoning. As soon as the Reformation Parliament met, grievances against the clergy came to the fore, and since the Church had failed to remedy its notorious abuses the Parliament, encouraged

[12] 4 Henry VII, c. 14.
[13] Esp. 4 Henry VIII, c. 2; 23 Henry VIII, c. 1; 28 Henry VIII, c. 1; 5 & 6 Edward VI, c. 10.
[14] Holdsworth, III, 299 ff.
[15] Above, p. 32. Sanctuary was also whittled away by acts which ordered those abjuring to be branded (21 Henry VIII, c. 2), substituted confinement in recognised sanctuaries for exile (22 Henry VIII, c. 14), excepted treason from the privilege (26 Henry VIII, c. 13), and provided for some supervision of sanctuary men (27 Henry VIII, c. 19).
[16] 32 Henry VIII, c. 12. On the whole subject cf. Thornley, *Tudor Studies*, 182 ff.
[17] It was possibly an accident. Cf. for these events Elton, *Reform and Reformation*, 50 ff.

rather by the withdrawal of royal restraint than by more positive proddings, took immediate action. Three acts of the 1529 session, prepared by Commons' committees (**115**), limited fees for the probate of wills, defined the proper mortuaries or burial dues, and legislated against clerical pluralism, non-residence and such extra-curricular employment as trading or farming.[18] Apart from dealing with these long-standing lay grievances, the Commons in all probability also began discussing the general problem of Church courts, discussions which emerged two sessions later (1532) as the Supplication against the Ordinaries (**170**).[19] This comprehensively attacked clerical legislation for its independence of royal control, clerical jurisdiction for its costs and capriciousness, and a variety of other misdemeanours on the part of the bishops' officials. It produced only one positive result in the clergy's surrender of their legislative independence,[20] but it showed the anticlerical temper of the laity, especially the gentry.

Thereafter lay grievances came for a time to be subsumed in the Crown's general policy against Church and papacy. However, it would be a mistake to think that the early Reformation settled these issues; nothing is more striking than the continued hostility to clerical pretensions and the continued dissatisfaction with the standards of the clergy. The complaints became almost a commonplace, repeated in barely changing terms down to the Civil War. Much of the effective appeal of Elizabethan and later Puritanism lay in the strength of the conviction that the Church of England, like its medieval predecessor, needed moral, spiritual and intellectual reform. Such complaints as Latimer's at the worldliness of bishops (**171**) or the attacks on insufficient ministers which were collected by the Puritans in 1583 (**173**) find many parallels elsewhere. That there was a serious problem remains plain when all *parti pris* and exaggeration have been allowed for; the hierarchy were aware of it and often tried to do something about it (**172**). The constitutional changes in the sixteenth-century Church took place against a background of lay dislikes and contempts, coupled often with a passionate despair on the part of the better members of the Church itself. The Reformation did not terminate the vigorous anticlericalism of the temporalty or the frequent insufficiency of the spiritualty which were among the more obvious factors that prepared its coming.[21]

[18] 21 Henry VIII, cc. 5, 6, 13.

[19] Ordinaries are the judges in the spiritual courts (i.e. the bishops or their deputies). For the Supplication cf. Elton, *Studies*, II, 107 ff., and *Reform and Reformation*, 150 n. 27. The Ordinaries' Answer is in Gee and Hardy, 154 ff.

[20] *Ibid.*, 176 ff.

[21] The subject really belongs more to the spiritual and moral history of the Church. Cf. Hill, *Economic Problems*, 39 ff.; O'Day, *Continuity and Change*, 55 ff. For an official expression of doubts cf. also Grindal's *Articles* of 1576 (*Remains*, 185 ff.).

169. Simon Fish, *A Supplication for the Beggars* (1528).

Most lamentably complaineth their woeful misery unto your Highness your poor daily bedemen, the wretched, hideous monsters (on whom scarcely for horror any eye dare look), the foul, unhappy sort of lepers and other sore people, needy, impotent, blind, lame and sick, that live only by alms, how that their number is daily so sore increased that all the alms of all the well-disposed people of this your realm is not half enough for to sustain them, but that for very constraint they die for hunger. And this most pestilent mischief is come upon your said poor bedemen by the reason for that there is, in the times of your noble pre-decessors passed, craftily crept into this your realm another sort, not of impotent, but of strong, puissant and counterfeit holy and idle beggars and vagabonds, which, since the time of their first entry by all the craft and wiliness of Satan, are now increased under your sight not only into a great number but also into a kingdom. These are not the herds[22] but the ravenous wolves going in herds' clothing devouring the flock— the bishops, abbots, priors, deacons, archdeacons, suffragans, priests, monks, canons, friars, pardoners, and summoners. And who is able to number this idle, ravenous sort which (setting all labour aside) have begged so importunately that they have gotten into their hands more than the third part of all your realm. The goodliest lordships, manors, lands and territories are theirs. Besides this they have the tenth part of all the corn, meadow, pasture, grass, wool, colts, calves, lambs, pigs, geese and chickens. Over and besides, the tenth part of every servant's wages, the tenth part of the wool, milk, honey, wax, cheese and butter. Yea, and they look so narrowly upon their profits that the poor wives must be countable to them of every tenth egg, or else she getteth not her rights at Easter, shall be taken as an heretic. Hereto they have their four offering days. What money pull they in by probates of testaments, privy tithes, and by men's offerings to their pilgrimages and at their first masses? Every man and child that is buried must pay somewhat for masses and *diriges* to be sung for him, or else they will accuse the dead's friends and executors of heresy. What money get they by mortuaries, by hearing confessions (and yet they will keep thereof no counsel), by hallowing of churches, altars, superaltars,[23] chapels and bells, by cursing of men and absolving them again for money? What a multitude of

---

[22] Shepherds.
[23] A portable stone slab consecrated for use upon an unconsecrated altar or table.

money gather the pardoners in a year? How much money get the summoners by extortion in a year, by citing the people to the commissary's court and afterwards releasing the appearance for money? Finally, the infinite number of begging friars; what get they in a year? ... Is it any marvel that the taxes, fifteenths and subsidies that your Grace most tenderly of great compassion hath taken among your people to defend them from the threatened ruin of their commonwealth have been so slothfully, yea, painfully levied, seeing that almost the utmost penny that might have been levied hath been gathered before yearly by this ravenous, cruel and insatiable generation? ... (pp. 1-3).

And what do all these greedy sort of sturdy, idle, holy thieves with these yearly exactions that they take of the people? Truly nothing but exempt themselves from the obedience of your Grace. Nothing but translate all rule, power, lordship, authority, obedience and dignity from your Grace unto them. Nothing but that all your subjects should fall into disobedience and rebellion against your Grace, and be under them. ... For the which matter your most noble realm wrongfully (alas, for shame!) hath stood tributary, not unto any kind temporal prince but unto a cruel, devilish bloodsupper, drunken in the blood of the saints and martyrs of Christ. ... (pp. 4-5).

... Yea, and what do they more? Truly nothing but apply themselves, by all the sleights they may, to have to do with every man's wife, every man's daughter, and every man's maid that cuckoldry and bawdry should reign over all among your subjects, that no man should know his own child. ... These be they that by their abstaining from marriage do let[24] the generation of the people, whereby all the realm at length, if it should be continued, shall be made desert and inhabitable[25]. ... (p. 6).

What remedy: make laws against them? I am in doubt whether ye be able. Are they not stronger in your own Parliament House than yourself? What a number of bishops, abbots and priors are lords of your Parliament? ... Who is he (though he be grieved never so sore) ... dare lay it to their charge by any way of action? And if he do, then is he by-and-by by their wiliness accused of heresy. ... So captive are your laws unto them, that no man that they list to excommunicate may be admitted to sue any action in any of your courts. If any man in

_____

[24] Hinder.   [25] Uninhabited.

your sessions dare be so hardy to indict a priest, . . . he hath, ere the year go out, such a yoke of heresy laid in his neck that it maketh him wish he had not done it. . . . (p. 8).

. . . This is the great scab why they will not let the New Testament go abroad in your mother tongue, lest men should espy that they by their cloaked hypocrisy do translate thus fast your kingdom into their hands, that they are not obedient unto your high power, that they are cruel, unclean, unmerciful and hypocrites, that they seek not the honour of Christ but their own, that remission of sins are not given by the pope's pardon but by Christ, for the sure faith and truth that we have in him. . . . Set these sturdy loobies abroad in the world to get them wives of their own, to get their living with their labour in the sweat of their faces according to the commandment of God, Gen. iii, to give other idle people by their example occasion to go to labour. Tie these holy, idle thieves to the carts to be whipped naked about every market town till they will fall to labour, that they by their importunate begging take not away the alms that the good Christian people would give unto us sore, impotent, miserable people your bedemen. Then shall as well the number of our foresaid monstrous sort, as of the bawds, whores, thieves and idle people decrease. Then shall these great yearly exactions cease. Then shall not your sword, power, crown, dignity and obedience of your people be translated from you. Then shall you have full obedience of your people. Then shall the idle people be set to work. Then shall matrimony be much better kept. Then shall the generation of your people be increased. Then shall your commons increase in riches. Then shall the gospel be preached. Then shall none beg our alms from us. Then shall we have enough and more than shall suffice us; which shall be the best hospital that ever was founded for us. Then shall we daily pray to God for your most noble estate long to endure (pp. 11, 14–15).

170. The Commons' Supplication against the Ordinaries, 1532.

* * * * * *

First, the prelates and other of the clergy of this your realm, being your subjects, in their Convocation by them holden within this your realm have made and daily make divers fashions of laws and ordinances concerning temporal things; and some of them be repugnant to the laws and statutes of your realm; not having ne requiring your most royal assent to the same laws by them so made, nor any assent or knowledge of your lay subjects is had to the same, nor to them published and known in the English tongue. . . . Declaring the infringers of the same laws so by them made not only to incur into the terrible censures of excommunication but also unto the detestable crime and sin of heresy; by the which divers of your most humble and obedient lay subjects be brought into this ambiguity whether they may do and execute your laws according to your jurisdiction royal of this your realm for dread of the same pains and censures comprised in the said laws. . . .

Also divers and many of your said most humble and obedient subjects, and specially those that be of the poorest sort within this your realm, be daily convented and called before the said spiritual ordinaries, their commissaries and substitutes, *ex officio*, some time at the pleasures of the said ordinaries . . . for displeasure without any provable cause, and sometimes at the only promotion and suggestion of their summoners and apparitors, being very light and indiscreet persons. . . . And some time upon their appearance *ex officio* at the only will and pleasure of the ordinaries . . . they be committed to prison without bail or mainprize, and there some lie (as it is reported) half a year and some more or they can come to their declaration. . . . Divers so appearing . . . shall be constrained to answer to many subtle questions and interrogatories only invented and exhibited at the pleasure of the said ordinaries . . . by the which a simple unlearned or else a wellwitted layman without learning some time is and commonly may be trapped and induced by an ignorant answer to the peril of open penance to his shame, or else to redeem the same penance for money, as it is commonly used. And if it rest upon witnesses, be they but two in number, never so sore defamed of little truth and credence, adversaries or enemy to the party, yet in many cases they may be allowed only by the discretion of the said ordinaries . . . to put the party accused or infamed *ex officio* to open penance and then to redemption for money. . . .

Also divers and many your most humble and obedient subjects be originally cited to appear out of the diocese that they dwell in, and many times be suspended and excommunicate for small and light causes upon the only certificate devised by the proctors of the adversaries made under a pretensed seal of an archdeacon (which any proctor hath at his pleasure); whereas the party suspended and excommunicate many times never had any warning. And yet, when he shall be absolved, if it be out of the court he shall be compelled to pay to his own proctor

20d. and to the proctor which is against him other 20d., and 20d. to the scribe, to the great impoverishing of your said poor lay subjects.

Also your said most humble and obedient subjects find themselves grieved with the great and excessive fees taken in the said spiritual courts, and in especial in the said courts of the Arches and Audience; ... Also in probate of testaments, notwithstanding the last statutes thereof made, there is invented new fashions to charge your subjects for probate of testaments, that is to say long delays and tracts or the proof thereof can be admitted, and also sometimes the executors be put to travel to far places out of the shires they dwell in (although the probate thereof belong not to the prerogative). And likewise since the statute made for mortuaries, there is exacted and demanded of your subjects in divers parishes of this your realm other manner of tithes than they have been accustomed to pay this hundred years past. ... And where any mortuary is due after the rate of the statute, sometimes curates, before they will demand it, will bring citations for it and then will not receive the mortuary till he may have such costs as he says he hath laid out for suit for the same. ...

And also, whereas divers spiritual persons, being presented as well by your Highness as by other patrons within this your realm to divers benefices and other spiritual promotions, the said ordinaries and their ministers do not only take of them for their letters of institution and induction many great and large sums of money and rewards, but also do long delay them without reasonable cause before they will admit, institute and induct them, because they will have the profits of the benefice during vacation, unless they will pact and covenant with them by temporal bonds after such fashions and conditions as they will; whereof some bonds contain that the ordinaries should have part of the profits of the said benefice after their institution. ...

And also the said spiritual ordinaries do daily confer and give sundry benefices unto certain young folks, calling them their nephews or kinsfolk, being in their minority and within age, apt ne able to serve the cure of any such benefice; whereby the said ordinaries do keep and detain the fruits and profits of the same benefices in their own hands ... and the poor silly souls of your people and subjects ... for lack of good curates do perish without good example, doctrine or any good teaching.

* * * * * *

State Papers Henry VIII (Theol. Tracts), vol. 1, no. 22

335

171. Hugh Latimer on the deficiencies of the clergy, 1548.

... This much I dare say, that since lording and loitering hath come up, preaching hath come down, contrary to the apostles' times, for they preached and lorded not, and now they lord and preach not. ... For ever since the prelates were made lords and nobles the plough standeth; there is no work done, the people starve. They hawk, they hunt, they card, they dice; they pastime in their prelacies with gallant gentlemen, with their dancing minions, and with their fresh companions, so that ploughing is set aside; and by their lording and loitering, preaching and ploughing is clean gone. ... But now for the fault of the un-preaching prelates. ... They are so troubled with lordly living, they be so placed in palaces, couched in courts, ruffling in their rents, dancing in their dominions, burdened with ambassages, pampering of their paunches, like a monk that maketh his jubilee. ... They are otherwise occupied, some in the King's matters, some are ambassadors, some of the Privy Council, some to furnish the court, some are lords of the Parliament, some are presidents and controllers of mints. Well, well, is this their duty? Is this their office? Is this their calling? Should we have ministers of the Church to be controllers of mints? ...

... And now I would ask a strange question: who is the most diligentest bishop and prelate in all England that passeth all the rest in doing his office? I can tell for I know him who it is; I know him well. But now I think I see you listening and hearkening that I should name him. There is one that passeth all the other, and is the most diligent prelate and preacher in all England. And will ye know who it is? I will tell you: it is the devil. He is the most diligent preacher of all other; he is never out of his diocese; he is never from his cure; ye shall never find him unoccupied; he is ever in his parish; he keepeth residence at all times; ye shall never find him out of the way, call for him when you will he is ever at home; the diligentest preacher in all the realm; he is ever at his plough; no lording nor loitering can hinder him; he is ever applying his business, ye shall never find him idle, I warrant you. And his office is to hinder religion, to maintain superstition, to set up idolatry, to teach all kind of popery. He is ready as he can be wished for to set forth his plough; to devise as many ways as can be to deface and obscure God's glory. ... O that our prelates would be as diligent to sow the corn of good doctrine as Satan is to sow cockle and darnel. ...

'Sermon on the Plough', *Sermons*, 66–7, 70–1

172. Matthew Parker to Edmund Grindal, 15 August 1560.

After our right hearty recommendations. Whereas, occasioned by the great want of ministers, we and you both, for tolerable supply thereof, have heretofore admitted unto the ministry artificers and others, not traded and brought up in learning, and, as it happened in a multitude, some that were of base occupations: forasmuch as now by experience it is seen that such manner of men, partly by reason of their former profane arts, partly by their light behaviour otherwise and trade of life, are very offensive unto the people, yea, and to the wise of this realm are thought to do great deal more hurt than good, the gospel there sustaining slander; these shall be to desire and require you hereafter to be very circumspect in admitting any to the ministry, and only to allow such as, having good testimony of their honest conversation, have been traded and exercised in learning, or at the least have spent their time with teaching of children. . . .   Parker, *Correspondence*, 120–1

173. The Puritan 'Survey of the Ministry' for Essex, 1586.

A survey of sixteen hundreds or thereabouts in the county of Essex, containing benefices . . . 335.

Wherein there are of ignorant and unpreaching ministers 173, of such as have two benefices apiece 61, of non-residents that are single beneficed 10, preachers of scandalous life 12.

*   *   *   *   *   *

Non-Residents.

Bartholomew Barefoote, very young in years, presented to his benefice by his father, a non-resident.

The parson of Quenden, double-beneficed, he lieth absent from his place where there has been neither divine service nor preaching since Christ-tide last past.

Bancks, parson of Moreton and canon of Christ Church in Oxon., who by reason of his age is not able to preach nor distinctly to read, yet he provideth none among his people to do good. Witness, Robert Ogley.

Preachers of Scandalous Life in Essex.

Mr Ampleforth, vicar of Much Baddow, had a child by his own sister and it doth appear to be true by his divers examinations and deposition taken as well before justices of peace as in the spiritual court before the high commissioners, as also by keeping of the child in sundry places at his charges; he is also suspected of popery, sometime a popish priest, and he is one that doth falsify the Scriptures.

Mr Goldringe, parson of Langdon Hill, he was convicted of fornication, a drunkard.

Mr Ocklei, parson of Much Burstead, a gamester.

Mr Durdent, vicar of Stebbing, a drunkard and a gamester and a very gross abuser of the Scriptures. Witnesses, Mr Denham, Mr Rogers, etc.

Mr Durden, parson of Mashbury, a careless man, a gamester, an alehouse haunter, a company keeper with drunkards and he himself sometimes drunk. Witnesses, Richard Reynolds, John Argent, etc.

Mr Cuckson, vicar of Linsell, unable to preach, he hath been a pilferer.

Mr Wilkinson, vicar of Stansted, Mountfitchet, a gamester.

Mr Fountaine of Much Brackstead, an alehouse haunter and gamester.

Mr Mason, parson of Rawrey, had a child by his maid and is vehemently suspected to have lived incontinently with others, and was brought for the same before a justice of peace.

Mr Glascock, parson of Willingdale Doe, sometime a popish priest, a gross abuser of the Scriptures.

Mr Glibberie, vicar of Halstead, a very ridiculous preacher.

Mr Buffin of Bulmer, an alehouse haunter and convicted for drunkenness before a justice of peace.

Mr Warener, vicar of West Mercy, a drunkard and accused of incontinency, ut supra.

Mr Ellis, parson of Bowers, a dicer, a carder, a pot companion, a company keeper of riotous persons, living very offensively to all men.

[There follows 'A Note of the sufficient, painful and careful preachers and ministers in Essex who have been sundry times molested and vexed, partly for refusing the late urged subscription and partly for not wearing the surplice and omitting the cross in baptism, and such like,' giving 38 names.]   *The Seconde Parte of a Register, II, 97, 162–3*

II. THE ROYAL SUPREMACY

The problem of establishing the king's undisputed authority over the spiritualty in his dominions involved two separate issues. The clergy had to be subjected to the royal will, and the ties which bound it to Rome had to be severed. The first was not only the easier but also the more obvious task, and long before Henry VIII grasped the full extent to which his claim to supremacy could be used against the pope he was busy eliminating all possible resistance from his own clergy.[26] The process began in 1529 with the parliamentary attack on abuses, but the real attack opened in the year after. The weapon to be used lay ready to hand, or rather Wolsey's recent exploitation of it suggested its employment not only against the cardinal himself but against the whole clergy. It was that of praemunire. Strictly the name of a writ designed to protect the royal rights of jurisdiction, the word had come to denote a complex of offences and penalties whose chief characteristic was that no one quite knew how far they might extend. Praemunire had been developed in the fourteenth century against the papal attempts to invade lay rights in the appointments of the Church, but though the purpose had been limited and application rare, the summarising statute of 1393 (16 Richard II, c. 5) could be read as punishing all invasions of 'the king's regality'— especially any activity of spiritual judges to the detriment of the royal courts—with loss of property and imprisonment at pleasure.[27] Wolsey surrendered at once to an indictment under this comprehensive and elastic law,[28] and this seems to have encouraged the Crown's lawyers to use the same instrument against other actual or potential opponents. At any rate, in 1530 some fifteen prelates and lesser clergy were indicted of praemunire (for participating in the illegal exercise of Wolsey's legateship), and early in 1531 the whole clergy in both provinces found themselves in the same predicament, though the charge against them was the even more devastating one that they had broken the king's law by the very use of their spiritual jurisdiction.[29] The Church gave in to the extent of buying a pardon for the offence,[30] but their surrender was far from complete. Henry had at first demanded that they should accept him as supreme head of the Church and clergy of England and recognise his claim to have cure of souls; in the outcome they altogether ignored the second and severely qualified the first by the addition of the words 'as far as the law of Christ allows'. It is, in fact, clear enough that

[26] For my latest views on the struggle over the king's policy cf. *Reform and Reformation*, ch. 6. Scarisbrick, *Henry VIII*, chs. 8–10, ascribed to Henry more control and initiative than I can find. It is important to remember that in 1521, when he defended the pope against Luther, Henry showed himself more papalist than any of his advisers.

[27] Cf. Davies, *History*, 1953, 116 ff.; Waugh, *Eng. Hist. Rev.*, xxxvii, 173 ff. The crucial act of 1393 is printed in Gee and Hardy, 122 ff.

[28] Pollard, *Wolsey*, 242 ff. He shows also (247 ff.) that praemunire was very much alive in the earlier part of Henry VIII's reign.

[29] Scarisbrick, *Camb. Hist. Journal*, xii, 22 ff.

[30] Embodied in statute: **174** (for the southern province); 23 Henry VIII, c. 9 (for the northern). Canterbury paid £100,000 and York £18,000, but much of these sums was later remitted (Elton, *Tudor Revolution*, 145). The laity, having also used the 'illegal' jurisdiction of the Church courts, obtained a free pardon (22 Henry VIII, c. 16).

Henry had not at this time decided on a policy of replacing the pope in England and that he got nothing from the great praemunire attack beyond a bit of money.

In 1532 the king (probably under Cromwell's guidance) turned from the law to Parliament. The Supplication against the Ordinaries[31] was exploited in the royal interest to secure the total surrender of the Church's legislative independence by the Submission of the Clergy,[32] given statutory confirmation in 1534 (**175**).[33] The clergy's collapse on this occasion saved them from an attack on the other grievances listed in the Supplication, but it also bestowed upon the king his first new positive powers in the Church. Moreover, since the control of canons belonged not to the English Church but to the pope, the Submission constituted also the first invasion of papal powers. In the same year the conditional Act in Restraint of Annates (**176**), later confirmed by letters patent and re-enacted in fuller form in 1534 (**178**), deprived the papacy of its major source of revenue from England and bestowed upon the Crown the initiative and the last word in appointments to sees and abbacies.[34] In 1533 the Act of Appeals (**177**) ended the judicial links between England and the court of Rome; intended in the first place to ensure that the divorce should be finally determined by Cranmer's archiepiscopal court, its scope in the end covered most jurisdiction by appeal from one of the parties or provocation at the suit of a party which gave Rome immense and detailed influence over private English concerns.[35] In 1534 a series of acts completed the destruction of papal and elaboration of royal powers by ending all payments to Rome and authorising Canterbury to issue all ecclesiastical licences and

[31] Above, pp. 333 ff.

[32] Gee and Hardy, 176 ff.

[33] The revision of the canon law envisaged by the Submission and ordered to be entrusted to a royal commission of thirty-two, sixteen clergy and sixteen from the two Houses of Parliament, never took place. It was, however, seriously contemplated, and even began in this reign (Logan, *Bull. Inst. Hist. Res.*, XLVII, 99 ff.); on two occasions Henry VIII secured further parliamentary authority for proceeding to the appointment of the commission (27 Henry VIII, c. 15, 35 Henry VIII, c. 16). In 1552 Cranmer got so far as to draw up a full *Reformatio Legum Ecclesiasticarum* (Hughes, *Reformation*, II, 128 ff.), but this did not receive the necessary parliamentary sanction. Nor have, so far, any of the later attempts to define the law of the English Church, though the canons of 1604 (accepted by the Crown and the Convocations) have in practice been in use till recent days. In 1535 Henry VIII prohibited the study of the canon law (which he thought popish) at Oxford and Cambridge, with the result that the civil law and civil lawyers grew dominant in the English Church courts; in 1545 a statute (37 Henry VIII, c. 17) authorised doctors of civil law to practise in the courts Christian even if they were lay and married.

[34] The problem of overlarge dioceses much exercised opinion at this time. Wolsey's legatine commission, which had empowered him to do something about it, had yielded no result (Pollard, *Wolsey*, 183 f.). An act of 1534 (26 Henry VIII, c. 14) contemplated the creation of suffragan bishops, and one of 1539 (31 Henry VIII, c. 9) authorised the king to create new sees by letters patent. The power was used to erect the bishoprics of Chester, Peterborough, Gloucester, Oxford, Bristol and Westminster, the last named being abolished in 1550.

[35] For the prehistory of the act cf. Elton, *Studies*, II, 82 ff. Doc. **175**, sect. iv, extended the prohibition to all kinds of cases.

faculties (Act of Dispensations: **179**), by confirming the cessation of annates and establishing a new method of appointing bishops which left the control entirely in the king's hands (**178**), by confirming the 1532 submission and elaborating the course of appeals so as to leave the last word with the king in Chancery (**175**), and by confirming the title of supreme head, originally accepted by the Church in 1531 but now free of all qualifications and full of the contents created by the work of 1533–4 (**180**). The Treasons Act of the same year (**30**) added the protection in law which the Act of Supremacy did not provide. An act of 1536 (**181**) summed up the new position by a long attack on papal usurpations and a general imposition of praemunire on any who would defend the authority of the bishop of Rome.

Therewith the royal supremacy in the Church was created and complete. It was claimed to be a restoration of the true position, and while it is patently absurd (except for propaganda purposes) to treat some four centuries of papal monarchy as a mere 'usurpation', it would be wrong to regard the historical arguments set out in the various preambles as entirely false. There was much in the past which justified the stand taken by Henry VIII—much history underlay the claim to 'true monarchy' or (as the Act of Appeals put it) 'empire'.[36] Long convinced of the greatness of his 'imperial crown', Henry VIII either put through, or more probably allowed Cromwell to put through, a reconstruction of the body politic which depended for its validity on the notion of national sovereignty embodied in the head and king. The political structure envisaged in the Act of Appeals (**177**) looks dualist only because there were in fact two systems of courts (lay and spiritual) in the realm and jurisdiction was the point at issue. But the doctrine of that confident preamble is essentially unitary: the important words are 'this realm of England is an empire'. Although it goes on to deal with the king's headship—with his possessing the 'dignity and royal estate of the imperial crown of the same'— it would be dangerous to overlook the primary stress on the polity, the commonwealth. The ruler may make that polity visible, but he is nothing without it.[37]

If it is hard to deny that, despite the distant precedents, the replacement of the pope by the king amounted to a revolution, the case is less clear when one looks at the practical issues involved. In practice Henry claimed (and Parliament confirmed) all those powers over the Church in England which the pope had exercised: he controlled its laws, its courts, its appointments, its

---

[36] 'Empire' in this sense means a territorial unit which has sovereignty, i.e. does not admit any authority over it from outside its borders. It is well defined in the preambles of **177** and **179**.

[37] For the political doctrines of the English Reformation, and especially its attempts at historical justification, cf. Koebner, *Bull. Inst. Hist. Res.*, XXVI, 29 ff.; Zeeveld, *Foundations*, 128 ff.; Elton, *Studies*, II, 221 ff.; Nicholson, 'Historical Arguments'.

revenues, and also its doctrine. For it was an essential aspect of the Henrician supremacy that the determination of doctrinal and liturgical disputes should rest with the supreme head.[38] He was, in fact, a bishop—a lay-bishop, like Constantine the Great—but no priest.[39] Hooker's description of the supremacy (185) puts the stress on the essential justification of the whole revolution: the English Church had no single head or organisation except the king— though Wolsey, as legate, had tried to provide one[40]—and therefore no existence at all without the monarch. But though even Henry VIII avoided all claims to sacerdotal powers, Hooker wrote under the supremacy of Elizabeth which was markedly less ecclesiastical than her father's, and one must remember the direct and personal authority of the first supreme head without thinking of later reductions in the office. Whilst it is true that kings of England had for long had a share in ecclesiastical taxation, had exercised some control over the Church courts and indirectly over cases, and had got pretty much the bishops they wanted,[41] the Reformation not only greatly augmented these powers and gave them the certainty of law,[42] but enormously added to them. Henry VIII's predecessors may have got episcopal sees for their nominees, but they had never been able to say what should be the law of the Church or what its doctrine. Even if the immediate impact of such new powers did not produce sweeping changes under a king who adhered to the teachings of the past, the Henrician Reformation still amounted in theory and in practice to a political and jurisdictional revolution.

The king claimed to hold his headship from God; in his view, at least, it was a personal one, to be exercised by his own mere authority. The Act of Supremacy took the supremacy for granted; it only ordered that it be recognised for the fact it was (180). As he proved when he made Cromwell his vicegerent, bestowing upon him the total powers of the supremacy (182), the king could delegate his authority without reference to anyone else. God had invested him, and no earthly power shared his eminence. There was, in fact, nothing parliamentary about the origin of the supremacy, nor (in this reign) anything parliamentary about its exercise. The acts consist of preambles and enacting clauses, of which only the latter describe what is being done by Parliament; the preambles may explain, justify, pretend—

---

38 Cf. the Injunctions of 1536 and 1538 (Gee and Hardy, 269 ff., 275 ff.), issued by Cromwell's authority as Henry's vicegerent or deputy.

39 This is an adaptation, in terms of office, of the well known distinction between *potestas ordinis* and *potestas iurisdictionis*; after the early days of 1531, Henry VIII never came near to claiming the former.

40 Pollard, *Wolsey*, 169 ff.

41 Harriss, *Past and Present*, XXV, 13 ff.

42 For an example of the sort of difficulties inherent in the pre-Reformation co-existence of authorities cf. Elton, *Star Chamber Stories*, 147 ff.

they may be a historical recital, an exposition, a piece of propaganda—but they can never tell of Parliament's doings. Invariably it is in the preambles that the great principles occur—that England is described as an empire or the king as supreme head—while the enactments draw certain consequences therefrom. There are two kinds of consequences: administrative details or the working out of the practical aspects of the rights mentioned in the preamble, and (when necessary) the appointment of pains and penalties to protect the state of affairs outlined in the preamble. Since only Parliament could create new offences carrying serious punishments (new treasons and felonies) the king could not hope to enforce his supremacy in the common-law courts unless he called in Parliament to provide these sanctions; and it is certainly true that both habit and necessity would make him want to see the supremacy settled in the law of the land. Thus the participation of Parliament was inescapable, but its part was to provide for the enforcement of a power in the making of which it had had no share. There is no sign that anyone in Henry VIII's reign regarded the king's rule over the Church as vested in the king in Parliament, though it was recognised that all sanctions other than spiritual must be provided by statute. The really remarkable thing was, of course, that statute was now permitted to concern itself with matters affecting the order of the Church and clergy.

However, up to a point this inferior position of Parliament relative to the supremacy was from the first more apparent than real. If the essence of a law lies in its sanction it could be said that Parliament had throughout an essential part to play; the difference between creation and enforcement would become academic. That it was not academic appears manifestly in the problem of execution: as long as the carrying out of the supremacy was the personal duty and prerogative of the supreme head, Parliament remained an assistant rather than a partner. However, things changed after Henry's death. Though Elizabeth maintained to the end of her days that her supremacy was personal (although she could, if she wished, ask Parliament to take part in it),[43] she was, compared with her father, in a weak position. Henry VIII exercised his supremacy in person; he delegated without parliamentary authority; when he used Parliament to assist in so fundamental a detail as the definition of doctrine he was careful, once again, to confine its task to the appointment of penalties (190). Admittedly even he devolved upon the Parliament the actual decision to abolish the lesser monasteries (186), but the same act also asserted that the real authority to discover and establish the necessity for this lay in the king.[44] Two developments in the reigns of Edward

[43] Cf. e.g. Nicholas Bacon's speech of 1559, cited Morris, *Political Thought*, 83.
[44] It seems likely that the decision to dissolve was made to appear as a request from Lords and Commons because it involved a transfer of property to the Crown which would seem less outrageous if done in response to an ostensible petition.

VI and Mary undermined the essentially personal character of the supremacy. In the first place, the Edwardian Acts of Uniformity (**191, 192**) went a very long way towards resting the liturgy and ceremonial of the Church on the authority of Parliament; the second act could speak of the first Prayer Book as 'a very godly order set forth by authority of Parliament' and of the second as annexed to the act. Instead of merely enforcing, by penalties, a personal decree of the supreme head, Parliament thus fully participated in the ultimate exercise of his power, the definition of the true faith. Secondly, Mary's desire to abrogate the Reformation called forth the inherent weakness of a personal power which depended for its effectiveness upon statute. Though Parliament, not having created the supremacy, was not required to render it null, only Parliament could remove the penalties in the law which alone gave the supremacy active force. Thus the reconciliation of the realm to Rome had to be the work of Parliament (**183**).

The Elizabethan settlement of 1559 necessarily embodied these compromises between a personal supremacy and one exercised by the queen in Parliament; it also added a few more points to weaken the liberty of the prerogative. The Act of Uniformity (**195**) again treated the Prayer Book as authorised by Parliament. The Act of Supremacy (**184**) admittedly spoke of restoring jurisdictions and powers which it described as anciently belonging to the Crown, and it would be wrong to suppose that anyone at this time held that the Crown's position in the Church could have been created by anyone other than by God. However, the Marian repeal had produced a situation in which only Parliament could clear the way for a resumption of these God-given powers, so that from the first Elizabeth's supremacy was much less independent of Parliament than her father's had been. Moreover, section viii of the act used language dangerous to a personal rule in the Church and very different from that employed by Henry VIII's Act of Supremacy. Here it is requested that all jurisdiction and power in matters ecclesiastical shall be 'annexed to the imperial crown of this realm' by authority of Parliament, and the right to delegate is expressly (though in the widest terms) conferred by statute. It is hard, therefore, to avoid the conclusion that in law and political theory the Elizabethan supremacy was essentially parliamentary, while Henry VIII's had been essentially personal.

This is not to deny the queen's right to govern the Church without the participation, in every detail, of some other authority, any more than she was prevented from ruling the state through her person and Council; but it does mean that in the Church, as in the state, the ultimate authority now rested with the queen-in-Parliament rather than the queen sole. In addition Elizabeth gave up the title of supreme head and called herself instead 'supreme governor . . . as well in all spiritual and ecclesiastical things or causes as temporal'. In the main this only answered doubts about the propriety of a woman being called *caput ecclesiae*; it also satisfied some moderate Catholic opinion that at least Elizabeth had not taken a title rightly belonging to the pope only. Contemporaries regarded the change as one without a difference.[45] No doubt they were right to think that Elizabeth would dominate and domineer as much as Henry VIII, but it is worth noting that as supreme governor she could not claim that quasi-episcopal position which had been his. She was not, so to speak, a semi-spiritual person but governed the spiritualty from outside. If one takes this fact together with the reception of Parliament into the supremacy, it becomes plain that Henry VIII's Constantinian rule in the Church—his 'caesaro-papism'—was by this time abandoned for the unquestioned triumph of the laity over the clergy.

Indeed, the ultimate essence of the supremacy, once it had settled down after these vicissitudes of the years 1534–58, lay in this triumph. One must not speak of the victory of the state over the Church, if only because the Tudor concept was rather of one commonwealth—a 'state' in matters temporal and a 'Church' in matters spiritual—in which certain men, the clergy, occupied themselves professionally with religion. However, the Reformation amounted to a triumph of the *regnum* over the *sacerdotium*, and in the process it defined the *regnum* as the king-in-Parliament. The Convocations of the clergy took no part in the Elizabethan settlement which was perfectly good in law though all the spiritual peers voted against the Act of Uniformity. Hooker (185) put his finger on the critical point when he stressed the need for a royal supremacy to provide unity and authority in the Church of England. Only the Crown, putting together the provinces of Canterbury and York and cutting them loose from the universal Church within which they had stood side by side with dozens of other metropolitan sees, could create that separate national Church. The Church of England only existed in and through the royal supremacy, and once that supremacy had lost the quasi-episcopal and highly personal character it possessed in Henry VIII's estimation,[46] the Church found itself the servant rather than the ruler of the lay commonwealth.

---

[45] Protestants and Catholics were agreed on this: *Span. Cal., 1558*, 55; Parker, *Correspondence*, 66.

[46] It is arguable that only Henry himself took so exalted a view of his supremacy, though it tended to be supported by ecclesiastical writers like Gardiner and Foxe (Elton, *Policy and Police*, 182, 187 f.; Allen, *Political Theory*, 160 ff.). More mundane interpretations are found even in his reign, as in St. German's *Answer* which gives greater weight to the parliamentary 'recognition' than to the inherent completeness of the supremacy. The common lawyers (and Cromwell possibly with them) never lost sight of law and statute even in the glaring light of divine right. The later divergence of high and low views on Church and supremacy can be traced to the reign of Henry VIII: Elton, *Reform and Reformation*, 197 ff.

174. An Act concerning the pardon granted to the King's spiritual subjects of the province of Canterbury for the Praemunire (1531: 22 Henry VIII, c. 15).

The King our sovereign lord, calling to his blessed and most gracious remembrance that his good and loving subjects the most reverend father in God the archbishop of Canterbury and other bishops, suffragans, prelates and other spiritual persons of the province of the archbishopric of Canterbury of this his realm of England, and the ministers underwritten which have exercised, practised or executed in spiritual courts and other spiritual jurisdictions within the said province, have fallen and incurred into divers dangers of his laws by things done, perpetrated and committed contrary to the order of his laws, and specially contrary to the form of the statutes of provisors, provisions and praemunire;[47] and his Highness, having always tender eye with mercy and pity and compassion towards his said spiritual subjects, minding of his high goodness and great benignity so always to impart the same unto them as justice being daily administered all rigour be excluded, and the great and benevolent minds of his said subjects largely and many times approved towards his Highness, and specially in their Convocation and Synod now presently being in the chapter house of the monastery of Westminster, by correspondence of gratitude to them to be requited: Of his mere motion, benignity and liberality, by authority of this his Parliament, hath given and granted his liberal and free pardon to his said good and loving spiritual subjects and the said ministers and to every of them, to be had, taken and enjoyed to and by them and every of them by virtue of this present act in manner and form ensuing, that is to wit: The King's Highness, of his said benignity and high liberality, in consideration that the said archbishop, bishops and clergy of the said province of Canterbury in their said Convocation now being have given and granted to him a subsidy of one hundred thousand pounds of lawful money current in this realm, to be levied and collected by the said clergy at their proper costs and charges and to be paid in certain form specified in their said grant thereof, is fully and resolutely contented and pleased that it be ordained, established and enacted by authority of this his said Parliament, That the most reverend father in God, William,[48] archbishop of Canterbury, metropolitan and primate of all England, and all other bishops and suffragans, prelates,

---

[47] See above, p. 339.
[48] Warham, archbishop of Canterbury, 1503–1532.

abbots, priors, and their convents and every person of the same convents, and convents corporate, . . . abbesses, prioresses and religious nuns, and all other religious and spiritual persons, deans and chapters and other dignities of cathedral and collegiate churches, prebendaries, canons and petty canons, vicars and clerks of the same and every person of the same, all archdeacons, masters, provosts, presidents, wardens of colleges and of collegiate churches, masters and wardens of hospitals, all fellows, brethren, scholars, priests, and spiritual conducts,[49] and every of the same, and all vicars-general of dioceses, chancellors, commissaries, officials and deans rurals, and all ministers hereafter generally rehearsed of any spiritual court or courts within the said province of Canterbury, that is to say: all judges, advocates, registers and scribes, proctors constituted to judgments, and apparitors, and all other which within the said province of the archbishopric of Canterbury at any time heretofore have administered, exercised, practised or executed in any jurisdictions within the said province as officers or ministers of the said courts or have been ministers or executors to the exercise or administration of the same; and all and singular politic bodies spiritual in any manner wise corporated, and all parsons, vicars, curates, chantry priests, stipendiaries and all and every person and persons spiritual of the clergy of the said province of Canterbury in this present act of pardon hereafter not excepted or to the contrary not provided for, by whatsoever name or surname, name of dignity, preeminence or office they or any of them be or is named or called, the successors, heirs, executors and administrators of them and of every of them, shall be by authority of this present pardon acquitted, pardoned, released and discharged against his Highness, his heirs, successors and executors, and every of them, of all and all manner offences, contempts and trespasses committed or done against all and singular statute and statutes of provisors, provisions and praemunire, and every of them, and of all forfeitures and titles that may grow to the King's Highness by any of the same statutes, and of all and singular trespasses, wrongs, deceits, misdemeanors, forfeitures, penalties and profits, sums of money, pains of death, pains corporal and pecuniary, as generally of all other things, causes, quarrels, suits, judgments and executions in this present act hereafter not excepted nor forprised, which may or can be by his Highness in any wise or by any means pardoned, before and to the

---

[49] I.e. spiritual guides or directors.

tenth day of the month of March in the twenty-second year of his
most noble reign. . . .

* * * * * *

Stat. Realm, III, 334–8

175. An Act for the submission of the clergy to the King's Majesty (1534: 25 Henry VIII, c. 19).

Where the King's humble and obedient subjects the clergy of this
realm of England have not only knowledged according to the truth that
the Convocations of the same clergy is always, hath been and ought to
be assembled only by the King's writ, but also submitting themselves
to the King's Majesty hath promised *in verbo sacerdotii* that they will
never from henceforth presume to attempt, allege, claim or put in ure,
or enact, promulge or execute any new canons, constitutions, ordinance
provincial, or other, or by whatsoever other name they shall be called,
in the Convocation, unless the King's most royal assent and licence may
to them be had to make, promulge and execute the same, and that his
Majesty do give his most royal assent and authority in that behalf:
And where divers constitutions, ordinance and canons, provincial or
synodal, which heretofore have been enacted, and be thought not only
to be much prejudicial to the King's prerogative royal and repugnant to
the laws and statutes of this realm but also overmuch onerous to his
Highness and his subjects, the said clergy hath most humbly besought
the King's Highness that the said constitutions and canons may be
committed to the examination and judgment of his Highness and of 32
persons of the King's subjects whereof 16 to be of the Upper and Nether
House of the Parliament of the temporalty, and the other 16 to be of
the clergy of the realm, and all the said 32 persons to [be] chosen and
appointed by the King's Majesty. . . . Be it therefore now enacted by
authority of this present Parliament, according to the said submission
and petition of the said clergy, that they nor any of them from henceforth shall presume to attempt, allege, claim or put in ure any constitutions or ordinances, provincial or synodal, or any other canons, nor
shall enact, promulge or execute any such canons, constitutions or
ordinance provincial, by whatsoever name or names they may be
called, in their Convocations in time coming, which alway shall be
assembled by authority of the King's writ, unless the same clergy may
have the King's most royal assent and licence . . . upon pain of every

one of the said clergy, doing contrary to this act and being thereof convict, to suffer imprisonment and make fine at the King's will.

II. And forasmuch as such canons . . . as heretofore hath been made by the clergy of this realm cannot now at the session of this present Parliament by reason of shortness of time be viewed, examined and determined by the King's Highness and 32 persons to be chosen and appointed. . . . Be it therefore enacted by authority aforesaid that the King's Highness shall have power and authority to nominate and assign at his pleasure the said 32 persons . . . and that the same 32 . . . shall have power and authority to view, search and examine the said canons . . . and such of them as the King's Highness and the said 32 . . . shall deem and adjudge worthy to be continued, kept and obeyed shall be from thenceforth kept . . . within the realm, so that the King's most royal assent under his great seal shall first be had. . . .

III. Provided alway that no canons, constitution or ordinance shall be made or put in execution within this realm by authority of the Convocation of the clergy which shall be contrariant or repugnant to the King's prerogative royal, or the customs, laws or statutes of this realm; anything contained in this act to the contrary hereof notwithstanding.

IV. And be it further enacted . . . that . . . no manner of appeals shall be had, provoked or made out of this realm or out of any of the King's dominions to the bishop of Rome nor to the see of Rome in any causes or matters happening to be in contention and having their commencement and beginning in any of the courts within this realm or within any of the King's dominions, . . . but that all manner of appeals . . . shall be made and had . . . after such manner, form and condition as is limited for appeals to be had and prosecuted within this realm in causes of matrimony, tithes, oblations and obventions, by a statute thereof made and established since the beginning of this present Parliament.[50] . . . And for lack of justice at or in any of the courts of the archbishops of this realm or in any the King's dominions, it shall be lawful to the parties grieved to appeal to the King's Majesty in the King's Court of Chancery, and that upon every such appeal a commission shall be directed under the great seal to such persons as shall be named by the King's Highness, his heirs and successors, like as in case of appeal from the Admiral Court to hear and definitively determine such appeals and causes concerning the same. . . .

[50] The Act in Restraint of Appeals (177).

v. And if any person or persons . . . provoke or sue any manner of appeals . . . to the said bishop of Rome or to the see of Rome, or do procure or execute any manner of process from the see of Rome or by authority thereof to the derogation or let of the due execution of this act or contrary to the same, that then every such person or persons so doing, their aiders, counsellors and abettors, shall incur and run into the dangers, pains and penalties contained and limited in the act of provision and praemunire made in the sixteenth year of . . . King Richard II against such as sue to the court of Rome against the King's crown and prerogative royal.

*   *   *   *   *   *

Stat. Realm, III, 460–1

176. An Act concerning restraint of payment of annates to the see of Rome (1532: 23 Henry VIII, c. 20).

Forasmuch as it is well perceived by long approved experience that great and inestimable sums of money be daily conveyed out of this realm to the impoverishment of the same, and specially such sums of money as the Pope's Holiness, his predecessors, and the court of Rome by long time have heretofore taken of all and singular those spiritual persons which have been named, elected, presented or postulated to be archbishops or bishops within this realm of England, under the title of annates, otherwise called first fruits; which annates or first fruits heretofore have been taken of every archbishopric or bishopric within this realm by restraint of the Pope's bulls for confirmations, elections, admissions, postulations, provisions, collations, dispositions, institutions, installations, investitures, orders holy, benedictions, palls, or other things requisite and necessary to the attaining of those their promotions, and have been compelled to pay before they could attain the same great sums of money, before they might receive any part of the fruits of the said archbishopric or bishopric whereunto they were named, elected, presented or postulated; By occasion whereof not only the treasure of this realm hath been greatly conveyed out of the same, but also it hath happened many times by occasion of death unto such archbishops and bishops so newly promoted within two or three years after his or their consecration, that his or their friends by whom he or they have been holpen to advance and make payment of the said annates or first fruits have been thereby utterly undone and impoverished; And for because the said annates have risen, grown and increased

350

by an uncharitable custom grounded upon no just or good title, and the payments thereof obtained by restraint of bulls until the same annates or first fruits have been paid or surety made for the same, which declareth the said payments to be exacted and taken by constraint, against all equity and justice; The noblemen therefore of this realm and the wise, sage, politic commons of the same assembled in this present Parliament, considering that the court of Rome ceaseth not to tax, take and exact the said great sums of money under the title of annates or first fruits as is aforesaid to the great damage of the said prelates and this realm, which annates or first fruits were first suffered to be taken within the same realm for the only defence of Christian people against the infidels, and now they be claimed and demanded as mere duty, only for lucre, against all right and conscience, insomuch that it is evidently known that there hath passed out of this realm unto the court of Rome since the second year of the reign of the most noble prince of famous memory King Henry the vijth unto this present time, under the name of annates or first fruits paid for the expedition of bulls of archbishoprics and bishoprics, the sum of eight hundred thousand ducats, amounting in sterling money at the least to eight score thousand pounds, besides other great and intolerable sums which have yearly been conveyed to the said court of Rome by many other ways and means, to the great impoverishment of this realm; And albeit that our said sovereign lord the King and all his natural subjects as well spiritual as temporal be as obedient, devout, Catholic and humble children of God and Holy Church as any people be within any realm christened, yet the said exactions of annates or first fruits be so intolerable and importable to this realm that it is considered and declared by the whole body of this realm now represented by all the estates of the same assembled in this present Parliament that the King's Highness before Almighty God is bound as by the duty of a good Christian prince, for the conservation and preservation of the good estate and commonwealth of this his realm, to do all that in him is to obviate, repress and redress the said abusions and exactions of annates or first fruits; And because that divers prelates of this realm be now in extreme age and in other debilities of their bodies, so that of likelihood bodily death in short time shall or may succeed unto them; by reason whereof great sums of money shall shortly after their deaths be conveyed unto the court of Rome for the unreasonable and uncharitable causes abovesaid, to the universal damage, prejudice and impoverishment of this realm, if speedy remedy be not in due time provided; It is therefore ordained, established and enacted by authority of this present Parliament that the unlawful payments of annates or first fruits . . . shall from henceforth utterly cease . . . and that no manner person or persons hereafter to be named, elected, presented or postulated to any archbishopric or bishopric within this realm shall pay the said annates or first fruits . . . upon pain to forfeit to our said sovereign lord the King, his heirs and successors, all manner his goods and chattels for ever, and all the temporal lands and possessions of the same archbishopric or bishopric during the time that he or they which shall offend contrary to this present act shall have, possess or enjoy the archbishopric or bishopric wherefore he shall so offend contrary to the form aforesaid.

[II. If the Court of Rome should delay or deny the 'bulls apostolic and other things requisite' for the consecration of any prelate to be hereafter appointed by the Crown, he is to be consecrated without them; if a bishop, by the archbishop in whose province the bishopric happens to be, and if an archbishop, by a commission of two bishops appointed by the King.]

* * * * * *

IV. And it is also further ordained and enacted by the authority of this present Parliament that the King's Highness at any time or times on this side the feast of Easter which shall be in the year of our Lord God 1533, or at any time on this side the beginning of the next Parliament, by his letters patent under his great seal to be made and to be entered of record in the roll of this present Parliament, may and shall have full power and liberty to declare by the said letters patent whether that the premises or any part, clause or matter thereof shall be observed, obeyed, executed, performed and take place and effect as an act and statute of this present Parliament or not . . . as though the same had been fully and perfectly established, enacted and confirmed to be in every part thereof immediately, wholly and entirely executed in like manner, form and effect as other acts and laws the which been fully and determinedly made, ordained and enacted in this present Parliament.

[V. Should the pope react by sentence of excommunication or interdict, it is further enacted that the King and his lay subjects may 'without any scruple of conscience . . . lawfully to the honour of Almighty God, the increase and continuance of virtue and good example within

this realm', continue to enjoy the sacraments, ceremonies and services
of Holy Church, any papal censures notwithstanding.]

Stat. Realm, III, 385-8

177. **An Act that the appeals in such cases as have been used to be
pursued to the see of Rome shall not be from henceforth had nor
used but within this realm (1533: 24 Henry VIII, c. 12).**

Where by divers sundry old authentic histories and chronicles it is
manifestly declared and expressed that this realm of England is an
empire, and so hath been accepted in the world, governed by one supreme head and king having the dignity and royal estate of the imperial
crown of the same, unto whom a body politic, compact of all sorts and
degrees of people divided in terms and by names of spiritualty and
temporalty, be bounden and owe to bear next to God a natural and
humble obedience; he being also institute and furnished by the goodness
and sufferance of Almighty God with plenary, whole and entire power,
preeminence, authority, prerogative and jurisdiction to render and
yield justice and final determination to all manner of folk resiants or
subjects within this realm, in all causes, matters, debates and contentions
happening to occur, insurge or begin within the limits thereof, without
restraint or provocation to any foreign princes or potentates of the
world: the body spiritual whereof having power when any cause of the
law divine happened to come in question or of spiritual learning, then
it was declared, interpreted and shewed by that part of the said body
politic called the spiritualty, now being usually called the English
Church, which always hath been reputed and also found of that sort that
both for knowledge, integrity and sufficiency of number, it hath been
always thought and is also at this hour sufficient and meet of itself, without the intermeddling of any exterior person or persons, to declare and
determine all such doubts and to administer all such offices and duties as
to their rooms spiritual doth appertain. For the due administration
whereof and to keep them from corruption and sinister affection the
King's most noble progenitors, and the antecessors of the nobles of this
realm, have sufficiently endowed the said Church both with honour and
possession. And the laws temporal for trial of propriety of lands and
goods, and for the conservation of the people of this realm in unity
and peace without ravin or spoil, was and yet is administered, adjudged,
and executed by sundry judges and administers of the other part of the
said body politic called the temporalty, and both their authorities and

353

jurisdictions do conjoin together in the due administration of justice the one to help the other. And whereas the King his most noble progenitors, and the Nobility and Commons of this said realm, at divers and sundry Parliaments as well in the time of King Edward I,[51] Edward III,[52] Richard II,[53] Henry IV,[54] and other noble kings of this realm, made sundry ordinances, laws, statutes and provisions for the entire and sure conservation of the prerogatives, liberties and preeminences of the said imperial crown of this realm, and of the jurisdictions spiritual and temporal of the same, to keep it from the annoyance as well of the see of Rome as from the authority of other foreign potentates attempting the diminution or violation thereof as often and from time to time as any such annoyance or attempt might be known or espied. And notwithstanding the said good estatutes and ordinances made in the time of the King's most noble progenitors in preservation of the authority and prerogative of the said imperial crown as is aforesaid, yet nevertheless since the making of the said good statutes and ordinances divers and sundry inconveniences and dangers not provided for plainly by the said former acts, statutes and ordinances have risen and sprung by reason of appeals sued out of this realm to the see of Rome, in causes testamentary, causes of matrimony and divorces, right of tithes, oblations and obventions,[55] not only to the great inquietation, vexation, trouble, costs and charges of the King's Highness and many of his subjects and resiants in this his realm, but also to the great delay and let to the true and speedy determination of the said causes, for so much as the parties appealing to the said court of Rome most commonly do the same for the delay of justice: and forasmuch as the great distance of way is so far out of this realm, so that the necessary proofs nor the true knowledge of the cause can neither there be so well known nor the witnesses there so well examined as within this realm, so that the parties grieved by means of the said appeals be most times without remedy. In consideration whereof the King's Highness, his Nobles and Commons, considering the great

---

[51] The Statute of Carlisle, 1307 (35 Edw. I, st. 1), an act against the abuses of papal patronage.
[52] The First Statute of Provisors, 1351 (25 Edw. III, st. 4) and the First Statute of Praemunire, 1353 (27 Edw. III, st. 1).
[53] The Second Statute of Provisors, 1390 (13 Rich. II, st. 2) and the Second Statute of Praemunire, 1393 (16 Rich. II, c. 5).
[54] 2 Henry IV, c. 3, confirmed and extended the Second Statute of Provisors and this was again confirmed by 9 Henry IV, c. 8; 2 Henry IV, c. 4, forbade bulls from Rome for exemption from tithe.
[55] 'Oblations' here include whatever is assigned to pious uses; 'obventions' in ecclesiastical law are fees occasionally received.

enormities, dangers, long delays and hurts that as well to his Highness
as to his said nobles, subjects, commons and resiants of this his realm in
the said causes testamentary, causes of matrimony and divorces, tithes,
oblations and obventions do daily ensue, doth therefore by his royal
assent and by the assent of the Lords spiritual and temporal and the Commons in this present Parliament assembled, and by authority of the
same, enact, establish and ordain that all causes testamentary, causes
of matrimony and divorces, rights of tithes, oblations and obventions, (the knowledge whereof by the goodness of princes of this realm
and by the laws and customs of the same appertaineth to the spiritual
jurisdiction of this realm) already commenced, moved, depending,
being, happening, or hereafter coming in contention, debate or question within this realm or within any the King's dominions or marches
of the same or elsewhere, whether they concern the King our sovereign
lord, his heirs or successors, or any other subjects or resiants within the
same of what degree soever they be, shall be from henceforth heard,
examined, discussed, clearly finally and definitely adjudged and determined, within the King's jurisdiction and authority and not elsewhere,
in such courts spiritual and temporal of the same as the natures, conditions and qualities of the causes and matters aforesaid in contention or
hereafter happening in contention shall require, without having any
respect to any custom, use or sufferance in hindrance, let or prejudice of
the same or to any other thing used or suffered to the contrary thereof
by any other manner person or persons in any manner of wise; any
foreign inhibitions, appeals, sentences, summons, citations, suspensions,
interdictions, excommunications, restraints, judgments, or any other
process or impediments of what natures, names, qualities or conditions
soever they be, from the see of Rome or any other foreign courts or
potentates of the world, or from and out of this realm or any other the
King's dominions or marches of the same to the see of Rome or to any
other foreign courts or potentates, to the let or impediment thereof in
any wise notwithstanding. And that it shall be lawful to the King our
sovereign lord and to his heirs and successors, and to all other subjects
or resiants within this realm or within any the King's dominions or
marches of the same, notwithstanding that hereafter it should happen
any excommengement, excommunications, interdictions, citations, or
any other censures or foreign process out of any outward parties to be
fulminate, provulged, declared or put in execution within this said
realm or in any other place or places for any of the causes before

rehearsed, in prejudice, derogation or contempt of this said act and the very true meaning and execution thereof, may and shall nevertheless as well pursue, execute, have and enjoy the effects, profits, benefits and commodities of all such processes, sentences, judgments and determinations, done or hereafter to be done in any of the said courts spiritual or temporal as the cases shall require, within the limits, power and authority of this the King's said realm and dominions and marches of the same, and those only and none other to take place and to be firmly observed and obeyed within the same: As also that all spiritual prelates, pastors, ministers and curates within this realm and the dominions of the same shall and may use, minister, execute and do, or cause to be used, ministered, executed and done, all sacraments, sacramentals,[56] divine services and all other things within the said realm and dominions unto all the subjects of the same as Catholic and Christian men owe to do; any foreign citations, processes, inhibitions, suspensions, interdictions, excommunications or appeals for or touching any of the causes aforesaid from or to the see of Rome or any other foreign prince or foreign courts to the let or contrary thereof in any wise notwithstanding. And if any of the said spiritual persons, by the occasion of the said fulminations of any of the same interdictions, censures, inhibitions, excommunications, appeals, suspensions, summons or other foreign citations for the causes beforesaid or for any of them, do at any time hereafter refuse to minister or to cause to be ministered the said sacraments and sacramentals and other divine services in form as is aforesaid, shall for every such time or times that they or any of them do refuse so to do or to cause to be done, have one year's imprisonment and to make fine and ransom at the King's pleasure.

II. And it is further enacted . . . that if any person or persons . . . do attempt, move, purchase or procure, from or to the see of Rome or from or to any other foreign court or courts out of this realm, any manner foreign process, inhibitions, appeals, sentences, summons, citations, interdictions, excommunications, restraints or judgments, of what nature, kind or quality soever they be, or execute any of the same process, or do any act or acts to the let, impediment, hindrance or derogation of any process, sentence, judgment or determination had, made, done, or hereafter to be had, done or made in any courts of this realm or the King's said dominions or marches of the same for any of the

---

[56] Rites or ceremonies analogous to a sacrament but not reckoned among the sacraments, e.g. the sign of the cross or the use of holy water.

causes aforesaid . . . that then every person or persons so doing, and
their fautors, comforters, abettors, procurers, executors and counsellors,
and every of them, being convict of the same, for every such default
shall incur and run in the same pains, penalties and forfeitures ordained
and provided by the statute of provision and praemunire made in the
sixteenth year of the reign of . . . King Richard II. . . .

III. And furthermore in eschewing the said great enormities, in-
quietations, delays, charges and expenses hereafter to be sustained in
pursuing of such appeals and foreign process . . . do therefore . . .
ordain and enact that in such cases where heretofore any of the King's
subjects or resiants have used to pursue, provoke or procure any appeal
to the see of Rome . . . they may and shall from henceforth take, have
and use their appeals within this realm and not elsewhere, in manner
and form as hereafter ensueth and not otherwise; that is to say, first
from the archdeacon or his official, if the matter or cause be there begun,
to the bishop diocesan of the said see . . . ; and likewise, if it be commenced before the bishop diocesan or his commissary, from the bishop
diocesan or his commissary, within fifteen days next ensuing the judgment or sentence thereof there given, to the archbishop of the province
of Canterbury, if it be within his province, and if it be within the province of York then to the archbishop of York; and so likewise to all
other archbishops in other the King's dominions as the case by the order
of justice shall require; and there to be definitively and finally ordered,
decreed and adjudged according to justice, without any other appella-
tion or provocation to any other person or persons, court or courts.
And if the matter or contention for any of the causes aforesaid be or
shall be commenced . . . before the archdeacon of any archbishop or
his commissary, then the party grieved shall or may take his appeal,
within fifteen days next after judgment or sentence there given, to the
Court of the Arches or Audience of the same archbishop or archbishops, and from the said Court of the Arches or Audience, within
fifteen days then next ensuing after judgment or sentence there given,
to the archbishop of the same province, there to be definitively and
finally determined without any other or further process or appeal
thereupon to be had or sued.

IV. . . . And in case any cause, matter, or contention . . . which hath,
doth, shall or may touch the King, his heirs or successors kings of this
realm, that in all and every such case or cases the party grieved . . .
shall or may appeal . . . to the spiritual prelates and other abbots and

priors of the Upper House assembled and convocate by the King's writ in the Convocation being or next ensuing within the province or provinces where the same matter of contention is or shall be begun; so that every such appeal be taken by the party grieved within fifteen days next after the judgment or sentence thereupon given or to be given. And that whatsoever be done or shall be done and affirmed, determined, decreed and adjudged by the foresaid prelates, abbots and priors of the Upper House of the said Convocation as is aforesaid, appertaining, concerning or belonging to the King, his heirs and successors, in any of these foresaid causes of appeals, shall stand and be taken for a final decree, sentence, judgment, definition and determination, and the same matter so determined never after to come in question and debate to be examined in any other court or courts. And if it shall happen any person or persons hereafter to pursue or provoke any appeal contrary to the effect of this act, or refuse to obey, execute and observe all things comprised within the same . . . that then every person and persons so doing, refusing or offending . . . their procurers, fautors, advocates, counsellors and abettors, and every of them, shall incur into the pains, forfeitures and penalties ordained and provided in the said statute made in the said sixteenth year of King Richard II, and with like process to be made against the said offenders as in the same statute made in the said sixteenth year more plainly appeareth. *Stat. Realm,* III, 427–9

178. An Act restraining the payment of annates etc. (1534: 25 Henry VIII, c. 20).

[I. Recites 23 Henr. VIII, c. 20, and its confirmation by the King's letters patent.]

II. And forasmuch as in the said act it is not plainly and certainly expressed in what manner and fashion archbishops and bishops shall be elected, presented, invested and consecrated within this realm and in all other the King's dominions: Be it now therefore enacted by the King our sovereign lord, by the assent of the Lords spiritual and temporal and the Commons in the present Parliament assembled, and by authority of the same, that the said act and everything therein contained shall be and stand in strength, virtue and effect: except only that no person nor persons hereafter shall be presented, nominated or commended to the said bishop of Rome, otherwise called the Pope, or to the see of Rome, to or for the dignity or office of any archbishop or bishop within this realm or in any other the King's dominions, nor shall send nor procure there for any manner of bulls, briefs, palls, or other things requisite for an archbishop or bishop, nor shall pay any sums of money for annates, first fruits, or otherwise, for expedition of any such bulls, briefs or palls; but that by the authority of this act such presenting, nominating or commending to the said bishop of Rome or to the see of Rome, and such bulls, briefs, palls, annates, first fruits and every other sums of money heretofore limited, accustomed or used to be paid at the said see of Rome for procuration or expedition of any such bulls, briefs or palls, or other thing concerning the same, shall utterly cease and no longer be used within this realm or within any the King's dominions; anything contained in the said act aforementioned, or any use custom or prescription to the contrary thereof notwithstanding.

III. And furthermore be it ordained and established by the authority aforesaid that at every avoidance of any archbishopric or bishopric within this realm or in any other the King's dominions, the King our sovereign lord, his heirs and successors, may grant unto the prior and convent or the dean and chapter of the cathedral churches or monasteries where the see of such archbishopric or bishopric shall happen to be void, a licence under the great seal, as of old time hath been accustomed, to proceed to election of an archbishop or bishop of the see so being void, with a letter missive containing the name of the person which they shall elect and choose; by virtue of which licence the said dean and chapter or prior and convent to whom any such licence and letters missives shall be directed, shall with all speed and celerity in due form elect and choose the said person named in the said letters missives to the dignity and office of the archbishopric or bishopric so being void, and none other; and if they do defer or delay their election above 12 days next after such licence and letters missives to them delivered, that then for every such default the King's Highness, his heirs and successors, at their liberty and pleasure shall nominate and present, by their letters patents under their great seal, such a person to the said office and dignity so being void as they shall think able and convenient for the same. ...

* * * * * *

[VI. If a prior and convent, or dean and chapter, fail to elect after receipt of licence, or if any archbishop or bishop fail to consecrate and invest any bishop so elected—in each case within twenty days of

receiving notice of licence of election—they shall be guilty of praemunire.]
Stat. Realm, III, 462–4

179. An Act for the exoneration of exactions paid to the see of Rome (1534: 25 Henry VIII, c. 21).

Most humbly beseech your most Royal Majesty your obedient and
faithful subjects the Commons of this your present Parliament assembled by your most dread commandment; That where your subjects of
this your realm, and of other countries and dominions being under your
obeisance, by many years past have been and yet be greatly decayed and
impoverished by such intolerable exactions of great sums of money as
have been claimed and taken and yet continually be claimed to be taken
out of this your realm and other your said countries and dominions, by
the bishop of Rome called the Pope, and the see of Rome, as well in
pensions, censes, Peter's pence, procurations, fruits, suits for provisions
and expeditions of bulls for archbishoprics and bishoprics, and for
delegacies, and rescripts in causes of contentions and appeals, jurisdictions legatine, and also for dispensations, licences, faculties, grants,
relaxations, writs called *perinde valere*, rehabilitations, abolitions, and
other infinite sorts of bulls, briefs and instruments of sundry natures,
names and kinds in great numbers heretofore practised and obtained
otherwise than by the laws, laudable uses and customs of this realm
should be permitted, the specialities whereof be over long, large in
number, and tedious here particularly to be inserted; wherein the bishop
of Rome aforesaid hath not been only to be blamed for his usurpation
in the premises but also for his abusing and beguiling your subjects,
pretending and persuading to them that he hath full power to dispense
with all human laws, uses and customs of all realms in all causes which
be called spiritual, which matter hath been usurped and practised by him
and his predecessors by many years in great derogation of your imperial
crown and authority royal, contrary to right and conscience. For where
this your Grace's realm, recognising no superior under God but only
your Grace, hath been and is free from subjection to any man's laws
but only to such as have been devised, made and ordained within this
realm for the wealth of the same, or to such other as by sufferance of
your Grace and your progenitors the people of this your realm have
taken at their free liberty by their own consent to be used amongst them,
and have bound themselves by long use and custom to the observance

of the same, not as to the observance of the laws of any foreign prince, potentate or prelate, but as to the accustomed and ancient laws of this realm originally established as laws of the same by the said sufferance, consents and custom, and none otherwise: It standeth therefore with natural equity and good reason that in all and every such laws human, made within this realm or induced into this realm by the said sufferance, consents and custom, your Royal Majesty and your Lords spiritual and temporal and Commons, representing the whole state of your realm in this your most High Court of Parliament, have full power and authority not only to dispense but also to authorise some elect person or persons to dispense with those and all other human laws of this your realm and with every one of them, as the quality of the persons and matter shall require; and also the said laws and every of them to abrogate, annul, amplify or diminish, as it shall be seen unto your Majesty and the Nobles and Commons of your realm present in your Parliament meet and convenient for the wealth of your realm, as by divers good and wholesome acts of Parliament made and established as well in your time as in the time of your most noble progenitors it may plainly and evidently appear. And because that it is now in these days present seen that the state, dignity, superiority, reputation and authority of the said imperial crown of this realm, by the long sufferance of the said unreasonable and uncharitable usurpations and exactions practised in the times of your most noble progenitors, is much and sore decayed and diminished, and the people of this realm thereby impoverished and so or worse be like to continue if remedy be not therfor shortly provided:

It may therefore please your most noble Majesty for the honour of Almighty God and for the tender love, zeal and affection that you bear and always have borne to the wealth of this your realm and subjects of the same, forasmuch as your Majesty is supreme head of the Church of England, as the prelates and clergy of your realm representing the said Church in their synods and Convocations have recognised, in whom consisteth full power and authority upon all such laws as have been made and used within this realm, to ordain and enact by the assent of your Lords spiritual and temporal and the Commons in this your present Parliament assembled and by authority of the same, that no person or persons of this your realm or of any other your dominions shall from henceforth pay any pensions, censes, portions, Peter's pence, or any other impositions to the use of the said bishop or of the see of

Rome, like as heretofore they have used by usurpation of the said bishop of Rome and his predecessors and sufferance of your Highness and your most noble progenitors to do; but that all such pensions, censes, portions and Peter's pence, which the said bishop of Rome otherwise called the Pope hath heretofore taken and perceived or caused to be taken and perceived to his use and his chambers which he calleth apostolic by usurpation and sufferance as is abovesaid within this your realm or any other your dominions, shall from henceforth clearly surcease and never more be levied, taken, perceived nor paid to any person or persons in any manner of wise; any constitution, use, prescription or custom to the contrary thereof notwithstanding.

II. And be it further enacted by the authority aforesaid that neither your Highness, your heirs nor successors, kings of this realm, nor any your subjects of this realm nor of any other your dominions, shall from henceforth sue to the said bishop of Rome called the Pope, or to the see of Rome, or to any person or persons having or pretending any authority by the same, for licences, dispensations, compositions, faculties, grants, rescripts, delegacies or any other instruments or writings of what kind, name, nature or quality so ever they be of, for any cause or matter for the which any licence, [etc.] . . . heretofore hath been used and accustomed to be had and obtained at the see of Rome or by authority thereof, or of any prelate of this realm, nor for any manner of other licences, [etc.] . . . that in causes of necessity may lawfully be granted without offending of the Holy Scriptures and laws of God. But that from henceforth every such licence, [etc.] . . . necessary for your Highness, your heirs and successors, and your and their people and subjects, upon the due examinations of the causes and qualities of the persons procuring such dispensations, licences, [etc.] . . . shall be granted, had and obtained from time to time within this your realm and other your dominions and not elsewhere in manner and form following and none otherwise, that is to say: the archbishop of Canterbury for the time being and his successors shall have power and authority from time to time by their discretions to give, grant and dispose by an instrument under the seal of the said archbishop unto your Majesty and to your heirs and successors kings of this realm, as well all manner such licences, [etc.] . . . for causes not being contrary or repugnant to the Holy Scriptures and laws of God, as heretofore hath been used and accustomed to be had and obtained by your Highness or any your most noble progenitors, or any of yours or their subjects, at the see of Rome or any person or persons by authority of the same, and all other licences, dispensations, [etc.] . . . in, for and upon all such causes and matters as shall be convenient and necessary to be had for the honour and surety of your Highness, your heirs and successors, and the wealth and profit of this your realm; so that the said archbishop or any his successors in no manner of wise shall grant any dispensation, licence, rescript, or any other writing afore rehearsed for any cause or matter repugnant to the law of Almighty God.

* * * * * *

XIII. Provided always that this act nor any thing or things therein contained shall be hereafter interpreted or expounded that your Grace, your nobles and subjects, intend by the same to decline or vary from the congregation of Christ's Church in any things concerning the very articles of the Catholic Faith or Christendom; or in any other things declared by Holy Scripture and the word of God necessary for your and their salvations; but only to make an ordinance by policies neces- sary and convenient to repress vice and for good conservation of this realm in peace, unity and tranquillity from ravin and spoil, ensuing much the old ancient customs of this realm in that behalf, not minding to seek for any reliefs, succours or remedies for any worldly things or human laws in any cause of necessity but within this realm at the hands of your Highness, your heirs and successors kings of this realm, which have and ought to have an imperial power and authority in the same and not obliged in any worldly causes to any other superior.

XIV. Provided alway that the said archbishop of Canterbury or any other person or persons shall have no power or authority by reason of this act to visit or vex any monasteries, abbeys, priories, colleges, hos- pitals, houses or other places religious which be or were exempt before the making of this act, anything in this act to the contrary thereof not- withstanding; but that redress, visitation and confirmation shall be had by the King's Highness, his heirs and successors, by commission under the great seal to be directed to such persons as shall be appointed re- quisite for the same, in such monasteries, colleges, hospitals, priories, houses and places religious exempt; so that no visitation nor confirma- tion shall from henceforth be had nor made in or at any such monas- teries . . . exempt, by the said bishop of Rome nor by any of his authority nor by any out of the King's dominions; nor that any person religious or other resiant in any the King's dominions shall from henceforth depart out of the King's dominions to or for any visitation, congregation or assembly for religion, but that all such visitations, congregations and assemblies shall be within the King's dominions.

* * * * * *

[XVI. Penalty for suing to Rome for licences is praemunire.]

XXI. And be it enacted by authority of this present Parliament, that the King our sovereign lord by the advice of his honourable Council shall have power and authority from time to time for the ordering, redress and reformation of all manner of indulgences and privileges thereof within this realm or within any the King's dominions heretofore obtained at the see of Rome or by authority thereof, and of the abuses of such indulgences and privileges thereof, as shall seem good, wholesome and reasonable for the honour of God and weal of his people. And that such order and redress as shall be taken by his Highness in that behalf shall be observed and firmly kept upon the pains limited in this Act for the offending of the contents of the same.

* * * * * *

Stat. Realm, III, 464–71

180. An Act concerning the King's Highness to be Supreme Head of the Church of England and to have authority to reform and redress all errors, heresies and abuses in the same (1534: 26 Henry VIII, c. 1).

Albeit the King's Majesty justly and rightfully is and oweth to be the supreme head of the Church of England, and so is recognised by the clergy of this realm in their Convocations; yet nevertheless for corroboration and confirmation thereof, and for increase of virtue in Christ's religion within this realm of England, and to repress and extirp all errors, heresies and other enormities and abuses heretofore used in the same, Be it enacted by authority of this present Parliament that the King our sovereign lord, his heirs and successors kings of this realm, shall be taken, accepted and reputed the only supreme head in earth of the Church of England called *Anglicana Ecclesia*, and shall have and enjoy annexed and united to the imperial crown of this realm as well the title and style thereof, as all honours, dignities, preeminences, jurisdictions, privileges, authorities, immunities, profits and commodities, to the said dignity of supreme head of the same Church belonging and appertaining. And that our said sovereign lord, his heirs and successors kings of this realm, shall have full power and authority from time to time to visit, repress, redress, reform, order, correct, restrain and amend all such errors, heresies, abuses, offences, contempts and enormities, whatsoever they be, which by any manner spiritual authority or jurisdiction ought or may lawfully be reformed, repressed, ordered, redressed, corrected, restrained or amended, most to the pleasure of Almighty God, the increase of virtue in Christ's religion, and for the conservation of the peace, unity and tranquillity of this realm: any usage, custom, foreign laws, foreign authority, prescription or any other thing or things to the contrary hereof notwithstanding.   *Stat. Realm*, III, 492

181. An Act extinguishing the authority of the bishop of Rome (1536: 28 Henry VIII, c. 10).

Forasmuch as notwithstanding the good and wholesome laws, ordinances and statutes heretofore enacted, made and established . . . for the extirpation, abolition and extinguishment, out of this realm and other his Grace's dominions, seignories and countries, of the pretended power and usurped authority of the bishop of Rome, by some called the Pope, used within the same or elsewhere concerning the same realm, dominions, seignories or countries, which did obfuscate and wrest God's holy word and testament a long season from the spiritual and true meaning thereof to his worldly and carnal affections, as pomp, glory, avarice, ambition and tyranny, covering and shadowing the same with his human and politic devices, traditions and inventions, set forth to promote and stablish his only dominion, both upon the souls and also the bodies and goods of all Christian people, excluding Christ out of his kingdom and rule of man his soul as much as he may, and all other temporal kings and princes out of their dominions which they ought to have by God's law upon the bodies and goods of their subjects; whereby he did not only rob the King's Majesty, being only the supreme head of this his realm of England immediately under God, of his honour, right and preeminence due unto him by the law of God, but spoiled this his realm yearly of innumerable treasure, and with the loss of the same deceived the King's loving and obedient subjects, persuading to them, by his laws, bulls and other his deceivable means, such dreams, vanities and fantasies as by the same many of them were seduced and conveyed unto superstitious and erroneous opinions; so that the King's Majesty, the Lords spiritual and temporal, and the Commons

in this realm, being overwearied and fatigated with the experience of
the infinite abominations and mischiefs proceeding of his impostures
and craftily colouring of his deceits, to the great damages of souls,
bodies and goods, were forced of necessity for the public weal of this
realm to exclude that foreign pretended power, jurisdiction and authority, used and usurped within this realm, and to devise such remedies
for their relief in the same as doth not only redound to the honour of
God, the high praise and advancement of the King's Majesty and of his
realm, but also to the great and inestimable utility of the same; and
notwithstanding the said wholesome laws so made and heretofore
established, yet it is come to the knowledge of the King's Highness and
also to divers and many his loving, faithful and obedient subjects, how
that divers seditious and contentious persons, being imps of the said
bishop of Rome and his see, and in heart members of his pretended
monarchy, do in corners and elsewhere, as they dare, whisper, inculce,
preach and persuade, and from time to time instil into the ears and heads
of the poor, simple and unlettered people the advancement and continuance of the said bishop's feigned and pretended authority, pretending the same to have his ground and original of God's law, whereby
the opinions of many be suspended, their judgments corrupted and
deceived, and diversity in opinions augmented and increased, to the
great displeasure of Almighty God, the high discontentation of our said
most dread sovereign lord, and the interruption of the unity, love,
charity, concord and agreement that ought to be in a Christian region
and congregation. For avoiding whereof, and repression of the follies
of such seditious persons as be the means and authors of such inconveniences, Be it enacted, ordained and established by the King our
sovereign lord and the Lords spiritual and temporal and the Commons
in this present Parliament assembled, and by authority of the same, that
if any person or persons, dwelling, demurring, inhabiting or resiant
within this realm or within any other the King's dominions, seignories
or countries, or the marches of the same, or elsewhere within or under
his obeisance and power, of what estate, dignity, preeminence, order,
degree or condition soever he or they be, after the last day of July which
shall be in the year of our Lord God 1536 shall, by writing, ciphering,
printing, preaching or teaching, deed or act, obstinately or maliciously
hold or stand with to extol, set forth, maintain or defend the authority,
jurisdiction or power of the bishop of Rome or of his see, heretofore
used, claimed or usurped within this realm or in any dominion or

country being of, within or under the King's power or obeisance, or by any pretence obstinately or maliciously invent anything for the extolling, advancement, setting forth, maintenance or defence of the same or any part thereof, or by any pretence obstinately or maliciously attribute any manner of jurisdiction, authority or preeminence to the said see of Rome, or to any bishop of the same see for the time being, within this realm or in any the King's dominions or countries, that then every such person or persons so doing or offending, their aiders, assistants, comforters, abettors, procurers, maintainers, fautors, counsellors, concealers and every of them, being thereof lawfully convicted according to the laws of this realm, for every such default and offence shall incur and run into the dangers, penalties, pains and forfeitures ordained and provided by the statute of provision and praemunire made in the sixteenth year of the reign of the noble and valiant prince King Richard II against such as attempt, procure or make provision to the see of Rome or elsewhere for any thing or things to the derogation, or contrary to the prerogative royal or jurisdiction, of the Crown and dignity of this realm.

* * * * * *

[VI–VII. An oath, renouncing the jurisdiction of Rome and supporting the royal supremacy is imposed on all officers ecclesiastical and temporal, as well as on all persons suing livery of lands, taking holy orders, or proceeding to a degree at the Universities.]

Stat. Realm, III, 663–6

182. From Edmund Bonner's Commission as bishop of London, 1538.

... Quandoquidem omnis jurisdicendi auctoritas, atque etiam jurisdictio omnimoda tam illa quae ecclesiastica dicitur quam saecularis, a regia potestate velut a supremo capite et omnium infra regnum nostrum magistratuum fonte et scaturigine primatus emanavit, sane illos qui jurisdictionem hujusmodi antehac non nisi precario fungebantur, beneficium hujusmodi sic eis ex liberalitate regia indultum gratis animis agnoscere, idque regiae munificenciae solummodo acceptum referre, eique, quotiens ejus majestati videbitur, libenter concedere convenit. Cum itaque nos praedilectum consiliarium nostrum Thomam Crumwell, nobilis ordinis Garterii militem, dominem Crumwell et de Wymolden, nostri privati sigilli custodem, nostrumque ad quascunque causas ecclesiasticas nostra auctoritate, uti supremi capitis dictae ecclesiae Anglicanae, quomodolibet tractandum sive ventilandum vicegerentem, vicarium generalem et officialem principalem per alias literas patentes sigillo nostro majori communitas constituerimus et praefecerimus. . . . Burnet, *Hist. of the Reformation*, IV, 411

[Translation:] Inasmuch as all authority to do justice, as well as all jurisdiction of all kinds both that which is called ecclesiastical and that which is secular, in the beginning arose from the King's power, he being supreme head and the source and origin of all authorities within our realm, it therefore behoves those who before this have exercised any jurisdiction of this sort by permission only to acknowledge with grateful minds this benefit allowed them by the King's generosity, to admit that they have received it but from his munificence, and freely to surrender it to him whenever his Majesty should deem it right. Whereas, therefore, we have appointed and made by other letters patent under our great seal, our dearly beloved councillor, Thomas Cromwell, knight of the noble order of the Garter, Lord Cromwell of Wimbledon, keeper of our privy seal, and by our authority as supreme head of the said Church of England vicegerent in treating and determining all causes ecclesiastical, vicar general and official principal. . . .

183. An Act repealing all statutes . . . made against the see apostolic of Rome since the 20th year of King Henry VIII, and also for the establishment of all spiritual and ecclesiastical possessions and hereditaments conveyed to the laity (1554: 1 & 2 Philip and Mary, c. 8).

Whereas since the 20th year of King Henry the Eighth of famous memory, father unto your Majesty our most natural sovereign and gracious lady and queen, much false and erroneous doctrine hath been taught, preached and written, partly by divers the natural-born subjects of this realm, and partly being brought in hither from sundry other foreign countries hath been sown and spread abroad within the same; by reason whereof as well the spiritualty as the temporalty of your Highness' realms and dominions have swerved from the obedience of the See Apostolic and declined from the unity of Christ's Church, and so have continued, until such time as your Majesty being first raised up by God and set in the seat royal over us, and then by his divine and gracious Providence knit in marriage with the most noble and virtuous prince, the King our sovereign lord your husband, the Pope's holiness and the See Apostolic sent hither unto your Majesties (as unto persons undefiled and by God's goodness preserved from the common infection aforesaid) and to the whole realm, the most reverend father in God the Lord Cardinal Pole, legate *de latere*, to call us home again into the right way from whence we have all this long while wandered and strayed abroad. And we after sundry long and grievous plagues and calamities, seeing by the goodness of God our own errors, have acknowledged the same unto the said most reverend father and by him have been and are the rather at the contemplation of your Majesties received and embraced into the unity and bosom of Christ's Church; and upon our humble submission and promise made, for a declaration of our repentance, to repeal and abrogate such acts and statutes as had been made in Parliament since the said 20th year of the said King Henry the Eighth against the supremacy of the See Apostolic, as in our submission exhibited to the said most reverend father in God by your Majesties appeareth: the tenor whereof ensueth:

We the Lords spiritual and temporal and the Commons assembled in this present Parliament, representing the whole body of the realm of England and the dominions of the same, in the name of ourselves particularly and also of the said body universally in this our supplication directed to your Majesties, with most humble suit that it may by your Graces' intercession and mean be exhibited to the most reverend father in God the Lord Cardinal Pole, legate sent specially hither from our most holy father the Pope Julius the Third and the See Apostolic of Rome, do declare ourselves very sorry and repentant of the schism and disobedience committed in this realm and dominions aforesaid against the said See Apostolic, either by making, agreeing or executing any laws, ordinances or commandments against the Supremacy of the said See, or otherwise doing or speaking that might impugn the same: offering ourselves and promising by this our supplication that for a token and knowledge of our said repentance we be and shall be always ready, under and with the authorities of your Majesties, to the utmost of our powers, to do that shall lie in us for the abrogation and repealing of the said laws and ordinances in this present Parliament as well for ourselves as for the whole body whom we represent: Whereupon we most humbly desire your Majesties, as personages undefiled in the offence of this body towards the said See, which nevertheless God by his Providence hath made subject to you, to set forth this our most humble suit that we may obtain from the See Apostolic by the said most reverend father, as well particularly as generally, absolution, release and discharge from all danger of such censures and sentences as by the laws of the Church we be fallen into; and that we may as children repentant be received into the bosom and unity of Christ's Church, so as this noble realm with all the members thereof may in this unity and perfect obedience to the See Apostolic and popes for the time being serve God and your Majesties to the furtherance and advancement of His honour and glory. We are at the intercession of your Majesties by the authority of our holy father Pope Julius the Third and of the See Apostolic assoiled, discharged and delivered from excommunication, interdictions and other censures ecclesiastical which hath hanged over our heads for our said defaults since the time of the said schism mentioned in our supplication. It may now like your Majesties that for the accomplishment of our promise made in the said supplication, that is to repeal all laws and statutes made contrary to the said supremacy and See Apostolic during the said schism, the which is to be understood since the 20th year of the reign of the said late King Henry the Eighth, and so the said Lord Legate doth accept and recognise the same.

[II repeals the clauses of 21 Henry VIII, c. 13 (in restraint of pluralities) which forbade the procuring from Rome of dispensations for pluralities or non-residence.]

[III repeals 23 Henry VIII, c. 9, in restraint of citations; 24 Henry VIII, c. 12, in restraint of appeals; 23 Henry VIII, c. 20, for the conditional restraint of annates; 25 Henry VIII, c. 19, for the submission of the clergy; 25 Henry VIII, c. 20, in absolute restraint of annates and for the election of bishops; and 25 Henry VIII, c. 21, the dispensations act.]

[IV repeals 26 Henry VIII, c. 1, the Act of Supremacy; 26 Henry VIII, c. 14, for the consecration of suffragans; 27 Henry VIII, c. 15, for the appointment of a commission of 32 persons for the making of ecclesiastical laws; 28 Henry VIII, c. 10, 'extinguishing the authority of the bishop of Rome'; 28 Henry VIII, c. 16, 'for the release of such as have obtained pretended licences and dispensations from the see of Rome'; 28 Henry VIII, c. 7, § 7, i.e. that part of the Second Succession Act which 'concerneth a prohibition to marry within the degrees expressed in the said act'; 31 Henry VIII, c. 9, authorising the King to erect new bishoprics and to appoint bishops to them by letters patent; 32 Henry VIII, c. 38, 'concerning pre-contracts of marriages and degrees of consanguinity'; and 35 Henry VIII, c. 3, concerning the King's style.]

[v repeals § 7 of 35 Henry VIII, c. 1, the Third Succession Act, which had imposed an oath of supremacy.]

[vi repeals 37 Henry VIII, c. 17, entitled 'An act that the doctors of the civil law may exercise ecclesiastical jurisdiction'.]

[vii repeals §§ 5 and 6 of 1 Edw. VI, c. 12, which had assigned penalties for preaching against the royal supremacy or affirming that the bishop of Rome is supreme head.]

viii. And be it further enacted by the authority aforesaid that all clauses, sentences and articles of every other statute or act of Parliament made since the said 20th year of the reign of King Henry the Eighth against the supreme authority of the Pope's Holiness or See Apostolic of Rome, or containing any other matter of the same effect only that is repealed in any of the statutes aforesaid, shall be also by authority hereof from henceforth utterly void, frustrate and of none effect.

ix. [Certain matters brought about since the schism, as new bishoprics, institutions to benefices, etc., to be confirmed by papal dispensation.] . . . And finally, where certain acts and statutes have been made in the time of the late schism concerning the lands and hereditaments of archbishoprics and bishoprics, the suppression and dissolution of monasteries, abbeys, priories, chantries, colleges and all other the goods and chattels of religious houses, since the which time the right and dominion of certain lands and hereditaments, goods and chattels, belonging to the same be dispersed abroad and come to the hands and possessions of divers and sundry persons who by gift, purchase, exchange and other means, according to the order of the laws and statutes of this realm for the time being, have the same: For the avoiding of all scruples that might grow by any the occasions aforesaid or by any other ways or means whatsoever, it may please your Majesties to be intercessors and mediators to the said most reverend father Cardinal Pole, that all such causes and quarrels as by pretence of the said schism or by any other occasion or mean whatsoever might be moved, by the pope's holiness or See Apostolic or by any other jurisdiction ecclesiastical may be utterly removed and taken away; so as all persons having sufficient conveyance of the said lands and hereditaments, goods and chattels, as is aforesaid by the common laws, acts or statutes of this realm, may without scruple of conscience enjoy them, without impeachment or trouble by pretence of any General Council, canons or ecclesiastical laws, and clear from all dangers of the censures of the Church.

* * * * * *

[XIII–XXVI are mainly concerned with saving the rights of the holders of the abbey lands.]

Stat. Realm, IV, 246–54

184. An Act restoring to the Crown the ancient jurisdiction over the state ecclesiastical and spiritual, and abolishing all foreign power repugnant to the same (Act of Supremacy, 1559: I Eliz. I, c. I).

Most humbly beseeches your most excellent Majesty your faithful and obedient subjects the Lords spiritual and temporal and the Commons in this your present Parliament assembled: that where in time of the reign of your most dear father of worthy memory, King Henry the Eighth, divers good laws and statutes were made and established, as well for the utter extinguishment and putting away of all usurped and foreign powers and authorities out of this your realm and other your Highness' dominions and countries, as also for the restoring and uniting to the imperial crown of this realm the ancient jurisdictions, authorities, superiorities and preeminences to the same of right belonging and appertaining; by reason whereof we your most humble and obedient subjects, from the five and twentieth year of the reign of your said dear father, were continually kept in good order and were disburdened of divers great and intolerable charges and exactions before that time unlawfully taken and exacted by such foreign power and authority as before that was usurped, until such time as all the said good laws and statutes by one act of Parliament made in the first and second years of the reigns of the late King Philip and Queen Mary, your Highness' sister [I & 2 Philip and Mary, c. 8], were all clearly repealed and made void, as by the same act of repeal more at large doth and may appear. By reason of which act of repeal your said humble subjects were eftsoons brought under an usurped foreign power and authority and yet do remain in that bondage, to the intolerable charges of your loving subjects if some redress by the authority of this your High Court of Parliament with the assent of your Highness be not had and provided. May it therefore please your Highness, for the repressing of the said usurped foreign power and the restoring of the rights, jurisdictions and preeminences appertaining to the imperial crown of this your realm, that it may be enacted by the authority of this present Parliament, That the said act . . . and all and every branch, clauses and articles therein contained (other than such branches, clauses and sentences as hereafter shall be excepted) may from the last day of this session of Parliament, by authority of this present Parliament, be repealed, and shall from thenceforth be utterly void and of none effect.

II. And that also for the reviving of divers of the said good laws and statutes made in the time of your said dear father, it may also please your Highness [that the following statutes may be revived by authority of this present Parliament: 23 Henry VIII, c. 9, Foreign Citations; 24 Henry VIII, c. 12 Appeals to Rome; 23 Henry VIII, c. 20, Payment of Annates; 25 Henry VIII, c. 19, Submission of the Clergy; 25 Henry VIII, c. 20, Consecration of Bishops; 25 Henry VIII, c. 21, Exactions from Rome; 26 Henry VIII, c. 14, Suffragans; 28 Henry VIII, c. 16, Dispensations] . . . And that the branches, sentences and words of the said several acts and every of them from thenceforth shall and may be judged, deemed and taken to extend to your Highness, your heirs and successors, as fully and largely as ever the same acts or any of them did extend to the said late King Henry the Eighth, your Highness' father.

* * * * * *

IV. And that it may also please your Highness that it may be further enacted by the authority aforesaid, that all other laws and statutes, and the branches and clauses of any act or statute, repealed and made void by the said act of repeal . . . and not in this present act specially mentioned and revived, shall stand, remain and be repealed and void in such like manner and form as they were before the making of this act; anything herein contained to the contrary notwithstanding.

[v revives 1 Edw. VI, c. 1 permitting communion in both kinds.]

[vi repeals the heresy laws revived by Mary, and the act which revived them.]

VII. And to the intent that all usurped and foreign power and authority, spiritual and temporal, may for ever be clearly extinguished and never to be used nor obeyed within this realm or any other your Majesty's dominions or countries: May it please your Highness that it may be further enacted by the authority aforesaid that no foreign prince, person, prelate, state or potentate, spiritual or temporal, shall at any time after the last day of this session of Parliament use, enjoy or exercise any manner of power, jurisdiction, superiority, authority, pre-eminence or privilege spiritual or ecclesiastical, within this realm or within any other your Majesty's dominions or countries that now be or hereafter shall be, but from thenceforth the same shall be clearly abolished out of this realm and all other your Highness' dominions for ever; any statute, ordinance, custom, constitutions or any other matter or cause whatsoever to the contrary in any wise notwithstanding.

VIII. And that also it may likewise please your Highness that it may be established and enacted by the authority aforesaid that such jurisdictions, privileges, superiorities and preeminences spiritual and ecclesiastical, as by any spiritual or ecclesiastical power or authority hath heretofore been or may lawfully be exercised or used for the visitation of the ecclesiastical state and persons, and for reformation, order and correction of the same and of all manner of errors, heresies, schisms, abuses, offences, contempts and enormities, shall for ever by authority of this present Parliament be united and annexed to the imperial crown of this realm. And that your Highness, your heirs and successors, kings or queens of this realm, shall have full power and authority, by virtue of this act, by letters patents under the great seal of England to assign, name and authorise, when and as often as your Highness, your heirs or successors, shall think meet and convenient, and for such and so long time as shall please your Highness, your heirs or successors, such person or persons being natural born subjects to your Highness, your heirs or successors, as your Majesty, your heirs or successors, shall think meet, to exercise, use, occupy and execute under your Highness, your heirs and successors, all manner of jurisdictions, privileges and preeminences in any wise touching or concerning any spiritual or ecclesiastical jurisdiction within these your realms . . . and to visit, reform, redress, order, correct and amend all such errors, heresies, schisms, abuses, offences, contempts and enormities whatsoever which by any manner spiritual or ecclesiastical power, authority or jurisdiction can or may lawfully be reformed, ordered, redressed, corrected, restrained, or amended, to the pleasure of Almighty God, the increase of virtue, and the conservation of the peace and unity of this realm. And that such person or persons so to be named, assigned, authorised and appointed by your highness, your heirs or successors, after the said letters patents to him or them made and delivered as is aforesaid, shall have full power and authority, by virtue of this act and of the said letters patents, under your Highness, your heirs or successors, to exercise, use and execute all the premises according to the tenor and effect of the said letters patents; Any matter or cause to the contrary in any wise notwithstanding.

IX. And for the better observation and maintenance of this act, may it please your Highness that it may be further enacted by the authority aforesaid that all and every archbishop, bishop, and all and every other ecclesiastical person and other ecclesiastical officer and minister, of what estate, dignity, preeminence or degree soever he or they be or shall be, and all and every temporal judge, justicer, mayor, and other lay or temporal officer and minister, and every other person having your Highness' fee or wages within this realm or any your Highness' dominions, shall make, take and receive a corporal oath upon the evangelist, before such person or persons as shall please your Highness, your heirs or successors, under the great seal of England to assign and name to accept and take the same, according to the tenor and effect hereafter following, that is to say: I, A. B., do utterly testify and declare in my conscience that the Queen's Highness is the only supreme governor of this realm and of all other her Highness' dominions and countries, as well in all spiritual or ecclesiastical things or causes as temporal, and that no foreign prince, person, prelate, state or potentate hath or ought to have any jurisdiction, power, superiority, preeminence or authority ecclesiastical or spiritual within this realm, and therefore I do utterly renounce and forsake all foreign jurisdictions, powers, superiorities and authorities, and do promise that from henceforth I shall bear faith and true allegiance to the Queen's Highness, her heirs and lawful successors, and to my power shall assist and defend all jurisdictions, preeminences, privileges and authorities granted or belonging to the Queen's Highness, her heirs and successors, or united or annexed to the imperial crown of this realm: so help me God and by the contents of this Book.

[x attaches to refusal to take the oath the penalty of loss of 'every ecclesiastical and spiritual promotion, benefice, and office, and every temporal and lay promotion and office' which the person so refusing holds 'at the time of such refusal made', 'and that also all and every such person and persons so refusing to take the said oath shall immediately after such refusal be from thenceforth during his life disabled to retain or exercise any office or other promotion which he at the time of such refusal hath jointly or in common with any other person or persons.' Persons hereafter preferred 'to any archbishopric or bishopric, or to any other spiritual or ecclesiastical benefice, promotion, dignity, office or ministry, or . . . to any temporal or lay office, ministry or service,' are required to take the oath before they 'receive, use, exercise, supply or occupy' such office.]

* * * * * *

[XII. Oath also to be taken by persons suing livery of lands and doing homage, and by anyone taking holy orders or degrees at the Universities.]

* * * * * *

XIV. And for the more sure observation of this act and the utter extinguishment of all foreign and usurped power and authority, may it please your Highness that it may be further enacted by the authority aforesaid that if any person or persons dwelling or inhabiting within this your realm or in any other your Highness' realms or dominions, of what estate, dignity or degree soever he or they be, after the end of thirty days next after the determination of this session of this present Parliament shall by writing, printing, teaching, preaching, express words, deed or act, advisedly, maliciously and directly affirm, hold, stand with, set forth, maintain or defend the authority, preeminence, power or jurisdiction spiritual or ecclesiastical of any foreign prince, prelate, person, state or potentate whatsoever, heretofore claimed, used or usurped within this realm or any dominion or country being within or under the power, dominion or obeisance of your Highness, or shall advisedly, maliciously and directly put in ure or execute anything for the extolling, advancement, setting forth, maintenance or defence of any such pretended or usurped jurisdiction, power, preeminence or authority, or any part thereof, that then every such person and persons so doing and offending, their abettors, aiders, procurers and counsellors, being thereof lawfully convicted and attainted according to the due order and course of the common laws of this realm, [shall be subject to the following penalties: for the first offence, forfeiture of goods, or if these are not worth £20, one year's imprisonment, the benefices and promotions of ecclesiastics becoming void; for the second offence, the penalties of praemunire; the third offence is to be deemed high treason].

* * * * * *

XX. Provided always and be it enacted by the authority aforesaid that such person or persons to whom your Highness, your heirs or successors, shall hereafter by letters patents under the great seal of England give authority to have or execute any jurisdiction, power or authority spiritual, or to visit, reform, order, or correct any errors, heresies, schisms, abuses or enormities by virtue of this act, shall not in any wise have authority or power to order, determine or adjudge any matter or cause to be heresy but only such as heretofore have been determined, ordered or adjudged to be heresy by the authority of the canonical Scriptures, or by the first four General Councils or any of them, or by any other General Council wherein the same was declared heresy by the express and plain words of the said canonical Scriptures, or such as hereafter shall be ordered, judged or determined to be heresy by the High Court of Parliament of this realm with the assent of the clergy in their Convocation; anything in this act contained to the contrary notwithstanding.

[xxi. Offences under this act shall be proved by two lawful witnesses, confronted with the accused.]

*   *   *   *   *   *

Stat. Realm, IV, 350–5

185. Richard Hooker on the Royal Supremacy, c. 1590.

... Touching the king's supereminent authority in commanding and in judging of causes ecclesiastical; first, to explain therein our meaning, it hath been taken as if we did hold that kings may prescribe what themselves think good to be done in the service of God; how the word shall be taught, how sacraments administered; that kings may personally sit in the consistory where bishops do, hearing and determining what causes soever do appertain unto these courts; that kings and queens in their own proper persons are by judicial sentence to decide the questions which rise about matters of faith and Christian religion; that kings may excommunicate; finally, that kings may do whatsoever is incident unto the office and duty of an ecclesiastical judge. Which opinion because we count as absurd as they who have fathered the same upon us, we do them to wit that thus our meaning is and no otherwise: There is not within this realm any ecclesiastical officer that may by the authority of his own place command universally throughout the king's dominions; but they of his people whom one may command are to another's commandment unsubject; only the king's royal power is of so large compass that no man commanded by him according to order of law can plead himself to be without the bounds and limits of that authority. . . . And that kings should be in such sort supreme commanders over all men, we hold it requisite as well for the ordering of spiritual as of civil affairs; inasmuch as without universal authority in this kind they should not be able when need serves to do as virtuous kings have done.

Ecclesiastical Polity, Bk. VIII, c. 8 (*Works*, III, 431–2)

III. SECULARISATION OF LAND

The triumph of the temporalty manifested itself most strikingly in the massive and prolonged transfer of ecclesiastical property into lay hands which took place in three main stages. Between 1536 and 1540 the Crown acquired, by dissolution and surrender, the whole lands and goods of all monasteries, friaries and nunneries (**186, 188**), as well as the less valuable commanderies of the Knights of St John (32 Henry VIII, c. 24). In 1547 the chantries—the very many small foundations for one or two priests saying prayers for the founders' souls, often with a school or hospital attached—went the same way (**189**).[57] And in the reigns of Edward VI and Elizabeth, a good many lands of bishops and other dignitaries were acquired by the Crown, the nobility and the gentry, by means of exchanges, forced leases, or even occasional surrender, especially under the notorious act of 1559 (**189a**).[58] In an era of fourfold inflation (1535–1603) the annual income of all episcopal sees dropped by about ten per cent to £27,000.[59] Thus over a quarter of all landed property in England changed hands in some sixty years. Although this was less drastic than a few real radicals seem to have wished,[60] and although the Dissolution should not be regarded as the main aspect of the Reformation, it yet was obviously the one most visible to the eye in all the changes that came over the Church in this century. Land secularisation had long been demanded by the laity; but while Wolsey and others had dissolved some monasteries in order to use the funds for such quasi-spiritual purposes as education, it was only after 1536 that the temporalty got their hands on the long-coveted properties.[61] On the whole, these events and their

[57] Their dissolution had been planned in 1545 (37 Henry VIII, c. 4) but was postponed by Henry VIII's death.

[58] Heal, *Prelates and Politics* (with an excellent bibliography).

[59] *Ibid.*, 328; moreover, the proportion of spiritualities (hard to collect and inflexible) rose from less than a tenth to over a third.

[60] Cf. a plan of *c.* 1534 to confiscate all Church property and pay salaries to the hierarchy, printed by Stone, *Bull. Inst. Hist. Res.*, XXIV, 9 ff. (and cf. also Elton, *ibid.*, XXV, 129, n. 2).

[61] Some of the earlier dissolutions had been for the use of the laity: Hibbert, *Dissolution*, 19 ff.

consequences belong less to the history of government than to that of society; nevertheless, a few points deserve special notice in the present context.

For the dissolution of the monasteries,[62] the main item in this programme of land-acquisition, the government proceeded by careful stages and put forward a number of propaganda reasons. A commission of early 1535 ascertained the wealth of the Church; its findings were assembled in the *Valor Ecclesiasticus*, a general register of all ecclesiastical income intended for the assessment of the first fruits and tenths granted to the Crown in 1534 (26). In the same year, Cromwell was also appointed the king's vicar-general to carry out a general visitation of the monasteries as envisaged in the Act of Supremacy (180). This, managed through a small group of prejudiced and in part unpleasant visitors, produced the notorious reports of insufficiency and depravity which were presented to Parliament in 1536 and underlie the preamble of the act dissolving the lesser monasteries (186). That the picture was painted much blacker than it deserved, that the visitors looked for scandal and distorted the truth, and that even when the surviving reports are added up nothing resembling universal collapse can be said to emerge—all this is true and well known. So is the fact that the general impression of worldliness, lack of zeal, internecine quarrelling, excessive laxity or excessive severity of superiors—the impression of an institution well out of joint—is borne out by pre-Reformation visitations. The monasteries were not sinks of iniquity, nor were they in any case rapidly passing away; though there had been few new foundations in recent decades—small wonder in a country which already harboured some 850 houses[63]—it would appear that they had shared in the general rise of the population which occurred from the last quarter of the fifteenth century onwards.[64] Nevertheless, one cannot escape the conclusion that monasticism was far from a living ideal in early Tudor England; far too many of the houses lacked sufficient inmates even to perform the services of religion which were their main justification, and far too many monks, professed before they understood the vows, showed themselves eager to return to the world when the chance offered.

[62] Cf. the best accounts in Knowles, *Religious Orders*, III, and Youings, *Dissolution*. For a summary of cause, events and effect cf. Elton, *Reform and Reformation*, ch. 10. The economic condition of the monasteries is analysed in Savine, *English Monasteries*. He shows that they were nothing like so backward (or considerate) in the exploitation of their lands as was once supposed; that links with the neighbouring gentry were very strong, many demesnes having been let to lease before the Dissolution; and that they played no great part in either education or poor relief.

[63] Knowles and Hadcock, *Medieval Religious Houses*, 364. Of these 143 were nunneries; in addition there were 563 hospitals.

[64] Knowles and Hadcock, *op. cit.*, 54 f., 364. A total of approximately 11,000 religious on the eve of the Dissolution (perhaps 0.3 per cent of the population owning nearly twenty-five per cent of the land), with about twice the number of servants to be added to the total (Savine, *English Monasteries*, 225 ff.), underlines the contemporary complaints about idle abbey-lubbers.

In any case, however, the pretended reason matters little, since we do not even know whether these charges of moral decay were required to persuade Parliament. The real reasons were two. In the first place, the government wanted the wealth of the monasteries, and the gentry hoped to obtain it from the Crown after confiscation. From the first, Cromwell was pestered by seekers after such bounty;[65] if he or Henry had ever intended to keep all the lands in Crown hands they could not have resisted such pressure. But it is clear anyhow that some judicious dispersal by gifts, lease or sale was part of the original plan. What had not been intended was the wholesale unloading, only modified by reserving a rent on lands sold and imposing tenure in knight's service with its fiscal burdens—and even these had to be given up later—which resulted from the financial embarrassment produced by war after 1542. What really happened—whether the Crown made a reasonable profit out of the sales—will never be completely worked out because the feverish land market swallowed the evidence,[66] but the old view, which spoke of 'squandering', cannot be maintained.[67] What is less in dispute is the final destination of the lands. The Crown acted only as a channel as recurrent financial crises in the 1540's, 1550's, 1560's and 1590's compelled it to sell off much of its landed property, and the landed gentry were the ultimate beneficiaries. Many lands went to established landed families, especially to those who had leased monastic demesnes before the Dissolution, continued to hold them on lease from the Crown, and acquired the freehold as soon as they were able. But more significant is the expansion of the landed gentry—that is, the number of middle-sized estates—produced by the fluid land-market. The new recruits came in part from classes that had never been in land before, such as merchants or lawyers who invested their wealth in this way, but the bulk would appear to have been gentlemen born whom the operation of primogeniture would have driven from the landed gentry if the Church lands had not enabled them to remain in the world of their origin. This expansion of the gentry had political consequences: the middling sort of landowner increased in influence both locally (in the shires) and at the

[65] As early as August 1537 the duke of Norfolk, writing to Cromwell about his desire for a share in the spoils, could say that 'the time of sowing is at hand, and every other nobleman hath already his portion' (State Papers, Henry VIII, vol. 106, fo. 157).

[66] Arguments based on mere figures of sales are misleading because they do not take into account such points as reserved rents or income from resales. There is some difficulty in accounting for a steady income in Augmentations despite heavy sales of land (Elton, *Tudor Revolution*, 225). The difficulties are well illuminated in Wyndham, *Bull. Inst. Hist. Res.*, LII, 129 ff.

[67] Cf. especially Habakkuk, *Econ. Hist. Rev.*, 1957–8, 362 ff., which also quite rightly disposes of the famous alleged speculators in land. In Devon, one-quarter of the new property had been given away by 1558 and another seventy per cent sold; i.e. the Crown had disposed of nearly all the new lands (Youings, *Eng. Hist. Rev.*, LXIX, 30, 34, 37). Yet while the value of the confiscated lands was £6,740 a year on acquisition, £2,413 was still obtained in 1558 (Youings, *Devon Monastic Lands*, 127, 136). That is to say, under one-twentieth of the property produced an income only two-thirds less than the lot.

centre (in Parliament), and it is possible that their collective wealth enabled them to stand up to Crown and nobility in a novel way. But such generalisations are suspect; for one thing, what, in practice, can 'collective wealth' mean? It should also be noted that the Crown did not so much lose as fail to gain; the only real loser was the Church.

It would, however, be wrong to suppose that there was nothing behind the assault on Church lands except the Crown's needs and the gentry's landhunger. In a sense it is true that the laity could look upon the ecclesiastical properties with such covetous eyes only because the whole notion of a wealthy and heavily endowed Church had ceased to carry conviction; more particularly, the monastic ideal no longer exacted the respect which alone could make up for the effect of so much monastic practice. The spread of opinion against 'superstitious practices'—a vital element in the growth of English Protestantism—hardened the attitude to the religious life. The Injunctions of 1536 came out against 'images, relics and miracles',[68] and those of 1538 ordered the removal of images 'for avoiding that most detestable offence of idolatry'.[69] Monasteries were not necessarily linked with image-worship, but on the other hand they were often associated with centres of pilgrimage and in general represented the same doctrines of intercession and mediation which, in other respects, led to idolatry. By the time the chantries came to be attacked the point stood out more starkly, and the act of 1547 (189) justified their dissolution in part because the money could be put to better educational and social uses but in part because they pandered to the 'vain opinions of purgatory and masses satisfactory'.[70] This is not to assert that the desire for land played a minor part in their disappearance. Nor can one be absolutely sure that Protestant notions lurked behind the Dissolution. But it is quite certain that the disappearance of the monasteries was necessary to the growth of Protestantism.

From the constitutional point of view, the greatest interest of the Dissolution lies in the manner in which it was carried out. It displays Tudor government at its most planned and efficient, for at no other time did it operate against so manageable—even helpless—a victim. Yet the task was enormous, and the ease and skill with which it was carried out (taking in its stride the outbreak of a great rebellion in the north) deserve respect. After the visitation of 1535, which collected the propaganda material and surveyed the ground, Cromwell[71] determined to make the task possible by proceeding

---

[68] Gee and Hardy, 271.   [69] *Ibid.*, 277 f.

[70] On chantries cf. Kreider, *Chantries*, and Kitching, *Church and Society*, 119 ff. Simon, *Education and Society*, chs. 8 & 9, has restored the reign of Edward VI to its traditional place as a period of school-founding and educational advance, against the tendentious attacks of Leach, *English Schools at the Reformation*.

[71] No one has ever disputed his primary share in this work because, after all, this is a point over which one may grow virtuously indignant.

in two stages. The act of 1536 (**186**) therefore divided the monasteries into the lesser (with an annual income below £200) and the greater; asserting that religion and morals were in a bad way among the former, it dissolved them and annexed their lands, buildings and movables to the Crown. Another act of the same year (**71**) set up the Court of Augmentations to administer the new property.[72] The actual task of disposing of the houses and inmates involved a hundred and one details of which the administrative 'treaty' between Augmentations and the Duchy of Lancaster gives a small indication **187**).[73] Big questions and small—from the survey of the lands, the collection of saleable property, or the pensioning of heads and lesser brethren, to debts to be paid[74] or bedding to be allowed to the departing monks—the commissioners appointed by Augmentations had to deal with them all. While this was going on, Cromwell set the second stage in motion: between 1536 and 1540 the remaining greater houses were gradually compelled to agree to a dissolution which the praise they had received in the act of 1536 made it difficult to secure by legislative enactment. Thus one body after another signed prepared statements of surrender presented to them by the vicegerent's commissioners;[75] threats and a few examples *in terrorem* removed all opposition;[76] and the Parliament of 1539 could be asked to confirm the process by vesting the additional lands in the Crown (**188**) even though not all the houses had yet been dissolved. The last house to go was Waltham Abbey, on 23 March 1540. The administration of this greater dissolution set bigger problems still than the first stage, if only because the properties involved were vastly larger and because the religious could now no longer be accommodated in undissolved houses of their order. But it was all carried out quite smoothly and with surprisingly little harshness or hardship, though some was, of course, involved in the very fact that a way of life was being destroyed. Pensions were paid, livings found for many who wanted them; the abbots and priors came off well, on the whole, though ordinary monks and especially nuns suffered more and sometimes came to destitution.[77] It is no longer held

---

[72] Above, p. 133.

[73] By the act of 1536 monasteries on Duchy lands were supposed to be dissolved by the Duchy officers; this led to overlapping and conflict (Elton, *Tudor Revolution*, 203 f., 208 ff.).

[74] The Crown not only inherited and paid annuities and other burdens resting on the confiscated lands (Youings, *Eng. Hist. Rev.*, LXIX, 26) but also became responsible for all debts owed by dissolved monasteries (**186**, section XII).

[75] One such is printed in Tanner, 89 ff.

[76] Abbots involved in the pilgrimage of grace were declared to have forfeited their abbeys to the Crown, and in 1539 the abbots of Woburn, Glastonbury, Reading and Colchester were hanged for treason, with the same consequences for their houses.

[77] Knowles, *Religious Orders*, III, 404 ff. But cf. Dickens, *Eng. Hist. Rev.*, LV, 384 ff., for a more critical view of the adequacy of pensions and the regularity with which they were paid. The ex-monks appear to have shared in the sufferings inflicted on all those who had claims on Edward VI's governments.

that the Dissolution was responsible for the problems of poverty and vagrancy which beset Tudor England; whether it even contributed to them remains at present an unresolved problem.

186. An Act whereby all religious houses of monks, canons and nuns which may not dispend manors, lands, tenements and hereditaments above the clear yearly value of £200 are given to the King's Highness, his heirs and successors, for ever (1536: 27 Henry VIII, c. 28).

Forasmuch as manifest sin, vicious, carnal and abominable living, is daily used and committed amongst the little and small abbeys, priories and other religious houses of monks, canons and nuns, where the congregation of such religious persons is under the number of 12 persons, whereby the governors of such religious houses and their convent spoil, destroy, consume and utterly waste as well their churches, monasteries, priories, principal houses, farms, granges, lands, tenements and hereditaments, as the ornaments of their churches and their goods and chattels to the high displeasure of Almighty God, slander of good religion, and to the great infamy of the King's Highness and the realm if redress should not be had thereof; and albeit that many continual visitations hath been heretofore had by the space of two hundred years and more for an honest and charitable reformation of such unthrifty, carnal and abominable living, yet nevertheless little or none amendment is hitherto had, but their vicious living shamelessly increaseth and augmenteth, and by a cursed custom so rooted and infested that a great multitude of the religious persons in such small houses do rather choose to rove abroad in apostasy than to conform them to the observation of good religion; so that without such small houses be utterly suppressed and the religious persons therein committed to great and honourable monasteries of religion in this realm, where they may be compelled to live religiously for reformation of their lives, there can else be no reformation in this behalf: In consideration whereof the King's most royal Majesty, being supreme head in earth under God of the Church of England, daily finding and devising the increase, advancement and exaltation of true doctrine and virtue in the said Church, to the only glory and honour of God and the total extirping and destruction of vice and sin, having knowledge that the premises be true, as well by the compts of his late visitations as by sundry credible informations, considering also that divers and great solemn monasteries of this realm wherein, thanks be to God, religion is right well kept and observed, be destitute of such full numbers of religious persons as they ought and may keep, hath thought good that a plain declaration should be made of the premises as well to the Lords spiritual and temporal as to other his loving subjects the Commons in this present Parliament assembled; whereupon the said Lords and Commons by a great deliberation finally be resolved that it is and shall be much more to the pleasure of Almighty God and for the honour of this his realm that the possessions of such spiritual religious houses, now being spent, spoiled and wasted for increase and maintenance of sin, should be used and converted to better uses, and the unthrifty religious persons so spending the same to be compelled to reform their lives; and thereupon most humbly desire the King's Highness that it may be enacted by authority of this present Parliament, that his Majesty shall have and enjoy to him and to his heirs for ever all and singular monasteries, priories and other religious houses of monks, canons and nuns, of what kinds or diversities of habits, rules or orders so ever they be called or named, which have not in lands and tenements, rents, tithes, portions and other hereditaments above the clear yearly value of two hundred pounds; and in like manner shall have and enjoy all the sites and circuits of every such religious houses, and all and singular the manors, granges, meses,[78] lands, tenements, reversions, rents, services, tithes, pensions, portions, churches, chapels, advowsons, patronages, annuities, rights, entries, conditions and other hereditaments appertaining or belonging to every such monastery, priory or other religious house not having as is aforesaid above the said clear yearly value of two hundred pounds, in as large and ample manner as the abbots, priors, abbesses, prioresses or other governors of such monasteries, priories and other religious houses now have or ought to have the same in the right of their houses; and that also his Highness shall have to him and to his heirs all and singular such monasteries, abbeys and priories which, at any time within one year next afore the making of this act, hath been given and granted to his Majesty by any abbot, prior, abbess or prioress under their convent seals, or that otherwise hath been suppressed or dissolved; And all and singular the manors, lands, [etc.] . . . to the same monasteries, abbeys and priories or to any of them appertaining or belonging; To have and to hold all and singular the premises with all their rights, profits, jurisdictions and commodities,

---

[78] Houses.

unto the King's Majesty and to his heirs and assigns for ever, to do and use therewith his or their own wills to the pleasure of Almighty God and to the honour and profit of this realm.

* * * * * *

IV. Provided always and be it enacted that forasmuch as divers of the chief governors of such religious houses, determining the utter spoil and destruction of their houses and dreading the suppressing thereof, for the maintenance of their detestable lives have lately fraudulently and craftily made feoffments,[79] estates, gifts, grants and leases under their convent seals, or suffered recoveries[80] of their manors, lands, tenements and hereditaments in fee simple, fee tail, for term of life or lives, or for years, or charged the same with rents or corrodies,[81] to the great decay and diminution of their houses, that all such crafty and fraudulent recoveries, feoffments, estates, gifts, grants and leases, and every of them, made by any of the said chief governors of such religious houses under the convent seals within one year next afore the making of this act, shall be utterly void and of none effect. . . .

V. And it is also enacted by authority aforesaid that the King's Highness shall have and enjoy to his own proper use all the ornaments, jewels, goods, chattels and debts which appertained to any of the chief governors of the said monasteries or religious houses in the right of the said monasteries or houses at the first day of March in the year of our Lord God 1535[82] or any time since, wheresoever and to whose possession soever they shall come or be found; except only such beasts, grain and woods, and such like other chattels and revenues, as have been sold in the said first day of March or since for the necessary or reasonable expenses or charges of any of the said monasteries or houses.

* * * * * *

VIII. In consideration of which premises to be had to his Highness and to his heirs as is aforesaid, his Majesty is pleased and contented of his most excellent charity to provide to every chief head and governor of

---

[79] A 'feoffment' is a mode of conveyance by which a person is invested with freehold land by livery of seisin. It could be used to effect a mortgage.

[80] A 'recovery' was a method of alienating land by a collusive action. By the Tudor period it had become a regular method of conveyance.

[81] A corrody, originally a grant of food, etc., made by a monastery, had to all intents become a purchasable annuity.

[82] I.e. 1536, modern style.

every such religious house during their lives such yearly pensions or benefices as for their degrees and qualities shall be reasonable and convenient; wherein his Highness will have most tender respect to such of the said chief governors as well and truly conserve and keep the goods and ornaments of their houses to the use of his Majesty, without spoil, waste or embezzling the same; And also his Majesty will ordain and provide that the convents of every such religious house shall have their capacities, if they will, to live honestly and virtuously abroad, and some convenient charity disposed to them toward their living, or else shall be committed to such honourable great monasteries of this realm wherein good religion is observed as shall be limited by his Highness, there to live religiously during their lives.

IX. And it is ordained by authority aforesaid that the chief governors and convents of such honourable great monasteries shall take and accept into their houses from time to time such number of the persons of the said convents as shall be assigned and appointed by the King's Highness, and keep them religiously during their lives within their said monasteries in like manner and form as the convents of such great monasteries be ordered and kept.

*   *   *   *   *   *

XII. And also the King's Majesty is pleased and contented that it be enacted by authority aforesaid that his Highness shall satisfy, content and pay all and singular such just and true debts which be owing to any person or persons by the chief governors of any of the said religious houses. . . .

XIII. Provided always that the King's Highness, at any time after the making of this act, may at his pleasure ordain and declare, by his letters patents under his great seal, that such of the said religious houses which his Highness shall not be disposed to have suppressed nor dissolved by authority of this act shall still continue, remain and be in the same body corporate and in the said essential estate, quality and condition, as well in possessions as otherwise, as they were afore the making of this act, without any suppression or dissolution thereof or any part of the same by authority of this act. . . .

*   *   *   *   *   *

XVII. And further be it enacted, ordained and established by authority aforesaid that all and singular persons, bodies politic and corporate, to whom the King's Majesty, his heirs or successors, hereafter shall give, grant, let or demise any site or precinct, with the houses thereupon builded, together with the demesnes of any monasteries, priories or other religious houses that shall be dissolved or given to the King's Highness by this act, and the heirs, successors, executors and assigns of every such person, body politic and corporate, shall be bounden by authority of this act, under the penalties hereafter ensuing, to keep or cause to be kept an honest continual house and household in the same site or precinct, and to occupy yearly as much of the same demesnes in ploughing and tillage of husbandry, that is to say, as much of the said demesnes which hath been commonly used to be kept in tillage by the governors, abbots or priors of the same houses, monasteries or priories, or by their farmer or farmers occupying the same, within the time of 20 years next before this act; and if any person or persons, bodies politic or corporate, that shall be bounden by this act, do not keep an honest house, household, husbandry and tillage in manner and form as is aforesaid, that then he or they so offending shall forfeit to the King's Highness for every month so offending £6. 13s. 4d. to be recovered to his use in any of his courts of record.[83]

*   *   *   *   *   *

Stat. Realm, III, 575–8

187. A Remembrance of the articles agreed between the chancellors of the Duchy of Lancaster and of the Augmentation at a meeting together at the White Hall at Westminster [5 July 1536].

*   *   *   *   *   *

First, upon the matter moved between both the said chancellors concerning their authorities of the suppression of religious houses etc.: it was there agreed between them that the said chancellor of the said Duchy of Lancaster had authority to make commissions of suppression of all manner of houses of religion in the County Palatine of Lancaster and the ordering both of their lands and tenements, goods and chattels.

Item, that the same chancellor of the Duchy had authority to assess and give pensions to the governors of the houses to have for their living during their lives; which pensions was extended to be after the rate of the tenth part of the yearly value of the revenues thereof or somewhat above, by the discretion of the said chancellor of the said Duchy or of the commissioners assigned for the same.

[83] Section XVII was added to the act in a separate schedule.

Item, in like wise to give part of the movable goods to the religious persons by the discretion of the said commissioners; that is to say, to such as have any continual disease or in extreme age or sickness, to give to them the more.

Item, they agreed that the said commissioners shall take the notes of all leases made and the same to be examined, so that it may be known how long the said leases shall continue and endure.

Item, of what value the lands so letten, over and above the yearly rents paid for the same.

Item, the said commissioners . . . to pay all true debts of every house, being under the value of £20.

Item, it is agreed that the said chancellor of Augmentations shall by commission suppress all houses to be suppressed by the act of the Duchy foundation out of the County Palatine of Lancaster, and to pay the debts of the same.

Item, that the officers of Augmentation shall declare the true value to the auditors of the Duchy of Lancaster and to deliver unto them all such rentals, books of accounts and other records and writings as they may come by concerning the said houses; and the same to make report thereof to the chancellor of the said Duchy.

Item, in every lease to be made by the King, that it be expressed in it that the lessee shall bear all the reparation of the houses except the tile and timber.

Item, all such persons to whom the King's Grace hath promised any lease shall have but only the demesnes that be temporal which the governors had in their own hands.

Item, the lessee of the demesnes of Conishead to find a friar and one officer continually to be abiding there, to ring the bell there accustomed when need shall require, according unto the old custom for the safeguard of passengers over the sands in those parts.

Item, the leases of Cartmel not to pass until they be bound in like wise to find a guide over the sands adjoining to the said house according to the old custom.

Item, the lessees of the demesnes of Cockersand to find one other guide over the sands adjoining thereunto.

Duchy of Lanc. Entry Books of Orders, vol. 6, fos. 204v–205

188. An Act for dissolution of abbeys (1539: 31 Henry VIII, c. 13).

Where divers and sundry abbots, priors, abbesses, prioresses and other ecclesiastical governors and governesses of divers monasteries, abbacies, priories, nunneries, colleges, hospitals, houses of friars and other religious and ecclesiastical houses and places within this our sovereign lord the King's realm of England and Wales, of their own free and voluntary minds, good wills and assents, without constraint, coaction or compulsion of any manner of person or persons, since the fourth day of February, the 27th year of the reign of our now most dread sovereign lord, by the due order and course of the common laws of this his realm of England, and by their sufficient writings of record under their convent and common seals, have severally given, granted and by the same their writings severally confirmed all their said monasteries, abbacies [etc.] . . . and all their sites, circuits, and precincts of the same, and all and singular their manors, lordships, granges, meses, lands, tenements, meadows, pastures, rents, reversions, services, woods, tithes, pensions, portions, churches, chapels, advowsons, patronages, annuities, rights, entries, conditions, commons, leets, courts, liberties, privileges and franchises, appertaining or in any wise belonging to any such monastery, abbacy [etc.] . . . or to any of them, by whatsoever name or corporation they or any of them were then named or called, and of what order, habit, religion or other kind or quality soever they or any of them then were reputed, known, or taken; to have and to hold all the said monasteries, abbacies [etc.] . . . sites, circuits [etc.] . . . and all other the premises to our said sovereign lord, his heirs and successors, for ever; and the same their said monasteries, abbacies, [etc.] . . . sites, circuits [etc.] . . . and other the premises, voluntarily as is aforesaid have renounced, left and forsaken, and every of them hath renounced, left and forsaken: Be it therefore enacted by the King our sovereign lord and the Lords spiritual and temporal and the Commons in this present Parliament assembled, and by authority of the same, that the King, our sovereign lord shall have, hold, possess and enjoy to him, his heirs and successors for ever all and singular such late monasteries, abbacies [etc.] . . . which since the said fourth day of February the 27th year of the reign of our said sovereign lord have been dissolved, suppressed, renounced, relinquished, forfeited, given up or by any other mean come to his Highness; and by the same authority and in like manner shall have, hold, possess and enjoy all the sites, circuits [etc.] . . . and other whatsoever hereditaments which appertained or belonged to the said late monasteries, abbacies [etc.] . . . or to any of them, in as large and ample manner and form as the late abbots, priors, abbesses, prioresses and other ecclesias-

tical governors and governesses of such late monasteries, abbacies [etc.]
... had, held or occupied, or of right ought to have had, holden or
occupied, in the rights of their said late monasteries, abbacies [etc.] ...
at the time of the said dissolution, suppression, renouncing, relinquish-
ing, forfeiting, giving up, or by any other manner of mean coming of
the same to the King's Highness, since the fourth day of February above
specified.

II. And it is further enacted by the authority abovesaid, that not only
all the said late monasteries, abbacies [etc.] ... sites, circuits [etc.] ...
and all other the premises, forthwith, immediately and presently, but
also all other monasteries, abbacies [etc.] ... which hereafter shall
happen to be dissolved, suppressed, [etc.] ... and also all the sites,
circuits [etc.] ... and other hereditaments, whatsoever they be,
belonging or appertaining to the same or any of them, whensoever and
as soon as they shall be dissolved, suppressed, [etc.] ... shall be vested,
deemed and adjudged by authority of this present Parliament in the very
actual and real seisin and possession of the King our sovereign lord, his
heirs and successors, for ever, in the state and condition as they now be
and as though all the said late monasteries, abbacies [etc.] ... so dissolved, suppressed [etc.] ... as also the said monasteries, abbacies [etc.]
... which hereafter shall happen to be dissolved, suppressed [etc.] ...
sites, circuits [etc.] ... and other the premises whatsoever they be and
every of them, were in this present act specially and particularly
rehearsed, named and expressed, by express words, names, titles and
faculties, and in their natures, kinds and qualities.

III. And be it also enacted by authority aforesaid, that all the said late
monasteries, abbacies [etc.] ... which be dissolved, suppressed [etc.]
... and all the manors, lordships, granges, lands, tenements and other
the premises, except such thereof as be come to the King's hands by
attainder or attainders of treason, and all the said monasteries, abbacies
[etc.] ... which hereafter shall happen to be dissolved, suppressed
[etc.] ... and all the manors, lordships, granges, lands, tenements,
meadows, pastures, rents, reversions, services, woods, tithes, portions,
pensions, parsonages, appropriate vicarages,[84] churches, chapels, advowsons, nominations, patronages, annuities, rights, interests, entries,
conditions, commons, leets, courts, liberties, privileges, franchises and
other hereditaments whatsoever they be, belonging to the same or to

---

[84] Benefices of which the fiscal rights had been acquired by someone other than the incumbent.

any of them (except such thereof which shall happen to come to the King's Highness by attainder or attainders of treason), shall be in the order, survey and governance of our said sovereign lord the King's Court of Augmentations of the Revenues of his Crown. . . .

* * * * * *

Stat. Realm, III, 733–9

189. An Act whereby certain chantries, colleges, free chapels and the possessions of the same be given to the King's Majesty (1547: 1 Ed. VI, c. 14).

The King's most loving subjects, the Lords spiritual and temporal and the Commons in this present Parliament assembled, considering that a great part of superstitution and errors in Christian religion hath been brought into the minds and estimation of men by reason of the ignorance of their very true and perfect salvation through the death of Jesus Christ, and by devising and phantasing vain opinions of purgatory and masses satisfactory to be done for them which be departed, the which doctrine and vain opinion by nothing more is maintained and upholden than by the abuse of trentals,[85] chantries, and other provisions made for the continuance of the said blindness and ignorance; and further considering and understanding that the alteration, change and amendment of the same, and converting to good and godly uses, as in erecting of grammar schools to the education of youth in virtue and godliness, the further augmenting of the Universities, and better provision for the poor and needy, cannot in this present Parliament be provided and conveniently done, nor cannot nor ought to any other manner person be committed than to the King's Highness, whose Majesty with and by the advice of his Highness' most prudent Council can and will most wisely and beneficially, both for the honour of God and the weal of this his Majesty's realm, order, alter, convert and dispose the same; And calling further to their remembrance [37 Henry VIII, c. 4, for the dissolution of the chantries]. It is now ordained and enacted by the King our sovereign lord with the assent of the Lords and Commons in this present Parliament assembled, and by the authority of the same, that all manner of colleges, free chapels and chantries, having being or *in esse* within five years next before the first day of this present Parliament, which were not in actual and real possession of the

---

[85] Requiem masses, usually collected in sets ot thirty.

said late King, nor in the actual and real possession of the King our sovereign lord that now is, nor excepted in the said former act ... and all manors, lands, tenements, rents, tithes, pensions, portions and other hereditaments and things above mentioned belonging to them or any of them, and also all manors, lands, tenements, rents and other hereditaments and things above mentioned, by any manner of assurance, conveyance, will, devise or otherwise had, made, suffered, knowledged or declared, given, assigned, limited or appointed to the finding of any priest to have continuance for ever, and wherewith or whereby any priest was sustained, maintained or found within five years next before the first day of this present Parliament, which were not in the actual and real possession of the said late King nor in the actual and real possession of our sovereign lord the King that now is, and also all annual rents, profits and emoluments at any time within five years next before the beginning of this present Parliament employed, paid or bestowed toward or for the maintenance, supportation or finding of any stipendiary priest intended by any act or writing to have continuance for ever, shall by authority of this present Parliament, immediately after the feast of Easter next coming, be adjudged and deemed and also be in the very actual and real possession and seisin of the King our sovereign lord and his heirs and successors for ever; without any office[86] or other inquisition thereof to be had or found, and in as large and ample manner and form as the priests, wardens, masters, ministers, governors, rulers or other incumbents of them or any of them at any time within five years next before the beginning of this present Parliament had, occupied or enjoyed, or now hath, occupieth and enjoyeth the same; and as though all and singular the said colleges, free chapels, chantries, stipends, salaries of priests, and the said manors, lands, tenements, hereditaments and other the premises whatsoever they be, and every of them, were in this present act specially, peculiarly and certainly rehearsed, named and expressed, by express words, names, surnames, corporations, titles and faculties, and in their natures, kinds and qualities.

*   *   *   *   *   *

VII. And furthermore be it ordained and enacted by the authority aforesaid that the King our sovereign lord shall from the said feast of Easter next coming have and enjoy to him, his heirs and successors, for ever, all fraternities, brotherhoods and guilds being within the realm of

---

[86] An enquiry by jury to discover Crown rights in any lands or goods.

England and Wales and other the King's dominions, and all manors, lands, tenements and other hereditaments belonging to them or any of them, other than such corporations, guilds, fraternities, companies and fellowships of mysteries or crafts, and the manors, lands, tenements and other hereditaments pertaining to the said corporations, guilds, fraternities, companies and fellowships of mysteries or crafts above mentioned, and shall by virtue of this act be judged and deemed in actual and real possession of our said sovereign lord the King, his heirs and successors, from the said feast of Easter next coming for ever, without any inquisitions or office thereof to be had or found.

[vIII–XII. The King may appoint commissioners under the great seal with power to survey all the lands, etc., vested in the King by this act. They are also empowered to assign lands for the support of a grammar school where such teaching was required by the foundation of the dissolved chantry; to appoint vicars where the parish church was a dissolved foundation; to assign chantry lands for the maintenance of additional priests in any parish; to make rules 'concerning the service, user and demeanours' of priests or schoolmasters appointed by them; and to grant pensions to the priests of dissolved chantries and to poor persons hitherto dependent on them for 'yearly relief'.]

XIII. And also be it ordained and enacted by the authority of this present Parliament that our sovereign lord the King shall have and enjoy all such goods, chattels, jewels, plate, ornaments and other moveables as were or be the common goods of every such college, chantry, free chapel or stipendiary priest, belonging or annexed to the furniture or service of their several foundations, or abused of any of the said corporations in the abuses aforesaid, the property whereof was not altered or changed before the 8th day of December in the year of our Lord God 1547.

[XIV. Debts of dissolved foundations to be paid by the King.]

XV. Provided always and be it ordained and enacted by the authority aforesaid that this act or any article, clause or matter contained in the same shall not in any wise extend to any college, hostel or hall being within either of the Universities of Cambridge and Oxford; nor to any chantry founded in any of the colleges, hostels or halls being in the same Universities; nor to the free chapel of St George the Martyr, situate in the Castle of Windsor; nor to the college called St Mary College of Winchester besides Winchester of the foundation of Bishop Wykeham; nor to the College of Eton; nor to the parish church commonly called the Chapel in the Sea, in Newton within the Isle of Ely in the county of Cambridge; nor to any manors, lands, tenements or hereditaments to them or any of them pertaining or belonging; nor to any chapel made or ordained for the ease of the people dwelling distant from the parish church, or such like chapel whereunto no more lands or tenements than the churchyard or a little house or close doth belong or pertain; nor to any cathedral church or college where a bishop's see is within this realm of England or Wales, nor to the manors, lands, tenements or other hereditaments of any of them, other than to such chantries, obits, lights and lamps, or any of them, as at any time within five years next before the beginning of this present Parliament have been had, used or maintained within the said cathedral churches or within any of them, or of the issues, revenues or profits of any of the said cathedral churches; to which chantries, obits, lights and lamps it is enacted by the authority aforesaid that this act shall extend.

[XVI-XXXVII deal largely with the administration details (the lands are put under the Court of Augmentations, except for those within the Duchy of Lancaster), with exceptions, and with saving the rights of those who have legitimate claims against chantry lands.]   *Stat. Realm*, IV, 24–33

189a. An Act for the Exchange of Bishops' Lands (1559: 1 Eliz. I, c. 19). The Lords Spiritual and Temporal and the Commons in this present Parliament assembled, perceiving how necessary it is for the imperial crown of this realm to be repaired with restitutions of revenue meet for the same, and having assented and fully accorded to restore to the same imperial crown the first fruits and tenths and parsonages impropriate[87] for the increase of the revenues thereof, be also desirous to devise some good means whereby the said revenue of tenths and impropriate benefices might be in the governance and disposition of the clergy of this realm . . . beseech your Majesty that it may be enacted by this present Parliament in manner and form hereafter following; That is to say:

1. Upon the vacation and avoidance of every archbishopric and Bishopric within this your realm of England and Wales and other your Highness' dominions it shall and may be lawful for your highness to elect and choose and to take into your hands and royal possession as

---

[87] Livings whose rectorial rights had been acquired by monasteries and which had thus passed to the Crown: the impropriator in particular drew the greater tithe but was supposed to appoint a vicar to serve the cure of souls.

much and as many of any the honours, castles, manors, lands, tenements and other hereditaments being parcel of the possessions of any archbishopric or bishopric so being void, as the clear yearly value of all your Majesty's parsonages appropriate and tenths within every such archbishopric or bishopric shall yearly amount and extend unto [and after assessment by royal commissioners and certificate into the Exchequer of all the property so taken] it shall and may be lawful for your Highness by your letters patent to give and assure unto such archbishop and bishop and his successors . . . so much and so many of your yearly tenths, tithes and parsonages appropriated, being within the same archbishopric or bishopric, as shall be of as much or of more yearly value as the said honours [etc.] . . . be certified . . .

Stat. Realm, IV, 381

IV. SETTLEMENT OF RELIGION

The Henrician Reformation began as a political and jurisdictional revolution, and the king himself at least never intended that it should involve any doctrinal changes beyond the denial of the pope's authority in England. It was significant enough that the only response made to the frequent complaints about the Church's treatment of heresy was a conservative act of 1533.[88] This reaffirmed the old legislation against Lollardy (which in effect included the new Lutheran doctrines); but it withdrew the rigour of the law from those who attacked the papacy and modified the forms of trial so as to hamper arbitrary action by the bishops. Until Wolsey's fall, 'heresy' both new and old had been little persecuted in England, but from 1529 to 1532 the bishops, supported by the new lord chancellor, Thomas More, acted more energetically. In these years the proto-martyrs of the Church of England suffered at the stake, while William Tyndale, the leader of the English Lutherans, chafed abroad.[89] The act of 1533 limited episcopal action by making it necessary for heresy trials to begin with an indictment at common law; partly for this reason and partly because the break with Rome required a virtual alliance with reformers at home and abroad, the later 1530's were almost free of the persecution of Protestants.[90] The Ten Articles of 1536,[91] followed up by the

---

[88] 25 Henry VIII. c. 14.

[89] On all this cf. Dickens, Reformation, ch. 4; Clebsch; Elton, Studies, I, 158 ff.

[90] An exception must be made for the reaction to the growth of Zwinglianism ('sacramentarianism'), especially at Calais. Even Cromwell (cf. Merriman, Life and Letters, II, 222 ff.) could only say that 'discreet and charitable punishment' should be applied to these sowers of sedition and division. This was also, of course, the time of the 'Catholic martyrs'.

[91] Burnet, History of the Reformation, IV, 278 ff.

Injunctions of that year, set out a formulary of faith (resting on the supreme head's authority) which made a few moves towards a compromise with the new ideas; the 'Bishops' Book' of 1537,[92] the Thirteen Articles of 1538 (which received no official authority),[93] and the Injunctions of that year may have marked a slightly greater distance from Wittenberg but were still far from Henrician orthodoxy. All this toing and froing, mingled with pamphleteering and diplomatic negotiations, produced a very unsettled atmosphere in the country; by 1539 Henry, always very sensitive to disturbances of the spirit which might undermine authority, had decided on a larger settlement; and prolonged discussions among bishops and divines resulted in victory for traditional orthodoxy. The outcome was a new heresy act—the Act of Six Articles (190).[94]

This act not only reasserted Catholic doctrine on disputed points,[95] but also established afresh the powers of episcopal courts to initiate trials for heresy without presentment by jury. The Commons, allegedly so hot against episcopal heresy trials some seven years before,[96] seem to have been convinced by this time that it was better for the ordinaries to be allowed a free hand than that the realm should be disrupted by religious dissension. Only in 1543 was it felt desirable again to limit prosecutions by laying down stricter rules as to procedure.[97] While Henry lived, the act remained the basis of the Church's faith; prosecutions for heresy started up again, though without much energy; in 1543 a new book of instruction, the 'King's Book', replaced the tentative Lutheranism of the 'Bishops' Book' by Catholic orthodoxy.[98] All these attempts to define doctrine rested entirely on the authority of the supreme head alone who promulgated them after taking advice from his spiritual counsellors and used Parliament only if he required the penal support of the law. The Act of Six Articles is directly in line with those heresy acts of Henry IV and Henry V which assisted a spiritual jurisdiction that had then derived from the pope.[99] It neatly illustrates Henry's quasi-papal position.

In 1547 the accession of Edward VI, brought up as an ardent Protestant and surrounded by a new generation of Protestant advisers, at once led to changes which, it would seem, his father had foreseen but determined to postpone until after his death. The Edwardian Reformation in religion pro-

---

[92] *Institution of a Christian Man*, a book of instruction and devotion. Cf. Hughes, *Reformation*, I, 355 f.; II, 30 ff.

[93] Rupp, *Protestant Tradition*, 117 f.

[94] For the making of the act cf. Elton, *Studies*, I, 206 ff.

[95] Some of its rigour was tempered a year later by 32 Henry VIII, c. 10.

[96] Cooper, *Eng. Hist. Rev.*, LXXII, 637 f.

[97] 35 Henry VIII, c. 5.

[98] *Necessary Doctrine and Erudition for any Christian Man*; cf. Hughes. *Reformation*, II, 46 ff.

[99] 2 Henry IV, c. 15; 2 Henry V, st. 1, c. 7.

ceeded in three stages. In 1547 Somerset got Parliament to permit communion in both kinds and to repeal the heresy laws (including the Act of Six Articles);[100] in the same year new Injunctions firmly pointed the Church in the direction of Protestantism.[101] Two years later Cranmer's labours produced the first Prayer Book of the Church of England, ushered in by an Act of Uniformity (191) which did not so much enforce its use as protect it from abuse. The Book was Protestant but moderately so—not enough to please the many continental advisers with whom Cranmer had surrounded himself.[102] This second stage was completed by an act permitting priests to marry,[103] another confirming the Prayer Book's monopoly by ordering the destruction of old service books;[104] and a third establishing a new ordination rite which denied full priesthood to the minister.[105] The fall of Somerset, the triumph of Northumberland and the extreme gentry, and Cranmer's steady move towards something very like Zwinglianism produced a last stage in the much more Protestant Prayer Book of 1552, enforced now by a vigorous and penal Act of Uniformity (192),[106] and supplemented by a formulary of faith in the Forty-two Articles of 1553.[107] Therewith the Church of England had been rendered officially Protestant: reformed, as later Puritans demanded it should be, by the example of the best reformed Churches, which in this case meant Zürich. It should be noted that the supremacy had now accepted parliamentary participation to a degree dangerous to the personal power of the supreme head, and that nearly all disputes and changes of the reign turned on the whole on essentials (doctrine and dogma). There was as yet no quarrel over Church government and little over externals.[108]

Whether the Edwardian Reformation could ever have been enforced in its uncompromising form on a country which was still predominantly attached to the old ways must remain an unresolved point. It was not given the chance: the accession of Mary in 1553 produced an immediate reaction. Her policy was simple enough: she returned to the condition of the Church before Henry VIII had begun all the trouble. The Protestant changes of her brother's reign were at once repealed (193) and in 1554 the old heresy laws were revived (194). In the same session the Parliament ratified England's reconciliation to Rome in the act which repealed the Henrician Reformation, though it safeguarded changes in landownership (183). For the rest the religious

---

[100] 1 Edward VI cc. 1, 12.   [101] Tanner, 101 ff.
[102] Hughes, *Reformation*, II, 105 ff.; Jordan, I, chs. 10 & 11.
[103] 2 & 3 Edward VI, c. 21 (Gee and Hardy, 366 ff.).
[104] 3 & 4 Edward VI, c. 10 (Tanner, 113 ff.).
[105] 3 & 4 Edward VI, c. 12 (cf. Hughes, *Reformation*, II, 113 ff.).
[106] Hughes, *Reformation*, II, 123 ff.; Jordan, II, ch. 9.
[107] Hughes, *Reformation*, II, 135 f.; Smyth, *Cranmer*, 257 ff.
[108] John Hooper raised the problem of vestments (Hughes, *Reformation*, II, 117 f.), and Ridley replaced altars by tables (Tanner, 115 f.).

policy of the reign concentrated on the suppression of heresy and restoration of Catholic uniformity in a wave of persecution which has marked Mary's name for ever—and not unjustly, for despite various apologetics the queen and her archbishop (Cardinal Pole) cannot be exonerated from a major share in the responsibility for the burnings.[109] If the capricious excesses of Edward's reign had done little to ensure the establishment of Protestantism in England, Mary's persecution created a general hatred of popery which, reinforced time and again, became the chief emotional (often irrational) factor in English politics for at least 150 years.

With Elizabeth's accession in November 1558 the country was once more called upon to change its course. The Elizabethan settlement of 1559 consisted of the Acts of Supremacy (**184**) and Uniformity (**195**), of which the second enforced the lasting Prayer Book of the Church of England. The settlement embodied the intentions of queen and Council, not a surrender to an extremer House of Commons.[110] The Prayer Book was essentially the more Protestant one of 1552 with certain modifications taken from that of 1549; especially it included a double definition of the sacrament of the altar which combined Catholic and Zwinglian forms of words, and a rubric on ornaments which authorised 'popish' ritual and vestments. The enforcement of the new order was, by the Injunctions of 1559 and the erection of an ecclesiastical commission,[111] entrusted to the bishops who proceeded to weed out objectors in the clergy by administering the oath of supremacy; the number deprived has been much disputed but was probably between 200 and 400 in a total of over 2000.[112] The promulgation of the Thirty-nine Articles, based on the Forty-two of 1553, in the Convocation of 1563 completed the basis of the Church of England.[113] It was a Church traditional (or Catholic) in structure, with its hierarchy of bishops and courts under the supreme governor, but in doctrine Protestant and indeed Calvinist. Its ritual owed much to the past, a fact which made it more readily accepted by the mass of the people though distasteful to those more eager Protestants whose desire to purify the Church earned them the name of Puritans. But it was a settlement grown out of politics and established by the queen in Parliament, and one which met attacks from several sides; except for Elizabeth herself, no one at

[109] The story of the reign may be read in Loades, *Mary Tudor*, esp. chs. 5 & 10; also Pogson, *Mid-Tudor Polity*, 116 ff.

[110] For the demolition of Neale, *Eng. Hist. Rev.*, LXV, 304 ff. cf. above, p. 310.

[111] Tanner, 104 f.; Gee and Hardy, 417. For the commissions, cf. above, pp. 221 f.

[112] Gee, *Elizabethan Clergy*, remains the authoritative review of this problem, but a new study would not come amiss.

[113] Haugaard, ch. 6. In 1566, the Commons tried to assert their part in the supremacy by promoting a bill to confirm the Articles; Elizabeth stopped them at the cost of losing several government bills (Neale, *Elizabeth and her Parliaments*, I, 166 ff.). In 1571 she let them proceed, and the Articles thus received statutory sanction (*ibid.*, 203 ff., 212). The act (13 Eliz. I, c. 12) is printed in Gee and Hardy, 477 ff.

first seems to have been attached to it without an air of apology—until time, enforcement and further study yielded up an intellectual and spiritual devotion best summed up in Hooker's *Ecclesiastical Polity* (**196**).[114]

190. An Act abolishing diversity in opinions (1539: 31 Henry VIII, c. 14).

Where the King's most excellent Majesty is by God's law supreme head immediately under Him of this whole Church and Congregation of England, intending the conservation of the same Church and Congregation in a true, sincere and uniform doctrine of Christ's religion, calling also to his blessed and most gracious remembrance as well the great and quiet assurance, prosperous increase and other innumerable commodities which have ever ensued, come and followed of concord, agreement and unity in opinions, as also the manifold perils, dangers and inconveniences which have heretofore in many places and regions grown, sprung and arisen of the diversities of minds and opinions, especially of matters of Christian religion; and therefore desiring that such an unity might and should be charitably established in all things touching and concerning the same, as the same so being established might chiefly be to the honour of Almighty God, the very author and fountain of all true unity and sincere concord, and consequently redound to the common wealth of this his Highness' most noble realm and of all his loving subjects and other resiants and inhabitants of or in the same: Hath therefore caused and commanded this his most High Court of Parliament for sundry and many urgent causes and considerations to be at this time summoned, and also a Synod and Convocation of all the archbishops, bishops and other learned men of the clergy of this his realm to be in like manner assembled; and forasmuch as in the said Parliament, Synod and Convocation there were certain articles, matters and questions proponed and set forth touching Christian religion. . . . The King's most royal Majesty, most prudently pondering and considering that by occasion of variable and sundry opinions and judgments of the said articles, great discord and variance hath arisen as well amongst the clergy of this his realm as amongst a great number of vulgar people his loving subjects of the same, and being in a full hope and trust that a full and perfect resolution of the said articles should make a perfect concord

[114] For the nation's experience of the Reformation cf. Palliser, *Church and Society*, 35 ff.; Luxton, *ibid.*, 57 ff.; and esp. Haigh, *Reformation and Resistance*.

and unity generally amongst all his loving and obedient subjects; of his most excellent goodness not only commanded that the said articles should deliberately and advisedly by his said archbishops, bishops and other learned men of his clergy be debated, argued and reasoned, and their opinions therein to be understood, declared and known, but also most graciously vouchsafed in his own princely person to descend and come into his said High Court of Parliament and Council, and there like a prince of most high prudence and no less learning opened and declared many things of high learning and great knowledge touching the said articles, matters and questions, for an unity to be had in the same; whereupon, after a great and long deliberate and advised disputation and consultation had and made concerning the said articles, as well by the consent of the King's Highness as by the assent of the Lords spiritual and temporal and other learned men of his clergy in their Convocation and by the consent of the Commons in this present Parliament assembled, it was and is finally resolved, accorded, and agreed in manner and form following, that is to say: First, that in the most blessed sacrament of the altar, by the strength and efficacy of Christ's mighty word, it being spoken by the priest, is present really, under the form of bread and wine, the natural body and blood of our Saviour Jesu Christ, conceived of the Virgin Mary, and that after the consecration there remaineth no substance of bread or wine, nor any other substance but the substance of Christ, God and man; Secondly, that communion in both kinds is not necessary *ad salutem* by the law of God to all persons, and that it is to be believed and not doubted of but that in the flesh under form of bread is the very blood, and with the blood under form of wine is the very flesh, as well apart as though they were both together; Thirdly, that priests after the order of priesthood received as afore may not marry by the law of God; Fourthly, that vows of chastity or widowhood by man or woman made to God advisedly ought to be observed by the law of God, and that it exempteth them from other liberties of Christian people which without that they might enjoy; Fifthly, that it is meet and necessary that private masses be continued and admitted in this the King's English Church and Congregation as whereby good Christian people ordering themselves accordingly do receive both godly and goodly consolations and benefits, and it is agreeable also to God's law; Sixthly, that auricular confession is expedient and necessary to be retained and continued, used and frequented, in the Church of God. For the which most godly study, pain and travail of his Majesty and determination and resolution of the premises, his most humble and obedient subjects, the Lords spiritual and temporal and the Commons in this present Parliament assembled not only render and give unto his Highness their most high and hearty thanks ... but also being desirous that his most godly enterprise may be well accomplished and brought to a full end and perfection, and so established that the same might be to the honour of God, and after to the common quiet, unity and concord to be had in the whole body of this realm for ever, most humbly beseechen his royal Majesty that the resolution and determination above written of the said articles may be established and perpetually perfected by authority of this present Parliament. It is therefore ordained and enacted by the King our sovereign lord, the Lords spiritual and temporal, and the Commons in this present Parliament assembled, and by authority of the same. . . .

[I. Any who after 12 July 1539 in word, writing or printing 'publish, preach, teach, say, affirm, declare, dispute, argue or hold' contrary to the first article, as well as their supporters, shall be guilty of heresy and burned.

II. Any who preach, teach or affirm publicly contrary to the other five articles, or any priest who, having vowed chastity, shall marry, shall be guilty of felony without benefit of clergy.

III. Any who shall otherwise maintain (in speech, writing, printing etc.) opinions contrary to the other five articles shall forfeit all their property and be imprisoned at the King's pleasure; for a second offence they shall be guilty of felony.

IV. Marriages of priests and persons who have taken vows of chastity and widowhood are void.

* * * * * *

VI. Persons refusing to confess or receive the sacrament at the normal times shall be fined and imprisoned by the Council; a second offence to be felony.

VII. Enforcement is committed to special periodic commissions directed by the King to archbishops and bishops.

VIII. This shall not bar the ordinary power of the ecclesiastical courts to enquire into offences under this act; and justices of the peace and others are also authorised to make enquiry by the verdict of a jury.]

* * * * * *

Stat. Realm, III, 739–43

191. An Act for the uniformity of service and administration of the sacraments throughout the realm (First act of uniformity 1549: 2 & 3 Ed. VI, c. 1).

Where of long time there hath been had in this realm of England and Wales divers forms of common prayer commonly called the service of the Church, that is to say, the use of Sarum, of York, of Bangor and of Lincoln; and besides the same now of late much more divers and sundry forms and fashions have been used in the cathedral and parish churches of England and Wales, as well concerning the matins or morning prayer and the evensong, as also concerning the holy communion commonly called the mass, with divers and sundry rites and ceremonies concerning the same and in the administration of other sacraments of the Church; and as the doers and executors of the said rites and ceremonies in other form than of late years they have been used were pleased therewith, so other not using the same rites and ceremonies were thereby greatly offended; and albeit the King's Majesty, with the advice of his most entirely beloved uncle the Lord Protector and other of his Highness' Council, hath heretofore divers times assayed to stay innovations or new rites concerning the premises, yet the same hath not had such good success as his Highness required in that behalf; whereupon his Highness by the most prudent advice aforesaid, being pleased to bear with the frailty and weakness of his subjects in that behalf, of his great clemency hath not been only content to abstain from punishment of those that have offended in that behalf, for that his Highness taketh that they did it of a good zeal, but also to the intent a uniform, quiet and godly order should be had concerning the premises, hath appointed the archbishop of Canterbury and certain of the most learned and discreet bishops and other learned men of this realm to consider and ponder the premises, and thereupon having as well eye and respect to the most sincere and pure Christian religion taught by the Scripture as to the usages in the primitive Church, should draw and make one convenient and meet order, rite and fashion of common and open prayer and administration of the sacraments, to be had and used in his Majesty's realm of England and in Wales; the which at this time, by the aid of the Holy Ghost, with one uniform agreement is of them concluded, set forth and delivered to his Highness, to his great comfort and quietness of mind, in a book entitled The Book of the Common Prayer and Administration of the Sacraments and other Rites and

Ceremonies of the Church after the Use of the Church of England. Wherefore the Lords spiritual and temporal and the Commons in this present Parliament assembled, considering as well the most godly travail of the King's Highness, of the Lord Protector, and other of his Highness' Council, in gathering and collecting the said archbishop, bishops and learned men together, as the godly prayers, orders, rites and ceremonies in the said book mentioned, and the considerations of altering those things which be altered and retaining those things which be retained in the said book, but also the honour of God and great quietness which by the grace of God shall ensue upon the one and uniform rite and order in such common prayer and rites and extern ceremonies, to be used throughout England and in Wales, at Calais and the marches of the same, do give to his Highness most hearty and lowly thanks for the same, and humbly pray that it may be ordained and enacted by his Majesty, with the assent of the Lords and Commons in this present Parliament assembled and by the authority of the same, that all and singular person and persons that have offended concerning the premises, other than such person and persons as now be and remain in ward in the Tower of London or in the Fleet, may be pardoned thereof; and that all and singular ministers in any cathedral or parish church, or other place within this realm of England, Wales, Calais and marches of the same, or other the King's dominions, shall from and after the feast of Pentecost next coming be bounden to say and use the matins, evensong, celebration of the Lord's Supper commonly called the mass, and administration of each of the sacraments, and all their common and open prayer, in such order and form as is mentioned in the said book and none other or otherwise.

II. Albeit that the same be so godly and good that they give occasion to every honest and conformable man most willingly to embrace them, yet lest any obstinate person who willingly would disturb so godly order and quiet in this realm should not go unpunished, that it may also be ordained and enacted by the authority aforesaid that if any manner of parson, vicar or other whatsoever minister that ought or should sing or say common prayer mentioned in the said book or minister the sacraments, shall after the said feast of Pentecost next coming refuse to use the said common prayers or to minister the sacraments in such cathedral or parish church or other places as he should use or minister the same, in such order and form as they be mentioned and set forth in the said book, or shall use, wilfully and obstinately standing in the same, any other rite, ceremony, order, form or manner of mass, openly or privily, or matins, evensong, administration of the sacraments or other open prayer than is mentioned and set forth in the said book (open prayer in and throughout this act is meant that prayer which is for other to come unto and hear, either in common churches or private chapels or oratories, commonly called the service of the Church); or shall preach, declare or speak anything in the derogation or depraving of the said book or anything therein contained or of any part thereof, and shall be thereof lawfully convicted according to the laws of this realm by verdict of twelve men, or by his own confession, or by the notorious evidence of the fact, shall lose and forfeit to the King's Highness, his heirs and successors, for his first offence the profit of such one of his spiritual benefices or promotions as it shall please the King's Highness to assign or appoint coming and arising in one whole year next after his conviction; and also that the same person so convicted shall for the same offence suffer imprisonment by the space of six months without bail or mainprize; and if any such person once convict of any offence concerning the premises shall after his first conviction eftsoons offend and be thereof in form aforesaid lawfully convict, that then the same person shall for his second offence suffer imprisonment by the space of one whole year, and also shall therefore be deprived *ipso facto* of all his spiritual promotions; and that it shall be lawful to all patrons, donors and grantees of all and singular the same spiritual promotions to present to the same any other able clerk in like manner and form as though the party so offending were dead. And that if any such person or persons, after he shall be twice convicted in form aforesaid, shall offend against any of the premises the third time and shall be thereof in form aforesaid lawfully convicted, that then the person so offending and convicted the third time shall suffer imprisonment during his life. And if the person that shall offend or be convict in form aforesaid concerning any of the premises shall not be beneficed nor have any spiritual promotion, that then the same person so offending and convict shall for the first offence suffer imprisonment during six months without bail or mainprize; and if any such person not having any spiritual promotion after his first conviction shall eftsoons offend in anything concerning the premises and shall in form aforesaid be thereof lawfully convicted, that then the same person shall for his second offence suffer imprisonment during his life.

III. And it is ordained and enacted by the authority above-said that if any person or persons whatsoever, after the said feast of Pentecost next coming, shall in any interludes, plays, songs, rhymes or by other open words declare or speak anything in the derogation, depraving or despising of the same book or of anything therein contained or any part thereof, or shall by open fact, deed, or by open threatenings compel or cause or otherwise procure or maintain any parson, vicar or other minister, in any cathedral or parish church or in any chapel or other place, to sing or say any common and open prayer or to minister any sacrament otherwise or in any other manner or form than is mentioned in the said book, or that by any of the said means shall unlawfully interrupt or let any parson, vicar or other ministers in any cathedral or parish church, chapel, or any other place to sing or say common and open prayer or to minister the sacraments or any of them in any such manner and form as is mentioned in the said book [he shall be fined £10 or suffer three months' imprisonment for the first offence, and £20 or six months for the second; and forfeiture of goods with imprisonment for life for the third].

* * * * * *

VI. Provided always that it shall be lawful to any man that understandeth the Greek, Latin and Hebrew tongue, or other strange tongue, to say and have the said prayers heretofore specified of matins and evensong in Latin or any such other tongue, saying the same privately as they do understand. And for the further encouraging of learning in the tongues in the Universities of Cambridge and Oxford, to use and exercise in their common and open prayer in their chapels, being no parish churches or other places of prayer, the matins, evensong, litany and all other prayers, the holy communion commonly called the mass excepted, prescribed in the said book, in Greek, Latin or Hebrew; anything in this present act to the contrary notwithstanding.

* * * * * *

[XII–XIII. Offences may be punished by the ecclesiastical courts using spiritual weapons, providing a first offence is punished only once, either by the spiritual or the temporal court.]   *Stat. Realm*, IV, 37–9

192. An Act for the uniformity of common prayer and administration of the sacraments (Second act of uniformity 1552: 5 & 6 Ed. VI, c. 1).

Where there hath been a very goodly order set forth by authority of Parliament for common prayer and the administration of the sacraments, to be used in the mother tongue within the Church of England, agreeable to the word of God and the primitive Church, very comfortable to all good people desiring to live in Christian conversation, and most profitable to the estate of this realm, upon the which the mercy, favour and blessing of Almighty God is in no wise so readily and plenteously poured as by common prayers, due using of the sacraments, and often preaching of gospel, with the devotion of the hearers; and yet this notwithstanding, a great number of people in divers parts of this realm, following their own sensuality and living either without knowledge or due fear of God, do wilfully and damnably before Almighty God abstain and refuse to come to their parish churches and other places where common prayer, administration of the sacraments and preaching of the word of God is used, upon the Sundays and other days ordained to be holy days: For reformation hereof be it enacted by the King our sovereign lord with the assent of the Lords and Commons in this present Parliament assembled, and by the authority of the same, that from and after the feast of All Saints next coming, all and every person and persons inhabiting within this realm or any other the King's Majesty's dominions, shall diligently and faithfully, having no lawful or reasonable excuse to be absent, endeavour themselves to resort to their parish church or chapel accustomed, or upon reasonable let thereof to some usual place where common prayer and such service of God shall be used in such time of let, upon every Sunday and other days ordained and used to be kept as holy days, and then and there to abide orderly and soberly during the time of the common prayer, preachings or other service of God there to be used and ministered; upon pain of punishment by the censures of the Church.

II. And for the due execution hereof the King's most excellent Majesty, the Lords temporal, and all the Commons in this present assembled, doth in God's name earnestly require and charge all the archbishops, bishops and other ordinaries that they shall endeavour themselves to the uttermost of their knowledge that the due and true execution hereof may be had throughout their dioceses and charges, as they will answer before God for such evils and plagues wherewith Almighty God may justly punish his people for neglecting this good and wholesome law.

III. And for their authority in this behalf, be it further likewise enacted by the authority aforesaid that all and singular the same archbishops, bishops, and all other their officers exercising ecclesiastical jurisdiction, as well in place exempt as not exempt within their diocese, shall have full power and authority by this act to reform, correct and punish by censures of the Church all and singular persons which shall offend within any their jurisdictions or dioceses after the said feast of All Saints next coming against this act and statute; any other law, statute, privilege, liberty or provision heretofore made, had or suffered to the contrary notwithstanding.

IV. And because there hath arisen in the use and exercise of the foresaid common service in the Church heretofore set forth divers doubts for the fashion and manner of the ministration of the same, rather by the curiosity of the minister and mistakers than of any other worthy cause; therefore as well for the more plain and manifest explanation hereof as for the more perfection of the said order of common service, in some places where it is necessary to make the same prayers and fashion of service more earnest and fit to stir Christian people to the true honouring of Almighty God, the King's most excellent Majesty, with the assent of the Lords and Commons in this present Parliament assembled and by the authority of the same, hath caused the foresaid order of common service entitled The Book of Common Prayer to be faithfully and goodly perused, explained and made fully perfect, and by the foresaid authority hath annexed and joined it so explained and perfected to this present statute, adding also a form and manner of making and consecrating archbishops, bishops, priests and deacons, to be of like force, authority and value as the same like foresaid book entitled The Book of Common Prayer was before, and to be accepted, received, used and esteemed in like sort and manner, and with the same clauses of provisions and exceptions to all intents, constructions and purposes, as by the act of Parliament made in the second year of the King's Majesty's reign was ordained and limited, expressed and appointed, for the Uniformity of Service and Administration of the Sacraments throughout the Realm,[115] upon such several pains as in the said act of Parliament is expressed: and the said former act to stand in full force and strength

[115] Doc. 191.

to all intents and constructions, and to be applied, practised and put in ure to and for the establishing of the Book of Common Prayer now explained and hereunto annexed, and also the said form of making of archbishops, bishops, priests and deacons hereunto annexed, as it was for the former book.

v. And by the authority aforesaid it is now further enacted, that if any manner of person or persons inhabiting and being within this realm or any other the King's Majesty's dominions shall after the said feast of All Saints willingly and wittingly hear and be present at any other manner or form of common prayer, of administration of the sacraments, of making of ministers in the churches, or of any other rites contained in the book annexed to this act than is mentioned and set forth in the said book or that is contrary to the form of sundry provisions and exceptions contained in the foresaid former statute, and shall be thereof convicted according to the laws of this realm before the justices of assize, justices of oyer and terminer, justices of peace in their sessions, or any of them, by the verdict of twelve men or by his or their own confession or otherwise, shall for the first offence suffer imprisonment for six months without bail or mainprize, and for the second offence being likewise convicted as is abovesaid imprisonment for one whole year, and for the third offence in like manner imprisonment during his or their lives.

vi. And for the more knowledge to be given hereof and better observation of this law, be it enacted by the authority aforesaid that all and singular curates shall upon one Sunday every quarter of the year, during one whole year next following the foresaid feast of All Saints next coming, read this present act in the church at the time of the most assembly, and likewise once in every year following; at the same time declaring unto the people by the authority of the Scripture how the mercy and goodness of God hath in all ages been shewed to his people in their necessities and extremities by means of hearty and faithful prayers made to Almighty God, especially where people be gathered together with one faith and mind to offer up their hearts by prayer, as the best sacrifices that Christian men can yield.   *Stat. Realm*, IV, 130-1

193. An Act for the repeal of certain statutes made in the time of the reign of King Edward VI (1553: 1 Mary, st. 2, c. 2).

Forasmuch as by divers and several acts hereafter mentioned, as well the divine service and good administration of the sacraments as divers other matters of religion which we and our forefathers found in this Church of England to us left by the authority of the Catholic Church, be partly altered and in some part taken from us, and in place thereof new things imagined and set forth by the said acts, such as a few of singularity have of themselves devised, whereof hath ensued amongst us in very short time numbers of divers and strange opinions and diversities of sects, and thereby grown great unquietness and much discord, to the great disturbance of the common wealth of this realm, and in very short time like to grow to extreme peril and utter confusion of the same unless some remedy be in that behalf provided, which thing all true, loving and obedient subjects ought and are bounden to foresee and provide to the uttermost of their power: In consideration whereof be it enacted and established by the Queen's Highness, the Lords spiritual and temporal and the Commons in this present Parliament assembled, and by the authority of the same, that [the following acts be repealed: 1 Edw. VI. c. 1, concerning the sacrament of the altar; 1 Edw. VI, c. 2, concerning the election of bishops; 2 & 3 Edw. VI, c. 1, the first act of uniformity; 2 & 3 Edw. VI, c. 21, concerning the marriage of priests; 3 & 4 Edw. VI, c. 10, concerning images; 3 & 4 Edw. VI, c. 12, 'An act for the ordering of ecclesiastical ministers'; 5 & 6 Edw. VI, c. 1, the second act of uniformity; 5 & 6 Edw. VI, c. 3, 'An act for the keeping of holy days and fasting days'; and 5 & 6 Edw. VI, c. 12, a declaratory act concerning the marriage of priests].

II. And be it further enacted by the authority aforesaid that all such divine service and administration of sacraments as were most commonly used in the realm of England in the last year of the reign of our late sovereign lord King Henry the Eighth, shall be, from and after the 20th day of December in this present year of our Lord God 1553, used and frequented through the whole realm of England and all other the Queen's Majesty's dominions; and that no other kind nor order of divine service nor administration of sacraments be after the said 20th day of December used or ministered in any other manner, form or degree within the said realm of England or other the Queen's dominions than was most commonly used, ministered and frequented in the said last year of the reign of the said late King Henry the Eighth.

* * * * * *

Stat. Realm, IV, 202

194. An Act for the renewing of three statutes made for the punishment of heresies (1554: 1 & 2 Philip & Mary, c. 6).

For the eschewing and avoiding of errors and heresies which of late have risen, grown and much increased within this realm, for that the ordinaries have wanted authority to proceed against those that were infected therewith: Be it therefore ordained and enacted by the authority of this present Parliament that the statute made in the fifth year of the reign of King Richard the Second concerning the arresting and apprehension of erroneous and heretical preachers,[116] and one other statute made in the second year of the reign of King Henry the Fourth concerning the repressing of heresies and punishment of heretics,[117] And also one other statute made in the second year of the reign of King Henry the Fifth concerning the suppression of heresy and Lollardy,[118] and every article, branch and sentence contained in the same three several acts and every of them, shall from the 20th day of January next coming be revived and be in full force, strength and effect, to all intents, constructions and purposes for ever. _Stat. Realm_, IV, 244

195. An Act for the uniformity of common prayer and divine service in the Church, and the administration of the sacraments (Act of Uniformity 1559: 1 Eliz. I, c. 2).

Where at the death of our late sovereign lord King Edward the Sixth there remained one uniform order of common service and prayer and of the administration of sacraments, rites and ceremonies in the Church of England, which was set forth in one book entitled The Book of Common Prayer and Administration of Sacraments and other Rites and Ceremonies in the Church of England, authorised by act of Parliament holden in the fifth and sixth years of our said late sovereign lord King Edward the Sixth, entitled An Act for the Uniformity of Common Prayer and Administration of the Sacraments;[119] the which was repealed and taken away by act of Parliament in the first year of the reign of our late sovereign lady Queen Mary,[120] to the great decay of the due honour of God and discomfort to the professors of the truth of Christ's religion: Be it therefore enacted by the authority of this

[116] 5 Ric. II, c. 5 (1382).
[117] 2 Henry IV, c. 15 (1401). [118] 2 Henry V, c. 7 (1414).
[119] Doc. 192. [120] Doc. 193.

present Parliament that the said statute of repeal and everything therein contained only concerning the said book and the service, administration of sacraments, rites and ceremonies contained or appointed in or by the said book shall be void and of none effect from and after the feast of the Nativity of St John Baptist next coming; and that the said book with the order of service and of the administration of sacraments, rites and ceremonies, with the alteration and additions therein added and appointed by this statute shall stand and be from and after the said feast . . . in full force and effect according to the tenor and effect of this statute; anything in the aforesaid statute of repeal to the contrary notwithstanding.

II. And further be it enacted by the Queen's Highness, with the assent of the Lords and Commons in this present Parliament assembled and by authority of the same, that all and singular ministers in any cathedral or parish church or other place within this realm of England, Wales and the marches of the same, or other the Queen's dominions, shall, from and after the feast of the Nativity of St John Baptist next coming, be bounden to say and use the matins, evensong, celebration of the Lord's Supper and administration of each of the sacraments, and all their common and open prayer, in such order and form as is mentioned in the said book so authorised by Parliament in the said fifth and sixth year of the reign of King Edward the Sixth, with one alteration or addition of certain lessons to be used on every Sunday in the year, and the form of the Litany altered and corrected, and two sentences only added in the delivery of the sacrament to the communicants, and none other or otherwise. And that if any manner of parson, vicar or other whatsoever minister that ought or should sing or say common prayer mentioned in the said book, or minister the sacraments, from and after the feast of the Nativity of St John Baptist next coming, refuse to use the said common prayers or to minister the sacraments in such cathedral or parish church or other places as he should use to minister the same, in such order and form as they be mentioned and set forth in the said book, or shall wilfully or obstinately (standing in the same) use any other rite, ceremony, order, form or manner of celebrating of the Lord's Supper openly or privily, or matins, evensong, administration of the sacraments, or other open prayers than is mentioned and set forth in the said book (open prayer in and throughout this act is meant that prayer which is for other to come unto or hear, either in common churches or private chapels or oratories, commonly called the service of the Church) or shall preach, declare or speak anything in the derogation or depraving of the said book or anything therein contained, or of any part thereof, and shall be thereof lawfully convicted according to the laws of this realm by verdict of twelve men, or by his own confession, or by the notorious evidence of the fact [he shall suffer penalties as follows: first offence, forfeiture of one year's profit of his 'spiritual benefices or promotions' and six months' imprisonment; second offence, one year's imprisonment and deprivation; third offence, deprivation and imprisonment for life. If not beneficed, for the first offence, one year's imprisonment, and for the second, imprisonment for life.]

III. And it is ordained and enacted by the authority abovesaid, that if any person or persons whatsoever after the said feast . . . shall in any interludes, plays, songs, rhymes, or by other open words, declare or speak anything in the derogation, depraving or despising of the same book, or of anything therein contained, or any part thereof, or shall by open fact, deed, or by open threatenings, compel or cause or otherwise procure or maintain any parson, vicar or other minister in any cathedral or parish church or in chapel or in any other place to sing or say any common or open prayer or to minister any sacrament otherwise or in any other manner and form than is mentioned in the said book, or that by any of the said means shall unlawfully interrupt or let any parson, vicar or other minister in any cathedral or parish church, chapel, or any other place to sing or say common and open prayer, or to minister the sacraments or any of them, in such manner and form as is mentioned in the said book, that then every such person being thereof lawfully convicted in form abovesaid [shall be subject to penalties as follows: first offence, 100 marks; second offence, 400 marks; third offence, forfeiture of goods and imprisonment for life; on non-payment of fines for the first and second offences, imprisonment for six and twelve months respectively]. And that from and after the said feast . . . all and every person and persons inhabiting within this realm or any other the Queen's Majesty's dominions, shall diligently and faithfully, having no lawful or reasonable excuse to be absent, endeavour themselves to resort to their parish church or chapel accustomed, or upon reasonable let thereof, to some usual place where common prayer and such service of God shall be used in such time of let, upon every Sunday and other days ordained and used to be kept as holy days, and then and there to abide orderly and soberly during the time of the common prayer, preachings or other service of God there to be used and ministered;

upon pain of punishment by the censures of the Church, and also upon pain that every person so offending shall forfeit for every such offence twelve pence, to be levied by the churchwardens of the parish where such offence shall be done, to the use of the poor of the same parish, of the goods, lands and tenements of such offender by way of distress.

* * * * * *

XIII. Provided always and be it enacted that such ornaments of the church and of the ministers thereof shall be retained and be in use as was in the Church of England by authority of Parliament in the second year of the reign of King Edward the Sixth until other order shall be therein taken by the authority of the Queen's Majesty, with the advice of her commissioners appointed and authorised under the great seal of England for causes ecclesiastical or of the metropolitan of this realm; and also that if there shall happen any contempt or irreverence to be used in the ceremonies or rites of the Church by the misusing of the orders appointed in this book, the Queen's Majesty may, by the like advice of the said commissioners or metropolitan, ordain and publish such further ceremonies or rites as may be most for the advancement of God's glory, the edifying of his Church, and the due reverence of Christ's holy mysteries and sacraments.

XIV. And be it further enacted by the authority aforesaid that all laws, statutes and ordinances wherein or whereby any other service, administration of sacraments, or common prayer is limited, established or set forth to be used within this realm or any other the Queen's dominions or countries, shall from henceforth be utterly void and of none effect.   *Stat. Realm*, IV, 355–8

196. Richard Hooker on the Church of England (*c.* 1590).

The Preface

. . . Under the happy reign of her Majesty which now is, the greatest matter awhile contended for was the wearing of the cap and surplice, till there came Admonitions directed unto the High Court of Parliament[121] by men who, concealing their names, thought it glory enough to discover their minds and affections, which now were universally bent even against all the orders and laws wherein this Church is found uncon-

[121] Cf. Docs. 203–4.

formable to the platform of Geneva. Concerning the defender of which Admonitions all that I mean to say is but this: *There will come a time when three words uttered with charity and meekness shall receive a far more blessed reward than three thousand volumes written with disdainful sharpness of wit.* But the manner of men's writing must not alienate our hearts from the truth, if it appears they have the truth . . . [c. 2, § 10].

. . . Weigh what doth move the common sort so much to favour this innovation, and it shall soon appear unto you that the force of particular reasons which for your several opinions are alleged is a thing whereof the multitude never did nor could so consider as to be therewith wholly carried; but certain general inducements are used to make saleable your cause in gross, and when once men have cast a fancy towards it any slight declaration of specialties will serve to lead forward men's inclinable and prepared minds. The method of winning the people's affection unto a general liking of 'the cause' (for so ye term it) hath been this. First, in the hearing of the multitude the faults especially of higher callings are ripped up with marvellous exceeding severity and sharpness of reproof; which being oftentimes done, begetteth a great good opinion of integrity, zeal and holiness to such constant reprovers of sin, as by likelihood would never be so much offended at that which is evil unless themselves were singularly good. The next thing hereunto is to impute all faults and corruptions wherewith the world aboundeth unto the kind of ecclesiastical government established. Wherein, as before by reproving faults they purchased unto themselves with the multitude a name to be virtuous, so by finding out this kind of cause they obtain to be judged wise above others. . . . Having gotten thus much sway in the hearts of men, a third step is to propose their own form of Church government as the only sovereign remedy of all evils, and to adorn it with all the glorious titles that may be. And the nature, as of men that have sick bodies so likewise of the people in the crazedness of their minds, possessed with dislike and discontentment at things present, is to imagine that anything (the virtue whereof they hear commended) would help them, but that most which they least have tried. The fourth degree of inducements is by fashioning the very notions and conceits of men's minds in such sort that when they read the Scripture they may think that everything soundeth towards the advancement of that discipline and to the utter disgrace of the contrary. . . . [c. 3, §§ 5–9].

The First Book : concerning laws and their several kinds in general

He that goeth about to persuade a multitude that they are not so well governed as they ought to be shall never want attentive and favourable hearers; because they know the manifold defects whereunto every kind of regiment is subject, but the secret lets and difficulties, which in public proceedings are innumerable and inevitable, they have not ordinarily the judgment to consider. And because such as openly reprove supposed disorders of state are taken for principal friends to the common benefit of all, and for men that carry singular freedom of mind, under this fair and plausible colour whatsoever they utter passeth for good and current. That which wanteth in the weight of their speech is supplied by the aptness of men's minds to accept and believe it. Whereas on the other side, if we maintain things that are established, we have not only to strive with a number of heavy prejudices deeply rooted in the hearts of men, who think that herein we serve the time and speak in favour of the present state because thereby we either hold or seek preferment, but also to bear such exceptions and minds so averted beforehand usually take against that which they are loath should be poured into them. [c. 1, § 1.]

The Second Book: concerning their first position who urge reformation in the Church of England, namely that Scripture is the only rule of all things which in this life may be done by men.

. . . There is no necessity that if I confess I ought not to do that which the Scripture forbiddeth me, I should thereby acknowledge myself bound to do nothing which the Scripture commandeth me not. For many inducements besides Scripture may lead me to that which, if Scripture be against, they all give place and are of no value, yet otherwise are strong and effectual to persuade . . . [c. 5, § 7].

The Third Book: concerning their second assertion, that in Scripture there must be of necessity contained a form of Church polity the laws whereof may in no wise be altered.

. . . Now as it can be to nature no injury that of her we say the same which diligent beholders of her works have observed, namely that she provideth for all living creatures nourishment which may suffice, that she bringeth forth no kind of creature whereto she is wanting in that which is needful; although we do not so far magnify her exceeding bounty as to affirm that she bringeth into the world the sons of men adorned with gorgeous attire or maketh costly buildings to spring up out of the earth for them. So I trust that to mention what the Scripture of God leaveth unto the Church's discretion in some things is not in anything to impair the honour which the Church of God yieldeth to the sacred Scripture's perfection. Wherein seeing that no more is by us maintained than only that Scripture must needs teach the Church whatsoever is in such sort necessary as hath been set down, and that it is no more disgrace for Scripture to have left a number of other things free to be ordered at the discretion of the Church than for nature to have left it unto the wit of man to devise his own attire and not to look for it as the beasts of the field have theirs . . . [c. 4, § 1].

. . . They which first gave out that *Nothing ought to be established in the Church which is not commanded by the Word of God*, thought this principle plainly warranted by the manifest words of the law. . . . Wherefore having an eye to a number of rites and orders in the Church of England, as marrying with a ring, crossing in the one sacrament, kneeling at the other, observing of festival days more than only that which is called the Lord's Day, enjoining abstinence at certain times from some kinds of meat, churching of women after childbirth, degrees taken by divines in universities, sundry Church offices, dignities and callings, for which they found no commandment in the holy Scripture, they thought by the one only stroke of that axiom to have cut them off. But that which they took for an oracle, being sifted was repelled . . . [c. 5, § 1].

. . . In the Church of the Jews is it not granted that the appointment of the hour for daily sacrifices, the building of synagogues throughout the land to hear the Word of God and to pray in when they came not up to Jerusalem, the erecting of pulpits and chairs to teach in, the order of burial, the rites of marriage, with such like, being matters appertaining to the Church, yet are not anywhere prescribed in the law but were by the Church's discretion instituted? What then shall we think? Did they hereby add to the law, and so displease God by that which they did? None so hardly persuaded of them. . . . Sundry things may be lawfully done in the Church, so as they be not done against the Scripture, although no Scripture do command them, but the Church, only following the light of reason, judge them to be in discretion meet. . . . So that free and lawful it is to devise any ceremony, to receive any order, and to authorise any kind of regiment, no special commandment being thereby violated, and the same being thought such by them to whom the judgment thereof appertaineth, as that it is not scandalous but decent, tending unto edification, and setting forth the glory of God . . . [c, 7, §§ 2–4].

The Fourth Book: concerning their third assertion, that our form of Church polity is corrupted with popish orders, rites and ceremonies, banished out of certain reformed Churches, whose example therein we ought to have followed.

. . . Concerning rites and ceremonies, there may be fault either in the kind or in the number and multitude of them. The first thing blamed about the kind of ours is that in many things we have departed from the ancient simplicity of Christ and his apostles, we have embraced more outward stateliness, we have those orders in the exercise of religion which they who best pleased God and served him most devoutly never had. For it is out of doubt that the first state of things was best, that in the prime of Christian religion faith was soundest, the Scriptures of God were then best understood by all men, all parts of godliness did then most abound; and therefore it must needs follow that customs, laws and ordinances devised since are not so good for the Church of Christ, but the best way is to cut off later inventions and to reduce things unto the ancient state wherein at the first they were. Which rule or canon we hold to be either uncertain or at leastwise insufficient, if not both. For in case it be certain, hard it cannot be for them to shew us where we shall find it so exactly set down that we may say without controversy, *These were the orders of the apostles' times, these wholly and only, neither fewer nor more than these.* . . . So that in tying the Church to the orders of the apostles' times they tie it to a marvellous uncertain rule, unless they require the observation of no orders but only those which are known to be apostolical by the apostles' own writings. But then is not this their rule of such sufficiency that we should use it as a touchstone to try the orders of the Church by for ever. Our end ought always to be the same; our ways and means thereunto not so. The glory of God and the good of his Church was the thing which the apostles aimed at and therefore ought to be the mark whereat we also level. But seeing those rites and orders may be at one time more which at another time are less available unto that purpose, what reason is there in these things to urge the state of our only age as a pattern for all to follow? It is not, I am right sure, their meaning that we should now assemble our people to serve God in close and secret meetings; or that common brooks or rivers should be used for places of baptism; or that the eucharist should be ministered after meat; or that the custom of church-feasting should be renewed; or that all kinds of standing provision for the ministry should be utterly taken away and their estate made again dependent upon the voluntary devotion of men. In these things they easily perceive how unfit that were for the present which was for the first age convenient enough . . . [c. 2, §§ 1–3].

The Fifth Book: Of their fourth assertion, that touching the several public duties of Christian religion there is amongst us much superstition retained in them; and concerning persons which for performance of those duties are endued with the power of ecclesiastical order, our laws and proceedings according thereunto are many ways herein also corrupt.

. . . But howsoever superstition do grow, that wherein unsounder times have done amiss the better ages ensuing must rectify as they may. I now come therefore to those accusations brought against us by pretenders of reformation. . . . For so it is judged, our prayers, our sacraments, our fasts, our times and places of public worship and service of God, our marriages, our burials, our functions, elections and ordinations ecclesiastical, almost whatsoever we do in the exercise of our religion according to laws for that purpose established, all things are some way or other thought faulty, all things stained with superstition . . . [c. 4, §1].
. . . That which inwardly each man should be, the Church outwardly ought to testify. And therefore the duties of our religion which are seen must be such as that affection which is unseen ought to be. Signs must resemble the things they signify. If religion bear the greatest sway in our hearts, our outward religious duties must shew it as far as the Church hath outward ability. Duties of religion performed by whole societies of men ought to have in them according to our power a sensible excellency correspondent to the majesty of him whom we worship. Yea, then are the public duties of religion best ordered when the militant Church doth resemble by sensible means, as it may in such cases, that hidden dignity and glory wherewith the Church triumphant in heaven is beautified. . . . Let our first demand be therefore that in the external form of religion such things as are apparently, or can be

sufficiently, proved effectual and generally fit to set forward godliness, either as betokening the greatness of God, or as beseeming the dignity of religion, or as concurring with celestial impressions in the minds of men, may be reverently thought of, some few, rare, casual and tolerable or otherwise curable inconveniences notwithstanding [c. 6, § 2].

Neither may we in this case lightly esteem what hath been allowed as fit in the judgment of antiquity and by the long continued practice of the whole Church, from which unnecessarily to swerve, experience hath never as yet found it safe. . . . In which consideration there is cause why we should be slow and unwilling to change, without very urgent necessity, the ancient ordinances, rites and long approved customs of our venerable predecessors. The love of things ancient doth argue stayedness; but levity and want of experience maketh apt unto innovations. . . . All things cannot be of ancient continuance which are expedient and needful for the ordering of spiritual affairs; but the Church, being a body which dieth not, hath always power, as occasion requireth, no less to ordain that which never was than to ratify what hath been before . . . [c. 7, §§ 1, 3; c. 8, § 1].

Ecclesiastical Polity (*Works*, I, 141–2, 146–7, 198, 308, 357–9, 361–3, 421–3; II, 26, 29–30, 32, 33)

V. THE CATHOLIC THREAT

The Elizabethan Church came under attack from two sides: neither Puritans nor Catholics could be satisfied with it. Of the two, the Catholic threat seemed the more serious at the time to most people, especially because it was linked with the succession problem and with international rivalries. From 1568 Mary Queen of Scots, exiled in England, provided a centre for disaffection; and increasingly, as the reign wore on, Spain came to be thought of as the national and religious enemy. Inasmuch as the threat came from outside it cannot here concern us; but since Elizabeth never solved the problem of a surviving minority of Catholics in England, issues of government were raised by the battle with Rome.[122] At first it looked as though there would

[122] For surveys cf. McGrath, *Papists and Puritans* and Pritchard, *Loyalism*. Meyer, *England and the Catholic Church* remains useful. For general interpretation cf. Bossy, *Past and Present*, XXI, 39 ff. Particular studies abound in the journal *Recusant History*; for Lancashire cf. Haigh, *Reformation and Resistance*, and for Yorkshire Aveling, *Northern Catholics*. The leadership abroad is studied in Loomie, *Spanish Elizabethans*. Trimble, *Laity* (to be used with care) emphasises the absence of serious conflict at the personal level. There is an argument over the degree to which post-Reformation Catholicism represented a continuation of pre-Reformation belief. Bossy, *Catholic Community*, sees 1570 as a virtually new start, but cf. Haigh's critique (*Hist. Journal*, XXI, 181 ff.) for an assertion of continuity.

be no need for strife. Elizabeth herself hoped to make her Church comprehensive and allow time to bring in those who still hankered after the old religion; the history of the Church since Henry VIII suggested that yet another tergiversation would prove possible. She had to rid the clergy of irreconcilables, among them all but one of Mary's bishops but only a minority of the lesser priesthood;[123] and the Act of Uniformity (**195**, section iii) provided a very modest weapon in the weekly 12*d*. fine for recusancy (failure to attend the services of the established Church) to force conformity on the laity. Enforcement even of this basic requirement remained patchy throughout the 1560's. The government prudently did not press the point, especially in the northern counties where the gentry remained in great part Catholic; for some years, they pursued a policy of allowing Catholicism to atrophy in a cold climate and without sustenance from its champions abroad. The Commons in Parliament, dominated by a stricter Protestantism, showed their temper and fears in sharpening the one measure of those years which touched the position of the Catholics.[124]

Whether the policy of drift could ever have been successful cannot be known; in was in any case stultified by a vigorous revival of the old religion among an ardent minority. In 1563 the closing of the Council of Trent left the Church of Rome organised for counter-attack. From 1567 when William Allen, exile and later cardinal, founded an English seminary at Douai in the Spanish Netherlands, the training of Catholic missionaries began in earnest. His college for secular priests, which later moved to Reims, and Jesuit colleges in Rome and Spain produced—usually from young men who had fled abroad in the course of the reign—a sizable group of men determined to return to England, to spread the faith, and to undergo martyrdom. The crisis of 1568–71—Mary's arrival in England, the northern rebellion, the Ridolfi plot—revealed the possible dangers and changed the mood of the government. Into all this dropped the papal bull of 1570, an unmistakable declaration of war (**197**). It may have had all the formal and practical weaknesses usually ascribed to it—there are technical errors, and Pius V's failure to consult Spain robbed the bull of an executor[125]—but it posed the fatal dilemma from which neither the Catholics nor the government could thereafter escape. Obedience to Rome now meant acceptance of the excommunication and deposition of Elizabeth, and therefore at least treason *in posse*.

[123] Only Kitchen of Llandaff could adjust his conscience to the second breach with Rome. On the deprived clergy cf. above, p. 398.

[124] 5 Eliz. I, c. 1. This made it praemunire for a first offence and treason for a second to maintain the pope's authority, and extended the application of the oath of supremacy as a test of allegiance to a wide range of lay and spiritual persons. A second refusal of the oath was punishable by death. The Commons may have been responsible for the real severities of the act (Neale, *Elizabeth and her Parliaments*, 1, 116 ff.).

[125] Meyer, *England and the Catholic Church*, 76 ff.

It may well be true that the national loyalties of English Catholics were not affected by the bull;[126] at least, except for a few hotheads who got involved in plots, they remained peaceful, and after the outbreak of war with Spain the majority demonstrated that they had chosen England before religion. But the government could not be expected to take this for granted. Nor could it be satisfied by the sophistical explanation offered by Gregory XIII in 1580 in response to an enquiry from the first Jesuit mission to England: that the bull, though always binding on heretics, was so on Catholics only when its execution became possible.[127] This was intended to liberate the English Catholics from the conflict of loyalties into which Pius V had thrust them, but it only served to confirm the English view that all things Romish were treacherous.

Thus Elizabeth, her Council and her Parliament were driven, in acts of self-defence which for the more ardent among them turned readily into eager attack, to tighten the measures against Catholics and to enact a number of increasingly severe penal laws. In 1571, in response to the bull, an act made it treason to bring in, seek out or publish any documents from Rome (**198**). Real battle, however, was not joined until the priests began to arrive from abroad. This invasion began in 1577 and soon grew to considerable strength. It ended the original hope of reconciling the English Catholics to the Elizabethan Church. Under the vigorous guidance of these highly trained missionaries the remaining Catholic families were confirmed in their faith and came to form a hard-core underground movement, known (as a rule) but able to survive because by and large they belonged to the well-to-do classes, in particular the gentry of the north and west. At the same time, popular adherence to the old religion also continued, especially in Wales and the north-west; this owed little to the missions. Half-dragged by the violently antipopish Commons, the government added to its armoury. Although it was possible to argue that all priests were by the simple fact of their allegiance to Rome traitors to the queen whose subjects, despite self-exile, they had remained,[128] convictions on such grounds required proof of overt acts; and while the Crown could maintain that all priests came to publish the bull (which would bring them within the scope of the 1571 act), it was usually impossible to convict them of an offence which they strenuously and truthfully denied they had committed. Thus an act of 1581 (**199**) extended the treason law to cover those who withdrew the queen's subjects from their allegiance to either queen or Church of England; it also increased the

[126] Pritchard. But cf. Holmes, *Resistance and Compromise*, who shows how Catholic opinion switched between resistance and accommodation in the wake of events and emphasises the role of Robert Persons.

[127] Meyer, *op. cit.*, 135 ff.

[128] Thus the first trials and executions of priests, especially of Edmund Campion in 1581, took place under the basic treason law of 1352.

recusancy fine to the prohibitive figure of £20. It was hoped both to catch the missionaries and to discourage conversions; for the missions had put an end to the easy practice of earlier days when Catholics had obeyed the law by attending the parish church, only to hear mass privately afterwards in their own homes. As passions increased, especially in Parliament,[129] and as the various plots against the queen were discovered, even this comprehensive attack seemed insufficient; and in 1585 it was not only made treason to be the cause for which others plotted treason (37) but another act (200) ordered the driving out of the priests from England and made it treason thereafter to be convicted simply of being a Jesuit or seminary priest. Legislation could do no more against the invaders from abroad, though Parliament recurred to the problem of the English Catholics in an act of 1593 which compelled avowed Catholics to remain within five miles of their domicile and register themselves there (201); the poorer sort, unable to pay fines and likely as prisoners to be a charge on the state, were to be exiled.

This, then, was the body of laws under which the government proceeded against the Catholic danger. The story of the persecution does not belong here: at its height in the 1580's, it was at all times far from universal. 187 priests are said to have suffered death, and a greater number were imprisoned under conditions which varied from tolerable to appalling. The trials were often harsh in the extreme, torture being regularly used on a captured priest to make him reveal the underground network of which he was part and which grew in strength all this time.[130] The most striking things about the story, revealed in some detail in the reports which some of the survivors rendered to their superiors in Spain,[131] are the close links between Catholic families, the vigour of the secret organisation which passed the priests through the country, the ingenious subterfuges into which they were forced, and the inefficiency of the Elizabethan police system. However, most of the missionaries were caught in the end. A debate on rights and wrongs yields little result. The priests always maintained that they had come only to preach the faith: they carried no political message and were organising no subversive action. There is no doubt that on the whole they did as they asserted. From the government's point of view, however, it was not only impossible to

---

[129] All the penal legislation against Catholics was pressed by the Commons, and sometimes the Council, against a reluctant queen who seems to have both appreciated the real danger more coolly and disliked the idea of persecution. Cf. Neale, Elizabeth and her Parliaments, I, 191 ff., 212 ff., 386 ff.; II, 37 ff., 53 f.; but the situation had changed completely in 1593 when the Commons were indifferent: ibid., II, 281, 285, 294 ff.

[130] For a detailed, though not unbiased, account of the persecution cf. Hughes, Reformation, III, 357 ff. More soberly, Meyer, England and the Catholic Church, 124 ff.

[131] Cf. e.g. the autobiographies of William Weston and John Gerard. The reader is advised to concentrate on their own stories and ignore the editor's introductions.

trust such claims, but it signified little whether they were true. Active membership of the Church of Rome inevitably involved, in the last resort, obedience to a pope who had declared war on England and her Protestant Church, was enlisting the help of Spain in the battle, and encouraged attacks on the queen in the interests of her Catholic cousin. Elizabeth always maintained that she was hunting out priests because they represented a political danger, and though undeniably many of her subjects joined in the chase with religious passion in their hearts, the persecution cannot be described as religious in the real sense. The queen did not want to save souls or make converts; she wanted to protect the safety of her realm.[132] The persecution slackened after 1590; not surprisingly, the failure of the English Catholics to live up to the part for which they were cast in Spanish plans tended to destroy the popular identification of papists and traitors.[133] After Allen's death in 1594, the unity of Catholicism in England broke down in quarrels between the Jesuits, who supported Spain, and the secular priests who with the laity had grown tired of the struggle. Thus when, under Bancroft's influence, the government exploited the breach by tentatively offering peace to those who would take it, the strife subsided. However, the actual making of a superficial peace was left to the reign of James I. Though Elizabeth had always been more ready than most to close her eyes to a little toleration in practice, she would not compromise with the principle of uniformity. The Catholic danger to the Church of England, never great but necessarily feared to be enormous, was manifestly over before she died.

197. The Papal Bull against Elizabeth, 1570.

Pius Episcopus servus servorum Dei: ad perpetuam rei memoriam.

Regnans in Excelsis, cui data est omnis in coelo et in terra potestas, unam sanctam Catholicam et Apostolicam Ecclesiam, extra quam nulla est salus, uni soli in terris, videlicet Apostolorum principi Petro Petrique successori Romano pontifici, in potestatis plenitudine tradidit gubernandum. Hunc unum super omnes gentes et omnia regna principem constituit qui evellat, destruat, dissipet, disperdat, plantet et aedificet, ut fidelem populum mutuae charitatis nexu constrictum in unitate Spiritus contineat, salvumque et incolumem suo exhibeat Salvatori.

1. Quo quidem in munere obeundo, nos ad praedicta Ecclesiae

---

[132] The strictly political threat emerges clearly enough from the writings of Robert Persons (cf. Clancy, *Papist Pamphleteers*, and Holmes, *Resistance and Compromise*).
[133] Meyer, *England and the Catholic Church*, 187.

gubernacula Dei benignitate vocati, nullum laborem intermittimus, omni opera contendentes, ut ipsa unitas et Catholica religio (quam illis auctor ad probandam suorum fidem et correctionem nostram tantis procellis conflictari permisit) integra conservetur. Sed impiorum numerus tantum potentia invaluit ut nullus iam in orbe locus sit relictus quem illi pessimis doctrinis corrumpere non tentarint, adnitente inter caeteros flagitiorum serva Elizabetha, pretensa Angliae regina, ad quam veluti ad asylum omnium infestissimi profugium invenerunt. Haec eadem, regno occupato, supremi ecclesiae capitis locum in omni Anglia, eiusque praecipuum auctoritatem atque iurisdictionem monstruose sibi usurpans, regnum ipsum iam tum ad fidem Catholicam et bonam frugem reductum rursus in miserum exitium revocavit.

2. Usu namque verae religionis, quam ab illius desertore Henrico VIII. olim eversam, clarae memoriae Maria regina legitima huius Sedis praesidio reparaverat, potenti manu inhibito, secutisque et complexis haereticorum erroribus, regium consilium ex Anglica nobilitate confectum diremit, illudque obscuris hominibus haereticis complevit, Catholicae fidei cultores oppressit, improbos concionatores atque impietatum administros reposuit, missae sacrificium, preces, cerciunia, ciborum delectum, coelibatum ritusque Catholicos abolevit, libros manifestam haeresim continentes toto regno proponi, impia mysteria et instituta ad Calvini praescriptum a se suscepta et observata etiam a subditis servari mandavit. Episcopos, ecclesiarum rectores, et alios sacerdotes Catholicos suis ecclesiis et beneficiis eiicere, ac de illis et aliis rebus ecclesiasticis in haereticos homines disponere, deque ecclesiae causis decernere ausa, praelatis, clero et populo ne Romanam Ecclesiam agnoscerent neve eius praeceptis sanctionibusque canonicis obtemperarent interdixit, plerosque in nefarias leges suas venire et Romani pontificis auctoritatem atque obedientiam abiurare, seque solam in temporalibus et spiritualibus dominam agnoscere iurisiurando coëgit, poenas et supplicia in eos qui dicto non essent audientes imposuit, easdemque ab iis qui in unitate fidei et praedicta obedientia perseverarunt exegit, Catholicos antistites et ecclesiarum rectores in vincula coniecit, ubi multi diuturno languore et tristitia confecti extremum vitae diem misere finiverunt. Quae omnia cum apud omnes nationes perspicua et notoria sint, et gravissimo quamplurimorum testimonio ita comprobata ut nullus omnino locus excusationis, defensionis aut tergiversationis relinquatur.

3. Nos multiplicantibus aliis atque aliis super alias impietatibus et

facinoribus et praeterea fidelium persecutione religionisque afflictione impulsu et opera dictae Elisabeth quotidie magis ingravescente, quoniam illius animum ita obfirmatum atque induratum intelligimus ut non modo pias Catholicorum principum de sanitate et conversione preces monitionesque contempserit, sed ne huius quidem Sedis ad ipsam hac de causa nuncios in Angliam traiicere permiserit, ad arma iustitiae contra eam de necessitate conversi, dolorem lenire non possumus quod adducamur in unam animadvertere cuius maiores de Republica Christiana tantopere meruere. Illius itaque auctoritate suffulti qui nos in hoc supremo iustitiae throno, licet tanto oneri impares, voluit collocare, de Apostolica potestatis plentitudine declaramus praedictam Elisabeth haereticam, et haeriticorum fautricem, eique adhaerentes in praedictis anathematis sententiam incurisse esseque a Christo corporis unitate praecisos.

4. Quin etiam ipsam praetenso regni praedicti iure necnon omni et quocumque dominio, dignitate, privilegioque privatam.

5. Et etiam proceres, subditos et populum dicti regni, ac caeteros omnes qui illi quomodocumque iuraverunt a iuramento huiusmodi ac omni prorsus dominii, fidelitatis et obsequii debito perpetuo absolutos, prout nos illos praesentium auctoritate absolvimus, et privamus eandem Elisabeth praetenso iure regni aliisque omnibus supradictis. Praecipimusque et interdicimus universis et singulis proceribus, subditis, populis, et aliis praedictis ne illi eiusve monitis, mandatis et legibus audeant obedire. Qui secus egerint, eos simili anathematis sententia innodamus.

6. Quia vero difficile nimis esset praesentes quocumque illis opus erit perferre, volumus ut earum exempla notarii publici manu et praelati ecclesiastici eiusve curiae sigillo obsignata eandem illam prorsus fidem in iudicio et extra illud, ubique gentium faciant, quam ipsae presentes facerent, si essent exhibitae vel ostensae.

Datum Romae apud S. Petrum, anno Incarnationis Dominicae 1570; 5 Kal. Maii; Pontificatus nostri anno quinto.

Magnum Bullarium Romanum, II, 303

[Translation:] Pius Bishop, servant of the servants of God, in lasting memory of the matter.

He that reigneth on high, to whom is given all power in heaven and earth, has committed one holy Catholic and apostolic Church, outside of which there is no salvation, to one alone upon earth, namely to Peter, the first of the apostles, and to Peter's successor, the pope of Rome, to be by him governed in fullness of power. Him alone He has made ruler over all peoples and kingdoms, to pull up, destroy, scatter, disperse, plant and build, so that he may preserve His faithful people (knit together with the girdle of charity) in the unity of the Spirit and present them safe and spotless to their Saviour.

1. In obedience to which duty, we (who by God's goodness are called to the aforesaid government of the Church) spare no pains and labour with all our might that unity and the Catholic religion (which their Author, for the trial of His children's faith and our correction, has suffered to be afflicted with such great troubles) may be preserved entire. But the number of the ungodly has so much grown in power that there is no place left in the world which they have not tried to corrupt with their most wicked doctrines; and among others, Elizabeth, the pretended queen of England and the servant of crime, has assisted in this, with whom as in a sanctuary the most pernicious of all have found refuge. This very woman, having seized the crown and monstrously usurped the place of supreme head of the Church in all England together with the chief authority and jurisdiction belonging to it, has once again reduced this same kingdom—which had already been restored to the Catholic faith and to good fruits—to a miserable ruin.

2. Prohibiting with a strong hand the use of the true religion, which after its earlier overthrow by Henry VIII (a deserter therefrom) Mary, the lawful queen of famous memory, had with the help of this See restored, she has followed and embraced the errors of the heretics. She has removed the royal Council, composed of the nobility of England, and has filled it with obscure men, being heretics; oppressed the followers of the Catholic faith; instituted false preachers and ministers of impiety; abolished the sacrifice of the mass, prayers, fasts, choice of meats, celibacy, and Catholic ceremonies; and has ordered that books of manifestly heretical content be propounded to the whole realm and that impious rites and institutions after the rule of Calvin, entertained and observed by herself, be also observed by her subjects. She has dared to eject bishops, rectors of churches and other Catholic priests from their churches and benefices, to bestow these and other things ecclesiastical upon heretics, and to determine spiritual causes; has forbidden the prelates, clergy and people to acknowledge the Church of Rome or obey its precepts and canonical sanctions; has forced most of them to come to terms with her wicked laws, to abjure the authority and obedience of the pope of Rome, and to accept her, on oath, as their only

lady in matters temporal and spiritual; has imposed penalties and punishments on those who would not agree to this and has exacted them of those who persevered in the unity of the faith and the aforesaid obedience; has thrown the Catholic prelates and parsons into prison where many, worn out by long languishing and sorrow, have miserably ended their lives. All these matters are manifest and notorious among all the nations; they are so well proven by the weighty witness of many men that there remains no place for excuse, defence or evasion.

3. We, seeing impieties and crimes multiplied one upon another— the persecution of the faithful and afflictions of religion daily growing more severe under the guidance and by the activity of the said Elizabeth —and recognising that her mind is so fixed and set that she has not only despised the pious prayers and admonitions with which Catholic princes have tried to cure and convert her but has not even permitted the nuncios sent to her in this matter by this See to cross into England, are compelled by necessity to take up against her the weapons of justice, though we cannot forbear to regret that we should be forced to turn upon one whose ancestors have so well deserved of the Christian community. Therefore, resting upon the authority of Him whose pleasure it was to place us (though unequal to such a burden) upon this supreme justice-seat, we do out of the fullness of our apostolic power declare the foresaid Elizabeth to be a heretic and favourer of heretics, and her adherents in the matters aforesaid to have incurred the sentence of excommunication and to be cut off from the unity of the body of Christ.

4. And moreover [we declare] her to be deprived of her pretended title to the aforesaid crown and of all lordship, dignity and privilege whatsoever.

5. And also [declare] the nobles, subjects and people of the said realm, and all others who have in any way sworn oaths to her, to be forever absolved from such an oath and from any duty arising from lordship, fealty and obedience; and we do, by authority of these presents, so absolve them and so deprive the same Elizabeth of her pretended title to the crown and all other the abovesaid matters. We charge and command all and singular the nobles, subjects, peoples and others aforesaid that they do not dare obey her orders, mandates and laws. Those who shall act to the contrary we include in the like sentence of excommunication.

6. Because in truth it may prove too difficult to take these presents

427

wheresoever it shall be necessary, we will that copies made under the hand of a notary public and sealed with the seal of a prelate of the Church or of his court shall have such force and trust in and out of judicial proceedings, in all places among the nations, as these presents would themselves have if they were exhibited or shown.

Given at St Peter's at Rome, on 27 April 1570 of the Incarnation; in the fifth year of our pontificate.

198. An Act against the bringing in and putting in execution of bulls and other instruments from the see of Rome (1571: 13 Eliz. I, c. 2).

Where in the Parliament holden at Westminster in the fifth year of the reign of our sovereign lady the Queen's Majesty that now is, by one act and statute then and there made, entitled An Act for the Assurance of the Queen's Majesty's Royal Power over all States and Subjects within her Highness' Dominions,[134] it is among other things very well ordained and provided, for the abolishing of the usurped power and jurisdiction of the bishop of Rome and of the see of Rome heretofore unlawfully claimed and usurped within this realm and other the dominions to the Queen's Majesty belonging, that no person or persons shall hold or stand with to set forth, maintain, defend or extol the same usurped power, or attribute any manner jurisdiction, authority or preeminence to the same, to be had or used within this realm or any the said dominions, upon pain to incur the danger, penalties and forfeitures ordained and provided by the statute of provision and praemunire made in the sixteenth year of the reign of King Richard the Second, as by the same act more at large it doth and may appear; And yet nevertheless divers seditious and very evil disposed people, without respect of their duty to Almighty God or of the faith and allegiance which they ought to bear and have to our said sovereign lady the Queen, and without all fear or regard had to the said good law and statute or the pains therein limited, but minding, as it should seem, very seditiously and unnaturally not only to bring this realm and the imperial crown thereof (being in very deed of itself most free) into the thraldom and subjection of that foreign, usurped, and unlawful jurisdiction, preeminence and authority claimed by the said see of Rome, but also to estrange and alienate the minds and hearts of sundry her Majesty's subjects from their dutiful obedience, and to raise and stir sedition and rebellion within this realm,

[134] 5 Eliz. I, c. 1.

to the disturbance of the most happy peace thereof, have lately procured and obtained to themselves from the said bishop of Rome and his said see divers bulls and writings, the effect whereof hath been and is to absolve and reconcile all those that will be contented to forsake their due obedience to our most gracious sovereign lady the Queen's Majesty, and to yield and subject themselves to the said feigned, unlawful and usurped authority, and by colour of the said bulls and writings the said wicked persons very secretly and most seditiously in such parts of this realm where the people for want of good instruction are most weak, simple and ignorant, and thereby farthest from the good understanding of their duties towards God and the Queen's Majesty, have by their lewd and subtle practises and persuasions so far forth wrought that sundry simple and ignorant persons have been contented to be reconciled to the said usurped authority of the see of Rome and to take absolution at the hands of the said naughty and subtle practisers, whereby hath grown great disobedience and boldness in many, not only to withdraw and absent themselves from all divine service now most godly set forth and used within this realm, but also have thought themselves discharged of and from all obedience, duty and allegiance to her Majesty, whereby most wicked and unnatural rebellion hath ensued, and to the further danger of this realm is hereafter very like to be renewed if the ungodly and wicked attempts in that behalf be not by severity of laws in time restrained and bridled. For remedy and redress whereof, and to prevent the great mischiefs and inconveniences that thereby may ensue, be it enacted by the Queen's most excellent Majesty with the assent of the Lords spiritual and temporal and the Commons in this present Parliament assembled, and by authority of the same, that if any person or persons after the first day of July next coming shall use or put in ure in any place within this realm or in any the Queen's dominions any such bull, writing or instrument, written or printed, of absolution or reconciliation at any time heretofore obtained and gotten, or at any time hereafter to be obtained and gotten, from the said bishop of Rome or any his successors, or from any other person or persons authorised or claiming authority by or from the said bishop of Rome, his predecessors or successors, or See of Rome; or if any person or persons after the said first day of July shall take upon him or them by colour of any such bull, writing, instrument or authority to absolve or reconcile any person or persons, or to grant or promise to any person or persons within this realm or any other the Queen's Majesty's dominions any such absolution or reconciliation by any speech, preaching, teaching, writing, or any other open deed; or if any person or persons within this realm or any the Queen's dominions after the said first day of July shall willingly receive and take any such absolution or reconciliation; or else if any person or persons have obtained or gotten since the last day of the Parliament holden in the first year of the Queen's Majesty's reign, or after the said first day of July shall obtain or get from the said bishop of Rome or any his successors or see of Rome any manner of bull, writing or instrument written or printed, containing any thing, matter or cause whatsoever; or shall publish or by any ways or means put in ure any such bull, writing or instrument; That then all and every such act and acts, offence and offences, shall be deemed and adjudged by the authority of this act to be high treason, and the offender and offenders therein, their procurers, abettors and counsellors to the fact and committing of the said offence or offences, shall be deemed and adjudged high traitors to the Queen and the realm; and being thereof lawfully indicted and attainted, according to the course of the laws of this realm, shall suffer pains of death, and also lose and forfeit all their lands, tenements, hereditaments, goods and chattels, as in cases of high treason by the laws of this realm ought to be lost and forfeited.

[II. 'Aiders, comforters or maintainers' after the fact are to be subject to the penalties of praemunire.]

III. Provided always and be it further enacted by the authority aforesaid that if any person or persons to whom any such absolution, reconciliation, bull, writing or instrument as is aforesaid shall after the said first day of July be offered, moved or persuaded to be used, put in ure, or executed, shall conceal the same offer, motion or persuasion, and not disclose and signify the same by writing or otherwise within six weeks then next following to some of the Queen's Majesty's Privy Council or else to the president or vice-president of the Queen's Majesty's Council established in the North Parts or in the Marches of Wales for the time being, that then the same person or persons so concealing and not disclosing or not signifying the said offer, motion or persuasion, shall incur the loss, danger, penalty and forfeiture of misprision of high treason; and that no person or persons shall at any time hereafter be impeached, molested or troubled in or for misprision of treason for any offence or offences made treason by this act other than such as by this act are before declared to be in case of misprision of high treason.

IV. And be it further enacted by the authority aforesaid that if any person or persons shall at any time after the said first day of July bring into this realm of England or any the dominions of the same any token or tokens, thing or things, called by the name of an *Agnus Dei*, or any crosses, pictures, beads or suchlike vain and superstitious things from the bishop or see of Rome, or from any person or persons authorised or claiming authority by or from the said bishop or see of Rome to consecrate or hallow the same, which said *Agnus Dei* is used to be specially hallowed and consecrated, as it is termed, by the said bishop in his own person, and the said crosses, pictures, beads and suchlike superstitious things be also hallowed either by the said bishop or by others having power or pretending to have power for the same, by or from him or his said see, and divers pardons, immunities and exemptions granted by the authority of the said See to such as shall receive and use the same, and that if the same person or persons so bringing in as is aforesaid such *Agnus Dei* and other like things as be before specified shall deliver or offer or cause to be delivered the same or any of them to any subject of this realm or any of the dominions of the same to be worn or used in any wise, that then as well the same person and persons so doing, as also all and every other person or persons which shall receive and take the same to the intent to use or wear the same, being thereof lawfully convicted and attainted by the order of the common laws of this realm, shall incur into the dangers, penalties, pains and forfeitures ordained and provided by the statute of praemunire and provision made in the sixteenth year of the reign of King Richard the Second.

* * * * * *

Stat. Realm, IV, 528–31

199. An Act to retain the Queen's Majesty's subjects in their due obedience (1581: 23 Eliz. I, c. 1).

Where since the statute made in the thirteenth year of the reign of the Queen our sovereign lady, entitled An Act against the bringing in and putting in execution of Bulls, Writings, and Instruments, and other superstitious things from the See of Rome,[135] divers evil affected persons have practised, contrary to the meaning of the said statute, by other means than by bulls or instruments written or printed, to withdraw divers the Queen's Majesty's subjects from their natural obedience to her Majesty to obey the said usurped authority of Rome, and in respect

[135] Doc. **198.**

of the same to persuade great numbers to withdraw their due obedience to her Majesty's laws established for the due service of Almighty God: For reformation whereof, and to declare the true meaning of the said law, be it declared and enacted by the authority of this present Parliament that all persons whatsoever which have, or shall have, or shall pretend to have power, or shall by any ways or means put in practice to absolve, persuade or withdraw any of the Queen's Majesty's subjects or any within her Highness' realms and dominions from their natural obedience to her Majesty, or to withdraw them for that intent from the religion now by her Highness' authority established within her Highness' dominions to the Romish religion, or to move them or any of them to promise any obedience to any pretended authority of the see of Rome, or of any other prince, state or potentate, to be had or used within her dominions, or shall do any overt act to that intent or purpose, and every of them, shall be to all intents adjudged to be traitors, and being thereof lawfully convicted shall have judgment, suffer and forfeit as in case of high treason. And if any person shall, after the end of this session of Parliament, by any means be willingly absolved or withdrawn as aforesaid, or willingly be reconciled, or shall promise any obedience to any such pretended authority, prince, state or potentate as is aforesaid, that then every such person, their procurers and counsellors thereunto, being thereof lawfully convicted, shall be taken, tried and judged, and shall suffer and forfeit as in cases of high treason.

II. And be it likewise enacted and declared that all and every person and persons that shall wittingly be aiders or maintainers of such persons so offending as is above expressed, or of any of them knowing the same, or which shall conceal any offence aforesaid and shall not, within twenty days at the furthest after such person's knowledge of such offence, disclose the same to some justice of peace or other higher officer, shall be taken, tried and judged, and shall suffer and forfeit as offenders in misprision of treason.

III. And be it likewise enacted that every person which shall say or sing mass, being thereof lawfully convicted, shall forfeit the sum of two hundred marks and be committed to prison in the next gaol, there to remain by the space of one year and from thenceforth till he have paid the said sum of 200 marks: and that every person which shall willingly hear mass shall forfeit the sum of one hundred marks and suffer imprisonment for a year.

IV. Be it also further enacted by the authority aforesaid that every person above the age of 16 years which shall not repair to some church, chapel or usual place of common prayer, but forbear the same contrary to the tenor of a statute made in the first year of her Majesty's reign for Uniformity of Common Prayer, [136] and being thereof lawfully convicted, shall forfeit to the Queen's Majesty for every month after the end of this session of Parliament which he or she shall so forbear, twenty pounds of lawful English money; and that over and besides the said forfeitures, every person so forbearing by the space of 12 months as aforesaid shall for his or her obstinacy, after certificate thereof in writing made into the court commonly called the King's Bench by the ordinary of the diocese, a justice of assize and gaol delivery, or a justice of peace of the county where such offender shall dwell or be, be bound with two sufficient sureties in the sum of two hundred pound at the least to the good behaviour, and so to continue bound until such time as the persons so bound do conform themselves and come to the church, according to the true meaning of the said statute made in the said first year of the Queen's Majesty's reign.

* * * * * *

IX. Provided also that every person which usually on the Sunday shall have in his or their house the divine service which is established by the law in this realm, and be thereat himself or herself usually or most commonly present, and shall not obstinately refuse to come to church and there to do as is aforesaid, and shall also four times in the year at the least be present at the divine service in the church of the parish where he or she shall be resident, or in some other open common church or such chapel of ease, shall not incur any pain or penalty limited by this act for not repairing to church.

* * * * * *

Stat. Realm, IV, 657-8

200. An Act against Jesuits, seminary priests and such other like disobedient persons (1585: 27 Eliz. I, c. 2).

Whereas divers persons called or professed Jesuits, seminary priests and other priests, which have been and from time to time are made in the parts beyond the seas by or according to the order and rites of the Romish Church, have of late years come and been sent, and daily do come and are sent, into this realm of England and other the Queen's

[136] Doc. **195.**

433

Majesty's dominions, of purpose (as hath appeared as well by sundry of their own examinations and confessions as by divers other manifest means and proofs) not only to withdraw her Highness' subjects from their due obedience to her Majesty but also to stir up and move sedition, rebellion and open hostility within her Highness' realms and dominions, to the great dangering of the safety of her most royal person and to the utter ruin, desolation and overthrow of the whole realm, if the same be not the sooner by some good means foreseen and prevented: For reformation whereof be it ordained, established and enacted by the Queen's most excellent Majesty and the Lords spiritual and temporal and the Commons in this present Parliament assembled and by the authority of the same Parliament, that all and every Jesuits, seminary priests and other priests whatsoever, made or ordained out of the realm of England or other her Highness' dominions or within any of her Majesty's realms or dominions by any authority, power or jurisdiction derived, challenged or pretended from the see of Rome since the feast of the Nativity of St John Baptist in the first year of her Highness' reign, shall within forty days next after the end of this present session of Parliament depart out of this realm of England and out of all other her Highness' realms and dominions, if the wind, weather and passage shall serve for the same; or else so soon after the end of the said forty days as the wind, weather and passage shall so serve.

II. And be it further enacted by the authority aforesaid that it shall not be lawful to or for any Jesuit, seminary priest or other such priest, deacon or any religious or ecclesiastical person whatsoever, being born within this realm or any other her Highness' dominions, and heretofore since the said feast of the Nativity of St John Baptist in the first year of her Majesty's reign made, ordained or professed, or hereafter to be made, ordained or professed, by any authority or jurisdiction derived, challenged or pretended from the see of Rome, by or of what name, title or degree soever the same shall be called or known, to come into, be or remain in any part of this realm or any other her Highness' dominions after the end of the same forty days, other than in such special cases and upon such special occasions only and for such time only as is expressed in this act; and if he do, that then every such offence shall be taken and adjudged to be high treason; and every person so offending shall for his offence be adjudged a traitor, and shall suffer, lose and forfeit as in case of high treason. And every person which after the end of the same forty days, and after such time of departure as is before limited and appointed, shall wittingly and willingly receive, relieve, comfort, aid or maintain any such Jesuit, seminary priest, or other priest, deacon, or religious or ecclesiastical person as is aforesaid, being at liberty or out of hold, knowing him to be a Jesuit, seminary priest or other such priest, deacon, or religious or ecclesiastical person as is aforesaid, shall also for such offence be adjudged a felon without benefit of clergy, and suffer death, lose and forfeit as in case of one attainted of felony.

III. And be it further enacted by the authority aforesaid, if any of her Majesty's subjects (not being a Jesuit, seminary priest or other such priest, deacon, or religious or ecclesiastical person as is before mentioned) now being or which hereafter shall be of or brought up in any college of Jesuits or seminary already erected or ordained or hereafter to be erected or ordained in the parts beyond the seas or out of this realm in any foreign parts, shall not, within six months next after proclamation in that behalf to be made in the City of London under the great seal of England, return into this realm, and thereupon, within two days next after such return, before the bishop of the diocese or two justices of peace of the county where he shall arrive, submit himself to her Majesty and her laws, and take the oath set forth by act in the first year of her reign;[137] that then every such person which shall otherwise return, come into or be in this realm or any other her Highness' dominions, for such offence of returning or being in this realm or any other her Highness' dominions without submission as aforesaid, shall also be adjudged a traitor and shall suffer, lose and forfeit as in case of high treason.

IV. And be it further enacted by the authority aforesaid, if any person under her Majesty's subjection or obedience shall at any time after the end of the said forty days by way of exchange or by any other shift, way or means whatsoever, wittingly and willingly, either directly or indirectly, convey, deliver or send, or cause or procure to be conveyed or delivered to be sent, over the seas or out of this realm or out of any other her Majesty's dominions or territories into any foreign parts, or shall otherwise wittingly and willingly yield, give or contribute any money or other relief to or for any Jesuit, seminary priest or such other priest, deacon, or religious or ecclesiastical person as is aforesaid, or to or for the maintenance or relief of any college of Jesuits or seminary already erected or ordained or hereafter to be erected or ordained in any

---

[137] The oath of supremacy ordered by the act of 1559 (Doc. **184**).

the parts beyond the seas or out of this realm in any foreign parts, or of any person then being of or in any the same colleges or seminaries and not returned into this realm with submission as in this act is expressed, and continuing in the same realm; that then every such person so offending, for the same offence shall incur the danger and penalty of praemunire mentioned in the statute of praemunire made in the 16th year of the reign of King Richard the Second.

v. And be it further enacted by the authority aforesaid, that it shall not be lawful for any person of or under her Highness' obedience, at any time after the said forty days, during her Majesty's life (which God long preserve) to send his or her child or other person being under his or her government into any the parts beyond the seas out of her Highness' obedience without the special license of her Majesty, or of four of her Highness' Privy Council, under their hands in that behalf first had or obtained; (except merchants, for such only as they or any of them shall send over the seas only for or about his, her or their trade of merchandise, or to serve as mariners, and not otherwise); upon pain to forfeit and lose for every such their offence the sum of one hundred pounds.

*   *   *   *   *   *

VIII. Provided also that this act or anything therein contained shall not in any wise extend to any such Jesuit, seminary priest or other such priest, deacon, or religious or ecclesiastical person as is before mentioned, as shall at any time within the said forty days, or within three days after that he shall hereafter come into this realm or any other her Highness' dominions, submit himself to some archbishop or bishop of this realm, or to some justice of peace within the county where he shall arrive or land, and do thereupon truly and sincerely before the same archbishop, bishop, or such justice of peace, take the said oath set forth *in anno primo*, and by writing under his hand confess and acknowledge and from thenceforth continue his due obedience unto her Highness' laws, statutes and ordinances made and provided, or to be made or provided, in causes of religion.

*   *   *   *   *   *

XI. And be it also further enacted by authority aforesaid that every person or persons being subject of this realm which after the said forty days shall know and understand that any such Jesuit, seminary priest or other priest abovesaid shall abide, stay, tarry or be within this realm or other the Queen's dominions and countries, contrary to the true meaning of this act, and shall not discover the same unto some justice of peace or other higher officer within twelve days next after his said knowledge, but willingly conceal his knowledge therein; that every such offender shall make fine and be imprisoned at the Queen's pleasure. And that if such justice of peace or other such officer to whom such matter shall be so discovered do not within 28 days then next following give information thereof to some of the Queen's Privy Council or to the president or vice-president of the Queen's Council established in the North or in the Marches of Wales for the time being, that then he or they so offending shall for every such offence forfeit the sum of two hundred marks.

* * * * * *

XIII. And be it also enacted that all such oaths, bonds and submissions as shall be made by force of this act as aforesaid, shall be certified into the Chancery by such parties before whom the same shall be made . . . And that if any person submitting himself as aforesaid do at any time within the space of ten years after such submission made come within ten miles of such place where her Majesty shall be, without especial license from her Majesty in that behalf to be obtained in writing under her hand, that then and from thenceforth such person shall take no benefit of the said submission, but that the said submission shall be void as if the same had never been.   *Stat. Realm*, IV, 706–8

201. An Act against popish recusants (1593: 35 Eliz. I, c. 2).

For the better discovering and avoiding of all such traitorous and most dangerous conspiracies and attempts as are daily devised and practised against our most gracious sovereign lady the Queen's Majesty and the happy estate of this common weal by sundry wicked and seditious persons, who terming themselves Catholics and being indeed spies and intelligencers, not only for her Majesty's foreign enemies but also for rebellious and traitorous subjects born within her Highness' realms and dominions, and hiding their most detestable and devilish purposes under a false pretext of religion and conscience do secretly wander and shift from place to place within this realm to corrupt and seduce her Majesty's subjects and to stir them to sedition and rebellion: Be it ordained and enacted by our sovereign lady the Queen's Majesty and the Lords spiritual and temporal and the Commons in this present Parliament assembled and by the authority of the same, that every person above the age of sixteen years, born within any the Queen's Majesty's realms or dominions or made denizen, being a popish recusant and before the end of this session of Parliament convicted for not repairing to some church, chapel or usual place of common prayer to hear divine service there, but forbearing the same contrary to the tenor of the laws and statutes heretofore made and provided in that behalf, and having any certain place of dwelling and abode within this realm, shall within forty days next after the end of this session of Parliament (if they be within this realm and not restrained or stayed, either by imprisonment, or by her Majesty's commandment, or by order and direction of some six or more of the Privy Council, or by such sickness or infirmity of body as they shall not be able to travel without imminent danger of life, and in such cases of absence out of the realm, restraint or stay, then within twenty days next after they shall return into the realm, or be enlarged of such imprisonment or restraint, and shall be able to travel) repair to their place of dwelling where they usually heretofore made their common abode, and shall not any time after pass or remove above five miles from thence. And also that every person being above the age of sixteen years born within any her Majesty's realms or dominions or made denizen, and having or which hereafter shall have any certain place of dwelling and abode within this realm, which being then a popish recusant shall at any time hereafter be lawfully convicted for not repairing to some church, chapel or usual place of common prayer to hear divine service there, but forbearing the same contrary to the said laws and statutes, and being within this realm at the time that they shall be convicted, shall within forty days next after the same conviction (if they be not restrained or stayed by imprisonment or otherwise as is aforesaid, and in such cases of restraint and stay then within twenty days next after they shall be enlarged of such imprisonment or restraint and shall be able to travel) repair to their place of usual dwelling and abode, and shall not at any time after pass or remove above five miles from thence: upon pain that every person and persons that shall offend against the tenor and intent of this act in any thing before mentioned shall lose and forfeit all his and their goods and chattels, and shall also forfeit to the Queen's Majesty all the lands, tenements and hereditaments, and all the rents and annuities of every such person so doing or offending, during the life of the same offender.

[II. Recusants 'not having any certain place of dwelling and abode' are to 'repair to the place where such person was born, or where the father or mother of such person shall then be dwelling,' and under like penalty 'shall not at any time after remove or pass above five miles from thence.']

*   *   *   *   *   *

IV. Provided always and be it further enacted by the authority aforesaid that all such persons as by the intent and true meaning of this act are to make their repair to their place of dwelling and abode, or to the place where they were born or where their father or mother shall be dwelling, and not to remove or pass above five miles from thence as is aforesaid, shall within twenty days next after their coming to any of the said places, as the case shall happen, notify their coming thither and present themselves and deliver their true names in writing to the minister or curate of the same parish and to the constable, headborough or tithingman[138] of the town; and thereupon the said minister or curate shall presently enter the same into a book to be kept in every parish for that purpose; and afterward the said minister or curate and the said constable, headborough or tithingman shall certify the same in writing to the justices of the peace of the same county at the next general or quarter sessions to be holden in the said county; and the said justices shall cause the same to be entered by the clerk of the peace in the rolls of the same sessions.

V. And to the end that the realm be not pestered and overcharged with the multitude of such seditious and dangerous people as is aforesaid, who having little or no ability to answer or satisfy any competent penalty for their contempt and disobedience of the said laws and statutes, and being committed to prison for the same do live for the most part in better case there than they could if they were abroad at their own liberty; the Lords spiritual and temporal and the Commons in this present Parliament assembled do most humbly and instantly beseech the Queen's Majesty that it may be further enacted that if any such person or persons being a popish recusant, not being a *femme covert*, and not having lands, tenements, rents or annuities of an absolute estate of inheritance or freehold of the clear yearly value of twenty marks above all charges, to their own use and behoof and not upon any secret trust

---

[138] These three are practically equivalent titles for the men in charge of the smallest units of government.

or confidence for any other, or goods and chattels in their own right and to their own proper use and behoof, and not upon any secret trust or confidence for any other, above the value of forty pounds, shall not within the time before in this act in that behalf limited and appointed repair to their place of usual dwelling and abode, if they have any, or else to the place where they were born or where their father or mother shall be dwelling, according to the tenor and intent of this present act, and thereupon notify their coming and present themselves and deliver their true names in writing to the minister . . . as is aforesaid; or at any time after such their repairing to any such place as is before appointed shall pass or remove above five miles from the same, and shall not within three months next after such person shall be apprehended or taken for offending as is aforesaid conform themselves to the obedience of the laws and statutes of this realm in coming usually to the church to hear divine service, and in making such public confession and submission as hereafter in this act is appointed and expressed, being thereunto required by the bishop of the diocese, or any justice of peace of the county where the said person shall happen to be, or by the minister or curate of the parish; that in every such case every such offender, being thereunto warned or required by any two justices of the peace or coroner of the same county where such offender shall then be, shall upon his or their corporal oath before any two justices of the peace or coroner of the same county abjure this realm of England and all other the Queen's Majesty's dominions for ever. And thereupon shall depart out of this realm at such haven and port and within such time as shall in that behalf be assigned and appointed by the said justices of peace or coroner before whom such abjuration shall be made, unless the same offenders be letted or stayed by such lawful and reasonable means or causes as by the common laws of this realm are permitted and allowed in cases of abjuration for felony; and in such cases of let or stay, then within such reasonable and convenient time after as the common law requireth in case of abjuration for felony as is aforesaid. And that every justice of peace and coroner before whom any such abjuration shall happen to be made as is aforesaid, shall cause the same presently to be entered of record before them and shall certify the same to the justices of assizes and gaol delivery of the said county at the next assizes or gaol delivery to be holden in the same county: and if any such offender which by the tenor and intent of this act is to be abjured as is aforesaid shall refuse to make such abjuration as is aforesaid, or after such abjuration made shall not go to such haven and within such time as is before appointed and from thence depart out of this realm according to this present act, or after such his departure shall return or come again into any her Majesty's realms or dominions without her Majesty's special licence in that behalf first had and obtained, that then in every such case the person so offending shall be adjudged a felon and shall suffer and lose as in case of felony without benefit of clergy.

VI. And be it further enacted and ordained by the authority aforesaid that if any person which shall be suspected to be a Jesuit, seminary or massing priest, being examined by any person having lawful authority in that behalf to examine such person which shall be so suspected, shall refuse to answer directly and truly whether he be a Jesuit or a seminary or massing priest as is aforesaid, every such person so refusing to answer shall for his disobedience and contempt in that behalf be committed to prison by such as shall examine him as is aforesaid, and thereupon shall remain and continue in prison without bail or mainprize until he shall make direct and true answer to the said questions whereupon he shall be so examined.

VII. Provided nevertheless and be it further enacted by the authority aforesaid that if any of the persons which are hereby limited and appointed to continue and abide within five miles of their usual dwelling place, or of such place where they were born or where their father or mother shall be dwelling as is aforesaid, shall have necessary occasion or business to go and travel out of the compass of the said five miles, that then and in every such case upon license in that behalf to be gotten under the hands of two of the justices of the peace of the same county, with the privity and assent in writing of the bishop of the diocese, or of the lieutenant or of any deputy lieutenant of the same county, under their hands, it shall and may be lawful for every such person to go and travel about such their necessary business, and for such time only for their travelling, attending and returning as shall be comprised in the same license; anything before in this act to the contrary notwithstanding.

* * * * * *

[x provides that offenders against the act may, before conviction, 'come to some parish church on some Sunday or other festival day and then and there hear divine service, and at service time before the sermon or reading of the gospel make public and open submission' according to a form provided, and so escape the penalties of the act; the minister of the parish being required to enter such submission 'into a book to be kept in every parish for that purpose,' and also within ten days to 'certify the same in writing to the bishop of the diocese'.]

* * * * * *

Stat. Realm, IV, 843-6

VI. THE PURITAN MOVEMENT

The problems of the Elizabethan Church have of late attracted a very great deal of attention; the sizable pamphlet literature has been more widely explored than before, and (more importantly) historians have begun to investigate what actually happened, in dioceses and parishes, in universities and colleges, and indeed in the inner minds of many devoted men.[139] The results have been distinctly disconcerting because virtually all the landmarks of a supposedly distinguishable 'Puritan movement' have disappeared. Who and what were the Puritans of Elizabeth's reign? Sensible scholars now fight shy altogether of a name which owes its all-pervasive appearance far more to later than to contemporary usage. Nevertheless, it is retained here because one needs some convenient term to comprehend the phenomenon of religious nonconformity, dissatisfaction and agitation, however unsatisfactory the traditional word, loaded with traditional meanings, may be. 'Puritans' here, therefore, means those members of the Church of England who, while accepting the concept of a national and comprehensive Church, found themselves in disagreement with official conformity in a variety of ways that ranged from dislike of allegedly popish ceremonies and details of the Prayer Book to desire for a totally reconstructed system of Church government. We now know how varied such nonconforming or protesting attitudes could be, but recent work has also demonstrated a degree of coherence among men —nearly always clerics—who believed that the Church set up in 1559 needed further reform. Thus the term 'moderate Puritan', though widely used today to describe those who asked for changes without revolution, disguises the fact that in doctrine and beliefs most of these moderates held views quite as extreme as those which characterised the genuine Presbyterians.[140] On the other hand, all attempts to distinguish between Anglicans and Puritans disguise the opposite truth, namely that Puritans were invariably Anglicans

---

[139] The recent literature is much too large to be fully rehearsed here; much of it, of course, is also not addressed to the problems of government. The outstanding work is Collinson, *Puritan Movement*; this first showed up the unclassifiable variety of attitudes, tenets and forms of behaviour comprehended under the term. Knappen, *Tudor Puritanism*, though much too schematic, retains some value as an analysis of Puritan writings.

[140] Cf. Lake, *Journ. Eccl. Hist.*, XXIX, 23 ff.; also his 'Laurence Chaderton'.

and that Calvinism, variously interpreted, formed the general foundations for the religion of all who accepted a Church of England.

The Puritans, therefore, were the active, zealous, proselytising Anglicans, especially forward in rooting out remnants—often sizable remnants—of the unreformed religion, and characterised by earnestness, dedication, inflexibility, narrowness and commonly youth.[141] Most of them accepted the episcopal government of the Church as well as the royal supremacy, and several bishops could be charged by equally narrowminded opponents of the precise sort with favouring the enemy within.[142] Many worried lay members of the ruling order—noblemen, country gentry, privy councillors —supported Puritan ministers and programmes.[143] In fact, any Elizabethan whose Protestant faith was strong and sincere was bound to respect the exhortations of manifestly ardent Protestant clergy and have his doubts about negligent, inadequate, ill-behaved conformists, even if this meant giving countenance to tenets which tended towards subversive inclinations; and they could feel that way the more readily because 'moderate' Puritans regularly and loudly disavowed all such leanings. The received view, which used to regard Puritanism in general as a dangerously subversive movement, rested on four misleading notions. For one thing, there was the manifestly revolutionary Puritanism of the 1640's and 1650's: but it is an error to read the mid-seventeenth century back into the reign of Elizabeth. For a second, the tendentious writings of Richard Bancroft, professional Puritan-hunter, for too long coloured later interpretations.[144] Thirdly, Elizabeth herself identified all failure to conform with revolutionary hostility to herself, a conviction which correctly judged the possibilities inherent in the movement but greatly exaggerated their reality. And lastly, certain Puritan propagandists did write more uncompromisingly, and certain phases of the movement did aim much further, than the generality of troubled Protestants would approve: the error here lay in treating the fringes as descriptive of the centre. Because the queen shared this false opinion and insisted on suppressing even non-revolutionary demands for change, the history of the government's involvement with Puritanism does in fact consist of those exceptional moments of crisis which tradition supposed were typical of the whole movement.[145]

From the first a considerable section of the English Church was not satisfied with the 1559 settlement. Led, to begin with, by some of those who had

---

[141] Haigh, *Eng. Hist. Rev.*, XCII, 30 ff.; Tyacke, *English Commonwealth*, 77 ff.

[142] Collinson, *Grindal*, and *Studies in Church History*, III, 91 ff.; Lake, *History*, LXIV, 182 ff.

[143] E.g. Collinson, *Bull. Inst. Hist. Res.*, Supplement V; Cross, *Puritan Earl*; Read, *Walsingham*, II, 258 ff.

[144] Babbage, *Puritanism and Richard Bancroft*.

[145] That Neale was wrong in regarding the House of Commons as deeply infected with revolutionary Puritanism has already been said (above, p. 310).

deepened their Protestantism in continental exile under Mary but later by a younger generation of clergy trained especially at Cambridge,[146] they held that the Elizabethan Church retained too many traces of popery and must be purified. The malcontents opened their first attack in the southern Convocation of 1563, with six articles demanding reforms in outward observances (202).[147] They were narrowly defeated, but Archbishop Parker was not content with this. From 1566, using his *Advertisements* on clerical dress and ceremonies,[148] he waged vigorous war on nonconformity in the clergy. The Vestiarian Controversy[149] ended in victory for the official Church and the bishops, and conformity seemed established. The battle was entirely over externals, but it had its ominous side. The queen, who was driving the reluctant bishops on to more energetic action, regarded these Puritan consciences as both needlessly precise and potentially subversive; and about the second of these she was right. For the consequences of the controversy were much more far-reaching than its occasion. The bishops' disciplinary action concentrated the attack on them. The second phase of Elizabethan Puritanism turned on the government of the Church and involved a wholesale assault on the institution of episcopacy. As Elizabeth rightly maintained, it therefore—and in spite of the never-ceasing avowals of loyalty—involved an attack on her supremacy. The phase began with the appointment, in 1569, of Thomas Cartwright as Lady Margaret professor of divinity at Cambridge. Cartwright, the pope of Elizabethan Puritanism, was in everything a complete Calvinist and Presbyterian.[150] The difference that his teaching made may be conveniently studied by a comparison between the 1563 articles (202), with their mild complaints about externals, and the brief list of nineteen points in which Bancroft, one of their chief enemies, accurately summed up the 'opinions and dealings of the precisians'.[151] Ceremonies, vestments and the like are still part of the issue, but discipline (the nature of Church government) is entirely to the fore. They 'condemn the authority of bishops and ecclesiastical officers as wicked, unlawful and not agreeable to God's word', and 'condemn all bishops, deans, and archdeacons, and desire to have certain elders or superintendents. . . . Some also refuse to pray for the queen as supreme governor in all causes ecclesiastical'. Resting themselves on their

[146] Cambridge remained the chief centre of Puritan teaching throughout the reign, though it had its conservatives (Porter, *Reformation and Reaction*, Part II). At Oxford, where Roman Catholicism retained a foothold (Knappen, *Tudor Puritanism*, 218), there were a few Puritan cells, notably Magdalen College under Lawrence Humphreys. The personalities of individual heads of houses—sometimes of individual tutors—were decisive; both Catholic and Puritan parents took care to place their sons with men of the right persuasion.

[147] The battles of this meeting are the chief subject of Haugaard, *Elizabeth*.

[148] Prothero, 191 ff. The *Advertisements* are a handy guide to the sort of nonconformity encountered at this stage.

[149] Primus, *Vestments Controversy*.

[150] Cf. Pearson, *Thomas Cartwright*.   [151] *Tracts ascribed to Bancroft*, 10 ff.

appeal to the Bible—which meant that they asked for every disputed institution or practice to be proved in Scripture before they would accept it—they had come to stand for a totally different Church from that established in 1559. They were now a fully revolutionary movement, but they were a small, though powerful, minority among all those whom one must call Puritan.

Between 1569 and 1572 the Presbyterians attempted to overthrow the bishops through a concerted attack in Parliament and the press. The failure of reform by statute in 1571 produced a major concentration of effort in 1572 with the two *Admonitions to the Parliament*, the first (**203**) written by two young London ministers, John Field[152] and Thomas Wilcox, and the second (**204**) almost certainly by Cartwright himself who had returned from abroad where he had gone after deprivation at Cambridge. The two documents give a full and clear conspectus of the Puritan plan, and the 1572 Parliament did consider a bill which would have slackened the enforcement of uniformity on deviant clergy, but the move encountered the hostility of the queen and collapsed.[153] The Puritan clergy were thus thrown back on their own resources and attempted for the next few years to convert the Church by persuasion and example. This they did in the so-called 'prophesyings' which were, on the face of them, no more than meetings of the clergy in the localities for the purpose of studying and expounding Scripture. They sought and obtained the approval, even the assistance, of some of the bishops who at first saw in this no more than a useful means of improving the general level of their clergy.[154] Edmund Grindal, who succeeded Parker at Canterbury in 1576, a man particularly aware of the deficiencies of the clergy, defended the prophesyings to Elizabeth as wholesome and harmless (**205**); but the queen saw deeper. From her point of view she was right to treat the movement as subversive, for these meetings could and did form nuclei for presbyterian cells; when Grindal refused to obey her order to suppress them (**206**) he was suspended. Most bishops did as they were told, and the Puritans found themselves once again under general attack.

Thus the policy of 'tarrying for the magistrate' had failed: while that magistrate was Elizabeth they would have a long wait. The Puritans therefore changed their tactics once more and fell back on conversion from below, bit by bit, and by stages. From the early 1570's onwards, but more commonly later in the decade, extreme ministers cooperated with sympathetic gentry and town councils to create local organisations—either incorporating or often bypassing the parish—in which 'the example of the best reformed

---

152 Coninson, *Government and Society*, 127 ff.
153 Neale, *Elizabeth and her Parliaments*, I, 298 ff. greatly exaggerates.
154 Collinson, *Movement*, 168 ff. Tanner, 179 ff., prints an example of the regulations for these 'exercises' approved by the bishop of Lincoln.

Churches' (read Geneva) might be followed. These local associations, called *classis* or conference, sometimes replaced the Prayer Book with Walter Travers's highly Genevan *Book of Discipline* (1574), enforced spiritual and moral discipline upon both ministers and laity, and in some place (especially in the county of Northampton) set up a secret Presbyterian Church within the episcopal structure of the official Church. However, this 'classical movement' manifested little coherence: it never embraced more than a part of the realm, varied in practices and intensity from place to place, and generally lacked the hallmark of true Presbyterianism—the appointment of lay elders to the government of the Church.[155] Though powerfully and purposely nonconforming, very few classes seem to have thought of revolution from within. Of course, the potential existed, especially when efforts were made, led by Field, to bring these various half-secret groups into cooperation by organising synods attended by representatives. The example of what the French Hugenots had managed to achieve with precisely such means—a state within a state—acted as a sufficient warning, and once Grindal was out of the way the government took countermeasures. It was the attack launched from 1583 by Archbishop Whitgift—a firm Calvinist but an implacable enemy to Presbyterianism—that changed the atmosphere. Whitgift energetically sought out nonconforming clergy, using the High Commission and the three articles framed in 1583 (**207**) to compel submission or, if that was denied, to deprive the irreconcilable.[156] The extremists, led by Field, reacted by attempting a true revolution in the Church: repression turned the bogey into a reality. Field's heyday came in 1587. He prepared the ground by compiling an indictment of the official Church ('Survey of the Ministry'),[157] convened a general synod in London of like-minded men from many parts of the country, and coordinated things with Anthony Cope who introduced his revolutionary proposal for setting up a Presbyterian Church into the parliamentary session of that year (**164**).[158] The attack turned out to be a comprehensive and revealing failure. Cope was easily blocked by the Speaker, while the synod, like that convened in 1589 at Cambridge, displayed not the strength of a movement but only the violent disagreements dividing the opinionated brethren.

Field died in 1588, and with him departed what force this much overrated

---

[155] The classical movement is both fully studied and reduced to its proper weight in Collinson, *Movement*, esp. 131 ff., 208 ff. The survival of the minute book of the Dedham classis in Essex used to mislead people into taking the peculiar for the typical (cf. Usher, *Presbyterian Movement*, Introduction).

[156] For an example of a High Commission investigation cf. the articles put to Cartwright in 1590 and his necessarily evasive answers: *Cartwrightiana*, 21 ff.

[157] Cf. **173** for an extract from this heavily biased survey.

[158] Cope's 'Bill and Book'—a bill to abolish bishops, and Travers's *Book* to replace the Book of Common Prayer.

movement had had. However, the panic, nurtured by queen, Whitgift and Bancroft, encouraged an ever more energetic purging of the clergy, with, in effect, total success. The revolutionary phase proved to have neither endurance nor substance. With the outbreak of the patriotic war the support which Puritan ambitions had secured from a more moderate but uneasy laity began to decline. Thirty years of usage were conferring stability on Church and Prayer Book; the Puritans no longer had a monopoly in intellectual and pastoral distinction; and some of their most active leaders died between 1588 and 1590. Cartwright, in exile till that last date, returned a markedly less incendiary preacher than he had left. The violently abusive, though often pointedly funny, Marprelate Tracts of 1589 alienated more opinion than they attracted, and this gave Whitgift grounds for further vigour.[159] By the early 1590's the bishops had won: the classis was in effect dead, the clergy nearly all conforming, and the Elizabethan Presbyterian movement had come to a real end even before it received an intellectual put-down from Hooker. What not even Whitgift could suppress, however, was that general dissatisfaction with a Church that did not measure up to the strenuous demands of prophecy-inspired believers. Reforming Puritanism—sometimes eirenic, sometimes embattled, usually millenarian, sometimes very sane but often pretty mad—survived the attack because it remained politically quiescent; its followers could conform sufficiently to maintain the Church of England's traditional tolerance for men of widely differing views under one institutional umbrella.

Quite apart from Puritans of whatever kind, all of whom held to a belief in one national Church (sinners as well as saints), there existed separatist splinter groups, small in number, at odds with one another, but interesting as representing a different spiritual and usually also social milieu. These sects were distinguished by their conviction that the true Church must consist of elect believers only and that they, in every case, were the only true believers.[160] These 'gathered churches' had ancestral links with Lollard and Anabaptist cells, owed something to the tolerated strangers' churches (French and Dutch) in London, but grew up in the main because in an age of chiliastic and splintered faith any prophet can attract seekers to his tabernacle.[161] The largest group was that which accepted Robert Browne's combative leadership at Norwich, and Brownist came to be the term most commonly applied to sectaries who, rejecting all external authority, drew everybody's hostility upon themselves. That there was much logic and piety in their notions (208) is obvious enough. But while the majority of men

---

[159] Pierce, *Historical Introduction* (from a nonconformist point of view); McGinn, *John Penry*.

[160] Knappen, *Tudor Puritanism*, 303 ff. provides a still acceptable outline—provided it is understood that separatists were *not* Puritans.

[161] Loades, *England and the Continent*, 59 ff.; Collinson, *ibid.*, 71 ff., and *Movement*, 87 ff.

agreed that in one realm there can be only one Church, the growth of sects was bound to be seen as the last word in disruption. Bancroft found a dozen heresies in Browne's works, ranging from papism and anabaptism to Priscillianism and Donatism.[162] Persecution and exile were the lot of these small, self-contained congregations, usually composed of the lower orders, though in the end many returned to the fold. The Parliament of 1593 was easily persuaded to pass a vicious act against sectaries (209); the London leaders Henry Barrow and John Greenwood were hanged for felonious sedition in 1593, and so was the most remarkable and perhaps finest spirit among the separatists, John Penry.[163] In the reign of Elizabeth, separatism like presbyterianism came to an abrupt end, though no doubt both left pieces of root in the ground.

202. The puritan articles in Convocation, 1563.

I. That all the Sundays in the year and principal feasts of Christ be kept holy days; and all other holy days to be abrogated.

II. That in all parish churches the minister in common prayer turn his face towards the people; and there distinctly read the divine service appointed, where all the people assembled may hear and be edified.

III. That in ministering the sacrament of baptism, the ceremony of making the cross in the child's forehead may be omitted, as tending to superstition.

IV. That forasmuch as divers communicants are not able to kneel during the time of the communion, for age, sickness and sundry other infirmities, and some also superstitiously both kneel and knock;[164] that order of kneeling may be left to the discretion of the ordinary within his jurisdiction.

V. That it be sufficient for the minister, in time of saying divine service and ministering of the sacraments, to use a surplice; and that no minister say service or minister the sacraments but in a comely garment or habit.

VI. That the use of organs be removed.   Strype, *Annals*, I, 502–3

203. The First Admonition to the Parliament, 1572.

. . . May it therefore please your wisdoms to understand, we in England are so far off from having a Church rightly reformed, according to the prescript of God's word that as yet we are not come to the outward face

---

[162] *Tracts ascribed to Bancroft*, 2 ff.
[163] For Penry cf. especially his *Notebook*.   [164] Beat their breasts.

of the same. For to speak of that wherein all consent and whereupon all writers accord: the outward marks whereby a true Christian Church is known are preaching the Word purely, ministering of the sacraments sincerely, and ecclesiastical discipline which consisteth in admonition and correction of faults severely. Touching the first, namely the ministry of the Word, although it must be confessed that the substance of doctrine by many delivered is sound and good, yet herein it faileth that neither the ministers thereof are according to God's word proved, elected, called or ordained, nor the function in such sort so narrowly looked unto as of right it ought and is of necessity required. . . .

. . . Now to the second point, which concerneth ministration of sacraments. In the old time the Word was preached before they were ministered; now it is supposed to be sufficient if it be read. Then, they were ministered in public assemblies, now in private houses. Then by ministers only, now by midwives and deacons equally. . . . To redress these, your wisdoms have to remove (as before) ignorant ministers. . . . To join assistance of elders and other officers, that seeing men will not examine themselves they may be examined and brought to render a reason of their hope. . . . That people be appointed to receive the sacrament rather sitting, for avoiding of superstition, than kneeling, having in it the outward show of evil from which we must abstain. That excommunication be restored to his old former force. That papists nor other, neither constrainedly nor customably, communicate in the mysteries of salvation. That both the sacrament of the Lord's Supper and baptism also may be ministered according to the ancient purity and simplicity. . . .

Let us now come to the third part, which concerneth ecclesiastical discipline. The officers that have to deal in this charge are chiefly three: ministers, preachers or pastors, of whom before; seniors or elders; and deacons. Concerning seniors, not only their office but their name also is out of this English Church utterly removed. Their office was to govern the Church with the rest of the ministers, to consult, to admonish, to correct and to order all things appertaining to the state of the congregation. Instead of these seniors in every Church, the pope has brought in, and we yet maintain, the lordship of one man over many churches, yea over sundry shires. These seniors, then, because their charge was not overmuch, did execute their offices in their own persons without substitutes. Our lords bishops have their under-officers, as suffragans, chancellors, archdeacons, officials, commissaries, and such like. Touching deacons, though their names be remaining, yet is the office foully perverted and turned upside down, for their duty in the primitive Church was to gather the alms diligently and to distribute it faithfully, also for the sick and impotent persons to provide painfully, having ever a diligent care that the charity of godly men were not wasted upon loiterers and vagabonds. Now it is the first step to the ministry, nay rather a mere order of priesthood. For they may baptise in the presence of a bishop or priest, or in their absence (if necessity so require) minister the other sacrament, likewise read the Holy Scriptures and homilies in the congregation, instruct the youth in the catechism, and also preach if he be commanded by the bishop. Again, in the old Church every congregation had their deacons. Now they are tied to cathedral churches only, and what do they do there? Gather the alms and distribute to the poor? Nay, that is the least piece, or rather no part of their function. What then? To sing a gospel when the bishop ministereth the communion. If this be not a perverting of this office and charge, let everyone judge. . . . The final end of this discipline is the reforming of the disordered and to bring them to repentance and to bridle such as would offend. The chiefest part and last punishment of this discipline is excommunication, by the consent of the Church determined, if the offender be obstinate, which how miserably it hath been by the pope's proctors and is by our new canonists abused, who seeth not? In the primitive Church it was in many men's hands; now one alone excommunicateth. In those days it was the last censure of the Church and never went forth but for notorious crimes; now it is pronounced for every light trifle. Then excommunication was greatly regarded and feared; now, because it is a money matter, no whit at all esteemed. . . .

Frere and Douglas, Puritan Manifestoes, 9, 13–14, 15–17

204. The Second Admonition to the Parliament, 1572.

. . . Next, you must repeal your statute or statutes whereby you have authorised that ministry that now is, making your estate partly to consist of lords spiritual (as you call them) and making one minister higher than another, appointing also an order to ordain ministers, which order is clean differing from the Scriptures; wherefore you must have the order for these things drawn out of the Scriptures, which order is this. When any parish is destitute of a pastor or of a teacher, the same parish may have recourse to the next conference and to them make it known that they may procure chiefly from the one of the universities, or, if otherwise, a man learned and of good report, whom, after trial of his gifts had in their conference, they may present unto the parish which before had been with them about that matter, but yet so that the same parish have him a certain time amongst them, that they may be acquainted with his gifts and behaviour, and give their consents for his stay amongst them if they can allege no just cause to the contrary; for he may not be sent away again which is so sent to a parish except a just cause of misliking, the cause alleged being justly proved against him either amongst themselves in their own consistory, so that he will appeal no further for his trial, or else in the next conference, or council provincial, or national, unto which from one to another he may appeal if he find himself clear; and if he give over they may proceed as afore for another. And when such an one is found to whom the parish must give consent because there is no just cause to be alleged against him, the next conference by whose means he was procured shall be certified of the parish's liking, whereupon they shall amongst themselves agree upon one of the ministers which shall be sent by them to the same parish, and after a sermon made according to the occasion, and earnest prayer to God with fasting, according to the example of the Scriptures, made by that congregation to God that it would please him to direct them in their choice and to bless that man whom they choose, he shall require to know their consent, which being granted he and the elders shall lay their hands on him, to signify to him that he is lawfully called to that parish to be pastor there or teacher. . . .

. . . This is the right way to bring the ministry into credit and estimation—their gifts given them of God and their painfulness and honest life amongst their congregations, and not to make some of them lords, graces, earls, prelate and register of the Garter, barons, suffragans, some of them rich deans, archdeacons, masters of Colleges, chancellors, prebends, rich parsons and vicars, and though some of them be poor enough to get them credit by their rochets, hoods, caps, cloaks, tippets and gowns, or such-like implements used by the Pharisees, which claimed high rooms and made large borders on their garments and loved to be greeted and to be called rabbi, which things by our Saviour are forbidden his ministers and an order enjoined that they which look for it should not have it but be least esteemed. . . .

. . . I have already made mention of a consistory which were to be had in every congregation. That consisteth first of the ministers of the

451

same congregation, as the guides and mouth of the rest, to direct them
by the Scriptures, and to speak at their appointment that which shall be
consented upon amongst them all, because of their gifts and place
amongst them, which maketh them more fit for those purposes. The
assistants are they whom the parish shall consent upon and choose for
their good judgment in religion and godliness, . . . using the advice of
their ministers therein chiefly . . . and also using earnest prayers with
fasting, as in the choice of the minister; and having made their choice,
thereafter they shall publish their agreement in their parish, and after
a sermon by their minister at their appointment and upon their consent
the minister may lay his hands upon every of them to testify to them
their admission. This consistory . . . shall examine all disordered ceremonies used in place of prayer and abolish those which they find evil or
unprofitable, and bring in such orders as their congregation shall have
need of, so they be few and apparent, necessary both for edifying and
profit and decent order, proving it plainly to the whole church that
it is so. . . .   Frere and Douglas, *Puritan Manifestoes*, 96–7, 102–3, 118–20

205. Edmund Grindal to Queen Elizabeth, 20 December 1576.

. . . Now for the second point, which is concerning the learned exercise and conference amongst the ministers of the Church. I have consulted with divers of my brethren the bishops by letters, who think the
same as I do, viz.—a thing profitable to the Church and therefore
expedient to be continued. And I trust your Majesty will think the
like when your Highness shall be informed of the manner and order
thereof; what authority it hath of the Scriptures; what commodity
it bringeth with it; and what incommodities will follow if it be
clear taken away. The authors of this exercise are the bishops of the
dioceses where the same is used, who both by the law of God and
by the canons and constitutions of the Church now in force have
authority to appoint exercises to their inferior ministers for increase of
learning and knowledge in the Scriptures as to them seemeth most
expedient. . . .

These orders following are also observed in the said exercise: First,
two or three of the gravest and best learned pastors are appointed of the
bishop to moderate in every assembly. No man may speak unless he be
first allowed by the bishop, with this proviso that no layman be suffered
to speak at any time. No controversy of this present time and state shall

be moved or dealt withal. If any attempt the contrary, he is put to silence by the moderator. None is suffered to glance openly or covertly at persons public or private, neither yet anyone to confute another. If any man utter a wrong sense of the Scripture, he is privately admonished thereof and better instructed by the moderators and other his fellow-ministers. If any man use immodest speech or irreverent gesture or be-haviour, or otherwise be suspected in life, he is likewise admonished as before. If any wilfully do break these orders, he is presented to the bishop to be by him corrected. . . .

Howsoever report hath been made to your Majesty concerning these exercises, yet I and others of your bishops whose names are noted in the margin hereof,[165] as they have testified unto me by their letters, having found by experience that these profits and commodities fol-lowing have ensued of them: 1. The ministers of the Church are more skilful and ready in the Scriptures, and apter to teach their flocks. 2. It withdraweth them from idleness, wandering, gaming, etc. 3. Some afore suspected in doctrine are brought hereby to open confession of the truth. 4. Ignorant ministers are driven to study, if not for conscience yet for shame and fear of discipline. 5. The opinion of laymen touching the idleness of the clergy is hereby removed. 6. Nothing by experience beateth down popery more than that ministers (as some of my brethren do certify) grow to such a good knowledge by means of these exercises that where afore were not three able preachers, now are thirty meet to preach at St Paul's Cross, and forty or fifty besides able to instruct their own cures; so as it is found by experience the best means to increase knowledge in the simple and to continue it in the learned. Only back-ward men in religion and contemners of learning in the countries abroad do fret against it; which in truth doth the more commend it. The dissolution of it would breed triumph to the adversaries, but great sorrow and grief unto the favours of religion. . . . And although some few have abused this good and necessary exercise, there is no reason that the malice of a few should prejudice all. . . .   Strype, *Grindal*, 566–9

206. The Queen's letter suppressing prophesyings, 1577.

Right reverent father in God, we greet you well. We hear to our great grief that in sundry parts of our realm there are no small number of

---

[165] Canterbury, London, Winchester, Bath, Lichfield, Gloucester, Lincoln, Chichester, Exeter and St David's.

persons, presuming to be teachers and preachers of the Church though neither lawfully thereunto called nor yet fit for the same, which, contrary to our laws established for the public divine service of Almighty God and the administration of His holy sacraments within this Church of England, do daily devise, imagine, propound and put in execution sundry new rites and forms in the Church, as well by their preaching, reading and ministering the sacraments, as well by procuring unlawful assemblies of a great number of our people out of their ordinary parishes and from place far distant, and that also some of good calling (though therein not well advised) to be hearers of their disputations and new devised opinions upon points of divinity far and unmeet of unlearned people, which manner of invasions they in some places call prophesying and in some other places exercises; by which manner of assemblies great numbers of our people, specially the vulgar sort, meet to be otherwise occupied with honest labour for their living, are brought to idleness and seduced and in a manner schismatically divided amongst themselves into variety of dangerous opinions, not only in towns and parishes but even in some families, and manifestly thereby encouraged to the violation of our laws and to the breach of common order, and finally to the offence of all our quiet subjects that desire to serve God according to the uniform orders established in the Church, whereof the sequel cannot be but over dangerous to be suffered. Wherefore, considering it should be the duty of the bishops . . . to see these dishonours against the honour of God and the quietness of the Church reformed, and that we see that . . . great danger may ensue, even to the decay of the Christian faith, whereof we are by God appointed the defender, besides the other inconveniences to the disturbance of peaceable government; we therefore, according to authority we have, charge and command you . . . to take order through your diocese . . . that no manner of public and divine service, nor other form of the administration of the holy sacraments, nor any other rites or ceremonies, be in any sort used in the Church but directly according to the orders established by our laws. Neither that any manner of person be suffered within your diocese to preach, teach, read, or any wise exercise any function in the Church but such as shall be lawfully approved and licensed as persons able for their knowledge and conformable to the ministry in the rites and ceremonies of the Church of England; and where there shall not be sufficient able persons for learning in any cures to preach or instruct their cures as were requisite, there you shall limit the curates to read the public Homilies, according to the injunctions heretofore by us given for like causes. And furthermore considering for the great abuses that have been in sundry places of our realm by reason of the foresaid assemblies called exercises . . . we will and straitly charge you that you also charge the same forthwith to cease and not to be used; but if any shall attempt, or continue, or renew the same, we will you not only to commit them unto prison as maintainers of disorders, but also to advertise us or our Council of the names and qualities of them and of their maintainers and abettors, that thereupon for better example their punishment may be more sharp for their reformation. And in these things we charge you to be so careful and vigilant, as by your negligence, if we shall hear of any person attempting to offend in the premises without your correction or information to us, we be not forced to make some example or reformation of you, according to your deserts. Given under our signet at our manor of Greenwich the 7th of May, 1577.

Cardwell, Documentary Annals, I, 373

207. Archbishop Whitgift's Articles, 1583.

*   *   *   *   *   *

Sixthly, that none be permitted to preach, read, catechise, minister the sacraments, or to execute any other ecclesiastical function, by what authority so ever he be admitted thereunto, unless he first consent and subscribe to these articles following, before the ordinary of the diocese wherein he preacheth, readeth, catechiseth, or ministereth the sacraments: *viz.*

I. That her Majesty, under God, hath and ought to have the sovereignty and rule over all manner of persons born within her realms and dominions and countries, of what estate ecclesiastical or temporal so ever they be. And that none other foreign power, prelate, state or potentate hath or ought to have any jurisdiction, power, superiority, preeminence or authority ecclesiastical or temporal within her Majesty's said realms, dominions and countries.

II. That the Book of Common Prayer, and of ordering bishops, priests and deacons, containeth nothing in it contrary to the Word of God. And that the same may be lawfully used; and that he himself will use the form of the said book prescribed, in public prayer and administration of the sacraments, and none other.

III. That he alloweth the book of Articles of Religion, agreed upon by the archbishops and bishops in both provinces, and the whole clergy in the Convocation holden at London in the year of our Lord 1562, and set forth by her Majesty's authority. And that he believeth all the articles therein contained to be agreeable to the word of God.

*   *   *   *   *   *

Strype, *Whitgift*, I, 229–30

208. Henry Barrow on the nature of the Church, 1590.

... The people, upon a superstitious reverence and preposterous estimation unto their teachers and elders, resigned up all things, even their duty, interest, liberty, prerogative, into their hands, suffering them to alter and dispose of all things after their own lusts, without inquiry or controlment; whereupon the true pattern of Christ's Testament, so highly and with so great charge incommended by the Apostles unto the fidelity of the whole Church, was soon neglected and cast aside, especially by these evil workmen these governors, who some of them affecting the preeminence, sought to draw an absolute power into their own hands, perverting those offices of more labour and care into swelling titles of fleshly pomp and worldly dignity. ... Then were these called bishops ... and had under them inferior or country bishops, as also deacons, subdeacons. Thus the whole Church growing remiss and negligent, both people and officers, that heavenly pattern left by the Apostles was soon violate, and upon new pretences more and more innovate. ... The pride of some could not herewith be satisfied until they had gotten them a new dignity, namely to be archbishops over all the bishops in a province or country. Here were also new deacons, archdeacons erected; yet was not the ambitious thirst of some thus staunched, but they aspired yet to a more high degree and preeminence, so that there must now be picked out four principal cities which must carry four patriarchs. These had yet higher power than the archbishops, and were erected to see to the government and discipline (as they call it) of all churches, in respect, or rather in despite of those four beasts which had so many eyes and wings and stood day and night about the throne of God, but they were rather those four angels which stood upon the four corners of the earth, holding the four winds of the earth, that the winds should not blow upon the earth, neither on the sea, nor on any tree. (pp. 3–4).

... The prince himself entereth by the same door of faith into the

456

Church, and is bound to the strait observation and obedience of God's laws in his calling as well as any other; and is for any transgression thereof liable and subject to the censures and judgments of Christ in his Church, which are without partiality or respect of persons. Which censures and judgments if the prince contemn, he contemneth them against his own soul and is thereupon by the same power of Christ to be disfranchised out of the Church and to be delivered over unto Satan, as well as any other offender. Now though by this sin he loseth his right to be a Christian or member of the Church, yet loseth he not his right to be a king or magistrate, and is so to be held and obeyed of all faithful Christians which are his subjects ... (pp. 14–15).

The poor parish or congregation where these priests serve may not meddle or have to do with the election, administration or deposing of these their ministers; for why, they are laymen and have no skill, neither ought to intermeddle with ecclesiastical affairs or with the Word of God. Be their minister never so blind, unsufficient or vile a wretch, detected of never so horrible sins, yet may not they remove him; their only help is to complain to their lord ordinary.[166] ... Let their minister preach never such damnable or heretical doctrine, wrest, pervert, corrupt, falsify the Scriptures never so violently and heinously, all the church ... hath no authority, nay is by express law forbidden, to reprove this doctrine presently or publicly, or yet to forbid him to deal with the Scriptures; their remedy is still to complain to their ordinary and until it please him to take order therein, the whole congregation is still bound to frequent his heretical sermons and ministry. ... But my purpose is ... to shew that every Christian congregation hath power in themselves, and of duty ought, presently and publicly to censure any false or unsound doctrine that is publicly delivered or maintained amongst them, if it be known and discerned unto them; yea, any one member in the Church hath this power, whatsoever he be, pastor or prophet, that uttereth it ... (p. 165).

The public censuring of any member, whether elder or other, is an action of the whole Church, whereunto (if it use the most fit members or officers) should such officers and members hereupon arrogate the whole action, interest and power to themselves, secluding the whole body of the Church, whose officers and members they are? ... What a dismembering of the body and rending of the Church would these

---

[166] I.e. the bishop or his official.

ambitious priests make, who the one would withdraw all public actions of the Church into their popish courts, the other into their conventicles and synods of priests?

As for reproof by admonition, any member of the Church hath free power also to reprove the greatest elder of the Church according to the quality of his offence; if his office be private, privately, if public, publicly: yea, he is bound by the law of God so to do . . . (p. 230).

We have shewed how this power of excommunication, election, ordination, etc., is not committed into the hands of one particular person, as the pope and his natural children our lord bishops now use it; nor yet into the hands of the eldership only or of the pastors of many particular congregations (as the reforming preachers would have it); so much as it is given and committed to the whole Church, even to every particular congregation, and to every member thereof alike . . . (p. 242).

A Brief Discovery . . .

209. An Act to retain the Queen's subjects in obedience (1593: 35 Eliz. I, c. 1).

For the preventing and avoiding of such great inconveniences and perils as might happen and grow by the wicked and dangerous practices of seditious sectaries and disloyal persons: Be it enacted by the Queen's most excellent Majesty, and by the Lords spiritual and temporal and the Commons in this present Parliament assembled, and by the authority of the same, that if any person or persons above the age of sixteen years which shall obstinately refuse to repair to some church, chapel or usual place of common prayer to hear divine service established by her Majesty's laws and statutes in that behalf made, and shall forbear to do the same by the space of a month next after without lawful cause, shall at any time after forty days next after the end of this session of Parliament, by printing, writing or express words or speeches, advisedly and purposely practise or go about to move or persuade any of her Majesty's subjects or any other within her Highness' realms or dominions to deny, withstand and impugn her Majesty's power and authority in causes ecclesiastical united and annexed to the imperial crown of this realm; or to that end or purpose shall advisedly and maliciously move or persuade any other person whatsoever to forbear or abstain from coming to church to hear divine service or to receive the communion according to her Majesty's laws and statutes aforesaid, or to come to or to be present at any unlawful assemblies, conventicles or meetings under colour of pretence of any exercise of religion, contrary to her Majesty's said laws and statutes; or if any person or persons which shall obstinately refuse to repair to some church, chapel or usual place of common prayer and shall forbear by the space of a month to hear divine service as is aforesaid, shall after the said forty days either of him or themselves, or by the motion, persuasion, enticement or allurement of any other, willingly join or be present at any such assemblies, conventicles or meetings under colour or pretence of any such exercise of religion, contrary to the laws and statutes of this realm as is aforesaid: That then every such person so offending as aforesaid, and being thereof lawfully convicted, shall be committed to prison, there to remain without bail or mainprize until they shall conform and yield themselves to come to some church, chapel or usual place of common prayer and hear divine service, according to her Majesty's laws and statutes aforesaid, and to make such open submission and declaration of their said conformity as hereafter in this act is declared and appointed.

II. Provided always and be it further enacted by the authority aforesaid that if any such person or persons which shall offend against this act as aforesaid shall not within three months next after they shall be convicted of their said offence conform themselves to the obedience of the laws and statutes of this realm in coming to the church to hear divine service and in making such public confession and submission as hereafter in this act is appointed and expressed, being thereunto required by the bishop of the diocese, or any justice of peace of the county where the same person shall happen to be, or by the minister or curate of the parish, that in every such case every such offender, being thereunto warned or required by any justice of the peace of the same county where such offender shall then be, shall upon his and their corporal oath before the justices of peace in the open quarter sessions of the same county, or at the assizes and gaol delivery of the same county before the justices of the same assizes and gaol delivery, abjure this realm of England and all other the Queen's Majesty's dominions for ever unless her Majesty shall license the party to return. And thereupon shall depart out of this realm at such haven or port and within such time as shall in that behalf be assigned and appointed by the said justices before whom such abjuration shall be made, unless the same offender be letted or stayed by such lawful and reasonable means or causes as by the common laws of this realm are permitted and allowed in cases of abjuration for felony;

and in such cases of let or stay, then within such reasonable and convenient time after as the common law requireth in case of abjuration
for felony as is aforesaid. . . . And if any such offender . . . shall refuse
to make such abjuration as is aforesaid, or after such abjuration made
shall not go to such haven and within such time as is before appointed
and from thence depart out of this realm according to this present act,
or after such his departure shall return or come again into any her
Majesty's realms or dominions without her Majesty's special licence in
that behalf first had and obtained, that then in every such case the person so offending shall be adjudged a felon, and shall suffer as in case of
felony without benefit of clergy.

[III. Offenders who, before they are required to make abjuration,
'repair to some parish church on some Sunday or other festival day and
then and there hear divine service, and at service time before the sermon or reading of the gospel make public and open submission,'
according to a form prescribed in the act, are discharged from the
penalties inflicted by the act. Such submissions are to be entered by the
curate in a book to be kept for the purpose in every parish, and within
ten days he is to 'certify the same in writing' to the bishop of the
diocese.]

*   *   *   *   *   *

v. And for that every person having house and family is in duty
bounden to have special regard of the good government and ordering
of the same: Be it enacted by the authority aforesaid that if any person
or persons shall at any time hereafter relieve, maintain, retain or keep in
his or their house or otherwise any person which shall obstinately refuse
to come to some church, chapel or usual place of common prayer to
hear divine service, and shall forbear the same by the space of a month
together, contrary to the laws and statutes of this realm, that then every
person which shall so relieve, maintain, retain or keep any such person
offending as aforesaid, after notice thereof to him or them given by the
ordinary of the diocese, or any justice of assizes of the circuit, or any
justice of peace of the county, or the minister, curate or churchwardens
of the parish where such person shall then be, or by any of them,
shall forfeit to the Queen's Majesty for every person so relieved,
maintained, retained or kept after such notice as aforesaid, ten pounds
for every month that he or they shall so relieve, maintain, retain or
keep any such person so offending.

VI. Provided nevertheless that this act shall not in any wise extend to punish or impeach any person or persons for relieving, maintaining or keeping his or their wife, father, mother, child or children, ward, brother or sister, or his wife's father or mother not having any certain place of habitation of their own, or the husbands or wives of any of them; or for relieving, maintaining or keeping any such person as shall be committed by authority to the custody of any by whom they shall be so relieved, maintained or kept; anything in this act contained to the contrary notwithstanding.

* * * * * *

x. Provided also that every person that shall abjure by force of this act, or refuse to abjure being thereunto required as aforesaid, shall forfeit and lose to her Majesty all his goods and chattels for ever, and shall further lose all his lands, tenements and hereditaments for and during the life only of such offender and no longer; and that the wife of any offender by force of this act shall not lose her dower; nor that any corruption of blood shall grow or be by reason of any offence mentioned in this act; but that the heir of every such offender by force of this act shall and may after the death of every offender have and enjoy the lands, tenements and hereditaments of such offender as if this act had not been made. And this act to continue no longer than to the end of the next session of Parliament.   *Stat. Realm*, IV, 841–3

CHAPTER 10

LOCAL GOVERNMENT

Local government under the Tudors can be described quite briefly; alternatively it requires a whole volume to itself. The first method, of necessity adopted here, gives a concise account of the instruments available; the second tries to show how that machinery actually worked in the great diversity of English regions—the highly complex interaction of local administration and politics, and the equally complex interaction of central institutions with the local agents of enforcement. The realities of what perhaps hardly deserves the name of a system involved a vast network of altogether informal relationships and arrangements because it was recognised that the locality had its own social structure upon which action would have to rely: social superiors naturally exercised rule over their inferiors, even if both remained ultimately responsible to king and Council. The carrying out of policy and even the enforcement of the law were liable to depend far more on the normal hierarchies of this society than on any bureaucratic channels of command. This is a theme, revolving around patronage and clientage, around social conventions and convictions, which cannot be usefully illustrated here: but its overriding importance should be remembered. A certain amount of work has by now been done to illumine the actual operation of law and government in shires and towns; any student of the Tudor constitution should be aware of that diffuse, highly variable and often obscure amalgam of formal government with social relationships, provided he does not fall into the error of supposing that so seemingly haphazard an arrangement could not possibly have worked effectively. Work it did, and dependence on the cooperation of the locality never induced monarch or Council to abate their authority or demand anything short of deference from the regions. If here we confine ourselves to the outline of the machinery, we shall nevertheless not forget that setting it to work involved a constant exchange of inquiries, reports, exhortations, appeals and reproofs— the mobilising of social duties generally accepted to derive from hierarchic function as much as from office.[1]

[1] For a detailed study of how the system actually worked cf. Elton, *Policy and Police*, chs. 3 & 8. A useful general account is provided in Williams, *Tudor Regime*, Part II. Studies of localities contain instructive discussions, often hidden behind social, economic or religious analyses. For counties cf.: Smith, *County and Court* (Norfolk); Clark, *English Provincial Society* (Kent); MacCulloch, 'Power, Privilege and the County Community' (Suffolk); Rowse, *Tudor Cornwall*; Dickens, *Lollards* and Smith, *Land and Politics* (Yorkshire); James, *Family, Lineage and Society* (Durham); Haigh, *Reformation and Resistance* (Lancashire); Hodgett, *Tudor Lincolnshire*. For London cf. Brigden, 'Early Reformation' and Foster, *Politics of Stability*. For other towns cf.

The agencies of local government in the sixteenth century were of three kinds: truly local courts, royal officials appointed in the localities, and local men commissioned by the Crown for purposes of government. Of the first it is here necessary to say only that neither the feudal (baronial) nor the popular (hundred and shire) courts retained much significant life. They dealt with a few very minor civil or criminal cases; but the only functions of consequence which remained to them were the economic administration of the manor through its court, and the election of knights for the Parliament in the shire court.[2] The number of royal officials increased at this time. To the old shire trinity of sheriff, escheator, and coroner were added not only familiar figures like lords lieutenant and their deputies, but also various receivers of royal revenue, customers and their underlings, and the feodaries of the Court of Wards.[3] The sheriff, once undisputed ruler of the shire, had long lost that place; in the fifteenth century, reliance on the local gentry and the difficulty of controlling sheriffs from the centre finally induced the Crown to deprive the office of all really important powers. As the officer responsible for certain unimportant revenues, for executing most judicial writs, for keeping the county gaol, and especially for supervising elections to the Parliament, the sheriff retained intermittent weight in administration; in the main, however, his office was a burdensome and expensive honour, only to be borne because it lasted only a year and came but once in a gentleman's life.[4]

The office of lord lieutenant, on the other hand, was an addition made by the Tudors.[5] It took its origin in military needs. Henry VIII, in particular, sometimes appointed temporary deputies in the north and west whom he called lieutenants; at the same time it became customary to commission local magnates to supervise the levying of shire musters and to be responsible for the military forces of a given district. Such commissions of array were used when need arose, but Northumberland, after 1550, reacted to the local disturbances of Edward VI's reign by regularly sending lieutenants into the shires year by year.[6] By the end of the century the whole country was divided into regular districts over which lords lieutenant presided,

MacCaffrey, *Exeter*; Phythian-Adams, *Coventry*; Howell, *Newcastle*, ch. 2; and more generally, Bond and Evans, *Eng. Hist. Rev.*, XCI, 102 ff.

[2] Holdsworth, I, 132 ff. says something about the survival of these old courts into recent times. The franchisal rights of certain lords encouraged them to maintain the jurisdiction of the court leet, once a sheriff's court but long since fallen into private hands (*ibid.*, IV, 127 ff.).

[3] The escheators were responsible for the king's rights over feudal tenures, though they were in effect superseded by the feodaries. Coroners were elected in the county court, but despite this they had started as royal officers intended to curb the independence of sheriffs. They already specialised in inquests on deaths.

[4] This may be quite inadequate. A study of the Tudor sheriff is badly needed.

[5] The fullest account is Scott Thomson, *Lords Lieutenants*; cf. also Cheyney, *History of England*, II, 359 ff.

[6] Scott Thomson, *Lords Lieutenants*, 30 ff.

though to the last the Tudors did not think it necessary or desirable to identify each shire with a single lieutenant. The men chosen were as a rule local magnates who had close links with the court. To assist them, they were usually allowed to appoint deputies, one or more to a shire.[7] This work remained, in the first place, military: the lieutenants were responsible for levying, mustering, equipping and commanding the militia upon which the defence of the country depended. They were also empowered to choose from among the musters any contingents picked for service abroad. The tasks involved in this were difficult, distasteful and hard to carry out with even a modicum of efficiency; military organisation and administration remained the gravest weakness of Tudor government.[8] However, officials so conveniently placed were bound, in Tudor conditions, to have other tasks laid on them as well. They played their part in administering taxation, religious uniformity and economic legislation.[9] Usually peers though sometimes commoners, they grew to be, under the watchful eye of the Privy Council, the formal heads of their localities.

However, despite the existence of such individual officers holding appointment by letters patent, the real sway over the regions was exercised by commissioning local gentlemen to carry out the orders of the central government. Such commissions were frequent and diverse, for the method was by its nature flexible: *ad hoc* general commissions, like those which saw to the dissolution of the lesser monasteries,[10] or *ad hoc* special commissions like those which empowered local men to investigate cases brought before the conciliar courts,[11] or more standing commissions like those of sewers, used in a half-organised way to make an attack on England's marshlands and waterways[12]— these and many other variants all rested on the power and willingness of the Crown to grant authority to act to certain chosen men of some social standing in their own neighbourhood. Of all these commissions, that of the peace was the most regular and most important. The justices of the peace, appointed shire by shire and year by year, were a well-established institution before the accession of the Tudors who greatly added to their administrative duties without really altering the nature of the office.[13] But while this is true, it is also true that during the sixteenth century this old system of local law-enforcement was vastly expanded and allowed to engross virtually all local government,

---

[7] Scott Thomson, *Trans. R. Hist. Soc.*, 1922, 150 ff.

[8] For the military organisation of Tudor England cf. Boynton, *Militia*; Cruickshank, *Elizabeth's Army*; Davies, *Econ. Hist. Rev.*, XVII, 234 ff.; Goring, *History*, LX, 185 ff.

[9] Scott Thomson, *Lords Lieutenants*, 117 ff.   [10] Above, p. 382.   [11] Above, p. 172.

[12] Regulated by statute in 1532 (23 Henry VIII, c. 5).

[13] Holdsworth, I, 29*. This fact should warn one against the sort of rhapsodies common on this subject; cf. Tanner, 452—the Tudors' 'reorganisation of the English system of local government is a monument to their constructive genius'. Gleason, *Justices*, still repeats such extravagances and is altogether not a satisfactory study of the institution.

to the exclusion of even older institutions. It became a principle with Tudor government to commit the carrying out of legislative reform to the justices, and this increase of work involved a refinement of organisation as well as the expansion of the commission. It is likely that this last reflects demand from below: as the justices took hold of the countryside, the gentry began to see in membership of the commission—work virtually unpaid and frequently tiresome—a necessary part of their lives and power. Numbers rose from less than ten to an average of forty or fifty to a shire, ranging from about fifteen in Rutland to about eighty in Kent; to all practical intents the commission included by the end of the century all the significant gentry.[14] For their instruction there appeared several handbooks, of which Lambarde's *Eirenarcha*, first published in 1581, was both the best and the most successful.[15] To obviate the most immediate dangers inherent in the employment of amateurs to administer complex legal problems, the Tudors developed three aspects of the institution. By the *quorum* clause in the commission they ensured that important things should not be done by the justices without the presence of one of a small group of trusted or expert members (210); by appointing the leading justice as keeper of the local records (*custos rotulorum*) they ensured the beginnings of organisation and some supervision over the rest; and by the regular appointment of a clerk of the peace to assist each commission they provided a small professional element in all that welter of amateurism.[16]

The powers and duties of the justices, as Lambarde remarked,[17] derived from two sources—the commission and certain statutes. The commission of the peace was issued every year. By the later middle ages it had assumed a fixed form of seven separate clauses which in the main authorised the justices to enforce the basic statutes concerning the peace and to enquire by jury into stated offences.[18] Although, from the reign of Henry VII onwards, their duties were much augmented, the commission remained unchanged and growingly unsatisfactory until it was thoroughly revised in 1590. The new form (212), in force for over 300 years, authorised the justices (1) to enforce all statutes concerning the peace,[19] to take sureties for good behaviour, and to imprison those who would or could give none; (2) subject to the presence of one of the quorum, to enquire by sworn inquest into a variety of felonies and offences, some common law and some statutory, including the insufficiencies of local officials from sheriffs to constables; (3) to try cases upon indictment; (4) to

---

[14] The commission was frequently a testing ground for faction strife, which could leave the losers out in the cold (e.g., Smith, *County and Court*, esp. Part II).

[15] Putman, *Early Treatises*.

[16] Cheyney, *History of England*, II, 326 ff.

[17] *Eirenarcha*, 33.   [18] Holdsworth, I, 27* f.

[19] I.e. especially the Statutes of Winchester (1285), Northampton (1328) and Westminster (1365), with later additions.

hear and determine a variety of offences; (5) (a proviso)—not to proceed to judgment in difficult cases arising out of the foregoing without the presence of a justice of either Bench or of assize; (6) to hold regular sessions. The last clauses ordered the sheriff to provide sufficient men on sessions days for the empanelling of juries and appointed one of the justices as *custos rotulorum*. The commission thus preserved the essentially judicial character of the office: it concerned itself with the enforcement of the law in cases of actual transgressions. In this work the justices, by practice rather than injunction, lost control over felonies (treason they never could try) to the more expert Assizes; they confined themselves to breaches of the peace and misdemeanours.[20]

However, several of the more comprehensive phrases of the commission—especially the one authorising enquiry in all matters in which justices of the peace may or shall lawfully enquire—remind one of the justices' second duty. They were charged by one statute after another to see to its proper execution. From the first—more particularly from the Parliament of 1495 onwards—a growing body of local administration as distinct from law-enforcement in the strict sense had been committed to them.[21] By the end of Elizabeth's reign Lambarde could list 309 statutes which in one way or another referred to the duties of justices of the peace; of these only 133 (going back to the thirteenth century) preceded 1485, 60 were made between 1485 and 1547, 39 under Edward VI and Mary, and 77 under Elizabeth.[22] Although quite a few of them would be insignificant, a vast number were complex and vital. The manner in which purely judicial officers came to concern themselves with the ordering of local affairs is well illustrated in such acts as those which bestowed upon them the licensing of ale-houses (**214**) or charged them with the fixing of wages as well as the punishment of breaches of the regulations which they had to enforce (**215**). They supervised the maintenance of bridges and highways; they enforced sumptuary laws, recusancy laws, and price regulations.[23] The developing poor law of the century gives perhaps the most extensive example: originally especially concerned with the punishment of rogues and vagabonds, the justices ultimately found themselves also supervising and enforcing the collection and administration of a compulsory rate for the relief of the deserving poor.[24] There cannot be any question that the sheer burden of

[20] Cockburn, *Assizes*, ch. 6.

[21] Pickthorn, 1, 65; Cheyney, *History of England*, II, 321. Holdsworth, IV, 137 ff., gives a detailed summary, arranged by the type of sessions, of the mixed judicial and administrative work imposed on justices.

[22] *Eirenarcha*, 589 ff.   [23] Tanner, 495 ff., 506 f.

[24] The subject of the Tudor poor law—too bulky and of too little constitutional interest to be illustrated here at length—is discussed by Tanner, 469 ff.; cf. *ibid.*, 473 ff. for extracts from the leading acts. Cf. further Leonard, *English Poor Relief*; Holdsworth, IV, 387 ff.; Elton, *Studies*, II, 137 ff. The standard accounts require revision and expansion. One interesting by-product of

work resting on the justices increased steadily and heavily. Up to a point
they could no doubt ease it by negligence, but throughout this period they
were controlled by a vigilant Council. Although local government by local
worthies was bound to leave the central authority with less power than a
genuine system of royal officials would have provided, the Council could and
did use expulsion from the commission as a weapon against inefficiency or
local opposition, and instructed the justices in their duties. Henry VII found
it necessary, in a remarkable statute designed to revive efficiency, to call
upon the justices to invite criticisms of themselves (213).[25] In 1542 justices of
assize were empowered to hear charges of negligence or abuse of powers
against justices of the peace, and from 1543 King's Bench received a tran-
script of proceedings before quarter sessions.[26] If the Crown could not do
without the justices, neither could the gentry do without the Crown from
whom alone they could obtain the powers which gave political reality to
their social eminence.

The increase of the justices' work raised questions of organisation. The
justices acted in two ways: in general sessions, with everyone expected to be
present, or out of them, in small groups. Sessions were called quarter sessions
because they were held four times a year in each shire in places fixed by the
justices (211). Only in them could the justices do everything they were
charged with, since only in sessions did they sit with a jury to enquire, hear
and determine in a great variety of offences. But quarter sessions were
cumbersome and much beset by formalities of the law.[27] Though they remained to the end of the system the essential and most formidable occasion
for action by the justices, many of the Tudor statutes which used justices for
their enforcement were content with action out of sessions by one or two
or more of them, sitting without a jury and dealing summarily.[28] The growing
burden of administration led in 1542 to an attempt to create other formal
sessions to be held by two justices for every hundred in the shire, six weeks
before the quarter sessions, at which acts concerning vagabonds, retaining,
archery, and so forth should be enforced. Three years later the reform was
abandoned as too inconvenient and rigid.[29] But although this last act envisaged that all the work would be done in quarter sessions, it is clear that the
justices exercised much freedom in the arranging of additional sessions of two
or more of them to suit their needs.[30] No further formal attempts at reorganisa-

---

the Tudor poor law was the adaptation of the ecclesiastical parish to secular uses; it replaced the
old hundreds, tithings and townships as the smallest unit of local government (Holdsworth, IV,
151 ff.; Tanner, 508 ff.).

[25] The act lapsed in 1510.   [26] 33 Henry VIII, c. 10; 34 & 35 Henry VIII, c. 14.

[27] For a good picture of the justices at work cf. Samaha, *Law and Order*, and *Hist. Journal*,
XXI, 763 ff.

[28] Holdsworth, IV, 138 ff.

[29] 33 Henry VIII, c. 10; 37 Henry VIII, c. 7.   [30] Holdsworth, IV, 147 f.

tion were made under the Tudors. The growing practice of keeping rolls and records was itself sufficient to turn quarter sessions into a regular court which handled the bulk of criminal jurisdiction below the level of felony.

Not many additions were made to the actual powers of the justices, beyond extending the scope of the commission. Statutes of 1487, 1554 and 1555 reformed their powers to take bail, a consequence of the practice which transferred to the justices the preliminary investigation of offences to be tried at sessions or before commissioners of oyer and terminer and gaol delivery.[31] The so-called Star Chamber act of 1487 (78) also empowered justices to enquire into earlier land inquests suspected of impropriety; and an act of 1496 temporarily went a long way to establish summary control over crime by authorising trial upon information without presentment by jury in all cases except treasons, murders and felonies.[32] In general, however, Tudor governments seem to have thought the traditional powers of the justices sufficient, especially if they were helped out by frequent special directions from above. The main issue involved the justices' power to order arrests.[33] In the ordinary course they would commit to prison or trial upon presentment by jury, and it seems to have been regarded as established that they could arrest anyone they themselves suspected of felony. Though they had developed a practice of issuing warrants for arrest upon suspicions laid before them by other persons, this was condemned as illegal in 1522 and did not become generally accepted until the later seventeenth century when the great age of the justices really began. As a rule, Tudor justices arrested suspects either upon proper indictment or by warrant from the Council; that they exercised any wide personal powers of granting warrants for arrests or house-searches seems at present unlikely.

210. Sir Thomas Smith on justices of the peace (1565).

... The justices of peace be men elected out of the nobility, higher and lower, that is the dukes, marquises, barons, knights, esquires and gentlemen, and of such as be learned in the laws, such and in such number as the prince shall think meet, and in whom for wisdom and discretion he putteth his trust, inhabitants within the county; saving that some of the high nobility and chief magistrates for honour's sake are put in all or in the most of the commissions of all the shires of England. These have no time of their rule limited but by commission from the prince alterable at pleasure.

[31] 3 Henry VII, c. 3; 1 & 2 Philip & Mary, c. 13 (Tanner, 464 f., 468 f.); 2 & 3 Philip & Mary, c. 10. Cf. Langbein, *Prosecuting Crime*, Part 1.
[32] 11 Henry VII. c. 3; repealed by 1 Henry VIII, c. 6 as too dangerous an innovation.
[33] Cf. Holdsworth, I, 294 f.

At the first they were but 4, after 8, now they come commonly to 30 or 40 in every shire, either by increase of riches, learning, or activity in policy and government. So many more being found which have either will or power or both, are not too many to handle the affairs of the commonwealth in this behalf. Of these in the same commission be certain named which be called of the Quorum, in whom is especial trust reposed, that where the commission is given to 40 or 30, and so at the last it cometh to 4 or 3, it is necessary for the performance of many affairs to have likewise divers of the Quorum. The words of the commission be such, *Quorum vos* A.B., C.D., E.F. *unum esse volumus.*

The justices of the peace be those in whom at this time for the repressing of robbers, thieves and vagabonds, of privy complots and conspiracies, of riots and violences, and all other misdemeanours in the commonwealth the prince putteth his special trust. Each of them hath authority upon complaint to him made of any theft, robbery, manslaughter, murder, violence, complots, riots, unlawful games, or any such disturbance of the peace and quiet of the realm, to commit the persons whom he supposeth offenders to the prison ... till he and his fellows do meet. A few lines signed with his hand is enough for that purpose. These do meet four times in the year, that is, in each quarter once, to enquire of all the misdemeanours aforesaid. ...

... The justices of the peace do meet also at other times by commandment of the prince upon suspicion of war, to take order for the safety of the shire, sometimes to take musters of harness and able men, and sometime to take order for the excessive wages of servants and labourers, for excess of apparel, for unlawful games, for conventicles and evil orders in alehouses and taverns, for punishment of idle and vagabond persons, and generally, as I have said, for the good government of the shire the prince putteth his confidence in them. And commonly every year or each second year in the beginning of summer or afterwards (for in the warm time the people for the most part be more unruly, even in the calm time of peace) the prince with his Council chooseth out certain articles out of penal laws already made for to repress the pride and evil rule of the popular and sendeth them down to the justices, willing them to look upon those points, and after they have met together and consulted among themselves how to order that matter most wisely and circumspectly, whereby the people might be kept in good order and obedience after the law, they divide themselves by three or four, and so each in his quarter taketh order for the execution of the said articles. And then within certain space they meet again and certify the prince or his Privy Council how they do find the shire in rule and order touching those points and all other disorders. There was never in any common wealth devised a more wise, a more dulce and gentle, nor a more certain way to rule the people, whereby they are kept always as it were in a bridle of good order, and sooner looked unto that they should not offend than punished when they have offended. . . .

De Republica Anglorum, 85-9

211. William Lambarde on the justices' sessions (c. 1580).

[Cap. 2] . . . The common . . . manner is, to call the officers and county together for [sessions] by a precept to the sheriff. . . . This precept may be made . . . by any two justices of the peace, so that the one of them be of the quorum, for two such may hold a session of the peace, as it doth plainly appear by the commission. . . . The place of holding them is arbitrable and at the pleasure of the justices themselves, so that it be meet for access. And although the precept do appoint the sessions to be holden in some one town by name, yet may the justices keep it in any other town, and all the presentments shall be good that shall be taken where they hold it; but then again no amercement can be set upon any man for his default of appearance there, because he had no warning of it. So if two such justices make a precept for a session to be holden in one town, and two other justices make another precept for another session to be holden at another town (or in another part of the same town) the same day, then the presentments taken before either of them shall be good. And then also it seemeth that he which serveth at the one session (as a juror or officer) shall be excused for his default at the other, because as they both be the Queen's courts and of equal authority so he cannot present himself in them both at once. . . .

[Cap. 3] Amongst the officers the *custos rotulorum* hath worthily the first place, both for that he is always a justice of the quorum in the commission, and amongst them of the quorum a man (for the most part) especially picked out either for wisdom, countenance or credit; and yet in this behalf he beareth the person of an officer, and ought to attend by himself or his deputy. . . . And now as this man is (by name and office) keeper of the records of the peace, so would it not a little amend the service if he were (in deed also) careful for the due preservation of them and would not loosely leave them (as commonly it is found) to the only custody of the clerk of the peace, without having any register of their number and sorts, and without appointing any convenient place certain for the more ready search and safe bestowing of them; whereby it falleth out very often that after the death of such a clerk these records are hardly recovered and that piecemeal from his widow, servants or executors, who at their pleasure may embezzle, misuse, or conceal what they will. . . . And this office of the *custos rotulorum* was of ancient time given by the discretion of the lord chancellor. . . .

The clerk of the peace oweth his attendance at the sessions also, for . . . he readeth the indictments and serveth the court, he enrolleth the acts of the sessions and draweth the process. He must record the proclamations of rate for servants' wages and enroll the discharge of apprentices, 5 Eliz. c. 4. . . . He keepeth the register-book of licences given to badgers[34] and laders of corn, 5 Eliz. c. 12, and of those that are licensed to shoot in guns, 2 Edw. VI, c. 14. And he is bound (under the pain of 40s.) to certify unto the King's Bench transcripts of indictments, outlawries, attainders and convictions had before the justices of the peace within the time limited by the statute 34 Henry VIII, c. 14. . . . The nomination and appointment of him hath long time belonged to the *custos rotulorum*, and he is to enjoy his office as long as the *custos rotulorum* keepeth his place. . . .

[Cap. 19] The general sessions of the peace be those which are provided for the general execution of the authority of the justices of peace. . . . These be moreover called the Quarter Sessions, because they be holden quarterly or four times in the year; and the statute 4 Henry VII, c. 12, termed them principal sessions, for that in them chiefly the power of justices of the peace doth shine and shew itself, in which respect 27 Eliz., c. 19 and some other statutes do give the name of open sessions also.

[Cap. 20] The special sessions of the peace do vary from the general in this chiefly, that they be holden at other times, when it shall please the justices themselves or any two of them (the one being of the quorum) to appoint them. . . . They be also (for the most part) summoned for some special business and not directed to the general service of the commission; and yet there is no doubt but that all the articles

---

[34] Itinerant dealers or hawkers.

within the commission of the peace are both inquirable and determinable at any special session of the peace.

Eirenarcha (Bk. IV), 366–9, 371–5, 376–8, 557–8, 579–80

212. The commission of the peace after 1590.

. . . Sciatis quod assignavimus vos, coniunctim et divisim et quemlibet vestrum, iusticiarios nostros, ad pacem nostram in comitatu nostro Kanciae conservandam; Ac ad omnia ordinationes et statuta pro bono pacis nostrae, ac pro conservatione eiusdem, et pro quieto regimine et gubernatione populi nostri edita, in omnibus et singulis suis articulis in dicto comitatu nostro, tam infra libertates quam extra, juxta vim, formam et effectum eorundem, custodiendum et custodiri faciendum. Et ad omnes contra formam ordinationum vel statutorum illorum, aut eorum alicuius in comitatu praedicto delinquentes, castigandum et puniendum, prout secundum formam ordinationum et statutorum illorum fuerit faciendum; et ad omnes illos qui alicui vel aliquibus de populo nostro de corporibus suis, vel de incendio domorum suarum minas fecerint, ad sufficientem securitatem de pace vel bono gestu suo erga nos et populum nostrum inveniendam coram vobis seu aliquo vestrum venire faciendum, et (si huiusmodi securitatem invenire recusaverint) tunc eos in prisonis (quousque huiusmodi securitatem invenerint) salvo custodiri faciendum.

Assignavimus etiam vos et quoslibet duos vel plures vestrum (quorum aliquem nostrum A. B. C. D. E. F, etc., unum esse volumus) iusticiarios nostros, ad inquirendum per sacramentum proborum et legalium hominum de comitatu praedicto (per quos rei veritas melius sciri poterit) de omnibus et omnimodis feloniis, veneficiis, incatationibus, sortilegiis, arte magica, transgressionibus, forstallariis, regratariis, ingrossariis, et extortionibus quibuscunque; ac de omnibus et singulis aliis malefactis et offensis (de quibus iusticiarii pacis nostrae legitime inquirere possunt aut debent) per quoscunque et qualitercunque in comitatu praedicto factis sive perpetratis, vel quae imposterum[35] ibidem fieri vel attemptari contigerit; ac etiam de omnibus illis qui in comitatu praedicto in conventiculis contra pacem nostram in perturbationem populi nostri, seu vi armata ierunt vel equitaverunt, seu imposterum ire vel equitare praesumpserint; ac etiam de omnibus hiis qui ibidem ad

[35] Hereafter.

gentem nostram mayhemandam[36] vel interficiendam in insidiis iacuerunt vel imposterum iacere praesumpserint; ac etiam de hostellariis et aliis omnibus et singulis personis qui in abusu ponderum vel mensurarum sive in venditione victualium contra formam ordinationum vel statutorum vel eorum alicuius inde pro communi utilitate regni nostri Angliae et populi nostri eiusdem editorum deliquerunt vel attemptaverunt seu imposterum delinquere vel attemptare praesumpserint in comitatu praedicto; ac etiam de quibuscunque vicecomitibus,[37] ballivis[38] seneschallis,[39] constabulariis, custodibus gaolarum, et aliis officiariis qui in executione officiorum suorum (circa praemissa seu eorum aliqua) indebite se habuerunt aut imposterum indebite se habere praesumpserint, aut tepidi, remissi vel negligentes fuerunt aut imposterum fore contigerit in comitatu praedicto; et de omnibus et singulis articulis et circumstantiis et aliis rebus quibuscunque, per quoscunque et qualitercunque in comitatu praedicto factis sive perpetratis vel quae imposterum ibidem fieri vel attemptari contigerit, qualitercunque praemissorum vel eorum alicuius concernentibus plenius veritatem.

Et ad indictamenta quaecunque sic coram vobis seu aliquibus vestrum capta sive capienda, aut coram aliis nuper iusticiariis pacis in comitatu praedicto facta sive capta (et nondum terminata) inspiciendum, ac ad processus inde versus omnes et singulos sic indictatos, vel quos coram vobis imposterum indictari contigerit (quousque capiantur, reddant se, vel utlagentur) faciendum et continuandum.

Et ad omnia et singula felonias, veneficia, incantationes, sortilegia, artes magicas, transgressiones, forstallarias, regratarias, ingrossarias,[40] extorsiones, conventicula, indictamenta praedicta, caeteraque omnia et singula praemissa, secundum leges et statuta regni nostri Angliae (prout in hujusmodi casu fieri consuevit aut debuit) audiendum et terminandum; et ad eosdem delinquentes et quemlibet eorum pro delictis suis per fines, redemptiones, amerciamenta, forisfacturas, ac alio modo (prout secundum legem et consuetudinem regni nostri Angliae aut formam ordinationum vel statutorum praedictorum fieri consuevit aut debuit) castigandum et puniendum.

Proviso semper, quod si casus difficultatis super determinatione aliquorum praemissorum coram vobis vel aliquibus duobus vel pluribus

---

[36] 'Mayhem' signifies, a maim, wound or bodily hurt by which a man is deprived of the use of any member which is or might be of use to him in defence.

[37] Sheriffs.　　　　　　　　　[38] Bailiffs.　　　　　　　　　[39] Stewards.

[40] Offences committed in dealing in foodstuffs: forestalling—buying on the way to market; regrating—selling for a rise; engrossing—cornering.

vestrum evenire contigerit, tunc ad iudicium inde reddendum (nisi in praesentia unius iusticiariorum nostrorum de uno vel de altero banco aut unius justiciariorum nostrorum ad assisas in comitatu praedicto capiendas assignatorum) coram vobis vel aliquibus duobus vel pluribus vestrum minime procedatur.

Et ideo vobis et cuilibet vestrum mandamus, quod circa custodiam pacis, ordinationum, statutorum, et omnium et singulorum caeterorum praemissorum diligenter intendatis; et ad certos dies et loca quae vos vel aliqui huiusmodi duo vel plures vestrum (ut praedictum est) ad hoc provideritis super praemissis faciatis inquisitiones, et praemissa omnia et singula audiatis et terminetis, ac ea faciatis et expleatis in forma praedicta facturi inde quod ad iustitiam pertinet secundum legem et consuetudinem regni nostri Angliae; salvis nobis amerciamentis et aliis ad nos inde spectantibus.

Mandamus enim tenore praesentium vicecomiti nostro Kanciae quod ad certos dies et loca (quae vos vel aliqui huiusmodi duo vel plures vestrum, ut praedictum est, ei, ut praedictum est, scire feceritis) venire faciat coram vobis vel huiusmodi duobus vel pluribus vestrum (ut dictum est) tot et tales probos et legales homines de balliva sua (tam infra libertates quam extra) per quos rei veritas in praemissis melius sciri poterit et inquiri.

Assignavimus denique te praefatum Edw. Hobby, militem, custodem rotulorum pacis nostrae in dicto comitatu nostro; ac propterea tu ad dies et loca praedicta brevia, praecepta, processus, et indictamenta praedicta coram te et dictis sociis tuis venire facias, ut ea inspiciantur et debito fine terminentur sicut praedictum est. In cuius rei testimonium etc. Datum decimo septimo die Novembris anno regni nostri quadragessimo primo.

Lambarde, Eirenarcha, 34–7

213. An Act for justices of the peace, for the due execution of their commissions (1489: 4 Henry VII, c. 12).

The King our sovereign lord considereth that by the negligence and misdemeaning, favour, and other inordinate causes of the justice of peace in every shire of this his realm, the laws and ordinances made for the politic weal, peace and good rule of the same, and for perfect surety and restful living of his subjects of the same, be not duly executed according to the tenor and effect that they were made and ordained for; wherefore his subjects be grievously hurt and out of surety of their bodies and goods, to his great displeasure; for to him is nothing more joyous than to know his subjects to live peaceably under his laws and to increase in wealth and prosperity. And to avoid such enormities and injuries, so that his said subjects may live more restful under his peace and laws to their increase, he will that it be ordained and enacted by the authority of this present Parliament, that every justice of the peace within every shire of this his said realm, within the shire where he is justice of peace, do cause openly and solemnly to be proclaimed yearly 4 times in a year in four principal sessions the tenor of this proclamation to this bill annexed; and that every justice of peace being present at any of the said sessions, if they cause not the said proclamation to be made in form abovesaid, shall forfeit to our said sovereign lord at every time 20s.

The Proclamation

Henricus Dei gratia, etc. The King our sovereign lord considereth how daily within this realm his coin is traitorously counterfeited, murders, robberies, felonies be grievously committed and done, and also unlawful retainers, idleness, unlawful plays, extortions, misdemeanings of sheriffs, escheators, and many other enormities and unlawful demeanings daily groweth and increaseth within this his realm, to the great displeasure of God, hurt and impoverishing of his subjects, and to the subversion of the policy and good governance of this his realm; For by these said enormities and mischiefs his peace is broken, his subjects inquieted and impoverished, the husbandry of this land decayed, whereby the Church of England is upholden, the service of God continued, every man thereby hath sustenance, every inheritor his rent for his land: For repressing and avoiding of the said mischiefs sufficient laws and ordinances be made by authority of many and divers Parliaments holden within this realm, to the great cost of the King, his Lords and Commons of the same, and lacketh nothing but that the said laws be not put in due execution, which laws ought to be put in due execution by the justice of peace in every shire of this realm, to whom his Grace hath put and given full authority so to do since the beginning of his reign; And now it is come to his knowledge that his subjects be little eased of the said mischiefs by the said justices, but by many of them rather hurt than helped. And if his subjects complain to these justices of peace of any wrongs done to them they have thereby no remedy, and the said mischiefs do increase and not subdued. And his Grace (considereth that a great part of the wealth and prosperity of this land standeth in that, that his subjects may live in surety under his peace in their bodies and goods, and that the husbandry of this land may increase and be upholden, which must be had by due execution of the said laws and ordinances), chargeth and commandeth all the justices of the peace of this his shire to endeavour them to do execute the tenor of their commission the said laws and ordinances ordained for subduing of the premises, as they will stand in the love and favour of his Grace, and in avoiding the pains that be ordained if they do the contrary. And over that, he chargeth and commandeth that every man what degree or condition that he be of, that let them in word or deed to execute their said authorities in any manner form abovesaid, that they shew it to his Grace; and if they do it not and it come to his knowledge by other than by them, they shall not be in his favour but taken as men out of credence and be put out of commission for ever. And over this, he chargeth and commandeth all manner of men, as well the poor as the rich, which be to him all one in due ministration of justice, that is hurt or grieved in anything that the said justice of peace may hear or determine or execute in any wise, that he so grieved make his complaint to the justice of the peace that next dwelleth unto him, or to any of his fellows, and desire a remedy; and if he then have no remedy, if it be nigh such time as his justices of assizes come into that shire, that then he so grieved shew his complaint to the same justices, and if he then have no remedy, or if the complaint be made long after the coming of the justices of assizes, then he so grieved come to the King's Highness or to his chancellor for the time being and shew his grief; and his said Highness then shall send for the said justices to know the cause why his said subjects be not eased and his laws executed, whereupon if he find any of them in default of executing of his laws in these premises according to this his high commandment, he shall do him so offending to be put out of the commission, and further to be punished according to his demerits. And over that, his said highness shall not let for any favour, affection, cost, charge, nor none other cause, but that he shall see his laws to have plain and due execution, and his subjects to live in surety of their lands, bodies and goods, according to his said laws, and the said mischiefs to be avoided, that his said subjects may increase in wealth and prosperity to the pleasure of God.   *Stat. Realm*, II, 536–8

214. An Act for keepers of ale-houses to be bound by recognisances (1552: 5 & 6 Ed. VI, c. 25).

Forasmuch as intolerable hurts and troubles to the common wealth of this realm doth daily grow and increase through such abuses and disorders as are had and used in common ale-houses and other houses called tippling-houses;[41] it is therefore enacted by the King our sovereign lord with the assent of the Lords and Commons in this present Parliament assembled, and by the authority of the same, that the justices of peace within every shire, city, borough, town corporate, franchise or liberty within this realm, or two of them at the least, whereof one of them to be of the quorum, shall have full power and authority, by virtue of this act, within every shire [etc.] where they be justices of peace to remove, discharge and put away common selling of ale and beer in the said common ale-houses and tippling-houses in such town or towns and places where they shall think meet and convenient. And that none . . . shall be admitted or suffered to keep any common ale-house or tippling-house but such as shall be thereunto admitted and allowed in the open sessions of the peace, or else by two justices of the peace, whereof the one to be of the quorum. And that the said justices . . . shall take bond and surety from time to time by recognisance of such as shall be admitted and allowed hereafter to keep any common ale-house or tippling-house, as well for and against the using of unlawful games as also for the using and maintenance of good order and rule to be had and used within the same, as by their discretion shall be thought necessary and convenient. . . . And the said justices shall certify the same recognisance at the next quarter sessions of the peace to be holden within the same shire [etc.] where such ale-house or tippling-house shall be; the same recognisance there to remain of record before the justices of peace of that shire . . . upon pain of forfeiture to the King for every such recognisance taken and not certified, £3. 6s. 8d.

* * * * * *

iv. Provided alway that in such towns and places where any fair or fairs shall be kept, that for the time only of the same fair or fairs it shall be lawful for every person and persons to use common selling of

[41] 'Tippler' was a technical term for a retailer of ale, and a 'tippling-house' was a place where ale was sold.

ale or beer in booths or other places there for the relief of the King's subjects that shall repair to the same, in such like manner and sort as hath been used or done in times past; this act or anything therein contained to the contrary notwithstanding. *Stat. Realm*, IV, 157

215. An Act touching divers orders for artificers, labourers, servants of husbandry, and apprentices (Statute of Artificers, 1563: 5 Eliz. I, c. 4)

Although there remain and stand in force presently a great number of acts and statutes concerning the retaining, departing, wages and orders of apprentices, servants and labourers, as well in husbandry as in divers other arts, mysteries and occupations, yet partly for the imperfection and contrariety that is found and do appear in sundry of the said laws, and for the variety and number of them, and chiefly for that the wages and allowances limited and rated in many of the said statutes are in divers places too small and not answerable to this time, respecting the advancement of prices of all things belonging to the said servants and labourers, the said laws cannot conveniently without the great grief and burden of the poor labourer and hired man be put in good and due execution: And as the said several acts and statutes were at the time of the making of them thought to be very good and beneficial for the common wealth of this realm, as divers of them yet are, So if the substance of as many of the said laws as are meet to be continued shall be digested and reduced into one sole law and statute, and in the same an uniform order prescribed and limited concerning the wages and other orders for apprentices, servants and labourers, there is good hope that it will come to pass that the same law, being duly executed, should banish idleness, advance husbandry, and yield unto the hired person both in the time of scarcity and in the time of plenty a convenient proportion of wages. Be it therefore enacted by the authority of this present Parliament. . . .

*　　*　　*　　*　　*　　*

[III. Persons unmarried, not having 40*s*. by the year nor being otherwise employed, shall be compellable to serve as yearly servants in the crafts in which they were brought up.]

IV. And be it further enacted that no person which shall retain any servant shall put away his or her said servant, and that no person retained according to this statute shall depart from his master, mistress or dame before the end of his or her term . . . unless it be for some reasonable and sufficient cause or matter to be allowed before two justices of peace, or one at the least, within the said county, or before the mayor or other chief officer of the city, borough or town corporate wherein the said master, mistress or dame inhabiteth, to whom any of the parties grieved shall complain; which said justices or justice, mayor or chief officer, shall have and take upon them or him the hearing and ordering of the matter between the said master, mistress or dame, and servant, according to the equity of the cause: and that no such master, mistress or dame shall put away any such servant at the end of his term, or that any such servant shall depart from his said master, mistress or dame at the end of his term, without one quarter warning given before the end of his said term, either by the said master, mistress or dame, or servant the one to the other. . . .

[v. All persons between the ages of 12 and 60, not being otherwise employed, are declared compellable to be yearly servants in husbandry.

vi. Penalty for masters improperly dismissing servants is 40s., for servants improperly leaving masters, imprisonment until they undertake to complete their service; enforcement is committed to justices of oyer and terminer, or of assize, or of peace in quarter sessions.]

* * * * * *

xi. And for the declaration and limitation what wages servants, labourers and artificers, either by the year or day or otherwise, shall have and receive; be it enacted by the authority of the present Parliament, that the justices of peace . . . shall yearly at every general sessions first to be holden and kept after Easter . . . assemble themselves together, and they so assembled calling unto them such grave and discreet persons of the said county or of the said city or town corporate as they shall think meet, and conferring together respecting the plenty or scarcity of the time and other circumstances necessary to be considered, shall have authority . . . to limit, rate and appoint the wages . . . of . . . artificers, handicraftsmen, husbandmen; or any other labourer, servant or workman . . . and shall . . . certify the same engrossed in parchment, with the considerations and causes thereof, under their hands and seals into the Queen's most honourable Court of Chancery, whereupon it shall be lawful to the lord chancellor of England, . . . upon declaration thereof to the Queen's Majesty, her heirs or successors, or to the lords and others of the Privy Council for the time being attendant on their persons, to cause to be printed and sent down . . . into every county to the sheriff and justices of peace there . . . ten or twelve proclamations or more, containing in every of them the several rates appointed by the said justices, . . . with commandment by the said proclamations to all persons in the name of the Queen's Majesty . . . straitly to observe the same, and to all justices, sheriffs and other officers to see the same duly and severely observed. . . . And if the said . . . justices . . . shall at their said general sessions . . . upon their assembly and conference together think it convenient to retain and keep for the year then to come the rates and proportion of wages that they certified the year before, or to change or reform them or some part of them, then they shall . . . yearly certify into the said Court of Chancery their resolutions and determinations therein, to the intent that proclamations may accordingly be renewed and sent down. And if it shall happen that there be no need of any reformation or alteration of the rates of the said wages, but that the former shall be thought meet to be continued, then the proclamations for the year past shall remain in force until new proclamations upon new rates concerning the said wages shall be sent down. . . .

[XII. Penalty on any justices, etc., absent from the sessions for rating wages, 'and not visited with any such sickness as he could not travel thither without peril and danger of his life, or not having any other lawful and good excuse,' £10.

XIII. Penalty on giving higher wages than are so rated, ten days imprisonment and £5; on receiving, twenty-one days imprisonment.]

*   *   *   *   *   *

XV. Provided always and be it enacted . . . that in the time of hay or corn harvest, the justices of peace and every of them, and also the constable or other head officer of every township, upon request and for the avoiding of the loss of any corn, grain or hay, shall and may cause all such artificers and persons as be meet to labour . . . to serve by the day for the mowing, reaping, shearing, getting or inning of corn, grain and hay, according to the skill and quality of the person; and that none of the said persons shall refuse so to do, upon pain to suffer imprisonment in the stocks by the space of two days and one night. . . .

*   *   *   *   *   *

XVII. And be it further enacted . . . that two justices of peace, the mayor . . . of any city, borough or town corporate and two aldermen . . . shall and may by virtue hereof appoint any such woman as is of the age of twelve years and under the age of forty years and unmarried and forth of service as they shall think meet to serve, to be retained or serve by the year or by the week or day, for such wages and in such reasonable sort and manner as they shall think meet: and if any such woman shall refuse so to serve, then it shall be lawful for the said justices of peace, mayor, or head officers to commit such woman to ward until she shall be bounden to serve as aforesaid.

*　*　*　*　*　*

XXVIII. And be it further enacted that if any person shall be required by any householder having and using half a ploughland at the least in tillage to be an apprentice and to serve in husbandry or in any other kind of art, mystery or science before expressed, and shall refuse so to do; that then upon the complaint of such housekeeper made to one justice of peace of the county wherein the said refusal is or shall be made, or [in a city or town corporate to the mayor] they shall have full power and authority by virtue hereof to send for the same person so refusing; and if the said justice or the said mayor . . . shall think the said person meet and convenient to serve as an apprentice in that art, labour, science or mystery wherein he shall be so then required to serve, that then the said justice or the said mayor . . . shall have power and authority by virtue hereof, if the said person refuse to be bound as an apprentice, to commit him unto ward, there to remain until he be contented and will be bounden to serve as an apprentice should serve, according to the true intent and meaning of this present act. And if any such master shall misuse or evil intreat his apprentice, or that the said apprentice shall have any just cause to complain, or the apprentice do not his duty to his master, then the said master or prentice being grieved and having just cause to complain shall repair unto one justice of peace within the said county or to the mayor . . . of the city, town corporate, market town or other place where the said master dwelleth, who shall by his wisdom and discretion take such order and direction between the said master and his apprentice as the equity of the cause shall require; and if for want of good conformity in the said master, the said justice of peace or . . . mayor . . . cannot compound and agree the matter between him and his apprentice, then the said justice or ... mayor ... shall take bond of the said master to appear at the next sessions then to be holden in the said county or ... town, ... and upon his appearance and hearing of the matter before the said justices or the said mayor, ... if it be thought meet unto them to discharge the said apprentice of his apprenticehood, that then the said justices or four of them at the least, whereof one to be of the quorum, or the said mayor ... with the consent of three other of his brethren or men of best reputation within the said ... town, ... shall have power by authority hereof in writing under their hands and seals to pronounce and declare that they have discharged the said apprentice of his apprenticehood, and the cause thereof, and the said writing so being made and enrolled by the clerk of the peace or town clerk amongst the records that he keepeth, shall be a sufficient discharge for the said apprentice against his master, his executors and administrators. ... And if the default shall be found to be in the apprentice, then the said justices or ... mayor ... with the assistants aforesaid shall cause such due correction and punishment to be ministered unto him as by their wisdom and discretions shall be thought meet.

* * * * * *

[xxx. Twice a year, the justices of the peace, dividing their shire amongst themselves, are to hold enquiries into the operation and effect of this statute.]

* * * * * *

Stat. Realm, IV, 414–22

LIST OF BOOKS

This list includes, in strictly alphabetical order, the full description of all the works referred to in this book. Any abbreviations employed in the text or footnotes are found in the alphabetically correct place, with a full expansion of their titles.

Allen, J. W., *A History of Political Thought in the Sixteenth Century*. London 1928

Alsop, J. D., 'The Revenue Commission of 1552', *Historical Journal*, XXII (1979), 511 ff.

Anglin, J. P., 'The Essex Puritan Movement and the "Bawdy" Courts, 1577–94', *Tudor Men and Institutions* (ed. A. J. Slavin; Baton Rouge 1972), 171 ff.

A.P.C. – *Acts of the Privy Council of England*, ed. J. R. Dasent. London 1880–1907

Arnold, R., *The Customs of London, otherwise called Arnold's Chronicle*. Reprint: London 1811

Aston, M., 'Lollardy and the Reformation: Survival or Revival?', *History*, XLIX (1964), 149 ff.

Aveling. H., *Northern Catholics: the Catholic Recusants of the North Riding of Yorkshire, 1558–1790*. London 1966

Aylmer, J., *An Harborowe for Faithful and True Subjects against the Late Blown Blast concerning the Government of Women*. Strassburg 1559

Babbage, S. B., *Puritanism and Richard Bancroft*. London 1962

Bacon, F., *Works*, ed. J. Spedding. London 1858

Baker, J. H., 'Criminal Courts and Procedure at Common Law', *Crime in England 1550–1800* (ed. J. S. Cockburn; London 1977), 15 ff.
'The Dark Age of English Legal History', *Legal History Studies 1972* (ed. D. Jenkins; Cardiff 1975), 1 ff.
An Introduction to English Legal History (2nd edn). London 1979
(ed.), *The Reports of Sir John Spelman*, 2 vols. London, Selden Society, 1977

Barnes, T. G., 'Due Process and Slow Process in the late Elizabethan–early Stuart Star Chamber', *American Journal of Legal History*, VI (1962), 221 ff., 315 ff.

Barrow, H., *A Brief Discovery of the False Church*. London 1590

Baumer, F. le Van, *The Early Tudor Theory of Kingship*. Cambridge, Mass. 1938

Bayne, C. G., and Dunham, W. H. (ed.), *Select Cases in the Council of Henry VII*. London, Selden Society, 1958

Bell, H. E., *An Introduction to the History and Records of the Court of Wards and Liveries*. Cambridge 1953

Bellamy, J. G., *The Law of Treason in the Later Middle Ages*. Cambridge 1970
The Tudor Law of Treason; an Introduction. London 1979
Beresford, M. W., 'The Common Informer, the Penal Statutes, and Economic Regulation', *Economic History Review*, 2nd Series, X (1957), 221 ff.
Blatcher, M., *The Court of King's Bench 1450–1550*. London 1978
'Touching the Writ of Latitat: an Act "of no great moment"', *Elizabethan Government and Society* (ed. S. T. Bindoff, J. Hurstfield, C. H. Williams; London 1961), 188 ff.
Bond, S., and Evans, N., 'The Process of Granting Charters to English Boroughs, 1547–1649', *English Historical Review*, XCI (1976), 102 ff.
Bossy, J. A., 'The Character of Elizabethan Catholicism', *Past and Present*, XXI (1962), 39 ff.
The English Catholic Community 1570–1850. London 1975
Bowker, M., 'The Commons' Supplication Against the Ordinaries in the light of some Archidiaconical *Acta*', *Transactions of the Royal Historical Society*, 5th Series, XXI (1971), 61 ff.
The Secular Clergy in the Diocese of Lincoln, 1495–1520. Cambridge 1968
Boynton, L., *The Elizabethan Militia*. London 1967
Bradshaw, B., *The Irish Constitutional Revolution of the Sixteenth Century*. Cambridge 1979
'Sword, Word and Strategy in the Irish Reformation', *Historical Journal*, XXI (1978), 475 ff.
Brigden, S. E., 'The Early Reformation in London, 1520–47: the Conflict in the Parishes', unpublished dissertation, Cambridge 1979
Brooks, C. W., 'Litigants and Attorneys in the King's Bench and Common Pleas, 1560–1640', *Legal Records and the Historian* (ed. J. H. Baker; London 1978), 41 ff.
Brooks, F. W., *The Council of the North*. London, Historical Association, 1953
Bryson, W. H., *The Equity Side of the Exchequer*. Cambridge 1975
Burnet, G., *The History of the Reformation of the Church of England*, ed. N. Pocock. Oxford 1865
[Caesar Sir Julius,] *The Ancient State, Authority and Proceedings of the Court of Requests*. London 1597
Camden, W., *Annals, or the History of the Most Renowned and Victorious Princess Elizabeth, late Queen of England*. London 1630
Canny, N. P., *The Elizabethan Conquest of Ireland: a Pattern Established, 1565–76*. Hassocks 1976
Cardwell, E., *Documentary Annals of the Reformed Church of England, 1546–1716*. Oxford 1839
Cartwrightiana, ed. A. Peel and L. H. Carlson. London 1951
Certain Sermons or Homilies, appointed by the King's Majesty to be declared and

read by all Parsons, Vicars or Curates every Sunday in their Churches where they have Cure. London 1547

Challis, C. E., *The Tudor Coinage*. Manchester 1978

Cheyney, E. P., *A History of England from the Defeat of the Armada to the Death of Elizabeth*, 2 vols. London 1926

Chrimes, S. B., *English Constitutional Ideas in the Fifteenth Century*. Cambridge 1936

An Introduction to the Administrative History of Medieval England. Oxford 1952

and Brown, A. L., *Select Documents of English Constitutional History 1307–1485*. London 1961

C.J. – Journal of the House of Commons

Clancy, T. H., *Papist Pamphleteers: the Allen–Parsons Party and the Political Thought of the Counter-Reformation in England, 1572–1615*. Chicago 1964

Clark, P., *English Provincial Society from the Reformation to the Revolution: Religion, Politics and Society in Kent, 1500–1640*. Hassocks 1977

Clebsch, W., *England's Earliest Protestants, 1520–1535*. New Haven 1964

Cockburn, J. S., *A History of English Assizes, 1558–1714*. Cambridge 1972

Coke, Sir Edward, *The Fourth Part of the Institutes of the Laws of England*. London 1644

Reports, translated into English. London 1658

A Collection of Ordinances and Regulations for the Government of the Royal Household. London, Society of Antiquaries, 1790

Collinson, P., *Archbishop Grindal, 1519–1583: the Struggle for a Reformed Church*. London 1980

'Calvinism with an Anglican Face: the Strangers Churches in Early Elizabethan London and their Superintendent', *Reform and Reformation: England and the Continent c. 1500 to c. 1750* (ed. D. Baker; Oxford 1979), 71 ff.

The Elizabethan Puritan Movement. London 1967

'Episcopacy and Reform in England in the Later Sixteenth Century', *Studies in Church History*, III (ed. G. J. Cuming: Leiden 1966), 91 ff.

'John Field and Elizabethan Puritanism', *Elizabethan Government and Society* (ed. S. T. Bindoff, J. Hurstfield, C. H. Williams; London 1961), 127 ff.

'The Letters of Thomas Wood, Puritan, 1566–1577', *Bulletin of the Institute of Historical Research*, Supplement V (1960)

Constable, R., *Prerogativa Regis*, ed. S. E. Thorne. New Haven 1949

Cooper, J. P., 'The Supplication against the Ordinaries Reconsidered', *English Historical Review*, LXXII (1957), 616 ff.

Cross, C., *The Puritan Earl: the Life of Henry Hastings third Earl of Huntingdon, 1536–1595*. London 1966

The Royal Supremacy in the Elizabethan Church. London 1969

Cruickshank, C. G., *Elizabeth's Army* (2nd edn.). Oxford 1966

Davies, C., 'The Statute of Provisors of 1351', *History*, xxxviii (1953), 116 ff.

Davies, C. S. L., 'Provision for Armies 1509–1560: a Study in the Effectiveness of Early Tudor Government', *Economic History Review*, 2nd Series, xvii (1964–5), 234 ff.

Davies, M. G., *The Enforcement of English Apprenticeship, 1563–1642.* Cambridge, Mass. 1956

Dawson, J. P., *A History of Lay Judges.* Cambridge, Mass. 1960

Deputy Keeper's Reports – Reports of the Deputy Keeper of the Public Records. London 1840–61

D'Ewes, Sir Simonds, *The Journals of all the Parliaments during the Reign of Queen Elizabeth, both of the House of Lords and House of Commons.* London 1682

Dickens, A. G., 'The Edwardian Arrears in Augmentation Payments and the Problem of the ex-Religious', *English Historical Review*, lv (1940), 384 ff.

The English Reformation. London 1964

Lollards and Protestants in the Diocese of York 1509–1558. Oxford 1959

Dietz, F. C., *English Government Finance 1485–1558.* Urbana, Ill. 1920

English Public Finance 1558–1642. New York 1932

The Exchequer in Elizabeth's Reign. Northampton, Mass. 1923

A Discourse upon the Exposicion & Understandinge of Statutes, ed. S. E. Thorne. San Marino, Calif. 1942

Dugdale, W., *A Perfect Copy of all Summons of Nobility to the Great Councils and Parliaments of this Realm.* London 1685

Duncan, G. I. O., *The High Court of Delegates.* Cambridge 1971

Dunham, W. H., jr., 'The Ellesmere Extracts from the "Acta Consilii" of King Henry VIII', *English Historical Review*, lviii (1943), 301 ff.

'Henry VIII's Whole Council and its Parts', *Huntingdon Library Quarterly*, vii (1943), 7 ff.

Lord Hastings' Indentured Retainers 1461–83. New Haven 1955

'Wolsey's Rule of the King's Whole Council', *American Historical Review*, xlix (1944), 64 ff.

Dyer, A. D., 'The Market Towns of Southern England 1500–1700', *Southern History*, i (1979), 123 ff.

Edwards, J. G., *The Commons in Medieval English Parliaments.* London 1958

' "Justice" in Early English Parliaments', *Bulletin of the Institute of Historical Research*, xxvii (1954), 35 ff.

Ellis, H. (ed.) *Original Letters Illustrative of English History.* 3 series. London 1824–46

Ellis, S. G., 'The Administration of Ireland under the Early Tudors', unpublished dissertation, Belfast 1979

'The Kildare Rebellion and the Early Henrician Reformation', *Historical Journal*, XIX (1976), 807 ff.

'Thomas Cromwell and Ireland, 1532–1540', *Historical Journal*, XXIII (1980), 497 ff.

'Tudor Policy and the Kildare Ascendancy in the Lordship of Ireland, 1496–1534', *Irish Historical Studies*, XX (1977), 235 ff.

Elsynge, H., *The Manner of Holding Parliaments in England*. London 1768

Elton, G. R., 'Arthur Hall, Lord Burghley and the Antiquity of Parliament', *History and Imagination: essays in honour of H. R. Trevor-Roper* (ed. H. Lloyd-Jones, V. Pearl, B. Worden; London 1981), 88–103

'The Early Journals of the House of Lords', *English Historical Review*, LXXXIX (1974), 481 ff.

'Parliament in the Sixteenth Century: Function and Fortunes', *Historical Journal*, XXII (1979), 255 ff.

Policy and Police: the Enforcement of the Reformation in the Age of Thomas Cromwell. Cambridge 1972

Reform and Reformation; England 1509–1558. London 1977

Reform and Renewal: Thomas Cromwell and the Common Weal. Cambridge 1973

'The Rolls of Parliament 1449–1547', *Historical Journal*, XXII (1979), 1 ff.

'The Sessional Printing of Statutes, 1484–1547', *Wealth and Power in Tudor England* (ed. E. W. Ives, R. J. Knecht, J. J. Scarisbrick; London 1978), 68 ff.

Star Chamber Stories. London 1958

Studies in Tudor and Stuart Politics and Government: Papers and Reviews 1946–1972, 2 vols. Cambridge 1974 (Nos. 3, 4, 7, 8, 10, 14, 16, 18, 19, 20, 21, 22, 24, 25, 26, 31)

'Taxation for War and Peace in Early-Tudor England', *War and Economic Development* (ed. J. M. Winter; Cambridge 1975), 33 ff.

'Tudor Government: the Points of Contact. I. Parliament; II. The Council; III. The Court', *Transactions of the Royal Historical Society*, 5th Series, XXIV (1974), 183 ff.; XXV (1975), 195 ff.; XXVI (1976), 211 ff.

The Tudor Revolution in Government. Cambridge 1953

Evans, F. M. G., *The Principal Secretary of State*. Manchester 1923

Fish, Simon, *The Supplicacyon of the Beggars*, ed. F. J. Furnivall. London, Early English Text Society, 1871.

Fortescue, Sir John, *The Governance of England*, ed. C. Plummer. Oxford 1885

Foster, F. F., *The Politics of Stability: a Portrait of the Rulers of Elizabethan London*. London 1977

Frere, W. H., and Douglas, C. E. (ed.), *Puritan Manifestoes*. London 1907; reprint 1954

Gardiner, Stephen, *Letters*, ed. J. A. Muller. Cambridge 1933

Gee, H., *The Elizabethan Clergy and the Settlement of Religion 1558–1564*. Oxford 1898

and Hardy, W. J., *Documents Illustrative of English Church History*. London 1896

George, M. D., 'Notes on the Origin of the Declared Account', *English Historical Review*, XXI (1916), 41 ff.

Gerard, J., *The Autobiography of an Elizabethan*, ed. P. Caraman. London 1951

Giuseppi, M. S., *Guide to the Manuscripts Preserved at the Public Record Office*, 2 vols. London 1923

Gleason, J. H., *The Justices of the Peace in England, 1558–1640*. Oxford 1969

Goring, J. J., 'Social Change and Military Decline in Mid-Tudor England', *History*, LX (1975), 185 ff.

Gras, N., *The Early English Customs System*. Cambridge, Mass. 1918

Graves, M. A. R., *The House of Lords in the Parliaments of Edward VI and Mary I: an Institutional Study*. Cambridge 1981

'Thomas Norton the Parliament Man: an Elizabethan M.P., 1559–1581', *Historical Journal*, XXIII (1980), 17 ff.

Gray, C. M., *Copyhold, Equity and the Common Law*. Cambridge, Mass. 1963

Grindal, Edmund, *Remains*. Parker Society. Cambridge 1843

Guth, D. J., 'Exchequer Penal Law Enforcement 1485–1509', unpublished dissertation, Pittsburgh 1967

Guy, J. A., *The Cardinal's Court: the Impact of Thomas Wolsey in Star Chamber*. Hassocks 1977

The Public Career of Sir Thomas More. Brighton 1980

Habakkuk, H. J., 'The Market for Monastic Property 1540–1603', *Economic History Review*, 2nd Series, X (1957–8), 362 ff.

Haigh, C. A., 'Puritan Evangelism in the Reign of Elizabeth I', *English Historical Review*, XCII (1977), 30 ff.

Reformation and Resistance in Tudor Lancashire. Cambridge 1975

'Some Aspects of the Recent Historiography of the English Reformation', *Stadtbürgertum und Adel in der Reformation* (ed. W. Mommsen; Stuttgart 1979), 88 ff.

Hall, Arthur, *Letter to F.A.* Reprint: London 1816

Hall, Edward, *Chronicle, or The Union of the Two Noble and Illustre Famelies of Lancastre and York*. Reprint: London 1809

Harcourt, L. W. Vernon, *His Grace the Steward and Trial by Peers*. London 1907

The Harleian Miscellany: A Collection of Scarce, Curious and Entertaining Pamphlets and Tracts . . . found in the late Earl of Oxford's Library, 8 vols. London 1745

Harpsfield, N., *The Life and Death of Sir Thomas More, knight, sometimes Lord*

High Chancellor of England, ed. E. V. Hitchcock and R. W. Chambers. London, Early English Text Society, 1932

Harriss, G. L., and Williams, P. H., 'A Revolution in Tudor History?', *Past and Present*, xxv (1963), 1 ff.; with answer by G. R. Elton, *ibid.*, xxix (1964), 26 ff.

Hastings, M., *The Court of Common Pleas in Fifteenth-Century England*. Ithaca, N.Y. 1947

Haugaard, W. P., *Elizabeth and the English Reformation: the Struggle for a Stable Settlement of Religion*. Cambridge 1968

Hawarde, J., *Les Reportes del Cases in Camera Stellata 1593–1609*, ed. W. P. Baildon. London 1894

Heal, F., 'Clerical Tax Collection under the Tudors', *Continuity and Change: Personnel and Administration of the Church of England, 1500–1642* (ed. R. O'Day and F. Heal; Leicester 1976), 97 ff.

Of Prelates and Princes: a Study of the Economic and Social Position of the Tudor Episcopate. Cambridge 1980

Heath, P., *The English Parish Clergy on the Eve of the Reformation*. London 1969

Heinze, R. W., *The Proclamations of the Tudor Kings*. Cambridge 1976

Hill, J. E. C., *Economic Problems of the Church from Archbishop Whitgift to the Long Parliament*. Oxford 1956

Hill, L. M., 'The Two-Witness Rule in English Treason Trials', *American Journal of Legal History*, xii (1968), 95 ff.

Hoak, D. E., *The King's Council in the Reign of Edward VI*. Cambridge 1976

Hodgett, G. A. J., *Tudor Lincolnshire*. Lincoln 1975

Holdsworth, W. S., *A History of English Law*, vol. 1 (7th edn by S. B. Chrimes, London 1956); vols. iv and v (3rd edn, London 1945)

Holinshed, R., *Chronicles of England, Scotland and Ireland*. Reprint: London 1808

Holmes, P. J., *Resistance and Compromise: the Political Thought of the Elizabethan Catholics*. Cambridge 1982

Homilies, see *Certain Sermons*

Hooker, J. R., 'Some Cautionary Notes on Henry VII's Household and Chamber "System"', *Speculum*, xxxiii (1958), 69 ff.

Hooker, R., *Works*, ed. J. Keble, revised by R. W. Church and F. Paget, 3 vols. Oxford 1888

Houlbrooke, R. A., *Church Courts and the People during the English Reformation, 1520–1570*. Oxford 1979

Howell, R., *Newcastle upon Tyne and the Puritan Revolution*. Oxford 1967

Hudson, W. S., *The Cambridge Connection and the Elizabethan Settlement of 1559*. Durham, N. C. 1980

Hughes, C., 'Nicholas Faunt's Discourse Touching the Office of Principal Secretary of Estate &c., 1592', *English Historical Review*, xx (1905), 499 ff.

Hughes, P., *The Reformation in England*, 3 vols. London 1950, 1953, 1954

Hurstfield, J., 'The Greenwich Tenures of the Reign of Edward VI', *Law Quarterly Review*, XLV (1949), 72 ff.

The Queen's Wards. London 1958

'The Revival of Feudalism in Early Tudor England', *History* XXXVII (1952), 131 ff.

Ives, E. W., 'The Common Lawyers in Pre-Reformation England', *Transactions of the Royal Historical Society*, 5th Series, XVIII (1968), 145 ff.

'The Genesis of the Statute of Uses', *English Historical Review*, LXXXI (1967), 673 ff.

'Promotion in the Legal Profession of Yorkist and Early Tudor England', *Law Quarterly Review*, LXXV (1959), 348 ff.

'The Reputation of the Common Lawyers in English Society, 1450–1550', *University of Birmingham Historical Journal*, VII (1960) ,130 ff.

James I, *Political Works*, ed. C. H. McIlwain. Cambridge, Mass. 1918

James, M. E., *Family, Lineage and Civil Society: a Study of Society, Politics, and Mentality in the Durham Region, 1500–1640.* Oxford 1974

Jones, N. L., *Parliament and the Settlement of Religion.* London 1982

Jones, W. J., *The Elizabethan Court of Chancery.* Oxford 1967

'The Exchequer of Chester in the last Years of Elizabeth I', *Tudor Men and Institutions* (ed. A. J. Slavin; Baton Rouge 1972), 123 ff.

Jordan, W. K., *Edward VI*, 2 vols. London 1968, 1970

Kitching, C. J., 'The Disposal of Monastic and Chantry Lands', *Church and Society in England: Henry VIII to James I* (ed. F. Heal and R. O'Day; London 1977), 119 ff.

'The Prerogative Court of Canterbury from Warham to Whitgift', *Continuity and Change: Personnel and Administration of the Church of England 1500–1642* (ed. R. O'Day and F. Heal; Leicester 1976), 191 ff.

Knappen, M. M., *Tudor Puritanism.* Chicago 1939

Knowles, M. D., *The Religious Orders in England*, vol. III. Cambridge 1959 and Haddock, R. N., *Medieval Religious Houses: England and Wales.* London 1953

Knox, D. A., 'The Court of Requests in the Reign of Edward VI', unpublished dissertation, Cambridge 1974

Koebner, R., ' "The Imperial Crown of the Realm": Henry VIII, Constantine the Great, and Polydore Vergil', *Bulletin of the Institute of Historical Research*, XXVI (1953), 29 ff.

Kreider, A., *English Chantries: the Road to Dissolution.* Cambridge, Mass. 1979

Labaree, L. W., and Moody, R. E., 'The Seal of the Privy Council', *English Historical Review*, XLIII (1928), 190 ff.

Lake, P., 'The Dilemma of the Establishment Puritan: the Cambridge Heads and the Case of Francis Johnson and Cuthbert Binbrigg', *Journal of Ecclesiastical History*, XXIX (1978), 23 ff.

'Laurence Chaderton and the Cambridge Moderate Puritan Tradition', unpublished dissertation, Cambridge 1977

'Matthew Hutton: a Puritan Bishop?', *History*, LXIV (1979), 182 ff.

Lambarde, W., *Archeion, or a Commentary upon the High Courts of Justice in England*. London 1635

Eirenarcha, or the Office of the Justice of the Peace. London 1602

Lambert, S., 'Procedure in the House of Commons during the Early Stuart Period', *English Historical Review*, XCV (1980), 753 ff.

Lander, J. R., 'Attainder and Forfeiture, 1453–1509', *Historical Journal*, IV (1961), 120 ff.

'The Yorkist Council and Administration, 1461–1485', *English Historical Review*, LXXIII (1958), 27 ff.

Lander, S., 'Church Courts and the Reformation in the Diocese of Chichester', *Continuity and Change: Personnel and Administration of the Church of England 1500–1642* (ed. R. O'Day and F. Heal; Leicester 1976), 215 ff.

Langbein, J., *Prosecuting Crime in the Renaissance*. Cambridge, Mass. 1974

Latimer, Hugh, *Sermons*, ed. G. E. Corrie. Parker Society. Cambridge 1844

Leach, A. F., *English Schools at the Reformation 1546–48*. London 1896

Leadam, I. S. (ed.), *Select Cases in the Court of Requests 1497–1569*. London, Selden Society, 1898

(ed.), *Select Cases in the Court of Star Chamber 1477–1509*. London, Seldon Society, 1903

Lehmberg, S. E., 'Early Tudor Parliamentary Procedure: Provisos in the Legislation of the Reformation Parliament', *English Historical Review*, LXXXV (1970), 1 ff.

The Later Parliaments of Henry VIII, 1536–1547. Cambridge 1977

The Reformation Parliament, 1529–1536. Cambridge 1970

'Supremacy and Vicegerency: a Reexamination', *English Historical Review*, LXXXI (1961), 225 ff.

Lemasters, G. E., 'The Privy Council in the Reign of Queen Mary I', unpublished dissertation, Cambridge 1971

Leonard, E. M., *The Early History of English Poor Relief*. Cambridge 1900

Letters and Papers Illustrative of the Reigns of Richard III and Henry VII, ed. J. Gairdner. London, Rolls Series, 1861

L.J. – Journal of the House of Lords

Lloyd, H. A., *The Gentry of South-West Wales, 1540–1640*. Cardiff 1968

Loach, J., 'Conservatism and Consent in Parliament, 1547–59', *The Mid-Tudor Polity* (ed. J. Loach and R. Tittler; London 1980), 9 ff.

Loades, D. M., 'Anabaptism and English Separatism in the Mid-Sixteenth Century', *Reform and Reformation: England and the Continent c. 1500 to c. 1750* (ed. D. Baker; Oxford 1979), 59 ff.

The Reign of Mary Tudor: Politics, Government and Religion in England, 1553–1558. London 1979

Logan, F. D., 'The Henrician Canons', *Bulletin of the Institute of Historical Research*, XLVII (1974), 99 ff.

Loomie, A. J., *The Spanish Elizabethans*. New York 1963

L.P. – Letters and Papers, Foreign and Domestic, of the Reign of Henry VIII, 32 vols., ed. J. S. Brewer, J. Gairdner, R. H. Brodie. London 1862–1932

Luxton, J., 'The Reformation and Popular Culture', *Church and Society in England: Henry VIII to James I* (ed. F. Heal and R. O'Day: London 1977), 57 ff.

Lyte, H. M., *Historial Notes on the Use of the Great Seal in England*. London 1926

MacCaffrey, W. T., *Exeter 1540–1640*. Cambridge, Mass. 1958

'Place and Patronage in Elizabethan Politics', *Elizabethan Government and Society* (ed. S. T. Bindoff, J. Hurstfield, C. H. Williams; London 1961), 95 ff.

The Shaping of the Elizabethan Regime. Princeton 1968

McConica, J. K., *English Humanists and Reformation Politics*. Oxford 1965

MacCulloch, D. N. J., 'Power, Privilege and the County Community: County Politics in Elizabethan Suffolk', unpublished dissertation, Cambridge 1977

McGinn, D. J., *John Penry and the Marprelate Controversy*. New Brunswick N.J. 1966

McGrath, P., *Papists and Puritans under Elizabeth I*. London 1967

McIlwain, C. H., *Constitutionalism Ancient and Modern*. Ithaca N.Y. 1947

Constitutionalism and the Changing World. Cambridge 1939

The High Court of Parliament and its Supremacy. New Haven 1910

McKisack, M., *The Parliamentary Representation of the English Boroughs during the Middle Ages*. Oxford 1932

Magnum Bullarium Romanum: Pius IV – Innocentius IX. Lyons 1692

Maitland, F. W., *English Law and the Renaissance*. Cambridge 1901

Equity, and the Forms of Action at Common Law. Cambridge 1909

Marchant, R. A., *The Church under the Law: Justice, Administration and Discipline in the Diocese of York, 1560–1640*. Cambridge 1969

Merriman, R. B., *The Life and Letters of Thomas Cromwell*, 2 vols. Oxford 1902

Metzger, F., 'The Last Phase of the Medieval Chancery', *Law-Making and Law-Makers in British History* (ed. A. Harding; London 1980), 79 ff.

Meyer, A. O., *England and the Catholic Church under Queen Elizabeth*, Eng. trans. London 1916

Miklovich, J. I., 'The Significance of the Royal Sign Manual in Early Tudor Legislative Procedure', *Bulletin of the Institute of Historical Research*, LII (1979), 23 ff.

Miller, H., 'Attendance in the House of Lords during the Reign of Henry VIII', *Historical Journal*, X (1967), 325 ff.

'The Early Tudor Peerage 1485–1547', *Bulletin of the Institution of Historical Research*, XXIV (1951), 88 ff.

The Mirror for Magistrates, ed. L. B. Campbell. Cambridge 1938

Morris, G. C., *Political Thought in England: Tyndale to Hooker*. London 1953

The Tudors. London 1955

Mosse, G. L., *The Struggle for Sovereignty in England from the Reign of Queen Elizabeth to the Petition of Right*. East Lansing 1950

Muller, J. A., *Stephen Gardiner and the Tudor Reaction*. London 1926

Narratives of the Days of the Reformation, ed. J. G. Nichols. London, Camden Society, 1849

Neale, J. E., 'The Commons Journals of the Tudor Period', *Transactions of the Royal Historical Society*, 4th Series, III (1920), 136 ff.

'The Commons' Privilege of Free Speech in Parliament', *Tudor Studies presented . . . to A. F. Pollard* (ed. R. W. Seton-Watson; London 1924), 257 ff.

'The Elizabethan Acts of Supremacy and Uniformity', *English Historical Review*, LXV (1950), 304 ff.

The Elizabethan House of Commons. London 1949

Elizabeth I and her Parliaments, 2 vols. London 1953, 1957

Essays in Elizabethan History. London 1958

'The Lord Keeper's Speech to the Parliament of 1592–3', *English Historical Review*, XXXI (1916), 128 ff.

Newton, A. P., 'The Establishment of the Great Farm of the English Customs', *Transactions of the Royal Historical Society*, 4th Series, I (1918), 129 ff.

'Tudor Reforms of the Royal Household', *Tudor Studies presented . . . to A.F. Pollard* (ed. R. W. Seton-Watson; London 1924), 231 ff.

Nicholson, G. D., 'The Nature and Function of Historical Argument in the Henrician Reformation', unpublished dissertation, Cambridge 1977

The Notebook of John Penry, ed. A. Peel. London 1944

O'Day, R., 'The Reformation of the Ministry, 1558–1642', *Continuity and Change: Personnel and Administration of the Church of England 1500–1642* (ed. R. O'Day and F. Heal; Leicester 1976), 55 ff.

Ogilvie, C., *The King's Government and the Common Law, 1471–1641*. Oxford 1958

Otway-Ruthven, J., 'The Constitutional Position of the Great Lordships of South Wales', *Transactions of the Royal Historical Society*, 5th Series, VIII (1958), 1 ff.

The King's Secretary and the Signet Office in the XV Century. Cambridge 1939

Palliser, D. M., 'Popular Reactions to the Reformation during the Years of Uncertainty, 1530–70,' *Church and Society in England: Henry VIII to James I* (ed. F. Heal and R. O'Day; London 1977), 35 ff.

Parker, Matthew, *Correspondence*, ed. J. Bruce. Parker Society. Cambridge 1853

Pearson, A. F. S., *Thomas Cartwright and Elizabethan Puritanism.* Cambridge 1925

Peck, F. (ed.), *Desiderata Curiosa.* London 1779

Phythian-Adams, C., *Desolation of a City: Coventry and the Urban Crisis of the Late Middle Ages.* Cambridge 1979

Pickthorn, K. W. M., *Early Tudor Government*, 2 vols. Cambridge 1934

Pierce, W., *An Historical Introduction to the Marprelate Tracts.* London 1908

Pike, L. O., *A Constitutional History of the House of Lords.* London 1908

Plowden, E., *The Commentaries or Reports* (English translation). Dublin 1792

Plucknett, T. F. T., 'The Lancastrian Constitution', *Tudor Studies presented . . . to A. F. Pollard* (ed. R. W. Seton-Watson; London 1924), 161 ff.

'Some Proposed Legislation of Henry VIII', *Transactions of the Royal Historical Society*, 4th Series, XIX (1936), 119 ff.

Pogson, R. H., 'The Legacy of the Schism: Confusion, Continuity and Change in the Marian Clergy', *The Mid-Tudor Polity* (ed. J. Loach and R. Tittler; London 1980), 116 ff.

Pollard, A. F., 'Council, Star Chamber, and Privy Council under the Tudors', *English Historical Review*, XXXVII (1922), 337 ff., 516 ff.; XXXVIII (1923), 42 ff.

'The "de facto" Act of Henry VII', *Bulletin of the Institute of Historical Research*, VII (1930), 1 ff.

The Reign of Henry VII from Contemporary Sources, 3 vols. London 1913

'Thomas Cromwell's Parliamentary Lists', *Bulletin of the Institute of Historical Research*, IX (1931–2), 31 ff.

Wolsey. London 1929

Pollock, F., and Maitland, F. W., *A History of English Law before the Time of Edward I*, 2 vols. Cambridge 1895

Porter, H. C., *Reformation and Reaction in Tudor Cambridge.* Cambridge 1958

Prest, W. R., *The Inns of Court under Elizabeth and the Early Stuarts, 1570–1640.* London 1972

(ed.), *Lawyers in Early Modern Europe and America.* London 1981

Price, F. D., 'The Abuses of Excommunication and the Decline of Ecclesiastical Discipline under Queen Elizabeth', *English Historical Review*, LVV (1942), 106 ff.

'The Commission for Ecclesiastical Causes for the Dioceses of Bristol and

Gloucester, 1574', *Transactions of the Bristol and Gloucestershire Archaeological Society*, LIX (1937), 61 ff.

'An Elizabethan Church Official – Thomas Powell, Chancellor of Gloucester Diocese', *Church Quarterly Review*, CXXVIII (1939), 94 ff.

Primus, J. H., *The Vestments Controversy: an Historical Study of the Earliest Tensions Within the Church of England in the Reigns of Edward VI and Elizabeth*. Kampen 1960

Pritchard, A., *Catholic Loyalism in Elizabethan England*. London 1979

Proceedings and Ordinances of the Privy Council of England, ed. N. H. Nicolas. London, Record Commission, 1837

Proceedings in the Court of Star Chamber, in the Reigns of Henry VII and Henry VIII, ed. G. Bradford. Somerset Record Society, vol. XXVII, 1911

Pronay, N., and Taylor, J. (ed.), *Parliamentary Texts of the Later Middle Ages*. Oxford 1980

Prothero, G. W. (ed.), *Select Statutes and other Constitutional Documents illustrative of the Reigns of Elizabeth and James I*, 4th edn. Oxford 1913

Pugh, T. B., *The Marcher Lordships of South Wales, 1415–1536*. Cardiff 1963

Pulman, M. B., *The Elizabethan Privy Council in the 1570s*. Berkeley 1971

Purvis, J. S., *Select XVI Causes in Tithe*. Yorkshire Archaeological Society, Record Series, vol. CXIV, 1949

Putman, B. H., *Early Treaties on the Practice of the Justices of the Peace in the sixteenth and seventeenth centuries*. Oxford 1926

Quinn, D. B., 'Anglo-Irish Local Government, 1485–1534', *Irish Historical Studies*, I (1939), 354 ff.

Read, C., *Mr Secretary Cecil and Queen Elizabeth*. London 1955

Mr Secretary Walsingham and the Policy of Queen Elizabeth, 3 vols. Oxford 1925

Reid, R. R., *The King's Council in the North*. London 1921

'The Rebellion of the Earls, 1569', *Transactions of the Royal Historical Society*, New Series, XX (1906), 171 ff.

Richardson, W. C., *The History of the Court of Augmentations*. Baton Rouge 1962

'The Surveyors of the King's Prerogative', *English Historical Review*, LVI (1941), 52 ff.

Tudor Chamber Administration. Baton Rouge 1952

Roberts, P. R., 'The "Act of Union" in Welsh History', *Transactions of the Honourable Society of Cymmrodorion* (1972–3), 49 ff.

'The "Acts of Union" and the Tudor Settlement of Wales', unpublished dissertation, Cambridge 1966

'The Union with England and the Identity of "Anglican Wales"', *Transactions of the Royal Historical Society*, 5th Series, XXII (1972), 49 ff.

Roper, W., *The Lyfe of Sir Thomas More, knighte*, ed. E. V. Hitchcock. London, Early English Text Society, 1935

Roskell, J. S., *The Commons in the Parliament of 1422*. Manchester 1954

'Perspectives in English Parliamentary History', *Bulletin of the John Rylands Library*, XLVI (1964), 448 ff.

'The Social Composition of the Commons in a Fifteenth-Century Parliament', *Bulletin of the Institute of Historical Research*, XXIV (1951), 152 ff.

Rotuli Parliamentorum ut et Petitiones et Placita in Parliamento, 6 vols. London s.a.

Rowse, A. L., *Tudor Cornwall*. London 1941

Rupp, E. G., *Studies in the Making of the English Protestant Tradition*. Cambridge 1947

Russell, C., 'Parliamentary History in Perspective, 1604–1629', *History*, LXI (1976), 1 ff.

St German, Christopher, *An Answer to a Letter*. London 1535

Doctor and Student, ed. T. F. T. Plucknett and J. L. Barton. London, Selden Society, 1974

Samaha, J. B., 'Hanging for Felony: the Rule of Law in Elizabethan Colchester', *Historical Journal*, XXI (1978), 763 ff.

Law and Order in Historical Perspective: the Case of Elizabethan Essex. New York 1974

Savine, A., *English Monasteries on the Eve of the Dissolution*. Oxford 1909

Scarisbrick, J. J., 'Clerical Tax Collection in England, 1485–1547', *Journal of Ecclesiastical History*, XI (1960), 41 ff.

Henry VIII, London 1968

'The Pardon of the Clergy, 1531', *Cambridge Historical Journal*, XII (1956), 22 ff.

Schofield, R. S., 'Parliamentary Lay Taxation, 1485–1547', unpublished dissertation, Cambridge 1963

Schramm, P. E., *A History of the English Coronation* (English translation). Oxford 1937

Scott Thompson, G., *Lords Lieutenants in the Sixteenth Century*. London 1923

'The Origin and Growth of the Office of Deputy-Lieutenant', *Transactions of the Royal Historical Society*, 4th Series, V (1922), 150 ff.

The Seconde Parte of a Register, ed. A. Peel. Cambridge 1915

Simon, J., *Education and Society in Tudor England*. Cambridge 1966

Simpson, A. W. B., *An Introduction to the History of the Land Law*. Oxford 1961

Skelton, E., 'The Court of Star Chamber in the Reign of Elizabeth', unpublished dissertation, London 1930

Slavin, A. J., *Politics and Profit: a Study of Sir Ralph Sadler, 1507–1547*. Cambridge 1966

Smith, A. G. R., 'The Secretariats of the Cecils, circa 1580–1612,' *English Historical Review*, LXXXIII (1968), 481 ff.

Servant of the Cecils: the Life of Sir Michael Hicks. London 1977

Smith, A. H., *County and Court: Government and Politics in Norfolk 1558–1603.* Oxford 1974

Smith, R. B., *Land and Politics in the England of Henry VIII: the West Riding of Yorkshire, 1530–46.* Oxford 1970

Smith, Sir Thomas, *De Republica Anglorum*, ed. L. Alston. Cambridge 1906 (To be replaced by a new edition by Mary Dewar, Cambridge 1982.)

Somerville, R., 'The Duchy of Lancaster Council and Court of Duchy Chamber', *Transactions of the Royal Historical Society*, 4th Series, XXIII (1941), 159 ff.

'Henry VII's "Council Learned in the Law"', *English Historical Review*, LIV (1939), 427 ff.

History of the Duchy of Lancaster, vol. I, London 1953

Span. Cal. – Calendar of State Papers, Spanish, 13 vols. London 1862–1945

Span. Cal. Eliz. – Calendar of State Papers, Spanish, Elizabeth, 4 vols. London 1892–9

Squibb, G. D., *The High Court of Chivalry.* Oxford 1959

Stanford, W., *An Exposition of the King's Prerogative.* London 1567

Starkey, D. R., 'The King's Privy Chamber, 1485–1547', unpublished dissertation, Cambridge 1973

State Papers of King Henry VIII, 8 vols. London, Record Commission, 1830–52

State Trials and Proceedings for High Treason, ed. T. E. Howell. London 1816–98

The Statutes of the Realm 12 vols. London, Record Commission, 1810–28

Steel, A., *The Receipt of the Exchequer 1377–1485.* Cambridge 1954

Stone, L., 'The Political Programme of Thomas Cromwell', *Bulletin of the Institute of Historical Research*, XXIV (1951), 1 ff.

Stow, J., *A Survey of London*, ed. C. L. Kingsford, 2 vols. Oxford 1908

Strype, J., *Annals of the Reformation and Establishment of Religion.* Oxford 1824
Ecclesiastical Memorials. Oxford 1822
The Life and Acts of Edmund Grindal. Oxford 1821
The Life and Acts of Matthew Parker. Oxford 1821
The Life and Acts of John Whitgift. Oxford 1822

Tanner, J. R., *Tudor Constitutional Documents, A.D. 1485–1603, with an Historical Commentary*, 2nd edn. Cambridge 1930

Thomson, J. A. F., *The Later Lollards 1414–1520.* Oxford 1965

Thorne, S. E., 'Dr Bonham's Case', *Law Quarterly Review*, LIV (1938), 543 ff.

Thornley, I. D., 'The Destruction of Sanctuary', *Tudor Studies presented . . . to A. F. Pollard* (ed. R. W. Seton-Watson; London 1924), 182 ff.

'Treason by Words in the Fifteenth Century', *English Historical Review*, XXXII (1917), 556 ff.

Tout, T. F., *Chapters in the Administrative History of Medieval England*, 6 vols. Manchester 1920–33.

Tracts Ascribed to Richard Bancroft, ed. A. Peel. Cambridge 1953

Trimble, W. R., *The Catholic Laity in Elizabethan England, 1558–1603*. Cambridge, Mass. 1964

Tudor Royal Proclamations, 3 vols., ed. P. L. Hughes and J. F. Larkin. New Haven 1964, 1969

Tyacke, N., 'Popular Puritan Mentality in Late Elizabethan England', *The English Commonwealth 1547–1640* (ed. P. Clark, A. G. R. Smith, N. Tyacke; Leicester 1979), 77 ff.

Usher, R. G., *The Presbyterian Movement in the Reign of Queen Elizabeth*. London, Camden Society, 1905

The Rise and Fall of the High Commission, reprinted with an Introduction by P. Tyler. Oxford 1968

Ven. Cal. – Calendar of State Papers . . . in the Archives and Collections of Venice, ed. R. Brown *et al.* London 1864–98

Vowell, J., alias Hooker, 'The Old and Ancient Order of Keeping of the Parliament in England', *Somers Tracts* (London 1809), I, 175 ff.

Waugh, W. T., 'The Great Statute of Praemunire', *English Historical Review*, XXXVII (1922), 173 ff.

Weikel, A., 'The Marian Council Revisited', *The Mid-Tudor Polity* (ed. J. Loach and R. Tittler; London 1980), 52 ff.

Wernham, R. B., 'The Disgrace of William Davison', *English Historical Review*, XLVI (1931), 632 ff.

Weston, W., *The Autobiography of an Elizabethan*, ed. P. Caraman. London 1955

Williams, G., *Welsh Reformation Essays*. Cardiff 1967

Williams, P. H., *The Council in the Marches of Wales under Elizabeth*. Cardiff 1958

The Tudor Regime. Oxford 1979

Wolffe, B. P., *The Crown Lands 1461 to 1536: an Aspect of Yorkist and Early Tudor Government*. London 1970

'Henry VII's Land Revenues and Chamber Finance', *English Historical Review*, LXXIX (1964), 225 ff.

'The Management of English Royal Estates under the Yorkist Kings', *English Historical Review*, LXXI (1956), 1 ff.

Woodcock, B. L., *Medieval Ecclesiastical Courts in the Diocese of Canterbury*. Oxford 1952

Woodworth, A., 'Purveyance for the Royal Household in the Reign of Queen Elizabeth', *Transactions of the American Philosophical Society*, New Series, XXXV, part 1. Philadelphia 1945

Wyndham, K. S. H., 'The Royal Estate in Mid Sixteenth-Century Somerset', *Bulletin of the Institute of Historical Research*, LII (1979), 129 ff.

Youings, J., 'The Council of the West', *Transactions of the Royal Historical Society*, 5th Series, x (1960), 41 ff.

Devon Monastic Lands: Calendar of Particulars for Grants 1536–58. Torquay, Devon and Cornwall Record Society, 1955

The Dissolution of the Monasteries. London 1971

'The Terms of the Disposal of the Devon Monastic Lands', *English Historical Review*, LXIX (1954), 18 ff.

Youngs, F. A., *The Proclamations of the Tudor Queens*. Cambridge 1976

Zeeveld, W. G., *Foundations of Tudor Policy*. Cambridge, Mass. 1948

GLOSSARY

Affeir: belong; assess

Censes: taxes

Cess: assess

Coarct: coerce

Demur: (1) stay, reside; (2) erect a defence on a point of law while refusing to plead to the facts alleged

Distress: confiscation of movables by court order

Eftsoons: a second time

Embracery: corruption of juries

Escheat: cf. p. 41

Essoin: lawful excuse for failure to appear in court

Femme covert: married woman (with husband living)

Inculce: inculcate

Indenture: a document used to record a contract or lease; the matter is written out twice on the same piece of parchment which is then cut in two along an 'indented' line, each party retaining one half

Let: hinder

Livery: surrender to the heir of lands in knight's service; also payment exacted for this

Mainprize: remission to friendly security, with guarantee that the person remitted will appear in court as ordered, the person to whom remission is made being held responsible (i.e. bail without money)

Maintenance: cf. p. 31

Misprision of treason: strictly, failure to reveal knowledge of a treason; more generally, association with treasonable activities without direct participation in them; a lesser but still serious offence

Odible: odious

Oyer and terminer: a commission 'to hear and determine', i.e. to try a stated criminal case and judge it

Peculiar: an ecclesiastical organisation exempted from the discipline of the diocesan and subjected to that of another

Perceive: receive

Praemunire: cf. p. 330

Prest : money advanced by one government department to another; imprest

Provocation: (in canon law) the calling of a case into a higher court

Provulge: promulgate

Resiant: resident

Ure: use

Vailable: effective

INDEX